WAYS OF WAR AND PEACE

WAYS OF WAR AND PEACE

REALISM, LIBERALISM, AND SOCIALISM

Michael W. Doyle

W. W. NORTON & COMPANY
NEW YORK / LONDON

Printed in the United States of America
First Edition

The text of this book is composed in Electra
with the display set in ITC Fenice
Composition and manufacturing by the Maple-Vail Book Manufacturing Group
Book design by JAM Design
Cartography by Jacques Chazaud

Library of Congress Cataloging-in-Publication Data

Doyle, Michael W.
Ways of war and peace : realism, liberalism, and socialism /
Michael W. Doyle.
p. cm.
Includes bibliographical references and index.
ISBN 0-393-03826-2. — ISBN 0-393-96947-9 (pbk.)
1. Peace. 2. International relations—Philosophy. 3. Politics
and war. 4. World politics—1989– I. Title.
JX1963.D687 1997
327.1'7—dc20 96-15090
CIP

W. W. Norton & Company, Inc., 500 Fifth Avenue, New York, N.Y. 10110
http://www.wwnorton.com

W. W. Norton & Company Ltd., 10 Coptic Street, London WC1A 1PU

4 5 6 7 8 9 0

to Amy Gutmann,
who inspired my effort to build a bridge between international politics
and political philosophy and whose advice and
affection sustained me along the way

Contents

PART FOUR
CONSCIENCE AND POWER

PART FIVE
FUTURES

Preface

THIS BOOK MAKES a case for the importance of the classical tradition of theoretical scholarship in interstate politics. I divide that tradition into Realism, Liberalism, and Socialism. I then explore a new way of thinking about how theorists differ within each family as well as how they fit into each family. Thucydides, Machiavelli, Hobbes, and Rousseau are among the Realists; Locke, Bentham, Smith, Schumpeter, and Kant are among the Liberals; Marx and Lenin are the Socialists. I try to do justice to the complexity of each theorist while showing how their association in a wider tradition of thought opens up valuable understandings of what makes for harmony, cooperation, and conflict, and thus for war and peace in world politics. The classical theorists examine explanatory and moral questions about the sources and strategies of war and peace, about when to intervene by force, and about when the global rich should feel bound to assist the global poor.

The world has changed a great deal in recent years, and some of what the classic theorists discovered is dated, since they failed to anticipate key aspects of the political universe we inhabit today. None of the theorists examined here anticipated the destructiveness of nuclear weapons or the speed of global communications. But much of what they argued for and about is timeless. Exploitation and chauvinism, human dignity and equality, oppression and autocracy, democracy and freedom, poverty and social welfare, national and transnational solidarities: These are phenomena with long pedigrees. As a whole, however, they are the travails and triumphs of the modern age. These are also ideas which—though some were foreign to their own times—the classic theorists envisaged in ways that helped make them understood and even a reality in ours. When one recalls the recent disasters in the streets of Mogadishu in the summer and fall of 1993 in which the United States and the United Nations seemed so lost amid factional violence and patriotic resistance, it is not too difficult to imagine that Machiavelli would have been much more at home than we who, having forgotten him, never quite understood the princely politics of Somalia. When one observes the end of cold war—the striking reduction in tensions between once-sworn enemies—it is not hard to imagine Kant smiling as he contemplates the beginnings of another widening of the pacific union of representative republics. New thinking on world politics, some of which I survey in the conclusion, may someday transcend these classic thinkers, but the problems that animated the classic work have yet to be resolved.

All of these theorists—even Thucydides in his own intention—are modern in a recognizable sense. Each begins with the modern predicament—masterless men in modern society—and tries to speak across history to all who share it. Their stories are tales grounded in this predicament but full of hope that we can work out a sort of peace, in all its varieties—more or, more often, less permanent. Peace, indeed, is the great challenge the human species faces before it can begin to tackle effectively the equally hard questions of global governance and justice. But peace in its turn depends on approaching an understanding of justice and governance capable of bridging borders.

It is the virtue of these classic philosophers that they appreciated these questions as parts of one whole. Their arguments plumb deep wells of human nature, the complicated play of how polities choose their policies, and the special condition of politics among states that lack a commonly accepted source of superior authority. They steadfastly confronted the full politics—empirical and analytic, normative and practical—of international relations.

This book has been many years in the making. It builds on the study of Liberalism I began in the early 1980s with a focus on Immanuel Kant's Liberal Internationalism. It seeks to expand that appreciation to the two other traditions of classic international thought and to the variety of ideas embodied in each of the three traditions.

ACKNOWLEDGMENTS

Many have assisted me in putting my thoughts into these chapters. Roby Harrington and Sarah Caldwell of Norton offered encouragement from the beginning, together with excellent editorial advice at every stage. Pearl Hanig expertly copyedited the manuscript.

Peter Katzenstein and Jack Snyder reviewed the manuscript as a whole and helped me rethink some key points of substance and presentation. Marshall Cohen, George Downs, Richard Falk, Peter Gellman, Felix Gilbert, Robert

Gilpin, Joseph Grieco, Albert Hirschman, Stanley Hoffmann, George Kateb, James Kurth, Arno Mayer, Thomas Romer, Judith Shklar, Richard Ullman, and Michael Walzer commented on earlier versions of the project and parts of the manuscript in ways that saved me from a number of mistakes. I received enthusiastic research assistance at various stages from Ethan Balogh, Michael Clementi, Amanda Dickins, Peter Furia, James Friel, Geoffrey Herrera, Arie Kacowicz, Jacob Levy, Robert Mayer, Tomoharu Nishino, Katia Pappagianni, Karthick Ramakrishnan, Chandra Sriram, Erica Strecker, and Hongying Wang. Ms. Philomena Fischer ably assisted the production of various drafts.

My arguments benefited from seminars and comments I received at Cornell University, from Richard Ned Lebow and Barry Strauss; Duke University, Joseph Grieco; Harvard University, Samuel Huntington, Robert Keohane, Joseph Nye, and Andrew Moravcsik; the Korean International Studies Association, David Kang, Woosang Kim, and Chaibong Hahm; McGill University, John Hall; New York University Law School, Lea Brilmayer; Ohio University, John Gaddis; the University of California, Los Angeles, Arthur Stein and Richard Rosecrance; the University of Chicago, Bruce Cumings, Stephen Walt, and John Mearsheimer; University of Cincinnati, Richard Harknett; University of Pittsburgh, Jeff Checkel and Frederick Thayer; and at the Yale Law School, from Paul Kahn. I have tried out many of the arguments in the pages that follow on students at Johns Hopkins and Princeton who furthered my thinking.

I first presented parts of the arguments appearing in these chapters elsewhere. Chapter 2 draws on "Thucydidean Realism," *Review of International Studies*, 16 (June 1990), pp. 223–37; and "Thucydides: A Realist?," in Barry Strauss and R. Ned Lebow, eds., *Hegemonic Rivalry* (Boulder, Colo.: Westview Press, 1991), pp. 169–88. Chapter 5 draws on "Balancing Power Classically: An Alternative to Collective Security?," in George Downs, ed., *Collective Security beyond the Cold War* (Ann Arbor: University of Michigan Press, 1994), pp. 133–65. Chapter 8 builds on "Kant, Liberal Legacies, and Foreign Affairs," Parts I and II, *Philosophy and Public Affairs*, XII, 3 and 4 (June and October 1983), pp. 205–35 and 323–53; "Liberalism and World Politics," *American Political Science Review*, 80, 4 (December 1986), pp. 1151–69; "The Voice of the People: Political Theorists on the International Implications of Democracy," in Geir Lundestad, ed., *The Fall of Great Powers: Peace, Stability, and Legitimacy* (Oslo: Scandinavian University Press/Oxford University Press, 1994), pp. 283–310; and on short essays in Michael Brown, Sean Lynn-Jones, and Steven E. Miller, eds., *Debating the Democratic Peace* (Cambridge, Mass.: MIT Press, 1996). Chapter 12 borrows parts of "Liberalism and the End of the Cold War," in Richard N. Lebow and Thomas Risse-Kappen, eds., *International Relations Theory and the End of the Cold War* (New York: Columbia University Press, 1995), pp. 85–108.

I am grateful for financial assistance from the Social Science Research Council/MacArthur Foundation Fellowship in International Peace and Security, the Pew Foundation, the Center for Science and International Affairs of Harvard University, and especially for the continuing support of the Center of International Studies of Princeton University.

None of these institutions or individuals bears responsibility for what I have written, but all of them helped improve the final product.

Princeton, New Jersey
January 1997

WAYS OF WAR AND PEACE

INTRODUCTION

The Politics of Peace and War

THE COLD WAR is over, and people are debating what kind of world order will replace it. Does the surprisingly peaceful conclusion of the Cold War after 1989—the dissolution of the Warsaw Pact, the unification of Germany, and the collapse of the Soviet Union—herald a safer new world order? Or do the breakup of Yugoslavia, the rise of an assertive nationalist China, and the wars and disasters in Africa in 1992 and 1993 warn us of a much more dangerous world? Will the spread of liberal democracies produce peace? Or will the globalization of the world economy and a shift in the center of world power to the Pacific make for war?

In a widely noted exchange in February 1992, one that exemplified many of the debates over policy at the end of the Cold War, former Secretary of State Henry Kissinger criticized Secretary James Baker III for the latter's willingness to accommodate Soviet President Mikhail Gorbachev. Baker, Kissinger opined, held a worldview assuming "that the only conflict in the world has been between communism and democracy and therefore if the Soviet Union abandons communism, they and we are practically comparable and have identical interests in preserving the peace." Kissinger added that this "is not borne out by history."[1] Kissinger's worldview was different. As he later explained, the new

[1] Thomas Friedman, "Fighting Words in a Genteel World," *New York Times*, February 1, 1992. Secretary Baker also noted, "Real democracies do not resort to war with one another," and President Bush averred, "Democrats in the Kremlin are a greater guarantee of security than nuclear weapons." See Jerry Sanders, "The Prospects for Democratic Engagement," *World Policy Journal* (Summer 1992), p. 367. President Clinton later argued, "The United States believes that an expanding community of market democracies not only serves our own security interests, it also advances the goals enshrined in this body's charter and its universal declaration of human rights," in his speech, September 1993, at the United Nations General Assembly.

world order—rather than the expanding democratic partnership envisaged by President Bush and Secretary Baker, and later President Clinton too—would be better conceived as a revival of the classical multipolar balance of power. The former secretary of state foresaw a new order resembling the foreign relations of eighteeth- and nineteenth-century Europe. The United States, Europe, China, Japan, Russia and probably India would in the years ahead engage in competitive relations in which power will balance against power.[2] Kissinger lamented that this was a game the United States, by both its ideological tradition and current expectation, was poorly equipped to play.

In the former Soviet Union, Gorbachev led the reevaluation of Cold War categories, which had become by 1988, he thought, utterly useless in an age threatened by nuclear destruction and deeply in need of "comprehensive security."[3] But Soviets too were cross-pressured. In speeches directed at fellow Communists, Gorbachev reaffirmed his and the Commmunist Party of the Soviet Union's identity as Marxist-Leninists and their fraternal solidarity with all other Socialist countries and revolutionary movements. He himself discounted the degree of change his restructuring and openness (perestroika and glasnost) portended, comparing them not to a new revolution but to a new "stage" in, or task for, Socialism: like victory in the Civil War (1918–1920), the Great Patriotic War (World War II), or the collectivization of Soviet agriculture (1928–1932). The revolutionary task (in 1988) was to achieve an international system of security that, on the one hand, promoted domestic glasnost and perestroika and, on the other, curbed and then reduced the danger of nuclear destruction.[4] To square international cooperation with Socialist ideology, Gorbachev and other Socialists tried to resolve historical contradictions by highlighting "reactionary circles of the bourgeoisie" and the "military-industrial complex" in the United States (borrowing the words of President Dwight D. Eisenhower!). Leaving acres of room for accommodation by others, only narrow cliques threatened alike the legitimate national interests of the American people, the world peace movement so especially prominent in Western Europe, and, of course, "universal human values."[5] President Boris Yeltsin resolved the contradictions differently, accepting the values of market democracy. But in doing so,

[2] Henry Kissinger, *Diplomacy* (New York: Simon and Schuster, 1994), p. 23.
[3] Mikhail Gorbachev, CPSU Report to the 27th Congress, 1988.
[4] Mikhail Gorbachev, interview in *L'Humanité*, 1988.
[5] Gorbachev, CPSU Report to the 27th Congress, 1988. Andrei V. Kozyrev, a senior official in the Foreign Ministry, echoed these views, while seeming to go even further in the rejection of the utility and "realism" of class struggle as a guide to international politics. In the Third World, he said, Moscow has repeatedly aligned itself with dubious military dictatorships professing revolutionary ardor against world imperialism. This alignment tended more to the polarization of the Third World than to social or economic progress, which was not incompatible with trade with the capitalist West. He advocated instead a foreign policy, rejecting dogma, based on "realism," the "interests of our fatherland," and yet, expressing the same tension found in Gorbachev's speeches, "a return to Leninism." "Why Foreign Policy Went Sour," *New York Times*, January 7, 1989, op-ed page.

he raised the hard question of just what place a weakened Russian nation would play in a fast-changing international order.

In the midst of global change, how can we figure out what outcomes are possible, which more or less likely, in order for us to make better policy choices in confusing times? One obviously bad way is to be myopic, driven by newspaper headlines, and focused on the present. Another bad way is to adopt a single abstract guide to war and peace, tortuously interpret the present (and reinterpret the past) in its beam, and march to its prescriptions. And a third bad way is to invoke the real complexity of world politics as an excuse not to try to interpret and prescribe. The first a kind of pragmatism, the second a kind of dogmatism, and the third a kind of excess skepticism; all three are recipes for missing opportunities and repeating past mistakes, for acting on impulse or surrendering to those who do.

A much better way is to reexamine the time-tested classics of ways of war and peace. Three main worldviews have shaped the modern perception of world politics: Realism, Liberalism, and Socialism. The three are rich, complex, deep and directly address the combination of explanation and prescription that we need to overcome a skeptical, passive resignation to the flow of events. Together they can shape a debate designed to avoid dogmatism. And each seeks to generate the longer perspective that can combat excess pragmatism. They put our current debates in a critical light and draw upon the intellectual capital of generations of statesmen and scholars.

Each of these worldviews shares a tradition whose common elements we can construct. Each also has been a self-conscious attempt at connected inquiry. In addition to sharing assumptions and arguments, theorists are engaged in shared projects in which they debate and strive to carry forward an agenda of interpretation and policy.[6]

Each worldview has combined two projects. Each has an empirical, analytic theory explaining political outcomes in both domestic and international politics. Each tells us about the causes of war and peace and their roots in conflict and cooperation, empire and independence. At the same time, they are normative theories corresponding to political values that they want to be and that

[6] Used in the sense of Alasdair MacIntyre, *Whose Justice? Which Rationality?* (Notre Dame: Notre Dame Press: 1988), pp. 324–26. This is a scheme that has analogues in the theory of international political economy. See, for example, Robert Gilpin, *The Political Economy of International Relations,* (Princeton: Princeton University Press, 1987). My description of the three differs from Gilpin's. I regard each as being both descriptive and normative and do not distinguish Realism and Marxism as descriptive and Liberalism as normative for reasons I suggest below. For two insightful normative interpretations of international theory, see Andrew Linklater, *Men and Citizens in the Theory of International Relations* (London: Macmillan, 1990), which focuses on the evolution of world history, and Chris Brown, *International Relations Theory: New Normative Approaches* (New York: Columbia University Press, 1992), which focuses on the cosmopolitan-communitarian debate. A recent valuable intellectual history of international relations theory can be found in Torbjorn Knutsen, *A History of International Relations* (Manchester: Manchester University Press, 1992).

have been chosen by actors in politics, both domestic and international. They prescribe when, if ever, one state should intervene militarily in another state. Should the United States have intervened as it did in Grenada (1983) or Panama (1989) or Haiti (1994)? They consider whether rich societies owe reparations for past exploitation to poor societies. Or, irrespective of blame, do the rich have a moral obligation to assist the poor? Or, instead, do international borders preclude international taxation, obligatory aid payments? Their choices on both intervention and redistribution reflect varying commitments to the state and the nation, to the free individual and his or her duties and rights, to class and solidarity within and between international borders. Political theories of international relations thus see goals as different and consequential.

Those two projects are closely related. A policy maker who wants to shape outcomes needs to understand how the world really does work. He or she particularly needs to know what worldviews are shaping the policies—reflecting their motives and capabilities—of allies and adversaries, or else the policy maker will not know the "levers" to pull. This information is usually opaque or complex and so calls out for theoretical simplification. We, as observers, seek to study how all sides employ their worldviews and, as citizens, are (however amateur) players in the policy-making game.[7]

Realism

The Realist's worldview was shaped by the ancient Greek historian Thucydides, writing twenty-five hundred years ago. Machiavelli in the sixteenth century, Hobbes in the seventeenth century, and Rousseau in the eighteenth century laid the modern foundations of the core of contemporary Realism. They hold in varying degrees that the best description of world politics is a "jungle" characterized by a "state of war," not a single continuous war or constant wars but the constant possibility of war among all states. Politics is gripped by a "state of war" because the nature of humanity, or the character of states, or the structure of international order (or all three together) allows wars to occur. This possibility of war requires that states follow "realpolitik": be self-interested, prepare for war, and calculate relative balances of power. This view is reflected in simple, and hard, attitudes, such as that of Prince Bernhard von Bülow (former German chancellor), who in 1914 declared: "In the struggle between nationalities, one nation is the hammer, the other the anvil; one is the victor, the other the vanquished." This attitude has led to violent campaigns of national aggrandizement and imperialism. But it also shapes desperate efforts to preserve peace through isolation and minimal conceptions of national security. Realist international political science has led the study of international relations for a genera-

[7] A valuable discussion of the policy and interpretive roles of theory can be found in Robert Jervis, *Perception and Misperception in International Politics* (Princeton: Princeton University Press, 1976) and Alexander George, *Presidential Decisionmaking in Foreign Policy: The Effective Use of Information and Advice* (Boulder, Colo.: Westview Press, 1980).

tion. It underlies Kissinger's criticisms of Baker. Although Realists often portray themselves as being free of idealism, accompanying Realist analysis is Realist moral philosophy, which holds that individuals should accept the "national interest" as an ideal, a one true guide to the formulation of the public policy of states in this dangerous international system. Failing to accept the national interest, or reason of state, is a prescription for national disaster, an increase in global violence, and an irresponsible act of statesmanship that places private interests or ideals above public needs. Science and morals are not separate endeavors. Realist moral philosophy makes Realist political science coherent; Realist political science provides an essential description that is needed to justify Realist ethics.

Liberalism

The Liberals draw on Machiavelli's view of republicanism but emerge with Locke's seventeenth-century view of a government of free individuals, defending law and property, and then, in the eighteenth century, a view of Liberal commercialism, pursuing the pacific implications of the free market. At the end of the eighteenth century Immanuel Kant's Liberal republicanism brought markets and rights and republican institutions together, reaffirming the centrality of Liberal politics and setting out the bases of modern theories of individual responsibility, representation, and Liberal internationalism. Rejecting the view of world politics as a "jungle," Liberals' view of word politics is that of a cultivable "garden," which combines a state of war with the possibility of a state of peace. In their view, the state is not a hypothetical single, rational, national actor in a state of war (as it is in the Realist ideal), but a coalition or conglomerate of coalitions and interests, representing individuals and groups. A state's interests are determined, not by its place in the international system, but by which of the many interests, ideals, and activities of its members captures (albeit temporarily) governmental authority. Differentiating between representative republics and autocratic dictatorships, Liberals regard representative states as reflections of individual consent; autocratic states, conversely, they regard as instances of the repression of individual rights. Liberals, as Secretary Baker argued, then hold that these domestic differences have international significance. (Liberals come in conservative, even Reaganite and Thatcherite, and not merely McGovernite and Social Welfareist, varieties.) Domestic values and institutions shape foreign policy, and thus representative and autocratic states are assumed to behave differently. The state of war for many of these Liberals only holds outside the separate peace that they have established among themselves.

Liberal moral theory supports many of those empirical insights with a prescriptive force. Foreign policy should, Liberals thus argue, reflect the rights and duties of individuals. It should serve to support whatever institutional measures would enhance the ability of moral equally human beings to live their own lives, here, there, everywhere. But Liberals greatly differ concerning the practical import of their principles, whether they dictate a strict observance of national sovereignty or permit the possibility of justified intervention and redistribution.

Socialism

Marxist Socialist international theory is by far the best defined of the three modern traditions. (Unlike the two other "churches," its apostles have had to answer to "bishops" and, occasionally, a "pope" or two.) From Marx and Engels's work we can follow a distinct dialogue through the democratic Socialists to Lenin, Stalin, Mao, and current-day interpreters of the canon. For them world politics is intraclass solidarities combined with interclass war waged both across and within state borders. Descriptively, they agree with the Liberals that domestic interests do define the political character of a state and that this definition then shapes the state's foreign policy. They disagree, in that the constitutive feature of the state is a matter not of consensus on domestic political regime that then shapes the international foreign policy of the state, but of a "war" between classes that takes place within and across national boundaries.

Despite an analytic tradition that (as do the Realists) explicitly describes normative questions as ideological, Marxists also rely upon an idealistic commitment to human welfare that makes the determination of international progress an essential feature of both their scientific explanation and their plan for revolutionary liberation.

THREE DISTINCTIONS

I make three distinctive choices that separate the approach of this study from many other theoretical studies of peace and war. It is distinctly political (leaving in all the hard choices politics presupposes). It explores the interests, identities, and institutions that are the philosophical underpinnings of these political choices. And it makes a case for theoretical pluralism separate from three well-established contemporary approaches to the theoretical study of the deep causes of peace and war, those of John Herz, Kenneth Waltz, and Martin Wight.

Clausewitz's Politics

"War is not a mere act of policy, but a true political instrument, a continuation of political activity by other means."[8] The great philosopher of war's famous dictum that we have heard so often was—and still is—more original than it can

[8] Carl von Clausewitz, *On War*, ed. and trans. Michael Howard and Peter Paret (Princeton: Princeton University Press, 1976), p. 87. See the commentary "The Continuing Relevance of *On War*." by Bernard Brodie, ibid., pp 45–60.

now seem. What Clausewitz meant is that war cannot be reduced to any abstract, or metaphysical, structure. It is not an autonomous game produced by fixed external or internal constraints; it is instead a matter of political choice, reflecting all the variety of political purposes that make wars into exterminations or minuets and interventions into liberations or oppressions.

Clausewitz demonstrates the necessarily political character of war by questioning the concept of war as an autonomous activity. He begins with war autonomously considered as a "duel," "an act of force to compel the enemy to do our will."[9] As a bilateral contest between two interdependent unitary actors, the duel leads to maximum use of force. Neither duelist has an interest in surrendering, and therefore neither has a limit short of his total capacity to his reciprocal competition. This is the first "extreme"—the reason why the conflict will become a total war. Victory, moreover, can be achieved only by disarming the enemy; otherwise he will return to the contest. Thus arises the second source of extreme war. Both parties then will exercise their maximum will as well as their total means, since it makes no sense to lose for failure to do so. This is the third extreme.

In practice, however, war is never an isolated act; it takes place in a known environment with known, not abstract, "duelists." War does not consist of a single blow; it spreads over time, leaving time for consideration and changes in resources, allies, and morale. Nor in real life is a war ever final; countries recover. Still, Clausewitz ruminates that war might be made again abstract and total, because nothing he has argued so far would explain how war would ever end. Real world factors might slow down the totalization of war, but if one state sought to postpone the contest, the other would have a reciprocal incentive to speed it up.

In the end war is removed from this abstract chain of totalization by the superiority of the defense over the offense, by the effect of imperfect knowledge (the fog of war), and by the play of chance. A state's decision to shift from offense to defense allows discretion to alter the balance of forces. The fog of war and chance prevent efficient exploitation of advantages. The three together remove war from the game of tight reciprocal interaction, moderate the contest, and slow it down. Freed from reciprocation, statesmen thus must—and now can—exercise choice, making war an instrument of their purposes rather than the tyrant over their polities. Ideas then can shape decisions, and decisions will reshape ideas. Ideology thus comes into play in Erik Erikson's sense of "an unconscious tendency underlying religious and scientific as well as political thought: the tendency at a given time to make facts amenable to ideas, and ideas to facts, in order to create a world image convincing enough to support the collective and individual sense of identity."[10]

[9] Clausewitz, p.77.
[10] Erik Erikson, *Young Man Luther* (New York: Norton, 1958), pp. 26–27. See also Robert

Interests, Identities, and Institutions: A Political Philosophy of World Politics

As political leaders and citizens seek to come to terms with the Clausewitzian "proof" of the necessity of choice, they confront a confusing present and uncertain future. They consider in various ways—usually implicitly—three sets of questions.

First, what should we want? What is required to promote justice or human welfare; or national security, welfare, prestige, and power; or class solidarity and social revolution?

Second, what threats exist to these goals? How might the factors that cause these threats change? Why do such threats arise? What are the most effective ways to achieve the changes we want or avoid the changes we do not? Or, more generally put, how does the relevant world work?

Third, in addition to a set of normative questions—what *should* we do?—and to a set of analytic questions—what *will* happen?—a third set bridges the two, an implicit question of identity: Who or what are *we?*

These questions of course are typical of any political choice.[11] They probe prospective political choices; political ends and means, causes and consequences. They are related: those who seek to guarantee American power see the Soviets as similarly driven; those who seek class solidarity and social revolution see class domination and capitalist imperialism as their leading threats; those who seek individual freedom and the enjoyment of democracy see authoritarian and totalitarian threats. But the connections are not inevitable, nor are they always so clear. Political actors, as the eighteenth-century philosopher Jean-Jacques Rousseau once said, make their political schemes "rotate"; they pursue power in order to become wealthy, wealth in order to exercise power, justice in order to be strong, and strength in order to protect just institutions.[12]

These questions also can help us understand important aspects of the pattern

---

Coles, *Erik Erikson: The Growth of His Work* (Boston: Little, Brown, 1970) and Judith Goldstein and Robert Keohane, eds., *Ideas and Foreign Policy* (Ithaca: Cornell University Press, 1993).

[11] Alexander George discusses fundamental beliefs about human nature and instrumental beliefs about effective strategy as two essential elements of the "operational code" method of analysis in "The Operational Code: A Neglected Approach to the Study of Political Leaders and Decision-Making," *International Studies Quarterly* 13 (1969), pp. 190–222.

[12] "The prince always makes his schemes rotate; he seeks to command in order to enrich himself, and to enrich himself in order to command." J.-J. Rousseau, A *Lasting Peace through the Federation of Europe*, trans. C. E. Vaughan (London: Constable, 1917), p. 99. The best account that I know of the strategies of statesmen involved in the ending of the Cold War is Don Oberdorfer's *The Turn* (New York: Simon and Schuster, 1991), which illustrates the complex mix of worldviews—interpretations and goals, some inspired by Realism others by Liberalism—that shaped the diplomacy of Reagan, Gorbachev, Shultz, and Shevardnadze, and Baker.

of events of the past, when other political actors attempted to interpret and change their worlds, to make political choices and succeeded or failed in them. With the advantage of hindsight, moreover, we as historians and social scientists can begin to do our own secondary analysis of their political ends and means. We can ask not just which policies were good but also which were most influential, when and for whom. We can ask which of the analyses the participants made were accurate and which were not and why. And we can of course judge the results of the ends pursued and the views held, as a way of refining our own political choices. History and historical analysis are different from contemporary politics and political analysis, but only in time.

International political judgments rely on assumptions about interests, moral and material, and institutions, which shape and are shaped by interests. If we want our international theories to help us interpret history in the present and past, what should our theories be able to do?

First, they will need to acknowledge the significance of competing ends—within and among individuals and states.[13] International politics, like all politics, is driven by interests, both material and moral. These wills are normative, expressing the political objectives Clausewitz found as the essence of strategy. They encompass both values and interests. Statespersons, like most individuals, have complex motivations; moral values mix with numerous competing as well as compatible material concerns, both personally and politically. We are driven by "a desire to be able to justify our actions to others on grounds they could not reasonably reject."[14] We cannot separate these drives from those that increase our power, profit, prestige. We uneasily combine these drives in our own wills, we contest over them with our fellow citizens, and representing our states, we compete and cooperate with other representatives of other states.

Second, theories should be able to interpret how we assess threats and opportunities, reflecting both interests and institutions. We especially need to know whether (and, if so, why) those assessments differ within and between states. Does the mere power of foreigners threaten us? Should capability be read as intention when we, lacking world law and order, necessarily lack any guarantee that capability will not be used against us? Or do we need to look at other indications that mix apparent intentions with capabilities?[15] We should be able

[13] Arnold Wolfers in "The Goals of Foreign Policy," in *Discord and Collaboration* (Baltimore: Johns Hopkins University Press, 1962), pp. 67–80, stresses the interrelations of goals and means, ultimate and proximate ends. Interrelating ends, explanations, and policies has long been recognized as being central to the project of international relations theory. See the report on the state of the field by Kenneth Thompson, "Toward a Theory of International Politics," in Stanley Hoffman, ed., *Contemporary Theory in International Relations* (Englewood Cliffs: Prentice Hall, 1960).

[14] Scanlon (1982), p. 116; and for discussion, see Walzer (1987), pp. 46–48.

[15] Walt (1988). Some of these assessments are of course also governed by particular interests. In 1994 the Pentagon considered the rationale justifying the F-22, a new fighter to be built

to analyze the institutional capacities of states. Which states have strong incentives to behave in certain ways because their bureaucracies, interest groups, classes, structure of public opinion, or federal or constitutional structure prejudice them in one direction or another? Do monarchies differ from democracies; capitalists from socialists? Theories need to give us an account of how the environment operates around us.

Third, in the process of answering the first and second, theories will inevitably wind up addressing questions of identity (who we are), simply because what we should want and how we see the world serve to define who we are. World politics is defined by the identity of actors who see themselves as representatives of nations, free citizens, members of a class, or some combination of all three, each of whom is acting in a world political environment that lacks a global source of law and order. This is what makes world politics different from national politics, urban politics, organizational politics, and family politics.[16] Yet within this shared realization of anarchy, identities differ according to differing assumptions about the content of interests and the meaning of institutions.

Theories that help us identify who the actors are by telling us what actors should want, do want, and actually do provide effective guides to explaining and changing world politics. They will cover the larger issues, but they will not enable us to retrace the exact process of decision that led to the end of the Cold War. What theory surrenders, in order to answer the broader questions, are the particularities of the moment and the individual. They miss insights into how individuals, groups, and states assess willingness to bear risk. Are we optimists, pragmatists, pessimists?[17] For example, some Liberals held that a decentralizing, reforming Soviet Union would be a moderate Soviet Union. The United States should thus, they argued, accommodate by freeing the Soviet Union from the Cold War restrictions on trade and welcoming it as a participant in

by Lockheed and Boeing for $70 billion (at $172 million per fighter). The current fighter—the F-15—now dominates all other fighters. The only states now in even a similar league to the United States are the UK, France, and Russia (and those to which they sell?). What is the threat? "Uncertainty is the threat," according to the U.S. Air Force. See "60 Minutes," October 16, 1994.

[16]This is why Raymond Aron and Stanley Hoffmann begin their discussion of international relations theory with the assumption of a "decentralized milieu" (Hoffmann, *Contemporary Theory*, p. 1), before proceeding to discuss the effects of differing domestic societies. For a valuable discussion of recent issues in the theory of international politics, see Alexander Wendt, "The Agent-Structure Problem in International Relations Theory," *International Organization* 413 (1987), pp. 335–70, and Barry Buzan, Charles Jones, and Richard Little, *The Logic of Anarchy* (New York: Columbia University Press, 1993).

[17]For personality factors, Burke and Greenstein (1989). For a discussion of the methodology of role analysis, Martin Hollis and Steven Smith, *Explaining and Understanding* (Oxford: Clarendon, 1990).

international institutions, such as the GATT and the IMF, in which it sought legitimate participation.[18] Others, however, with a similar interest in liberalizing reform argued that the Soviet "leopard" may have changed its spots but that it was still a leopard.[19] Former German Chancellor Helmut Schmidt thus queried: "Am I mad? Will I give Gorbachev a Marshall Plan so that his successor can resume Russian expansionism with a strong economy behind him?"[20] For this group, a protracted crisis and a reversion to Brezhnev stagnation or a military coup were the more likely outcomes of the nationalist rebellion both in Eastern Europe and within the Soviet Union that perestroika, glasnost, and democratization were likely to bring.[21] Factors such as these can influence policy judgments, making Liberals sometimes prescribe like Realists, and vice versa.

Nor do theories give us accounts of the particular capacities of states in a specific international setting. Which state is more powerful, where, on what issues—now and here? As the USSR collapsed, former Secretary of State Kissinger and former National Security Adviser Brzezinski recommended balancing against Russian power by aiding Ukraine against Russia, in a classic balance of power logic.[22] Other Realist views emphasized a supposed increase in Asian power (Japan and China), leading to a relative decline in Soviet and American power. Following the logic of traditional Realist balancing of power, this provided an incentive for a realignment of interests and allegiances, with the United States and the Soviet Union joining to contain the new Asian center of world power.[23] Also in a Realist spirit, however, were very different views perceiving a need to end the Cold War with Russia. The most straightforward

[18] The clearest expression of this widely shared Liberal viewpoint I have found is Richard Ullman's insightful essay (1988). I summarize its major claims in the paragraph above. The spiritual ancestor of these analyses is George Kennan's "America and the Russian Future," *Foreign Affairs* (April 1951), which sets forth the conditions needed for a "peace" in the Cold War. There he stressed three changes: (1) the lifting of the iron curtain, or allowing for an openness and moderation in Soviet foreign policy, (2) the detotalitarianization of Soviet domestic society, particularly refraining from enslaving its own labor, and (3) the freeing of oppressed nationalities both within and without the Soviet Union. Forty years later, Kennan's conditions were more modest; see next.

[19] Richard Nixon (1988) quotes Simes to this effect, p. 45.

[20] *Economist* (December 1988), p. 40. The Group of Seven Meeting in France on July 15, 1989, achieved a compromise of progressive and conservative views when it offered aid to the democratizing Soviet bloc while asserting that complete democratization and liberalization, together with "commercial" relations, were prerequisites of economic aid and peaceful relations (*New York Times*, July 16, 1989).

[21] Brzezinski, *The Grand Failure* (1989).

[22] See a good account of these debates in U.S. foreign policy in Alexander Dallin, "America's Search for a Policy toward the Former Soviet Union," *Current History* (October 1992).

[23] Liska, (1986).

stressed that the Soviet Union no longer posed a subversive threat to Western Europe, as it may have in the immediate postwar period. The two nuclear superpowers had (and have) rational, overwhelmingly mutual interests in arms control and curbing their arms race, eminent Russian expert George Kennan advised in 1989. Security, he argued, is necessarily mutual in the nuclear age; it requires accommodation, not confrontation. Without the specific content, policy has no referent.[24] Theory therefore can never serve as a history or a recipe; it is a guide to how to analyze and justify policy, now and in the past, and not a replacement for strategy.

Still, theories can help structure the interpretation of history. Ends pursued, threats and means assessed: An ideal interpretation would cover all these considerations and perhaps more.[25] And theories should lend themselves to being combined and reconstructed so that they can become as close to the reality experienced as possible.

That, however, is only one role of theory. Theory can lend coherence to observations and thereby make them the interpretations that make sense of otherwise meaningless or at least confusing events, such as the endings and beginnings of cold wars. But even as it does that, it necessarily begins to do something more, which is to explain why one interpretation is more apt than another.

To interpret choices—whether today, in 1989, or in 1945—we will need to compare and contrast implications drawn from the differing interpretations of ends, interests, and institutions that seek or sought to shape what states should do in order to see which explains better when and where. Interpreting history thus leads us into theory. Realism, Liberalism, and Socialism reflect three possible combinations of normative and cognitive worldviews. They neither are nor were the only three worldviews. But they are three classic choices whose global competition shaped the twentieth century.

Skinning Cats, Blooming Flowers, and Basketing Eggs: The Value of Theoretical Pluralism

This approach attempts to be genuinely pluralist, exploring the strengths as well as the weaknesses of three traditions holding that at the end of the twenti-

[24] Richard Ned Lebow's study of international crises draws useful distinctions between context and event that parallel the differences between general theory and reconstructing specific policy choices. See *Between Peace and War* (Baltimore: Johns Hopkins University Press. 1981).

[25] For example, an empirical statistical demonstration of the limitations of single factor analysis can be found in Bruce Bueno do Mesquita and David Lalman, "Empirical Support for Systemic and Dyadic Explanations of International Conflict," *World Politics* XLI, 1 (October 1988), pp. 1–20; and a formal demonstration in James D. Morrow,"Social Choice and System Structure in World Politics," *World Politics* XLI, 1 (October 1988), pp. 75–97.

eth century, each is necessary for our comprehension of world politics. In doing so, it steps aside from three leading theoretical approaches, each of which privileged a chosen path.

Idealism versus Realism. Scholars in the field have drawn a classic distinction between "Idealist" and "Realist" theory. Following the collapse of internationalism, international law, and the League of Nations during the Great Depression of the 1930s, post–World War Two scholars sought to separate international theory from its supposed interwar "idealism." The classic criticism of "idealism" by John Herz in 1950 was subtle and balanced.[26] Herz focused on three forms of utopian internationalism: Mazzinian nationalism, Marxist Socialist internationalism, and Cobdenite commercial pacifism. For each, whether a world of free nations, liberated working classes, or competitive capitalism, fulfillment meant peace. But each neglected, Herz charged, the "security dilemma," which consists of the dilemma all states face. Realists warn us that without a world government, no state will be able to trust other states because it cannot be assured of their peaceful intentions. Whether those intentions appear to be satisfied nationalism, Socialist internationalism, or commercial pacifism, each state's defenses appear to be potential offensive preparations to other states. The result: "A vicious circle will arise—of suspicion and countersuspicion, competition for power, armament races, ultimately war."[27]

We will reconsider the accuracy of this important indictment of Liberalism and Socialism later, but for now let us consider if this is a useful way to categorize theory. Are some theories idealistic while others are realistic? Herz is aware that Realism can be transformed into an ideological glorification of power politics (such as it was by Nazism) and warns us of these dangers.[28] But is even the prudent version that he favors free from ideational—ideological and moral—foundations?

Is a consistent Realism possible? If we assume a state as the self-interested Realistic actor, we must ask, What makes a state a unit, what unifies it? If the head of state himself (or herself) is incapable of alone wielding coercive authority, what holds it together? If a coalition of factions, what holds each group together? If a group is a coalition of individuals, what makes them adhere long enough and reliably enough to constitute an actor themselves? And individuals are not—indeed cannot be, Realists tell us—independent actors in world politics. Somewhere along the way, we need solidarity (at least among "thieves"?),

[26] John Herz, "Idealist Internationalism and the Security Dilemma," *World Politics* 2, 2 (January 1950), pp. 157—80; and more extensively in *Political Realism and Political Idealism* (Chicago: University of Chicago Press, 1951).
[27] From the Introduction to Herz's *The Nation State and the Crisis of World Politics* (New York: McKay, 1976), p. 10, which contains a reprint of his essay "Idealism and the Security Dilemma."
[28] Ibid., pp. 95–98.

shared values, or legitimacy to make groups cohere. In just this way, rational corporate strategy presupposes corporate hierarchy, a ladder of authority from CEO to organization, employer to employees, which in turn rests on a law of incorporation. Market behavior presupposes an agreement on property.[29]

As we shall see, one of the substantial virtues of the classical approach to international theory is that it was the classical theorists (unlike often their modern counterparts and followers) who made these ideal presuppositions behind Realist theory explicit. Differing "ideal" presuppositions accounted for differing types of Realism, from Machiavelli's entrepreneurialism to Hobbes's statism and Rousseau's nationalism. At the same time, the supposed idealists, such as Cobden and Marx, in fact rested their arguments on material, very "realistic" portrayals of social conflict.

Levels of Analysis. A second approach addresses the classic debate on the levels of analysis ranging from the individual to the structure of domestic society to the structure of the international system. The most influential application of this approach has been Kenneth Waltz's magisterial *Man, the State and War.* It has shaped a generation of scholarship in the field with an analysis of the "state of war" through an examination of the adequacy of three "images." The first sought to explain war by human nature; the second, by the internal structure of states; and the third, by international anarchy.[30] The accomplishments of the work lay not merely in the range of theorists that he analyzed but in the incisive criticism of the first two images.

The first image holds that, to simplify, good men—the Gandhis of the world—preserve peace; bad men—the Hitlers—create war. Human nature, furthermore, is either fixed—and therefore individual men are (if evil) irredeemable or in mass (for the religious-minded) damned—or changeable, and we can reform or at least learn.[31]

Waltz found this image inadequate for four reasons that reveal his criteria of what constitutes explanatory merit.[32] First, the human nature explanation is *empirically* weak. Too many "good" statesmen have engaged in war; too many bad statesmen have maintained peace (in their conduct of foreign relations). Second, it was *logically* contradictory. If human nature is fixed, and if the empirical contradictions above held, then the opposite cause produced identi-

[29] Good surveys of these issues can be found in "Individualism and Social Thought," chapter 3 of *Forms of Explanation* by Alan Garfinkel and Abba Lerner, "The Economics and Politics of Consumer Sovereignty," *American Economic* Review 62 (1972), p. 258.

[30] Kenneth Waltz, *Man, the State and War: A Theoretical Analysis* (New York: Columbia University Press, 1954); see also for a related approach, J. David Singer, "The Level of Analysis Problem in International Relations," *World Politics* 14 (October 1961).

[31] Waltz, chaps. 2 and 3.

[32] The criteria employed are essentially straightforward applications of Popper's falsification method as a way of eliminating weak theories.

cal effects. And if the same statesmen are sometimes at war and sometimes at peace (in otherwise similar circumstances, we should add), then the same cause is producing opposite effects. Third, even if the first two criteria were met to some minimally satisfactory degree, we might hesitate before adopting changes in human nature as a *practical* approach to international reform. Given the pervasiveness of war in history and the constancy of human nature, the human image of war would be the equivalent of mere resignation or of waiting for divine retribution. If human nature is in fact changeable and if war is a product of masses of human beings whether similar or differentiated in character, we then should seek out the social, not the individual psychological, causes of learning or elite replacement. And fourth, even if all the above criteria were satisfied, we should still want to ask whether any proposed reforms suggested by adherents of the particular image were *morally* desirable. Were their indirect consequences or methods morally reprehensible, as would, for example, be coercive reeducation camps as purges for aggressive instincts?

Waltz applies similar criticisms to Image II, the internal structures of states as the causes of war. Richard Cobden, a nineteenth-century British Liberal, once argued that because democratic states represent citizens who bear the harmful consequences of war, democratic states are inherently repelled by the idea of engaging in war. So, too, some Socialists have held that capitalist profit mongering is a fundamental cause of war. Under Socialism, they added, all aggressive impulses would disappear, leaving a peaceful world. But, as Waltz notes, both democracies and Socialist (or Communist) regimes have and do continue to fight many wars.

Having refuted, or disconfirmed, the first two images, Waltz thus adopts Image III, "War," or international anarchy, as his model of the essential cause of war. Individual leaders sometimes provoke a war, some wars are started because of domestic pressures within states, but the fundamental reason why interstate relations are in a state of war—a "condition wherein the will to battle is sufficiently known," in Hobbes's phrase—is that international anarchy means there is nothing to prevent it. Unlike the hierarchical domestic order, the anarchic international system contains no regular monopoly of violence. Many disputes arise, and they readily escalate to the ultimate arbitration of war.

The coherence, the clarity, the seeming escape from political polemics into structural analysis: These are traits of the Waltzian argument that are the more obvious sources of its influence on the field. But there are many reasons that make it less than a sufficient, general foundation for international political theory. Most obviously, like human nature and domestic structure (which produced both peace and war), international anarchy produces both peace and war. Anarchy per se, moreover, is compatible with a considerable degree of order and even social equality. Among anarchic ("acephalous") tribal societies order results from community and equality.[33] We need more to explore the effects of international anarchy and to develop a theory of peace and war.

Another problem bears on how we categorize theorists. Dividing the arguments of the philosophers according to whether they emphasize the sources of war in man, the state, or the structure of the international system was obviously a productive strategy for categorizing a wide variety of views bearing on international politics. But dividing the philosophers along those analytical lines distorts their conceptions of the coherence and integrity of the political life of man. That political life is composed of the relation between his nature, the opportunities and constraints of the domestic politics of states, and the conditions of world politics. The major philosophies embody assumptions about all three levels of analysis.

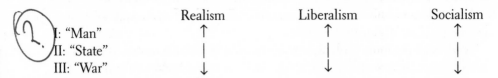

	Realism	Liberalism	Socialism
I: "Man"	↑	↑	↑
II: "State"	|	|	|
III: "War"	↓	↓	↓

Although political philosophers have focused their attention at different "horizontal" levels of analysis, they have not created separate "man," "state," and "war" philosophies.[34]

In this book I would like to explore what we can learn from the "vertical" relations among views of man, the state, and war embodied in each of Realism, Liberalism, and Socialism. Does Realism's emphasis on the condition of anarchy presuppose a certain kind of state or a certain view of human nature? Does Liberalism's focus on domestic constitutional arrangements or Marxism's attention to class struggles presume a special view of world politics, a different view of human nature? What difference within Realist, Liberal, or Socialist philosophies do more particular differences in each of the assumptions make for their understandings of international relations? Can we fill in the gaps in Image III (Structural) Realism and counter the weaknesses allegedly found in Liberalism and Socialism?

Worldviews. If philosophers cannot be well categorized as either Idealists or

[33] See Michael Taylor, *Community, Anarchy and Liberty* (Cambridge: Cambridge University Press, 1982), pp. 65–94.

[34] Waltz notes that his categories override these more thorough views of the theorists—"Introduction" to *Man, the State, and War*—but he concentrates on the three images in order to develop a model of the causes of war in general. For a survey of a large number of political philosophers and their views on international relations, see F. Parkinson, *The Philosophy of International Relations* (Beverly Hills: Sage, 1977). And for an excellent collection and commentary on approaches to international relations theory, see Paul Viotti and Mark Kauppi, eds., *International Relations Theory* (New York: Macmillan, 1993).

Realists and they do not neatly trisect according to whether they are theorists of human nature, domestic structure, or international structure, how effective is an alternative—grouping them by worldview, by programs and consequences rather than by causes? This was just the categorization adopted by Martin Wight and followed by Hedley Bull as they sought to organize what (despite their initial skepticism) they found in international theory.[35] Wight divided theorists into three groups: Revolutionaries, Realists, and Rationalists.

The *Revolutionaries* think international anarchy is, could, and should be transcended by moral unities of a cosmopolitan and "missionary" character. Revolutionaries, include religious zealots of the sixteenth-and seventeenth-century Protestant Reformation and Catholic Counter-Reformation, French Jacobins, Joseph Stalin and Adolf Hitler. Their philosophers are Jean Calvin, J. J. Rousseau, and Karl Marx, but their essential embodiment is Immanuel Kant, the philosopher of universal republicanism. Their mode of reasoning is preeminently ethical, an argument for reform.

The *Realists* are more familiar. For the Realists, international anarchy means a necessary engagement in power politics and warfare. Doubting the reality of international norms, they regard normative claims from a sociological point of view, as reflections of the interests of those who at the time dominate international politics. Machiavelli and Hobbes are their preeminent theorists; Carr Kennan and Morgenthau, their modern followers. Their reasoning is sociological: how the world does (and must) work.

The *Rationalists* are Wight's preferred and most distinctive contribution. A *via media* in between the cosmopolitanism of the Revolutionists and the power politics of the Realists, they portray international relations as a society governed by a set of consensual rules among independent and mutually self-respecting states, all tied together with treaties and commerce. Reason for them is a cardinal source of knowledge, of rights and duties, each of which concords with interests—when rationally perceived. Wight attaches Locke and Grotius to it as the central figures. Earlier Thomas Aquinas and the Spanish jurists Francisco Vitoria and Francisco Suarez, and later Edmund Burke, Richard Cobden and J. S. Mill, Alexis de Tocqueville and Abraham Lincoln all played roles. Kant too

[35] Martin Wight's most famous essay on international theory was "Why Is There No International Theory?" in Herbert Butterfield and M. Wight, eds., *Diplomatic Investigations* (London: Allen and Unwin, 1966), chap. 1. Despite the unpromising title (which really said there was no world polis to theorize about), in *International Theory*, Gabriele Wight and Brian Porter (New York: Holmes and Meier, 1992) have offered Wight's own lifelong reflections on international theory. It is an edited version of Wight's lecture notes, which were very influential in shaping the British tradition of international studies. See also Hedley Bull, *The Anarchical Society* (New York: Columbia University Press, 1977), which adopts Wight's categorization, and Hedley Bull, Benedict Kingsbury, and Adam Roberts, eds., *Hugo Grotius and International Relations* (Oxford: Clarendon, 1990).

appears, and so does Wilson and the League. Indeed, as Wight acknowledges, it is the "broad middle road" that meanders and sometimes narrows and often loses its edges.[36] Their reasoning is teleological, how the world can and will evolve.

Like Kenneth Waltz's three "images" of world politics, Wight's three "traditions" contribute to an insightful catalog of policy choices in world politics. They acknowledge the "vertical" integrity of philosophical perspectives that combine insights on "man," "state" and "war." But have we been offered a useful key to categorizing international thought?

Many share the respect for moderation that drives Wight's view of the world and of what is possible and just within it. But has he created "straw men" in his depictions of the Realists and Revolutionists? No modern interpretation of Hobbes corresponds to the "Realist"; none of Kant or Marx truly fits "Revolutionist." All, on the other hand, share significant features of rationalism, differing in their reasons for it. Hobbes, as we shall see, was a firm believer in the virtue of reasonable prudence and duty to seek peace (where possible), an advocate of the balance of power, and a defender of the efficacy of international commerce. Kant firmly defended an international order of independent states and utterly opposed the idea of world state (his *foedus pacificum* was limited to a mutual security treaty, hospitality and commerce), rejected missionary interventions as almost always morally wrong and prudentially dangerous, and found world empire mongering repulsive (if that is not too weak a word). (Marx too shares these strictures against premature one-worldism.)

Moreover, can one really find three streams throughout the history of international thought that give us room for a coherent, significant, and convenient middle of the sort Wight describes? At various points in the discourse of international relations some theorists have defined themselves against a real debate having relevant extremes. In particular, in the early modern period scholars of international law reacted against the two prevalent imperialisms: Dante's universal Christian monarchy, on the one hand, and Machiavelli's imperialist, nationalist republicanism, on the other. Wight's mistake is to regard these as equivalent to continuous modern projects of "Revolutionism" and "Realism." The stretch just doesn't work.

[36] *International Theory*, p. 15. For a perceptive study of the Wight *via media*, see "The Idea of International Society," a dissertation by Dr. Ursula Vollerthun (Australian National University, 1992). But the difficulty of discerning just what the *via media* might be is nowhere better illustrated than in Hedley Bull's critical review of Michael Walzer's *Just and Unjust Wars*, the outstanding attempt to combine the practical reasoning of Realism and Liberalism. Bull criticizes Walzer for failing to find a principled *via media*, a logical foundation that combines individualist and collectivist conceptions of obligation. Bull, the preeminent expositor of Grotianism, himself suggests no such foundation. See "Recapturing the Just War for Political Theory," *World Politics* 31 (1979), pp. 588–99.

Ironically, Wight, who pointedly derided the idea of an autonomous international theory,[37] has himself created an unduly internationalist set of categories. Acknowledging the absence of a world state, he began by advocating an idea of international theory that must remain inherently derivative—political theory with secondary international implications. That was an insight worth retaining, and one I gratefully borrow.

PLAN

Thus this book focuses on political theories of world politics. It will explain the view each theoretical tradition takes of world politics—whether as a state of war, a state of peace, or a mixture of both. The chapters that follow will examine why each theory holds the view it does. They also will explore the causes of particular wars and particular peaces and outline the strategy of peace each theory proposes. Each section of the book thus assesses the strengths and weaknesses of the explanation that each theoretical tradition offers and the value of the strategies for peace that the traditions present.

My approach will build on Waltz's assumption of international anarchy and Wight's integral (vertical) perspective on political philosophy. The work critically examines Realism, Liberalism, and Socialism as philosophies that address our competing identities, interests, and institutions. These traditions make claims about both the way that world politics does work and the way it should. I will therefore evaluate each theory not only on its own analytical terms but also on its capacity to explain significant regularities, trends, and episodes in peace and war among states. I will also consider what each theoretical tradition tells us about crucial issues of contemporary international policy: international intervention, international redistribution, and the prospects for the transformation of world politics.

Part One examines the theory of Realism. Beginning with the classic text of international relations (Thucydides's *Peloponnesian War*), I identify what is at the core of the Realist worldview of the "state of war" among independent states. I explore the reasons Thucydides advances for the constrained role that moral choices can play in the options available to responsible heads of state. I then examine three modem variants of Realism: the entrepreneurial view of Machiavellian leadership, the structural theory of Hobbesian balance of power, and the tragic perspective of the Rousseauian sociology of the state of war.

I illustrate the power of their insights in historical examples and in an extensive case study of the core insight of Realist theory, the balance of power. I

[37] Wight, "Why Is There No International Theory?"

develop a set of indicators for whether states are actually balancing power (considered as capabilities) and then test these indicators against the self-understanding and actions of statespersons in the era when the conditions for balance of power politics were better met than they had ever been before or have been since—during, that is, the classical age of the balance between 1713 and 1789. I examine what statespersons such as Frederick the Great thought of the balance of power. I then consider whether the alliances they actually formed corresponded to the implicit rules of "counterpoise" and "equipoise," measures that I derive from eighteenth-century theories of the balance of power. I find that balancing behavior does explain international alignments in that century (including the famous Diplomatic Revolution of 1756), and consider why the theory of balance does so much less satisfactorily as a complete model of international politics in the period before and after its "classic" age.

Part Two analyzes international Liberalism. Examining the wide variety of Liberal theory, including Locke's Liberal legalism, Smith's (and Schumpeter's) Liberal pacifism, and Kant's Liberal internationalism, I employ historical examples to illustrate each of these traditions. More extensive case studies and comparisons investigate the two most significant legacies of Liberalism in foreign affairs: the zone of peace among Liberal states, which Kant first recognized, and the tendency of Liberal states to engage in imprudent (often aggressive) policy toward non-Liberal states.

In Part Three, I discuss Socialism, focusing on Marx's ideas on the effects of class solidarity and class conflict on international relations. I trace Lenin's transformation of Marx's theory of capitalist solidarity into a theory of capitalist war and explain how Lenin turned Marx's observations on the economic and political effects of imperialism into a coherent (not necessarily correct) theory of imperialism. Again, I analyze these ideas in historical context as I reassess the "Great Betrayal" of August 1914, when the Socialist parties seemed to abandon international class solidarity by voting with their national governments for war.

The overall purpose of these parts is to explore the following general hypothesis: When we hold these theories up to more rigorous standards of explanation and examine them in the light of historical experience, each has a comparative advantage in explaining certain kinds of international events and the foreign policy of different types of actors. In the course of testing the general hypothesis, I illustrate the particular comparative advantages of each theory.

Part Four takes up two difficult problems confronting citizens and politicians in international politics today. By focusing on intervention and redistribution, I evaluate the potential policy guidance within each theory.

In these chapters I investigate the guidance Realism, Liberalism, and Socialism provide for international intervention and redistribution. Here I examine the explicit and implicit recommendations that the three traditions offer concerning the significance of political and economic borders.

I shall assess the implications of their remarks for the choices U.S. officials and citizens had to make when they decided whether to invade or, as citizens, to endorse the U.S. invasion of Grenada. What moral criteria were employed to explain the intervention? Did the security of the United States or the promotion of human rights actually justify the invasion? In an interdependent world can any government that does not meet the standards of human rights (including civil liberties, political democracy, and various welfare rights) be said to have a secure right to political independence and territorial integrity?

Taking up the global distribution of income, I discuss what criteria are, and what criteria should be, used to weigh the merits of the legislation designed to fund international development through bilateral foreign aid and multilateral institutions (such as the World Bank and the Inter-American Development Bank). Is such funding designed to promote the security and prosperity of the United States or to enhance democracy overseas or solely to further the basic human needs of the disadvantaged, and should it be? Does the suffering of the world's poor impose a duty to alleviate global poverty on the world's rich? If so, are there any just limits to this duty, short of global equality?

The purpose of these chapters is to explore the differing standards for assessing ends, means, and consequences that the three traditions identify. But I also want to determine how severe the different choices need to be. To what extent can moral statesmanship reduce the trade-offs among national security, human rights, and global social progress that the traditions highlight?

I conclude with a discussion of the future of world politics. What are the competing conceptions of world peace? Is Liberalism, as some have recently claimed, about to triumph by "ending history"? Is Marxism "dead"? Will the nation-state become obsolete? Doubting the proximity of a Liberal triumph and the demise of Socialism, I explore how statesmen can try to manage their foreign affairs in an age of political diversity. In the end, they are bound not to be sufficient, even in combination: real political choice is too complex and arbitrary to be determined by theoretical speculation. Modern world politics reflect Realist, Liberal, and Socialist tendencies. Modern individuals have divided political souls, tugged by the competing claims of nation, class, and individual rights. But, taking stock of the existing repertoire of thought about the ways of peace and war, we should prepare to perceive what is familiar and what is truly new, what consequences can follow which choices and which are truly unknown. This is as much as we can expect from theory, and we would be unwise to settle for less.

But why, you ask, focus on these three, Realism, Liberalism, and Socialism? Are they perennial? Will they endure? All three of the paradigms are time-bound. Two hundred years ago there obviously was no Marxist Socialist paradigm. The Liberal tradition was just, with the American and French revolutions, beginning to move from the philosophers' studies to the assemblies of power. Then a study such as this one would have focused on the debate between Realism and Christianity, making Machiavelli and Hobbes, on the one hand, and the Counter-Reformation, on the other, the central divide. Or perhaps the focus would have been on the rising "West" against the "rest" (of the world). Today some say Marxist Socialism is about to disappear altogether (much too premature a judgment, I will argue). These paradigms are also space-bound. Each is Western.

Thus the clear answer is that there is no reason other than either convention or convenience to stop at three. Today scholars are exploring philosophers of the warring states period in China, Talmudic scholarship on war and peace, Islamic international theory and the impact of differing civilizations. A gender-sensitive interpretation opens new aspects of world politics, as do approaches that explore the integrity of planetary ecology. Many of these new approaches do not claim to be comprehensive worldviews, adopting instead perspectives that critically enhance the traditional political paradigms. But some do make the larger claims. Should Khomeini's followers succeed in transforming the Middle East, we shall need a chapter on Shiite Islamic thought and institutions. If Medvedev and Gorbachev and their followers had succeeded in replacing Marxist-Leninism with whatever they meant by global humanism and market economics, more chapters still will be or would have had to be written. We shall all learn something if they succeed.

Realism, Liberalism, and Socialism have long been dominant in the West. Yet with the spreading influence of nationalism, industrialism, and individualism around the world, each has come to have significant influence far from their European genesis. Philosophers, moreover, have successively transformed our understandings in part in response to historical events. (The nuclear revolution of the postwar period has significantly enhanced the significance of "enemy" and subtly undermined the significance of "ally.")

The argument of the book is designed to show the usefulness of these integral conceptions of international political theories. It examines how descriptive claims about human nature, domestic politics, and world politics are related to one another. And it seeks to restore a focus on normative political choice. I place competing views of human capacities, domestic political ends, and the opportunities of world politics at the center of the study of world politics. In particular, I focus on three choices that have been the predominant sets of alternatives for secular politics in the modern world: Realism, Liberalism, and Socialism.

In doing this, I think I shall be coming closer to the competing understandings of world politics that characterize the actual political contests that take place within a very large number of modern states. I do not attempt to impose an overarching model of world politics on these separate claims to political allegiance. Theory does not and should not track the detailed and highly specific debates that have influenced the actual course of international diplomacy. It thus cannot provide a recipe for the conduct of either just or effective foreign policy. Subject to critical empirical assessment, a guide to moral argument in international politics, theory has tended to shape the general concepts within which particular debates are framed.

Arnold Wolfers wrote what should be a credo for the international political theorist: "If there is any difference between today's political scientist and his predecessors (the classical political theorists)—who, like himself, were confronted with such problems as alliance policy, the balancing of power, intervention in the affairs of other countries, and the pursuit of ideological goals—one would hope it might lie in a keener realization of the controversial and tentative nature of his reply, in a greater effort to consider alternative answers, and in a more conscious attempt to remain dispassionate and objective."[38]

[38]Arnold Wolfers, "Political Theory and International Relations," introduction to Arnold Wolfers and Laurence Martin, eds., *The Anglo-American Tradition in Foreign Affairs* (New Haven: Yale University Press, 1956) and in *Discord and Collaboration*, p. 237.

PART ONE

REALISM

INTRODUCTION

The Range of Realism

REALISM IS OUR dominant theory. Most international relations scholars are either self-identified or readily identifiable Realists. Most of our scholarship examines concepts derived from Realist models. In one exhaustive study of the development of the Realist "paradigm" since World War II, almost three-quarters of all the phenomena noted, and over 90 percent of the hypotheses tested, were identifiably Realist in inspiration.[1] Realism, moreover, is our most distinctive theory, the theory that, for some, promises an explanation of international politics grounded in nothing below or beyond the anarchy of interstate relations itself. And Realism, our oldest theory, newly inspires creative work in applications of game theory, political psychology, and political economy.

Yet its philosophical foundations in Thucydides, Machiavelli, Hobbes, and Rousseau are unduly obscure. On the one hand, we too readily integrate its competing basic tenets into a comprehensive causal model and philosophy of life, the Structural-Realist model.[2] Or we tend to define Realists as the sum of

[1] John Vasquez, *The Power of Power Politics: A Critique* (New Brunswick, N.J.: Rutgers University Press, 1983), chap. 5, especially tables 5.1 (indicating that 74.9 percent of the indicators in the field were Realist), 6.1, 6.2 and 6.3 (indicating that 92 percent of the hypotheses and 94 percent of the variables tested were Realist). A wider survey of the field taken in 1972 (which included those more historically inclined) identified the American Realist Hans Morgenthau as the leading scholar of international relations and his *Politics among Nations* as the leading book (Vasquez, pp. 43–44). The overwhelming majority of other postwar general theorists have worked inside the Realist tradition.

[2] For example, Robert Jervis, in a recent account comparing Realism and game theory, captures the conventional practical wisdom well when he describes Realism unproblematically and in shorthand as "structural, strategic, and rational unitary" (1988, p. 318). For a discussion of Realism in the context of the interdependence literature, see Weltman (1974).

their criticisms: the opponents of idealism or the critics of moralism, legalism, cosmopolitanism, or rationalism.[3] Realists are sometimes reduced to a single identification, the philosophers of force. One important stream of popular culture grasps Realism by that "hard nose." In between descents into the 1993 violences of Bosnia and Rwanda, Christiane Amanpour, the ubiquitous CNN war correspondent, declared herself for the Realist stereotype: "I believe in the law of the jungle. There are strong and there are weak; there is an order in our species and our world. What's happening now is that no one seems to know what the order is. . . . Whatever anyone says, it's just about power."[4]

On the other hand, Realists are too readily dichotomized by others into tangential distinctions between, for example, traditional Realists and Neo-Realists, adherents of scientific-statistical or interpretive-historical methods. The most vociferous group of these critics draws a line between the structural and scientific Structural "Neo-Realism" of today, and the interpretive and historical "classical Realism" of Morgenthau and his predecessors back to Thucydides.[5] Structural Neo-Realism the critics decry as statist, utilitarian, and positivistic ("an ideological move toward the economization of politics").[6] Classical Realism, on the other hand, though incomplete, respects political judgment and the politics of the historical, traditional practice of international politics, according to the same critics.

In this part, I attempt three tasks:

First, I would like to retrieve the political arguments made by the Realists.[7] I want to rescue the Realists from the charge of "economism" by examining the political values and choices that have shaped the arguments made by Realist philosophers of interstate politics. I also want to rescue them from the charge of irrationalism (aggressiveness for its own sake) by showing how their political analysis portrays politics as a means designed to advance the ends they posit.

Second, I would like to rescue Realism from the charge of monolithism. I

[3] I think George Kennan's conception of Realism, described in the essays in *American Diplomacy*, is best understood as practical criticism of what he considers various excesses of American diplomacy. In this respect, he follows the Thucydidean tradition.

[4] Stephen Kinzer, "Where There's a War There's Amanpour," *New York Times Magazine* (October 9, 1994), p 58.

[5] Ashley (1984), and Walker (1987).

[6] See Alker (1981) for a similar criticism in which he focuses on the dialectical logic of world politics. Stanley Hoffmann (1977, p. 44) also defended a discontinuity thesis in the social scientific variant of international relations. But he placed the break at, not after, Morgenthau. Hoffmann noted Morgenthau's claim to having discovered a set of laws of power, which established a scientific field of endeavor that took root in postwar America in the new discipline of international relations—"An American Social Science."

[7] Thus I am not considering Realism in the philosophical sense of a philosophy "adequate to reality" of Berki (1981, pp. 67–69) or Navari's (1982) definition of real Realism based on the ontology of historical forces (in distinction to Hobbes, the nominalist and philosophical rationalist).

Realism = World is a "jungle".
War is continuous due to political insecurity.

want to distinguish what divided the philosophic founders and still divides influential strands of contemporary Realism. I do this by showing how, even though each concentrates on one of the three levels of analysis, or Waltzian "Images"—the individual (1), the domestic constitution (2), or the international system (3)—each requires some set of necessary assumptions drawn from the other levels in order to make its argument complete and coherent.

Third, and on the other hand, I would also like to rescue the Realists from radical dichotomization, or extreme fragmentation, or incoherence. Here I explore what unites Realism.[8] What is it that despite their differences makes Realists part of a single approach toward the hard choices that arise in world politics?

Realists, I plan to show, are united in a set of views about reality. These views distinguish them from other analytic traditions, and their differences as measured against other worldviews establish a common identity. They share a skeptical attitude toward schemes for pacific international order.[9] They also share analytical assumptions. Realists, unlike Socialists, assume that state interests should and in most cases do dominate class interests. Unlike Liberals, they assume that state interests should and can be distinguished from individual rights. As theorists they hold that generalization is both possible and useful.

Beyond these political and scientific goals, their most important source of unity is a distinctive view of what constitutes international politics (their "dependent variable"). They are the theorists of the "state of war." They discount any claims to system-wide international order other than that based ultimately on power or force, finding instead that among independent states, or other international actors, international society is best described as a condition of international anarchy. This is a condition that places all states in a warlike situation of reciprocal insecurity in which every alliance is temporary and every other state is a possible enemy, which makes, Hobbes argued, the possibility of war continuous. All states face in varying degrees a "security dilemma": self-help is the only route to political security, and self-help makes other states insecure.

Their causal and normative routes to these conclusions differ markedly. While some of the differences among Realist theorists are illusory, others are real. Some search for, and claim to have found, deeply grounded or structurally

[8] I want to differ from a too-natural skepticism such as that casually expressed in Stanley Hoffmann's skeptical remark ". . . we are all realists now, but there are not two realists who agree either in their analysis of what is, or on what ought to be, or on how to get from here to there" (1981, p. 659).

[9] John Vincent has called the attitude Realist "cold water." It consists of admonitions: "International politics is a struggle for power; war is inevitable in the international anarchy; there is no right and wrong, only competing conceptions of right; there is no society beyond the state; international law is an empty phrase" (1981, p. 93).

Directions of Realist Thought

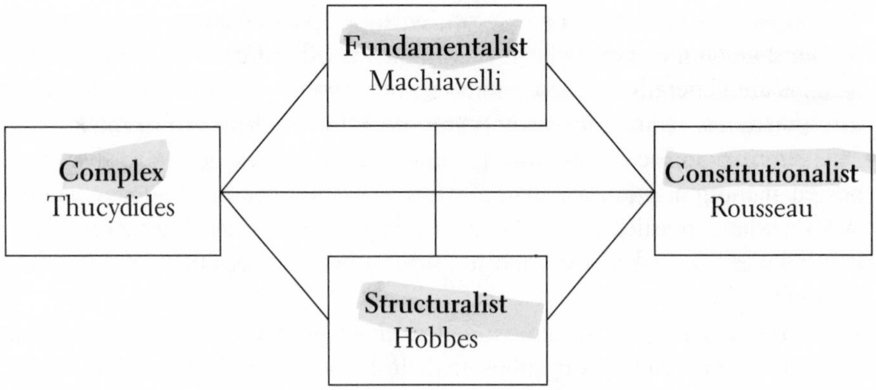

determined scientific generalizations; others deny the possibility of anything but contingently generalizable insight severely limited by contextual diversity. Some base their Realism directly on the competitive drives of human nature; others, primarily on international anarchy; still others, only on a particular combination of the two that stresses the varying effects of domestic social institutions. These differences lead to differing conclusions on the prospects for peace and war, cooperation and conflict, and empire and independence, as well as to differing judgments on how states can best pursue their interests. When these considerations are taken together, three elective affinities of assumptions, arguments and conclusions—three schools of interpretation—emerge. They all derive from historically contingent, or Complex, Realism. I call the three theoretical interpretations Fundamentalist, Structuralist, and Constitutionalist Realism. I will suggest that they correspond with four traditional discourses begun by Thucydides and developed by Machiavelli, Hobbes, and Rousseau.

In order to explore these similarities and differences, I will focus on three questions addressed to each of the three traditions.

What causes the "state of war"?

What causes particular wars and particular peaces?

What strategy of peace is explicit or implicit in the work of each of the three traditions?

I do this in order to sort out the analytical differences among these four perspectives on realism. I also hope to lay the groundwork for an assessment of the empirical validity of the laws and moral coherence of the advice that each theory promulgates, explicitly or implicitly.

REALISMS

1. *Complex*, like all forms of Realism, portrays a worldview or an explanation of interstate politics as a state of war. Unlike the other Realisms, its interpretive insights are generally implicit, wrapped in historical accounts and contingent interpretations. Its insights are premised on three minimal assumptions. First, "the international scene is properly described as an anarchy—a multiplicity of powers without a government."[10] Second, the primary actors are independent states whose domestic hierarchy (sovereignty) complements international anarchy.[11] Third, the lack of a legitimate international source of controlling authority means no restraint—whether moral, social, cultural, economic, or political—is sufficiently strong or general either to eliminate completely or to manage reliably conflicts of interest, prestige, or value. Together these three tenets generate the state of war, an omnipresent threat of war.

Mutual mistrust characterizes interstate politics so that, even with the best will in the world, no power can surrender any part of its security or liberty to another. But this view, common to a number of writers in the contemporary field, assumes nothing about the rationality of states, their pursuit of power or their "national interest," or the way they set their various goals.[12] Indeed, it assumes that the processes and preferences of states vary and are open to choice influenced by both domestic and interstate considerations. And it includes the possibility of an international society and international law providing some constraints on state behavior. The quality of political judgment is thus often seen as crucial because interstate action is not tightly constrained by the system or by human nature, and it may or may not be strictly determined by local or domestic politics. Political choice includes moral choices, but this variant of Realism assumes that ethical choices cannot be categorical or absolute—that is, that they necessarily depend upon a prior consideration of strategic security. Given the lack of international security, states seeking to maintain their independence must provide for their own security, and this calls for an attention to relative power.

[10] Wight (1978), p. 101.

[11] Alternatively put, the state is at least relatively autonomous. It faces no significant challenges to its authority from either "below" domestically or "above" internationally.

[12] For example, this view appears to fit Arnold Wolfers's *Discord and Collaboration* (especially chaps. 1, 2, and 4); Kenneth Waltz's *Man, the State and War* ("anarchy is the framework of world politics," but the "forces that determine policy" are located within the nation, p. 238); Martin Wight: "Power politics means the relations between independent powers. This implies two conditions: independent units which acknowledge no political superior, and continuous and organized relations between them" (*Power Politics* [Royal Institute of International Affairs, 1946], p. 68). It also follows Vasquez's basic description of Realism (1983, p. 28).

The dominant inference of Complex Realism is the continuity of the state of war. Interstate politics thus constitutes a field in which generalization, when placed in proper context, can be useful. Particular wars have many causes, ranging from blunder to cold calculation and ideological crusades, from the pursuit of gain to the fear of defeat. The permanent context of anarchy makes fear an especially powerful cause of war, as G. F. Hudson notes in his discussion of the Second World War in the Pacific: "There is perhaps no factor which drives a state into war so inexorably as a steady loss of relative power. Sooner or later a desperate now-or-never mood overcomes the calculations of prudence, and the belief that a war may be won today, but cannot be won tomorrow, becomes the most convincing of all arguments for an appeal to the sword."[13]

Only changing one of the basic assumptions changes the essence of interstate politics. World government or empire or a very unlikely perfect normative consensus or harmony of interest: Any one would remove states from the international state of war. Societies then would experience international civil politics, a cessation of interstate politics, a universal empire, or a "security community." Failing these, the state of war persists.

The descriptive virtue (and theoretical vice) of the Complex model of Realism is its accuracy. It is the model whose complexity most effectively allows us to re-create the actual process of world politics.

2. *Fundamentalism* characterizes all social interaction as fundamentally rooted in mankind's psychological and material needs that result in a drive for power.[14] State behavior, like all social behavior from the family through all other organizations, can thus best be understood as a reflection of interest-oriented, power-seeking activity.[15] The struggle for power changes form, but not substance, when we move from a consideration of domestic to international politics and, as Hans Morgenthau notes, "politics, like society in general, is governed by objective laws that have their roots in human nature."[16] The drive for power produces the state of war.

The Fundamentalist accepts the anarchy assumption of the Complex Realists but questions the differentiation between domestic and interstate politics. Fundamentalism specifies both the means and ends (both power) left open by the minimalist assumptions of Complex Realism. Rooted in human nature itself, the drive for power leaves statesmen no choice other than power politics. Power, moreover, can be translated. Leadership can reshape one endeavor into resources available for other, as, following Machiavelli, "good arms make good laws; good laws, good arms."

[13] G. F. Hudson, *The Far East in World Politics* (London: Oxford University Press, 1937), p. 198.
[14] Hans Morgenthau (1949 / 1967), p. 4.
[15] Ibid., p. 32.
[16] Ibid., p. 6.

In the first edition of *Politics among Nations*, Morgenthau notes this theory's dominant inference that "all nations actively engaged in the struggle for power must actually aim not at a balance—that is, equality—of power, but at a superiority of power in their own behalf."[17] This same logic applies to individuals, who seek to maximize the satisfaction of their internal drives. Leaders can of course make mistakes. They should pursue power rationally, but human passions, prejudice, and error will ensure that some will fail to do so.[18]

The great virtue of the Fundamentalist model is that, with its focus on individual leadership, it helps us trace the mechanisms of change in world politics as it reveals the difficult policy choices statespersons regularly confront.

3. *Structuralism* also explains the state of war. Like the Complex version, Structuralism assumes international anarchy and the predominance of state actors. Unlike that model, Structuralism also assumes that state actors are "functionally similar units" differing in capabilities but not on ends, as Kenneth Waltz notes in his *Theory of International Politics*.[19]

Rational process, fungibility of power resources, and a strong preference for power as a means to security form necessary parts of the model.[20] But unlike Fundamentalists, Structuralists see these features, not as assumptions about human nature or social organization, but as derivations from the structure itself. State behavior is homogenized—made rational and power-seeking—through competition and socialization.[21] Only the rational and power-seeking will survive the competition to dominate and thus educate their rivals.

Specific Structural inferences, such as the hypothesized stability of a bipolar world,[22] the instability of multipolarity, and the weaknesses of transnational restraints, are deduced from the model, once one specifies the number and capabilities of the states that compose the system. And scientific Structuralism offers the promise of regularities that can be falsified or confirmed.

The great promise of the elegance of Structuralism, with its sparse set of causal variables, is laws that are potentially disconfirmable and, therefore, scientifically rigorous prediction.

[17] Ibid., p. 210.

[18] Morgenthau (1951), pp. 12–15. Thus, according to Morgenthau and Kenneth Thompson, the balance of power is really a doctrine of *prudence* for a "rationally conducted policy . . . for those nations which wish to preserve their independence" (*Principles and Problems of International Politics*, p. 104).

[19] Kenneth Waltz, *Theory of International Politics* (Reading, Mass.: Addison Wesley, 1979), pp. 96–97.

[20] Robert Keohane (1986), p. 172.

[21] Waltz, *Theory*, p. 75. The Structural determination depends, we need to add, on the systemic interaction's being sufficiently intense to select very efficiently for appropriate behavior, such as would be observed under the economist's model of perfect competition. See the valuable discussion in Keohane (1986, pp. 171–75).

[22] Bipolarity (the economists's "bilateral monopoly") may, however, strain against the assumption of perfect competition.

Varieties of Realist Thought

	Complex Thucydides	**Fundamentalist** Machiavelli	**Structuralist** Hobbes	**Constitutionalist** Rousseau
Human Nature	xx	xx	x	x
Domestic Society	xx	x	x	xx
Interstate System	xx	x	xx	x

4. *Constitutionalism* examines the effects of variation in cultural, social, economic, and political institutions; otherwise it is most like the Complex interpretation of Realism. For like the Complex Realism of Thucydides, it allows for variation in all the major determinants of interstate relations, holding only to the assumptions of state action and international anarchy. But unlike Thucydidean Realists, the Constitutionalists explore variation systematically and make explicit the historically contingent factors that Thucydides leaves implicit in his narrative. Rousseau best exemplifies this strain of Realism as he focuses on the effects of European culture and commercial civilization and examines the effects of democracy and monarchy, unjust and just states. In modern scholarship, Raymond Aron's study *Peace and War* exemplifies the power of systematic generalization contained within a framework that portrays world politics as a semiautonomous realm shaped by diplomats and warriors.

The great virtue of the Constitutionalist model of Realism is that it offers us a powerful sociology of world politics, identifies large and general constraints, and suggests the consequences of domestic reform or revolution.

Complex Realism can best trace its ancestry back to Thucydides. The closest philosophical roots of the Fundamentalist interpretation lie in Machiavelli's studies of the politics of both private and public life. The Structuralist's theory is based on assumptions and arguments best articulated in political philosophy by Hobbes. And Rousseau best articulates the assumptions and arguments of the Constitutionalists.

I explore each of these theorists as different routes to an understanding of why world politics can be seen as a state of war, different routes to an awareness of the fundamental forces that shape war and peace, cooperation and conflict, empire and independence, and differing prescriptions for how statesmen should manage a world where danger is so prevalent and opportunity so fleeting. I also lay the groundwork for a test of its central claim—that states engage in self-help by balancing power against power—as a way of determining when we should regard the Realists as realistic.

CHAPTER ONE

Complex Realism: Thucydides

> I propose first to give an account of the causes of complaint which they had against each other and of the specific instances where their interests clashed: this is in order that there should be no doubt in anyone's mind about what led to this great war falling upon the Hellenes. But the real reason for the war is, in my opinion, most likely to be disguised by such an argument. What made war inevitable was the growth of Athenian power and the fear which this caused in Sparta.[1]

TO MOST SCHOLARS in international politics, to think like a Realist is to think as the philosophical historian Thucydides first thought. Realists invoke Thucydides in order to establish a continuous tradition and to say that their worldview dates back to the actual emergence of regular interstate politics more than two thousand years ago. We begin our articles and books with "Even as long ago as the time of Thucydides, political realism" or "Thucydides, the founding father of Realism," or "Ever since Thucydides."[2] Theorists as influential as Martin

[1] Thucydides, *The Peloponnesian War,* trans. Rex Warner, intro. M. I. Finley (Harmondsworth: Penguin, 1972) Book I: Paragraph 23. I will refer to *The Peloponnesian War* as his *History* and cite by book: paragraph—e.g. I:23.

[2] See Keohane (1986), p. 7; Nye (1988), p. 235; Jervis (1988), p. 317. Kenneth Waltz in his influential *Theory of International Politics* notes the contemporaneity of Thucydides as evidence of the "enduring anarchic character of international politics" (1979, p. 66). Robert Gilpin describes Thucydides in ways that most in the field would find uncontroversial when he calls him the first political scientist and first Realist, noting Thucydides's attention to the vital significance of shifts in international power (Gilpin [1981], p. 93).

Wight describe Thucydides as "the only acknowledged counterpart [to the classics of political philosophy] in the study of international relations. . . ."[3]

But was Thucydides a founder of Realism? Given the influence of Thucydides, the question may seem to invite a tautology. Was Thucydides Thucydidean? Is Realism Realist? As I noted in the introduction to this discussion of Realism, the variety of contemporary Realisms complicates any answer to that question. So too does the gap between Thucydides's time and our own. Many thus reject the unity and continuity theses underlying the claim of a Thucydidean paternity for Realism. Critics draw a line between the Structural and scientific "neo-Realism" of today and the interpretive and historical "classical Realism" that goes back to Thucydides. Structural Neo-Realism is statist, utilitarian, and positivistic, while classical Realism respects political judgment and the traditional practice of international politics.[4]

In this chapter I propose to defend the continuity thesis but reject the unity thesis. Realism does hark back to Thucydides, but he is not a Structuralist, a Fundamentalist, or a Constitutionalist. Each strand of Realism can trace some of its crucial elements to Thucydides's *History*. But only Complex Realism follows his methods and lessons, what Thomas Hobbes translated as his "everlasting possession." This "everlasting possession," moreover, is both a set of empirical lessons on how to understand what does happen in world politics and a set of moral lessons for statespersons seeking to preserve the security of their states in dangerous times.

Eminent practitioners of Realist diplomacy regularly invoke Thucydides's authority, as Secretary of State George C. Marshall did at Princeton University in February 1947: "I doubt seriously whether a man can think with full wisdom and with deep convictions regarding certain of the basic international issues today who has not at least reviewed in his mind the period of the Peloponnesian Wars and the fall of Athens."[5] Astute journalists have also been known to catch statesmen in some less apt invocations as when Secretary of State Kissinger famously described the Cold War as a new "Peloponnesian War" between a United States "Athens" and a Soviet "Sparta," and the journalist asked whether

[3] Wight, "Why Is There No International Theory?" p. 32.

[4] Richard Ashley (1986), pp. 260–63, with quote from p. 297. And see Alker (1988) for a similar criticism in which he focuses on the dialectical logic of Thucydides's Melian Dialogue. Stanley Hoffmann (1977, p. 44) also defended a discontinuity thesis in the social scientific variant of international relations. But he placed the break at, not after, Morgenthau. Hoffmann noted Morgenthau's claim to have discovered a set of laws of power that established a scientific field of endeavor that took root in postwar America in the new discipline of international relations—"An American Social Science."

[5] Referred to by David Ignatius, "They Don't Make Them Like George Marshall Anymore," *Washington Post*, National Edition, June 8, 1987, p. 25.

that meant that we were bound to lose.[6] Strategists have followed Thucydides's *History* to learn about the roles of sea and land power. Political scientists have studied him for insights concerning the dilemmas of alliance with powers much stronger than oneself, the sources of the informal imperialism of the Athenian, imperial Delian League and of the interstate hegemony of the Spartan-led Peloponnesian League. Political theorists focus on his work to learn of the difficulties of moral action in international politics and of the typical strengths and weaknesses of democratic and oligarchic polities. (For it was in this *History* that democracy first acquired the reputation for disastrous factionalism and international insecurity that has dogged it through the centuries.)[7] And Thucydides himself makes a demanding claim upon our continuing attention when he says: "It will be enough for me, however, if these words of mine are judged useful by those who want to understand clearly the events which happened in the past and which (human nature being what it is) will at some time or other and in much the same ways, be repeated in the future. My work is not a piece of writing designed to meet the taste of an immediate public, but was done to last forever" (I:22).[8]

As a theorist of world politics Thucydides holds our attention for the depth of his insight, the range of his vision of interstate relations, and the "thickly described" complexity of his presentation. Born about 460 B.C., he came from the Athenian elite, a wealthy family owning mining property in Thrace. The war broke just as he was entering adult life, fully capable, he notes, of understanding its importance (V:26). He rose to *strategos* (general) in 424, but he then suffered a defeat at Amphipolis that led to his exile, an exile that he matter-of-factly says, allowed him better to obtain information from both sides (IV:104–07). He died about 404, soon after the defeat of Athens.

Thucydides is essentially a Realist, who believed that none of the traditional moral norms linking individuals across state boundaries have reliable effect. Interstate relations in his view exist in a condition where war is always possible, a state of war such as that "hard school of danger" that persisted between Athens and Sparta during the "peace" that preceded the actual outbreak of hostilities (I:19). To Thucydides, as to later Realists, international anarchy precludes the effective escape from the dreary history of war and conflict that are the consequences of competition under anarchy. Thucydides, after all, is the explicator of the "truest cause" of the great war between Athens and Sparta—the real

[6]One reference to Kissinger's use of the metaphor can be found in Elmo Zumwalt, *On Watch* (New York: Quadrangle, 1976), p. 319.

[7]Madison's No. 10, for example, addresses the dangers of factionalism through the virtues of size. Kennan's essays in *American Diplomacy* continue to indict democratic foreign policy.

[8]All translations are from the Rex Warner translation of Thucydides, *The Peloponnesian War.*

reason that it was "inevitable"—which lay in competitive power politics or, in modern parlance, the "security dilemma."[9] Efforts of each side to protect its security made the other side insecure. Severely complicating the normal systemic competition was a shifting power distribution: "—the growth of Athenian power and the fear which this caused in Sparta" (I:23).[10] Whatever goals and means political actors might choose in the conduct of foreign relations among states, their foreign politics, Thucydides suggested, had to be constrained by the need to preserve their security independently.

Thucydides's Complex Realism

Human Nature	xx
Domestic State and Society	xx
Interstate System	xx

But unlike some later Realists, Thucydides did not seek to reduce world politics to some causal essence. For him, world politics was caught in a web of antinomies. He did not think that states were the only significant actors in international politics. Individuals, such as Alcibiades, played important and sometimes independent roles in the determination of the course of international events; but their characters, mistakes, and misperceptions did not independently or essentially define world politics. Nor did Thucydides think that state interests could or should be defined solely in terms of the rational pursuit of power. No abstraction or structurally determined model of political behavior could successfully supersede a more complex explanation drawing on the actual variety of ends ("security, honor, and self-interest") that animated political leaders and citizens. Polities did systematically differ, but their differences did not allow for a transformation of the state of war.

Nor, of course, did Thucydides conceive of his work as a work of science, a subject that could readily yield both universal laws and unique predictions of events, whether prospectively or retrospectively. Nonetheless, relations among states were and are subject to certain generalizations, lessons that could be derived from a careful study of the past, such as his own history of the great war between Athens and Sparta. Thucydides as a historian was not merely a chronicler or entertainer (as he implied that Herodotus had been). Historical interpreters are capable of generating meaningful, contingent generalizations. He carefully reports opposing interpretations and then argues for—explicitly or

[9] See John Herz, "Idealist Internationalism and the Security Dilemma," and Robert Jervis, "Realism, Game Theory and Cooperation," pp. 317–49.
[10] For insightful views on the importance of shifting power distributions, see Robert Gilpin, *War and Change in World Politics.*

implicitly—the view that he finds most persuasive. In the classical world, which lacked archives and detailed records, it was only because he was writing contemporary history—and thus could do field research and interview participants—that he could find the evidence to make those analytical and empirical determinations. Beyond that, the generalizability of Thucydidean history rests upon the assumption that human nature was constant (I:22).[11] He wanted, moreover, his *History* to be "judged useful" because we can learn from it (I:22).

Thucydides reasoned that pressures of war and civil disorder would create the same effects in similar circumstances anywhere because all would follow the impulses of fear and self-interest and prestige (III:82). Circumstances, however, often differed. Fear of war yielded futile resistance in Melos, surrender in Mytilene, and successful defense in Sicily. His lessons, therefore, are embedded in the narration.

THE COMPLEXITY OF REALISM

The "complexity" of Thucydidean Realism suggests that the important events of interstate politics can be explained by examining the roles of leadership, state regimes, and international structures. At the same time, it cannot be explained by any one factor alone—not by the character of individual leaders or the proclivities of certain types of states or the imperatives of the balance of power. Only by considering all together can we gain a sense of why wars and peace occur, why some states achieve victory, and some are defeated.

Thucydides tells about each of these features of world politics in the course of his history of the Peloponnesian War between Athens and its allies and Sparta and its allies. His history of the war—the origins, conduct, and outcome of this war, these particular alliances, empires, and hegemonies—is explicitly an invitation to learn about the way interstate politics works in general. But his lessons are not simple or straightforward; instead he asks us to learn through a critical rethinking of each historical development and the careful consideration of the various interactions of all the actual participants.

[11] Charles Cochrane, *Thucydides and the Science of History* (London: Oxford University Press, 1929), pp. 7–13, and Peter Pouncey, *The Necessities of War* (New York: Columbia University Press, 1980), p. 20. Thucydides seems to accept Hippocrates's argument that since the human physical constitution was sufficiently the same, the same symptoms occurring across the human population would signify the same disease (II:48). Ironically, Thucydides, who is said to have borrowed his methods of analysis from medicine, may have been a better diagnostician than even the professional medical men of his time. See Oswyn Murray, "Greek Historians," in John Boardman, Jasper Griffin, and O. Murray, eds., *Greece and the Hellenistic World* (Oxford: Oxford University Press, 1988), p. 189.

THE ORIGINS OF THE WAR

The background history to the war was familiar to all Thucydides's public. He nonetheless took the time to repeat it, from the origins of Greek society to his present, perhaps so that we, his later audience, would truly understand the context from which he drew his lessons. It was, he noted, a period of "great war" when both sides were at the height of their power and the Greek world was divided into two great alignments, one about Athens, the other about Sparta (I:1–20).

The two antagonists represented two different ways of life. Athens was a commercial society, almost forced to be such by the poor quality of its soil and the geographic advantage of a central position on the Aegean Sea. The wealth supplied by commerce, together with an unusually ethnically homogeneous population, allowed Athens to complete the democratization of its institutions by the middle of the fifth century. The citizens, composed of about forty to fifty thousand males, were divided by class into a landed elite, merchants, and artisans. But all citizens were distinguished from metics (resident foreigners) and slaves (who worked in the mines and in households). The citizens, however, met one another as equals in the sovereign Assembly, which convened at least forty times a year and generally drew an attendance of about six thousand. The majority in the Assembly formed the government. It directly made all the vital decisions, but it was assisted by a council (of five hundred, chosen by lot) that prepared an agenda, and it delegated military leadership to ten annually elected archons, of whom Pericles became the dominant figure.[12]

Sparta was almost Athens's opposite: agrarian rather than commercial, isolationist rather than cosmopolitan, disciplined where Athens was free, and oligarchic where Athens was democratic. Unkindly described as a military barracks, Sparta separated its young men from their families at seven and educated them in packs for the military life. Sparta was ruled by a mixed constitution. At thirty, males became full and equal citizens and members of the Spartan Assembly. But a hereditary monarchy of two kings held the right to military leadership, the supreme court was elected from among a small aristocracy, and five ephors elected by the Assembly served as the executive agent with wide powers. The Assembly acted only by acclamation, unlike the Athenian Assembly, which depended on debate. Stability was Sparta's strong suit, but its stability rested on a precarious domination over masses of other Greeks, the helots, enslaved to work Spartan plantations.[13]

[12] See Geoffrey de Ste. Croix, *The Origins of the Peloponnesian War* (Ithaca: Cornell University Press, 1972) and Donald Kagan, *The Outbreak of the Peloponnesian War* (Ithaca: Cornell University Press, 1969).
[13] W. G. Forrest, *A History of Sparta, 950–192 BC* (London: Hutchinson, 1968).

GREECE AT THE OUTBREAK OF THE PELOPONNESIAN WAR

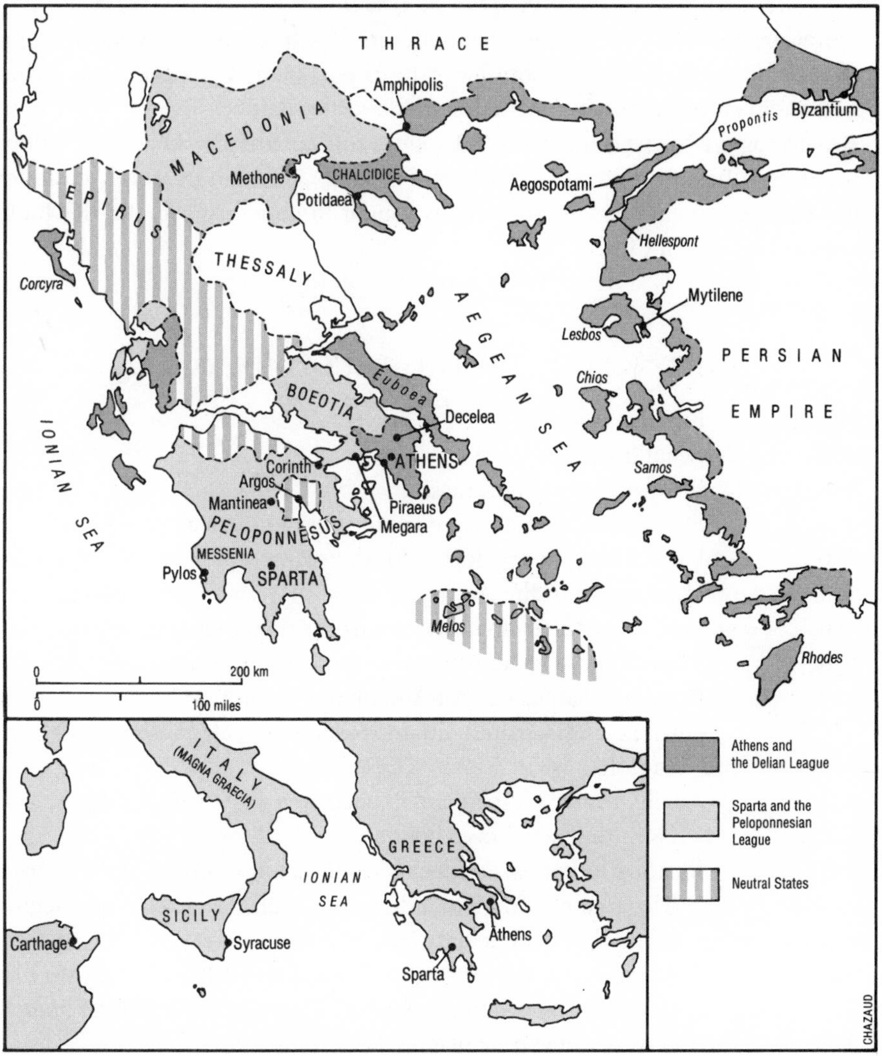

Athens and Sparta cooperated to defeat the Persian invasion in 480, but soon thereafter their interests diverged. Sparta resented the leadership Athens began exercising over the Greek states liberated from Persia. Because it was suspicious of Athens's decision to build long walls to its port (which made the city invulnerable to siege), Sparta's anxiety festered and then grew as Athens turned an alliance against Persia, the Delian League, into an empire in which Athens taxed its "allies" to fund an Athenian fleet and an Athenian treasury. Yet under the lead of the archon Cimon, Athens sought to conciliate Sparta, the traditional hegemon of the Greeks.

CHRONOLOGY OF THE THUCYDIDEAN ERA

490 B.C.	First Persian War
480	Second Persian War
479	Revolts against Pausanias; Sparta abdicates strategic leadership of Greek allies
476	Delian League develops into Athenian empire
464	Helot revolt in Sparta
460	First Peloponnesian War; Athens is stripped of key colonies
446	Thirty Years' Peace; Athenian expansion resumes
440	Revolt on Samos against Athenian control
435	Corcyra and Corinth quarrel over colonial possession of Epidamnus
433	Athens assists Corcyra in its victory over Corinth; Athens and Corinth quarrel over Potidaea
432	Sparta supports a Potidaean revolt against Athens; Athens bans Megarians from its harbors; Corinth, Megara, and Aegina lobby Sparta to declare war on Athens
431	Thucydides's narrative begins; Thebes and Athens battle over Plataea (Athens is victorious); Pericles delivers his funeral oration
430	Athens is stricken by plague; Pericles is deposed
429	Pericles is reinstated but dies shortly thereafter
428	The Athenian Assembly splits into moderate and "war party" factions led by Nicias and Cleon respectively. After defeat in the north, Thucydides is exiled
427	Athens takes Mytilene; Sparta takes Plataea
421	The Peace of Nicias (albeit hostilities never fully abate)
416	Athens conquers Melos; Athens embarks on the Sicilian Expedition
411	Sparta allies with Persia: The government of the 400 takes over in Athens; four months later the 400 is deposed in favor of the 5000

410	Thucydides's narrative ends; Athenian democracy is restored; with the war party ascendant (now led by Cleophon); Athens rejects a Spartan offer of peace on the basis of the status quo
409–405	Sparta and its allies continue to recover territory and raise revolts in Athenian colonies; Athens rejects a second Spartan offer of peace
404	Cleophon is tried and executed; Athens surrenders to Sparta; the Thirty Tyrants come to power in Athens
403	The Thirty Tyrants are deposed with Sparta's cooperation; Athenian democracy is again restored

Relations deteriorated. In 465, following a devastating earthquake and the revolt of the helots, Athens sent an expedition to assist the Spartans, but fearing that Athens would assist the oppressed helots instead, Sparta sent them home. Discredited, Cimon fell. Athens then did assist a group of helot refugees, establishing them at Naupactus, a strategic site on the north coast of the Peloponnesus. When two Spartan allies, Megara and Corinth, came to blows, Athens accepted Megara's request for assistance. In addition to enraging Corinth, Athens now seemed to threaten Spartan hegemony: Megara's territory across the isthmus closed Sparta off from the rest of Greece. The First Peloponnesian War resulted as Sparta's allies dragged it into a long campaign against the dominating threat posed by Athens.

Athens lost the land-based portion of its empire in the Thirty Years' Peace, which ended the war in 446–45. Both hegemons seemed to have accepted a modus vivendi between the recognized land power of Sparta and the sea power of Athens. Each agreed to negotiate disputes and not to interfere in the affairs of the other alliance. Athens was careful not to provoke the Spartans and their allies in the west and carefully avoided imperial expansion in Sicily. In the north and east, remote from Spartan and Corinthian interests, Athenian expansion continued into the Aegean and the Black Sea granaries.

A crisis in 440 demonstrated how uneasy the peace was. Two Athenian allies—Miletus and Samos, the first dependent on Athens, the second autonomous—quarreled. Athens sided with Miletus and sent an expedition that crushed and then democratized Samos. Samian refugees turned to the Persians, and this became the signal for two other Athenian allies to revolt. This was an opportunity for Sparta to crush Athens, so it called a meeting of the Peloponnesian League. But Corinth later claimed (I:40) the credit for preventing war, implying for some that Sparta had sought war.[14] Saved, Athens took the opportunity to consolidate its imperial rule.

[14]This episode is one of the key differences between de Ste. Croix and Kagan on the origins of the Second Peloponnesian War. It raises the issue of whether the war nine years later was an accident or, as Thucydides says, forced by the growing power of Athens. de Ste. Croix, pp. 201–3. See below.

Five years later a crisis over the remote Adriatic city of Epidamnus led to the Second Peloponnesian War, the great war that Thucydides chronicles. Epidamnus—a colony of the dynamic, and neutral, Corcyra—experienced a democratic rebellion against its aristocrats. The aristocrats crushed the rebellion; the democrats appealed to Corcyra. When Corcyra refused assistance, the Epidamnian refugees appealed next to Corcyra's founder, Corinth. Corinth, angered by years of rivalry with Corcyra, its disrespectful daughter colony, decided to assist the Epidamnians and, not coincidentally, thereby advance its commercial and strategic interests in the northwest. Sparta sought to moderate the actions of its Corinthian ally by refusing to intervene and urging the parties to negotiate. The Corinthians rejected negotiation, hired a fleet, but then were defeated by the Corcyreans, the second naval power in Greece.

Wealthy Corinth spent the next two years (to 433) preparing for revenge, recruiting a large fleet, and raising the alarm throughout the Peloponnesian League. Corcyra, outside the established alliances, then took its case to Athens. Arguing before the Athenian Assembly, Corinth appealed to law and morals. It invoked the provisions of the Thirty Years' Peace (which did not include Corcyra) and Athenian gratitude to Corinth (for holding out against war in 440). Corcyra appealed to fear. It warned the Athenians that war with the entire Peloponnesian League was on its way and asked if Athens would want to fight Sparta with both the second (Corcyrean) and third (Corinthian) strongest navies on the Spartan side. This threat to Athenian naval dominance was inevitable should Corcyra be defeated and its fleet absorbed by Corinth.

Persuaded by Corcyra, the Athenians sought a limited involvement in order to avoid war. They sent a small "defensive" fleet to back up the Corcyreans in case they were in danger of losing. At Sybota, Corinthians, supported by two Peloponnesian allies (Elis and Megara), attacked, and in the confusion of battle the Athenians were eventually drawn in. The ensuing defeat of the Corinthian fleet raised tensions a significant notch higher.

Athens decided to punish Corinth's ally Megara by imposing a trade embargo. It also tightened control in the empire, insisting that Potidaea (a subordinate Athenian "ally," though settled by Corinthians) pull down its walls. Potidaea appealed to Corinth. Corinth and Megara demanded that Sparta call a meeting of the Peloponnesian League and declare for war.

A debate before the Spartan Assembly decided the issue. Corinthian envoys goaded the Spartans with the increasing power of Athens and threatened that the alliance would collapse unless Sparta acted now. The conservative Spartan king Archidamus urged a delay of a few years in order to build up Spartan forces. An ephor, Sthenelaidas, demanded war to uphold Spartan honor. The Assembly saw war as inevitable—as did the Athenian Assembly, according to Thucydides—and viewed the growing power of Athens as a great danger. Archidamus lost the vote but gained a delay in order to negotiate. But Sparta's demands—even the most moderate demand that the Megarian decree be lifted—were unacceptable to Pericles, who persuaded the Athenians that the demands were designed to weaken them in the face of inevitable war (I:140). Their empire, he assured the Athenian Assembly, was both readily defensible and too dangerous to let go.

CONTROVERSIES AND CAUSES

The war broke out in the summer of 431, when Thebes, an ally of Sparta's, attacked Plataea, an ally of Athens's, and thereby violated the provisions of the Thirty Years' Peace. The Spartans blamed Pericles, Athens's great democratic leader, for the war. Many of the Greek city-states blamed Athenian imperialism and commercial greed. Popular opinion also charged that Pericles, the leader of the anti-Spartan faction of Athenian politics, had a political stake in the war.[15]

But Thucydides obviously means to tell us that none of these popular impressions was correct. No one state should be singly blamed for the war; no one leader caused it. Nor was the war a necessary feature of interstate politics. It was, however, explicable—that is, caused—and the"truest cause" was both generalizable and contextualized, likely to recur yet not permanent. Thucydides wanted to teach future statesmen how to recognize the dangers and perhaps to avoid, mitigate, or manage them.

Pericles led the anti-Spartan faction, so the Spartans insisted in a final message to the Athenian Assembly that the Athenians purge themselves of an ancient curse by throwing out those affiliated with the cursed clan (Pericles's). Plutarch, rather than Thucydides, gives us the background. According to charges then current, Pericles had fanned the flames of war in order to divert the citizenry from his own domestic political problems, specifically, the charges of impiety launched against Aspasia (his mistress) and of peculation against Pheidias, the sculptor (Pericles's friend). But the attempt to discredit Pericles backfired, and the Athenians rallied even more strongly behind him, whom they saw as the most steadfast defender of their public interests. Although Pericles led the Athenians, it is also important to remember that they chose demo-

[15]Valuable background interpretation in addition to Thucydides can be found in Plutarch, "Pericles," in *The Rise and Fall of Athens: Nine Greek Lives*, trans. Ian Scott-Kilvert (London: Penguin, 1960); Donald Kagan, *The Outbreak of the Peloponnesian War* and *On the Origins of War* (New York: Doubleday, 1995); de Ste. Croix, *The Origins of the Peloponnesian War* and Robert Connor, *Thucydides* (Princeton: Princeton University Press, 1984); Laurie Bagby, "The Use and Abuse of Thucydides," *International Organization* 48, 1 (Winter 1994), and Robert Gilpin, "Peloponnesian War and Cold War" and Richard Ned Lebow, "Thucydides, Power Transition Theory and the Causes of War," in Richard Ned Lebow and Barry Strauss, eds., *Hegemonic Rivalry* (Boulder, Colo.: Westview Press, 1991).

cratically to follow him. Some votes in the Assembly (such as the vote to come to the aid of Corcyra) were apparently close, but all the votes supported the actions that led to the outbreak of the war.

On the Spartan side, Sthenelaidas played an analogous but different role in moving Sparta toward war. In contrast with Pericles's cool argument, Sthenelaidas made a heated harangue, appealing to Sparta's pride in its military prowess and sense of fidelity to its allies. He, too, succeeded in moving the Spartan Assembly to vote for war (I:86). But, as with Pericles, his individual role may not have been that decisive. Sthenelaidas's rival, the king Archidamus, also thought that war with Athens was likely; he simply and for logistic reasons preferred to fight later, when Sparta would be better equipped, rather than sooner. After extensive consideration and debate the Spartans allowed themselves to be swept up by Sthenelaidas.

Thucydides's own explanation of the war is clear, straightforward, and dismissive of the charges against specific individuals. War, as he and most Realists argue, is usually a product of larger causes. For Thucydides, the real cause was the "growth of Athenian power and the fear which this caused in Sparta" (I:23). But does he mean that Athens or Sparta or Corcyra (which appealed to Athens) or Corinth (which strove to ignite Spartan fear) was the cause and deserves the blame for the war?

Corinth and Corcyra certainly sought to embroil the two bigger powers. In 435 Corinth decided to support the Epidamnians in their rebellion against Corcyra. Corinthian involvement sent the Corcyraeans to Athens to request Athenian support. The Corcyraeans helped enlist Athens by threatening to take the Corcyraean fleet, the second-largest in the Greek world, over to the Spartans if Athens refused to support them. Later, in 432, it was the Corinthians who argued before the Spartan Assembly the case for war against Athens, detailing an Athenian record that they charged was an implacably imperialist course of expansion. The long-standing rivalry between Corinth and Athens for control of the trade to the west serves as a backdrop to their hostility and to this series of escalating crises.[16] But Corinth does not appear to have been aggressively bent on war with Athens. Earlier, in 440, it had been the voice holding out against Samos's request for Peloponnesian League support in the Samian rebellion against Athens. Corinth too tried to persuade Athens to stay out of its quarrel with Corcyra over Epidamnus.

[16] Francis Cornford, *Thucydides Mythhistoricus* (London: Routledge & Kegan Paul, 1907 / 1965).

MAJOR STATESMEN OF THE PELOPONNESIAN WAR

Pericles	Preeminent democratic leader of Athens from approximately 460 B.C. until his death in 429 B.C. Pericles forged an Athenian empire out of states formerly in the pan-Hellenic Delian League.
Cleon	Imprudent, aggressive, cruel but not unpatriotic Athenian general, most influential after the rule of Pericles. Cleon lobbied the Athenian Assembly to punish the Mytilenian rebels harshly.
Nicias	The most prudent and least warlike of the Athenian generals. Thucydides questions his abilities as a strategist yet offers a rare eulogy on how among the war dead, Nicias least deserved the "butchering" he received.
Alcibiades	Traitorous and imprudent but brilliant Athenian general. Just as he set out from Athens to lead the ill-fated Sicilian expedition, Alcibiades was called back to Athens for trial on a charge of sacrilege. He escaped to Sparta and informed the Spartans of Athenian military secrets (upon learning that Athens had condemned him to death). Later, shifting loyalties once again, Alcibiades enjoyed a brief return to favor in Athens upon the overthrow of the Athenian democracy, yet eventually fell out of favor again and had to flee to Persia, where it was the Spartans who finally ordered him killed.
Archidamus	Spartan king from approximately 470 B.C. until approximately 426 B.C., but only mentioned once in Thucydides's history after Book I. Archidamus advocated a prudent Realism, characteristic of Spartan conservatism, and sought to postpone the war with Athens until a more suitable moment. His influence with the aristocratic Spartan Assembly was not absolute, however, and his advice was not heeded.
Sthenelaidas	Spartan leader who successfully argued a case for aggressive Realism against Archidamus and for immediate war with Athens.

Diodotus	Athenian leader who successfully argued for prudent moderation against Cleon's advocacy of cruel punishment in the treatment of Mytilene. As there is little historical record of Diodotus besides that of Thucydides, some have speculated that "Diodotus" ("soft speaker") was a convenient voice for a view expressed in the Athenian debate that Thucydides wanted to highlight.
Hermocrates	Sicilian leader whose strong leadership forged military and civil unity out of the factionalism of his state, thereby contributing to its defeat of Athens.

Sparta, of course, bore formal responsibility for the war. In 431 it reduced the prospects for a reasonable arbitration by requiring that Athens lift the embargo on Megara as a precondition, and it added purely provocative demands, such as that the curse attached to Pericles's clan be purged (I:127). It then, together with its Peloponnesian League, declared war. Spartan rage and pride also played a part in the war's origins, as the reception Sthenelaidas's harangue received at the Spartan Assembly indicates. Sparta's honor, the growth of Athenian power, and fidelity to allies were each invoked by the enraged Spartans, who by a "great majority" voted with the ephor Sthenelaidas (I:86). But it would be wrong to see Sparta as the aggressive party driving all to war. Its reputation for caution, indeed excess delay, was more than demonstrated in the crises leading up to the declaration. It sought to restrain Corinth. Corinth repeatedly stressed Spartan procrastination and warned the hegemon of the Peloponnesian League of (or did Corinth threaten Sparta with?) defections (I:71) unless it backed up the interests of the members and confronted Athenian"aggressions." These aggressions included attacks on Corinth (the Corcyraean affair); Potidaea (a Corinthian colony in rebellion from but allied to Athens); Megara (whose citizens were banned from Athenian ports as punishment for a border transgression); and Aegina (which accused the Athenians of restricting its freedom [I:67]).

Thus, to many Greeks, Athens seemed the oppressively and aggressively expanding empire. According to the Peloponnesians, its refusal to give "freedom" back to the Hellenes was the root cause of the war (I:125 and I:139). Indeed, though acting completely within the legal confines of the peace, Athens had interfered in the affairs of neutrals (Epidamnus-Corcyra), forcibly disciplined its allies (Potidaea), and settled bilateral disputes in a heavy-handed manner (Megara). Under Pericles, the Athenian demos profited from and gloried in the expansion of the empire, which (though once a freely chosen alliance against the Persians) had become a coercive restriction on the freedom of at least the nondemocratic members of the Delian League. Pericles, moreover, had accepted Corcyra's warnings and its alliance and had come to think that war with Sparta was inevitable (I:33 and I:44).

Pericles and the majority of the Athenians had come to believe that they had no choice. Athens had done nothing unusual, nothing beyond what was necessary, as the Athenian "ambassadors" at a prewar Spartan Assembly argued. Now they must prepare for a war that seemed bound to arrive (I:44). The Athenians in the debate at Sparta argued that no particular blame should be attached to Athens (I:75–76). Athens acquired an empire that began as a free alliance whose declared purpose was to liberate the Greeks from Persian domination (following the victories at Salamis and Plataea in 480–479). All shared the fear of Persia, and the Spartans were not prepared to lead the Greeks. Afterward self-interest and honor also came to play a role in the transformation of the league into an expanding empire. But these motives too were common to most states, Thucydides's *History* seems to imply. Moreover, any state that left Athens's Delian League / empire would merely have defected to the Peloponnesian League; that, after all, was the fear upon which Corcyra had played. Security too affirmed the primacy of self-interest. And so Pericles warned the Athenians that even if their empire had been wrong to acquire, it would now be more dangerous to let it go than to defend it.[17]

THE END OF THE WAR

We see a similarly complex story in Thucydides's account of the end of the war and the defeat of Athens. At the simplest level, Athens was finally defeated in 404 because Sparta and the Peloponnesian League turned out to be the more powerful coalition. From this perspective the revival of Persia, temporarily eclipsed by civil war, and its decision to provide financial and naval support to Sparta and against the dominant Athenian naval power, tipped the balance against the Athenian empire and led to the string of naval defeats that culminated in the Spartan occupation of Athens.

Thucydides, however, really wanted to tell us a more complicated story, despite the fact that his work remained incomplete at his death and his death came before the final defeat of Athens. He wanted to explain why Athens was losing. The tip in the balance of forces was to him a symptom, or intermediate

[17] For discussion, de Ste. Croix, p. 290ff.

cause, of a deeper problem that explained how Athens had wasted its resources.

A failure of strategy formed part of the explanation of how Athens had squandered what Pericles (and Thucydides) saw as its initial superiority in power. Pericles persuaded the Athenians to follow a prudent sea strategy, emphasizing a war of attrition. Athens, invulnerable to a land attack because of its dominance of the sea and the massive fortifications that linked its seaport Piraeus to the mother city, was to focus its naval forces on amphibious raids against Sparta and its allies. Eschewing any expansion of the empire, even abandoning Attica to Sparta's land campaign, and relying on its control of Aegean commerce to provide needed supplies, the Athenians were persuaded by Pericles that they would wear Sparta out (I:144).

Tragic fate, or chance, decreed otherwise. Sparta's land campaign, even though it could not dent Athens's true naval dominance, may have contributed to the flight from Attica into Athens that led to the outbreak of the plague in the besieged and overcrowded city. And the plague seems to have contributed, Thucydides argues, to the undermining of public morale that led to a deterioration of leadership, which led to a deterioration of strategy. Leaders such as Pericles combined brilliance, prudence, and patriotism, John Finley has argued in his influential study of Thucydides's *History*.[18] Their authority also stemmed from the willingness of the populace to trust their judgment. The plague eroded public trust: None of the citizens could trust one another as those who helped the plague victims seemed to be the first to be punished by the baffling disease (II:53). Leaders then seemed to exploit the resulting fear and self-interest. Some, such as the hard-line demagogue Cleon, were patriotic but neither brilliant nor prudent. Others, such as the promoter of the Sicilian expedition Alcibiades, were brilliant, but neither prudent nor patriotic. Still others resembled the general in command of the Sicilian expedition, Nicias, who was patriotic and prudent (indeed excessively so) but not brilliant. Strategy began to reflect each of these tendencies. It became rash and cruel under Cleon, rash and brilliant under Alcibiades with the disastrous decision to expand the empire by conquering Sicily, and prudent and halting under Nicias, who frittered away the Athenian advantages in Sicily and helped produce the utter defeat of this vast expenditure of Athenian resources.

The other and deeper cause of Athens's defeat was factionalism. Even with poor leadership Athens would have won if it had remained united, Thucydides claims (II:65). The "internal strife" of oligarch against democrat, rural landowner against urban artisan fractured Athenian resources. The Spartan invasions of Attica destroyed the estates of the rural oligarchs first, making Athenian reliance on a naval strategy seem excessively democratic. The factions escalated

[18] John Finley, *Thucydides* (Ann Arbor: University of Michigan Press, 1963), chap. 5.

beyond this, however, until, in the end, the democratic fleet fought alone as oligarchs plotted with Sparta and surrendered Athens to Spartan fellow conservatives in order to avoid domestic Athenian revolution. (Here one almost sees a foreshadowing of the French right's dictum in the 1930s: "Better Hitler than Léon Blum.")

No single individual, no single state could account for the war or Athens's defeat, Thucydides thus suggests. But where are we to find the underlying causes he urged us to search for? Our three later variants—human Fundamentalism, interstate Structuralism, and domestic Constitutionalism—distill theories of such underlying factors. Let us see whether any one of the theoretical distillations captures Thucydides's Complex interpretation.

HUMAN FUNDAMENTALISM

The Thucydidean view of politics shares important similarities with the Fundamentalist view. But we can also distinguish Thucydides's views from the core tenets of Fundamentalist Realism.

Fundamentalist Realists see all society, all politics—domestic as well as interstate—as being rooted in a human nature that gives rise to contests of competing interests, struggles for power, and drives toward domination. That is the way human beings fundamentally are. Moral choice is irrelevant because for the Fundamentalists, life is an unrelenting struggle for individual political power. Politics is governed as much by chance and accident as by necessity and plan.

In this model, war derives from aggressive instincts, calculated or miscalculated. Using war to promote their interests, individual leaders exploit states and their publics. Or driven by fear and prejudices, confusion and misperception, leaders push their states to war, irrespective of true, rational, public interests.[19]

Classical political thought was preoccupied with psychological causation.[20] An essential aspect of Thucydidean thought, moreover, was the continuity of politics that rests on the continuity of human nature. It is "human nature being what it is" that made it possible to understand clearly the past and the future—

[19] A valuable survey of the individual drive literature can be found in James Schellenberg, *The Science of Conflict* (New York: Oxford University Press, 1982) and Samuel Kim, "The Lorenzian Theory of Aggression and Peace Research: A Critique," *Journal of Peace Research* 13, 4 (1976), pp. 253–76. Classic sources include: Robert Ardrey, *The Territorial Imperative* (New York: Atheneum, 1966), Konrad Lorenz, *On Aggression* (New York: Harcourt, 1966), Joseph De Rivera, *The Psychological Dimensions of Foreign Policy* (Columbus: Merrill, 1968), and Sigmund Freud, "Why War?," *Collected Papers*, ed. James Strachey (New York: Basic Books), vol. 22, pp. 204–11.
[20] Cornford, *Thucydides Mythistoricus*, pp. 64–65.

by its similarities to the past (I:22).[21] In this respect Thucydides's famous trinity of security, honor, and interest applied fundamentally to both personal and political motivation. Commentators on Thucydides have employed the connection between personality and politics to construct general theories of international change that span his time to our own.[22] But there is a significant difference for Thucydides between intrastate and interstate politics that does not allow us to assimilate the two into one continuous struggle for power as the Fundamentalists would have us do.

Thucydides used personification ("Athens") somewhat less than modern scholars do (he more frequently used "Athenians"). He saw factions within the state as contributing to choices of foreign policy (Archidamus's peace party at Sparta, the rural versus the urban inhabitants of Athens, the demos and the oligarchy). But with the striking exception of Alcibiades, individual leaders throughout the Peloponnesian War acted in the name of the public interest and through their control over state resources. Domestic factions, moreover, were not fixed in their influence or preferences. Thucydides meant politics to be understood as relatively autonomous public deliberation: choosing among competing interests and values.[23]

The Complex interpretation of Thucydides's Realism has been challenged by scholars (inspired by Fundamentalist views) who question the assumption of states as relatively autonomous actors. These critics question the notion that the state, the people, or their leadership could make politically responsible choices.[24] An aggressive policy, some say, had been forced on Pericles by the domestic commercial faction within Athens that sought to promote its private business prospects overseas. The merchants were the group with the most to benefit from an imperialist policy in the west and from the destruction of their Megarian commercial rivals, and both these actions were the ones that embroiled Athens with Corinth and thus with Corinth's ally Sparta.

[21] Robert Gilpin (1986) makes this biological-psychological continuity an important part of the reason that justifies the extension of Thucydidean and Realist thought into the present.

[22] Peter Pouncey (1980, p xii) and William Bluhm (1962, pp. 32–33) have shown how much of a contribution to our understanding of the Thucydidean state of war can be achieved with this method. Their theories of Athenian imperialism work through a "progress of pessimism": from fundamental human aggressiveness, through political organization, to imperial conquest, to interstate resistance, to domestic strain, to civil war, and collapse into a war of all against all.

[23] Marc Cogan (1981).

[24] Cornford, chaps. 2 and 3, has challenged that core Realist assumption (which underlies all Realist considerations of foreign policy) in favor of an interpretation of the war stressing the determinant role of instrumental class interests. Cornford's point is not that Thucydides held that class interests explained the war (were "the truest cause") but that Thucydides lacked altogether an explanation of the war in terms of state rivalry and that his failings are revealed in the patent superiority of a materialist, economic explanation (pp. 68–69).

Critics reject the strategic rivalry between Athens and Sparta as a sufficient explanation because neither state was best served by an aggressive policy.[25] But for a Realist—for Thucydides—the failure to achieve what would be the best outcome for each state considered separately is hardly a sufficient indication that the states were not acting according to their strategic interest. Nor is it an indication that they were instead being manipulated by particularistic domestic factions. Athens may well have preferred continued peace with its empire intact; Sparta, continued peace with its equality guaranteed. But if continued peace involved the steady increase in Athens's imperial power and Sparta preferred war to inferiority (as its Assembly in fact chose), then Thucydides is offering a strategic analysis and a Realist explanation of why Sparta chose war over peace, since no arrangement of international anarchy could lead to a stable peace other than the balanced power resources of the two sides. For him, unlike for the later Marxists, class interests do not provide a coherent, alternative way to organize political life. Individuals shaped but also were shaped by the state and the interstate system.

Still other Fundamentalist scholars have challenged the analysis of changing interstate power underlying Thucydides's explanation of the war. In making this challenge, these scholars attack another primary tenet of Complex Realist explanations. The continuity of interstate anarchy for the Realist provides the grounds for a comparative explanation of international events. The influence of changes in relative interstate power gives evidence of the underlying symmetry of interstate anarchy.

Thucydides asserts a Realist, power-oriented "truest cause" for the war—"what made the war inevitable was the growth of Athenian power and the fear which this caused in Sparta" (I:23 and see also I:44, I:88, and I:128)—and in doing so, he initiated what has since become a Realist staple.[26] But Thucydides failed—the critics argue—to offer a truly Realist explanation for the origins of the war. According to the critics, this is because he never fully demonstrated and explained the growth of Athenian power; instead he described a crisis in which allies embroiled the two antagonists and fear led one of them (Sparta) to declare war.[27] Critics argue that his *History* shows that Corinth, not Athens, forced Sparta into war.[28] Or it shows the significance of differences in political institutions, rules, and conventions,[29] which in its turn draws us into all the

[25] Ibid., pp. 8, 13.
[26] Hudson (1937) for the Second World War in the Far East, p. 198. Robert Gilpin, *War and Change in World Politics*, p. 201.
[27] In classics literature the charge was made by Meyer, Schwartz, Momigliano, and others (see the account by Kagan [1969] pp. 357–64, of these views) and in the political science literature, recently in a valuable article by Garst (1989).
[28] Meyer and Schwartz.
[29] Garst.

nonstructural and contingent crises and complaints from Epidamnus onward.[30]

Clearly, these critics are identifying something important. Thucydides's *History* showed that differences in political culture between Athens and Sparta as well as Corinth's incitement to action exacerbated Spartan fear. But Thucydides did not think they were the predominant, or truest, cause of Sparta's fear or of the war, which was the growth in Athenian power. Furthermore, he attempted to demonstrate this carefully.

The "Archaeology" (I:1–19) with which Book One begins is a long account of why the Peloponnesian War was the greatest of all wars. Great suffering and various prodigies made it noteworthy, of course, but likely a more important reason was that the two main combatants were at the height of their power, which was greater than any ever before exercised in Greece. The "Archaeology" further explains the growth of power among the city-states and notes, in particular, the emergence of states in place of tribal societies, the development of shipping, and the increase in money (which together led to colonization), the growth in size of territory, and the replacement of unstable and personalistic tyrannical rule by more unified public rule.

Differences in just these dimensions of power—ships, money, and size—identified the growth in Athenian power relative to that of Sparta. By the time of the outbreak of the war, neither the "great majority" (pro-war) nor the minority (anti-war) of the Spartans disagreed with that proposition. King Archidamus, arguing for negotiation and peace, urged caution in the face of the already superior power of Athens and delay in the hope that financial and naval aid would in a few years tilt the balance of power to Sparta's advantage (I:80–95). (But as a patriotic Greek he could not bring himself to utter the name of Persia, its only significant prospective source.) The ephor Sthenelaidas, arguing for war, played upon the military honor and sense of military superiority of the Spartan Assembly and warned it that it was better to have a war now—joining with its allies—against Athens than a war later, after having lost its allies, against an even stronger Athens (I:86). Thucydides then said that it was not so much that the allies persuaded or forced the Spartans, but that the Spartans, who made up their own minds, decided on war "because they were afraid of the further growth of Athenian power" (I:88).

Thucydides in the immediately following passages, the "Pentecontaetia" (I:89–117), proceeded to show how it was that Athenian power grew, stressing

[30] On the other hand, if Spartan fear developed independently of the actual growth of Athenian power, Thucydides's explanation would not be Realist, following the logic of self-help security; it would not be constrained by the continuity of international anarchy and conditioned by the evolution of the balance of power. If the war occurred inevitably through power dynamics and without the addition of Spartan fear, Thucydides's explanation would be Realist, but purely Structuralist and not Complex. It would also, if Kagan and Gruen are correct, be much less persuasive.

the crucial sources of power the "Archaeology" had identified. The growth in the relative power of Athens was a function both of its own success and of Spartan stagnation. Despite Sparta's traditional military preeminence among the Greeks, its institutions, its economy, and its culture were not conducive to a growth in power following the defeat of Persia. Its conservative, subsistence agriculture precluded the commerce needed to sustain seafaring and thus naval power. Its leader and its forces were too boorish and overbearing to lead the pan-Greek coalition then liberating Ionia from the weakened Persian empire (I:94–95). Its helots were prone to revolt, thereby tying down Spartan forces for domestic security. Athens, conversely, had the seafaring capacity to undergird specifically naval power, the sophistication to lead the other Greeks, and all the domestic security that a well-walled maritime city could enjoy. Taking over the lead from Sparta in liberating the Ionians, it expanded its maritime activities, established the leadership of a league of other states, which it transformed into an empire, and imposed a tribute on its "allies" (I:96–97). The increase in Athenian ships, money, and imperial expansion—the dimensions of power stressed in the "Archaeology"—now made for the growth in power that alarmed Sparta (see Thucydides's summary, I:118).

Differences in institutions and culture provoked tension and contributed to the failure of postwar cooperation.[31] Athenian conflicts with Sparta's most significant ally, Corinth, and Athenian ties to Sparta's traditional enemy, Argos, also increased tension. And the growth in Athenian power was not continuous. Athens sustained setbacks during the expedition to Egypt and in the loss of Boeotia following the First Peloponnesian War. But the fundamental sources of Athenian power that Thucydides stresses—seafaring, the navy, and the empire—remained intact and continued to grow until, in Thucydides's own words, Sparta felt its position "to be no longer tolerable" (I:118).[32] It was this

[31] The abortive Athenion mission to help Sparta put down a helot revolt serves as an ironic example.

[32] A second set of critics has conceded that Thucydides attempted a power-oriented explanation but argues that Thucydides's explanation is simply historically incorrect. This was the charge made by F. E. Adcock (1927, pp. 190–91) and supported by Donald Kagan's revisionist history of the causes of Peloponnesian War (1969, pp. 373–74). The crux of Kagan's revision was that the truest cause according to Realist explanation was *clearly* not true. Athens's power was not growing between the end of the First Peloponnesian War (446) and the diplomatic crises leading to the Second (435) (1969, chap. 19). The growth of Athenian power in the 450s would have justified a Spartan preventive war. The peace of 446–45, however, settled the first war following Athenian losses that radically reduced its power and according to terms that were acceptable to both Athens and Sparta. The actual outbreak of the second—Thucydides's—war was in 431. Athens's power did not increase between the two, so power cannot be used to explain the war or Sparta's fear. Athenian power in 431 probably did not match its power in the 450s, when its fleet fought in Egypt, it occupied its seafaring rival Megara, and it controlled most of central Greece (Boeotia). But Athens did improve its strategic position after the peace of 446—that is, after the defeat in the first war that saw the loss of each of those possessions. Thucydides may have exaggerated when he

shift in power that constrained policy choice. The Spartans were not free to ignore interstate politics without suffering decline; they were forced to fight or appease.

INTERSTATE STRUCTURALISM

Structuralism explains the necessity of the state of war by focusing on international anarchy. Structuralism finds the complexity and contingency of Complex Realism unnecessary. For the Structuralist, the important questions can be explained parsimoniously via international structure—not through difficult political or moral choice but through the unrelenting competition of independent states.[33] Thucydides respected Structural parsimony. That is what the "truest cause"—"the growth of Athenian power and the fear which this caused in Sparta" (I:23)—was all about. But his theory was not Structural.

According to the proponents of Structuralism, competition and socialization under anarchy select for power-seeking ends and rational decision-making processes in the way a competitive market selects for profit maximization.[34] States that do not operate according to these standards of power maximization will simply be eliminated; we should thus assume that complex political and moral choices are irrelevant. States naturally balance power against power, rather than "bandwagon" toward the powerful. They fight when they think they can win. States can be assumed to be basically similar "units," and international politics can thereby be understood primarily in reference to the number and relative power of the states—to the "structure" of the international system.

called 431 the high summer of Athenian power (I:1), but in the preceding fourteen years there is some evidence of real strategic advance on the part of Athens. Athens, as Romilly and more recently de Ste. Croix have noted, consolidated its naval preeminence and establishing complete command of the eastern Mediterranean. It shifted to a coherent imperial strategy by shedding its least defensible landed possessions while colonizing the more defensible island of Euboea. In 441–40 Athens crushed the strategically well-sited Byzantium and Samos (the single largest among its Delian "allies") and thereby absorbed them as subordinate tribute-paying states. Athens thus completed the transformation of the hegemonic alliance of Greek states it had inherited from Sparta after the Persian War into a true maritime empire (arche) effectively controlled from the imperial center (Romilly [1963], pp. 19–20; de Ste. Croix [1972], p. 60). In 437 it sent major colonial expeditions to the Black Sea shore (Sinope and Nymphaeum in the Crimea). This enhanced its commercial presence in that important granary, which was now more secure than Boeotia had been, as long as Athens maintained naval predominance. Athens then secured its northern sea route by planting colonies and forts in Thrace (437–36). It stocked a war chest of six thousand talents drawn from surplus tribute. And in the prewar crisis Athens added a defensive alliance with Corcyra, the second naval power of Greece.

[33] For example, Kenneth Waltz made structural factors the decisive reasons in his arguments against the significance of economic interdependence and for the stability of bipolar systems (1979, chaps. 7 and 8).

[34] Ibid.

We can therefore reconstruct what a purely Structural account of the war would look like. After the great battles of Salamis and Plataea (480 B.C.), which crushed the Persian invasion of Greece, the Spartan general Leonidas led the Greek campaign to eject the Persians from the Aegean. His overbearingness, however, soon led the Greek allies to replace Sparta and entrust the Athenians with the leadership of a league of Greek city-states whose treasury they placed at Delos. Sparta and its allies dropped out. The successful liberation of Persia's Greek colonies led to the growth of Athenian power. Step by step, Athens transformed the Delian League into an Athenian empire, fortified itself with long walls, and established a dominance over the commerce of the eastern Mediterranean. Sparta's allies struck against Athenian power in a First Peloponnesian War, but this war resulted in only a temporary setback to the growth of the Athenian empire.

By the 430s, just before the outbreak of the Second Peloponnesian War, the distribution of power in the Greek world was what we would call quasi-*bipolar*, in that, as Thucydides says, the states of Greece were divided up between two "alliances": the Peloponnesian League led by its hegemon, Sparta, one of the two "poles"; and the Delian League, an empire directed by Athens, the other pole (I:1). Both Athens and Sparta stood out as the militarily leading states; no one state—other than one of the two poles—could readily contemplate an attack on either of the two poles.[35] In the 430s the composition of power was not identical. Sparta, the great land power, could in an emergency draw on fifty thousand of its unequaled frontline hoplites (elite troops). Sparta's Peloponnesian League mustered 140 ships, mostly Corinthian, at the naval Battle of Sybota, which preceded the war, against Corcyra's 110 ships, but the destruction on both sides eliminated those two powers as factors in the naval balance of power. Athens, the great naval power, kept thirteen thousand hoplites under arms and could draw on sixteen thousand in reserve; but its real strength lay at sea, where it could launch 300 ships and rely on a revenue of one thousand talents (six hundred of which derived from the empire alone).[36]

The Structuralist logic of a *static* bipolar system suggests a stable balance of power since no small power can rationally challenge one of the two large powers and (given a normal advantage for the defense over the offense) neither of the two more equal large powers can contemplate successful aggression. Change, however, can be extremely disruptive in such a system. As Thucydides says, it was the "growth" of Athenian power that caused the war (I:23). To see how, we can compare it to a multipolar system. A bipolar system lacks one of

[35] This is one of the criteria that Waltz (1979) employs to define a bipolar relationship; see also the discussion in Hopf, (1991).
[36] N. G. L. Hammond, A *History of Greece* (New York: Oxford University Press, 1986) assembled these figures, relying on contemporary evidence.

the *dynamic* stabilizing tendencies of a multipolar system. In a multipolar system the increase in the power of one state can be met in either of two ways. State A balances *internally* when it matches the rising power of state B with increases in spending on arms in the short run or investment in the long run. State A balances *externally* when it matches the rising power of state B by forming a coalition against B from among states—C, D, E, etc.—which were previously neutral or previously allied with B. Bipolar systems, by definition, lack effective sources of external balancing since the only other significant strategic power is the other pole. The only dynamic stabilizing factor of a bipolar system is *internal* balancing—increased investment in arms. Given Sparta's traditional and complete dedication to military preparedness, the increase in Athens's power meant surrender, resignation to subordination, or a war of resistance. War in turn meant war now or war later, when Athens would be even more powerful.

As a *quasi*-bipolar, on the other hand, some of the logic of multipolar politics applied. Before their fleets were destroyed, the threat of the combined Corcyrean and Corinthian fleets would have nearly matched that of Athens's own fleet. Bipolar systems presume an indifference to the defection of allies—from the purely military point of view. This is what helps keep them stable. But neither Athens nor Sparta could be indifferent; they were not superior enough. In multipolar systems, on the other hand, alliances shift to reflect multiple changes in relative power.[37] But Athens and Sparta were each too large to be readily balanced by marginal shifts in alliances. Quasi-bipolar systems suffer the evils of both systems; Corinthian and Corcyrean threats of defection helped drag in their superior allies, but they were insufficient to balance the power of the two leaders.

Of course, Thucydides does not explain the exact timing, in 431, in this way. For that we need his account of the expressed complaints from Epidamnus and Potidaea. These disputes spread the conflict from the minor powers, Corcyra and Corinth, to Athens and Sparta (I:36). But war was likely—if not at that time, then sooner rather than later—because of the systemic (Structural) slide in the key, bilateral balance of forces against Sparta and its Peloponnesian League. Thus the rise in Athenian power rationally compelled (explained) the war, both its occurrence and its timing.

But important as these Structuralist observations are, they are not the essence of Thucydides's argument. Thucydides's work is a testament to the fact that he held that a state's ends, its means, and (therefore) its choices could not be

[37] Karl Deutsch and J. David Singer, "Multipolar Systems and International Stability," *World Politics* 16, 3 (April 1964), pp. 390–406. I return to these issues of relative stability in chapter 3.

adequately determined through an analysis of international structure. Structure was not enough to determine the political choices that shaped the war, the Athenian empire, or the Spartan hegemony. Structure, for him, was both *too narrow* and *too shallow*.

Did narrow power competition alone make the war "inevitable"? Thucydides notes that Sparta's "fear," one of the root causes of the war, was a product, not just of Athenian power, but of the mood that Sthenelaidas exploited in the Spartan Assembly.[38] The growth in Athenian power was not in itself sufficient to make the war "inevitable."[39] Thucydides says in the famous verdict of I:23: "What made the war inevitable was the growth of Athenian power and the fear which this caused in Sparta." The trend toward an increase in Athenian power did seem to make a war rationally preferable now rather than later. But if Archidamus's rationalistic analysis (I:80–81) was correct, Athens was already more powerful (possessed more strategic resources) than Sparta. War thus was not clearly the rational response. It was the addition of Sthenelaidas's persuasive harangue (I:86) against Athenian power and his evocation of Spartan honor, hatred, and fear that overwhelmed Archidamus's rational discourse on Athenian power and Spartan prudence. Athenian power did not compel or produce an inevitable result without Spartan fear and honor, both of which were stimulated by Sthenelaidas. This fear was produced not merely by Athenian power, but also by Spartan vulnerability and Spartan pride. Specifically, Sparta believed that it was vulnerable to a helot uprising, inspired and, perhaps, assisted by democratic Athenians.[40] It also felt threatened by a loss of its leadership of the Peloponnesian League, which would have been set in motion had Corinth defected out of frustration with Sparta's failure to overturn the Corcyraean alliance with Athens. Sparta's pride shaped Sthenelaidas's ferocious harangue and his demand that the assembled Spartans vote for "the honor of Sparta and for war." Would Sparta be subordinate to Athens or, as it had once been, superordi-

[38] Donald Kagan has introduced persuasive reasons for us to believe that each of the major participants—Sparta, Athens, Corinth—had a significant range of choice that was in part domestically determined (1969, pp. 351–56).

[39] Supporting both Kagan's history and Thucydides's interpretation, Erich Gruen has suggested that the proper translation of Thucydides's passage is "forced them to go to war," which is less mechanical a compulsion than is suggested by "inevitable" (1971, p. 331). W. R. Connor translates this passage similarly, ending with "drove them into war" rather than employing "inevitability" (1984, p. 126). Thucydides. we should note, was contrasting not the underlying or remote as against the surface or immediate causes, but the real reasons or truest causes actually compelling Sparta as against the expressed or superficial excuses and complaints. Athens's power grew (a real and an underlying cause), and this helped explain fear in Sparta (also a real but an immediate cause). Together these factors caused the war.

[40] In 462 Sparta sent home the Athenians who had volunteered to help them suppress a helot rebellion (I:102).

nate to Greece? That was the question he asked them.[41] Their answer was not a simple rational response; their pride responded to Sthenelaidas's superior harangue.

So too Thucydides found that Athens's mistakes and final defeat could not be attributed to a simple decline in its relative power resources, for both its ends and means had changed. Athenian policy too had become subject to something other than rational, national, strategic calculation. Thucydides would have agreed that statesmen should, as Pericles did, calculate their security with close attention to the threats posed by other states and to the resources available to meet those threats. But states could become corrupted, as did Athens, through the strains of war, plague, and factionalism. In the debate over the decision to send an expedition to Sicily, private interests, not public security, governed policy, as I discuss below. Mass religious panic had an equivalent effect in the decision to prosecute the brilliant (though rash) general Alcibiades. Factionalism intensified, and soon Athenians fought Athenians, making the eventual Spartan victory a product more of Athenian disunity than of Spartan superiority. "In the end it was only because they had destroyed themselves by their own internal strife that finally they were forced to surrender" (II:65).

Thucydides also rejected shallow interpretations of power. He agreed that "We have no right, therefore, to judge cities by their appearances rather than by their actual power" (I:11). But power too had to be explained. One response to the increase in Athens's power should have been internal balancing on the part of Sparta, including investment in a fleet, a larger expeditionary force, and its own empire, in order to match the Athenian empire. But Sparta's social structure, which was equivalent to a massive penal colony designed to control and exploit the oppressed Messenian helots, resisted innovation. According to Thucydides, conservative, agrarian, aristocratic Sparta was simply incapable of stimulating growth through commerce and economic innovation.

Actualized power, also according to Thucydides, was not merely a function of similar categories of power, fungibly distributed in quantity across the interstate system. For Thucydides, Athens differed from Sparta not only in quantity of power but also in differences in the nonequivalent functions of power.[42] At the outset of the war Athens's army could no more invade and occupy Sparta than the Spartan Navy could blockade Piraeus.

Imperial power, moreover, differed from hegemonic power. The Athenian empire *(arche)* rested on the far-flung outposts and material benefits that an expansive commercial society could readily provide to its collaborating subordinates. Sparta's conservative noncommercial society could not provide the exten-

[41] For a discussion of Sparta's traditional preeminent ranking, see W. Robert Connor, *Thucydides*, pp. 33–34.

[42] See Klaus Knorr, *Power and Wealth* (New York: Basic Books, 1973) for these distinctions.

sive range of material and psychological benefits that sustained imperial collaboration. Spartan hegemony (*hegemonia*) correspondingly rested on its military prowess.[43]

Some polities, like the Greek remnants of the Persian empire liberated by Athens in the 480s, were vulnerable to imperial conquest, and others were much less so. Some were racked by deep social fissures. Their democrats became a trans-statal faction favoring Athens, just as their oligarchs favored Sparta. Each faction preferred to collaborate with foreigners in order to balance against domestic rivals, rather than to adhere to domestic unity in order to balance against external threats and preserve state independence. Indeed, this was exactly Alcibiades's insightful point when, just before the expedition to Sicily, he assured the Athenians that no one should overestimate Sicilian power. Despite Sicilian numbers and wealth, their factionalism meant that they were "scarcely likely either to pay attention to one consistent policy or to join together in concerted action" (VI:17). The mistake of Alcibiades and Athens was not in failing to estimate the numbers of the Sicilians, but in failing to realize that under Hermocrates's brilliant leadership the states of Sicily were more like the Athenians themselves than like the weak and divided islands Athens had absorbed from the Persian empire.[44] Sicily was not a Structurally determined power center; Hermocrates made the Sicilians a power committed to their own defense.

For Thucydides, rational unitary action was a goal and a key to survival in an anarchic world. Balancing power against power was not a Structurally determined necessity. Rational strategic action relied on both domestic and international circumstances.[45] The necessities that states, empires, and hegemonies claimed for themselves represented political choices made by statesmen and citizens.

INTERSTATE CONSTITUTIONALISM

Lastly, Constitutionalism makes the simple claim that domestic structures and institutions make a difference in the formulation of foreign policy and the shape of international politics. Actors, preferences, and information do not constitute themselves naturally; instead they are defined by rules and conventions that are

[43] I attempt to provide support for and some qualifications to these propositions in *Empires* (1986, chap. 3, pp. 54–81).
[44] They were "democracies like themselves," of a considerable size, "well-equipped," and polities against whom "fifth columns" (collaborators) were ineffective (VII:55).
[45] Bagby, "The Use and Abuse of Thucydides," pp. 131–153, offers a valuable examination of these issues.

primarily domestic, social constructs.[46] The Realist version of Constitutionalism makes modest claims because it assumes that no institution is sufficient to take states out of the condition of war. Neither international law nor domestic law, neither norms nor institutions, can make state behavior sufficiently trustworthy to end the insecurity, interest, and prestige that make states natural enemies of one another.

International institutions, both formal and informal, appeared to have very little influence in Thucydides's *History*. The Corinthian case for international law and norms of gratitude held little weight against the Corcyraean argument in favor of the naval balance of power. The Delphic oracle showed up largely as a curiosity, reported coolly, as were various religious signs that occasionally influenced soldiers and citizens.

Domestic institutions had more regular effects. The cultural divide between (Athenian) Ionians and (Spartan) Dorians shaped the diplomacy of the entire war. Sparta's existence as a slave economy and Athens's as a dynamic commercial economy governed much of their initial distrust and fouled their attempts at cooperation, as when Athens attempted to rescue Sparta from a slave rebellion before the wars, merely resulting in heightening Spartan suspicions and anti-Athenian sentiments (I:102).

Do democratic and aristocratic republics, as birds of different feathers, each flock to their own kind and express hostility toward their opposites?[47] Majority self-interest, expressed through representative government and solidarity toward those defined as similar to oneself, seemed to help account for the tendency that made democrats the allies of democrats and aristocrats the allies of aristocrats. And some evidence supports the hypothesis. The Delian League was predominantly democratic; the Peloponnesian League, predominantly aristocratic (or oligarchic).[48]

But this hypothesis falters on what Thucydides observed to be the subversive effects of complex self-interest, honor, and insecurity, together with the dynamic effects of corruption and leadership. There were, for example, oligarchic members of the Delian League (Chios, Lesbos, and for a while Samos) and democratic members of the Peloponnesian League (Elis, Mantinea). While *force majeure* may have kept them allied (and there is evidence for this with regard to Samos and others), so too did *force majeure* play a role in regard

[46] James March and Johan Olson, "Organizing Political Life: What Administrative Reorganization Tells Us about Government," *American Political Science Review* 77, 2 (June 1983), pp. 281–96.

[47] Spencer Weart, "Peace among Democratic and Oligarchic Republics," *Journal of Peace Research* 31, 3 (August 1994), pp. 299–313.

[48] Bruce Russett and William Antholis "The Imperfect Democratic Peace of Ancient Greece," in Bruce Russett, ed., *Grasping the Democratic Peace* (Princeton: Princeton University Press 1992).

to all of Athens's allies, however popular the empire may have been with some of the demos, some of the time, on some of the subordinate islands.[49] In crises the players were often driven in disparate directions by the search for security and honor: oligarchic Corinth turned out to be the protector of the democratic Epidamnians against the more democratic Corcyraeans. Athens attacked Syracuse, though Syracuse was a quasi-democracy, because it saw the Sicilians as weak, ridden with both class and factional divisions (as they were to some extent [I:20]). If Thucydides had found democratic institutional solidarity and automatic hostility to aristocracy to have been the governing principle of Athenian policy, he would have pointed it out. It would have violated his sense of rational prudence, and he had no sympathy for the excesses of democracy.

More important, Thucydides took pains to point out the changeability of institutions. Athens could become corrupted by private self-interest, causing the abandonment of its plan to wage a war of prudent attrition. Instead, the Assembly chose to expand its empire aggressively by means of the Sicilian expedition. As Periclean leadership disappeared, domestic distrust and demoralization favored leaders who appealed to single virtues that thus became vices: Alcibiades's brilliance; Nicias's caution; Cleon's patriotism. Each lacked the combined and balanced virtues of Pericles. Athens came apart under the stress of war, plague, and poor leadership, and in the end this was the ultimate cause of the Athenian defeat (II:65). Some states fractured completely, as did Corcyra during its revolution. And some, equally important, were constructed during the war, as Hermocrates forged a unified Sicily to meet and then, with Spartan help, to defeat the Athenian expedition.

At root these republics may have been too similar for their institutional differences to have been decisive factors in interstate politics. Or perhaps the ancient democracies lacked the fundamental perceptions of human rights and equal human dignity that later made Liberal societies come to feel a significant degree of mutual respect. Human equality was still at best a matter for philosophic speculation, a matter still eloquently rejected by the great minds of Plato and Aristotle as a principle with which to govern the actions of states.

Another Thucydidean view of the effects of democratic institutions on relations among states serves as a valuable counterpoint to the modern view that attributes both power and peace to democracy.[50] Rather than peace or restraint, power and imperial growth, followed by excess, factionalism, and collapse, were the traits that Thucydides associated with democracy. This association leaves us with two puzzles. The larger one is why we see democracy as peace-loving

[49] See M. Finley, "The Fifth Century Athenian Empire: A Balance Sheet," in P. D. A. Garnsey and C. R. Whittaker, eds., *Imperialism in the Ancient World* (Cambridge: Cambridge University Press, 1978), pp. 103–26.

[50] For an interesting discussion of these issues, see David Lake, "Powerful Pacifists," *American Political Science Review* 86, 1 (1992), pp. 24–37.

when he saw it as empire-making (this I postpone to the conclusion of Part II). The smaller puzzle, the Athenian puzzle, is how an institution so useful in making an empire could be so prone to overextension.

Democracy meant that power was in the hands not of the minority but of the "whole people." Citizens enjoyed equality before the law, a political career open to talents, and a special freedom and tolerance in private matters (I:37). In actual practice, of course, Athens was a slave society depending on forced labor for its profitable mines at Laurium and for some of its agriculture. Still, for the forty to fifty thousand male citizens democratic self-rule was real, the Assembly and its democratically elected Council of Five Hundred being the dominant voice in legislative affairs of the state just as the ten democratically elected strategoi were in military and executive affairs.

For Thucydides, states are driven by "honor, security and self-interest" (I:76). States cannot escape from constant danger because "when tremendous dangers are involved no one can be blamed for looking to his own interest" (I:76). Since weakness always means subjection, only independent strength guarantees independent security, so states must look to their own relative power or accept the dangers of strategic dependence (II:62).

The most straightforward connection between democracy and power lies in the importance of naval power. When naval power relies upon oared galleys, a navy of free rowers is inherently superior to a navy of slave rowers, since in the heat of battle the former can be called upon to defend their ships. As Pseudo-Xenophon notes, "the poorer classes and the demos rightly possess more authority than the well-born and the rich because it is the demos that rows the ships and keeps the city powerful."[51]

A second democratic source of power comes from the resources that are freed up when citizens have a stake in the survival and success of the state. Rather than spend resources in coercing the citizenry, the state can draw upon citizens' resources for what are regarded as public purposes. A free society generates an "adventurous spirit," producing a willingness to take risks, to increase production, and to trade far and wide. A free society, furthermore, is a society in which deliberation in public can guide and, through the exercise of reason, improve public policy. As Pericles so eloquently explained in his funeral oration for the Athenian war dead (II:34–46), a democratic polity is the necessary expression of a free society, and only in a free society are the creative energies of the populace allowed full play to develop.

Third, democratic participation also provides a large part of the motive force—both material and ideal—that drives policy. By the 440s paid jury duty provided valuable sources of additional income to approximately half the citi-

[51] Pseudo-Xenophon, *The Constitution of Athens*, I:2.

zenry.[52] Colonial settlement on the confiscated lands of recalcitrant "allies" offered a livelihood to smaller numbers. Of the one thousand talents of annual state revenue in 431, six hundred were derived from imperial taxation, fees, and tariffs.[53] Equally important (according to Pericles) was the authority public magistrates derived from the Athenian respect for law (II:37). Moreover, the freedom of Athens produced a confidence in one's ability to overcome dangers that contributed to the Athenian patriotism underlying the empire (II:39–40).

Fourth, those domestic traits together made Athens an attractive center for all the Ionian peoples and offered the material basis that permitted it to "make friends by doing good to others" (II:40). The Athenian empire was, Pericles acknowledged, a tyranny, but it also had popular mass support, even in the subordinated colonies. Athens's subordinate allies sought access to the economy it controlled. The masses sought association with the Athenian demos; indeed, they could be counted on as allies in many cases against their own oligarchic rulers. Athenian liberality, together with manifest productivity of its economy and cultural vitality of its society, also produced the international "popularity" that made association with the Athenian polis, even in its imperial form, attractive to the masses throughout much of the Greek world.[54]

Democracy, however, is also a source of eventual weakness. Indeed, it is here, in Thucydides's *History*, that democracy first acquired its reputation for such disastrous factionalism that, more than two thousand years later, the authors of the *Federalist Papers* still thought it necessary to try to rebut the charge. Athenian democracy fractured under stress. The great plague of 430 undermined trust (those first to help others became the most likely to be infected [II:51]). Afterward the patriotism, respect for the laws, caution, courage, and brilliance that had led the citizens to follow the wise strategy of attrition prescribed by Pericles (who embodied all those virtues) broke down into passion, suspicion, and greed. The citizens let themselves be led by lesser men who had some but not all his virtues; they followed the cautious (Nicias), or courageous (Cleon), or brilliant (Alcibiades).[55] Each of these leaders and the

[52] Hammond, p. 301.
[53] Ibid., p. 347.
[54] The demos on Samos and other leading colonies stayed surprisingly loyal to the demos of Athens, even after Athens began to lose the war. (See Russell Meiggs, *The Athenian Empire* [Oxford: Oxford University Press, 1972], pp. 371–72.) Earlier in the war the demos of Mytilene, for example, resisted the efforts of the oligarchic faction to liberate Mytilene from the Athenian empire, so that when the oligarchy mistakenly armed them, they forced the oligarchy to surrender to Athens (III:27). But for a thorough treatment of the complex issue, see the debate on this issue between de Ste. Croix and Bradeen in *Historia*, in 1954 and 1960. For current scholarship on the international implications of Thucydides's history, see Lebow and Barry Strauss, *Hegemonic Rivalry*.
[55] John Finley's *Thucydides* suggests this interpretation.

policies of appeasement, brutality, and adventurousness that they advocated became the public policy of the majority of the democratic citizenry. Nowhere better than in the debate over whether to send an expedition to conquer hitherto neutral Sicily do the effects of factionalism and majority tyranny emerge. Thucydides sums up the debate and fateful decision in this way:

> There was a passion for the enterprise which affected everyone alike. The older men thought they would either conquer the places against which they were sailing or, in any case, with such a large force, could come to no harm; the young had a longing for the sights and experiences of distant places, and were confident that they would return safely; the general masses and the average soldier himself saw the prospect of getting pay for the time being and of adding to the empire so as to secure permanent paid employment in the future. The result of this excessive enthusiasm of the majority was that the few who actually were opposed to the expedition were afraid of being thought unpatriotic if they voted against it, and therefore kept quiet [VI:24].

Domestic institutions thus are fluid, not determinate. In a world that required that states look to their relative power in order to maintain security, democracy was valued because it contributed to state power and, in particular, helped create imperial power. But more than simply adding to resources and influence, democracy shaped and continuously reshaped public goals and visions. It engendered unnecessary reasons for expansion: to maintain employment; to enhance glory; to stir up adventures; to expand commerce; to educate other peoples in democratic civilization. These new goals, each chosen by a temporary majority, led to unnecessary wars, which then undermined the security of the state. That is the democratic tragedy of which Thucydides warns us.

THUCYDIDEAN METHODOLOGY

How, then, can a Realist draw everlasting lessons expressing the actual continuity of international anarchy if interests, security, and honor are contingent on both international structure (shifting balances) and domestic politics? The answer, if this analysis is persuasive, is "The way Thucydides did." According to Hobbes, one should interpret Thucydides in the "narration."[56] Thucydides himself did not formulate general laws, though the speakers whose words he recounts often did. He, however, did seek truest causes and the exact truth, "an accurate view" (V:26). He reported competing explanations, but he only offered multiple interpretations of the same event in his own voice when he could offer nothing better and suffered from lack of information. His own method was a

[56] Schlatter (1975), p. 18.

combination of direct explanations of the "truest cause" variety and indirect explanations implied by his placing events in multiple contexts—interstate, domestic, and personal.

What are our interpretive options? We find general observations made by speakers whose words we must place in their context and then try to translate into ours. We find warnings in extreme situations.[57] And we are shown typical, generalizable situations that confront statesmen in interstate politics.[58] Thucydides provided direct warnings of the need to avoid the common and uncritical acceptance of popular stories (I:20) and of how parallels could be abused. This was what the Athenians did when they applied their memory of the conspiracy of Harmodius and Aristogiton to Alcibiades (VI:53–59).[59] Thucydides also showed how history could be properly used. His lengthy demonstration of the comparative pettiness of previous Greek wars was designed to demonstrate the importance of the Peloponnesian War (I:1–21). Lessons learned from recognizing the plague and its social effects might warn us of what to expect in a recurrence (II:48). Together these methods—akin to those of medical diagnosis—made the history as a whole "useful" to "those who want to understand clearly the events which happened in the past and which (human nature being what it is) will, at some time or other and in much the same ways, be repeated in the future" (I:22).[60]

Thucydides believed, just as the Realists do, that no reliable order exists above the sovereign city-states. It is therefore interstate anarchy, as well as human nature, that makes interstate relations similar enough to be explicable. Both produce and reproduce, through the actions of states, a "state of war" which is mutual mistrust and a concern with the balance of power. Even with the best will in the world, no power will surrender any part of its security or liberty to another unless it is forced to do so by conquest or the need to counter an even greater, mutual threat (such as Persia). Shifts in relative power together with provokable fears make mistrusts into wars.

THUCYDIDEAN ETHICS

A long tradition of Realist thought in international politics says that one cannot be both realistic and moralistic. Realists have demonstrated little patience with statements such as that made by President Woodrow Wilson in the course of his declaration of war when he looked forward "to the beginning of an age in

[57] Hayward Alker (1981) has analyzed the Melian Dialogue using (appropriately) dialectical methods to uncover Thucydides's interpretation of how force can govern logic.
[58] Kateb (1964).
[59] See Rawlings (1981), pp. 103–17.
[60] Cochrane, chap. 3.

which it will be insisted that the same standards of conduct and of responsibility for wrong shall be observed among nations and their governments that are observed among individual citizens of individual states."[61]

Moral philosophers, however, have shown that Realist criticisms of "moralism," persuasive as they often are, have little bearing on whether ethical judgments should apply to international politics. A sophisticated conception of morality, they also argue, should be preferred over a crude or simple moralism. States should not follow simpleminded rules when the security of their own population or human welfare more broadly considered demands the recognition of conflicts in moral duties. That leaders of states should arm, train, and send soldiers into battle to kill when necessary in a just cause no more corresponds to murder than lying to save a friend from a known assassin is a culpable lie. For the philosophers, the resolution of moral conflict is the essence, not the refutation, of ethical reasoning.[62]

But the Realists have profound criticisms of the relevance of moral standards in international politics. Three of these criticisms together constitute Realist moral skepticism. The fourth develops a specifically Realist ethics of the international situation.

The first is that the structure of the international system leaves no room for choice. The necessity of states precludes even strategic choices—*a fortiori* moral choices. This can most clearly be associated with the Structuralist (or Hobbesian) view. The second, a Constitutionalist view, is that the competitive necessities of all politics preclude moral choices. All power corrupts (and absolute power, as Lord Acton opined, does so absolutely). The third highlights the pervasive human struggle for power and advantage, private or public, at home and overseas, which derogates all moral considerations. This associates itself of course with the Fundamentalist (or, some say, Machiavellian) condition.[63]

The fourth acknowledges the existence of authentic moral choices, but argues that the circumstances of world politics severely limit the range of justifiable rules just as they limit the scope of individual and political choice. This is Thucydides's own Complex Realism, an attempt both to explain the war and Athens's defeat, as discussed above, and to probe the relationship between political necessity and moral choice.[64]

[61] Morgenthau (1952), p. 242.
[62] Marshall Cohen (1985).
[63] These correspond with three images of international politics. My views on these parallels were improved by a comment by Peter Furia. Both Hobbesian and Machiavellian forms of Realism are discussed in this way in the author's "Thucydidean Realism," *Review of International Studies* 16, 3 (July 1990). Machiavelli's own views are more complicated, as the next chapter will suggest.
[64] The Constitutionalist view of Rousseau, as the most direct inheritor of Thucydides's own Complex position, is quite close to Thucydides's in this regard and will be considered in a later chapter.

Just as empirical Realists invoke Thucydides to establish a continuous tradition, so Realist moralists look to classical Greece to discover an ethics of world politics not constrained by what they regard as inappropriate religious or cosmopolitan moralities.[65] I would like to show that Realists seeking to learn from Thucydides should realize that his views correspond to none of the Realist skepticisms outlined above but that he does develop the fourth argument. He does not reject ethical standards although he does instruct political leaders in the importance of circumscribing radically the range of moral choice in international politics. If we judge Thucydides's views both by his few but important direct statements and by the lessons that the *History* considered as a whole teaches, he offers guidelines to a distinct Realist ethics of interstate politics.[66] He rejects the idea that we can have categorical moral duties in international politics, such as those some liberals sometimes advocate, without rejecting the idea that we can have moral duties that should sometimes override both the political advantages of particular leaders and the material interests of particular states. For Thucydides, the range of moral choice should be circumscribed only by strategic necessity, the essential security of the state.

The Structural balance of power, the Constitutionalist conception of state interests, and the Fundamental power struggle of ambitious leaders did not eliminate political choice, according to Thucydides. Politics for him was open to responsible choice. But would the possibility of a responsible politics include moral considerations, and would they carry over to international politics? Could the foreign policy of a Thucydidean statesman join moral choice with the political "necessities" of Realism?

The outlines of Thucydides's conventional Realism are hardly in doubt. After all, he was the explicator of the "truest cause" of the great war between Athens and Sparta: the pressures of power politics (I:23). Interstate relations in his view existed in a condition where war was always possible, a state of war such as that "hard school of danger" that persisted between Athens and Sparta during the "peace" that preceded the actual outbreak of hostilities (I:19). We all recall the stark warning the Athenian officials gave the Melians: "The strong do what they have the power to do and the weak accept what they have to accept" (V:89). Thucydides also recognized that the struggle of factions that competed over policy could also threaten the domestic unity of every state. But he saw that statesmen—necessarily situated in both domestic politics and interstate competition—made choices among both values and interests.

In assessing the role played by values and interests in political choice, recent

[65] For a careful interpretation of the modern Realist consciousness, covering in particular the reaction of modern Realists, through Niebuhr, to the problem of Christianity, see Michael Smith (1986).

[66] Good examples of this style of interpretation applied to Thucydides's politics can be found in Kateb (1964) and Robert Connor (1984).

scholarship suggests that Thucydides was much more of a categorical moralist than conventional Realism would allow. Many of his "amoralisms" were necessary rhetorical deceptions, we are told.[67] Consider the following example. Thucydides recounts the Mytilenian debate in the Assembly when the Athenian citizens decided to reconsider their decision to execute all the Mytilenians as a punishment for their rebellion against Athens. Cleon demanded that the Assembly stick to its harsh sentence as a just punishment for the rebellious criminals he claimed the Mytilenians were. Diodotus told the Athenians that their Assembly was a political body, not a court of law (III:44). He then persuaded them that Athenian self-interest—the stable acceptance of their imperial rule by their colonies—required moderation. Diodotus may have been tempted to speak deceptively in order to persuade the war-weary Athenians (III:43). But deception did not require him to cater to the Assembly's self-interest, disguising his own (and Thucydides's) moral repugnance at Cleon's "monstrous" but legalistic defense of vengeance.[68] The Athenian populace itself had already come to regret the harshness of its previous decision.[69]

We should not identify moral choice with the application of categorical rules. The debate between Cleon and Diodotus not only expresses Thucydides's preference for Diodotus's rhetoric of prudent self-interest over Cleon's categorically moral, legal punishment, but also expresses Thucydides's preference for Diodotus's prudent morality over Cleon's legalistic vengeance. Prudent self-interest can thus be read as an authentic expression of Thucydides's views and not merely as a rhetorical tactic in a disguised morality.

The mainstream interpretation of Thucydides argues for another view, holding that, for him, every instance of strategic necessity eliminated moral or religious duty. Thucydides, on this account, saw military necessity as eroding all restraints—whether religious or moral—on Athenian imperialism.[70] The example in question runs as follows: In the course of driving an Athenian force from their land, the Boeotians defeat the Athenian Army and then refuse to grant the

[67] A recent article by David Cohen focusing on the events of Book III at Plataea, Corcyra, and Mytilene has rejected the standard view of Thucydides as an "amoral realist" (1984), p. 37. See also the valuable and differing discussions of this issue in M. I. Finley, "Introduction" to the Penguin edition ("a moralist's work," p. 32), de Ste. Croix (1972, p. 11), and Kagan (1975). Cohen is revising earlier accounts such as Cochrane's, which argued that the views of both Diodotus and Cleon reflected expediential reasoning (Cochrane, pp. 105–06).

[68] We have good reason to believe that Diodotus *did* speak deceptively. He seems to have misled the Assembly into believing that only the local oligarchs were rebellious when it appeared that many more were involved. But we need not assume that his entire argument was deceptive, any more than we need to agree that Cleon made a true case for just punishment. See W. R. Connor (1984), pp. 87–88.

[69] Thucydides also finds this reflected in the attitude of the Athenian expedition sent to punish the Mytilenians; they rowed slowly, expressing their reluctance (III:49). See the discussion in Walzer (1977), pp. 10–11.

[70] For background, see Orwin (1989), p. 217.

return of the Athenian dead for burial. When Athens demands the return of its dead according to traditional international law, the Boeotians demand the evacuation of the last spot of Boeotia, the temple at Delium, which Athens has fortified and retains. The Boeotians denounce the fortification as an act of impiety. Athens pleads necessity to justify the fortification of the temple and use of the sacred waters (for drinking), claiming that military necessity compelled the use and that sovereignty over temples goes to those who conquer the territory (IV:97–99).

Thucydides refused to judge this issue explicitly. In the lack of explicit judgment, however, he seemed to acknowledge the weight of the arguments each side advanced—and thus the importance of necessity. But he did not seem to be saying that necessity eliminated all restraints. Both parties claimed necessity. On the one hand, Athens could justify its invasion of Boeotia as a matter of strategic necessity. Athens invaded in order to take the pressure off the repeated Spartan-Boeotian invasions of Attica. On the other hand, Boeotians could claim, as did their general Pagondas, that Athens was a continuously aggressive imperial power. Athens was a revolutionary state; it could not be treated as a normal state. Athens might no longer be threatening the survival of Boeotia, but its army had to be defeated wherever and whenever it was met in battle (IV:92).

The tragedy of war is that two incommensurate necessities can clash. When they seemed necessary for each party, necessities ruled and created impiety and injustice. But not every pressure of war eliminated moral and religious standards. Earlier in the campaign, abiding by the traditional laws of war in a cavalry skirmish, Athens returned the Boeotian dead (IV:72). And following the defeat of the Athenians at the temple-fortress of Delium, the Boeotians returned the Athenian dead, according to traditional religious and moral norms (IV:101).

Rejecting both extremes, Thucydides placed the questions of just what range of action was available for moral choice, and what range was governed by necessity, at the core of Realist morality. Thucydides's accounts of the major speeches, including those of the Corinthians and Corcyraeans at Athens, the Corinthians and Athenians at Sparta, Cleon and Diodotus at Athens, Euphemus and Hermocrates at Camerina, all displayed a combination of moral-legal and self-interested, prudential reasoning.

He also seemed to disapprove of all the simple justifications for the extreme choices. He rejected views such as those of Cleon in the debate over Mytilene and those of the Corinthians in Athens at the outbreak of the war who argued that "right makes might" (that the moral course of action inherently builds strategic support or strength). Neither did he endorse the untrammeled pursuit of "might makes might." Didn't Thucydides think that Euphemus's failure to persuade the Sicilians of Athens's moderate intentions during Athens's Sicilian intervention (VI:82–87) could be attributed to the Sicilians' awareness of the barbarous treatment of the Melians, whom the Athenians had mercilessly slaughtered and enslaved (V:116)? If so, the Athenian defeat in Sicily is the strategic lesson of the massacre at Melos and "might" made failure.[71]

Thucydides equally rejected the "might makes right" doctrine; a wanton massacre is a wanton massacre, whether it be of the Mycalessians by the Athenian mercenaries (who slaughtered its inhabitants, including a school full of children [VII:29]), Thebans by Plataeans (III:63–67), Plataeans by Spartans (III:52), or Athenians by Sicilians—such as occurred in the killing of the defeated general Nicias, "who least deserved to come to so miserable an end, since the whole of his life had been devoted to the study and practice of virtue" (VII:86). But "right makes right" (the categorical moral and legal view) cannot govern state behavior when necessity speaks clearly. Safety required Athenian imperialism, and none can be blamed for this self-interest, Thucydides has the Athenian ambassadors say (I:75).

Nor did Thucydides follow the views of what is now called the ethics of a moderate patriot. Just as a parent observing two children (one her own) in mortal danger and, being unable to save both, can justly choose to save her own instead of the other, so a moderate patriot may, we are assured (if forced by circumstances to choose), prefer the *survival* of her own country to that of another.[72] Thucydides, on the other hand, said that the ethical Realist may perform what would otherwise be unjust acts of imperial oppression and war for the sake of enhancing the *security* of—avoiding danger to—his or her own country. That is, the Realist statesman had to be prepared to plan the *certain death* of foreigners today for the sake of decreasing the *risk* that the lives of fellow citizens might someday in the future have to be sacrificed in battle. Thus the death of Nicias was a "miserable end" inflicted on a man who "least deserved" it, but Thucydides does not condemn the Syracusans and Corinthians who ordered it to avoid "more harm in the future" (VII:86).

Thucydides viewed as necessary violence that was instrumental in promoting the security of the state. But he condemned unnecessary violence. The slaughter of all the men, women, and children of Mycalessus was "horrible," "pitiable," a "butchery," not because a war of attrition against Boeotia was morally wrong (it was strategically useful), but because the slaughter was not a necessary part of waging a war of attrition (VII:29).

Although contemporary Greeks would have found Thucydides's spare use of moral rhetoric unusual, they would not have found his standards of judgment totally unfamiliar. Athenians could have seen a parallel situation in Aeschylus's tragedy *Agamemnon*. Agamemnon has to sacrifice his daughter, Iphigenia, in

[71] I have found the discussion in W. R. Connor (1984), pp. 154–56, helpful on this issue.
[72] Nathanson (1989).

order to secure the favor of the gods and guarantee the success of the expedition against Troy. He does not, however, have to sacrifice her as if she were a sacrificial animal, and so the chorus excoriates him: "That pollution never grows old."[73] Polemarchus too, in Plato's *Republic*, describes a constrained conception of justice when he explains to Socrates that to be just is to "do good to friends and evil to enemies."[74]

Thucydides similarly showed how the Athenians present during the prewar debate at Sparta rejected legalistic rhetoric, noting, as later did Diodotus at the Mytilenian debate, that a political assembly was not a court of law (I:73).[75] The Athenians admitted that Athens, like all states, pursued its security, honor, and self-interest in the establishment of its empire. At first the Delian League was a voluntary alliance and a liberation from Persian rule; later most of the Greeks (the oligarchy, if not the demos) saw the empire that the league had become as a tyranny. Furthermore, they noted that the weak usually became subject to the strong in interstate politics, where there was no international state that could forcibly prevent the strong from exercising their might.

Nevertheless, rather than rest the argument on a purely skeptical reading of interstate standards of moral judgment, the Athenians added two moral justifications. First, abandoning control over the empire would create great danger for Athens by enabling the former colonies to join the Spartan alliance against Athens. They therefore assert, "[w]hen tremendous dangers are involved no one can be blamed for looking to his own interests" (I:75). Given the need for self-help, authentic dangers to national security should allow one to escape blame and justify what would otherwise be immoral wrongs, like imperial oppression. Second, given the usually self-interested motives of competing states, "[t]hose who really deserve praise are the people who, while human enough to enjoy power, nevertheless pay more attention to justice than they are required to do by the situation" (I:76).

Conditions of Realist Ethics

Thucydides offered no set of rules for how to be an ethical Realist. The pressures of strategic necessity and political advantage continually threatened Realist ethics. Instead he sought to justify and teach Realist ethics. He thought he could justify Realist ethics by the accuracy of its interpretation of international

[73] Martha Nussbaum (1986), p. 41.

[74] Plato, *The Republic*, I:332.

[75] Thucydides regularly undercut traditional, religious, and moral rhetoric. At the outset of the war he appeared to approve of the Athenian Assembly's rejection of Corinth's legalistic condemnation of Corcyra's actions. And by noting that the war seemed inevitable to both the Athenians (I:44) and the Spartans, he seemed to endorse the strategic reasons the Corcyreans offered for why the Athenians should support their cause against Corinth (I:31–I:34).

danger, by the prudence of the choices statesmen made among uncertain alternatives, and by the ethical value of the state. He thought he could teach it through his *History*.

First, in order for security to preempt moral rules, security had at least to be shown to be at risk. The "hard school of danger" Thucydides described was an education that a polis seeking to maintain its independence could not avoid. If interstate justice can hold only among equals, as the Athenians at Melos tell the hapless and inferior Melians, interstate justice must mean that only equals have the power to make sure that they receive what is their due from other states, not that states have effective interstate obligations to abide by international norms (V:84–113). Nothing in Thucydides's *History* contradicted the views of the Athenians who argued that Athens did nothing unusual in acquiring its empire (I:76). All states, they said, are motivated by self-interest, fear, and glory. Despite Sparta's condemnation of this Realist (Athenian) ethic in favor of an international ethic of established law, Sparta at the outset of the war refused to arbitrate its dispute with Athens (I:144), as the treaty between them required. Despite its demands that the Athenians liberate the subordinate states of the Athenian empire, Sparta maintained its own oppressive tyranny over Greek Messenians and other helots in the Peloponnese.

Second, to say that Realism could be ethical also presupposed that statespersons could be skillful—that is, display competence in determining when security was endangered and in deciding what measures could best reduce the danger to the state. No rules could adequately encompass Realist prudence. Instead the best leaders could do would be to follow the practice of the best doctors in diagnosing a disease.[76] They should compare symptoms in order to reveal diagnoses in order, in turn, to prescribe what seemed to work, even when one could not fully understand the reasons for the ills that one observed. The purpose of Thucydides's entire history of the Peloponnesian War should be read as an education in just that kind of therapeutic statesmanship (I:22). It is not, however, a simple tale of ready cures, either prudential or ethical.[77]

Strategic ends and moral choice were and (for Realists sharing Thucydides's views) still are only indirectly connected. We cannot, for example, infer from the final defeat of Athens that the Sicilian expedition, which expended so much treasure and lost so many lives, was morally wrong because it was strategically counterproductive. Nor can we infer that because the Sicilian expedition failed, the slaughter of Melos—word of which seemed to stiffen Sicilian resistance to Athenian intervention—was correspondingly immoral. Athens might have conquered Sicily, Thucydides indicates, if a surprise attack had been attempted against Syracuse, or if the leadership had not been divided between Nicias and Alcibiades, or if the public at home had provided fresh reinforcements. And

[76] See Cochrane, chap. 3.
[77] W. R. Connor (1984) demonstrates the uncertainties Thucydides describes.

Athens fell because of "internal strife" (II:65), Thucydides notes, eight years after the Sicilian expedition. Chance (the plague), many other decisions (including the disaster in Sicily), and the frailty of human nature under stress led to the strife that caused the final loss of Athenian security.

As Thomas Hobbes once noted, the genius of Thucydides's teaching lies "in the narration"—in the opportunity to reconstruct hard choices as they were experienced by the participants in the war. Both security and morality were matters for judgment. We can infer from his comments and the course of the events that, to Thucydides, Athenian security required the empire, the Corcyraean alliance, and war with Sparta (which Sparta chose). Pericles's strategy of attrition also served Athenian security by best promoting a victory at tolerable Athenian costs. These strategies called for what would otherwise be immoral killings, which a categorical moralist or modern "just war" moralist would condemn. But the Sicilian expedition was a simple waste of resources, a looting expedition chosen by a divided, contentious, self-interested Assembly. It distracted Athens from the war of attrition that should have been directed against Sparta. The slaughter at Melos added an island that was not clearly necessary, during the middle of truce, in a manner that would alarm neutrals at least as much as it would deter colonial rebellion. For Thucydides, necessary violence in a strategically valuable conquest was excusable, but Sicily and Melos were neither.

Third, though Thucydides's sense of the constraints of strategic necessity and the opportunities for moral action hold in both domestic and international politics, the moral difference between them was crucial. It was not true that interstate politics was the absolute realm of necessity, and intrastate politics the pure realm of ethical life. Mycalessus would have been a butchery wherever it occurred. But there was a striking difference in the structural opportunities for ethical behavior, in the practice of wise politicians, and therefore also in their ethical responsibility in the two realms. This difference justified placing the security of the polis over the rules of universal morality.

Civil war (the Corcyraean stasis) could make a state of war of domestic politics. Ethical restraint dissolved as trust, and even language, lost their meanings (III:82).[78] During the plague at Athens natural disease destroyed social security. Those who tried to help others died first (II:51). Empire, conversely, could make a nearly secure state of peace out of "interstate" politics, thereby increasing the prospect of impartial justice administered by regular courts. That, together with necessity, was the justification the Athenians at the conference at Sparta could offer for their empire (I:77).[79]

Moreover, there is a significant difference for Thucydides between intrastate and interstate politics that does not allow us to assimilate the two into one

[78] Ibid., pp. 95–105.
[79] Christopher Bruell (1974).

continuous struggle for power, as the Fundamentalists would have us do. Leo Strauss's discussion of Machiavelli's princely politics identified but oversimplified the contrast: "Contemporary readers find in both authors [Thucydides and Machiavelli] the same 'realism,' that is to say, the same denial of the power of the gods or of justice and the same sensitivity to harsh necessity and elusive chance. Yet Thucydides never calls into question the intrinsic superiority of nobility to baseness. . . . ."[80]

Part of the ethical difference between "Machiavellianism" and Thucydidean Realism lies in their different views of baseness, and the relations between interstate and intrastate baseness, and of its opposite, virtue.[81] Machiavellianism, according to some, allows to princes and those who would become princes license to achieve power over and above the interests of the state. Thucydides may admire Alcibiades, but he also condemns him. Thucydides also showed that ethical or legal standards were not sufficient in interstate politics. However ethical and law-abiding a citizen Nicias was, he was also a disastrously poor general (VII:6).[82] The Melians suffered the fate of the weak in interstate politics, and their appeals to law and justice fell on deaf ears. But in the polis, laws could make the weak equal. Domestic security made moral virtues, justice, and legality efficacious. It therefore made sense to try to shape policy according to a public interest. Thus Pericles in the funeral oration (II:37) told the Athenians to be proud and to honor the Athenian dead for their virtues and sacrifices, to which, he added, the present citizens owed their lives, welfare, and freedom.

Authentic security excused moral blame. Doing good, where safe and feasible, was morally praiseworthy. Ethical statesmanship and virtuous citizenship consequently consisted of finding ways to reduce the conflict between national security and universal good, as Pericles explained when he described how Athenians had "organized our State in such a way that it is perfectly well able to look after itself both in peace and war" (II:36) and could therefore "make friends by doing good to others" (II:40).[83]

THUCYDIDEAN REALISM

The importance of Thucydides's *History* extends beyond Realism. Marxists have been fascinated by the little that Thucydides says about class conflict. And

[80] Leo Strauss, *Thoughts on Machiavelli* (Chicago: University of Chicago Press, 1958), p. 292.
[81] De Ste. Croix, pp. 18–19; Arlene Saxonhouse (1978).
[82] De Ste. Croix, p. 19.
[83] David Grene suggests a similar conclusion when he says, "[T]he area where moral comment is in order is only that in which human beings can be regarded as in some sense operating with a freedom to choose between one alternative and another without the direct force of necessity constraining them" (1965), p. 78.

what political society has ever been so subordinate to its mode of production as Sparta was to the suppression of its helot labor force? But Marxism does not rest its analysis of social development on the slave mode of production. The great transformation of modern life followed the classical world by two millennia. Industrialism has reshaped the daily life of human beings and added a vastly enhanced dynamism to world politics that magnifies both uncertainty and opportunity.

Liberal democrats cannot fail to consider Thucydides's indictment of the Athenian democrats for the irresponsible rashness of their decision to launch, as well as for the subsequent mismanagement of, the expedition to Sicily, which contributed to the eventual defeat and collapse of Athenian democracy. But Liberalism, however much it concerns itself with the democratic determinants of foreign policy, has as its central and distinctive contribution a view of the moral equality of all human beings. Liberals are committed to ensuring that the interests of the constitutional majority become public policy, whether foreign or domestic. They are equally concerned that the rights of individuals shape the definition of the public's interests whether at home or abroad. By those criteria, few societies have been more democratic and less Liberal than Thucydides's Athens. The public triumph of the Liberal ideal postdates Thucydides and his contemporaries.

Realism embraces the continuity of interstate anarchy. Thucydides belongs to the Realists. They belong to him. Henry Kissinger's harking back to Thucydides is not altogether wrong. We can see there a quasi-bipolar system, not too unlike the one we have just survived with its tendencies toward overextension, whether in Sicily or in Vietnam. We fortunately, it appears, lived for most of the Cold War in a bipolar world with two and not one dynamic superpower, and when the Soviets did decline in the 1980s, some of its leadership saw the possibility of an accommodation with a Liberal world. Both superpowers, moreover, possessed nuclear weapons, which left them less vulnerable to the defection of allies. The United States felt the "loss of China" in 1949 much less than Sparta would have felt the loss of Corinth, and the United States acted differently. But to the extent that we sometimes, in some of our foreign relations, live in a world without reliable law and order, we will need Thucydides's complex insights into the constraints the international "state of war" places on domestic orders and individual leadership.[84]

Although Thucydides is a Realist, he is not a Fundamentalist or a Structuralists or a Constitutionalist. Paternity suits tend to be messy, for each version of Realism can identify its views in Thucydides's *History*. Fundamentalists, Structuralists and Constitutionalists can each draw upon the events of Thucydides's *History* to analyze the Peloponnesian War in particular, and international his-

[84] Robert Gilpin draws these contrasts in "Peloponnesian War and Cold War," Lebow and Strauss, eds., *Hegemonic Rivalry* (1991).

tory in general. But to borrow Thucydides's judgments in order to support their conclusions, they will need to put their conclusions in his contexts, both domestic and international.

A Thucydides writing today would see the importance of the changes a Gorbachev or a Reagan has made, but he or she would also not assume that leaders can transform their polities according to their own interests and goals. Rejecting the Fundamentalist view, he or she would recognize the constraint on choice maintained by the historical compromises that have shaped the institutions and cultures of particular states. Rejecting extremes of the Constitutionalist perspective, he or she would also recognize that international anarchy makes national power and effective national independence go hand in hand. A modern philosophic historian with Thucydidean views, while noting the Structuralist trend away from bipolarity in the international system, would not assume that those changes in international structure would be either necessary or sufficient to end the hostility of the Cold War. At the same time such a historian would reject the view shared by many modern Liberals and Marxists that changes in the domestic structure (e.g., moves toward democratization or social equality) of the two superpowers could be sufficient to end the insecurity they share.

To be a Thucydidean Realist today is to see that states are not, as the Structuralist would claim, equivalent and without choice and that their differences are of real consequence. States are not reliably conditioned by the international system to behave rationally and nationally. These are *ideals* achieved only through outstanding leadership, such as that exercised by Pericles, and by unusual national unity, such as that manifested by Athens at the outset of the war and by its enemies at the end. To be a Thucydidean and Realist is to recognize that interstate and intrastate politics are not the same, even though human beings play out their hopes and fears in both. It is to realize that the continuity of the state of war is based on the persistence of interstate anarchy, just as the chance of either peace or war is contingent on domestic choice and international opportunity.

It is also to realize that, because the statesmen Thucydides described had choices, they could and should have made ethical choices. For a Realist, these choices were, and should have been, constrained by the "school of danger" that the persistence of interstate anarchy required states to attend. Security, prestige, and self-interest eroded all treaties and promises, dissolved gratitude and generosity, and did so according to the harsh logic of national egoism under conditions of international anarchy. Doing good to others was nonetheless still possible; avoiding unnecessary harm was morally required. Realism narrowed the range of moral choice. It did not eliminate it.

CHAPTER TWO

Fundamentalism: Machiavelli

Prudent men are wont to say—and this not rashly or without good ground—that he who would foresee what has to be, should reflect on what has been, for everything that happens in the world at any time has a genuine resemblance to what happened in ancient times. This is due to the fact that the agents who bring such things about are men, and that men have, and always have had, the same passions, whence it necessarily comes about that the same effects are produced.

—Niccolò Machiavelli, *The Discourses*, III:43

The grave and natural enmities that exist between the men of the people and the nobles, caused by the wish of the latter to command and the former not to obey, are the cause of all evils that arise in cities. . . . For the enmities between the people and the nobles at the beginning of Rome that were resolved by disputing were resolved in Florence by fighting. Those in Rome ended with a law, those in Florence with the exile and death of many citizens; those in Rome always increased military virtue, those in Florence eliminated it altogether. . . .

—Niccolò Machiavelli, *Florentine Histories*, III:1[1]

MACHIAVELLI'S REALISM RESTS causally and directly—fundamentally—on the individual leader, citizen, or subject and his or her ambitions, fears, and interests. Whether leaders lead well or ill determines whether we live in a

[1] Niccolo Machiavelli, *The Discourses*, trans. Leslie Walker, ed. Bernard Crick (Harmondsworth: Penguin, 1970), p. 517, and *Florentine Histories*, trans. Laura Banfield and Harvey Mansfield, Jr. (Princeton: Princeton University Press, 1988), p. 105.

glorious and secure "Rome" or an oppressed and dangerous "Florence." He takes what was one element in Thucydides's view of interstate politics and distills from it a practical guide to the behavior of new princes and the leaders of expansionist republics. Machiavelli thus can be seen as limiting a "Thucydides" to the mind of Alcibiades as a prospective tyrant or possible archon of a polis. Machiavelli, to be sure, draws his examples not from Greece but from the princes of contemporary Europe and the imperial republic of classical Rome. Where Thucydides explains by means of thickly described historical context, Machiavelli presents general lessons, often in dichotomies and antinomies ("whether it is better to be loved or feared"). He validates these lessons by providing two sorts of evidence. For supporting or contradicting example, he offers his contemporary European experience: the successes and failures of, among others, Ferdinand of Aragón, Cesare Borgia, Louis XII, and the players in the history of his own Florentine Republic. For integrated, or definitive and digested, exemplary experience, he offers the glorious experience of Rome, whose successful use as interpreted by Livy validates any procedure.[2]

Machiavelli's Fundamentalism	
Human Nature	xx
Domestic Society	x
Interstate System	x

Machiavelli (1469–1527) also shares some personal characteristics with Thucydides. Like Thucydides the unsuccessful Athenian general, Machiavelli was a public official forced by the vagaries of political life into a premature retirement. He rose to be an official and emissary, a sort of special assistant for national security affairs, a Henry Kissinger or Tony Lake of the Florentine Republic. Sent on a mission to Cesare Borgia in 1502, he was in Rome when Cesare lost his gamble to control the papacy. In Florence, Machiavelli established a citizen militia and led his new force to the conquest of Pisa in 1509. After the Medici coup of 1512, he was imprisoned and tortured. Following his release, he was forced into retirement on his farm in the hills above Florence. From there each day, after supervising his farm workers and dropping in at the local tavern for a few hours, he retired to his study and put on his former robes of state. There and then he communed with the ancients and wrote his treatises, distilling in *The Prince* and *The Discourses* the lessons of Roman statecraft and of his own diplomatic experience. He hoped, it appears, to persuade the

[2]Quentin Skinner, *Machiavelli* (New York: Hill and Wang, 1981), chap. 2.

Medici to offer him his old job, which makes *The Prince* the most brilliant job application in history.[3]

Machiavelli's great contribution is to provide historical depth, beginnings and endings, dynamics to the analysis of the state of war. He tells how individual political entrepreneurship makes states as well as how states expand and why they fall.

His state of war is both various and pervasive. This variety results from differences both in human character and in international and political, or constitutional, circumstance. Fundamentalist Realists need, he implied, to put their characters in a social context. His state of war is *various*, because it does not affect hereditary principalities or conservative republics to the same degree as it affects new princes and expansionist republics, and *pervasive* because it makes itself felt not only between states but within them. Hereditary princes, like the duke of Ferrara, can rely upon custom to secure the love of their subjects. That love poses formidable hurdles to the ambitions of conquerors, who would find these principalities not only difficult to conquer but even more difficult to hold against all those who prefer a return of the ancient ruling family.[4] Conservative aristocratic republics like Venice and Sparta try to limit their insecurity by limiting their ambitions. By choosing isolation and autonomy, Sparta kept its citizens poor and powerless. Spartan kings ruled over citizens whose modest but adequate standard of living stimulated few appetites, either material or political, domestic or foreign.[5] But neither hereditary princes nor conservative republics fully escape insecurity because they cannot completely escape new princes and expansionist republics.

PRINCELY *VIRTÚ*

Virtú[6]—the glorious exercise of an individual's courageous ambition—depends on circumstances. But it faces a nearly constant danger, Machiavelli explains

[3] The standard life of Machiavelli is Roberto Ridolfi, *The Life of Niccolo Machiavelli,* trans. Cecil Grayson (Chicago, University of Chicago Press, 1963). Machiavelli's "Letter to Vettori" (translated in the Mansfield edition of *The Prince*) described the composition of *The Prince.* In 1520 he eventually succeed in being appointed official historiographer of Florence.

[4] Niccolo Machiavelli, *The Prince,* trans. Harvey Mansfield, Jr. (Chicago: University of Chicago Press, 1985), p. 6–7.

[5] Niccolo Machiavelli, *The Discourses* in *The Prince and the Discourses,* trans. Christian Detmold (New York: Modern Library, 1950), pp. 122, 126.

[6] Isaiah Berlin catalogs the virtues of *virtú* as "courage, vigour, fortitude in adversity, public achievement, order, discipline, happiness, strength, justice, above all assertion of one's proper claims and the knowledge and power needed to secure their satisfaction." See his "The Originality of Machiavelli," in *Against the Current* (Penguin, 1980), p. 45.

in *The Prince*, his brilliant treatise on how a prince could achieve "greatness."[7] New princes both cause and respond to the threat of violence that surrounds them, Machiavelli warns. Both new principalities (an enterprising individual stages a coup and seizes power) and "mixed" principalities (an old prince attempts to conquer a new province) create enemies of all those displaced in the conquest. At the same time, they gain little security from the support of their followers, whom they could not fully reward without further alienating the conquered population.[8] Conquests that are similar in culture, have been previously governed by another prince rather than by a free republic, or are organized bureaucratically rather than feudally may be easier to hold than their opposites, but all conquests call for ruthless methods.[9] Early, swift, ruthless violence—such as assassinating the previous ruling family—can economize on violence that might otherwise be needed later, but because some violence is necessary in order to avoid more violence, in no case can traditional moral standards tame the insecurity princes and subjects alike suffer.[10]

So why would an ambitious person enter this violent contest? Are new princes simply seekers after "power for its own sake"?[11] Machiavelli said that princes seek war and military conquest despite all the dangers for two reasons: first, in order to demonstrate and obtain the rewards fortune bestows on *virtú* (courageous ambition) and second, in order to protect *their* state from predation.

"It is a very natural and ordinary thing to desire to acquire, and always, when

[7] Machiavelli, from the "Dedicatory Letter" of *The Prince*, offered to Lorenzo de Medici.
[8] Machiavelli, *The Prince*, p. 8.
[9] Machiavelli distinguishes between conquest-resistant and conquest-prone situations much as we now distinguish between offense-dominant and defense-dominant international systems. See Robert Jervis, "Cooperation under the Security Dilemma," *World Politics* 30, 1 (January 1978).
[10] Sheldon Wolin, *Politics and Vision* (Boston: Little, Brown, 1960), pp. 200–02. Some commentators argue that Machiavelli subscribed to traditional moral standards in *The Prince* and *The Discourses* but that he said they caused more harm than good if they were applied to politics (Bernard Crick, "Introduction" to *The Discourses*, p. 62). However, Machiavelli also seems to endorse the utility, if not necessity, of the betrayal of all forms of trust in his play about love (or lust), the *Mandragola*.
[11] A number of modern commentators on or critics of Realism suggest that this best characterizes the essence of the Realist motivation. See, for example, Brian Porter's description of Martin Wight's views on the power motivation underlying Realism (in Michael Donelan, ed., *The Reason of States* [London: Allen Unwin, 1978], p. 65), and E. H. Carr's discussion of the importance of a "grounds for action" in E. H. Carr, *The Twenty Years' Crisis* (London: Macmillan, 1951), chap. 6, and Robert W. Tucker, "Professor Robert Morgenthau's Theory of Political Realism," *American Political Science Review* 46 (1952). For a postmodern reading of these issues, see R. B. J. Walker, *Inside/Outside: International Relations as Political Theory* (Cambridge: Cambridge University Press, 1993), chap. 2. For a thoughtful discussion of a variety of differing perspectives on this type of Realism, see Peter Gellman, "Hans J. Morgenthau and the Legacy of Political Realism," *Review of International Studies* 14, 4 (October 1988).

men do it who can, they will be praised or not blamed,"[12] Machiavelli so matter-of-factly notes. Indeed, it is so ordinary—so fundamental a part of human nature—that even we common folk are not free from the drive, and this is what allows us to understand the great. For in love, as in war, human freedom allows aggressiveness and our too-extensive desires engender competition.[13]

Machiavelli's comedy the *Mandragola* depicts the strategy of war applied to war between the generations—between some of us, the common folk, fighting over sex. The young, wily Callimaco, deeply in love, tricks the foolish old Nicias to allow him to sleep with the old man's beautiful young wife, Lucrezia, by persuading him that the first man to sleep with her will immediately suffer a horrible death. Nicias falls into this trap and thus bribes the wily Callimaco to "suffer" for him.

But many of us prefer the quiet life, safe in our private gardens, with our own wives or husbands and free from princely ambition. Thus Machiavelli's true claim to originality begins in chapter 15 of *The Prince,* where he describes his new science of "effectual truth," a realistic politics that applies to all of us, replacing "imagined," idealistic politics. Here too is where Machiavelli outlines his new morality of civic life.[14]

In addition to satisfying the human (or, at least, princely) drive for glory, the practice of war helps secure the "state." Rather than an abstract sovereign institution, the state, for Machiavelli, was nothing less—or more—than the government, the prince himself at home and abroad.[15] By securing himself, however, the successful prince can then provide us with some security too. "A wise Prince," Machiavelli said, "knows how to do wrong when it is necessary and it is very often necessary to act contrary to charity, contrary to humanity, contrary to religion if the Prince wishes to sustain his government."[16] This is the Machiavellian justification for our modern metaphors of Realist ethics: what we call "dirty hands," the "cracked eggs" that, Lenin said, an omelet requires, and Hamlet's excuse: "I must be cruel to be kind."[17] Politics has a

[12] Machiavelli, *The Prince,* p. 14.

[13] Generalizing in the same vein, Machiavelli notes: "Men Jump from One Ambition to Another and First They Seek Not to Be Injured, Then They Injure Others"—a title from the *Florentine Histories.*

[14] The most powerful evocation of Machiavellian ethics I have read is Isaiah Berlin, "The Originality of Machiavelli," pp. 25–79. For an insightful application of these ideas to international ethics, see Stanley Hoffmann, *Duties beyond Borders,* chap. 1.

[15] Hanna Gray, "Machiavelli: The Art of Politics and the Paradox of Power," in I. Krieger and Fritz Stern, eds. *The Responsibility of Power* (Garden City: Doubleday, 1967), pp. 40, 51.

[16] Machiavelli, *The Prince,* chap. 18.

[17] The classic moral dilemma of "dirty hands" is explored by Jean-Paul Sartre in his play of the same title and by Michael Walzer in "Political Action: The Problem of Dirty Hands," *Philosophy and Public Affairs* 2, 2 (Winter 1973).

moral logic of its own, an independent value in the common life of the citizens, separate from Christian moral teachings. Certain crimes, like the many murders committed by Agathocles, were simply unnecessary for the security of the state and the prince, and they were doubly wrong. But princes will often have to engage in necessary crimes—to lie, steal, and kill for the life of the state—if they are to succeed. In getting their hands dirty, they may also be saving the lives of their citizens, who, if left to their Christian ethics, would be "weak," easy prey to "wicked men."[18] "Cesare Borgia," Machiavelli noted of a prince he admired, "was held to be cruel; nonetheless his cruelty restored the Romagna, united it, and reduced it to peace and to faith. If one considers this well, one will see that he was much more merciful than the Florentine people, who so as to escape a name for cruelty, allowed Pistoia to be destroyed."[19]

In order to succeed, Machiavelli advised that princes had to be both "lions" and "foxes." Through lionlike military leadership, the prince can turn uncertainty into confidence, despair into courage. For populations having little in common except their subjection to him, the prince can offer a promise of success through strategic brilliance.[20] Success in turn generates solidarity. Eschewing the defenses of fortresses, the prince should build a militia army, which can also become the womb of the nation. Through fox-like diplomacy the prince can economize on the use of violence, whether at home or abroad. Internally he should exercise financial parsimony, avoid the creation of divisions, and instead seek to create law and order, but above all avoid contempt and, should he fail to win the love of the people, make sure he enjoys their fear. *Virtú*-ous leaders provide themselves with good arms, and they win the fear (or love) of the people or the great, Machiavelli declares in chapter 24 of *The Prince*.

Princes achieve the vital "esteem" (chapter 21) that *virtú* craves by "great enterprises" and "rare examples." The first great enterprise is the imperial acquisition of new provinces, as Ferdinand of Aragón (more below) did. Externally princes should be "true friends and true enemies," as called for, and should neither declare neutrality nor, unless necessary, what we now call col-

[18] See also *The Discourses*, 2:2. This view (Berlin's) of two, partly overlapping moralities, Christian and political, differs from the view expressed by Strauss and others, that Machiavelli is simply a pure egoist or pure skeptical immoralist. There are passages that support the latter view, and it was the interpretation I (I now think incorrectly) argued for in "Thucydidean Realism," *Review of International Studies* (1989). But for an extensive defense of the latter interpretation, see Steven Forde, "Varieties of Realism: Thucydides and Machiavelli," *Journal of Politics* 54, 2 (May 1992).

[19] Machiavelli, *The Prince*, chap. 17, p. 65.

[20] Shakespeare captured this *virtú* well in *Henry V*. When the frightened English, Welsh, Scots, and Irish gather around Henry at Agincourt on the morning of St. Crispin's Day, young Henry inspires them with the sense of their glory and gives them unity and confidence by the confidence in victory he displays.

laborate or "bandwagon" by subordinating oneself or aligning with stronger foreign princes.[21] Active "balancing" is both more prestigious and more secure, since aligning against the more powerful can make the difference needed for victory and failing to align with the weaker can leave you victim to the designs of the winner, now without the support of that weaker state. Beyond these the prince should ensure that his acts become well-known, "rare examples." Rewarding good civic acts that serve to increase the power or wealth of the state and punishing harmful ones that hurt it: Both, when done in striking ways, contribute to the glory princes seek.

Machiavelli gave us many important reflections on the requisites of successful statecraft. He also offered many examples of mistaken policies[22] Machiavelli saw that the vigorous contest of world politics rested on good fortune and virtuous leaders. Some unfortunate leaders were both unfortunate and unwise and thus doubly disadvantaged, such as was Ludovico Sforza, who (appropriately) lost Milan, twice. Another who was fortunate but not wise was Louis XII, who invaded Italy at the invitation of the Venetians. Despite initial great advantages, he soon lost all his conquests, having made "five errors: he had eliminated the lesser powers; increased the power of a power in Italy; brought in a very powerful foreigner; did not come to live there; did not put colonies there."[23] In his most famous example, a lack of good fortune—illness and a failure to anticipate the resentment that the new pope, Julius II, would bear—caused the downfall of Cesare Borgia, who otherwise was a most "prudent and *virtú*-ous" prince (chapter 7).

Ferdinand of Aragón was, on the other hand, doubly advantaged. Prince of Aragón, husband of Isabella of Castile, hence king of a united Spain, conqueror of Granada, Naples, Navarre, and North Africa, sovereign of the Americas, Ferdinand was the one contemporaneous Christian prince who could measure his *virtú* head to toe against the great founders of antiquity whom Machiavelli so admired: Moses, Cyrus, and Romulus (chapter 6). Unlike the bumbling Sforza, he captured the Machiavellian state—in the sense of authoritative sta-

[21] See Machiavelli, *The Prince*, chap. 21, pp. 89–90. For contemporary advice of a similar sort, see Morgenthau, *Politics among Nations*, chap. 12, on different methods of the balance of power; and Waltz, *Theory of International Politics*, p. 126.

[22] But he does not pursue just what necessities or failures of *virtú* would compel collaboration or bandwagoning. For a discussion of the literature on collaboration, see Doyle, *Empires*; for "bandwagoning" toward "threats" (not necessarily power), Walt, *Origins of Alliances*. Machiavelli recognized that threats arise from inside as from outside a polity. He thus expected and gave examples of what Steven David has called omnibalancing, balancing against the most dangerous threat whether internal or external ("Explaining Third World Alignment," *World Politics* 43, 2 [January 1991]), but he recommended overwhelming, where possible, internal threats rather than calling in external support against internal threats, since the latter strategy threatened escalating dependence and imperialized collaboration.

[23] Machiavelli, *The Prince*, chap. 3, p. 15.

tus *(stato)*. He grasped both *dominio*, an effectively controlled territory, and *imperio*, a right of command.[24]

Understanding Ferdinand also requires us to understand the character of his leadership. Opportunity is not enough; there must be an entrepreneur to seize it. His action cannot be reduced to the simple Structural, "rational unitary state actor" variant of Realism. Although he was a rational calculator without compare and the founder of the Spanish state, his personal ambitions went much beyond the primacy of state security.

Ferdinand of Aragón's conquests, beginning with Granada, made him "the first king among the Christians" (chapter 21).[25] He succeeded both in enlarging his kingdom at the expense of foreign rivals and, more important, in securing himself at home. He kept the barons of Castile (his domestic rivals) occupied in foreign war. He employed the riches of the people and the church to create his own army. He acquired great fame and wealth in an act of "pious cruelty," whose victims were the hapless Marranos.[26]

Although born in 1452 as the son of King John II of Aragon, he learned that to become great, one had to think like a new prince, as he proceeded to do. He helped his father destroy his older brother (from a first marriage), the prince of Viana, who led the nationalist faction in Aragón. With the help of the bribes funded by the great Jewish financiers of Castile and Aragón, he succeeded in winning the hand in marriage of Isabella of Castile.[27] After trying a coup against his wife, he learned to appreciate her talents and ruled with her, suppressing the ancient independence of the noble magnates of Castile and Aragón, strengthening the bureaucratic discipline of the state, and then setting about great conquests.[28]

[24] See Sebastian de Grazia, *Machiavelli in Hell* (Princeton: Princeton University Press, 1989), p. 158, and Harvey Mansfield, "On the Impersonality of the Modern State: A Commentary on Machiavelli's Use of *Stato*," *American Political Science Review* 77 (1983), pp. 849–57.

[25] Although Machiavelli criticizes Ferdinand in his letters for "cunning and good luck, rather than superior wisdom" (*Letters*, trans. Allan Gilbert [Chicago: University of Chicago Press, 1961], p. 111), he praises Ferdinand at considerable length in chapter 21 of The *Prince*. Machiavelli's friend the Florentine historian Francesco Guicciardini describes Ferdinand as a "*Re di eccellentissimo consiglio, e virtú*" (a king of excellent wisdom and *virtú*) in *History*, vol. 6, lib. 12.

[26] Machiavelli, *The Prince*, p. 88.

[27] John Elliott, *Imperial Spain 1469–1716* (New York: New American Library, 1963), p. 21.

[28] W. H. Prescott in his classic *History of the Reign of Ferdinand and Isabella* (New York: AMS, 1904/1968) exaggerates Ferdinand's virtues: "impartial justice in the administration of the laws; his watchful solicitude to shield the weak from the oppression of the strong; his wise economy, which achieved great results without burdening his people with oppressive taxes; his sobriety and moderation; the decorum, and respect for religion, which he maintained among his subjects; the industry he promoted by wholesome laws and his own example; his consummate sagacity, which crowned all his enterprises with brilliant success, and made him the oracle of the princes of his age" (vol. IV, p. 255). But Prescott also notes his propensity toward "vicious galantries" which disturbed both Isabella and the stability of the kingdom (p. 251). One natural son, Alonso, having been made archbishop of Saragossa at

Internationally his success first appeared in the reconquest of Muslim Spain, Granada, in 1492. By "keeping the minds of the barons of Castile occupied," the war against Granada put them under his power (chapter 21). This increase in his power allowed him to turn against former allies and reward new ones, so he ruthlessly expelled the Jews and Moors in order to reward his new allies: the missionary orders, the soldiers, and the great nobles. (He appears to have known that this was an economically foolish policy—that it would destroy finance and agriculture—because he refused to expel the Moors from his personal kingdom of Aragón.) He then turned his new domestic authority to more foreign conquest and went after Naples (a traditional arena of Aragonese expansion), a halfhearted conquest of North Africa, and, at Isabella's urging, exploration of the Americas. Domestically his success in refounding the state was evidenced by his being able to raise public revenues from less than 900,000 reals in 1474 to 26 million in 1504.[29]

Ferdinand created an effective diplomatic service but repeatedly abused its members by requiring them to tell the most apparent lies. (The lies nonetheless successfully clouded his intentions, as Machiavelli noted in his letter to Vettori of 1513.[30]) He also created a great army under the leadership of Gonzalo Fernández de Córdoba, composed of a modern infantry of mixed forces—halberd, sword, and arquebus.

His end honored him little. After a life spent struggling to create a great and independent Spanish empire dominating the western Mediterranean, he was forced to recognize his daughter Juana the Mad and her hostile husband, the Habsburg archduke Philip, as his sole heirs.[31]

For Ferdinand, the balance of power was not an end or a policy but a tactic of "divide and rule" in an imperial strategy of conquest. His *virtú* was reflected in a willingness to take risks much beyond those someone attempting to maximize personal or national security would have been willing to assume. The state was an entity as yet uninstitutionalized and unpurposed. It was in Burckhardt's phrase a "work of art" yet to be fashioned, whether well or ill, by "artists" such as Ferdinand or Cesare.[32]

age six, did, however, serve with considerable worldly success as regent of Aragón at Ferdinand's death.

[29] Elliott, *Imperial Spain*, p. 90.

[30] Machiavelli, *Letters*, pp. 115–16. He made them famous for perfidy, as Guicciardini noted in his *History* (lib. 12, p. 273) and Machiavelli (*Letters*, letter 6, and see Machiavelli, *The Prince*, chap. 18, on lying).

[31] Elliott, *Imperial Spain*, p. 133.

[32] Burckhardt notes, "The feeling of the Ferrarese toward the ruling house was a strange compound of silent dread, of the truly Italian sense of well-calculated interest, and of the loyalty of the modern subject: personal admiration was transferred into a new sentiment of duty," in *The Civilization of the Renaissance in Italy* (1965), p. 32. And E. R. Hale comments, "National feeling and a national foreign policy were the consequence and not the cause of an age of dynastic wars," in *The New Cambridge Modern History*, vol. 1, p. 263.

Eliminating insecurity is impossible, for even hereditary princes have to fear the threat of "perpetual revolution" that the new princes pose.[33] Managing the insecurity prudently is necessary, but managing is also the cause of insecurity for others, creating a "security dilemma." Good arms (militias, not mercenaries) and good laws (being feared more than loved) will provide some self-help security against domestic and foreign foes (chapters 12–14, 15–19). Prudent conquest requires the crushing of overmighty subjects and never succumbing to the temptation to "balance" against them with the aid of foreign support (chapter 3). Effective, active aligning will help secure glory and security too. Above all, there is the core of Realism, "self-help": "[A] prince should have enough state to support himself, if need be, by himself."[34]

In contemporary international relations, Machiavelli's preferences would run to the patriotic founders: Churchill, Roosevelt, de Gaulle, Ho Chi Minh, Mandela. But Machiavelli's princely politics also echo in the career of Saddam Hussein, with whom Cesare Borgia or Ferdinand, one suspects, would have felt very much at home. A reputation for ruthlessness, the rapid execution of oppressive acts, a delicate domination of rival factions among Sunni Moslems, a tight cadre of followers from his home village, strict control over Shiite and Kurdish areas, together with a policy of prestige and imperialism directed toward his neighbors in Iran and Kuwait, and, above all, his remarkable survival: All resonate with the *virtú* of a Machiavellian prince. His failure to estimate the determination of the Iranian revolutionaries and the readiness of the U.S.-led coalition to protect the oil of the Gulf are not atypical failings; Cesare, after all, underestimated the determination of the new pope, Julius II.[35]

Machiavelli warned that eliminating insecurity in Italy as a whole may be possible only for that prince of outstanding *virtú* who can free Italy from the barbarians—that is, unite—that is, conquer—Italy (chapter 26).[36] But having done so, he will face new and larger threats and more difficult (because more

[33] See Grant Mindle, "Machiavelli's Realism," *Review of Politics* 47, 2 (1985), p. 217. This is the reason for Frederick II's very interesting condemnation of Machiavellianism in the *Anti-Machiavel.* Machiavelli's revolutionary ruthlessness, Frederick argued, was the product not of *raison d'état* but of the extension of *raison d'état* rationalizations to individuals who "should" be behaving as private persons (because they were not born sovereigns). See Frederick of Prussia, *Anti-Machiavel*, trans. Paul Sonino (Athens: Ohio University Press, 1981), pp. 159–81.

[34] Quoted in de Grazia, *Machiavelli in Hell,* p. 171.

[35] For excellent accounts of Saddam Hussein's career, see Samir al'Khalil, *Republic of Fear* (New York: Pantheon, 1989) and Judith Miller and Lauie Mylroie, *Saddam Hussein and the Crisis in the Gulf* (New York: Times Books, 1990). On Saddam Hussein's misestimation of U.S. policy, see Janet Gross Stein, "Deterrence and Compellence in the Gulf, 1990–91," *International Security* 17, 2 (Fall 1992), pp. 147–79.

[36] Some have argued that this chapter's patriotism is out of place and that the chapter is not Machiavelli's but a corrupted text. But the patriotism is very much a part of Machiavelli's purpose, as I discuss below.

disparate) future conquests. All courses are dangerous; one picks the "less bad as good" (chapter 21). The struggle for power is continuous, fundamental, irremediable. That is the state of war.

MORE SECURITY THROUGH REPUBLICAN IMPERIALISM

States, Machiavelli says, are either princely or republican. Both can be warlike, for he argues that not only are republics not pacifistic, but they are the best form of state for imperial expansion. Establishing a republic fit for imperial expansion is, moreover, the best way to guarantee the survival of a state that can overawe domestic enemies and overcome foreign foes.

Machiavelli's own preferences were then and are now clear. He is republican by conviction, a true lover of civic freedom: "Of all men who have been eulogized, those deserve it most who have been the authors and founders of religions: next comes such who have established republics or kingdoms." Republics, moreover, are better because—among other reasons—they are more lasting: "And if princes show themselves superior in the making of laws, and in the forming of civil institutions and new statutes and ordinances, the people are superior in maintaining those institutions, laws, and ordinances, which certainly places them on a par with those who established them."[37]

Machiavelli's republic is a classical mixed republic. It is not a democracy, which he thinks would quickly degenerate into a tyranny, but it is characterized by social equality, popular liberty, and political participation (*The Discourses*, bk. I, chap. 2, p. 112).[38] The Consuls serve as "kings"; the Senate as an aristocracy managing the state; the people in the Assembly as the source of strength.

Liberty results from the "disunion," the competition and necessity for compromise required by the division of powers among Senate and Consuls and tribunes (the last representing the common people). Liberty also results from the popular veto. The powerful few, Machiavelli says, threaten tyranny because they seek to dominate; the mass demands not to be dominated. Their veto thus

[37] Machiavelli, *The Discourses*, bk. I, chaps. 10 and 58. But this raises a problem. How then can we motivate a prince to found a republic when a Caesar has great glory despite the great evil of having destroyed a republic? The inspirational motivation seems to be the task of true historians, those understanding and sharing Machiavelli's *verita effetuale*, and is the task of Machiavelli's own histories, *The Discourses* on Rome and *Florentine Histories*. My understanding of Machiavelli's republicanism has been improved by discussions with Maurizio Viroli.

[38] Harvey Mansfield, "Machiavelli's New Regime," *Italian Quarterly* 13 (1970), pp. 63–95; Skinner, *Machiavelli*, chap. 3; Mark Huliung, *Citizen Machiavelli* (Princeton: Princeton University Press, 1983), chap. 2. And see J. G. A. Pocock, *The Machiavellian Moment* (Princeton: Princeton University Press, 1975) for the wider significance of Machiavellian republicanism.

preserves the liberties of the state (I:5). But since the people and the rulers have different social characters, the people need to be "managed" by the few in order to avoid having their recklessness overturn, or their fecklessness undermine, the ability of the state to expand (I:53). Thus the Senate and the Consuls plan expansion, consult oracles, and employ religion to manage the resources that the energy of the people supply. Lacking ordered management and the clever employment of patriotic religion, republics can become, as Florence became, prey to faction and coups. But no regime surpasses a well-managed republic.

Strength, and then imperial expansion, result from the way liberty encourages increased population and property, which grow when the citizens know that their lives and goods are secure from arbitrary seizure. Free citizens equip large armies and provide soldiers who fight for public glory and the common good, because they are in fact their own (II:2). If you seek the honor of having your state expand, Machiavelli advises, you should organize it as a free and popular republic like Rome, rather than as an aristocratic republic like Sparta or Venice. Expansion thus calls for a free republic.

"Necessity"—political survival—calls for expansion. Sparta and Venice each lasted a long time. They did so by restricting the entrance of new citizens (Sparta and Venice) and the expansion of their states (Sparta). This appears to be a tempting strategy if one seeks longevity. But Machiavelli rejects it. It is neither safe nor "honorable."

Chance undermines the conservative, self-contained republic. If a stable aristocratic republic is forced by foreign conflict "to extend her territory, in such a case we shall see her foundations give way and herself quickly brought to ruin." If domestic security, on the other hand, prevails, "the continued tranquility would enervate her, or provoke internal dissensions, which together, or either of them separately, will apt to prove her ruin" (I:6). The latter is what happened to Florence, where a failure to expand eroded social solidarity, morale, courage, and endurance and thereby provoked corruption and factionalism, which in turn destroyed public stability and respect for the laws.[39] Machiavelli therefore believes also that it is necessary to take the constitution of Rome, rather than that of Sparta or Venice, as our model.

Republican imperialism, however, contains one obvious flaw. To protect and glorify the freedom of one people, it crushes the freedom of others. What are the options? Machiavelli describes three. One could crush and enslave neighboring populations, as did the Spartans. Or one could form a league of "companions"—free and equal republics. This is what the ancient Etruscans and in his time the Swiss and the German free cities did. Or one could absorb free

[39]This argument is made well by Neal Wood, "Introduction" to *Art of War* by Machiavelli (New York: Da Capo/Bobbs Merrill, 1965), p. iii. And see Harvey Mansfield, *Machiavelli's New Modes and Orders* (Ithaca: Cornell University Press, 1979), pp. 51–53.

cities as "companions," but make sure that one retains effective control, as the Romans did.

Enslavement is exhausting and costly. A free league is tempting. It avoids unnecessary wars and offers security through unity against outside threats (II:4). Leagues tend to have a maximum size because difficulties of coordination limit their ability to expand. These limits unfortunately make them vulnerable to more powerful invaders, as the Etruscans were destroyed by the Gauls. Leagues are also stable only in special circumstances, as the German free cities depended on the imperial authority of the Holy Roman Empire for settling disputes and external protection (II:19). The best route to security and glory thus is the Roman way, expanding through "companions" (we would now call them collaborators), taking advantage of "empire by invitation" to extend effective rule.[40]

Hence republican as well as princely imperialism. We are lovers of glory, Machiavelli announces. We seek to rule or at least to avoid being oppressed. In either case we want more for ourselves and our states than just material welfare. Because other states with similar aims thereby threaten us, we prepare ourselves for expansion. Because our fellow citizens threaten us if we do not allow them either to satisfy their ambition or to release their political energies through imperial expansion, we expand. In doing so, we create a state of war—insecurity abroad as a way of mitigating, but never successfully eliminating, insecurity at home.

All this poses a challenge to republican strategy: "For as a free city is generally influenced by two principal objects, the one to aggrandize herself, and the other to preserve her liberties, it is natural that she should occasionally be betrayed into faults by excessive eagerness in the pursuit of either of these two objects" (I:29). Machiavelli then warns us of the danger of being ungrateful to those with virtue or suspicious of those who should be trusted. At the same time, we must be aware of the need to maintain social equality and avoid the development of a landed nobility, who can live without work, for they corrupt republican patriotism (I:55). The other danger is "daring enterprises" that risk the state by allowing the populace to become drunk with glory and booty, rather than prudent in the pursuit of security (I:53).

MODERN FUNDAMENTALISM

Modern Fundamentalists rest their analysis on similar basic human drives, but few are as consistent as Machiavelli. Like Machiavelli, Hans Morgenthau, the

[40] I have explored this theme in *Empires*. For a provocative interpretation of U.S. power in the postwar period, see Geir Lundestad, *The American "Empire"* (Oxford: Oxford University Press, 1990), whose phrase "empire by invitation" I borrow here.

preeminent modern Fundamentalist Realist, traces the "struggle for power," which he finds characteristic of all politics, whether domestic or international, to basic "elemental bio-psychological" drives in human nature.[41] "The essence of international politics is identical with its domestic counterpart," he says. It is modified only by different conditions under which the same struggle takes place, for the "tendency to dominate" is "an element of all human associations from the family . . . to the state" (p.32). Like Machiavelli, Morgenthau notes that statesmen pursue various distinct types of struggle for power—policies of the status quo (chapter 4), imperialism (chapter 5), and prestige (chapter 6) among them. He presents us with an insightful picture of the breadth of balance of power policies, which range from "dividing and ruling" potentially threatening coalitions to "compensations" designed to distribute territories and populations in a stabilizing (balancing) fashion to the more traditional "armaments" and "alliances" (chapter 12).

Like Machiavelli, Morgenthau finds moral considerations unfit for the necessities that characterize politics, particularly international politics. Traditional moral considerations are real, but they should (can) restrain otherwise expedient policy only where necessity does not override them (as in restraining international assassinations of threatening heads of state during peacetime).[42]

Unlike Machiavelli, however, Morgenthau fails to connect his domestic to his international struggles for power. We do not really learn why some states are imperialistic, others status quo–oriented. Morgenthau writes of the struggle for power without distinguishing Borgia's from Ferrara's (new from old princes) or Sparta's from Rome's (aristocratic from free republics). He thereby loses the analytic power of Machiavelli's insights concerning how variations in the distribution of human nature (few or many, with more or less *virtú*) make for variations in states and variations in foreign policies. He, unlike Machiavelli, therefore seems to suggest that statesmen pursue power for its own sake.

Morgenthau's own purpose, it emerges, is actually moral—"peace through accommodation." Since peace cannot now be achieved through "limitation"

[41] Morgenthau, *Politics among Nations*, p. 31.

[42] Ibid., p. 225. Morgenthau's position on moral restraints is, if anything, even more contradictory than Machiavelli's. Morgenthau consistently denies that he is a "Machiavellian" (by which he seems to mean a thoroughgoing moral skeptic). Morgenthau himself endorses what he sees as Hobbes's views (international moral skepticism) in his *Defense of the National Interest*, p. 34. But this does not square well with the international moral restraints he discusses in chapter 16 of *Politics among Nations* or with his transcendental ideal of a realm of absolute and universal ethical norms caught in an "ineluctable tension" with the world of actual politics. See Robert C. Good, "National Interest and Moral Theory," in *Statecraft and Moral Theory*, pp. 285–86. (Hobbes bridges that tension by having the sovereign define ethical standards within the state.) Moreover, Morgenthau privately subscribes to an unexplained affinity for evolutionary (Hegelian) conceptions of political ethics (see Michael Smith, "Hans Morgenthau and the American National Interest in the Early Cold War," *Social Research* 48, 4 [Winter 1981], p. 778).

(disarmament, collective security, or international law) or through "transformation" (a world state or world community), diplomacy is the best we can do, and corrupted by ideology and the quest for electoral popularity, we are not doing that well (chapter 32).

Machiavelli's Fundamentalism provides an intriguing and distinct view of the state of war within and between states that should not fall from the Realist vocabulary and catalog of insights. Princely *virtú* and republican imperialism rest on views on the nature of man and what they can create that preserve an entrepreneurial feature in Realist political analysis. But how would we know if Machiavelli and the Fundamentalists are correct? In a world dominated by new princes and Roman-style republics, we might be able to model state behavior as rational, self-interested, and power-maximizing (and nonnuclear). If we did, we might expect the emergence of balancing and a steadily increasing size of empires and steadily decreasing number of other states (as lesser powers were conquered).[43] These hypothetical imperial results are characteristically Machiavellian.

In a world dominated by no single form of state, we might look for systematic differences in the behavior of new and old princes. Are the Hitlers and Mussolinis on average more aggressive (because more glory-seeking and risk-prone) than the traditional monarchs were? (On the whole, though, military dictatorships are not very expansionist.)[44] Are more free, more egalitarian republics (Rome's) more expansionist than more conservative, aristocratic republics (Sparta's or late Venice's)? There is of course considerable historical evidence for republican imperialism. Machiavelli's own Rome and Thucydides's Athens both were imperial republics in the Machiavellian sense. Were the aristocratic republics of the Middle Ages more or less aggressive than their Roman predecessor? Today, if the United States qualifies as a new Rome, the historical record of numerous U.S. interventions in the postwar period supports Machiavelli's argument.[45] But an equally notable feature of it is the lack of enthusiasm the people seem to show for it.

The Strategic Balance

The Machiavellian model adds an important perspective to national security. Machiavelli prefers glorious imperialism to balancing. He nonetheless illuminates an important facet of the theory of the balance of power. While some theories of the balance (as we shall see in the next two chapters) assume that it

[43] See Richard Stoll (1987).

[44] For interesting speculation on these issues, see Stanislav Andreski, "On the Peaceful Disposition of Military Dictatorships," *Journal of Strategic Studies* 3 (1980), pp. 3–10.

[45] Raymond Aron, *Imperial Republic*, trans. Frank Jellinek (Englewood Cliffs: Prentice Hall, 1973), chaps. 3 and 4, and Richard Barnet, *Intervention and Revolution* (New York: Meridian, 1968), chap. 11.

is an automatic result of Structural anarchy or the product of Constituted or sociological conditions, a Machiavellian perspective develops a "strategic balance" focusing on leadership. It holds that the balance of power is maintained only by (1) the special *virtú* of great Machiavellian princes, (2) the special vigilance of "statesmen" rather than "prophets," or (3) a particular strategy. Here the balance is neither a mechanical artifact nor a sociological circumstance but a work of art, a product of finesse, and history is made by great men (and great women).[46]

Machiavelli offers the classic explanation for why and how princes play the game of balance of power politics, considered as a contest in political entrepreneurship. Leaders, as we have seen, go for power in order to enhance personal glory and maintain national security. Machiavelli, we should recall, warns against both neutrality and what we now call collaboration, bandwagoning, or omnibalancing, subordinating oneself to or aligning with stronger foreign princes.[47] Active interstate balancing is both more prestigious and more secure, since aligning can make the difference needed for victory and, in case of a loss, having failed to align with the weaker can leave you victim to the designs of the winner without the support of the weaker. More generally, Machiavelli illustrates the capacity of entrepreneurship to overcome Structural and Constituted constraints.[48]

Henry Kissinger offers us an eloquent portrait of a more developed strategic model with the statesman as the architect of the balance of power. Stability is a product of a consensus on legitimacy among states, according to Kissinger. Legitimacy is not natural or automatic but created. In legitimate orders disputes are settled diplomatically and alliances are appropriately flexible and pragmatic, because the legitimacy of the international order is not also up for dispute. "That Europe rescued stability from seeming chaos (at the close of the Napoleonic Wars) was primarily the result of the work of two great men: of Castlereagh, the British Foreign Secretary, who negotiated the international

[46] We should note, however, that Machiavelli focused on strategies of "divide and conquer" that displayed no clear conception of the balance of power as a general system of relations among states. See Herbert Butterfield, "The Balance of Power," in H. Butterfield and M. Wight, eds., *Diplomatic Investigations* (London: George Allen and Unwin, 1966), p. 134. His own strategic approach was closer to a simple policy of "divide and rule" *(divide et impera)*, a policy pursued by any rational actor seeking to reduce potential threats to its ambitions, whether it is balancing power or aggressively seeking to expand an empire. See also Morgenthau, *Politics among Nations*, chap. 31, and Henry Kissinger, *A World Restored* (Boston: Houghton Mifflin, 1964), chap. 17.

[47] For omnibalancing, see David, "Explaining Third World Alignment."

[48] For an interesting example of how leadership and doctrinal innovation can, for good and ill, overcome the advantages associated with offense/defense balances, see Jonathan Shimshoni, "Technology, Military Advantage, and World War I: A Case for Military Entrepreneurship," *International Security* 15, 3 (Winter 1990–91), pp. 187–215.

settlement, and of Austria's foreign minister, Metternich, who legitimized it."[49] Great statesmen succeed in creating international orders within the balance of power by reconciling what their societies regard as just with what the resources of their nation and its allies make feasible. Metternich sought to create a transnational order that would deter revolutionary domestic change by international intervention; Castlereagh, to create an international order that limited aggressive domestic revolution by international alliance. The Congress of Vienna, Kissinger tells us, reflected the combined success of those two projects. Metternich established a concert system that would intervene against revolutionary change. Castlereagh fulfilled Pitt's vision of a European balance that would employ an internally divided but externally stable German center as well as "great masses" of neighboring territory to contain the possibility of an imperial revival of France, all without turning Europe over to the Russians.

Bismarck adopted a similar creative role between 1870 and 1890. Then, by playing upon the fears of the three conservative monarchies against revolutionary democracy, he kept Russia, Austria, and Germany linked, despite their rivalries over the Balkans. By exacerbating Anglo-French tensions over Egypt and West African colonies and Franco-Italian tensions over the control of Tunisia and the naval balance in the Mediterranean, he kept France (deeply hostile because of its resentment over the loss of Alsace-Lorraine) isolated from its "natural" allies and dependent on Germany for diplomatic support. In 1890 the kaiser very unwisely dropped this "pilot" who had so successfully steered the international system.

Machiavelli's Legacy

Princely *virtú* and republican imperialism rest on views on the nature of human beings and what they can create that preserve an entrepreneurial feature in Realist political analysis. They provide the motives and ends that so many critics of Realism fail to find in modern abstractions. Fundamentalism provides a model for how states are created or expanded or preserved where there is little in the way of strong institutions or nationalism to hold them together. In a powerful invocation of prudence, Machiavelli tells us that "fortune is arbiter of half of actions" (*The Prince,* chapter 25). More striking—especially to modern social scientists—is the other half of his claim: "[B]ut . . . she [fortune] leaves the other half, or close to it, for us to govern."

Fundamentalist Realism also serves as a warning. Machiavelli's new princes both preserve themselves and realize their ambitions through glorious expansion. (Old princes, beware! Political creativity may not be dead.) And Machiavelli's republican imperialism warns us of tendencies in republican free

[49] Kissinger, *A World Restored,* p. 5.

government. Extending the rule of the dominant elite or avoiding the political collapse of their state, each calls for imperial expansion, at least when there is no sense of fundamental human rights to guarantee us against those tendencies either at home or abroad.[50]

[50] Unlike Machiavelli's republics, some modern Liberal (Kantian) republics are capable of achieving peace among themselves because they exercise democratic caution and because they are capable of appreciating the international rights of foreign republics. See the discussion in chapter 7.

CHAPTER THREE

Structuralism: Hobbes

> Out of civil states, there is always war of every one against every one.[1]
>
> —Thomas Hobbes

ALTHOUGH THUCYDIDES WAS the first of what we now call the Realists, he left much of what more theoretical Realists have wanted to understand caught up in historical contingency. His great themes—war, leadership, and democracy—were deeply embedded in his history of the Peloponnesian War. Machiavelli focused on one part of Thucydides's lesson—the roots of violence in individual ambition—and told us how a prince might achieve glory and a republic security, but his lessons too were highly contextual.

Thomas Hobbes (1588–1679)—Thucydides's most famous modern disciple and the preeminent philosopher of the modern sovereign state—has given us a more theoretical—that is, a less historically or circumstantially contingent—treatment of Realist thought.[2] Hobbes's *Leviathan* broke with Machiavellian Fundamentalism and began a strikingly different version of Realism, a Struc-

[1] *Leviathan*, ed. Michael Oakeshott (London: Collier, 1962, [1651]), p. 100. All page cites in the text come from this edition unless otherwise noted.

[2] Hobbes also shares many of the basic presuppositions of Liberalism: rationality, suspicion of tradition, and scientific modernism. He employs *methodological* individualism and rejects essentialist, purely traditional, or paternal arguments for autocracy. Yet he expresses great hostility to cultural and political individualism. For the modernist Liberal element in Hobbes, see John Dunn, *Western Political Theory in the Face of the Future* (Cambridge: Cambridge University Press, 1979), pp. 31–32, and also Robert Kraynak, "Hobbes's Behemoth and the Argument for Absolutism," *American Political Science Review* 76, 4 (December 1982).

tural view that sees interstate anarchy as the defining cause of the state of war. He also provided two key foundations that contemporary Structuralism lacks (or neglects).

1. He explained why states should and could be treated as rational unitary actors, despite all their actual diversity.

2. He explained why international anarchy could and should be considered a state of war, despite all the actual variety of state motives and relations. He achieved both of these by drawing in considerations of human nature and the nature of the state (Image I and II features).

Hobbes was the first of the great translators of Thucydides into English. Hobbes was drawn to Thucydides by his admiration for the "most politic historiographer that ever writ" and because of what he saw as Thucydides's effective refutation of radical claims, the sort of claims that were also being made in the 1620s.[3] Many of his basic insights concerning human motivation (fear, honor, self-interest) and the dangers of civil war formed the core of Thucydides's *History*. Indeed, the anarchy, destruction, and social collapse that occurred during the Corcyraean civil war were the closest analogue to what Hobbes describes in *Leviathan* as the "state of nature" without government. Writing his major political works in the 1640s, he addressed, directly and indirectly, the causes of the English Civil War, which he judged to be a result of religious dissent and the ambition of overmighty subjects. The horrible destruction of the war added force to his arguments concerning the dangers of anarchic confusion and fired his determination to discover a path to peace.[4] Unlike both Thucydides and Machiavelli, Hobbes played no direct role in public affairs and earned his living instead as a tutor to members of the aristocratic Cavendish family and, briefly, to Charles II. Scholarly and unworldly, he (and his arguments for absolute sovereignty) managed to offend both the parliamentarians and the royalists in the course of the strife of the English Civil War.

His most distinctive contributions, however, were less his conclusions and more his methods. The spirit of the new mathematics of geometry and of the new science of mechanics added an especially abstract and forcefully scientific twist to his political arguments. Hobbes sought the essential, universal, and absolute truths of politics just as his near contemporaries Galileo, Descartes, and Newton did in mechanics, geometry, and calculus. He assimilated the contingent insights of politics to the rigor and certainty of science and geometry as a way of refuting once and for all and forever what he saw as the vicious arrogance of those who would challenge the authority of the state and inflict

[3] Schlatter, *Hobbes' Thucydides*, and Richard Peters, *Hobbes* (Harmondsworth: Penguin, 1956), pp. 18–22.

[4] Peters, *Hobbes*, p. 36.

the miseries of war on their fellow citizens. He reasoned that the necessary truths contained in the basic concepts of the human appetites, which form the foundations of interest, duty, and right, were just as absolutely true as was the geometrical truth that any straight line passing through the center of a circle bisects it into two identical halves. Introspection thus can tell us what we need to know about human nature. He supports, rather than empirically tests, those truths with ad hoc examples. (We fear our fellowmen; why else would we lock our houses at night?)

Hobbes's Structuralism

Human Nature	x
Domestic Society	x
Interstate System	xx

For international relations theorists, Hobbes's most important contribution was his laying systematic and complete foundations for what is now the dominant model of international theory, Structural Realism. His argument was systematically *Structural*. Having assumed certain features of individuals (that they are rational but sometimes envious egoists), he showed how their interaction in anarchic conditions would lead them to want to form a truly sovereign state. He then showed how such states interacting in anarchic conditions would maintain a state of war. So, unlike the later Structuralists, who simply assumed, he *explained* why we should think of states as rational and unitary actors. Also, rather than simply assume, he *explained* why anarchy could lead to a state of war by explaining why it was that states would lack trust in one another and why strategies of cooperative security available within an anarchic international system would fail. Having done this, he could then argue that, for all essential purposes, effective states could be treated as like units. States seeking to preserve their security could, therefore, measure the threats posed by their neighbors by their neighbors' capacities. He thus laid the analytic foundations of the systemic balance of power and showed that it was the best order sovereign states could hope to maintain.

NATURAL CONDITIONS

The "State of Nature" as a "State of War"

Hobbes's description in *Leviathan* of the hypothetical "natural condition of men living together without a common power to keep them in awe" as a "state of war" is duly famous. The state of war is a war of all against all, not a single battle but a tract of time "wherein the will to contend by battle is sufficiently known" (p. 100). In the state of nature there is "no place for industry, because the fruit thereof is uncertain: and consequently no culture of the earth; no navigation, nor use of the commodities that may be imported by sea; no commodious building; no instruments of moving and removing, such things as require much force; no knowledge of the face of the earth; no account of time; no arts; no letters; no society; and which is worst of all, continual fear, and danger of violent death; and the life of man, solitary, poor, nasty, brutish, and short." (p. 100).

Hobbes sees the state of nature as a state of war because all men are equal in body, ambitions, and reason and there is no common power to restrain them. Traditionalism and Realism clearly, despite frequent association, are wrongly paired in Hobbes. Hobbes is one of the first of the radical individualists, one of the first and most extreme of the true moderns. For Hobbes, all human beings are created equal. Differences in strength exist, but no differences are so significant that a man can go without fear of being killed by his fellows. All must sleep at times; a few can gang up on the most able. All humans seek roughly the same things: shelter, food, sex, esteem, security. And the things they do seek they seek with an equal intensity. We all have roughly the same intelligence. After all, as Hobbes famously noted, through introspection we can discover that no one thinks he or she is dumber than his or her fellows: "[E]very man is contented with his share."[5] And reason serves as an efficient scout and spy for our needs and desires. We are not identical. Some men are more fearful; they have "feminine" characters.[6] Others are more aggressive and enjoy domination for its own sake. But these differences are swamped by our basic similarities.

"From equality proceeds diffidence," that is, fear.[7] We compete for needs and desires and are unwilling to cede them to a rival. Our competition makes us fearful of preventive or preemptive attack, and our equality gives us no confidence in our being able to maintain security alone, so we too choose to strike first for safety's sake. Even if we ourselves have no such acquisitive desires, we know that there are those who do, so we strike, and we give the same impression to all others. Our competition also extends to matters of prestige, for prestige might translate into deference. In any case, no one has authority to decide who is more worthy, and no one is prepared to cede preeminence to a mere equal.[8]

[5] Hobbes, *Leviathan*, p. 98.

[6] Hobbes refers to "men" rather than "human beings," and he draws some distinctions between men and women. Since the substantial differences among men do not swamp their basic similarity of human beings, there is not enough in Hobbes's argument to support a view that differences between men and women are sufficiently large to swamp their basic similarity.

[7] Hobbes, *Leviathan*, p. 98.

[8] See David Gauthier, *The Logic of Leviathan* (Oxford: Clarendon, 1969), p. 208; Gregory S. Kavka, "Hobbes's War of All against All," *Ethics* 93, 2 (January 1983), pp. 292–93. Among

Competition, diffidence (fear), and glory thus drive all against all into a "state of war," a tract of time wherein the possibility of battle is continuous. Hobbes derives "laws"—normative precepts—for the state of nature which flow from our fundamental right of self-defense and the rational desire for security. The first is to seek peace where possible but, where it cannot be found, to use all the "helps and advantages" of nature for self-preservation. We should keep a promise to keep the peace if others have fulfilled their half first. But all promises under these circumstances are "covenants without the sword." Since we cannot be sure that any promise will be enforced in a manner that can permit us to rely upon it, our own security must be the paramount rule of our conduct (chapter 15). Thus for Hobbes, as for so many contemporary social scientists, human beings should be considered rational egoists, at least in the sense that they rationally calculate the satisfaction of their passions.

The second law of nature is to be willing to lay down all our rights insofar as our safety requires if others are willing to do the same and on an equal basis. We thus can escape from this desperate condition of war by two means. Either we accept a state through conquest—we are conquered and pledge allegiance to a Leviathan in order to preserve our lives—or we establish a state, a commonwealth by institution and mutual contract. We institute a commonwealth by pledging one to another to cede all our rights except the right of self-preservation.

Driven by the terror of the state of natural war, we thereby accept or create the Leviathan, an "Artificial Man." The people and their wealth, Hobbes suggests, are its muscles; government agents are its joints; rewards and punishments are its nerves; laws and principles of equity are like reason; and the sovereign is the soul, which should govern all. The Leviathan then is sole sovereign; it governs as it sees fit. Its authority is inalienable, once granted. It can do no injustice since it defines what is just and unjust. Its authority is indivisible. It can judge the guilt of a man according to the laws it has decreed, and all citizens are required to carry out the sentence. The sovereign thus has all the personal rights of an individual in the state of nature in addition to all the rights of the citizens who have agreed to establish it. Subject citizens retain only one right, the basic right of nature, the right not to have to kill themselves, the right to self-preservation (chapters 17 and 18).

Here is the hypothetical "single rational unitary actor" the Structuralist theorists conceived of and justified as a rational ideal. Hobbes's reasoned intuition provides moral reasons why we should be prepared to cede to the state those characteristics. All Leviathans are equivalent in their absolute authority; hence

the best discussions of the neglected factor of "glory" are the chapters by Jean Hampton, William Sacksteder, and Andrew Altman in Peter Caws, ed., *The Causes of Quarrel* (Boston: Beacon, 1989). Also valuable on this important theme is Arthur Ripstein's "Hobbes on World Government and the World Cup," in Timo Airaksinen and Martin Bertman, eds., *Hobbes: War among Nations* (Aldershot: Gower, 1989), pp. 112–29.

the international lawyer's "sovereign equality." The Leviathan can be either one person or a group of persons—a monarch or a republic—and neither makes a fundamental difference because it is the amount of authority, not the management of the authority, that counts for individuals desperate to escape natural anarchy. So we have also established the "like units" posited by the Structuralists. But they are also, we infer, alike in a special way. The Hobbesian sovereign, whether one person or a committee, is a Hobbesian individual—another rational egoist driven by competition, diffidence, and glory. Driven by terror and desire for security we surrendered all authority to such an individual. But is there something in the structure of interstate anarchy that tames or re-structures the Leviathan?

INTERNATIONAL CONDITIONS

Sovereigns in interstate politics are, by analogy, somewhat like individuals in the state of nature: They exist in a state of war in which there is not effective international law or morality; all have unrestrained rights, none has enforceable duties. Or, put differently, all have a duty to follow "international law," but international law is nothing more than the same natural law of self-defense that was binding on individuals in the state of nature. "In all times," Hobbes explains, "kings, and persons of sovereign authority because of their independency are in continual jealousies and in the state and posture of gladiators; having their weapons pointing, and their eyes fixed on one another; that is, their forts, garrisons, and guns upon the frontiers of their kingdoms; and continual spies upon their neighbors; which is a posture of war" (p. 101).

Like Hobbesian individuals, they are caught up in competition for goods, fear of attack, and struggles for prestige. Competition, fear, and glory: Each is a reason for conflict and possibly war.

Persistent Anarchy?

Yet the international state of war is not as "nasty, brutish, and short" as the natural condition of mankind, for four reasons involving the artificiality of the sovereign personality.[9]

1. "[B]ecause they uphold thereby the industry of their subjects, there does not follow from it that misery which accompanies the liberty of particular men"

[9] See Stanley Hoffmann, "Rousseau on War and Peace," *The State of War* (New York: Praeger, 1965), pp. 45–87; Mark Heller, "The Use and Abuse of Hobbes," *Polity* 13, 1 (Fall 1980), pp. 24–25; Narvari, "Hobbes and the Hobbesian Tradition in International Thought"; and Vincent, "The Hobbesian Tradition in Twentieth Century International Thought," p. 95. For a valuable collection of essays on the theme, see Airaksinen and Bertman, *Hobbes: War among Nations.*

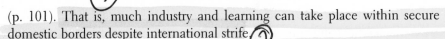

(p. 101). That is, much industry and learning can take place within secure domestic borders despite international strife.

2. Soldiers retain the right to self-preservation, and so in a battle there is much running away on either side. According to Hobbes, subjects can hire substitutes if they are called up in a draft and suffer from a "natural timorousness." Sergeants and officers of course have the right and duty to threaten a soldier with death if he runs away, and all soldiers must obey their officers in training and maneuvers up to the actual field of battle. In a national emergency, where the defense of all is required for the defense of each, soldiers will feel an especially strong incentive to stay and perhaps have a duty to do so. Volunteers especially have promised to stay, and Hobbes says they should. But even criminals retain the right to try to preserve their lives.

Soldiers will run away in dangerous battles. Knowing this, sovereigns are likely to be restrained in their aggressiveness and in their otherwise unfettered pursuit of their private and personal advantages. They will limit wars either to a lot of maneuvering or to campaigns against much inferior forces.

3. Sovereigns are not like individuals in important respects. Sovereigns, unlike individuals, are not mortal. The death of a king or a president does not end the state, so potential bushwhackers should be deterred.

4. Nor are sovereigns equal. Unlike natural men, artificial men can grow in disproportionate ways. Their inequality may even allow them to reflect differences in taste. In any case, the fear of the larger for the smaller is likely not to result in great insecurity; the fear of the smaller, to result in more deference. War, it has thus been argued, "is usually the outcome of a diplomatic crisis which cannot be solved because both sides have conflicting estimates of their bargaining power."[10]

Hobbes thus leaves the international state of war ambiguous. It is a state of war, but it is less brutal than the state of war of the natural condition. But being less brutal, it seems also to lack the terror that drives individuals to create a peace within the sovereign Leviathan. Thus the international condition may indeed be sufficiently safe and commodious that we would not be willing to establish a global Leviathan as a means of ensuring a truly global peace. The lesser danger of international war ironically seems to preclude the "sovereign" solution analogous to domestic peace. In the seventeenth century sovereigns provided enough security (and were themselves secure enough behind their armies) that no global sovereign was necessary. Today even the most extreme threats to survival—nuclear threats—under conditions of mutually assured

[10] The clarity of an unequal distribution of power thus contributes to peace, Geoffrey Blainey suggests in his insightful rumination, *The Causes of War* (New York: Free Press, 1973), p. 114.

destruction (stable second-strike capability) are deterred in ways that no individual in the natural condition can possibly count upon natural deterrence to work (individuals sleep at night, can be ambushed, etc.)[11] Therefore, we continue to suffer international insecurity.

International Cooperation?

Does the persistent anarchy of the international condition allow for cooperation, stability, and perhaps international legal order? One suspects that Hobbes, with his analytic individualism, would have found the modern analysis of cooperation and conflict found in game theory especially congenial as a way to imagine the possibilities of cooperation and conflict among Leviathans that lack authoritative international order.

Many of the sources of cooperation and conflict may really be, the game theorists tell us, the harmony or discord of simple decisions. A and B are in a "deadlock" if each prefers conflict to any form of cooperation. If both the United States and the USSR preferred to conduct an arms race rather than to control arms, then conflict was inevitable. Or A and B are in "harmony" if neither would choose conflicting policies.[12] If both trading states prefer free trade no matter what tariffs the other might impose, free trade is harmoniously determined.

More complicated causes of cooperation and conflict result from decisions in which cooperation is preferred to deadlock and in which coordination is necessary to achieve cooperation.[13] In contemporary international relations theory, "games" can model the competition, fear, and glory that Hobbes saw as the continuous roots of conflict, ranging from the natural condition to the international state of war. Games too are anarchic: outcomes depend not on authoritative decision but on the interdependent strategies, the decisions, of the players.

Some situations are, we imagine, completely competitive, in that what one person wins the other must lose (a zero-sum game). Prestige (who is to be king, who subject) or a unique resource (the only dry cave in a region) may not be shareable among Hobbesian individuals or families (a natural unit, for Hobbes). Strategies of victory therefore rely first on relative power and then, often, on deception, as in the famous case of the attack game used to model some of the

[11] For an argument that nuclear weapons do reconstitute the original insecurity of the natural condition, see Gauthier (pp. 207–09). Interestingly, even if one accepts the anarchy-enhancing logic of mutually assured destruction deterrence, the onset of first-strike capabilities should revive an interest in global sovereignty.

[12] Kenneth Oye, "Explaining Cooperation under Anarchy," *World Politics* 38, 1 (October 1985), pp. 1–24.

[13] Not all interdependent decisions need raise the possibility of conflict. A and B may be "altruistic" if each wants the other to have what it wants. In international relations altruistic decisions are assumed to be so rare as not to warrant much attention.

famous battles of World War II, such as the Battle of Leyte Gulf, between the nearly equal forces of Admirals Halsey and Yamamoto, or the Normandy landing, contested between Eisenhower and Rommel. If the attacker (Eisenhower) can land (or strike) unopposed and achieve surprise, he wins; if the defender (Rommel) anticipates the time and location of the attack, the defender (given

Zero-Sum Games

NORMANDY ATTACK
Rommel

		North	South
Eisenhower	North	100 −100	−100 100
	South	−100 100	100 −100

Variable Sum Games

COORDINATION GAME
Player One

		Right	Left
Player Two	Right	1 1	−1 −1
	Left	−1 −1	1 1

STAG DILEMMA
One Hunter

		Cooperate	Defect
Other Hunters	Cooperate	3 3	2 0
	Defect	0 2	1 1

PRISONER'S DILEMMA

First Prisoner

Second Prisoners	Cooperate	Defect
Cooperate	−2, −2	−10, 0
Defect	0, −10	−5, −5

CHICKEN DILEMMA

First Driver

Second Driver	Cooperate	Defect
Cooperate	−1, −1	−10, 10
Defect	10, −10	$-\infty$, $-\infty$

Mixed-Motive Games

BATTLE OF THE SEXES

Husband

Wife	Mountain	Shore
Mountain	2, 4	0, 0
Shore	0, 0	4, 2

the usual advantages of the defense) wins. Here the payoffs for each strategy of either attack or defense (concentrating forces, let us say, north [N] or south[S]) depend on the choice made by the other player. In the illustration, the attacker's (row) payoffs are in the lower left and the defender's (column) payoffs are in the upper right of each quadrant. The attacker thus prefers outcomes SN or NS; the defender, complementarily, SS or NN.

But conflicts need not be so completely competitive in order to generate strife. Even when both parties share some common interests, and both can lose or both can gain (as in variable sum games), conflicts can result. Even when states share an interest in a common good that could be attained by cooperation, the absence of a source of global law and order may mean that no one state can count upon the cooperative behavior of the others. Coordination games, for example, presuppose a shared and equivalent interest in cooperation, as occurs when both seek to coordinate outcomes, such as requiring that either all drive on their right (RR) or all drive on their left (LL) side of the street. Each prefers RR or LL to RL or LR. Established conventions usually solve these problems. Yet misperception and a lack of authoritative determination can produce "defections"—crashes.[14]

So-called Stag Dilemmas (after a story first elaborated by Jean-Jacques Rousseau) prove even more troubling. In a woods populated with deer and rabbits, a group of hunters stalk a stag, which only their combined skills can capture. Each hunter values his share of the stag (CC) at more than the value of an entire rabbit. But a rabbit can be caught by individual effort alone (DC). A rabbit appears as the hunters stalk the deer. If one hunter defects from the common enterprise of deer hunting, the other (that is, all the rest) will go hungry (CD) or be left scrambling for possible shares of other rabbits (DD). Can—should—any hunter rationally forgo the rabbit? The hunter's preference ordering is CC>DC>DD>CD. The problem is that the hunter—by analogy, a state—has a rational incentive to defect from the cooperative enterprise if he cannot trust his fellow hunters to be rational. Here accurate information, transparency, is crucial to cooperation: If all the hunters truly recognize that all the other hunters recognize the superiority of shared venison, cooperation should be forthcoming. The "dilemma" arises because under anarchy, hunters wonder whether these understandings can be made clear to the dim-witted or enforceable against the perverse.

Correspondingly, in international politics, even though each state knows that security is relative to the armaments level of potential adversaries and even though each state seeks to avoid excess arms expenditure (CC), it also knows that because there is no global guarantee of security, being caught unarmed by a surprise attack (CD) is worse than bearing the costs of armament. Each therefore tries to arm alone (DC); all are worse off (DD). This is typical of arms race situations.[15]

[14] See David Kreps, *Game Theory and Economic Modelling* (New York: Oxford University Press, 1990); Avinash Dixit and Barry Nalebuff, *Thinking Strategically: The Competitive Edge in Business, Politics, and Everyday Life* (New York: Norton, 1991); and Steven Brams, *Superpower Games: Applying Game Theory to Superpower Conflict* (New Haven: Yale University Press, 1985).

[15] George Downs, David Rocke, and Randolph Siverson, "Arms Races and Cooperation," *World Politics* 38, 1 (October 1985), p. 135.

Another situation under anarchy, illustrating rational preemption, may be the Prisoner's Dilemma. Two suspects are captured by the police. Interrogated separately, each is offered his freedom if he "rats" (DC) on his partner, who would then be convicted, become the "sucker" (CD), and receive the maximum sentence. If both rat (DD, both "defect"), both are convicted, though with tainted evidence and so receive a large sentence, but fewer years than the sucker would receive. If both stick to their claim of innocence (and thus CC, "cooperate"), both are convicted of some much lesser offense for which the prosecutor has some evidence. The suspects' preference ordering is again the same: DC>CC>DD>CD. Thus in colonial competition a cooperative scheme of exploitation (CC) would reduce strategic competition among the imperial metropoles and curb colonial wars (DD) in the peripheries and, above all, avoid the danger of losing out on the opportunity to claim resources (CD). But each metropole prefers even more to be the first and unchallenged claimant (DC). A "Scramble" (DD) ensues. This too is the situation in so-called Security Dilemmas, in which island nation A's need for a fleet (DC) for defensive reasons so threatens B's colonies (CD) that although both would prefer arms control (CC) to an arms race (DD), an arms race ensues.[16] In one-shot Prisoner's Dilemma play, the rational "criminal" or state will defect, making all worse off. Improvements in reliable information, transparency, merely increase the certainty of mutual defection. Only authoritative coordination, "sovereignty," will prevent defection in one-shot play. Only the likelihood of repeated play raises the prospects of arriving at stable mutual cooperation (CC).

This brings us to the risk of war from glory. Under anarchy, heavily armed states confront one another and must rely on self-help for security. They rely upon their prestige (glory), their credibility, to deter states from testing the true quality of their arms in battle, and credibility is measured by a record of successes. In the game theory literature, 1950s teenage "rebels without a cause" model the situation in the game of chicken. To determine prestige, two drivers confront each other on a narrow road and roar directly toward each other to see who will be the first to swerve, thereby losing face. If both fail to swerve, the result is death. If they "cooperate" and both swerve, they save their lives, but swerving leaves both drivers with tarnished prestige (but not as stained as that of the single "chicken" who continues to cooperate by swerving while the other defects and flashes to glory down the center line). Their preference orderings are DC>CC>CD>DD.

So too for states armed with extremely destructive weapons (nuclear weapons, for example), once a posture of confrontation has been assumed, backing down, although rational for both together, is not rational (first best) for either

[16] John Hertz, *Political Realism and Political Idealism* (Chicago: University of Chicago Press, 1951).

individually if one has an expectation that the other will back down first.[17] Here more information may increase the chances of avoiding disaster. But each side has a powerful incentive to fake—engage in "brinkmanship," risk-prone determination. The classic strategy is to throw a (one hopes, fake and spare) steering wheel out the window or make wild threats.

Not all games involve simple, equivalent payoffs. Some are also mixed-motive and raise the problem of power as a means to gain competitive goods, reduce fear, or acquire glory. "Battle of the Sexes" illustrates a common dilemma. A husband and wife like to vacation together. She, however, prefers the seashores; he, the mountains. Unlike in the previous games, the preference orderings differ: He prefers MM>SS>(MS or SM); she prefers SS>MM>(SM or MS). Here more reliable information or trust will not solve the conflict. Over the longer run, in healthy marriages, trade-offs take place—he gets the sports car, they go to the seashore—or they alternate vacation sites. But in a single decision only power (or altruistic love?) will rule. And in international relations love is in short supply.[18] States are also concerned that although cooperation is valuable, they may benefit differently from the cooperative scheme. This becomes an especially large concern when, given the self-help assumption, differences in resources may be translated into coercive capacities and possible conquest.[19]

States under international anarchy are thus insecure but not sufficiently terrified to form a global Leviathan. Are states in the international condition then safe and prudent enough to respect international law and thus create the minimum foundations needed for an interdependent international society?

Hobbes's answer was that international law is nothing more than the laws of nature. Sovereigns have all the rights to pursue the security of their states that individuals in the natural condition have to pursue the security of their persons. Should a Hobbesian expect that the changed conditions of international relations create conditions sufficient for international cooperation and perhaps legal order?[20]

Two arguments suggest grounds for a Hobbesian pacification. One is a matter of moral duty; the other, of rational egoism. A Hobbesian Realist could

[17] Jervis, "Cooperation under the Security Dilemma."

[18] Stephen Krasner, "Global Communications and National Power: Life on the Pareto Frontier," *World Politics* 43, 3 (April 1991), pp. 336–66.

[19] Joseph Grieco, *Cooperation among Nations* (Ithaca: Cornell University Press, 1990), p. 10.

[20] Recent arguments that this indeed may be the case are, with many qualifications, Vincent (1981) and, most extensively, Donald Hanson, "Thomas Hobbes's 'Highway to Peace' " *International Organization* 8, 2 (Spring 1984). See also Murray Forsyth, "Thomas Hobbes and the External Relations of States," *British Journal of International Studies* 5 (1979), pp. 196–209; and Hedley Bull, "Hobbes and the International Anarchy," *Social Research* 48, 4 (Winter 1981), pp. 717–38, for more traditional views.

argue that peace could be the outcome of prudent diplomacy guided by effective moral duties. Hobbes argues that sovereigns have a natural duty not to act against "the reasons of peace. . . . Dominions were constituted for peace's sake, and peace was sought for safety's sake."[21] The natural duty of the sovereign is therefore the safety of the people. But prudent policy cannot be an enforceable right of citizens because Hobbesian sovereigns, who remain in the state of nature with respect to their subjects and other sovereigns, cannot themselves be subjects. The sovereign nonetheless, according to some interpreters of Hobbes, has duties to God to uphold the natural laws, including that of peace, when they prudently can.[22] But also according to Hobbes, individuals had such duties in the natural condition, yet succumbed to "natural passions of partiality, pride, revenge, and the like" (p. 129).

The natural passions of states may be more disciplined by the duty to preserve security. But, Hobbes notes, the international laws of nature are also undermined by the duty of the Leviathan to promote security. "[C]ities and kingdoms" also "for their own security" undertake invasions out of fear of being invaded and seek to weaken or destroy neighbors as a way of reducing foreign threats (p. 130). For even if one sovereign is dutiful (peaceful), its duties to its subjects include taking those possibly warlike measures against other sovereigns who, because of the very lack of guarantee that they are not also dutiful, cannot be assumed to be.

Security under anarchy would then for Hobbes and modern Structural Realists have to rely on more contingent, rational egoistic considerations. Recent additions to game theory specify some of the circumstances under which prudence could lead to cooperative peace. Experience, geography, expectations of cooperation and belief patterns, and the differing payoffs to cooperation (peace) or conflict associated with various types of military technology all appear to influence the calculus.

Differing military technologies can alter the payoffs of the "Security Dilemma": making the costs of noncooperation high, reducing the costs of being unprepared or surprised, reducing the benefits of surprise attack, or increasing the gains from cooperation. In this regard, Robert Jervis has examined the differing effects of situations in which the offense or the defense has the advantage and in which offensive weapons are or are not distinguishable from defensive weapons.[23] When the offense has the advantage and weapons are indistinguishable, the level of insecurity is high, an arms race ensues, and incentives for preemptive attack correspondingly are strong. When the offense

[21] Hobbes, *De Cive*, in *The English Works of Thomas Hobbes* (London: J. Bohn, 1847), vol. 2, pp. 166–67.
[22] This has come to be called the Taylor-Warrender thesis; see Keith C. Brown, ed., *Hobbes Studies* (Oxford: Blackwell, 1965), chaps. 2 and 3.
[23] Jervis, "Cooperation under the Security Dilemma," pp. 167–214.

does not have an advantage and offensive weapons are distinguishable, the incentives for preemptive attack are low, as are the incentives for arms races. Capable of signaling with clarity a nonaggressive intent and of guaranteeing that other states pose no immediate strategic threat, statesmen should be able to adopt peaceable policies and negotiate disputes, further cooperation, and abide by international law. If motivated solely by security, states will not need to maximize their power (a needless expense in these circumstances), nor will they be concerned about relative gains from cooperation (because the extra assets of their rivals cannot be used to undermine security).[24]

Hobbes, however, is skeptical of so secure a picture of the international condition. Systemic anarchy alone does not produce the Realist's homogeneous "state of war." Only when anarchy is combined with Hobbesian human nature, and the nature of state Leviathans, does it systematically produce and reproduce the Security Dilemma of a state of war.

Hobbes thus finds a wide range of cooperative cures insufficient. States, he argues, are not solely motivated by security. Leviathans are artificial constructs that are like ourselves, motivated by competition, fear, and glory. They thus also have aggressive motives, and even if they themselves do not have aggressive motives, they must assume that some other states do.

He finds alliances prudent, even necessary, but he does not regard either small or large alliances as reliable sources of security. Small alliances are feasible because no rational self-interested actor would continually betray commitments. They are also necessary, for continual betrayal would leave the soon-notorious culprit isolated and exposed to the attack of effective "confederations" (p. 115). But small alliances do not provide security by deterring attacks because small-number coalitions are vulnerable to attack by the many coalitions that are only slightly larger (if offense equals defense) or much larger (even if the defense is superior). Large coalitions demonstrate that states are rationally, self-interestedly capable of cooperation in a single short-term endeavor in order, for example, to defeat a common enemy in a war (pp. 130–31). On the other hand, they too fail to establish security because their large numbers hinder effective decision making. As soon as the common enemy is defeated, they break apart over their particular interests (p. 130).

Cooperation under anarchy can be enhanced when the factors of learning and time and established patterns of cooperation—what we now call regimes—are taken into account. Drawing analogies to biological systems, Robert Axelrod and William Hamilton have found that multiple-play Prisoner's Dilemmas have rational long-run strategies that can produce long-run cooperation (CC)

[24] For a valuable extension of Jervis's argument along these lines, see Charles Glaser, "Realists as Optimists: Cooperation and Self-Help," *International Security* 19, 3 (Winter 1994–95), pp. 50–90.

by clearly signaling competitors that failure to cooperate will be punished (CD or DD).[25] For these scholars, prudential rules for cooperation in extended play Prisoner's Dilemma games are embodied in the superior strategy "Tit for Tat." They include "don't be envious" (seek absolute, not relative, gains), "don't be the first to defect," "reciprocate cooperation and defection," "don't be too clever (adopt simplicity)."[26] But states, Hobbes takes pains to point out, are not capable of long-term, rationally self-interested cooperation, like "bees, ants," or other sociable insects (p. 131)—the biological analogues made popular by Axelrod and Hamilton.

Hobbes's objection to extended rational cooperation is threefold. First, if states cooperated over an extended time, the distribution of benefits might add to the power of some states and thus threaten the security of the less advantaged—the relative gains problem.[27] Security, Hobbes noted, should always be "measured by comparison with the enemy we fear," (p. 130) because eventually states under anarchy will experience changes in military technology (implying uncertain but likely shifts in the offense-defense balance), and so they will find that capabilities will count. Their present awareness of that possibility should constrain cooperation, by raising concerns for relative gains.

Second, there is a long-run rationality problem, for Hobbes holds that such schemes would be unlikely to persist long enough to generate benefits. He finds the rules of rational cooperation unrealistic for humans, however useful they may well be for bees. Bees and ants, Hobbes thinks, may be naturally harmonious and not merely cooperative.[28] But apart from that, desires for "honor" and prestige mean that relative gains are more valuable for humans than absolute gains in cooperative schemes (humans *are* envious). Men and women are also driven by passion and fear. Substantive (long-run) rationality is an ideal; instrumental (calculating) rationality may simply serve the immediate passions. We share the instincts represented by the slogan of certain fans of British rugby teams in the 1990 season: "Get Your Retaliation in First!"[29]

Third, there are misperception and uncertainty problems. The ability of men

[25] Robert Axelrod, *The Evolution of Cooperation* (New York: Basic Books, 1984); Michael Taylor, *Community, Anarchy and Liberty* (Cambridge: Cambridge University Press, 1976); and Robert Axelrod and Robert Keohane, "Achieving Cooperation under Anarchy," *World Politics* 38, 1 (October 1985), pp. 226–54. But see Joanne Gowa, "Anarchy, Egoism and Third Images," *International Organization*, 40, 1 (Winter 1986), pp. 167–86, for a critical review.

[26] Axelrod, *Evolution of Cooperation*, chap. 6.

[27] Joseph Grieco, "Anarchy and the Limits of Cooperation," *International Organization* 42, 3 (Summer 1988).

[28] See Robert Keohane, *After Hegemony: Cooperation and Discord in World Political Economy* (Princeton: Princeton University Press, 1984), chap. 4, for a discussion of differences between harmony and cooperation.

[29] As reported in the *Economist* 27 (October 1990).

to reason and communicate means that disputes arise over interpretation and a desire for improvement (men are too clever—perhaps, as Axelrod would say, even for their own good). Lastly, men in anarchic circumstances (without a judge) cannot distinguish between injury and accident, and cooperative strategies rely very heavily on accurate signaling, an excessively demanding condition in interstate politics.[30] Even the "clearest" technical messages appear subject to garbling. The pre-1914 period, which objectively represented a triumph of the distinguishable defense (machine guns, barbed wire, trench warfare) over the offensive, subjectively, as Jervis notes, was a period that appeared to military leaders to place exceptional premiums on the offensive and thus on preemptive war.[31]

The purely Structural approach to Realism contains an important limitation. The two key Structural assumptions—anarchy and independent units—are *not* sufficient to generate a strong preference for power and a balance of power system. Anarchy can be contingently benign and stable. Anarchy also characterizes an interaction that turns into an imperial relationship.[32] Both anarchy and independent "actors," moreover, also characterize the units that, when they come into contact with one another, form, as we shall later see, a Liberal community or a "security community."[33]

In order, therefore, for Structure to serve as a foundation for Realism, we need to offer an additional argument to explain a strong, homogeneous preference for power, unrelenting competition, rational policy making, and an indifference to political regimes. This is what Hobbes's Structuralism—a "state of war"—gives us, for Thomas Hobbes explains why states would *always* oppose power against power. States balance power, he says, because individuals create absolute, all-powerful, functionally equivalent "Leviathans" (rational unitary actors) in order to escape the terror of anarchy and achieve domestic law and order.[34] Security will dominate all—"Clubs are Trumps," Hobbes claims—and relative position dominates absolute welfare because Leviathans cannot be made responsible to their citizens. Even if they could, both Leviathans and

[30] George Downs and David Rocke, "Tacit Bargaining and Arms Control," *World Politics* 39, 3 (April 1987), pp. 297–325.

[31] Jervis (1978), pp. 186–210, 212.

[32] These actors—usually either tribal or patrimonial societies—eventually tend to collaborate (bandwagon) rather than balance. Tribal societies destabilize under the impact of transnational forces, such as trade or missionaries. Patrimonial societies fracture and, after a period of crisis, their elites collaborate. Both tend to mount meager resistance to imperial aggression (see the argument and sources cited in Doyle, *Empires*, chap. 6 and ff).

[33] See Karl Deutsch and Sidney Burrell, *Political Community in the North Atlantic Area* (Princeton: Princeton University Press, 1957) and chapter 8 on Kantian Internationalism, below.

[34] Hobbes, *Leviathan*, chaps. 17 and 18. And see Forsyth, "Thomas Hobbes and the External Relations of States," pp. 196–209.

their citizens pursue aggressive passions (glory and interest) that make all insecure.[35] Born out of terror, Hobbes concludes, such states would accept no external constraints apart from the opposition of power to power.

The international condition for Hobbes remains, therefore, a state of war. Safety enjoins a prudent policy of forewarning (spying) and of forearming oneself to increase security against other sovereigns, who, lacking any assurance that you are not taking these measures, also take them. Safety as well requires (as a duty) taking actions "whatsoever shall seem to conduce to the lessening of the power of foreigners whom they [the sovereign] suspect, whether by slight or force."[36] If preventive wars are prudent, the Realist's prudence obviously cannot establish a firm foundation for peace or international law.

CONTEMPORARY STRUCTURALISM

The insightful contribution of the Structuralists lies in a parsimonious argument that anarchy can rule. The effects of differing domestic regimes (e.g., whether Liberal or Socialist or not) are overridden, they claim, by the structure of international anarchy under which all states live. Hobbes, we noted, does not bother to distinguish between "some council or one man" when he discusses the sovereign. Differing domestic regimes do affect the quantity of resources available to the state and the quality of its morale. But the effective ends that shape policy are determined for the Structuralist by the competitive structure of the international system.

Domestic state structures are hierarchic and centralized (sovereign). Hierarchy allows for differentiated functions and capabilities. Police and courts specialize in security, allowing finance ministers, private entrepreneurs, and laborers to concentrate on generating wealth; the clergy and the religious, on salvation; etc. The international structure of anarchy precludes differentiation and specialization. Because there is no global source of law and order, all states must make security their prime concern; none can safely specialize in wealth alone, or art or salvation without bearing the imprudent risk of turning themselves into the prey of the militarily powerful. This, if you will, is the contemporary lesson of the invasion of the oil sheikhdom of Kuwait, which had specialized in wealth, by Iraq, which had specialized in military power. Capabilities thus must be translatable—capable of generating security through military power—and they must be measured relative to the capabilities of other

[35] Grieco (1988) explores the resulting "positional" choices of states accepting these assumptions.

[36] Hobbes, "De Cive," vol. 2, p. 171.

states. States learn the necessity of self-help—national egoism—through either socialization or competition (defeat).

Once we add Hobbes's explanation for the sovereignty (unity) of states and his account of the preferences they hold (security, interest, glory), we can see how international politics can be explained merely by the *number* and *power* of the states. States can be considered "like units," socialized or selected to pursue security as a primary goal.[37] State behavior is homogenized—made rational and power-seeking—through competition and socialization.[38] Only the rational and power-seeking will survive the competition to dominate and thus to teach their rivals. These are the conditions that allow one to infer the universality of power balancing that the Structural approach assumes.

Structural Stability

International stability, or order, for the contemporary Structuralist then depends on the structure of the international system, whether it is unipolar, bipolar, tripolar, or multipolar.[39] Stable order—in the sense of an absence of great power war—is by definition present in a unipolar system such as the Pax Romana (where there is only one great power). There is widespread agreement that tripolar systems are unstable because they are prone to forming aggressive, ganging-up coalitions of two against one.[40] The interesting debate revolves about claims for bipolar versus multipolar systems.

The traditional argument appeared in Thucydides's *History*. Bipolar systems are more unstable. Threats can be met only through "internal balancing" (domestic rearmament), there being no third power of sufficient weight to deter an attack through "external balancing" (alliance realignment). Bipolar rivalries, moreover, tend to exacerbate hostilities through a continuous focus on a single

[37] Waltz, *Theory of International Politics*, pp. 75, 101. Interestingly, Waltz supports his theory very much as Hobbes does, by making analytic arguments (based primarily on microeconomic reasoning rather than geometry) and illustrating, rather than testing, propositions—for example, for competitive balancing, Germany and Russia in the 1920s (pp. 127–28).

[38] Ibid., p. 75. The structural determination depends, we need to add, on the systemic interaction being sufficiently intense to select very efficiently for appropriate behavior, such as would be observed under the economist's model of perfect competition. See the valuable discussion in Robert Keohane, "Realism, Neorealism, and the Study of World Politics," pp. 171–75.

[39] There is some dispute in the field over the meaning of "stability." For some, it seems to mean structural stability, or stasis, found when the rank order of the powers is maintained. For others, it means persistence of international regimes or rules of order. For still others, it means an absence of major war among the great powers. The last is the clearest, the one central to the major debate, and the one adopted recently by Kenneth Waltz, the topic's leading controversialist.

[40] This, of course, need not necessarily result in an aggressive war if the single power can balance, or deter, the two lesser powers. There are also inherent restraints against one small power's joining with a dominant power against another smaller power. As Machiavelli warned, the next victim is likely to be the now-helpless single small power.

enemy. Here Jonathan Swift's brilliant satire in *Gulliver's Travels* on the Anglo-French rivalry highlights the tendency in the contest between tiny Liliput and Blefuscu, each of which extends its political rivalry to include the correct manner of opening soft-boiled eggs—large end or small.[41] The modern analog presumably was the Cold War rivalry between the "free world" and "international communism"—the two ends of the eggs—which reflected the rivalry between U.S. and Soviet power. Multipolar systems, by contrast, offer both forms of balancing, external and internal, and they offer crosscutting cleavages as a means of muting hostilities.[42] Mathematicians have even made interesting arguments that among multipolar systems, pentagonal, or five-power, systems are especially likely to be stable, offering the opportunity for the fifth state to play a special role as a balancer between two two-state alliances.[43]

The new Structuralist argument, developed by Kenneth Waltz, argues just the opposite. Bipolar systems are the more stable. They resist "chain ganging" and "buck-passing"—two of the alleged weaknesses of multipolar systems. "Chain ganging" refers to the tendency to be drawn into wars as a means of protecting vital allies from defeat (as, for example, Germany was drawn to protect Austria in the crisis that led up to World War One). Bipolar great powers, however, have no allies that are that vital. "Buck-passing," on the other hand, refers to the tendency to neglect remote crises. Great powers sometimes assume that some other great power will make the effort needed to curb a menacing but distant aggressor state. By passing the responsibility, great powers fail to deter aggressors, who then have the opportunity to increase their strength through aggression and provoke eventually a large-scale systemic war. Great powers in a bipolar system, by contrast, either can readily crush small power aggressors or, facing a great power aggressor, have no other pole to which they could pass the responsibility for deterrence. They tend therefore to be eternally vigilant.[44] They also economize on the monitoring of threats, since they have to keep well informed about only one other serious rival.

In short, the alleged systemic virtues of each polarity are portrayed as alleged systemic vices of the other, and vice versa. The issue seems therefore to be empirical: Which claim is better supported by the historical record? Bipolar stability drew support from the stability of the Cold War. But critics decried

[41] Jonathan Swift, *Gulliver's Travels* (New York: New American Library, 1960), pp. 58–59.

[42] See Deutsch and Singer, "Multipolar Power Systems and International Stability," and Duncan Snidal, "Relative Gains and the Pattern of International Cooperation," *APSR*, 85, 3 (September 1991).

[43] Reinhard Selten, "A Simple Model of Imperfect Competition: Where 4 Are Few and 6 Are Many," *International Journal of Game Theory* 2, 3 (1973).

[44] Kenneth Waltz, "The Stability of a Bipolar World," *Daedalus* (April 1964) was the classic article. He reformulates the arguments in chapter 6 of *Theory of International Politics*. For the development of these themes, see Thomas Christensen and Jack Snyder, "Chain Gangs and Passed Bucks," *International Organization*, 44, 2 (1990).

resting arguments on a single case. They noted the equally compelling effect of nuclear deterrence as an alternative explanation of Cold War stability, and they cited the opposite effect in the Peloponnesian War and the Habsburg-Valois rivalry.[45] The bipolarists counter persuasively that at least the Peloponnesian system was not truly bipolar (as we saw), and they decry the instability of multipolar systems, pointing at the sorry record of two world wars in our own century. Clearly a more complex answer is warranted. System structure alone will not decide.

Structural Regimes

A second focus of analytic effort by the Structuralists centers on the theory of international regimes. States that regard themselves as caught in a state of war necessarily place supreme importance on national security and rely primarily on self-help. Trade therefore would be encouraged only to the extent that it produced relative advantages over other states and avoided strategic dependence on other states. If all states pursued this agenda, however, opportunities for widespread multilateral trade would be few. Instead mercantilism and the trade and monetary wars of the 1930s would presumably be the norm.

Hobbes's contemporaries indeed argued for regarding trade as a form of war in which princes had to be concerned about acquiring plenty to maintain their power and power to preserve and expand their plenty.[46] Mercantilists especially sought a favorable balance of trade (exports exceeding imports) as a way to encourage a steady inflow of gold specie. Indeed, during the seventeenth and eighteenth centuries, before the rise of efficient taxation, tariffs on international trade were one of the surest means to raise the ready state revenue that armies required.

Later mercantilists, including Friedrich List, identified the political roles embodied in seemingly neutral economic relations, which are in principle twofold. First, economic exchange can always be used as a tool of political power through boycotts, bribery, and the manipulation of trade incentives. Second, economic relationships can operate on a more fundamental level, shaping the political-economic growth of a weaker, less developed economy through the opportunity offered to it in the form of trade and finance. The weaker country in an economic relationship (like a weaker class) then becomes not just a group

[45] An article developing these themes is by Ted Hopf, "Polarity, the Offense-Defense Balance, and War," *American Political Science Review* 85, 2 (June 1991). For a more historical-sociological discussion of system effects, see Gordon Craig and Alexander George, *Force and Statecraft*, chaps. 1–3. For valuable discussions of the debate, see Waltz (1979, chap. 8); Jeffrey Hart, "Power and Polarity in the International System," in Alan Ned Sabrosky, ed., *Polarity and War: The Changing Structure of International Conflict* (Boulder, Colo.: Westview Press, 1985); and Manus Midlarsky, *The Onset of World War* (Boston: Unwin, 1988).
[46] Jacob Viner, "Power versus Plenty as Objectives of Foreign Policy in the Seventeenth and Eighteenth Centuries," *World Politics* 1 (1948), pp. 1–29.

of assorted individuals but a particularized, isolated, and dependent participant in the world economy—e.g., a single-crop exporter, an economy split into largely self-contained export and domestic sectors, or a "hewer of wood." Mercantilists see nations, as Marxists see classes, becoming alienated in the process of production and exchange.

These normative nationalistic concerns are far from new; they were eloquently addressed by U.S. Secretary of the Treasury Alexander Hamilton in his *Report on Manufactures* of 1790, in which he expresses the opposition of American nationalists to their country's assuming the role of a raw material exporter to Britain. Nationalists feared and opposed two aspects of this role: the tying of American economic development to the British economy and the growing dependence on Britain for goods vital to national defense. Friedrich List, inspired by Hamilton's observations of American trade policy, outlines in *American Political Economy* what he saw as the proper object for a developing country's commercial policy: "This object is not to gain matter, in exchanging *matter for matter*, as it is in individual and cosmopolitical [Liberal] economy, and particularly in the trade of a merchant. But it is to gain *productive and political power* by means of exchange with other nations; or to prevent the depression of productive and political power, by restricting that exchange."[47] At the earliest stages of development, List later argued, a free trade policy designed to encourage new commodities and techniques may be advantageous, but at later stages, and in order to develop a national culture and a national system of industry, protection, the mercantilists argue, will be needed to stimulate the growth of infant industries and avoid foreign-dominated dependence.

But, the Structuralist argues, multilateral regimes of stable economic interdependence, including free trade, can arise. These could be explained by hegemonic or unipolar concentrations of power. For then the dominant pole would have a reduced security concern and could therefore maximize such secondary objectives as wealth, and secondary states, having no prospect of matching the dominant power, would have little choice (or be coerced) into maximizing trade, which might or might not be to their advantage, depending on the balance of economic productivities. So, the argument runs, we should expect open trade in periods of unipolar hegemony, trade wars during periods of multipolar

[47] Friedrich List, *Outlines of American Political Economy* (Philadelphia: S. Parker, 1827), p. 18. Also in *National Gazette*, August 18–November 27, 1827. Before List returned to Germany to write his great work *The National System of Political Economy*, he was considerably influenced by the American nationalist political economists. I draw this passage from Fred Hirsch and Michael Doyle, "Politicization in the World Economy: Necessary Conditions for an International Economic Order," in Fred Hirsch, Michael Doyle, and Edward Morse, *Alternatives to Monetary Disorder* (New York: Council on Foreign Relations/McGraw-Hill, 1977), pp. 9–64.

competition,[48] and trade and monetary blocs corresponding to bipolar blocs.[49] Although critics question whether free trade was established coercively as well as whether hegemony is a logically necessary condition, the freer trade eras of the Pax Britannica and the ("free world") Pax Americana offer some support (at least a correlation) for this thesis.

The connection between interdependence and international structure, however, seems indeterminate: Would a few large great powers trade less because as large markets they need trade less[50] or trade more because their more stable security gives them less to fear from economic coercion, much to gain from system-wide trade, and more capability to bear the costs of open markets?[51]

If we seek evidence that might confirm (or, in the negative, disconfirm) other even more basic propositions drawn from Structural Realism, we would want to look at whether states successfully restrict interdependence; whether, when they subscribe to international law as a norm, they neglect its norms in practice; and, above all, whether they actually balance power against power.

Can we confirm Hobbes's views that general coalitions will be brief and that alliances will form and remain small? Here a great deal of diplomatic historiography implicitly supports Structural theses, but there are few systematic studies.[52] There is strong empirical support for one Hobbesian proposition: Wartime alliances tend to last little beyond the war.[53] There is some support as well for a trend that Hobbes would find congenial; as the great power system aged (and sovereignties became more perfect and stable?), the frequency of great power war fell.[54] Also tending to confirm, though weakly, Structural propositions are studies indicating a tendency toward rational resource-based trade-

[48] This literature builds on the theory of public goods and the work of Mancur Olson, *The Logic of Collective Action*. A thorough, Realist interpretation of political economy is argued by Robert Gilpin in *U.S. Power and the Multinational Corporation* (New York: Basic Books, 1975). It was further developed by Stephen Krasner, "State Power and the Structure of International Trade," *World Politics* 28, 3 (April 1976). Critics such as Robert Keohane have argued that institutions can sometimes sustain a regime after hegemony has eroded, in *After Hegemony*. Duncan Snidal argues that small cooperating groups, "k groups," can substitute for single hegemony, "The Limits of Hegemonic Stability Theory," *International Organization* 39 (1985), pp. 579–614.

[49] For the monetary case, see Hirsch, Doyle and Morse, *Alternatives to Monetary Disorder*. For the trade case, see Joanne Gowa, "Power, Politics and International Trade," *American Political Science Review* 87, 2 (June 1993), pp. 408–20.

[50] Waltz (1979), p. 145.

[51] Gilpin (1975); Krasner (1976).

[52] For a systematic critique of some of those structural assumptions, see Walt, *Origins of Alliances*.

[53] K. Holsti et al., *Unity and Disintegration in Alliances* (London: Wiley, 1973), chap. 3.

[54] Jack Levy, *War in the Modern Great Power System, 1495–1975* (Lexington: University of Kentucky Press, 1983), p. 148.

offs between alignment and defense expenditure and a thoroughly Hobbesian tendency for wars to be more likely between equals than between nonequals.[55]

Structural Strategy—The Balance of Power

The strictest test—and also the key prescription—of Structural Realism is the balance of power against power. Do states align themselves according to a function that minimizes threats conceived of as power divided by distance?[56] The balance would be regulated as if it were a market: autonomous individual decisions driven by egoistic motives produce social results that may differ from what any single actor intended. An "invisible hand," to borrow Adam Smith's famous market metaphor, coordinates action.[57]

The Structural model also holds that the balance of power should be the essential strategy of world politics. Hume's assertion that the balance was founded on "common sense and obvious reasoning" (p. 63) argues for it in these terms and accounts for why it was familiar to the famously "perspicacious" ancients. Kenneth Waltz's Structural Realism also presupposes a structured tendency toward balancing: "Balance of power politics prevail wherever two, and only two, requirements are met: that the order be anarchic and that it be populated by units wishing to survive."[58] Under those circumstances the tendency to oppose power with power, through either domestic efforts or interstate alliances, will prevail.

Four elements are said to constitute the sufficient foundations of the Structural tendency to balance power against power.[59] First among them is international anarchy, a "state system" of independent states whose security is interdependent (potentially affected by one another). This results in the need for self-help simply because it assumes that there is no world empire managing internal security.

Second, individual states are coherent units, each seeking at the minimum to survive, at the maximum to expand in capabilities. No state is so riven by faction that its leadership prefers to collaborate with the enemy rather than resist foreign aggression. This serves to distinguish interstate from imperial sys-

[55] David Garnham, "War Proneness, War Weariness and Regime Type: 1816–1980," *Journal of Peace Research* 23, 3 (September 1986), pp. 279–84; M. Altfeld, "The Decision to Ally," *Western Political Quarterly* 37, 4 (December 1984), pp. 523–44.
[56] Kenneth Boulding, *Conflict and Defense* (New York: Harper Torch, 1962).
[57] Nye, "Neorealism and Neoliberalism," pp. 235–51.
[58] Waltz (1979), p. 121. Waltz highlights the centrality of balance of power thinking when he suggests (for a Structural Realist): "If there is any distinctly political theory of international politics, balance-of-power theory is it" (p. 117). Other influential postwar Realists, including Martin Wight and Hans Morgenthau, regard the conjunction of Realism with the balance as essential and prudent, if not always necessary and obvious.
[59] Two works that explore these issues are Edward Gulick, *Europe's Classical Balance of Power* (New York: Norton, 1967), and Inis Claude, *Power and International Relations* (New York: Random House, 1962).

tems.[60] Structural Realism assumes not only international anarchy but also the predominance of state actors that are "functionally similar units" (making them the "coherent units"), differing in capabilities but not ends.[61] States are therefore best conceived of as rational egoists.

Third, states, it is assumed, will rely on self-help for security, and in the absence of any global source of law and order, security and therefore estimations of power will tend to be relative.

Fourth is a "rational system of estimating power," a measurable or comparable appreciation of capabilities, such that statesmen can weigh the balance at any given time, employing either simple (size of armies or navies) or more complex capability measures.[62]

Given these four conditions, Structuralists argue, states will form and re-form balances of power. They will balance internally by acquiring the arms they need and balance externally by forming and re-forming alliances they need against threats defined in terms of the capabilities of other states. The balance of power is the set of relationships—alignments and alliances—that result from states' trying to maximize their security, as defined by relative power.

Some individual case studies, however, suggest that the world is not so straightforward; states are not functionally equivalent units. States tend to balance perceived threats rather than objective threats. And perceptions include political, social, ideological, and other factors in addition to the power resources and distance of the threatening state.[63] Less decisive tests then would assess whether other things being equal, there is a tendency to restore threat balances once they are upset or whether states tend to coalesce, balancing against a single hegemon rather than bandwagoning in its direction.[64] In chapter 6, I illustrate how we can identify the operation of a balance of power and assess whether the Structural model is sufficient to explain it.

Structural Legacy

Realist Structural insight thus provides a significant step toward scientific parsimony beyond the contingent generalizations advanced by Machiavellian Fundamentalism. Contemporary Structuralists, such as Kenneth Waltz, have focused on explaining a few important things well (parsimoniously). But as some of their critics have argued, they leave the character of international politics indeterminate. Abstract anarchy, reason, and egoism are compatible with cooperation under certain conditions, and thus anarchic self-help need not create a security dilemma. By examining individual motives and accounting for

60 For discussion of these issues, see Doyle, *Empires*.
61 Waltz (1979), pp. 96–97.
62 Gulick (1955), pp. 24–29.
63 Walt (1987).
64 Waltz (1979), p. 128.

absolute sovereignty, Hobbes explains *why* modern rational egoistic individuals, concerned for their security, would want to think of their state as a unitary rational actor yet not want their state to form a world government or to be bound by international law. Hobbesian citizens thus condemn their Leviathans and thus themselves to the state of war. Hobbes thus showed how Structural theory can be politically meaningful as well as potentially elegant.

CHAPTER FOUR

Constitutionalism: Rousseau

> As individuals we live in the civil state, under the control of law; as nations, each is in the state of nature . . . we find ourselves exposed to the evils of both conditions, without winning the security we find in either . . . so long as the prince is regarded as absolutely uncontrolled, it is force alone which speaks to the subject under the name of law and to the foreigner under the name of reason of state: so taking from the latter the power and from the former the very will, to offer resistance . . . brute force reigns under the empty name of justice.[1]

THE AUTHORS OF the *Encylopédie* exaggerated when they said, "The philosophy of M. Rousseau of Geneva is almost the reverse of Hobbes's."[2] But Rousseau, writing a century later, did seek, albeit indirectly, to answer the "hard-nosed," authoritarian-leaning arguments that Hobbes had so effectively made. Rousseau made a case for the importance of justice and domestic political choice. He was the great democratic interlocutor of Hobbes and the democratic critic of his views on the state. He was and is the democratic Realist. He identified the *national* interest and made it something more than a slogan.

Rousseau's international theory differs from Hobbes's much less than his domestic theories would lead one to expect. Rousseau holds optimistic expectations of human nature. He believes in the justice of a state governed by self-determining free citizens. Yet he too sees an exceptionally dangerous interna-

[1] J.-J. Rousseau, *State of War* (1756), in A *Lasting Peace*, trans. C. E. Vaughan (London: Constable, 1917), p. 127.
[2] *Encyclopédie* (Paris: Breton, 1751–1765), vol. 92, p. 589.

tional state of war, some of whose danger is contributed by just those optimistic features of trust and solidarity carried onto the battlefield. He is a Realist who, though systematically theoretical, returns to the variety and complexity of Thucydides, seeing important causes of the state of war in the nature of human beings (Image I) and the structure of the international system (Image III).[3] But both of these operate through differing domestic constitutions, and thus his most distinctive contribution is an understanding of the impact of the varying domestic structure of states (Image II). Rousseau is a Realist, but a remarkably complicated one. If Thucydides was wise; Machiavelli, brilliant; and Hobbes, rigorous; Rousseau is profound.

Rousseau's Constitutionalism

Human Nature	x
Domestic Society	xx
Interstate System	x

Rousseau thus develops a third view of the state of war. For him, as for Machiavelli, the state of war is variable, not constant and homogeneous, as it was for Hobbes. But like Hobbes and unlike Machiavelli, Rousseau sees it as an international condition. War is an act among states from which international boundaries protect the domestic political life of a state.[4]

Unlike both Hobbes and Machiavelli, he traces its roots to variations in the constitution of the state. Like the other two, though, he also finds important sources in psychological and international structural variables. In making this

[3] In Kenneth Waltz's terms, Images I, II, and III are operating together (Waltz, 1954). For this point and many others, see Stanley Hoffmann's classic essay on Rousseau, "Rousseau on War and Peace" (1965). Other secondary sources that have influenced my reading of Rousseau's international thought include C. J. Carter, *Rousseau and the Problem of War* (New York: Garland, 1987); F. H. Hinsley, *Power and the Pursuit of Peace* (Cambridge: Cambridge University Press, 1963); W. Gallie, *Philosophers of Peace and War* (Cambridge: Cambridge University Press, 1978); Waltz, *Man, the State, and War*; Maurizio Viroli, *Jean Jacques Rousseau and the Well-Ordered Society* (Cambridge: Cambridge University Press, 1988); Judith Shklar, *Men and Citizens* (Cambridge: Cambridge University Press, 1969); and Michael Williams, "Rousseau, Realism, and Realpolitik," *Millennium* 18 (1989), pp. 185–203. The best collection of Rousseau's writings on international relations together with a coauthored revision of Stanley Hoffmann's interpretation can now be found in Stanley Hoffmann and David Fidler, eds., *Rousseau on International Relations* (Oxford: Clarendon, 1991). I have also benefited from conversation with Richard Matthew and from reading his fine dissertation on the evolution of world order principles, from Augustinean Christianity to Rousseauian nationalism.

[4] Rousseau is not completely consistent on this point. He describes the relation of master and slave as a "state of war" when he discusses Spartan oppression of the helots; in most contexts, however, he distinguishes and narrows "war" to policide (see below).

complex analysis, he takes us back to the range of insight embodied in the historical work of Thucydides. But he differs from Thucydides too in the systematic quality of the political philosophy with which he explains the origin and nature of the state—and the resultant state of war—and in his explicit moral critique of the various forms of oppression.

Descriptively he offers a truly systematic sociological account of the stability of the balance of power as well as an insightful political economy of interdependence and dependence. Normatively, keeping fully within Realism, he gives us the first meaningful analysis of the national interest and makes valuable contributions to how we can think about mitigating, at least for a while, the constant risk of war that is the state of war. He portrays a modern morality that does not shrink from nationalism. He tells what happens when the fully national state takes over. He confronts the moral dilemma of establishing a livable, albeit fragile and temporary, order in the face of international anarchy and thus as a fellow Realist seeks to promote international peace while acknowledging the force of the Realist challenge, later articulated so well by E. H. Carr: "Any so-called international order built on contingent obligation assumed by national governments is an affair of lath and plaster."[5]

Correcting Stereotypes

Jean-Jacques Rousseau, who lived from 1712 to 1778, is in many respects an unlikely candidate for Realist social philosopher. Although many today identify Realism with conservatism, Rousseau reverses the association. He was the preeminent theorist of popular sovereignty and revolution, the theorist who inspired but is not responsible for much of the handiwork of Robespierre during the French Revolution. His revolutionary views made him obnoxious to the established monarchies of eighteenth-century Europe and earned him an early place in the revolution's pantheon. Alternately charmed by his genius and outraged by his views, the monarchs no sooner tried to give him pensions than they expelled him from their kingdoms.

Rousseau's personal characteristics hardly square with the tough-minded image cultivated by some contemporary proponents of Realist doctrine. After a peripatetic and unstable childhood, he developed an extremely high-strung personality, one given to great psychological dependence on friends and his many mistresses. He wandered across Europe, living off these friends and mistresses, leaving at least five children at foundling homes and failing to support their long-suffering mother, his former housekeeper Thérèse Levasseur. He revealed late in life the deep psychological and sexual frustrations from which he had long suffered in his extraordinarily frank psychological memoir, *Confessions*. Can you imagine Henry Kissinger or Alexander Haig or some other con-

[5] E. H. Carr, *Nationalism and After* (New York: Macmillan, 1945), p. 32.

temporary proponent of Realism confessing in public that he went through life craving to be spanked?

A bit of a con artist, he proceeded to set himself up as a teacher of music to young girls in Geneva before he could read a note. But above all, he was a genius; he quickly taught himself music, created a new system of musical notation, and proceeded to compose original operas.

THE STATE OF WAR

The international condition among states is a state of war characterized by "social misery."[6] In the natural condition of mankind before the institution of states, there are many quarrels and fights, but war is a social creation of states, an act expressing an intention to destroy or weaken an enemy state. The "state of war" is characterized by a "mutual, constant, and manifest intention to destroy the enemy state, or at least to weaken it by all possible means"—that is, the continuing intention of policide, temporarily lacking the act.[7] "War then is a relation not between man and man, but between State and State, and individuals are enemies only accidentally, not as men, nor as citizens, but as soldiers; not as members of their country, but as its defenders."[8]

The state of war, moreover, is inherently unjust. Justice calls for a union of force and law, with force controlled by law. In most (corrupt) states we suffer the worst of both worlds because we suffer the evils of two conditions: domestic tyranny and international insecurity (see the quotation with which this chapter begins). But even if we had a just state internally, international politics would remain the mere exercise of force without the control of law, for international law is a mere "illusion"—for want of any global sanction to make it an effective replacement for the exercise of force.

Describing the condition of all states in an anarchic international system, Rousseau thus appears to some to be a strikingly Structural interpreter of world politics.[9] But he differs from Hobbes's route to these conclusions, and in the end he leaves a more varied set of possibilities open to the political struggle of rulers and citizens within and among political societies. The choices between a corrupt Europe and an ideal Social Contract are complemented by two case studies of partly imagined, partly real partial escapes: an isolated "Corsica" and a defensively constituted "Poland."

[6] Rousseau, *State of War* (1917), p. 128.
[7] *Ibid.*, p. 1
[8] J. J. Rousseau, *Social Contract*, chap. IV, in *The Social Contract and the Discourses* (1762), trans G. D. H. Cole (New York: Dutton, 1950), p. 10.
[9] See, for example, F. H. Hinsley (1967), chap. 3.

STATES OF NATURE

Where Hobbes portrays the Leviathan both as a natural man and his domestic tamer, Rousseau portrays the typical state as natural man's ultimate oppressor. In the original state of nature (SoN1), stripped of all the attributes of civilization, man is a gentle animal, according to Rousseau.

Rousseau's Constitutional Sociology of World Politics

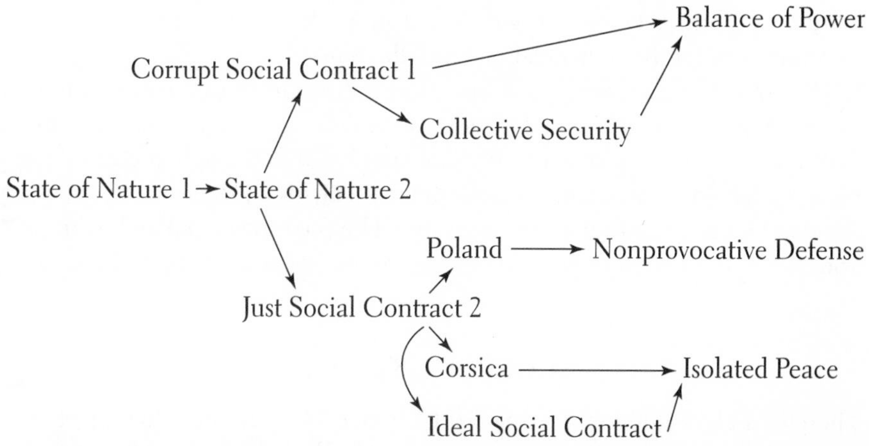

Man is naturally equal, and his social relations are completely casual and neither cooperative nor warlike. "I see him satisfying his hunger at the first oak, and slaking his thirst at the first brook; finding his bed at the foot of the tree which afforded him a repast; and with that all his wants supplied."[10] Lacking in language, he has few thoughts. Reason guides his pursuit of simple wants. He experiences few fears, which include fear of pain and cold but not of death. He experiences natural compassion for the sufferings of others.[11]

Soon scarcity arises as the numbers of men increase. This leads to a second state of nature (SoN2), which is both progressive and regressive. It is progressive because increased interdependence leads to stable relationships, the first "expansion of the human heart." Families are organized, and love comes to characterize human relations within them. Language evolves and reason develops as careful calculation rewards its practitioners with increased material benefits. Here we develop what we think of as specifically human consciousness beyond that which we share with the animals.

At the same time, scarcity is the origin of property, possession, rivalry, pride, hatred, and jealousies. Individualism and familism now replace natural happiness. Identities come to be dominated by *amour propre* (jealous status) rather

[10] Rousseau, *Second Discourse* (1950), p. 200.
[11] *Ibid.*, pp. 231–32.

than *amour de soi* (respect for oneself). Cooperation becomes inherently problematic. We become actors in Rousseau's fable of the stag hunt, caught in a problem of uncertain cooperation. It takes five hunters to catch a stag, Rousseau explains, and one to catch a rabbit, but one-fifth of a stag is more greatly valued than a whole rabbit. Rational hunters form groups of five and cooperate, but what happens when a rabbit appears? Do the groups stick together or do they break up, as each hunter runs after the rabbit—before his fellow hunters do—and seizes the less attractive but more certain game? Motivated by rational self-interest, but lacking trust and pulled by pride, the hunters abandon the common prey for the individual target of the hare.[12]

The spread of metallurgy and agriculture thus create extensive mastery of nature, more intensive social dependence, and fiercer competition. The more skillful at these more productive technologies became the rich; the less skillful became the poor. Inequality breeds more inequality. Deceit and pretension come to characterize human relationships. The poor then react and try to steal from the rich; the rich oppress in order to protect themselves from the poor.[13]

CORRUPT STATES

Then the rich decide to form a Social Contract (SCI). In order to protect their property, they trick the poor into accepting a legal equality of rights in property that in effect secures the rich's unequal superiority in possessions and influence. Armed with the power of the state, the rich and the domestically powerful pursue their particular interests at home and abroad.[14] Wars are then waged for the classic trinity of "land, money, and men"—that is, for territory, booty, commerce, slaves, power, religion, and glory.[15] The rich and powerful create more violence and mayhem among states in pursuit of their wealth and prestige than had ever characterized the original state of nature. Conflict now occurs between organized armies and not between individual quarrelers.

MITIGATING THE STATE OF WAR

Balancing the Power of Corrupt States

Like Hobbesian Leviathans, most of Rousseau's states owed their survival to their balancing of power. Unlike Hobbesian sovereigns, however, the sovereigns

[12] *Ibid.*, p. 238.
[13] *Ibid.*, p. 249.
[14] *Ibid.*, p. 252.
[15] See Grace Roosevelt's valuable retranslation of *State of War*, in *Reading Rousseau in the Nuclear Age* (Philadelphia: Temple University Press, 1990), pp. 193–94. For ideology as a source of war, Rousseau cites the Greek republics that attacked one another to change their enemies' "forms of governments."

described by the Abbé St.-Pierre (whose *Project for Perpetual Peace* Rousseau summarizes and then criticizes) share a common civilization and the widespread interdependence of commerce and other transnational ties. They are not homogeneous units, like any other state in any other international system: "The Powers of Europe constitute a kind of whole, united by identity of religion, of moral standard, of international law; by letters, by commerce, and finally by a species of balance, which is the inevitable result of all those ties and, however little any may strive consciously to maintain it, is not to be destroyed so easily as many men imagine."[16]

Their social interdependence and cultural homogeneity (not simply considerations of their own security) make the balance sufficiently important that states naturally want to reproduce it. Lacking these, Rousseau seems to be implying, states might not pay enough attention to balancing or might not perceive a need for competition. They succeeded in doing so because defenses (fortresses etc.) have the advantage over the offense and because national, particularistic preferences disrupt and stir up opposition to hegemony.[17] Lacking these characteristics, a single hegemon might come to rule the whole in an escalating, unstoppable aggregation of power, prestige, and perhaps imperial legitimacy. Emperors, such as Constantine, restored Roman imperial unity in just that way, relying in part on economies of military scale and a sentiment of imperial unity. Economic interdependence complements cultural ties in supporting the political independence of Europe's states by spreading the equalizing force of economic development. If, on the other hand, interdependence were continuously to concentrate economic capacity, the independence of states might soon fall victim to coercion or the economic incentives of joining the dominant market.

All these foundations of the European balance of power rely as well on a very special, contingent European circumstance: on a geography (the Pyrenees, the Alps) favoring division and on the existence of the Germanic confederation, whose size and central location present a formidable obstacle to continental conquest yet whose internal balance makes it incapable of itself conquering the continent.

Transnational ties establish interdependence and promote the political, social and economic foundations of the balance of power, which serves to pro-

[16] Rousseau, *Critique of the Peace Project of the Abbé de St. Pierre* (1756/1917), p. 40.
[17] *Ibid.*, p. 52. This is one of the earlier presentations of the significance of offense-defense advantages, which nonetheless are very difficult to distinguish in advance. For valuable discussions of this balance, see Steve Van Evera, "The Cult of the Offensive," *International Security* 9 (1984); Jack Snyder, *The Ideology of the Offensive* (Ithaca: Cornell University Press, 1984); and Jack Levy, "The Offense/Defense Balance of Military Technology," *International Studies Quarterly* 28 (1984), pp. 219–38. For a study that distinguishes "conquest-resistant" from "conquest-prone" situations—corresponding to Rousseau's consideration of fortresses—see Hopf, "Polarity, the Offense-Defense Balance, and War," pp. 475–93.

tect the independence of states. But they do not produce peace. They merely exacerbate conflict, giving more occasions—points of contact—for strife. Other social factors also influence the propensity toward war. Large undeveloped territories (low-population-to-area ratios) become vulnerable to predatory attack.[18] Christian soldiers seem to be less effective than pagan ones. States weak in material resources need to compensate with national morale. Unscrupulous leaders will therefore exploit sentiments of *amour propre* (jealous nationalism akin to jealous personal egoism). They will promote diversionary wars as a means of fostering popular support for unpopular regimes.[19]

Peace through Collective Security—the International Organization of Corrupt States

These are the corrupt states for which the good Abbé de St.-Pierre is attempting to construct a league of peace, which will protect its sovereigns from both international conquest and domestic revolution. The balance of power can mitigate international tyranny, but it does so only through the threat of war. Therefore, says St.-Pierre, sovereigns need to combine their separate and fundamental interests in security and subordinate their private interests to an organized league of peace. St.-Pierre's plan was just one of a series of early-eighteenth-century attempts to perfect the balance of power that were written by both scholars and politicians. In 1735, for example, Giulio Cardinal Alberoni (prime minister of Spain) had proposed a not-too-dissimilar unified diet of European princes (both Catholic and Protestant) joined in a project to dismember the Ottoman Empire.[20]

In his critique of St.-Pierre's peace project, Rousseau shows how peace is impossible for the protagonists. This is because (Image I) monarchs prefer their apparent interests (military prestige and relative superiority) to their real interests in security. And even if the monarchs were sensible (Image II), their ministers of state are the very individuals who gain from the existence of wars. These ministers are hardly likely to abolish the wars that are their greatest source of profit and influence.[21] And (Image III) even if both monarchs and ministers became committed to cooperation and all concerned adopted the good of all as the highest good of each, how would one ensure that all states came to the same realization at once, except through force? If force was required, should peace then be more desired or feared?[22] As a sign of the significance of these

[18] Rousseau, *Social Contract,* bk. II, chap. 10.
[19] Rousseau, *State of War.*
[20] Described by W. Evans Darby, "Cardinal Alberoni's Proposed European Alliance for the Subjugation and Settlement of the Turkish Empire," Grotius Society, *Transactions*, V, 7 (1920), p. 83.
[21] Rousseau, *Critique of the Peace Project* (1756/1917), p. 101.
[22] Ibid., pp. 100–02.

systemic forces, peace plans tend to be more a product of aggressive coalitions directed, as was the French king Henry IV's, against convenient enemies (e.g., the Turks) than the result of peaceable attempts to achieve mutual security.

REFORMED STATES

Having dismissed international organization as a system-wide route to peace, Rousseau considers the route to peace through domestic political revolution. Adding to the above, he considers three revolutionary routes to peace: democratic revolution and the just Social Contract; isolationism and autarky; and nationalism and nonprovocative defense.

The Social Contract—Democratic Revolution as a Route to Peace

Rousseau imagines the hypothetical creation of a just Social Contract (SC2) that would liberate citizens from their subjection and inequality. Sometime early in the history of a people, before corruption has become deeply ingrained in its character and institutions, a great moral legislator might be inspired to break the chains that bind a people and set them on the path to self-government.

Each citizen would be asked to pledge all not to a corrupt monarch, his ministers, or a Hobbesian Leviathan but to each other. Sovereignty would be made secure at home since no one could justly challenge the authority of the laws. The citizens, moreover, then would escape from the strife of the state of nature. Each citizen would also become both equal to all others and free. Inalienable, indivisible, infallible as an expression of the true interests of the people as a whole, and therefore all-encompassing, the people assembled would decide laws applying to all on an equal basis, absolutely, and thus constitute the General Will. The aim of the General Will is justice.[23] It secures justice, autonomy, and fair play. Each citizen receives his just due—the protection of life, liberty, and property—when each and all together, autonomously, make laws for themselves that apply fairly to all as equal citizens.[24] Justice, Rousseau adds, is the right way to constrain the natural propensity of individuals or groups to act in their own selfish particular interests. The General Will constrains particular wills by taking away (in Rousseau's famous and not altogether clear phrase) the "pluses and minuses that cancel one another, and the general will remains as the sum of the differences."[25] Citizens discover the general, just interest that is the sum of all the just interests that are held in

[23] This is the central idea of George Kateb's illuminating essay, "Rousseau's Political Thought," pp. 519–43.
[24] Rousseau, *Social Contract*, bk. 1, chap. 6, p. 14.
[25] Ibid., bk. 2, chap. 3.

common by means of a twofold process: by equal, autonomous participation in the democratic decision and by a preference for public justice that guides the general choice, a preference that is inculcated through civic education. Democratic institutions—the legislature and democratic education in schools and the arts—make all the difference. Rousseau thus gives us a powerful, moral, and democratic conception of the nation, the General Will. This General Will, or national interest, would thus be inherently general (meaning national, or coextensive with the polity) and rational; it is the people rightly understanding their long-term general interests.[26]

Discovering in practice what was in the national interest would nonetheless be a daunting task. A perfectly operating, directly democratic decision would, Rousseau suggests, ipso facto produce the national interest; the pluses and minuses of individual interests would cancel in the voting process, leaving what was truly general.[27] In a less than perfect democracy, however, the concept still has moral and political force. What would be the sort of interest for which the public resources and citizen lives should be risked; what meets the "blood and treasure" test? A private or group interest—a foreign commercial contract or financial investment or a personal quarrel—foisted on to the public agenda clearly would not qualify. Even if it had some fraction of public benefit, the private or group benefit would be unlikely to justify the direct expenditure of public resources, not to speak of lives. Nor can we assume that a pattern of foreign policy, however long and consistently pursued, necessarily reflects the national interest—again, in anything less than a just democracy.[28]

"Territorial integrity and political independence" are two conventional guideposts because they are prerequisites to any political authority. They make the exercise of just authority possible. Interests that affect all might be another indicator. But neither of those two indicators is free from problems. Citizens subject to an oppressive state might find a violation of "their" territorial integrity a precondition of their liberation. And general public policies, such as tariffs or industrial development policies, often have distributional implications that are not usually (if ever) balanced by systematic efforts to ensure that the losers are not made worse off. (For example, even if workers displaced by imports receive job retraining assistance, the psychic and social costs of dislocation can be

[26] Ibid., pp. 28–29.

[27] ". . . general will is always right and tends to the public advantage." Ibid., bk. 2, chap. 3. But the General Will can be "deceived"—when citizens mistakenly pursue their private rather than the public interest.

[28] It could better be said to reflect state interests than national interests. State interests could be identified by their length and consistency and their having a public standing more significant than transitory interests. For a discussion of interests, see Stephen Krasner, *Defending the National Interest: Raw Material Investments and U.S. Foreign Policy* (Princeton: Princeton University Press, 1978).

severe.) Nonetheless, political prerequisites and all-around benefit (Pareto optimality or compensation) are valuable starting criteria.

Together these considerations serve to emphasize Rousseau's revolutionary thesis. Although we can and must try to conceptualize a national interest, the very idea is murky, short of the direct democracy and simple similarity of egalitarian circumstance that Rousseau found essential to free democracy. Diverse interests are hard to weigh, and bureaucratic or elite rule weighs interests at best hypothetically.

In foreign policy the democratic Social Contract, unlike Hobbes's Leviathan or the monarchs St.-Pierre tried to save, would pursue no whims or private interests that would lead the state into possibly frequent battles. Wars would be fought only for national purposes that expressed the long-term rational interests of the people. But soldiers would volunteer for any war the Social Contract required and fight until the death. Wars would be fought only if necessary, but if fought, they would be unrestrained in their degree of violence except by the natural sympathies for fellow human beings that were part of the natural human condition. Wars would be fought only among states—among the soldiers who fight for states, not against noncombatants—and soldiers would become noncombatants as soon as they surrendered.[29]

But would wars be necessary in a state of war inhabited by just Social Contracts? Clearly, in a world in which Social Contracts were but one of many forms of regime, Social Contracts would find themselves fighting at least defensive wars against aggressive monarchies and other corrupt states. But in a world homogeneously composed of Social Contracts would war disappear? Would the compassion of the original state of nature translate into a sympathetic General Will? Or would the spirit of jealousies (the family rivalries) of the late state of nature translate into a jealous General Will? Would the true general interests of one nation be compatible with the true general interests of their neighboring nations?

Probably, unfortunately, the state of war would continue. Sympathy would lead to the protection of noncombatant (for wars are fought only against states) and to the avoidance of unnecessary cruelty (for General Wills are rational). But even if jealousy did not rule, a state of war would be difficult to avoid, for Rousseau notes that even if the ministers St.-Pierre describes were not privately interested in war, the very independence of states precludes a stable solution to international cooperation. Even just General Wills, each reflecting true long-term national interests, can have competitive interests over, for example, who has the right to exploit a particular fishery or has unimpeded access to a waterway. There is no global institution to define and shape a global General Will. Disappointment breeds rivalry, and furthermore, the very artificiality of

[29] Rousseau, *Social Contract*, pp. 9–10.

the state (which, unlike natural individuals, has no fixed limits) together with the anarchy of the international system results in a ceaseless struggle for relative power: "Its security, its defense, demand that it try to appear more powerful than its neighbors; and it can only grow, feed itself, and test its strength at their expense."[30]

For a state to have a "safe foundation," it must thus be small, so that the laws can be efficiently enacted and applied. It must have neither too much land, which makes it vulnerable to attack, nor too little, which requires it to depend on "commerce" or "war," a dependence that makes its existence "short and uncertain."[31] Rousseau concludes that "all peoples have a kind of centrifugal force that makes them continually act one against another, and tend to aggrandize themselves at their neighbours' expense, . . . thus the weak run the risk of being soon swallowed up; and it is almost impossible for any one to preserve itself except by putting itself in a state of equilibrium with all, so that the pressure is on all sides practically equal."[32]

Here, tragically, in order to account for horrible dangers of the state of war, Rousseau invokes not extreme or chauvinistic nationalism but a purely rational democratic nationalism. Although more stable states would be less dependent on commerce and war, these states would play the desperate game of nations more efficiently.[33] Historically, moreover, quasi-democratic republics have sometimes found that it is war that defines and develops a national interest, rather than the national interest's restricting the occasion of war. Thus Albert Gallatin, President James Madison's secretary of the treasury, remarked on the War of 1812, "The war has renewed and reinstated the national feelings and character which the Revolution had given, and which daily lessened. The people have now more general objects of attachment with which their pride and political opinions are connected. They are more Americans; they feel and act more as a nation; and I hope the permanency of the Union is thereby better secured."[34]

Although we cannot imagine national reform achieving global peace, Rousseau suggests it might allow particular states to mitigate or even to escape, at least for a while, the general state of war. The Social Contract is an ideal. What possibilities exist for real states? Rousseau explored two democratic-leaning reforms—those of Corsica and Poland—and considered other conditions favorable toward peace.

[30] Rousseau, *State of War*, p. 191 in the Roosevelt translation.
[31] Rousseau, *Social Contract*, bk. 2, chaps. 9 and 10.
[32] Ibid., bk. 2, chap. 9, p. 46.
[33] Rousseau, *State of War.*
[34] Letter to Mathew Lyon, May 7, 1816, in Henry Adams, ed., *The Writings of Albert Gallatin* (New York: Antiquarian Press, 1960), vol. 1, p. 700.

Peace through Isolationism and Autarky

Under anarchy, contact—even among just states—is the problem, so Rousseau explored a model for an isolationist peace. Corsica is his model of the small, undeveloped society capable of sufficient democratic virtue to escape the international system through autarky. (An eighteenth-century version of the antidependency role claimed by Tanzania, Albania, Eritrea, or Myanmar (Burma) in our times?)[35] The Genoese had blockaded the island, devastated the coasts, and slaughtered the native nobility. This tragedy offered a fortunate opportunity for authentic reform. From devastation, a wise Corsican leadership, Rousseau argued, could establish a society and republic of free farmers and small manufacturers, restricting trade with the outside world to the barest essentials. As a new "Sparta," it could cultivate its virtue with its small farms tilled by robust soldiers.[36] Here, while rural simplicity persists, "Everyone will make a living, and no one will grow rich."[37] Enjoying isolation and guaranteed by the unity a similarity of social circumstances brings, Corsica would present little temptation to and great resistance against any great power seeking a colonial conquest.[38] The Corsicans gain security in their time. National security then lasts until the increase in population creates a need for extensive manufactures and foreign commerce, and with them an end to virtue, simplicity, and the international self-dependence that might have made Corsica strong and safe in the surrounding state of war.[39]

Peace through Nonprovocative Defense

Rousseau also considered the establishment of what we now call nonprovocative defense.[40] Not all eighteenth-century states were of Corsican dimensions or potential democratic virtue. For the larger, more developed (more complex) states, Rousseau offered the example of Poland (an eighteenth-century Egypt, Brazil, or India perhaps). Introducing rustic equality and democratic virtue (not to speak of island isolation) was out of the question in a traditional society dominated by aristocratic landowners, afflicted with the odd domestic disability of the anarchic Polish Diet and its *liberum veto,* and surrounded by imperialistic great powers.

Instead Rousseau recommended a step-by-step progressive reform, creating as a surrogate for Corsica's island isolation a nonprovocative defense of Polish

[35] None of these states, however, was a democracy.
[36] Shklar (1969), pp. 28–29.
[37] J. J. Rousseau, "Constitutional Project for Corsica" (1765), in Frederick Watkins, ed., *Political Writings* (Edinburgh: Nelson, 1953), p. 308.
[38] Ibid., pp. 279–80, 281–83.
[39] Ibid., p. 328.
[40] A very good introduction to these arguments can be found in Dietrich Fischer's *Preventing War in the Nuclear Age* (Totowa, N.J.: Rowman and Allanheld, 1984).

independence. By cultivating education, cultural festivals, and a political system rewarding patriotic participation in public life, the Polish nationalists, Rousseau argues, could make Poland indigestible for any foreign conqueror.[41] Since the strength of states was a function of both their capacities and their will, Rousseau hoped to supplement Poland's undeveloped resources with a vibrant national will. Eschewing the chauvinistic *amour propre* of the corrupt, with their diversionary wars, the Poles should develop an *amour de soi*, a self-respect, cultivated through a pervasive, universal, free, and public education.[42] Elementary schools for the young and civic festivals for the adults would teach the nation's life, its heroes, achievements, almost to the exclusion of all else. Patriotic Americans soon after the separation from Britain expressed similar concerns and offered similar nationalistic recipes. In a letter of 1794 from a Virginia friend James Madison was urged: "No nation is really an independant one, unless their country, their Laws, Government, & Manners are, taken collectively, far preferable in the View of the people to those of any other nation whatsoever. . . . [T]he moment hostilities ceased, we relapsed into our old opinions & Habits, concerning Britain and her productions. It is this charm of inveterate Habits founded in former Subjection & political Nothings, that every American would wish to break & dissipate."[43]

Rousseau hoped to avert political dependence in even more vulnerable Poland. Combining patriotism, confederalism, central sovereignty, and a militia army, he hoped that Poland's enemies would find it neither an offensive threat (because its militia army could not engage in long-range conquests) nor an easy prey to invasion (because the army would be a formidable guerrilla force on the home territory). Beyond that, especially during the vulnerable period when it began to undertake the reforms it needed, Poland could rely on the natural checkerboard of the balance of power (see next chapter), the natural support of Turkey, which was Russia's and Austria's rival to the south.[44]

CONTEMPORARY REALIST CONSTITUTIONALISM

Testing the basic tenets of Realist Constitutionalism (as of Complex Realism) means confirming the continuing existence of a state of war. The significance of this form of Realism would be confirmed by the weaknesses of international law and order and the continuing insecurity of the international system considered as a whole. If all order is transient, all states in all their relations are subject

[41] J.-J. Rousseau, "Poland" (1772), in Watkins, ed., *Political Writings*, pp. 169–81, 183.
[42] I have found Roosevelt's discussion of these points in chapter 5 of her book to be persuasive.
[43] Walter Jones to Madison, March 25, 1794, *Papers of James Madison* (Richmond: University of Virginia Press, 1986), vol. 15, pp. 293–94.
[44] Ibid., p. 236, pp. 244–54, 268–70.

to the state of war, yet the state of war systematically varies with changes in the domestic structure of states; this type of Realism is confirmed.[45]

Tests are complicated, however, because specific propositions of Constitutionalist theorists themselves suggest ways in which the state of war can be mitigated and controlled for some states and for some period of time. Some of these theorists portray international hegemony as a source of imposed order. Studies of stability in balance of power systems stressing its necessary social and cultural foundations tend to confirm Rousseau's arguments, as we shall see in the next chapter.[46]

Rousseau's own specific propositions also call for examination. Do small democracies resembling his Social Contract actually behave more rationally but fight, when they fight, more fiercely? Do small islands of isolationist temper avoid foreign entanglements? Do nonprovocative force postures founded on balanced confederal constitutions deter attacks and restrain aggression?

Modern Constitutionalists, such as Raymond Aron, Henry Kissinger, Stanley Hoffmann, Robert Gilpin, Stephen Krasner, and Peter Katzenstein and other "statists," develop sociological models of the international system that build indirectly on Rousseau.[47] They assume the Realist state of war and thus consider whether the distribution of power is unipolar, bipolar, or multipolar, highly concentrated or loosely dispersed. But, as does Rousseau, they also give important explanatory weight to whether the system's domestic societies and cultures are heterogeneous or homogeneous, whether state and societal capacities are strong or weak and whether the international system accepts regimes as rules of order and tolerates nongovernmental actors as alternative sources of cooperation, conflict, and influence.[48] Together, not separately, this wider range of factors determines the stability or instability of international politics.

International systems thus vary not only according to the number and power

[45] Siverson (1980), Gilpin (1981).

[46] See, for example, Gulick (1967) and Jervis (1988), p. 345.

[47] They also thus build on Montesquieu, who influenced Rousseau's approach to political sociology, and their more direct source of insight is Weber's sociology, which operates in the field Rousseau's politics opens. See, for example, Wight (1977), Aron (1966), Hoffmann, "The Limits of Realism," *Social Research* (1981). For valuable surveys of recent contributions to this literature, sometimes called Soft Realism, see Zakaria (1992) and Rose (1996).

[48] Thus power becomes not merely "relational power" (whether state A can get state B to do something it otherwise would not) but also "meta-power," whether actor A can influence the rules of the system, the regime, so that other actors are required to respond to the agenda and rules the regime specifies. See Robert Keohane and Joseph Nye, *Power and Interdependence* (Boston: Little, Brown 1977), Robert Gilpin, *War and Change in World Politics* (Cambridge: Cambridge University Press, 1981), and Stephen D. Krasner, *Structural Conflict* (Berkeley: University of California Press, 1985), chap. 1. Much of this literature contrasts Realist interpretations with neoclassical economistic interpretations, arguing that political, power-oriented considerations influence policy and not merely profit-oriented considerations stressed by neoclassical economics. Contemporary international political economics does not yet seem to have Liberal models of international political economy that reflect Liberal political theory.

of the actors (the Structural view) but also according to the domestic constitutional characteristics of the states that compose the system and the social density of the "regimes"—the rules and international organizations—that constitute international society.[49] Homogeneous systems, Raymond Aron and Stanley Hoffmann explain, sharing similar domestic state and societal structures (e.g., all monarchies or all aristocracies) should have less to quarrel over and fewer misperceptions.[50] They are precluded from ideological wars over the best regime. They share a culture and set of assumptions that should reduce mistakes. Whether the society and its leadership are revolutionary, charismatic, or bureaucratic, Henry Kissinger argues, also influences the construction of foreign policy and the capacity for cooperation among states.[51] Revolutionaries seek purity; charismatics, glory; and bureaucrats, order. The first mixes well only with its own kind (even then there will be occasions for doctrinal strife), and both of the first two mix poorly with bureaucrats. Rousseau thus credited to Europe's common Christian culture and monarchical structure the efficacy of the balance of power, even if they did not, as St.-Pierre hoped, establish a sufficient basis for collective security and effective international organization. (I return to these arguments in the next chapter.)

Contemporary state Constitutionalists narrow our focus to the institutional structure of the state. Is it "weak" or "strong," meaning centralized or decentralized, capable of changing its society or subject to the interests of societal interest groups, a sculptor or a cash register? Rousseau offered us paradoxical advice on the role of state strength in international stability. On the one hand, weak states are vulnerable to easy invasion (as was Poland), to factionalized foreign policy (ministers start wars in order to promote their private interests), and to diversionary nationalistic wars (when desperate state leaders provoke war in order to build nationalistic support). On the other hand, it was the very weakness of the Holy Roman Empire at the center of Europe that permitted the European balance of power to be so stable, since its defensive mass deterred any attack on it and its internal weakness inhibited any aggressive capacity of its own.

Contemporary Constitutionalists, variously self-described as statists or institutionalists, agree on the importance of political structures. The first focuses on domestic state institutions, and the latter on international institutions. State elites seek to enhance their own power (sometimes simply measured by the

[49] Hedley Bull, *The Anarchical Society* (New York: Columbia University Press, 1977); Friedrich Kratochwil and John Ruggie, "International Organization: A State of the Art on the Art of the State," *International Organization* 40 (Autumn 1986), pp. 753–75; and Oran Young, "International Regimes: Problems of Concept Formation," *World Politics* 32 (April 1980).

[50] Raymond Aron, *Peace and War* and Stanley Hoffmann, *The State of War* (New York: Praeger, 1965). Hoffmann (p. 10) attributes the earliest contemporary formulation of this issue to Panaysis Papaligouras, *Théorie de la société internationale* (Geneva: Kundig, 1941).

[51] Henry Kissinger, in *American Foreign Policy* (New York: Norton, 1977).

budget), and existing state structures determine the capacities of government. But few scholars think that state structure is the sole cause or even the primary explanation of policy outcomes. Graham Allison examined U.S. state structure during the Cuban missile crisis of 1962 in order to show that even in a national emergency, when we would expect internal organizational and bureaucratic factors to be subordinated to unitary rational action, organizational routines and bureaucratic rivalries did shape policy, limiting some options that should (rationally) have been available (such as the surgical strike on Soviet missiles installed in Cuba).[52] In foreign economic policy Peter Katzenstein and Stephen Krasner have shown how the weakness of the U.S. state (its federalism and division of powers) has resulted in less than optimal outcomes, compared with the results achieved by stronger state structures, such as those of Japan and France. The necessity of compromise with entrenched societal interests, bureaucratic stalemate, delay, inappropriate but entrenched institutions and routines all come into play. But increasingly, scholarship in this subfield has come to emphasize contingency. State strength seems to vary according to the issue and to international pressure and to societal strength or weakness.[53]

Institutionalists have recently revived a debate on the effectiveness of collective security, asking how much difference do explicit commitments, established legal provisions, and international organizations make. Responding to the Realist skeptics, they show how more modest definitions of collective security do moderate strategic competition and enhance national security.[54]

[52] Graham Allison, *Essence of Decision* (Boston: Little, Brown, 1971).

[53] For the foundational contributions, see Peter Katzenstein, ed., *Between Power and Plenty* (Madison: University of Wisconsin Press, 1978) and *Small States in World Markets* (Ithaca: Cornell University Press, 1986), Evangelista (1989), and Stephen Krasner, *Defending the National Interest* (Princeton: Princeton University Press, 1978). Krasner distinguishes the raw material policy issue, where the United States is strong, from commercial policy, where it is weak. A recent volume of *International Organization* displays a range of contingencies: Some issues are more "public," as is monetary policy in which all firms and consumers suffer the same foreign exchange rate; others are subject to being captured by special interests, as is commercial policy with its many private special exceptions, Joanne Gowa has argued. Distinctions between the executive and legislative branches of the state are also significant (with the executive more national and strength-oriented), David Lake and Stephan Haggard have recently demonstrated. Michael Mastanduno adds that even the executive, if internally divided, will hamper state strength. Judith Goldstein indicates how entrenched institutions have ongoing effects, weakening or strengthening the state, despite the fact that the original circumstances that gave rise to the institutions have changed. And John Ikenberry shows how the executive when pressured by the international shock of the oil crisis can employ the market (usually a societal force) to change society through price-borne reallocations, when bureaucratic and regulatory means fail. See John Ikenberry, David Lake, and Michael Mastanduno, eds., *The State and American Foreign Economic Policy* (Ithaca: Cornell University Press, 1988).

[54] See the volume edited by George Downs, *Collective Security beyond the Cold War* (Ann Arbor: University of Michigan Press, 1994) and *International Security* (Summer 1995), which contains a valuable exchange between "institutionalists" and their critics.

Contemporary theorists of societal structure draw our attention to the impact of culture and the corporate structure of society. Which modes of legitimacy characterize society? Is civil society pluralistic or monistic, consensual or dissensual, organized or amorphous, stratified by class, industry, ethnic, religious, or regional identity? For rational, prudent security, Rousseau stressed the importance of democratic unity (the General Will) achieved through participatory legislating and civic education. Contemporary Realist scholars also decry societal factionalism. Jack Snyder blames overexpansionism on logrolling among diverse factions in a weak state. Each has some interest in expansion, but when society as a whole bears the expense, the factions resolve their differences over particular interests in expansion by implementing them all.[55] A stalemate of factions can also prevent state leadership, as seems to have occurred during the Great Depression, when, despite U.S. economic power, conflicts between nationalist and internationalist economic interest groups precluded coherent state policy. And contemporary proponents of nonprovocative defense consider both military organization and defensive technologies. This search has led some to explore inherently nonprovocative defense structures, such as defensive militias.[56] Others explore the once-intriguing suggestion that a kilometer-wide belt of trees planted on the inter-German border would have denied (thus deterred) NATO's greatest strategic concern, a Warsaw Pact tank invasion, without posing any direct offensive threat in the other direction.[57]

The Political Economy of Hegemony

One of Realism's most important contributions is to have outlined a perspective on the governance of the world economy. The Structuralists make an argument for hegemonic stability based on the existence of a dominant power that enforces openness to trade on weaker powers. The Constitutionalists develop that view based upon a more complicated sociology of national political economy.

"The governance of international systems," Robert Gilpin notes, "has been provided by empires, hegemonies, and great powers that have arisen and fallen over the millennia."[58] Rather than be anarchic orders, shaped by a competitive balance of power, international systems are hierarchically governed, Gilpin argues, by empires, hegemonies, or great powers that enforce order on the

[55] Jack Snyder, *Myths of Empire* (Ithaca: Cornell University Press, 1991).
[56] See, for example, Gene Sharp, *Making Europe Unconquerable: The Potential of Civilian-Based Deterrence and Defense* (London: Taylor and Francis, 1985). Also interesting in this connection is John Grin and Lutz Unterseher, "The Spiderweb Defense," *Bulletin of the Atomic Scientists*, 44, 7 (September 1988), pp. 28–30.
[57] An idea I once heard expounded separately by Lutz Unterseher and James Kurth.
[58] Robert Gilpin, *War and Change in World Politics* (Cambridge: Cambridge University Press, 1981), p. 156.

other, the weaker, states. Rules and regimes are created by underlying hierarchy. Free trade in the nineteenth century reflects the interests and power of Great Britain. The Bretton Woods agreements of the post–World War Two period—establishing fixed exchange rates, multilateral free trade, and convertibility of currencies—similarly reflected the interests and power of the dominant economy of the time, the United States. The international system remains Realist, "a state of war," but it is tamed, as it was for Rousseau, not by isolation or common civilization or particular structures of the balance of power but by dominance, by international governance.

Governance, however, raises a fundamental problem. Its underlying material foundations change, eroding the capabilities of the empires and hegemons that established and maintained the existing order. States establish empires or hegemonies over the international system in order to profit through imperial plunder and taxation or hegemonic trade and seigniorage (the value of being able to print international reserve currency). They expand their rule until the costs of exercising control equal the revenues derived from control. But an equilibrium does not last. Soon the difference between the benefits and costs of rule tend to become increasingly negative, producing a fiscal crisis for the dominant power.

Benefits fall and costs rise for both internal and external reasons. Internally, economies experience slowing growth as technologies age and supplies of inputs become more costly to acquire. Over time expenditure on consumption crowds out investment, the costs of military technologies tend to increase, and affluence decreases the martial spirit of the dominant people. Externally the costs of political dominance increase as subordinate states increase in power. Subordinate states borrow the technology of the dominant power and, enjoying the "advantages of backwardness," incorporate those techniques quickly and efficiently into their growing economies. Under these circumstances the international system enters "disequilibrium," a "disjuncture between the existing governance of the system and the redistribution of power in the system.[59] Such disequilibriums tend to be resolved by hegemonic war, as hegemons refuse to yield and challengers refuse to defer.[60]

Historically, empires, like that of Athens described by Thucydides, and great powers, like France, Austria, and Britain, do appear to rise and fall.[61] Some great powers do appear to have exercised hegemon-like influence, as the United

[59] Gilpin, p. 186.

[60] Robert Gilpin notes: ". . . there do not appear to be any examples of a dominant power willingly conceding dominance over an international system to a rising power in order to avoid war. Nor are there examples of rising powers that have failed to press their advantage and have refrained from attempts to restructure the system to accommodate their security and economic interests," p. 209.

[61] Paul Kennedy, *The Rise and Fall of the Great Powers* (New York: Random House, 1987).

States did following World War Two over the Western bloc.[62] (The USSR exercised empirelike influence over the internal and external affairs of its bloc, while neither the United States nor the Soviet Union controlled the international system as a whole.) Thus, while empires do establish governance over their colonies, it is much less clear that ordinary great powers, such as France in the seventeenth century or Britain in the nineteenth century, actually "govern" their international systems. Each great power enjoyed prestige and influence, but it is unclear how we would decide whether or not it governed. Did they control foreign policies—hegemonically, as did Sparta? Were the rules of the system imposed by the great power, or were they negotiated among the powers? The evidence is not clear. But it seems that France's and Britain's rivals—Austria and Spain in the seventeenth century and France and Germany in the nineteenth—would have denied that the two preeminent powers governed. Instead, during both centuries, the powers saw themselves in a multipolar balance of power in which no one power governed. Diplomatic historians suggest that they appeared to balance against each other, rather than being governed by a hegemon or even balancing against a single pole that threatened hegemonic control. (We shall examine these propositions in the next chapter.) International systems often do end violently, as did the nineteenth century in the cataclysm of World War One. Did war break out because Britain refused to cede preeminence to Germany? If so, why did Britain find itself at war with Germany and not with the other two rising powers, Russia and the United States? Would Britain have had to fight the United States (and vice versa) in 1914, if Germany and Russia had been growing less quickly?[63]

The Constitutional Realists thus offer us numerous pictures of international order, ranging from isolation to hegemony. But the modal picture, as it was for the Structuralists, is the balance of power in which states are strategically interdependent because they are capable neither of isolation nor of domination.

Strategy: Socially Constituting a Balance of Power

For most states, most of the time, the best a strategy premised on Realism can achieve is a stable balance of power. The Constitutionalists have developed a second version of the balance of power, a "sociological" model. It incorporates a set of special conditions in addition to those of the Structural model, in order

[62] But the United States did have to accommodate the interests of many of its allies, such as Britain, and offer considerable incentives to persuade them to adopt the rules the United States most preferred. Indeed the Europeans and the Japanese were exempted from the convertibility and free trade rules until well after they had recovered from the war.

[63] Robert Gilpin distinguishes the United States from Germany as being (following E. H. Carr) "tolerant and unoppressive" and draws our attention to the importance of "shared values and interests" in successful peaceful change, Gilpin's preferred form of international adjustment; see p. 209, *War and Change.*

to control aberrant behavior. They include such characteristics as a cultural commitment to European constitutionalism or social interdependence, technological stability and a sense of shared legitimacy, a sense of common interest in the continuation of the state system, or a recognition of a special position held by a "balancer" (e.g., Britain) or a "keystone" (Germany).[64] Since states seek more than just security or power, this "semiautomatic" model identifies the preferences and social conditions conducive to balancing behavior while excluding those that undermine it. It introduces three additional assumptions that together significantly redefine the preferences and behavior of the balance of power system. They create a sociology of the balance of power to match its Hobbesian political mechanics.

To the four requirements raised by the Structuralists—anarchy, coherent state units, a focus on relative power, and a rational system of estimating power—the Constitutionalists add three more:

First, in addition to a measurable scheme of power, the Constitutionalist model assumes that the measure of power remains technologically stable. That is, it should not be subject to large and radical shifts in military capacity, a stability that is closely related to the following.

Second, the Constitutionalists highlight the importance of a relative homogeneity of domestic structures among the leading members of the system, so that all, for example, are monarchies or aristocratic landlord societies. One need not assume identical domestic structures (this being remarkably unlikely). For example, in the eighteenth century structures ranged from parliamentary monarchies resting on aristocratic, landlord-dominated societies, such as Britain, to absolute monarchies, such as Prussia, resting on a similar base.

Third, this model rests on a shared transnational culture—in Europe, the common heritage of Christianity and Greco-Roman civilization—that provides a shared set of assumptions about values, norms, standards of taste, and even the very vocabulary of politics.

Together, by controlling for diverse goals and radical misperceptions, these assumptions transform the balance from an economistic, mechanical process into a diplomatic politics governed by a shared sense of destiny, a system that can be described as a "Christian Commonwealth" or a "Europe-wide Republic."[65] A "diversity in ideal unity" shapes the interaction of the states by providing a cultural foundation to the legal norms of international law. Specifically,

[64] See, for example, Stanley Hoffmann, "The Balance of Power," in David Sills, ed., *The International Encyclopedia of the Social Sciences* (New York: Macmillan, 1968), vol. 1, pp. 506–09, and Martin Wight, "The Balance of Power and International Order," in Alan James, ed., *The Bases of International Order* (London: Oxford University Press, 1973) and Alfred Vagts, "The Balance of Power: Growth of an Idea," *World Politics*, 1 (1948), pp. 82–101.

[65] These are the terms of the Abbé de Pradt writing in 1800, the international legal scholar Emmerich de Vattel, and Friedrich Gentz in his *Fragments on the Balance of Power*, p. 69. See the discussion in Edward Gulick, *Europe's Classical Balance of Power* (Norton, 1967), p. 11.

diplomats then can come to form a sort of *Internationale* (not unlike the Socialist International posited by Marx) in which their (often) aristocratic social origins create a dense web of mutual ties of family, marriage, and material interests and a community of respect for the institutions each of the separate states shares.

The Constitutional model thus adds more cooperative (not necessarily harmonious) expectations to the operation of the balancing system. States, most important, are presumed to have *no alliance handicaps*, so that each is an acceptable ally of any other and ideological definitions of threats are precluded. Their similarity excludes the ostracism of revolutionary powers, such as occurred during the early phases of the French Revolution, or the religious, ideological, or ethnic divisions of the fifth-century B.C. Peloponnesian system, in which democrat faced oligarch, and Ionian confronted Dorian. Henry Kissinger in his classic study of the creation of the coalition against Napoleon thus argues that "Diplomacy in the classic sense, the adjustment of differences through negotiation, is possible only in 'legitimate' international orders."[66] The minimal version of legitimacy posits a diplomacy of balancing achieved through homogeneity, which, by precluding social diversity, removes a potent source of alliance handicaps.

A maximal version of legitimacy makes a stronger claim. Common standards of civilization and legitimacy create a set of bounds on acceptable practice in the balancing system prohibiting the destruction of other members. This might have been what led the allies to restore the Bourbons to the throne in 1814 and 1815 and revive a coherent France as a full and equal member of the European system. Antagonisms thus tend to be muted by common standards of behavior in war.

None of these norms solves the security dilemma or therefore precludes competition for relative power, material interests, and prestige. Indeed, the Constitutional model assumes they enhance the prospect that states will effectively join together to confront and war against a potential hegemon by reinforcing individual security calculations with a sense of a common stake in the international system and the independence of all states that it protects. Nor, of course, does homogeneity necessarily make for systemic peace, which remains, in Gulick's apt phrase, a "barnacle on the boat" of the balance of power.

Just as Hobbes provided the foundations that explain why any state would balance power, Rousseau explained how states could overcome various ideological handicaps operating against balancing and adopt balancing within an international commonwealth.[67] Rousseau saw important determinants of the state

[66] Henry Kissinger, *A World Restored* (New York: Grosset and Dunlap, 1964), p. 2.

[67] Inis Claude, *Power and International Relations* (1962), regards Rousseau as an exemplar of the "automatic" (or Structural) approach because the balance works without direct human guidance, but I think the idea of sociological semiautomatism better describes what Rous-

of war in the structure of the system, the nature of mankind, and especially the varying domestic structure of states. Unlike Hobbesian sovereigns in a Structural or "automatic" balance of power, the sovereigns described by the Abbé de St.-Pierre shared a civilization and the widespread interdependence of commerce and other transnational ties. They were "a kind of whole, united by identity of religion, of moral standard, of international law; by letters, by commerce, and finally by a species of balance, which is the inevitable result of all those ties."[68] These ties do not, however, produce happiness or tranquillity. Indeed, these very ties are the "entanglements" that, without an international government to maintain law and order, produce rivalry, distrust, conflict, and a state of war that makes peace a mere truce and balancing both feasible and necessary. How well states have actually done in balancing power and how we can explain their successes or failures are the subjects of the next chapter.

The Constitutionalist Legacy

Reforms alter the state of war, mitigate its particular effects for particular states. The rational prudence of the General Will removes the factional, ideological, or purely chauvinistic aspect of conflict and war caused by monarchical and ministerial caprice. Isolation reduces the dangers of interdependence. Nonprovocative defenses assuage conflicts caused by fear of preemptive attack and deters attacks prompted by the likely success of easy conquest.

Each reform reduces the danger or offers a temporary (perhaps even for a generation or more) respite from the worst miseries of the state of war. No one of them promises "perpetual peace" or removes states from that state of war. Yet Rousseau presents us with a variety of options for mitigating and reducing international misery, each one suitable for a different political or social condition. The solution to which Hobbes condemns all states, a perpetual balancing of power, sustained the independence of most states. The balance is the best developed states—manufacturing economies, ruled by corrupt monarchies and oligarchies—could achieve, despite well-meaning efforts to establish collective security.

Rejecting Machiavelli's advocacy of republican imperialism—acquiring new territory, new people, and glory as the best route to long-run security (Rome's path)—Rousseau recommends that reformed developing states, small and agrarian, should attempt isolation and autarky. This constituted his advice to Corsica (another "Sparta"). Large and vulnerable, but undeveloped, states such as Poland should build nationalism through civic education and a nonprovoca-

---

seau saw as the source of the effective balance in Europe, characterized as it was by a particular geography, society, and culture, implying that without such features the balance would not succeed in maintaining itself.

[68] J.-J. Rousseau, "Criticism of St.-Pierre" (1761), in *A Lasting Peace*, p. 40.

tive militia defense. For individuals, seeking peace yet caught in a corrupt developed society, no moral option remained except private virtue, educated, as was Émile, to be as free as possible from the need to imitate the ways of a corrupt society.[69]

[69] *Émile* was Rousseau's version of Voltaire's "cultivating one's own garden."

CHAPTER FIVE

Balancing Power Classically

AS WE HAVE SEEN, the balance of power is the very heart of Realist strategy in world politics. Some, including Rousseau, have hoped for a temporary escape through isolation, as he proposed for Corsica. Others, among them Machiavelli, have dreamed of imperial glory. But all recognize that the balance of power is a result that all prudent states should aim to achieve if they cannot do better. Many Structuralist commentators, following Hobbes, have, moreover, argued that it is the best a rational state can do and that it is in any case deeply ingrained in the anarchic logic of interstate politics. Despite its centrality, however, the core Realist prediction of a balance of power is among the most discussed and the least examined aspects of world politics.

A good place to begin the study of the balance of power is to examine what it meant to balance power (when balancing was truly the dominant mode of world politics). In this chapter I first define how statespersons and scholars have identified the balance of power and then recall three explanations of it, drawing on Structuralist, Constitutionalist, and Fundamentalist—Hobbesian, Rousseauian, and Machiavellian—variants of Realism. I survey some contemporary empirical and theoretical work. In order to show what the balance can achieve and what causes can be associated with those achievements, I assess the theory of the balance of power in light of the historical evidence of the eighteenth century, the classical period when, if ever (for reasons I shall explain), the balance should have been working and working at its best. On the basis of the evidence, I conclude with a discussion of what should and should not be expected of the balance of power.

FEARFUL SYMMETRIES

Balancing power has by no means been a self-evident concept. Indeed, it has meant many different things to many people. In contemporary scholarship Ernst Haas describes eight distinct meanings covering its use as policy, concept, and propaganda, and Dina Zinnes describes eleven.[1] Martin Wight has variously recounted nine and fifteen different uses in the historical literature.[2] Its most optimistic proponents have claimed that it is the surest route to peace. Its critics have called it both a chimera and a provoker of war. And Realists adopt it most wholeheartedly, regard it as the necessary result of the very independence of states, and think it is the best states can do in an anarchic world.

Despite the variations, there is a core of meaning to the concept on which most definitions converge. The single most frequent definition of the balance of power portrays it as the interaction among states that assures the survival of the system by preventing the empire or hegemony of any state or coalition of states. Emmerich de Vattel and Friedrich von Gentz offer the best-known short definitions of the balance of power. "The balance of power . . . an arrangement of affairs so that no State shall be in a position to have absolute mastery and dominate over others" is how Vattel described it.[3] Gentz added, "What is usually termed a *balance of power* is that constitution which exists among neighboring states more or less connected with each other, by virtue of which none of them can violate the independence or the essential rights of another without effective resistance from some quarter and consequent danger to itself."[4] This too is the notion of the balance that informed David Hume's famous eighteenth-century essay in which he traced the original idea to Demosthenes's "Oration on the Megalopolitans."[5] Viscount Palmerston, the nineteenth-century British prime minister, developed a similar theme in a clear definition: " 'Balance of power' means only this—that a number of weaker states may unite to prevent a stronger one from acquiring a power which should be dangerous to them, and which should overthrow their independence, their liberty, and their freedom of action. It is the doctrine of self-preservation."[6]

[1] Ernst Haas, "The Balance of Power: Prescription, Concept or Propaganda," *World Politics* 5, 4 (July 1953), pp. 442–77. Dina Zinnes, "An Analytical Study of the Balance of Power Theories," *Journal of Peace Research* 3 (1967).

[2] Martin Wight, "The Balance of Power," in H. Butterfield and M. Martin, eds., *Diplomatic Investigations* (London: George Allen and Unwin, 1966) and "The Balance of Power and International Order."

[3] Emerich de Vattel, "Balance of Power" (1758), in *Theory and Practice of the Balance of Power: 1486–1914* (Totowa, N.J.: Rowman and Littlefield, 1975), p. 72.

[4] Friedrich von Gentz (1806), "The True Concept of a Balance of Power," ibid., p. 94.

[5] David Hume (1752), "Of the Balance of Power," *Essays: Moral, Political, and Literary* (Oxford: Oxford University Press, 1962).

[6] House of Commons, March 31, 1854, *Parliamentary Debates*, 3d ser., vol. cxxxii, col. 279, cited in Wight (1973).

Keeping that core in mind, we can help clarify the meaning of the balance of power by distinguishing results from causes, indicators from policies. Categorizing first the putative *results* (operational indicators) of balance of power systems, we can develop a list ranging from less to more order in the international system:

1. ***Counter-hegemonic Coalitions.*** The least orderly result can be considered the mere survival of international anarchy. Wars may be chronic, and some states will fail and be conquered, but we can expect states to league against a predominant hegemon, no matter what intentions it announces.[7]

When the system is not threatened by an hegemon, relations among states are indeterminate. The repeated failures of attempts at systemic empire over the anarchic international system of independent states thus best identifies this minimalist form of balancing.

Discussing the efficacy of balancing against systemic hegemony, historians have noted that when Queen Elizabeth I announced that she would support the kingdom of France against the great Habsburg empire of Spain and Austria because "whenever the last day of France came it would also be the eve of the destruction of England," she could be said to have been operating according to the antihegemonial, coalition-forming logic suggested by balance theory. So too was Churchill when he announced his support for Russia against Germany on the floor of Parliament in 1941.[8]

2. ***Geopolitical Counterpoise.*** This core result treats all states as potential friends or enemies. It is demonstrated by systematic alignments in which all states balance against the power of all other independent states. This indicator takes into account proximity as a component of effective power and thus threat, thereby discounting power by distance.[9] Counter-hegemonic coalitions are thus special cases of counterpoise in which the power distribution is concentrated in one "pole" having half or more of the power in the international system. Counterpoise and the next trait (equipose) are what we seem to mean when we say that we see a systematic pattern of states balancing power against power.

Kautilya's *Arthasastra*, a compendium of classical fourth-century B.C. Indian doctrine, first drew up a distinctly geopolitical model of alternating concentric

[7] Kenneth Waltz, *The Theory of International Politics*, pp. 126–27.

[8] Paul Kennedy, *The Rise and Fall of the Great Powers* (New York: Random House, 1987), p. 61. And see Waltz (1979) on coalition formation, p. 125.

[9] In the contemporary literature, Nicholas Spykman and Kenneth Boulding have discussed the "power gradient" in which power should be discounted by distance. See Spykman's *America's Strategy in World Politics* (New York: Harcourt Brace, 1942) and Boulding's *Conflict and Defense*. The discount factor could also be considered as state efficiency, national morale, or some other measure. Distance is conventional and in the period examined here especially important.

circles of hostility (nearest neighbors) and friendship (the neighbors of the enemy), as illustrated in Figure 1.[10] Martin Wight attributes a somewhat different European version of the same insight to Philippe de Commynes, who, writing in the fifteenth century, described the significance of a *checkerboard* pattern of European rivalries.[11] Sir Lewis Namier's description of European international politics in the interwar period as a "system of odd and even numbers"—geographically distributed (north-south) lines of allies and enemies alternating east to west across Europe—reflects these insights.[12]

A simple geometry of the balance of power distinguishes these folk models. If we assume that states balance against threats defined in terms of power and that power declines with increasing distance, then Kautilya's circles (Figure 1) will be produced whenever we think of all states but one as equally powerful (same-size circles), whose power is represented by area and whose centers are concentrically arranged about some one state that is larger than the rest. (If all states have the same power, radius, the pattern of relations is indeterminate.) Commynes's checkerboard (Figure 2), on the other hand, will dominate whenever we think of states as equally powerful (sized) squares, arranged side by side into larger squares or rectangles. Diagonal squares (states) will be allies, and orthogonal squares enemies, because the centers of the diagonal squares are the square root of two times more remote—hence less threatening—than the orthogonal squares. Lastly, smaller powers may form Namier's "lines" of allies

Geopolitical Counterpoises

FIGURE 1
Kautilya's Circles

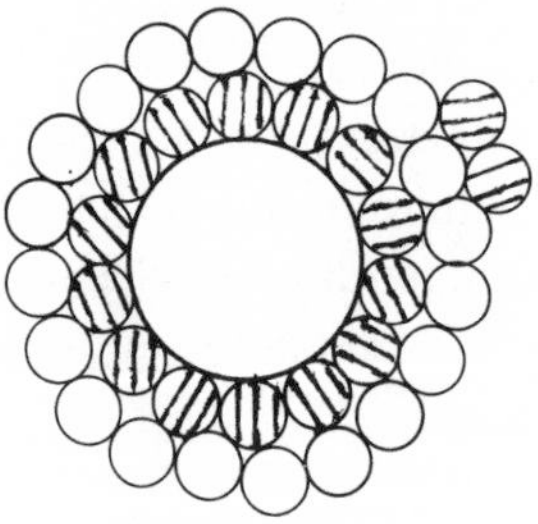

[10] Kautilya, *Arthasastra*, ed. and trans. R. Shamasastry, 4th ed. (Mysore: Sri Raghoveer Printing Press, 1951), pp. 289–91. It is discussed in George Modelski, "Kautilya," *American Political Science Review* 58 (September 1964), pp. 554–57. As was pointed out to me by Ms. Hongying Wang, the Indian doctrine resembles the ancient Chinese doctrine of "befriending those far away and attacking those nearby."
[11] Wight (1973), p. 90.
[12] Sir Lewis Namier, *Conflicts* (London: Macmillan, 1942).

FIGURE 2
Commynes's Checkerboard

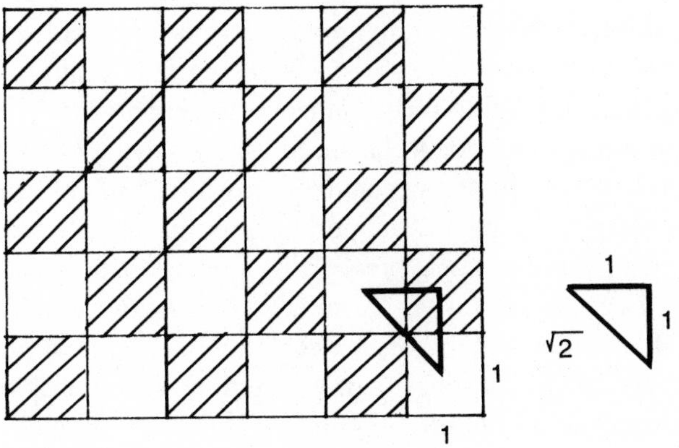

FIGURE 3
Namier's "Lines"

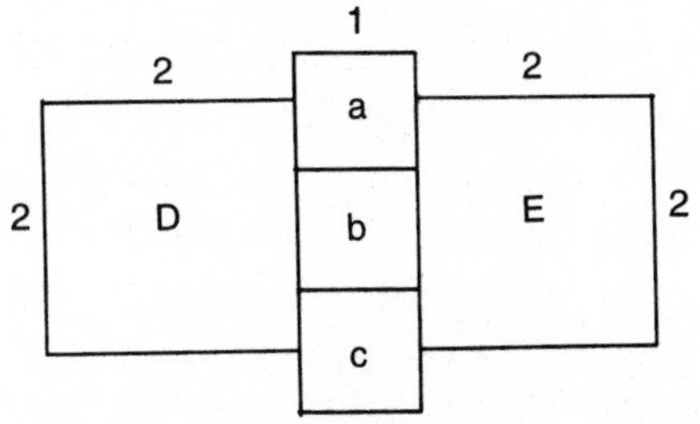

If we assume that area represents power, three states in geographic "line" (a, b, and c) will ally with one another in preference to allying with some other large square (D or E) tangent to them all, if and only if the power of the next "line" state divided by the distance between the centers of the two "line" states is less than the power of the large "tangent" state divided by the distance between the center of any "line" state and the center of the large "tangent" state. In the example above, with area equivalent to power, *a* will ally with *b* if and only if $\text{Power}_b/\text{Distance}_{a\text{-}b} < \text{Power}_D/\text{Distance}_{a\text{-}D}$. In Figure 3, the power of *b* is 1, the distance a–b is 1, the power of *D* is 4, and the distance a–D is 1.8. With 1 being less than 2.2, *a* allies with *b*, and by the same argument *c* allies with *b*.

(Figure 3) when tangent states of the same power and size all are tangent to some other state of much greater power.[13]

[13]The East European Little Entente formed in the 1920s, for example, is often said to have been patterned in "line" between Germany and Russia. A better explanation of the Little Entente is, however, "checkerboarding," in that Hungary was not a "line" member and

3. ***Equipoise.*** Equipoise involves the formation of two or more balanced coalitions among states.[14] The first indicator of equipoise is that each alliance contains the same total power resources as the other alliance or alliances.[15] The second allows for the advantage of interior lines (this is a measure I examine in the eighteenth-century case when distance was especially tyrannical). The third takes into account the utility of the alliance for each state in the alliance, comparing the sum total of threats balanced against—what I call the comparative threat quotient, which then generates a measure of *alliance stability*.

Unlike counterpoise, equipoise is purely a result, not a strategy. No state seeks balanced coalitions. Each presumably prefers to dominate a superior coalition, but the value of allies is presumably higher in the weaker coalition, encouraging the members of the weaker coalition to offer the incentives necessary to strip away allies from the superior coalition. When all play this game, balanced coalitions should result.

4. ***Equality.*** States balance not only *externally* (by shifting alliances) but also *internally* (by devoting more resources to security). Like the pressure of free market competition among independent firms that produces a tendency toward wage, rent, interest, and profit equalization, the pressures of state competition under conditions of anarchic insecurity should ensure that states will attempt to keep up with the latest in military capacity. Equality is manifested when, for example, military budgets demonstrate a tendency toward equalization, either absolutely or, that failing, proportionally (to national resources). This condition, however, is not fully compatible with alliance equipoise, since external balancing and internal balancing are in certain respects trade-offs.[16]

5. ***Great power stability*** (or essential actor stability) is indicated by the survival of the major states, that they are not eliminated in the course of balance of power wars.

Czechoslovakia, Yugoslavia, and Romania were balancing against it. An even more accurate interpretation would need to examine not only power variables but also the expressed aim of aligning the "satisfied" states of Eastern Europe with France against the "dissatisfied," which consisted of Hungary, Italy, and Germany.

[14] R. B. Mowat stresses the importance of this attribute: "The States System of Europe depends upon an equipoise, a balance of power, so adjusted that each State can keep what it already possesses, and that no one state State or group of States shall be able to coerce and despoil the rest," in *The European States System* (London: Oxford University Press, 1923), p. 18. This can allow for the emergence of a special role for any state outside the coalitions as a *balancer* correcting any tendency toward hegemony attempted by either coalition, the role occasionally played by Britain between the late sixteenth century and the twentieth century.

[15] We should note that this may not produce system stability. See the discussion below.

[16] See the valuable discussions in Benjamin Most and Harvey Starr, "International Relations Theory, Foreign Policy Substitutability and Nice Laws," *World Politics* 36 (April 1984), pp. 383–406, and James D. Morrow, "Arms vs. Allies," *International Organization* 47, 2 (Spring 1993), pp. 207–33.

6. ***System stability*** is the survival of all the states, whether great powers or small powers, that participate within the system.[17]

7. ***Peace.*** Strikingly (but infrequently) some have argued that the true glory of balance of power will be demonstrated by a system-wide peace. Threats of hegemonic conquest will be so deterred that all states will rationally remain at peace and enjoy "tranquillity" with one another. Niou and Ordeshook describe this as resource stability: that the balancing will lead to a continuous reproduction of the status quo, implying a peace in which no actor experiences a loss of resources or power. Antoine Pecquet, writing at the high point of the "classical balance of power" of the eighteenth century, described the balance thus: "I believe it to exist whenever I see states living together at peace and not threatening one another with destruction."[18] And Leckie in his highly regarded history of the balance of power commented that "the peace of Europe will be durable only in proportion to the perfection of its political balance."[19]

This list of indicators runs from manifestations of the least order (counterhegemony) to the most (system-wide peace), from primary indicators of balancing behavior 1–4, to putative secondary effects 5–7. Although some steps presuppose the former (as peace presupposes system stability; and system stability, great power stability), the list does not constitute a coherent ladder in which each step presupposes the former (some are trade-offs, as are counterpoise and equipoise and as are both those alliance outcomes and equality). Here I focus on demanding indicators of balancing behavior, especially counterpoise and equipoise. Counterhegemonic coalitions are not demanding enough (see the following paragraphs) and the secondary effects ask the balance to achieve what the majority of Realist theorists find chimerical.

A balance of power system should first be distinguished from three close analogues.

1. A balance against *threat* is not a balance against *power*.[20] We need to bear in mind that every rational international policy seeks to balance threats (constrain or minimize enemies).[21] This is also why systemic resistance to actual,

[17] "Essential actor stability," "system stability," and "resource stability" are the terms employed by Emerson Niou and Peter Ordeshook, "A Theory of the Balance of Power in International Systems," *Journal of Conflict Resolution* 30, 4 (December 1986), pp. 689–715. And see R. Harrison Wagner, "The Theory of Games and the Balance of Power," *World Politics* 39, 4 (July 1986), pp. 270–320.

[18] Antoine Pecquet (1757), quoted in Wright, p. 66.

[19] G. F. Leckie, *Balance of Power* (London: Taylor, 1817), p. 242.

[20] See Walt, *The Origins of Alliances*, for a Middle East case study that explores the significance of this distinction.

[21] Thus the widely quoted Arab saying "The friend of my friend is my friend, the enemy of my friend is my enemy, the enemy of my enemy is my friend" is not a balance of power

aggressive attempts at hegemony (by Louis XIV or Napoleon or Wilhelm II or Hitler), though frequently cited, do not constitute strong evidence for the Realist theory of the balance of power. It merely suggests, *post hoc*, that when states are attacked, they will defend themselves. The balance of power doctrine makes the special claim that power—capacity—is the valid and complete measure of threat and that we need to balance against capacity, whatever the intentions that other states are currently expressing.[22] This allows us to explain and predict, not just describe, alignments. Liberal and Marxist scholars expect, as we shall see, their states or classes to balance against threats but not against power per se. Liberal states balance against threats in the view of certain Liberal models, but they define threats in institutional, economic, and ideological terms (Liberals versus non-Liberals) rather than in power terms (capabilities versus capabilities). Liberal states therefore balance against the political threats that non-Liberal states seem to pose, not against the capabilities of fellow Liberals. Analogous considerations might be also found in certain Marxist models of international class warfare.[23]

2. A balance system also needs to be distinguished from a collective security system, which presupposes a collective commitment to defend all its members from aggression, no matter who the aggressor is.[24] A balancing system is directed against capabilities, not aggression, and it does not presuppose anything but individualistic decisions. Balancing indeed presupposes the possibility of "aggressive war" as an instrument in righting an imbalance of power.

3. A balancing system is closer to, though still different from, a concert system. The latter presupposes continuous coordination and collective decision making, in effect a single preponderant alliance; the former, multiple, competitive, and shifting alliances.[25] The two are identical only when a counterhege-

---

doctrine but (as stated) a balance of *threat* doctrine. Its dominant inference is *consistency* but not necessarily a balance of power. See Robert Jervis, "Systems Theories and Diplomatic History," in Paul Lauren, ed., *Diplomacy* (New York: Free Press, 1979), pp. 212–44. Even as such, the doctrine was controversial in the Muslim world, where aligning with Christians even against Christian enemies was regarded as abhorrent by some of the faithful; see Bernard Lewis, *The Muslim Discovery of Europe* (New York: Norton, 1982), p. 45.

[22] Thus balance of power theory differs from models of the utilities of allies and enemies based on the structure of patterns of international cooperation and conflict that is the foundation of models such as those of Brian Healy and Arthur Stein, "The Balance of Power in International History," *Journal of Conflict Resolution* 17, 1 (March 1973), pp. 33–61; Altfeld, "The Decision to Ally"; Alan Alexandroff, *The Logic of Diplomacy* (Beverly Hills: Sage, 1981); and James D. Morrow, "Social Choice and System Structure in World Politics," pp. 75–97. These are threat-balancing theories and thus compatible with all rational models of interstate behavior.

[23] See below, Parts II and III.

[24] Claude offers a clear discussion of these distinctions in chapter 4 of *Power and International Relations.*

[25] See Gulick (1967) for a discussion of the concert system and Charles Kupchan and Clif-

monic coalition is formed against a single power (such as was formed against France under Louis XIV and Napoleon) that threatens to take control of the entire system.

MODELS OF BALANCING

Three causal models characterize the literature on why and how states balance power. All three rest, as the preceding chapters have explained, on the Realist worldview of world politics. The first is Structural and can be rooted in Structural Realist, or Hobbesian, conceptions of international politics. The second is Constitutional—or sociological—Realist—and finds a thorough expression in Rousseau's thoughts on international politics. The third is Fundamental Realist and is best conveyed in the writings on statecraft and diplomatic strategy and well exemplified in Machiavelli's writings.[26] It is possible to conceive of these as separate models of the balance of power, in which strategic leadership, for example, compensates for a lack of sociological homogeneity, but the approach adopted here in the sociological presupposes the structural and the strategic presupposes the sociological. Thus the issue becomes one of how parsimonious we can be in answering the question of why states balance power: Do we need all three or can we explain as well with the first two or even just the first?

As we have seen, the Realist worldview forms the central foundation for balance of power thinking. Realists are the theorists of the state of war. They discount any claim to system-wide international order other than that based ultimately on force, or capability—the balance of power. They find instead that among independent states international society is best described as a condition of international anarchy that places all states in a warlike situation of reciprocal insecurity. Self-help is the only route to state security, yet self-help can make other states insecure.[27]

Drawing on Edward Gulick's and Inis Claude's studies of the balance of power, we can suggest that the following eight assumptions imply a tendency to balance power against power.[28] The first four draw on the Structural,

ford Kupchan, "Concerts," *International Security* (1991), and Richard Rosecrance, "Regionalism," *International Journal* (1991) for analyses of contemporary world politics in these terms.

[26] Inis Claude developed an instructive and similar catalog that characterizes the literature on why states balance power (1962, chap. 3). He classified the first as "automatic," the second as "semiautomatic," and the third as "manual."

[27] Keohane (1986), p. 172.

[28] The two works are Edward Gulick, *Europe's Classical Balance of Power* and Claude, *Power and International Relations*.

Hobbesian, view of Realism and claim that the balance is an "automatic" result of interstate anarchy. The next three draw on Constitutional, Rousseauian, Realism and portray the balance as "semiautomatic" dependent of favorable social conditions in the international system. The eighth draws on Fundamentalist, Machiavellian, Realism and holds that the balance also requires strategic leadership.

Structural

Assumption 1. The international system is "anarchic," a system of independent states whose security is interdependent (potentially affected by one another) and that lack world government.

Assumption 2. The individual states are coherent units, each seeking at the minimum to survive, at the maximum to expand in capabilities. No state is so riven by faction that its leadership prefers to collaborate with the enemy rather than resist foreign aggression. States are therefore best conceived of as rational egoists. This assumption serves to separate interstate anarchy from the world systemic anarchy that gives rise to empires.

Assumption 3. States will rely on self-help for security, and in the absence of any global source of law and order, security and therefore estimations of power will tend to be relative. They will adopt something like Morton Kaplan's first two rules for international behavior: "1. Act to increase capabilities, but negotiate rather than fight. 2. Fight rather than pass up an opportunity to increase capabilities."[29]

Assumption 4. Statesmen can estimate the balance of power rationally, by measuring and comparing capabilities, employing either simple (size of armies or navies) or more complex capability measures.[30] Modern scholars measure "critical mass" (population and territory), economic capability (GNP and special sectoral liabilities or strengths), and military capability as objective determinants of power, to which they also add force postures, "strategic purpose," and "national will," considerably less objective, less measurable attributes of perceived power.[31] Even so, the measure of power can become radically unpredictable.[32] The more, however, that one needs to take into account the less

[29] Morton A. Kaplan, *System and Process in International Politics* (New York: Wiley, 1962), p. 23.

[30] Gulick (1967), pp. 24–29.

[31] See Ray Cline, *World Power Assessment 1977* (Boulder, Colo.: Westview Press, 1977) and Barry Posen, *The Sources of Military Doctrine* (Ithaca: Cornell University Press, 1984), pp. 17–18.

[32] Democratization, nationalism, and industrialism, for example, rendered the pre–World War One balance remarkably ambiguous. Democratization questioned the very existence of tsarist power: Would the Russian people fight for the tsar or revolt? Nationalism equivalently

materially measurable, less objective factors, the more ambiguous and the less consistent and "automatic" (Structural) the power calculation will be and the more one will rely on Constitutional (sociological) considerations of the sort described in the next model.

Constitutional

Assumption 5. In addition to a measurable scheme of power, this model assumes that the measure of power remains technologically stable. That is, it should not be subject to large and radical shifts in military capacity, a stability that improves the capacity for calculation and is closely related to the following.

Assumption 6. The international system is characterized by a relative homogeneity of domestic structures among the leading members of the system. One need not assume identical domestic structures (this being remarkably unlikely), but a substantial similarity is assumed.

Assumption 7. A shared transnational culture—in Europe, the common heritage of Christianity and Greco-Roman civilization—provides a shared set of assumptions about values, norms, standards of taste, and even the very vocabulary of politics.

The Constitutional model (assumptions 5–7) thus adds more cooperative (not necessarily harmonious) expectations to the operation of the balancing system.[33] A *minimal version* holds that homogeneity permits a diplomacy of balancing by removing a potent source of alliance handicaps. Only in homogenous systems will one find systematic power balancing. A *maximal version* of legitimacy then may also create a set of bounds on acceptable practice in the balancing system prohibiting, for example, the destruction of other members. The rules of war then become operative. Legitimacy may also begin to work

---

undermined the Austro-Hungarian Empire. Industrialism produced destabilizing changes-with unpredictable speed. In 1870 France and Germany produced about the same amount of steel (a crucial component of modern military force), and Britain produced about twice the amount of either considered alone. In 1900, only thirty years later, Germany produced more than Britain and four times as much as France, yet Germany produced only two-thirds the amount produced by the United States (which had no role in the balance of power in 1870). A dreadnought naval arms race of strategically offensive weapons was under way between Britain and Germany; both were also developing the untested technology of strategically defensive submarines. Railroads appeared to give a great advantage to the strategic offensive at the same time, as the record of the U.S. Civil War suggested the defensive potential of trench warfare (to which the machine gun and barbed wire would add a considerable fillip). See A. J. P. Taylor, *The Struggle for Mastery in Europe* (Oxford: Oxford Unisity Press, 1954), pp. xxvii–xxxvi.

[33] Kissinger, *A World Restored*, p. 2.

against power balancing, leading states to form alliances against "revolutionary" states, defining them as threats irrespective of power considerations.

Fundamentalist

Assumption 8. A balance requires strategic leadership (Machiavellian Fundamentalism) by some statesman or other actor with both the motivation and the capacity to enforce a particular balance of power through a constellation of interests.

THE INCIDENCE OF BALANCING

The preceding list of indicators of the balance of power and the cascading model of causes leaves us with two categories of questions. First, has the international system actually balanced power (displayed the indicators) and, if so, which ones? Second, when the indicators were present, what was the most parsimonious version of the model that accounted for the balancing observed? That is, do we need all eight assumptions (the Strategic), seven (the Constitutional), or merely four (the Structural)?

Current scholarship offers only partial support for many of the propositions of balance of power theory. Few scholars doubt the prudence of balancing against attempts at systemic hegemony. The historical record seems to confirm the existence of counterhegemonic balancing against both France's and Germany's two attempts each at systemic hegemony.[34] But in those cases the counterhegemonic coalition was at least as much a counterthreat alliance as a balance of power alliance in that the power calculations were ambiguous and the coalition coalesced in response to actual attacks by the aspiring hegemon. Some have devised rigorous arguments elaborating the logic of structural stability in balance politics.[35] Some even suggest the theoretical prospect of systemwide peace.[36] But the evidence is only loosely tied to basic theoretical proposi-

[34]This is the major theme of Ludwig Dehio's *The Precarious Balance* (New York: Vintage, 1965).

[35]For valuable surveys of this literature see Harvey Starr, *War Coalitions* (Lexington, Mass.: Lexington Books, 1972); Roger Dingman, "Theories of, and Approaches to, Alliance Politics," in *Diplomacy* (New York: Free Press, 1979), pp. 245—56; Michael Ward, *Research Gaps in Alliance Dynamics*, Monograph Series in World Affairs, vol. 19, bk. 1 (Denver: University of Denver Press, 1982) and Roslyn Simowitz, *The Logical Consistency and Soundness of Balance of Power Theory*, Monography Series in World Affairs, vol. 19, bk. 3 (Denver: University of Denver Press, 1982).

[36]Emerson Niou, Peter Ordeshook, and Gregory Rose, *The Balance of Power: Stability in International Systems* (New York: Cambridge University Press, 1989) and Wagner (1988)

tions of international politics, or the theory tends to disconnect from historical evidence.

What we do not find in the literature are simple tests of the central principles of the balance of power, the principles of multilateral counterpoise and equipoise, the simple and fundamental claim that alliances are formed that balance power against power.

There is good reason for the paucity of tests. Much of the historical evidence does not at first sight appear to support this view. Niou, Ordeshook, and Rose need to add a series of ad hoc alliance "handicap variables" to study stability patterns in the late nineteenth century. Healy and Stein found that the basic principles of balance do not work for the 1870s.[37] Morrow's balancing model

allow us to obtain tentative answers to other systemic outcomes of automatic balancing. Their consideration of egoistic incentives both for aggressive minimum winning coalitions (Riker, 1962) and for defensive security-dominant coalitions models Hobbesian Leviathans eager to obtain additional resources, provided that doing so does not result in their own destruction. Their applied game also assumes that information is complete; the game is constant sum (or rates of growth are the same); resources transfer instantaneously among coalitions or states by negotiation or following defeat; the vanquished lose all their resources to the victors, who share the spoils according to their coalition agreement; any superiority in resources guarantees a victory over the inferior state or coalition; and all states prefer negotiation to conquest if they yield equivalent transfers of resources (Niou and Ordeshook, pp. 690–91). Together these assumptions mean that who would win a war between given coalitions is known as well as how much would be won (all the resources of the vanquished) and therefore how much the potential victims would need to offer to persuade some states to defect from the otherwise successful aggressive coalition. Their most important conclusion is that a Structural balance of power can produce the seventh effect, peace and "resource stability" (no transfer of resources). If one state comes to control exactly half the entire resources of the system (R/2), no coalition can conquer it and no other state will have an incentive to abandon the coalition that will form to balance the leading state out of fear that the leading state would then be able to attack an isolated state and acquire more than half the total resources and thereby be able to conquer the entire system. Deadlock equipoise in the sense of one coalition (consisting of one power) balanced by another coalition is associated with resource stability and peace. Power (resource) distributions such as (100, 100); (100, 50, 50); (100, 25, 70, 5), etc. thus are both resource-stable and peaceful (Niou and Ordeshook, p. 707; Wagner, p. 554). Only a few other distributions are assuredly peaceful and resource stable (p.561). The vast majority of distributions include the likelihood of resource transfers from the vulnerable to the victorious either "peacefully" through coercive negotiations or through defeat.

[37]The Niou and Ordeshook study is a modified balance of *threat* test that defines feasible coalitions in terms of threat perceptions and constrained coalition choices—following standard diplomatic history in, for example, excluding France as an acceptable partner for Germany after 1870 because of French revanchism (p. 236). Healy and Stein, "The Balance of Power in International History." In 1989 Jack Levy assessed the social scientific status of the balance of power literature quite negatively: "[T]he more basic question concerns the logical coherence of the theory and its validity in *any* historical era." "The Causes of War," in Philip Tetlock et al., eds., *Behavior, Society, and Nuclear War* (New York: Oxford University Press,

for the 1860s incorporates substantial estimates of perceived threat, determined by both domestic and international factors.[38]

We have not yet done enough careful studies to reach a firm conclusion. But in a preliminary judgment, we can conclude that the Structural model does not seem sufficient, that relative power does not explain alignment. Coherent, rational egoistic, states in a system of strategic interdependence do (we think) balance against perceived threats, but they perceived those threats in the sixteenth century as Protestantism or Catholicism as much as, if not more than, as measurable capacity, or power. In the nineteenth century they balanced as much against the threat of revolution, or the fear of reaction, or against colonial rivals for trade and prestige, or against affronts to national dignity. This overcomplicated the power balance during the age of the Concert of Europe between 1815 and 1848 and during the wars of national unification in the mid-century.[39] In the 1920s and 1930s ideological divides among liberalism, fascism, and communism again overcomplicated the power-balancing process, as they did after 1945 in the Cold War.

The Fundamentalist strategic model can raise similarly complicating problems. The very success of a great diplomat, such as a Metternich or a Bismarck, is a success against the natural logic of the balance. Entrepreneurial diplomacy is directed at overcoming as much as enhancing the simple logic of balancing against power. So Metternich united the conservative powers—Russia and Austria and France and Spain—against revolution rather than have them balance against one another and perhaps open the door to revolution. Bismarck united the conservative Three Emperors League against French radicalism and then united Austria and Italy against Russia and France: serving at one and the same time to prevent European balancing against a now-predominant Germany and to isolate France.[40]

Given the striking departures from power balancing of significant episodes of international history, two leading candidates for a closer look are the classical balance of the eighteenth century, and the prospective balance of the future, when, some say, we will relive those classical eighteenth-century times.

1989), vol. 1, p. 240. For the nineteenth century, a valuable assessment of measures of the balance of power can be found in William B. Moul, "Measuring the Balance of Power," *Review of International Studies* 15, 2 (April 1989).

[38] Morrow (1993) bases part of his argument concerning alliances on Michael Barnett and Jack Levy, "Domestic Sources of Alliances and Alignments: The Case of Egypt, 1962–1973," *International Organization* 45 (Summer 1991), pp. 369–95.

[39] See the evidence in Kupchan and Kupchan.

[40] Jervis, "Systems Theories and Diplomatic History."

THE CLASSICAL EIGHTEENTH-CENTURY BALANCE OF POWER

The eighteenth century presents us with an especially appropriate era for testing the balance of power theory. Between the 1730s and the outbreak of the French Revolution (1789), Europe constituted as perfect a laboratory of classical balance of power politics as history is likely to afford.[41] The troubles of the sixteenth- and seventeenth-century wars of religion had by and large been settled in favor of the status quo, yet the nineteenth- and twentieth-century wars of nationalism and liberalism had yet to materialize.[42] For the first time the European states system operated as a strategically interdependent whole, rather than as separate "northern" and "southern" systems, as it had earlier.[43] The measure of power was more stable than it would be when the industrial age stepped up the pace of change.[44] After a long seventeenth century of warfare, state institu-

[41] The period between 1714 and 1731 was shaped by the Anglo-French entente organized by Stanhope and Cardinal Dubois. Rather than by a balancing logic, the cooperative relationship between the two proximate great powers can better be accounted for by what has been called omnibalancing. The domestic vulnerability of the Hanoverians to a Stuart rebellion, the equivalent vulnerability of the Orleanist regency to a Spanish Borbón coup made the French and British governments eager to engage in international alliance against their domestic enemies. See Derek McKay and H. M. Scott, *The Rise of the Great Powers* (London: Longmans, 1983), pp. 101–35.

[42] "Religion was no longer and modern liberal ideas were not yet the mainspring of political action." Walter Dorn, *Competition for Empire, 1740–1763* (New York: Harper, 1940), p. 1. By this I do not mean that "medieval" institutions disappeared in 1730. The Holy Roman Empire persisted until 1806, when Napoleon abolished it. One of the considerable attractions to Frederick of Silesia was that it was a Protestant province of Austria. The Borbóns of Spain pursued a dynastic policy in Italy, sacrificing the interests of Spain in order to acquire patrimonies for the younger sons of Elizabeth Farnese, wife of Philip V. But after 1713 the flavor of European politics was modern. Dynastic inheritances provoked wars (as we can see by their titles), but the interests were statal, not personal. In the first half of the eighteenth century Protestant Prussia readily allied itself with Catholic France. Prussia and Austria behaved as independent great powers rather than as Holy Roman electorates. They consolidated their statal resources in competition with each other, Frederick having thoroughly rejected the deferential policy of his father, Frederick William. The Treaty of Utrecht (1713) was, moreover, the *first* general peace treaty to mention explicitly the balance of power, and *later* treaties, beginning with the Treaty of Vienna (1815), attempted to institutionalize international peace.

[43] Mowat, *The European States System*, pp. 33–34, whence the famous comment by Macaulay on Frederick II in the War of the Austrian Succession: ". . . and in order that he might rob a neighbor whom he had promised to defend, black men fought on the coast of Coromandel, and red men scalped each other by the Great Lakes of North America." Macaulay, *Frederick the Great*.

[44] Gulick p. 28, argues that in this era all a statesman truly needed to know was the size of the armies, the men who led them, and the size of the national revenues.

tions had become centralized and coherent.[45] There were few, if any, "alliance handicaps"—barriers other than security and power calculations, to changes in alliances through external balancing.

All the assumptions of the Structural model were in place: international anarchy, coherent states as rational positionalists, and a multipolar distribution with Britain, France, Russia, Prussia, and Austria constituting a classic system of five great powers. Power was measurable and, more important, technologically stable. Territory, subjects, wealth, and military forces combined to weigh power. All the assumptions of the Constitutional sociological model were also present. The states were homogeneously aristocratic, with varying relationships between monarchs and aristocracies in parliament or the bureaucracy. All shared a European culture, now deepening into a spreading self-awareness as a joint project of the Enlightenment, a transnational "party of humanity." Many too would argue that the diplomatic statesmanship that the Fundamentalist strategic model highlights was abundantly provided by Maria Theresa and Kaunitz (Austria), Fleury (France), Walpole and Pitt (Britain), and, above all, Frederick the Great (Prussia),[46] although no one statesperson dominated the era as Metternich did the 1820s and Bismarck the 1870s and 1880s.

Indeed, if the balance of power works anywhere at any time, it should have worked there and then. Let us examine the historical record and see whether it did and which of the indicators can be confirmed.

1. *Counterhegemonic balancing*, the most common feature of balancing power (as well as threats), was not relevant for this period. France's (Louis XIV's) first bid for hegemony had ended in 1713, when a coalition of Britain, Austria, and Holland had imposed the Peace of Utrecht.[47] France's military power continued to decline (relatively) throughout the century (until the Revolution). France's (Napoleon's) second bid for hegemony followed this period. This period was thus an ideal period for more complex multipolar dynamics driven by resources and position.[48]

[45] Robert E. Osgood and Robert W. Tucker, *Force, Order and Justice* (Baltimore: Johns Hopkins University Press, 1967), pp. 44–45.

[46] The effects of the opposite of statesmanship are also well illustrated in, for example, the confused diplomacy of the Duke of Newcastle.

[47] The period of French predominance is well surveyed in John B. Wolf, *Toward a European Balance of Power, 1620–1715* (Chicago: Rand McNally, 1970) and McKay and Scott, *The Rise of the Great Powers*, and William Doyle, *The Old European Order, 1660–1800* (Oxford: Oxford University Press, 1978).

[48] Kennedy, *The Rise and Fall of the Great Powers* describes the entire era as the maturing of a "genuinely multipolar system of European states" and focuses on the role of financial power and geopolitics as the dynamic elements in the shifting balance of power (p. 73). No army of this century, until the French Revolution, attained the preponderant size of the armies maintained by Louis XIV (four hundred thousand with field armies ranging up to

2. Geopolitical *counterpoise* is the most scientifically demanding test that this or any other historical period of the balance of power faces. Did eighteenth-century states balance against power, discounted by distance?

In a simple but crude inspection we can see that an obvious pattern exists in which the closer one great power is to another, the more likely that power is considered a threat. These five great powers form something close to a checkerboard pattern in the Old System of the first half of the century. France is an enemy of—sandwiched between—both Britain and Austria (whose Austrian Netherlands border on France). France is then an ally of Prussia, which in turn is an enemy of Austria (with which Prussia disputes the ownership of Silesia) and Britain (whose Hanover abuts Prussia). Russia is an enemy of Sweden (whose Baltic provinces touch it) but otherwise separated from the European balance by the passive mass of Poland. Small powers, such as the declining Holland, Spain, and Saxony/Poland, emerge as dependencies of the less threatening (less nearby) great power. Holland balances against France and depends on Britain, and Saxony balances against Prussia and depends on Austria, as Bavaria leans toward Prussia and France as it balances against Austria.[49] Only Spain balks against this simple checkerboarding, as it either pursues a dynastic policy or "bandwagons" toward France (following the ascension of the Bourbons to the throne after the Peace of Utrecht and the later formation of the Family Compact).[50]

How then do we explain that great event of the eighteenth-century balance of power, the Diplomatic Revolution of 1756? In 1756 Austria switched from its long tradition of enmity to France in order to join it and Russia in a war against the upstart Prussia, France's former ally. Britain correspondingly shifted its traditional Continental alliance from Austria to Prussia, in part to reduce the threat to its vulnerable Hanoverian dependency but also and more importantly because Austria was no longer prepared to balance against France, Britain's major, if not sole, rival. Russia entered the European balance against Prussia. The only constants were the enmity (and eventual war) between France and Britain and between Prussia and Austria.

The diplomatic strategy of this reversal is intriguing.[51] It involves mispercep-

---

one hundred thousand); statistics cited in Osgood and Tucker, p. 48. For a thorough analysis of the hegemonic periods preceding and following the classic multipolar balance of power periods, see Charles Doran, *The Politics of Assimilation: Hegemony and Its Aftermath* (Baltimore: Johns Hopkins University Press, 1971).

[49] McKay and Scott offer a good account of these relationships in chaps. 4–6.

[50] Dorn, chap. 4 is a good account of these arrangements. The dynastic ambitions involved finding territories (in Italy) for the sons of Elizabeth Farnese, Philip V of Spain's second wife.

[51] Valuable secondary sources for the origins of the Seven Years War include the extensive classic by R. Waddington, *Louis XV et le renversement des alliances* (Paris: 1896); Patrice

EUROPE: 1720–1756

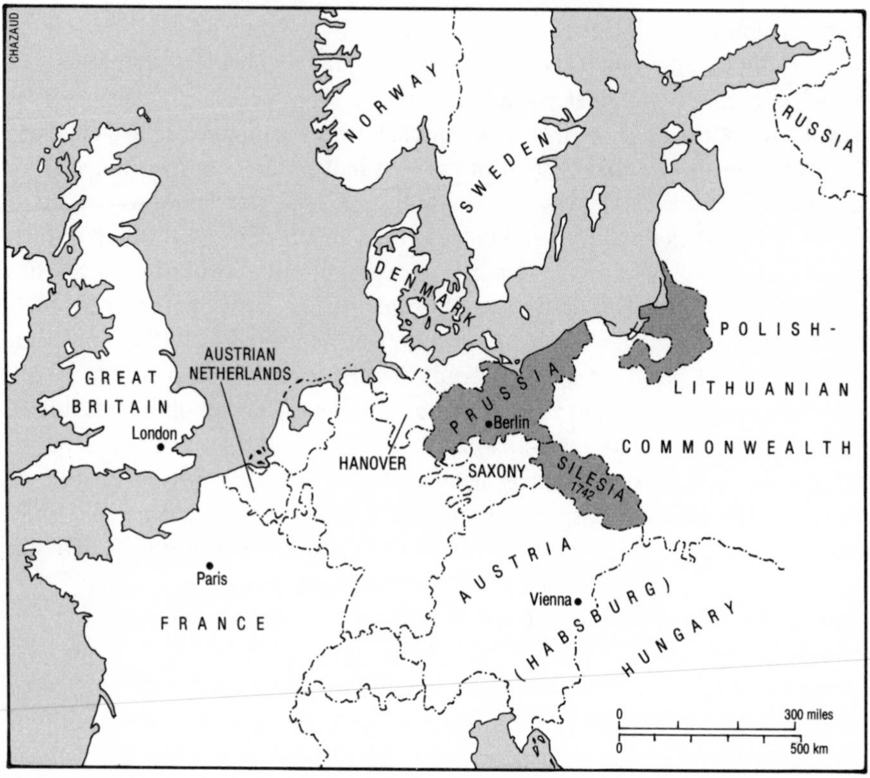

European Alliances of the Eighteenth Century

The Old System

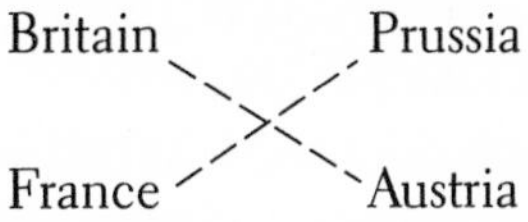

The Diplomatic Revolution

Britain ----- Prussia

France ----- Austria

--- = alliance

tions, deceptions, shrewd conceptions, and daring gambles.[52] Maria Theresa (later much encouraged by her brilliant minister Count Kaunitz) had not reconciled herself to the loss of the rich province of Silesia, won by Prussia in the War of the Austrian Succession, when the newly crowned Frederick had shown himself to be the most successful of all the poachers on her patrimony. Indeed, before the signing of the Peace of Aix la Chapelle (1748), ending that earlier war on terms that awarded Silesia to Frederick, Austria had already (1746)

Higonnet, "The Origins of the Seven Years War," *Journal of Modern History* 40, 1 (March 1968); D. B. Horn, "The Duke of Newcastle and the Origins of the Diplomatic Revolution," in J. E. Elliot and H. G. Koenigsberger, eds., *The Diversity of History* (London: Routledge and Kegan Paul, 1970); Herbert Butterfield's brilliant historiographic polemic "The Reconstruction of an Historical Episode: The History of the Enquiry into the Origins of the Seven Years War," *Man on His Past* (Cambridge: Cambridge University Press, 1954); W. J. McGill, "The Roots of Policy: Kaunitz in Italy and the Netherlands," *Central European History* 1 (1968) and "The Roots of Policy: Kaunitz in Vienna and Versailles," *Journal of Modern History* 43 (1971); David Ziegler's discussion of the balance of power in this era in *War, Peace, and International Politics* (1981); and Herbert Kaplan, *Russia and the Outbreak of the Seven Years War* (Berkeley: University of California Press, 1968). But curiously, the supposed Russian origins, which Butterfield found to dominate nineteenth-century historiography, do not seem after the fact to have misled Frederick II himself, who clearly attributed to Austria a design to regain Silesia, at the cost of war, if need be (see *History of the Seven Years War*, Part I, *Posthumous Works II* [London: Robinson, 1789], p. 55).

[52] There is also a gender dimension to the international politics of the time that I do not pursue here. But one should note that the War of the Austrian Succession was occasioned by the failure of the Pragmatic Sanction, which attempted to assure (against the dictates of traditional law) the right of a female, Maria Theresa, to inherit the Habsburg throne. The leadership of the international system in the 1750s and 1760s was also unusual: three "empresses" (Maria Theresa, Elizabeth [later Catherine], and Madame de Pompadour), one suspected homosexual (Frederick), and a manic depressive (Pitt).

entered a defensive alliance with Russia, the secret provisions of which entailed a partition of Prussia that would have restored Silesia to Austria. Saxony, concerned about the increase in Prussian power, acceded to the same treaty. Britain, Austria's traditional ally, concerned about the Prussian threat to Hanover, acceded to the public parts of the treaty in 1750.

Unbeknownst to other states and the ministers of the French government, Kaunitz, Austrian ambassador in Paris, had been assiduously wooing the members of the French court in order to persuade King Louis XV to abandon his alliance with Prussia in favor of an alignment with Austria. Frederick, like all the other statespersons of the period, assumed that such a realignment was most unlikely. After all, "Lorraine [the French acquisition from Austria by the Treaty of 1748] and Silesia are like two sisters, of whom one has married the King of Prussia, the other the King of France. This connection forces them to pursue a common policy."[53] Frederick failed to realize that Kaunitz had come to the firm conviction that Austria had to withdraw from its overstretched commitments in the Austrian Netherlands (perennial hostages to French ambition) and consolidate itself as a Central European power.

In 1755 Maria Theresa and Kaunitz induced Newcastle, the British prime minister, to sign a subsidy treaty with Russia, placing fifty thousand Russian troops on Frederick's eastern frontiers as a guarantee of Frederick's respect for the safety of British Hanover. In June 1755 bumbling and misperceptions escalated into an inadvertent colonial war in North America between France and Britain. In order to add further guarantees for Hanover, Newcastle (January 1756) negotiated the neutrality Convention of Westminster with Prussia.

This convention was all that Kaunitz needed to persuade Russia of Britain's perfidy (after all, the Russians saw their subsidy treaty as aimed at an offensive war against Prussia) and France of Prussia's perfidy (because a Prussian attack on Hanover was the prime value of the traditional French alliance with Prussia). Still, France, like Britain, was reluctant to enter a war—especially another Continental war—and would sign only a defensive treaty with Austria in May 1756.

Frederick, however, though poorly informed of Austro-French diplomacy, was well informed through various spies of Austro-Russian plans for a partition of Prussia, which he learned would begin with a coordinated invasion in 1757 through Saxony, Austria's ally immediately to Prussia's south. Armed with a large field-ready force of 150,000 and a war chest of thirteen million crowns, fearing Austrian aid to Saxony that would more than double the small Saxon army of 18,000 and, most importantly, a coordinated attack by Austria, Russia,

[53] Frederick II, *Political Testament of 1752*.

and Saxony, Frederick struck in a preemptive attack in August 1756 and easily overran his Saxon neighbor.[54]

"Political Arithmetick." Do these diplomatic affinities simply reflect the operation of the balance of power—geopolitical counterpoise and equipoise?

First, a justification of the measures involved.[55] (See Table 5-1.) They are crude, involving as they do just military forces, population, and distance. To many they will also be radically ahistorical. But I want to suggest that they are not ahistorical. They are indeed most historical, though still crude.

Statesmen *measured* power in this age, and they measured very much in these terms. Chancellor Hardenberg's plans for Prussian compensation were measured down to the last "subject." In 1815 he submitted a detailed account of Prussian losses and gains in the Napoleonic Wars as part of an argument justifying reciprocal compensations. He found a deficit for Prussia in a comparison of 1815 with 1805 of 3,411,715 "subjects," for which he demanded that Prussia be compensated. Count Kaunitz presented his diplomatic strategy to the Austrian cabinet as an example of "political algebra." Popular journals, such as the *Almanach de Gotha*—the *People* magazine of the eighteenth century—kept the aristocracy up with political statistics in the same pages in which it trumpeted the latest Paris fashions. After claiming to have increased Prussia's state revenue by 1.2 million crowns and its population to 5 million subjects in 1756, Frederick concluded: "Prussia might be estimated as two times as *powerful* [emphasis supplied] as it had been during the latter part of the reign of Fredick William I, the father of the king."[56]

Nor were these crude measures of armies, population, and revenue unreasonable. We can assume that statesmen really want security, wealth, and productive resources, but these are very hard to measure. For Continental Europe, population was probably the most measurable, reliable, and known indicator of long-run economic capacities in what were primarily agrarian societies of similar technology and widely differing soil and climate. Existing military capacities were probably the single best measure of security threat since citizen armies were unreliable and professional armies and navies in this era took a very long time to train.

Frederick the Great's appreciation for measurement was most famously revealed in 1760 in his statement to the countess von Gotha that "God is Always on the side of the Big Battalions." Every ten years or so after 1739,

[54] Frederick II, *History of the Seven Years War* (London: Robinson, 1789), pp. 60–62.

[55] For a contemporary discussion of the complexities of measuring power, see Aaron Friedberg, "The Assessment of Military Power," *International Security* 12, 3 (Winter 1987–88), pp. 190–202.

[56] Frederick II, *History of the Seven Years War*, p. 7. Hardenberg's tables are reproduced in Gulick, pp. 249–51.

reflecting an education in European political geography acquired in his training for the throne, he prepared his own strategic estimates of the states that surrounded Prussia.[57] In 1740, for example, he discussed the relative power of states, addressing resources, soldiers, revenue, population, and character. But he warned that in any measure of power one had to consider the tyranny of distance: "I observe that all wars carried far from the frontiers of the people by whom they are undertaken, have not equal success with those which are made nearer home." He noted the obviously increased difficulty of transporting supplies and obtaining local provisions as well as subtle psychological factors, which included the greater willingness to defend one's own hearth and home than to rob someone else's.[58]

So these measures are crude. Frederick seems to have measured better than he actually did. (Some of his figures are inaccurate—his estimate of the population of Prussia is one-third too high in 1740—and it is unclear whether he meant them as anything more than approximations.) As importantly, I have not been able to obtain comparable figures for all the great powers, in the range of years we need. I would like better revenue measures, but I have not obtained them.[59]

But we do have comparable estimates of army, navy, and population (Table 5.1). These were factors that counted a great deal, seemingly indeed most in

[57] "... Prussia, the revenues of the kingdom amounted only to seven millions four hundred thousand crowns; population, in the various provinces to three millions ... the balance of trade annually lost one million two hundred thousand crowns, which money enriched foreign nations ... the army was seventy six thousand strong, and about twenty-six thousand of the soldiery were foreigners ... [Austria], Charles VI ... his mind was limited, and destitute of penetration... a superstitious bigot, like all the princes of the house of Austria ... [France] her military forces consisted in a hunded and eighty battalions, each of six hundred men; two hundred and twenty four squadrons, of a hundred men each, which together amount to one hundred and thirty thousand four hundred men, beside thirty six thousand militia ... eighty vessels ... revenue, sixty million crowns." *A History of My Own Times*, Part 1, trans. Thomas Holdcroft (London: Robinson, 1789), pp. 1–17. This work was written in 1750, revised in 1775.

[58] "Preface," ibid., Part 1, p. xxi.

[59] Ideally I would like also to compare the perceptions of power of the major actors in each state against the objective power measures, as William Wohlforth, "The Perception of Power," *World Politics* 39, 3 (April 1987), pp. 353–81, does in his analysis of the balance of power before World War One. There is a danger that perceived power inadvertently incorporates assumptions about preferences and intentions by weighing the institutional routines and expectations that embody those intentions. Nonetheless, the additional measure would be valuable. In the eighteenth century both the haphazard data and the records of cabinet debates make this more difficult. Moreover, data in this era are subject to considerable qualification. Paul Kennedy has explained that we cannot use established military force levels as a measure for power in the sixteenth and seventeenth centuries because sovereigns could readily hire mercenaries. State budgets were no better guide because they were subject to large-scale embezzlement, and tax revenues were at best maximum estimates of real financial resources for the monarchies of these periods (Kennedy, p. 60).

TABLE 5.1

Eighteenth-Century Power Resources: Population (in Millions), Army (in Thousands), and Navy (in Ships)*

	Austria		*Prussia*		*Britain*			*France*			*Russia*		
	Pop.	Army	Pop.	Army	Pop.	Army	Navy	Pop.	Army	Navy	Pop.	Army	Navy
1700	8	100	2	39	9	75		19	400		17.5	220	
1720			2.3	80	9			20	350			300	
1740	15	100	2.3	80	9	120	124	21.5	140	50	20		30
1750	18	200	6	195	10.5	200	105	24	330	70		330	
1780	23	200	9.5	160	16	40		28	236		37	300	

TABLE 5.2

Distances between Capitals (in Km)

	Vienna	*Berlin*	*London*	*Paris*	*Moscow*
Vienna	0	524	1238	1038	1673
Berlin		0	934	880	1612
London			0	341	2506
Paris				0	2492
Moscow					0

* Sources: Kennedy (1987), p. 99; Brewer, *The Sinews of Power* (London: Unwin, 1989), Table 2.1; A. W. Woodruff, *Impact of Western Man* (New York: St. Martin's Press, 1967); *Almanach de Gotha*, various dates.

their—the contemporary—estimates. For a measure of distance (Table 5.2), I take the simplest: the distance between capitals. It may also be the most realistic, tapping the psychological dimension of where decisions are made.

Let us first examine the change, over the first half of the century, in the *Viennese* counterpoise *threat matrix*—the *power discounted by (divided by) distance* of each of Austria's great power neighbors. (See Tables 5.3 and 5.4.) Consider first the military threat (Table 5.4), measured by the size of the army divided by distance (T). (For comparison, I also include the best measure of basic resources, population, in Table 5.3.) In 1720 (Table 5.4), France, the traditional enemy, was clearly the most threatening with a T = 0.337—more than twice the Prussian T of 0.153. By 1740—at the time of the War of the Austrian Succession, when the powers descended on unfortunate Maria Theresa—Austria faced a separated set of threats, ranging from a low of 0.097 (Britain) to a high of 0.179 (Russia).

Then note the 1750s as events led up to the Diplomatic Revolution of 1756. Suddenly Prussia emerged as Austria's leading threat and outranked France in this respect, despite the considerable revival of French military strength in this period.

In terms of generalized resources (here measured as population, Table 5.3), no such clear pattern is observable, but in terms of dedicated and mobilized

TABLE 5.3

Vienna Threat Matrices: 1720s–1750s; T = Power/Distance; Power = Pop.

	Berlin	*Paris*	*London*	*Moscow*
1720	0.004	0.019	0.007	
1740	0.004	0.021	0.007	0.012
1750	0.011	0.023	0.008	

TABLE 5.4

Vienna Threat Matrices: 1720s–1750s; T = Power/Distance; Power = Army

	Berlin	*Paris*	*London*	*Moscow*
1720	0.153	0.337		0.179
1740	0.153	0.135	0.097	
1750	0.372	0.318	0.162	0.197

TABLE 5.5

Paris Threat Matrices: 1720s–1750s; T = Power/Distance; Power = Army or Navy

	Vienna	*Berlin*	*London*	*Moscow*
1720	0.096	0.091	0.22	0.12
1740	0.096	0.091	0.352	0.12
1740 navy*			0.182	
1740 both†			0.534	
1750	0.193	0.222	0.587	0.132
1750 navy				0.154
1750 both	0.193	0.222	0.7405	0.132

* "navy" counts each naval ship as 500 soldiers.
† "both" includes army and navy (as discounted).

resources, military power, Berlin had clearly emerged as Vienna's leading threat.

Now if we turn to Paris, the other major actor in the Diplomatic Revolution, we see complementary developments (Table 5.5). In 1720 Britain was France's leading threat, and it remained overwhelmingly so throughout the century. But there is a significant switch in the secondary threat: Prussia replaces Austria by the 1750s.

Here we see the makings of a revolution. Austria's resources were slightly larger than those of Prussia, yet it posed a somewhat lower threat. By the 1750s France was to gain more and balance against more by joining with Austria.

From the Austrian perspective, the case for an accommodation with France and opposition to Prussia is even stronger. Prussia now poses a vastly larger threat, and French subsidies might make the difference needed to defeat and then to dismember Prussia.

A complementary set of relationships emerged in Berlin and London. Vienna became Berlin's most serious threat as early as the 1740s. Paris remained London's permanent enemy. (See Tables 5.6 and 5.7.)

These transformations should be seen as the strategic background to the plot to partition Prussia that Austria arranged with the Russians. Crucially they are the heart of the arguments that Kaunitz, the brilliant Austrian chancellor, made in his cabinet and then sold to the French via the King's Secret (the back-channel negotiating scheme devised by the king and Madame de Pompadour). Despite the secrecy of Kaunitz's plot, Frederick was fully aware of the mounting Austrian fear and hatred directed against him; Maria Theresa had made no secret of her rage at the loss of Silesia. In the 1750s Frederick desperately went

TABLE 5.6

Berlin Threat Matrixes: 1720s–1750s; T = Power/Distance; Power = Army

	Vienna	*Paris*	*London*	*Moscow*
1720	0.191	0.398	0.08	0.186
1740	0.191	0.159	0.128	0.186
1750	0.382	0.375	0.214	0.205

TABLE 5.7

London Threat Matrices: 1720s–1750s; T = Power/Distance; Power = Army, or Navy

	Vienna	*Paris*	*London*	*Moscow*
1720	0.081	1.026	0.086	0.12
1740	0.081	0.411	0.086	0.12
1740 navy*		0.073		
1740 both†		0.484		
1750	0.162	0.968	0.209	0.132
1750 navy		0.103		
1750 both	0.162	1.07	0.209	0.132

shopping for new allies. Hoping to manipulate the rivalries to his own advantage, he negotiated with Britain for a subsidy at the same time as he struggled to reassure France, while trying to soothe Austria and Russia. All this collided with Britain's strained stratagem to protect its very vulnerable stake in Hanover from a Franco-Prussian attack. It offered to subsidize Frederick in a war against France at the same time as it subsidized Russia in a possible war against Frederick. Word, of course, leaked out (eighteenth-century spies were a most enterprising group, working for two or three sides at a time).

In the summer of 1756, Frederick realized that Austria and Russia were assembling a coalition to dismember Prussia, with a simultaneous invasion planned for the spring of 1757, and that he was about to lose his traditional French ally in the West. He struck with a preemptive attack while the British promises of a military subsidy made in the Convention of Westminster were still operative and before his enemies had a chance to mobilize.[60] Both the

[60] The rise of Prussian power is interestingly confirmed by Resmi Effendi, the Ottoman ambassador to Vienna in 1757 and later to Berlin in 1763, who explained Prussia's triumph by drawing Ibn Khaldun's views on the superiority of new states (Bernard Lewis, p. 116).

TABLE 5.8

Equipoise Measures

	Pop.	*Navy*	*Army*	*Army, adj**	*Difference†*
1740 Old Alliance					
Austria and Britain	24	124	220		
France and Prussia	23.8	50	220		
1740 "*Diplomatic Revolution*"					
Austria and France	36.5	50	240		
Britain and Prussia	16.5	124	200		
1756 Diplomatic Revolution					
Austria and France	42	70	530	1.021	0.175
and Russia	62	100	860	0.634	0.212
Prussia and Britain	16.5	105	395	0.846	
1756 "*Old Alliance*"					
Austria and Britain	28.5	105	400	0.646	0.547
France and Prussia	30	70	525	1.193	

* Adjusts the army strength of the alliance by dividing the total by half the distance between the capitals, in order to reflect costs of cooperation.
† Compares the differences in adjusted alliance strength by subtracting their adjusted armed strength.

diplomatic history and the evolution of the measured balance of power support the pattern of counterpoise quite well.

3. Now let us examine systemic *equipoise*. Were the *alliances* themselves balanced, reflecting a rational equilibrium of power?

Let us compare the Diplomatic Revolution pattern of France and Austria (with Russia allied in the background), against Prussia and Britain with the Old Alliance pattern of Austria and Britain against Prussia and France. Which pairing was better balanced? (See Table 5.8.)

The two systems (excluding Russia) are not surprisingly quite close. Balance of power systems are supposed to balance power. And Diplomatic Revolutions should therefore reflect marginal changes. The more balanced, however, is the Old Alliance—except the inclusion of Russia made the Austro-French alliance into a massive coalition aligned against Frederick.

Equipoise calculations, however, neglect distance, a particularly troublesome neglect given the state of logistics in the eighteenth century. If, therefore, we take into account the advantage of interior lines for military cooperation, a different story emerges, as does a possible additional motivation for the Diplomatic Revolution. Let us discount the sum of the armies—the operative allied resources—by a factor that measures the distance between their strategic centers. We can now see what equilibrist pressure might have been at work in the Diplomatic Revolution. Discounted in this fashion, the Diplomatic Revolution reduces by half the gap in distance-discounted military resources compared with a continuation of the old system. (The Old Alliance produces a gap of 0.547; the Diplomatic Revolution, a gap of 0.175 or, including Russia, 0.212.)

Another measure of equipoise, one that incorporates threat considerations (distance-discounting), is the *threat quotient* each alliance embodies. (See Table 5.9.) Alliance threat quotients measure the total threat experienced by the member states that is balanced against by their common alliance. Given the flexibility, hence contingent reliability, of all alliances, threat quotients have the advantage of measuring the sum of the individual strategic values of the alliance for the allied states. Threat quotients also generate the best measure of the *alliance stability* of an international system, conceived of as the difference between the sums of the threat quotients of the most valuable and next most valuable sets of possible alliances. This is because the higher the alliance threat quotient, the greater its strategic value; and the larger the difference between the threat quotients of the existing and any other potential alliance, the more resistant the system should be to a change in partners. Conversely, the smaller the difference of threat quotients, the more vulnerable the system should be to a Diplomatic Revolution. International systems in which military resources change should, if states play according to Realist rules, therefore experience Diplomatic Revolutions. (This may be what the traditional "flexibility" of alliance patterns means.) Conversely, international systems that, from a balance of power view, embody alliances strategically inferior to possible alliances suggest that the game is not being played by Realist rules.

In the 1750s (Table 5.9), the Old Alliance embodied a threat quotient of 1.5295 for Berlin and Paris; 1.969 for Vienna and London, for a total of 3.4985. The Diplomatic Revolution, on the other hand, balanced against 1.989 for Berlin and London; 1.4965 for Paris and Vienna, for a total of 3.4855. There is no reason to suspect that the states were not playing realpolitik. But the Diplomatic Revolution was not a necessary stabilization of the international system, since the 0.013 gap was within any reasonable error margin and leaned against the revolution.[61]

[61] For that matter, the Diplomatic Revolution could also have been arranged in 1740, judging from a purely systemic point of view. The differences in alliance threat quotients between the Old Alliance and a Diplomatic Revolution in 1740 was only 18 points in favor of the Old Alliance.

TABLE 5.9

Threat Quotients and Alliance Stability

"Old Alliance" in 1750s

	Berlin		*and*	*Paris*			
T's	0.214	0.382		0.7405	0.193	=	1.5295
	Vienna		*and*	*London*			
T's	0.372	0.318		1.07	0.209	=	1.969
				Alliance Total		=	3.4985

Diplomatic Revolution in 1750s

	Berlin		*and*	*London*			
T's	0.375	0.382		1.07	0.162	=	1.989
	Paris		*and*	*Vienna*			
T's	0.222	0.7405		0.372	0.162	=	1.4965
				Alliance Total		=	3.4855
Stability (Alliance Difference vs. Old Alliance in T's)						=	−0.013

"Grand Reconciliation" in 1750s

	Berlin		*and*	*Vienna*			
T's	0.375	0.214		0.318	0.162	=	1.069
	Paris		*and*	*London*			
T's	0.222	0.193		0.209	0.162	=	0.786
				Alliance Total		=	1.855
Stability vs. Old Alliance						=	−1.6435
Stability vs. Diplomatic Revolution						=	−1.6305

The superior account of the actual "revolution" lies in each state's own counterpoise calculations—in (to borrow Thucydides's phrasing) the rise of Prussia and the fear this incited in Vienna. Despite the systemic pressures of the balance, this was Kaunitz's "revolution"; leadership still made a difference. Leadership, however, could not overcome all possible differences. "Grand Reconciliations" between Austria and Prussia, on the one hand, and France and Britain, on the other (with each pair allied against the other), would have been, for example, impossible strains against the logic of equipoise and alliance stability (producing gaps of 1.6435 against the Old Alliance and 1.6305 against the Diplomatic Revolution).

4. A tendency toward *equality*—internal balancing—was manifested in the system considered as a whole. In the tension-ridden late 1750s we can see a convergence toward a mean, as France proved unable or unwilling to bear the burdens it had carried in the War of the Spanish Succession at the beginning of the century and the other powers found the will and resources to begin to increase to near French levels of armaments.

But it is also interesting to note that internal balancing served to stoke the arms race. With overall military forces at 834,000 at the beginning of the century and 1,255,000 at mid-century, we see an increase of about 50 percent in these fifty years.

5. What about *great power stability?* Interestingly, no great power is eliminated in this period. Sweden, Holland, and Spain had already been demoted as great powers in the aftermath of the Northern War and the War of the Spanish Succession at the beginning of the century. And none of the great or middle powers was eliminated altogether. During the rest of the century the great power club remained stable, after Prussia joined it in 1740 with the defeats it inflicted on Austria.

6. "*System stability*," however, in the sense of the preservation of all the political units, was not maintained. The skeleton in the closet of the balance of power in this century is the Partition of Poland, in three separate dissections by Prussia, Austria, and Russia in 1772, 1793, and 1795. Poland had long been recognized as a "sick man" of Central Europe. Frederick's remarks from the 1740s are dismissive, despite his admiration for the *dolce vita* that the Saxon electors enjoyed while ruling over their Polish kingdom.

Clearly social homogeneity and a common culture were an inadequate foundation for a set of norms sufficiently strong to prevent this naked aggression. Norms existed that condemned the unprovoked dismemberment of a legitimate state. Maria Theresa, well regarded for her sensitive soul, lamented the partitions. Frederick, with his usual wit, responded, "*Elle pleur mais elle prend.*"[62] It is also worth remembering that while Poland was the most striking partition of the century, it was not the only partition. Both Spain and Austria had experienced dissections (though not complete destruction) following their wars of succession, and Austria and Russia planned to inflict a radical partition of Prussian lands had Frederick lost the Seven Years War, begun in 1756.

7. Nor do we find a tendency toward *peace* ("resource stability"). The balance of power, as all the actors realized, often called for war to protect the fundamental interests of the states. Peace at best was a "barnacle" on this boat.

[62] "She cries, but she takes."

Great Power Warfare[63]

Period	States	Wars*	BoP Wars	GP Wars	Length†	Battles†
1550–1600	19	31	12	0		
1600–1650	34	34	13	1		
1650–1700	22	30	14	3	14	86 (Thirty Years War)
1700–1750	20	18	13	4		
1750–1800	32	20	10	3	8	111 (Seven Years War)
1800–1850	43	41	17	1		
1850–1900	45	47	22	1	6	332 (Napoleonic Wars)
1900–1945	57	24	14	2	4.5	615 (World War One)

* "Wars" includes "Balance of Power Wars" (in Europe), which includes "Great Power Wars." "Wars" also includes various imperial wars.

† Average length of great power wars and number of battles in the war noted, figures for the entire century.

None of the calculations of the statesmen could be so fine or so neglect the role of accident and strategic generalship that they could know in advance the outcome of a war and therefore decide rationally to appease the superior coalition.

Interestingly, the eighteenth century stands out as a period when there were fewer *wars*, but *more* wars among the great powers (lasting two or more years) than there were in earlier or later centuries.

CLASSICAL RESULTS

A simple model of the balance of power includes an objective set of systemic indicators ranging from the minimal to the maximal, from counterhegemony (which in practice is hard to distinguish from a balance of threat) to the core and distinguishing traits of counterpoise, equipoise, and equality to the more optimistic claims of great power stability, system stability, and peace. The model relies on Realist assumptions of Structure (anarchy and coherent states), Constitutional sociological assumptions (stable measures of power, regime homogeneity, and cultural communality), and Fundamentalist strategic (entrepreneurial) calculations to generate a cascading causal chain for balancing behavior. We can draw tentative conclusions from the historical record of the eighteenth century:

[63] Comparisons made in Hinsley, pp. 277–79, drawn from Quincy Wright, *A Study of War* (Chicago: 1942), I, app. XX, pp. 636–51. And see Jack Levy, *War in The Modern Great Power System, 1495–1975* (Lexington: University of Kentucky Press, 1983).

1. Even though we seem to have no evidence that states regularly and multilaterally balanced power in either earlier or later centuries and there is anecdotal evidence against the balance of power in those centuries, there is substantial evidence that states did balance power in the eighteenth century, making it truly a classical period of the balance of power. Statespersons not only thought they should balance against power but also appear to have done so. The actual distribution of alliance partners indicates that states balanced externally, demonstrating both geopolitical counterpoise and, to a lesser extent, systemic equipoise in the formation of their alliances.[64] States balanced internally through arms acquisitions, creating a tendency toward equality among the great powers.

2. The great powers were preserved (primarily through self-help and alliance); small powers were partitioned. Wars were not as frequent as in earlier or later centuries, and this may be a mark of enhanced order at the cost of increased great power wars, which were more frequent. Norms against aggression and favoring system stability had little apparent effect, despite the homogeneity of the international system.

3. If we assume that the characteristics of the Structural model were present during the entire post-Westphalian (post-1648) international system and that Strategic leadership has emerged in varying degrees throughout international history, then the singularity of the eighteenth century highlights the significance of the Constitutional sociological model. *In order to achieve counterpoise and equipoise, the Structural model (anarchy, coherent states, self-help security, measurable power) is not sufficient and the Fundamentalist strategic model (leadership) is not necessary. The Constitutional model (which adds technological stability, homogeneous regimes, and common culture to the Structural conditions) does, however, appear to be necessary.*[65] Though far from creating an international regime of law and order (the *maximal* claim), homogeneity did, we can infer, remove alliance handicaps and allow the balance to adjust rationally through alliance and war (the *minimal* claim).

The balancing of power against power thus *has* worked, but only partially and only during its classical age, the eighteenth century. Although strategic leadership contributed to the classical balance, both structural conditions and sociological conditions characterized the international system when states succeeded in balancing power against power.

[64] Of course states also balanced against hegemonic power (or against aggressive acts and threats) at both the beginning and end of the century (against Louis XIV and the French Revolution). This is compatible with either a balance of power or balance of threat model.
[65] But even with both present in the 1750s statespersonship (that of Kaunitz and Maria Theresa) played a demonstrable role in determining which of the coalitions was actually formed.

This result seems to have two implications. First, the balance of power can provide some form of order and do so while operating under all the inherent confusion and insecurity of the state of war. International law and a common Christian civilization did little to curb the prevalence of aggressive attacks that sought to dismember Austria and Prussia, but the simple competitive pressure of self-help, internal and external balancing, seems to have contributed to the survival of these great powers and may have reduced the overall number of wars.

But second, the balance of power, even at its best, is a poor form of international order to rely upon for international security. It may have ensured the survival of the great powers and somewhat reduced the number of wars, but it did so at the cost of a large investment in arms, the destruction of small powers, and a series of devastating great power wars.

This raises an obvious next question: If we grant that homogeneity was necessary to the formation of the balance of power, is it also sufficient? What are the alternatives to Realism? Can they also demonstrate a capacity to explain the reality of world politics? Statespersons have done and should continue to try to do better. The next two parts, examining Liberalism and Marxism, consider whether there is reasonable ground to expect that sometimes they can succeed.

Conclusion: Realists: Explaining Differences

INVESTIGATING THE CLASSICS of Realism for insights concerning contemporary international politics makes one vulnerable to two kinds of trouble. Some of their arguments may simply be anachronistic—the details of the fifth-century trireme balance are not as important as they once were—or we may misinterpret what the classical theorist said, creating a misleading, spurious relevance, discovering in Thomas Hobbes an apologist for the alleged contemporary virtues of authoritarian commercial capitalism or in Jean-Jacques Rousseau a twentieth-century totalitarian. But neglecting the classics can be equally perilous. They became classics by trying, as did Thucydides so explicitly, to speak across the generations. They have influenced how the influential formulate actual problems of political choice. However entertaining it may be to discover that we moderns have simply reinvented the wheel, we have a better reason to study the classics: We may have failed to "reinvent" the wheels they invented.

This survey suggests the value of retaining a varied conception of the Realist tradition. If Realists want to retain the range of insight embodied in the works of Thucydides, Machiavelli, Hobbes, and Rousseau, we need to reject a monolithic conception of a Realist model. There are three distinct strands of Realism, each finding an origin in Thucydides's interpretive history. Only Hobbesian Structuralism should be described (and even it with qualification) as "structural, strategic and rational unitary." Only the Machiavellian Fundamentalists specify the predominance of power-oriented preferences.

This survey nonetheless also suggests the value of retaining a coherent conception of the Realist tradition. We need to be wary of accepting epistemological eras: contemporary "neo"—that is, Structural and scientific—against traditional—that is, historicist and interpretive styles. Hobbes's Structuralism and mathematical enthusiasm surpass that of most modern Structuralists. Instead we see an evolving tradition and three strands of Realism.

This more complicated and theoretically grounded Realism contributes to our understanding by addressing some of the most frequent criticisms of Realist thought.

Realism need not be economistic. It did and does not lack "a motive for action," as its many critics have charged. Motives for action are an essential part of their theoretical foundations. They vary across forms of Realism from Thucydides's trinity of security, honor, and self-interest to Machiavelli's glory, liberty, and security to Hobbes's competition, diffidence, and glory to Rousseau's security and then, if reformed, national or, if corrupt, factional interests and passions.

Nor should the Realists be contrasted so starkly with the rationalists. The Realists have their reasons, and they are instrumental means toward the ends they find compelling. The awareness of the force of these reasons—and not merely a taste for the passions and aggression—drives them toward a consensus on the prevalence of the state of war.

Nor, should we contrast the Realist vision of international anarchy and a state of war with a "society of states."[1] If we conceive of the "society of states," as does Hedley Bull, as a set of common interests in the preservation of the system of states, common rules of behavior, including a norm of peace and a recognition of state sovereignty, and a set of common institutions, including the balance of power, diplomacy, international commerce, and international law, then the Realists too are social theorists. Hobbes, to be more specific, did not think that the international state of war was the direct equivalent of the state of nature. Leviathans were just those institutions that created the order that permitted commerce and that managed their international security through the balance of power. Peace was their first duty. Rousseau, moreover, explicitly premised his study of the European balance of power on the existence of a transnational European society. What the Realists deny, on the other hand, is that this society removes states from a state of war. International law exists; it simply does not protect states or princes that cannot protect themselves through self-help and balancing power, whether Machiavellian "omnibalancing" or Hobbesian or Roussseauian internal and external balancing. International law regulates very well the actual common interests of states (in uniform postal laws, for example); it helps facilitate agreements where compromises are possible by assigning responsibility and providing focal points for bargains (as in international commercial law). But, the Realists claim, it does not protect states from direct or indirect threats to their security, not Sparta or Athens in 431

[1] See the extensive discussion in Hedley Bull, *Anarchical Society*.

B.C.E. despite their carefully negotiated Thirty Years peace; not Austria in 1740 despite the web of international agreements sustaining the Pragmatic Sanction; not Kuwait in 1991 despite the explicit outlawry of international aggression embodied in the UN Charter.

REALISMS

Despite his complexity, Thucydides, we saw, is essentially a Realist. None of the traditional moral norms linking individuals across state boundaries have regular effect. Interstate relations in his view exists in a condition where war is always possible, a state of war such as the "hard school of danger" that persisted between Athens and Sparta during the "peace" that preceded the outbreak of hostilities (I:19). To Thucydides, as to later Realists, international anarchy precludes the effective escape from the dreary history of war and conflict that is the consequence of competition under anarchy. Thucydides, after all, is the explicator of the "truest cause" of the great war between Athens and Sparta—the real reason that made it "inevitable"—which "was the growth of Athenian power and the fear which this caused in Sparta" (I:23).[2] Therefore, whatever goals and means political actors might choose in the conduct of foreign relations among states, their foreign policies, he argues, should be constrained by the need to preserve their security independently.

But unlike later Realists, Thucydides does not think that states are the only significant actors in international politics. Individuals, such as Alcibiades, play important and sometimes independent roles in the determination of the course of international events. Nor does he think that state interests can or should be defined solely in terms of the rational pursuit of power or of any other abstract or structurally determined model of political behavior that reduces the variety of ends ("security, honor, and self-interest") or the significance of differing polities that have characterized the political determination of policy. Nor, of course, does Thucydides conceive of his work as a work of science, a subject that can readily yield both universal laws and unique predictions of events, whether prospectively or retrospectively.

Relations among states are subject to certain generalizations, lessons that can be derived from a careful study of the past, such as his own history of the great war between Athens and Sparta. Thucydides, though a historian, is not a historicist. Historical interpreters are capable of generating meaningful, contingent generalizations. The comparable quality of Thucydidean history arises from the constancy of human nature (I:22,4), the strongest binding concept in

[2] Thucydides, *The Peloponnesian War.*

his work.[3] He wants, moreover, his history to be "judged useful by those who want to understand clearly the events which happened in the past and which (human nature being what it is) will at some time or other and in much the same ways, be repeated in the future" (I:22). Thucydides reasons that pressures of war and civil disorder would create the same effects in similar circumstances everywhere because all would follow the impulses of fear and self-interest and honor (III:82,2).

Circumstances, however, often differ. Fear of war yielded futile resistance in Melos, surrender in Mytilene, and a successful defense in Sicily. His lessons therefore are embedded in the narration.

Thucydides develops a complex worldview of Realist politics that combined insights from international structure, domestic constitutions, and individual statesmanship. Together they accounted for the state of war he observes, the state of war all Realists since have found central to world politics. In specific applications he finds that those three factors could account for the origins of the Peloponnesian War and the defeat of Athens.

The modern Realists have differentiated his heritage. Modern Realism's philosophical foundations arose in Machiavelli, Hobbes, and Rousseau. Machiavelli inaugurated an emphasis on Fundamental, individual sources of the Realist state of war. Hobbes refined the Structural model of the international

Variants of Modern Realism

	Machiavellian Fundamentalists	Hobbesian Structuralists	Rousseauian Constitutionalists
State of War	Domestic/ International	International/ Homogeneous	International/ Heterogeneous
Actors	Individuals	States	States
Source of State of War	Ambition	Anarchy	Interests
Strategy of Peace	Imperialism	Balance of power	Isolation/ defense/ revolution

[3] Thucydides seems to accept Hippocrates's argument that since the human physical constitution was sufficiently the same, the same symptoms occurring across the human population would signify the same disease (II:48). See also Pouncey, p. 20.

system. Rousseau most closely followed the complex heritage of Thucydides, while highlighting the powerful effects of domestic Constitutional differences.

Modern Fundamentalism as first defined by Machiavelli roots social interaction in mankind's psychological and material needs.[4] State behavior, like all social behavior from the family through all other organizations, can thus best be understood as a reconstruction of interest-oriented, power-seeking activity.[5] The struggle for power changes form but not substance when we move from a consideration of domestic to international politics. The drive for power produces the state of war.

While accepting the anarchy assumption of all Realists, they question the differentiation between domestic and interstate politics. This means, on the one hand, that Fundamentalists leave open whether the state should be assumed to be a rational unitary actor. On the other hand, Fundamentalists specify both the means and preferences (both power) left open by the Complex Thucydidean view. Rooted in human nature itself, the drive for power leaves statesmen no choice other than power politics. Hans Morgenthau thus infers that "all nations actively engaged in the struggle for power must actually aim not at a balance—that is, equality—of power, but at a superiority of power in their own behalf."[6] States can, of course, make mistakes. The need to pursue power rationally, therefore, has a prudential and not necessarily a descriptive significance.[7]

Hobbesian Structuralism, like the other forms of Realism, assumes international anarchy. But modern Structuralism (like Hobbes) also assumes that state actors are "functionally similar units" differing in capabilities but not ends.[8] Rational process, fungibility of power resources, and a strong preference for power as a means to security form a necessary part of the model.[9] But unlike Fundamentalists, Structuralists see these features not as variables derived from assumptions about human nature or social organization but as derivations from the structure itself. State behavior is homogenized—made rational and power-seeking—through competition and socialization.[10] Only the rational and power-seeking will survive the competition. Inferences, such as the hypothe-

[4] Morgenthau, *Politics among Nations*, p.4.
[5] Ibid., p. 32.
[6] Morgenthau (1949), p. 210. A Complex Constitutionalist Realist, such as Wight, would disagree. The heterogeneity of the system means that the only shared trait among states is sovereignty and territory (1978, p. 106); all else, including motivations and methods of decision, differs among states.
[7] Morgenthau (1951), pp. 12–15.
[8] Waltz, *Theory of International Politics*, pp. 96–97.
[9] Robert Keohane (1986), p. 172.
[10] Waltz (1979), p. 75.

sized stability of bipolar or multipolar balances[11] and the weaknesses of transnational restraints, are deduced from the model, once one specifies the number and capabilities of the states that compose the system. And scientific Structuralism offers the promise of testable regularities.

Constitutionalism, like all forms of Realism, portrays a worldview or explanation of interstate politics as a state of war.[12] This view, common to a number of writers in the contemporary field, assumes nothing about the rationality of all states, their pursuit of power or the "national interest," or the way they set their various goals.[13] Indeed it assumes that the processes and preferences of states vary and are open to choice influenced by systematic differences in domestic considerations.

The dominant inference of Constitutional Realism (like Thucydidean Complex Realism) is the continuity of the state of war. Interstate politics thus constitutes a field in which generalization, when placed in proper context, can be useful. For the Constitutionalists, the state of war takes a wide variety of forms, from isolationism to the balance of power in a society of states.

Why do the separate strands all arrive at a state of war? What makes them all Realist? When one compares Machiavelli, Hobbes, and Rousseau, it appears that whatever the differences in their views of man and the nature of domestic politics, all agree that the prince or state either does or should command all force (Machiavelli and Hobbes) or command all loyalty (Rousseau). Differences in states and personal values are then contained by their similar degree of authority. There is thus no room for other loyalties and other interests to acquire sufficient strength to transform relations among states. They remain in a state of war.

But must that state of war be real? For some it has been seen as a myth, convenient for elites, responsive to passions, a nostalgia that limits human potential rather than protects it. Yeats brilliantly raised these doubts in his ironic poem "The Realists":

> Hope that you may understand!
> What can books of men that live
> In a dragon-guarded land,
> Paintings of the dolphin-drawn
> Sea-nymphs in the pearly wagons
> Do, but awake a hope to live

[11] Robert Keohane (1986), pp. 170–74.
[12] Wight (1978), p. 101.
[13] See Raymond Aron's *Peace and War* and Stanley Hoffmann's "Theory and International Relations" (1965, see esp. pp. 15–17).

That had gone
With the dragons?[14]

Whether Yeats is right partly depends on whether there are true alternatives to Realism. The Liberals, whether individualist (such as Locke), commercial (such as Schumpeter and his precursors), or internationalist (such as Kant), offer us a different vision of world politics, one that corresponds to a different set of combined conceptions of the human nature, society, and interstate relations. They are the subject of Part Two.

[14] W. B. Yeats, *The Collected Poems of W. B. Yeats,* ed. Richard Finneran (New York: Collier, 1983), p. 120.

PART TWO

LIBERALISM

INTRODUCTION

The Varieties of Liberalism

PROMOTING FREEDOM WILL produce peace, we have often been told. In a speech before the British Parliament in June 1982, President Reagan proclaimed that governments founded on a respect for individual liberty exercise "restraint" and "peaceful intentions" in their foreign policy. But he then announced a "crusade for freedom" and a "campaign for democratic development."[1] President Bush, similarly, on October 1, 1990, in an address before the United Nations General Assembly, declared: "Calls for democracy and human rights are being reborn everywhere. And these calls are an expression of support for the values enshrined in the Charter. They encourage our hopes for a more stable, more peaceful, more prosperous world."[2] In a UN address ("Pax Universalis," September 23, 1991), he stated equally unequivocally: "As democracy flourishes, so does the opportunity for a third historical breakthrough: international cooperation" (the first two were individual enterprise and international trade). Perhaps most consequentially, the President justified the large cuts in U.S. tactical nuclear forces as a product of the decline in hostility that stemmed from the survival of democratic forces in the USSR after the 1991 coup. President Clinton continued this tradition, making "democratic enlargement" the doctrinal centerpiece of his administration's foreign policy.

In making these claims, these presidents and other Liberal politicians joined a long list of Liberal theorists (and propagandists) and echoed an old argument: The aggressive instincts of authoritarian leaders and totalitarian ruling parties

[1] President Reagan's speech is printed in the *New York Times*, June 9, 1982.
[2] He earlier announced as a "plain truth: the day of the dictator is over. The people's right to democracy must not be denied." *Department of State Bulletin* (June 1989).

make for war. A modest version of this view led the authors of the U.S. Constitution to entrust Congress, rather than the presidency, with the authority to declare war. A more fiery American revolutionary, Thomas Paine, in 1791 proclaimed: "Monarchical sovereignty, the enemy of mankind, and the source of misery, is abolished; and sovereignty is restored to its natural and original place, the nation. . . . Were this the case throughout Europe, the cause of war would be taken away."[3]

Liberal states, the argument runs, founded on such individual rights as equality before the law, free speech and other civil liberties, private property, and elected representation, are fundamentally against war. When the citizens who bear the burdens of war elect their governments, wars become impossible. Furthermore, citizens appreciate that the benefits of trade can be enjoyed only under conditions of peace. Thus the very existence of Liberal states, such as the United States, Japan, and our European allies, makes for peace.

This is a large claim. The Realists described for us a state of war that could be mitigated but not overcome short of a world Leviathan. The Liberals, with important variations, announce to us the possibility of a state of peace among independent states.

In Part Two, we look at three distinct theoretical traditions of Liberalism, attributable to three theorists: John Locke, the great founder of modern Liberal individualism, who together with the later Utilitarian Jeremy Bentham, provided the Liberal foundations of international law; Adam Smith and Joseph Schumpeter and other Commercialists, explicators of the Liberal pacifism invoked by the politicians; and Immanuel Kant, a Liberal republican who calls for a demanding internationalism that institutes peace among fellow Liberal republics.

Human rights–based Liberalism provides us crucial moral foundations for international law. Commercial Liberalism identifies emerging sources of commercial pacifism in Liberal democracies. For some, Locke demands too little of Liberal republicans, and Schumpeter expects too much. Kant and other Liberal internationalists hold that Liberalism does leave a coherent legacy concerning foreign affairs. Liberal states are different. They are indeed peaceful. But they are also prone to make war. Liberal states, as Kant argued they would, have created a separate peace. They also, as he feared they might, have discovered Liberal reasons for aggression.

Principles of Liberalism

There is no canonical description of Liberalism. What we tend to call Liberal resembles a family portrait of principles and institutions, recognizable by certain characteristics—for example, individual freedom, political participation,

[3]Thomas Paine, *The Rights of Man*, in *Complete Writings*, ed. Eric Foner (New York: Oxford University Press, 1995), vol. I, p. 342.

private property, and equality of opportunity—that most Liberal states share, although none has them all.

Political theorists, however, identify Liberalism with an essential principle, the importance of the freedom of the individual. Above all, this is a belief in the importance of moral freedom, of the right to be treated and a duty to treat others as ethical subjects, not as objects or means only. A commitment to this principle has generated rights and institutions.

A threefold set of rights forms the foundation of an ideal version of Liberalism. Liberalism calls for freedom from arbitrary authority, often called negative freedom, which includes freedom of conscience, a free press and free speech, equality under the law, and the right to hold, and therefore to exchange, property without fear of arbitrary seizure. Liberalism also calls for those rights necessary to protect and promote the capacity and opportunity for freedom, the "positive freedoms." Such social rights as equality of opportunity in education and such economic rights as health care and employment, necessary for effective self-expression and participation, are thus among Liberal rights. A third Liberal right, democratic participation or representation, is necessary to guarantee the other two. To ensure that morally autonomous individuals remain free in those areas of social action where public authority is needed, public legislation has to express the will of the citizens making laws for their own community.

Ideal Liberalism is thus marked by a shared commitment to four essential institutions. First, citizens possess juridical equality and other fundamental civic rights, such as freedom of religion and the press. Second, the effective sovereigns of the state are representative legislatures deriving their authority from the consent of the electorate and exercising their authority free from all restraint apart from the requirement that basic civic rights be preserved. Most pertinently for the impact of Liberalism on foreign affairs, the state is subject to neither the external authority of other states nor the internal authority of special prerogatives over foreign policy held, for example, by monarchs or military bureaucracies. Third, the economy rests on a recognition of the rights of private property, including the ownership of means of production. Property is justified by individual acquisition (for example, by labor) or by social agreement or social utility. This excludes state Socialism or state capitalism, but it need not exclude market Socialism or various forms of the mixed economy. Fourth, economic decisions are predominantly shaped by the forces of supply and demand, domestically and internationally, and are free from strict control by bureaucracies.

These principles and institutions have shaped two high roads to Liberal governance. In order to protect the opportunity of the citizen to exercise freedom, laissez-faire Liberalism has leaned toward a highly constrained role for the state and a much wider role for private property and the market. In order to promote the opportunity of the citizen to exercise freedom, welfare Liberalism has expanded the role of the state and constricted the role of the market. Both nevertheless accept the four institutional requirements and contrast markedly with the colonies, monarchical regimes, military dictatorships, and Communist Party dictatorships with which they have shared the political governance of the modern world.[4] (See Table 8-1 in chapter 8 for a list of Liberal regimes.)

Uncomfortably paralleling each of the high roads are "low roads" that, while achieving certain Liberal values, fail to reconcile freedom, equality, and order. An overwhelming terror of anarchy and a speculation on preserving property can drive laissez-faire Liberals to support a law-and-order authoritarian rule that sacrifices democracy. Authoritarianism to preserve order is the Realist argument of Hobbes's Leviathan, and it finds an echo in Locke's Liberal concept of "tacit consent." It also shapes the argument of right-wing Liberals who seek to draw a distinction between "authoritarian" and "totalitarian" dictatorships. The justification sometimes advanced by Liberals for the former is that they can be temporary and can educate the population into an acceptance of property, individual rights, and, eventually, representative government.[5] Other Liberals focus solely on freedom of property and market relations and portray the state as a simple rational agent of property rights or as a firm ready for entrepreneurial capture, as do Bentham and Schumpeter. Lastly, some Liberals on the left make revolutionary dictatorship a vehicle for democratic education.

Liberalism and International Theory

For international relations theory, the political theorist's high and low views of Liberalism have ambiguous implications. Defined by the centrality of individual rights, private property, and representative government, it is a domestic theory. Realism, on the other hand, is an international theory, defined by the centrality of the state of war. There appears to be no simple theoretical integra-

[4]The sources of classic laissez-faire Liberalism can be found in Bentham, Cobden, the *Federalist Papers*, Kant, Spencer, Hayek, Friedman, and Robert Nozick, *Anarchy, State and Utopia* (New York: Basic Books, 1974). Expositions of welfare Liberalism are in the work of the later Mill, T. H. Greene, the Fabians and John Rawls, *A Theory of Justice* (Cambridge, Mass.: Harvard University Press, 1971). Amy Gutmann, *Liberal Equality* (Cambridge: Cambridge University Press, 1980) discusses variants of Liberal thought.

[5]See Jeane Kirkpatrick, "Dictatorships and Double Standards," *Commentary* 68 (November 1979), pp. 34–45, and Samuel Huntington, *Political Order in Changing Societies* (New Haven: Yale University Press, 1968). Complementarily, when social inequalities are judged to be extreme, the Welfare Liberal can argue that establishing (or reestablishing) the foundations of Liberal society requires a non-Liberal method of reform, a second "low road" of redistributing authoritarianism. Aristide Zolberg reports a "Liberal left" sensibility among U.S. scholars of African politics that was sympathetic to progressive autocracies. See *One Party Government in the Ivory Coast* (Princeton: Princeton University Press, 1969), p. vii. A recent example is the confused reaction in Europe and the United States to the decision by the Algerian government to abort an election that would have turned the state over to anti-Liberal Islamic fundamentalists and the subsequent warming of European Community relations with the Moroccan monarchy (*Economist* [January 9, 1993], pp. 37–38).

tion of the two. Realist theory would be falsely portrayed, indeed caricatured, if it were "domesticized" by being limited to authoritarian or totalitarian domestic politics or even purely unitary states. Correspondingly, Liberal theory would be caricatured if it were "internationalized" by being limited to assertions about the natural harmony of world politics. Some Realists are totalitarian; Hobbes justified authoritarian states. Some are democratic communitarians, such as was Rousseau. Machiavelli was a republican Realist. Some Liberals, such as Bentham or Cobden or Schumpeter, were homogeneously pacific. Others, such as John Stuart Mill, justified imperialism under some circumstances and intervention under others. No simplification well represents the actual philosophical and historical richness of their worldviews.

Instead, for the sake of expanding our analysis of the range of world politics, we need a conception of world political Liberalism that identifies what is special about the international relations of Liberal states but that neither caricatures nor whitewashes them. Worldviews align themselves on spectrums; they do not fall into neat boxes. We should be looking for a world politics in which Liberal individualism makes a difference, in which the good of individuals has moral weight against the good of the state or the nation. From the other side, we should be looking for a world politics in which the state of war is not the general characteristic of international relations (or individualism might not be making a difference, or adding something to Realism). In order to make sure that we have not created a circle of cause and effect, we will then need to make sure that our models are disconfirmable and that we are able to account for theoretical perimeters by distinguishing our Liberals from their philosophic cousins, the near Liberals. We will need to do this by accounting for differences in both causes and effects.

The core of Realism (to simplify) portrayed world politics as follows: a state of war among all states and societies, which is a condition in which war was regarded as a continuous possibility, a threatening prospect, in which each state had to regard every other state as presenting the possibility of this threat.

This was because:

1. Relations among states were anarchic, in that they lacked a global state. Trade, culture, even institutions and international law could still exist under anarchy, but none altered its anarchic and warlike character.

2. States were independent units that could be treated as strategic actors. The variations in state structure range from the abstractly unitary sovereign rationality of Hobbes to the ideally unitary moral rational of the General Will and sociologically diverse nonideal states of Rousseau, to the rational princes and imperial republics of Machiavelli, to the diverse states of Thucydidean Greece. Despite the variation, each theorist conceptualizes the state as struggling for a monopoly of effective or legitimate power. No one, no group other than the

state itself (prince, people as a whole, Senate, or Assembly) had a legitimate claim on authority. If a nonstate group had an effective counterclaim, then the state collapsed or collaborated and became subject to another state, ending anarchy, substituting hierarchy.

3. Some of these states sought to expand; others, merely to survive. None was prepared to engage in long-term accommodation or cooperation.

The perception that some societies would have good reasons to want to expand, that the sovereign similarity of all states made them functionally similar egoists, and that the international system itself lacked a global sovereign together, though in various combinations for each theorist, made rational states at least fear one another. They feared one another even if they were not inclined to aggress on one another, because they could not be sure that their neighbor was not prepared to aggress on them. Each was in a state of war that we call a security dilemma. The net result was that international goods have only relative value. They are relative because, as Hobbes opined, "clubs are trumps." At the extreme every good thus has to be measured first by the extent to which it contributes to security in a world where only self-help secures one's existence. Within an alliance absolute values can be appreciated, but only because they contribute to the relative superiority of the alliance over a rival alliance. And alliances are easy to break.

The Liberals are different.

World politics, rather than being a relatively homogeneous state of war, is at the minimum a heterogeneous state of peace and war and might become a state of global peace, in which the expectation of war disappears. If two or more Liberal societies coexist in the international system, then rather than have a security rationale governing all interaction—as it must for rational states in a state of war—other criteria of policy come into play. Liberal societies compete to become rich, glorious, healthy, cultured, all without expecting to have to resolve their competition through war. Formal and informal institutions such as international organization and law then take on a greater role in competition with the warriors and diplomats who dominate the Realist stage.[6]

This is because:

[6] Raymond Aron, *Peace and War*, chap. 1 identifies the centrality of the two for international politics, as Realism. Transnational complexity, though under the label of "Complex Realism," is well described by Joseph Nye and Robert Keohane in *Power and Interdependence* (Boston: Little, Brown, 1989). For an enlightening overview of the Liberal tradition, see Michael Howard, *War and the Liberal Conscience* (London: Temple Smith, 1978). And for a useful survey of current political science approaches to Liberal international theory, see Mark Zacher and Richard Matthew, "Liberal International Theory," in Charles Kegley, ed. *Controversies in International Relations Theory* (New York: St. Martin's Press, 1995), pp. 107–50.

1. Although states live under international anarchy, meaning the absence of a global government, they do not experience a general, state of war.

2. States are inherently different "units," differentiated by how they relate to individual human rights. So Liberals distinguish Liberal from non-Liberal societies, republican from autocratic or totalitarian states, capitalist from communist, fascist, and corporatist economies. Differences in international behavior then reflect these differences.

3. The aims of the state, as do the aims of the individual, go beyond security to the protection and promotion of individual rights.

Thus for Liberals, states behave differently and are not homogenized by the international system by being either competed out of existence or socialized into structural strategies. Some Liberals argue that Liberal states are inherently respectful of international law. Others argue that Liberal states are inherently peaceful, while authoritarians are inherently aggressive. Still others argue that Liberals are peaceful, but only toward one another.

Liberal states exist under anarchy (there is no world government), but their anarchy is different. Rather than being overwhelmingly a relative contest, a zero-sum game, their contest is a positive- or negative-sum game. They can win or lose together. A failure to inform may undermine coordination when Liberals are seeking compatible goals. In more competitive situations, a failure to trust may undermine cooperation when each would prefer at least one alternative to a failure to cooperate. This is because their insecurities can be solved by stable accommodation. They can come to appreciate that the existence of other Liberal states constitutes no threat and instead constitutes an opportunity for mutually beneficial trade and (when needed) alliance against non-Liberal states.

Liberals thus differ from the Realists. But they also differ from one another, and they do so in systematic ways. Each of the Liberal theorists, like the Realists, must make some assumptions about international structure, domestic society, and human nature. Liberals pay more attention to domestic structures and diverse human interests than do Realists. They all think that the international system has less than an overriding influence and so distinguish themselves from not only Structural Realists but also from almost all Realists. Still, compared with one another, we can identify "Image I" (human nature), "Image II" (domestic society), and "Image III" (international system) Liberals on the basis of where each variant locates predominant causes.

Locke we can identify as an Image I Liberal, who contributes an elaboration of human rights and consequent international duties. Schumpeter and the other commercial pacifists, Image II Liberals, focus on the effects of variations in domestic society, economy, and state structure. Kant, an Image III Liberal, tells us about the interaction of states–that is, about the effects of dyads and systems, about the genesis of a "Pacific Union" of Liberal states.

Close Cousins

This leaves us with a dilemma. How do we distinguish the Liberals from Realists who are democrats, republicans, and fellow analysts and advocates of popular sovereignty and human rights? Realists predict an inescapable state of war, Liberals, a heterogeneous state of peace and war. How do we explain the differing conclusions reached by three democratic or republican Realists—Thucydides, Machiavelli, and Rousseau?

Ranked by longevity, the earliest view of popular government is democratic imperialism. Democracies, it was said, are an effective, perhaps even the best means to launch imperial aggression. This is the view of Thucydides, which influenced classical political thought up to and including Machiavelli. Rather than peace, rather than restraint, power and imperial growth, excess and factionalism were the traits that Thucydides saw associated with democracy. Machiavelli's republic is characterized by social equality, popular liberty, and political participation.[7] The consuls serve as "kings"; the Senate as an aristocracy managing the state, the people in the Assembly as the source of liberty and strength. All three are expansionist.

The second view is that democracy should be associated with effective defense in all directions, a policy of isolationism within a pervasive and generalized state of war. In order to be completely self-determining, the General Will requires of its international relations independence above all else. This is Rousseau's vision.

In this part I shall examine what each of the Liberal traditions tells us about peace, war, and cooperation. I shall also explain how the Liberals distinguish themselves from the two types of democratic or republican Realists, who are also advocates and analysts of free and popular government.

[7] Machiavelli, *The Prince and the Discourses*, bk. I, chap. 2, p. 112. And see Quentin Skinner, *Machiavelli* (New York: Hill and Wang, 1981), chap. 3, and Harvey C. Mansfield, "Machiavelli's New Regime," *Italian Quarterly*, p. 52, for analyses of *The Discourses*.

CHAPTER SIX

Rights and Interests . . . and Institutions: Locke and Bentham

> Men living together according to reason, without a common Superior on Earth, with Authority to judge between them, is *properly the State of Nature*. But force, or a declared design of force upon the Person of another, where there is no common Superior on Earth to appeal for relief, *is the State of War*.
>
> —John Locke, *Second Treatise*

> Measures of mere self-defense are naturally taken for projects of aggression. The same causes produce on both sides the same effects; each makes haste to begin for fear of being forestalled. In this state of things, if on either side there happen to be a Minister, or a would-be Minister, who has a fancy for war, the stroke is struck, and the tinder catches fire.
>
> —Jeremy Bentham, *Plan for an Universal and Perpetual Peace.*[1]

THE THEORISTS OF this chapter and the next—Locke and Bentham, as founders of Liberal institutionalism, and Smith and Schumpeter, as founders of commercial pacifism—share the distinction of defining the ordinary reputation of Liberalism in world politics. Despite their many differences, Liberals, it is said, protect human rights, support international cooperation, profess international law, and support international norms. Liberal commerce and capitalism are inherently pacific. Indeed, these theorists serve well to foster both sets of

[1]John Locke, "*Second Treatise,*" in *Two Treatises on Government,* ed. Peter Laslett (New York: Cambridge University Press, 1690/1988), para. 19, and Jeremy Bentham, *Plan for Universal and Perpetual Peace* (London: Sweet and Maxwell, 1789/1927), p. 43.

impressions, but their arguments are well worth examining, being more sophisticated, complicated, and interesting than we often assume them to be.

The Liberals also need to be interpreted in their theoretical context. Unlike the Realists, the Liberals emerged in a political and philosophical space that was both secular and modern and was already occupied. Thucydides of course competed against a taste for the classical pantheon, and Machiavelli, Hobbes, and Rousseau wrote in the shadow of Christianity. (More than half the *Leviathan* was an antitheological theological tract.) But the Liberals also compete against the Realists. Locke reacts to Hobbes. The Commercialists react to the Realist Mercantilist view that foreign trade should be an instrument of war, and Schumpeter, as we shall later see, targets Lenin.

Like the Realists, the Liberals build upon one another. Locke draws upon the ideas of Protestant theologians and the traditions of the seventeenth-century English Puritan Revolution. Bentham builds on Locke and on classical market and democratic theory.

LOCKE'S LEGAL INSTITUTIONALISM

Locke's focus is on human rights and statesmanship as the motive forces of laws and institutions. His analogue among the Realists is Machiavelli, though Locke's is a work less of patriotic glory and more of Liberal moral strategy. But its most direct referent among Realist political philosophers is Hobbes. Indeed, Locke, among all the Liberals, is the closest theoretically to the Realists.

Liberal Institutionalists

Human Nature	xx
Domestic Society	x
Interstate System	x

Locke, who lived from 1632 to 1704, was a revolutionary. Yet in a Liberal society, such as the United States or Britain or France today, his ideas seem utterly commonplace. He employed an ordinary language clarity, rejecting all obscurantism and claims to mathematical certainty (no Hobbesian geometry here). He judged our passions and aesthetics by utility and the quality of explanations by their correspondence to the natural observation of the evidence they purported to explain. He saw the duty of the state to protect national security and uphold the "life, liberty, and property" of its subjects, for these are what the citizens set up the state for.

His ideas seem commonplace today, but only because of the success of the revolutionary philosophical and political movements for which he spoke and which he inspired. His great work, *An Essay Concerning Human Understanding*, established the epistemological foundation on which the Enlightenment was erected. His ordinary politics shaped the substance and even the political discourse of the American Revolution and the British evolution. Locke's "life, liberty, and property" became Jefferson's "life, liberty, and the pursuit of happiness."[2] Jefferson's justification of rebellion by citing a "long train of abuses, evincing a design," is also Locke's formula for justified rebellion in the *Second Treatise*.[3]

The record of Locke's life also makes it curious that he has been regarded as a conservative. Suspected of involvement in one coup, he was also identified, but not directly involved, with those in the organization and planning of a revolution, the Glorious Revolution of 1688, which established the supremacy of Parliament and reaffirmed the traditional rights of the individual subject. Although his *Two Treatises of Government* were not mere justifications for the revolution that established constitutional government in England (indeed, these were written, it seems, almost a decade before),[4] his work was characterized by what we would now call engaged intellectualism. It was scholarly but involved in commenting on and shaping the well-informed "insider's" view of current politics. In the end it earned him a position as the senior adviser and intellectual ornament of the Whig party, the urban and oligarchical faction that opposed the absolute government of the monarchy with its traditional Tory allies among the squirearchy.

As a young scholar at Oxford, Locke chose training as a physician primarily, it seems, to avoid religious orders (his alternative as a college tutor at Christ Church, Oxford). He nonetheless practiced little medicine other than as a private physician to his aristocratic patrons, the wealthy Shaftesbury family.[5] He first came to fame by means of a nearly miraculous operation on a liver abscess that saved the life of his patron, but his main preoccupation remained politics

[2] The actual translation took place through the Scottish Enlightenment, according to Garry Wills, *Inventing America: Jefferson's Declaration of Independence* (Garden City: Doubleday, 1978).

[3] Locke, "*Second Treatise*," para. 225.

[4] Laslett, "Introduction" to the *Two Treatises*, p. 33. See also C. B. Macpherson, *The Political Theory of Possessive Individualism: Hobbes to Locke* (Oxford: Clarendon, 1962) for the connections between Locke and Hobbes and the conservative bias of Locke's thought. For additional intellectual and historical background on the Second Treatise, John Dunn, *The Political Thought of John Locke: An Historical Account of the Argument of the Two Treatises* (London: Cambridge University Press, 1969) and Raymond Polin, *La Politique Morale de John Locke* (Paris: Presses Universitaire, 1984).

[5] On Locke's life, I have found Maurice Cranston, *John Locke: A Biography* (London: Longmans, 1957), Richard Ashcraft, *Revolutionary Politics and Locke's Two Treatises* (Princeton: Princeton University Press, 1986), and Peter Laslett, "Introduction" to the *Two Treatises* especially helpful.

and scholarship, both scientific and philosophic. He briefly served as secretary of the Council on Trade and Plantations, which was involved in colonial administration. In his middle years he became the political philosopher and occasional strategist of the Whig Party. And his final years were crowned by the publication of the great *Essay Concerning Human Understanding*, his political treatises, and the intellectual leadership of the constitutional, Liberal cause.

In those later years his aim in political philosophy, expressed both in *A Letter Concerning Toleration* and in the two treatises, was to expose the errors of religious oppression, divine right monarchy, and every other claim to absolute rule. He sought to justify the right to rebel and to have a government under law that protects civil liberties and property. Government for Locke meant the making of laws, the execution of those laws, and the defense of the commonwealth against foreign threats. Each of these functions was a trust held from the people. He advocated representative government without at the same time justifying all revolutions or democracy. To do this, he described the fundamental rights of all men, together with how those rights would both justify and limit the just exercise of state authority at home and abroad. His arguments reflected the consequent tension between universal human rights, on the one hand, and national prudence, on the other. Individuals had global natural duties, but they were bound to obey the laws of their commonwealth, the one to which they had consented either explicitly or tacitly. Prudent action by commonwealths then established a problematic world politics, one governed both by rights and prudence, by law and national security. By explicitly countering Hobbes's argument that free men would choose a Leviathan and remain in a state of war with other states, Locke makes a bridge to the Realists for the rest of the Liberal tradition.

THE LOCKEAN STATE OF NATURE

Like Hobbes, Locke planned to discover the just authority of the state by considering man in the hypothetical original state of nature. The state's rights and duties would simply be those the original owners—individuals—ceded to it. Conversely, politics among commonwealths would resemble the politics of individuals in the absence of a commonwealth.

Lockean man (just as is the Hobbesian and Rousseauian man) is morally equal, rational, and independent.[6] Locke also assumed that the original condition is anarchic, that there is no system of government. Unlike either Hobbes's or Rousseau's idea of human nature, Locke's man is obliged to obey a clear set of natural laws that confer natural rights and duties. The rights include the

[6] Locke, "*Second Treatise*," para. 4–7, 95.

classic rights to life, liberty, and property; and duties correlate to the extent that one has a natural duty not to violate the rights of others. Individuals, moreover, have a natural right to enforce those rights and to punish those who violate the rights of others. Murder, slavery, and theft therefore are categorically condemned even in the state of nature.

Why does (should) the individual have these broad rights? Life and liberty, the basic two, derive from a secular, rational appreciation of the equal personhood of all human beings. We should show to others the respect that we want shown for ourselves, irrespective of our special talents or relationships. We are not "made for another's use," and so we should treat one another as ends.[7] As significantly, God created us all. We are therefore all his "property," and we have no right to violate his property in either others or ourselves (i.e., suicide). Originally we justly acquire our own property, the third basic right, by mixing through our labor what we own (ourselves) with what no one else but God owns (nature), provided we do not waste and we leave "enough and as good" left over for others. (I shall return to the complications, including the invention of money, later.)

Individuals obtain the right to enforce natural law and punish violators simply because the law should be upheld and there is no one else or no institution to do it in the state of nature. Furthermore, we have a right to punish violators in order to help deter future violations and to extract just reparations from the guilty, provided we do so in proportion to the crime.

If in fact the laws were obeyed, one wonders whether anyone would voluntarily leave the state of nature for citizenship in the state of civil society. But the state of nature is rife with "inconveniences." These center on the imperfection of natural law as a source of law and order, including the inevitable partiality that flows from having judges judge their own cases.[8] But the state of nature is not, as it was for Hobbes, a state of war. "Men living together according to reason, without a common Superior on Earth, with Authority to judge between them, is *properly the State of Nature*. But force, or a declared design of force upon the Person of another, where there is no common Superior on Earth to appeal for relief, *is the State of War*."[9]

Rights are known and binding on moral individuals; reliable treaties (such as the famous example of those between "a Swiss and an Indian in the woods of North America") are possible and do create a degree of order that makes war a distinct violation of those rights. Laws are known; justice and duty, while subject to corruption, are not inherently subjective and arbitrary (mere words). War thus rests not on a condition, an inference, a possibility, as it did for Hob-

[7] Ibid., para. 6.
[8] Ibid., para. 90.
[9] Ibid., para. 19.

bes, but on an act or a declaration of intent. Yet the Lockean state of nature deteriorates into a series of possibly bloody conflicts when the laws are poorly known, partially judged, and inadequately enforced.[10] To avoid these ills and to obtain the conveniences of just and effective government, individuals consent to civil society, a commonwealth.

Unlike Hobbesian individuals, they will not "consent" to just any government; nor do they regard surrender to superior force as "consent." Hobbesian men are so terrified by the natural state of war that any form of order is an improvement. Lockean individuals seek to protect their fundamental rights and must consent to civil society for it to be legitimate. Indeed, any exercise of force, whether within the state of nature or within a tyranny, without right creates a right to reenter a state of war, a right to *rebellare*.

Civil society then is constituted and maintained by an implicit contract among all individuals to one another and governed by majority consent. Individuals form a commonwealth in order to protect the fundamental rights of life, liberty, and property. They choose a form of government—democratic, oligarchical, or monarchic—and allocate functions among a supreme "legislature" and a subordinate "executive" (administrative) power and a "federative" (foreign relations) power.[11] Individuals agree to obey the laws, and they cede the right to punish to the state, as long as the state protects the fundamental rights of individuals and abides by the provisions of its constitution. Locke prefers and praises (a qualified version of) representative democracy. But clearly the specific form of the state makes little difference to its legitimacy, provided the officials who compose it abide by the constitution and their obligations to protect life, liberty, and property.

Only foreign conquest dissolves a civil society. Governments, however, are dissolved by tyrannical acts: "Whenever the Legislators (or the Supreme Executor) endeavor to take away, and destroy the property of the People, or to reduce them to slavery under Arbitrary Power, they put themselves into a state of War with the People, who are thereupon absolved from any farther Obedience, and are left to the common refuge, which God hath provided for all Men, against force and violence."[12]

[10] These issues are informatively discussed by Richard Cox in *Locke on War and Peace* (Oxford: Oxford University Press, 1960), but I think he overestimates the degree of necessary convergence between the Lockean and the Hobbesian states of nature.

[11] "Federative" for the making of treaties *(foedera)* etc. in chaps. 8, 9, and 12 of the *Second Treatise*.

[12] Locke, "*Second Treatise*," para. 222. Liberal rebels mix with striking regularity the rhetoric of justification and explanation. Like Locke, they explain rebellions by "Arbitrary Power." Václav Havel, for example, stresses the exceptional character of the totalitarian regime and the arbitrariness of its power when he tries to explain to Westerners the origins of the Eastern liberations in the oppressive quality of daily life: "at the mercy of the all-powerful bureaucracy, so that for every little thing they have to approach some official or other . . . the

Locke's apparent radicalism, however, is tempered by the breadth of his conception of consent. In addition to explicit consent, silence presumes tacit consent. In the absence of rebellion, steady social interaction, obeying the laws, the ownership of property, and the mere use of money all imply consent.

LOCKEAN INTERNATIONAL POLITICS:
The Natural Law of Nations

"'Tis often asked a mighty Objection, *Where are,* or ever were, there any *Men in such as State of Nature?* To which it may suffice as an answer at present; That since all *Princes* and Rulers of *Independent* Governments all through the World, are in a state of Nature, 'tis plain the World never was, nor ever will be, without Numbers of Men in that State."[13] So Locke, like Hobbes, answers skeptics who doubt the existence of states of nature. But Locke has carefully distinguished the state of nature from the state of war. The international condition is not, if we follow the analogy, inherently warlike, a tract of time when the will to do battle must be assumed. Nothing short of world government removes Hobbesian states from the state of war. Instead, for Locke, it is a troubled peace where war is a clear act of aggression violating rights to life, liberty, or property or a stated declaration of intent to do so. All else is peace. And in peace, natural law—now international law—should rule.

The analogy raises four troubling questions about Lockean international politics and, more generally, about the Liberal foundations of international law.

1. ***Liberal Foreign Policy—"Federative Power."*** The commonwealth makes the "Legislative Power" "supream" because it enables the representatives of citizens to express the continuing consent of the majority to the laws of the state. The executive implements the law within the commonwealth and exercises the "prerogative" of emergency and delegated powers for the public good. And the executive exercises the federative power, the power to make *foedera* (treaties) with foreign powers and manage "the security and interest of the publick without."[14] This calls, above all, for prudence and requires, even more than the executive power, a degree of independent discretion in order to respond to the strategic interdependence of interstate politics. "For the *Laws* that concern subjects one amongst another, being to direct their actions, may

---

gradual destruction of the human spirit, of basic human dignity . . . lives in a state of permanent humiliation." Quoted in Zbigniew Brzezinski, *The Grand Failure* (New York: Scribners, 1989), p. 111. For an interesting application of Lockean ideas to Eastern Europe, see Zbigniew Rau, "Some Thoughts on Civil Society in Eastern Europe and the Lockian Contractarian Approach," *Political Studies* 35, 4 (December 1987), pp. 573–92.

[13] Locke, *Second Treatise*, para. 14

well enough *precede* them. But what is to be done in reference to *Foreigners*, depending much upon their actions, and the variation of designs and interests, must be *left* in great part *to* the *Prudence* of those who have this Power committed to them, to be managed by the best of their Skill, for the advantage of the Commonwealth."[15]

In short, the foreign relations of Liberal commonwealths should thus institutionally resemble those of Realist rational unitary actors and not be constrained directly by popular government or legislation. Liberal commonwealths will be governed by prudent strategists pursuing general interests, skillfully engaging in anticipatory games of strategy, all for the "advantage" of the commonwealth. They differ only in that they remain constrained by the duty not to violate natural law. They are rational *legal* egoists, bound to abide the law but also bound to exercise prudent advantage when they doubt that others are upholding the law.

2. ***Just and Unjust Wars.***[16] In the original state of nature we all have the right to enforce rights to life, liberty, and property against those who are guilty of transgressing them and creating a state of war. So too in international relations, states (to which we have ceded our enforcement rights) have themselves rights derived from our own to life and liberty (political independence) and property (territorial integrity). Any aggressor state that violates the natural rights of states or individuals makes itself the target of a just war of defense and even conquest.

As in the state of nature, a just conqueror and its allies have the right to punish transgressors (for murder, slavery, and theft) in order to deter future such acts and to exact just reparations. Locke thus goes considerably beyond what modern international law has been prepared to countenance. Sir Humphrey Waldock, president of the International Court of Justice, described three conditions permitting and limiting a just intervention to protect nationals: "1. an imminent threat of injury to nationals; 2. a failure or inability on the part of the territorial sovereign to protect them; and 3. measures of protection strictly confined to the object of protecting them against injury."[17] Modern law thus allows such interventions as the raid on Entebbe, Uganda, designed to free Israeli hostages, but it precludes the punishment and occupation Locke includes. Modern law reserves occupation and punishment for transgressions against state rights, such as Iraq's invasion and occupation of Kuwait, which led

[14] Ibid., para. 147.

[15] Ibid.

[16] This is the title of the leading monograph on the international ethics of war, by Michael Walzer. Locke discusses just and unjust wars extensively and with these titles.

[17] Humphrey Waldock, "The Regulation of the Use of Force by Individual States in International Law," *Recueil des Cours* 81 (1952), pp. 451, 467, cited in Lloyd Cutler, "The Right to

to a wide range of sanctions,[18] and against gross violations of human rights, such as genocide (which might justify occupation).

Jumping beyond the traditional legal standards of sovereign immunity, Locke advocated what are now the modern standards of individual accountability, the post-Nuremberg principles of international criminal law.[19] Indeed, Locke's standards are again, if anything, more demanding. They apply to the crimes of war and conquest but also to infringements on the rights of property. The first two are punishable by death ("Second Treatise," para 18, 178); the latter presumably by some lesser penalty. The penalties apply to all those who have "assisted, concurred, or consented" in the act of war, a considerable widening of what is called the circle of responsibility to all who planned (the criminal conspiracy) and assisted (soldiers) as well as to all who have concurred (Nazi voters, for example, if the Nazi party plan could be said to have been known in 1933).[20]

That said, Locke's restrictions on just punishment are even more important for the modern conception of the right of self-determination and of the rights of noncombatants in war. Conquest, even just conquest, gives no title to territory. The territory is worth more than any due compensation, and the people retain their right to self-government and self-determination, just as, Locke notes, the Greeks retained a right of rebellion against the Turks despite the centuries of imperial occupation (para. 192). Moreover, no punishment can be inflicted on any but those responsible for the war. No one who did not plan, assist, or concur can be harmed in any way whatsoever. Locke thus bars all collective punishment and explicitly excludes reprisals against women and children. Although property may be seized to exact reparations, no property belonging to wives may be touched, and the rights of legatees to a fair subsistence limit even the proportionate reparations that may be justly seized from a war criminal (para. 181–183).

So we see Locke provides a powerful moral Liberal foundation for the precepts of contemporary international law. At the same time, certain ambiguities in his principles illustrate a contemporary dilemma in international law. Any violation of natural law inflicted on anyone, anywhere in the original condition can be punished by anyone. We cede the right of punishment to the state. Can one state then punish the violations of natural law inflicted by another state on the second state's own population? Is there a right of forcible "humanitarian

Intervene," *Foreign Affairs* 64 (Fall 1985), p. 111.

[18] See Ian Johnstone, *Aftermath of the Gulf War: An Assessment of UN Action* (Boulder, Colo.: Lynne Rienner, 1994).

[19] See the London Charter of 1945 and the limitation of the "superior orders" and "act of state" defense. For discussion and excerpts, see Herbert Briggs, ed., *The Law of Nations* (New York: Appleton-Century-Crofts, 1966), pp. 1018–21.

intervention"? Could, for example, the United States have justly claimed the right to intervene to overthrow the governments of Grenada, Panama, Haiti, and perhaps Cuba for the violations they inflicted on their own populations?

The federative power and tacit consent together complicate global enforcement for a true Lockean. Although violations should be punished, only the members of a state have a right to rebel against their state. Short of rebellion, we must presume tacit consent, and tacit consent delegates the conduct of foreign policy to the state, which would then, to take it another step, have the right to call upon its citizens to defend itself from the foreign humanitarian intervention. The citizens have a right to refuse, and even to rebel, if they think the state has violated natural law. And a foreign intervention presumably could justly support them. But other citizens, not holding the same view, would have a right and a duty to defend the state against the foreign intervention. The "appeal to heaven" would be made. Prudent sovereigns would, we would hope, refrain from intervention until it was evident by a "long (and large) train of abuses" or mobilization of popular resistance that a just revolution was under way. Thus we see once more why the international condition would indeed be full of "inconveniences."

3. ***The International Distribution of Property.*** In the state of nature individuals have a right to acquire property by mixing their labor with it. So long as they (1) do not waste and (2) leave "enough" and (3) "and as good" for others, all others must respect those property rights.[21] The "tacit and voluntary" establishment of money alters all three restrictions, just as it alters the incentives to acquire that individuals experience.

The value of primitive commodities, such as apples picked from trees in the state of nature, has limits. There are only so many apples that an individual can want to acquire because our demand (use value) for them is limited and an excess will rot. The incentive to save, invest, and develop productive capacities is consequently also limited. But the value of money is unlimited. Money (e.g., gold and silver) neither can rot nor is subject to the inherent limits of use value; it has exchange value. Accumulating money produces no inherent "waste," and its accumulation has social effects that can generate "enough and as good" for others. Money can turn into savings, and savings into investment, which can generate employment. Provided an individual can find employment (at a living wage), then there is "enough" and, with enterprise and hard work, presumably as "good" an opportunity to acquire wealth as the original possessor.[22]

[20] For a contemporary discussion, see Walzer, *Just and Unjust Wars*, chap. 18.

[21] This applies to "acorns" and "apples." It also applies to "As *much land* as a Man Tills," and to "The Grass my Horse has bit; the Turfs my Servant has cut" (para. 28–33).

[22] Locke, "Second Treatise," para. 50. I borrow the Marxist anachronisms of use and exchange value simply because Locke's exposition of his labor theory of value becomes clearer with the terminology. There is in the literature on Locke an exceptionally interesting

What are the implications for international relations and the justice of the international distribution of property? Curiously, we find a contradiction, an odd combination of Liberal conservatism and radicalism.

a. On the one hand, the informal tacit process of justification of both physical and monetary property indicates that the lack of global institutionalization is little bar to just differences in distributions of wealth and income that are large. The rich can justly enrich themselves while the poor remain therefore justly poor. There are no barriers here that would not also be present in the state of nature, so both can be justified. Demands for redistribution based on egalitarianism or gaps in the standard of living have no place in a Lockean ethic.

b. On the other hand, the priority of the right to life makes superior demands. Individuals have a right to life, effectively a right to employment somewhere, and if that is not available at home, they would have right to emigrate to find work at a living wage. Barriers to immigration from the poorest of the developing countries, where starvation is rife, would on the surface be suspect in this Lockean ethic.

c. On top of that, that absolute prohibition of waste offers a powerful, moral foundation for an environmental ethic. Either God or we collectively own the "commons" unless they are justly appropriated by individuals—that is, without waste. Pollution and other forms of waste violate our rights. It is then *our* commons that are being polluted, and this gives us a right, whenever and wherever it occurs, to defend the health of the earth.

4. ***Grand Strategies of Lockean Peace?*** Lockean states remain at peace with other states unless they have been attacked or find their rights violated. Wars are thus created by criminals in the first instance, but the international condition is fraught with "inconveniences" that provoke even just states into war. Nowhere, therefore, do Lockean states find a state of secure peace or untroubled peace. Avoiding or mitigating the occasions of war is then the Lockean Liberal strategy of peace. It corresponds to contemporary conceptions of peace through improved regulation.

a. That *bias* and *ignorance* can cause war among well-meaning Liberals, Locke warns us, is the first "inconvenience" of the state of nature. Even though the laws of nature are clear, we will fail to reflect on their implications or be biased in their consideration in our own case.

b. That *partiality*, passion, and revenge can corrupt the adjudication of even clear law, biasing its application in one's own interest, is the second

debate on his status as a bourgeois apologist for modern capitalism. C. B. Macpherson launched the indictment. Valuable responses and additions include Peter Laslett, "Market Society and Political Theory," *Historical Journal* VII (1964); Alan Ryan, "Locke and the

"inconvenience." *Negligence* will make individuals remiss in the consideration of the others. Adjudication will lack, therefore, the *authority* it needs to be effective.

c. That *weakness* and *fear* will erode effective execution of the law is the third "inconvenience," Locke concludes. The power to enforce just judgments will thereby be absent.

In contemporary Liberal legalism, the "functional theory of regimes" developed by Robert Keohane addresses analogous problems.[23] The failure of cooperation (abiding by the law) out of weakness and fear (c) echoes in the Liberal theory of hegemonic cooperation.[24] If we begin with the Liberal assumption of international relations as a state of troubled peace, rather than a Realist state of war, then international law and order, rather than a competitive balance of forces, is a quasi-public good from which all benefit (like a higher wage for employees). If, none, however, find it advantageous to provide order through individual organizing effort, in the absence of a world state (a closed shop union, in the analogy illustrated by Mancur Olson), then law and order will not be provided although all would be better off if it were. Even an individual who might be able to bear alone the costs of enforcement may well shirk if she believes someone else in an equivalent position will do it (she will buck-pass). It fails because of the "weakness" of enforcement.

International collective goods, such as collective security against aggression, similarly fail out of "fear" when the sense of solidarity among the law-abiding states is insufficient to enable them to form an overwhelmingly large coalition against the aggressor.[25] A Liberal hegemon can resolve the dilemma of cooperation by providing the collective good if its private benefit from the collective good is larger than its private costs. It thus takes either hegemony or solidarity to redress this third "inconvenience."

Not all cooperation problems involving collective goods involve such daunting tasks of coordination among many actors as does the formation of an effec-

Dictatorship of the Bourgeoisie," *Political Studies* (1965); and Dunn (1969), chap. 17.

[23] Robert Keohane, *After Hegemony*, chap. 6.

[24] The landmarks in this political economy literature are Olson, *The Logic of Collective Action* and Charles Kindleberger, *The World in Depression* (Berkeley: University of California Press, 1973) and two excellent edited collections: Stephen Krasner, ed., *International Regimes* (Ithaca: Cornell University Press, 1983) and Kenneth Oye, ed., *Cooperation under Anarchy* (Princeton: Princeton University Press, 1985). And see the valuable collection of essays edited by David Rapkin, *World Leadership and Hegemony* (Boulder, Colo.: Lynne Rienner, 1990).

[25] Inis Claude, *Swords into Plowshares* (New York: Random House, 1957). Of course collective security would also fail if the aggressor or aggressors were simply more powerful than the united effort of the law-abiding states. For modern defenses of modified collective security, see George Downs and Keisuke Iida. "Assessing the Theoretical Case against Collective Security" (pp. 17–39) and Charles Kupchan, "The Case for Collective Security" (pp. 40–

tive labor union or collective security. Some could be resolved efficiently by free bargaining, provided there was an established legal framework of liability and ownership, perfect information, and low transaction costs.[26] These are the issues addressed by Locke's first two "Inconveniences"—(a) and (b). "Ignorance" of the law touches on perfect information, liability, and unsettled ownership. "Bias" and "partiality" refer to failures of settled authority, ownership, and transactions costs.[27] States, Keohane argues, establish regimes, international legal commitments, to help resolve these problems.

Locke's "Inconveniences" too might be mitigated by addressing ignorance through codification of the law.[28] Bias and partiality might be addressed through the development of a multilateral, institutionalized court and arbitration regime, such as the International Court of Justice, which allows for the intersubjectivity of a panel of judges to decide cases. And weakness should be met through collective security (or would be met through Liberal hegemony).

Each of these solutions should mitigate the problem, at least when they are compared with noninstitutionalized anarchic interaction. But human passions and interests, Locke thought, were resilient enough to transfer their action to the newly regulated arena. Indeed, that is why individuals, in order to escape the "Inconveniences" of the state of nature and enjoy the benefits of society, established sovereign commonwealths. And that too, at the international level, is what we can assume is the ultimate Lockean solution to international "Inconveniences." Unlike Hobbes, Locke gives us no firm reason why rational, law-abiding states—once their interdependence became sufficiently developed—would not want to take a next step toward supranational organization.

Short of such a transformation, Locke provides states with an important foundation for effective international law. But he also limits the authority of international law that makes it less than a sufficient solution to international order. Many international jurists (for example, the seventeenth-century Dutch jurist Hugo Grotius) argued that international law is authoritatively constituted by the agreements states reached. Locke agreed that promises made in the state of nature among individuals (and states) should be kept, since truth telling is an important virtue. But such promises could not, and should not, override the national interest ("advantage") of the state. The only law that has that standing

67), in George Downs, ed., *Collective Security beyond the Cold War.*

[26]The theoretical arguments are in George Akerlof, "The Market for Lemons: Qualitative Uncertainty and the Market Mechanism," *Quarterly Journal of Economics* 84 (August 1970), pp. 488–500, and Ronald Coase, "The Problem of Social Cost," *Journal of Law and Economics* 3 (October 1960), pp. 1–4. Keohane presents a clear application to international cooperation on pp. 85–98.

[27]High transactions costs allow time and occasion for partiality to have a sway over the outcome that might be absent in a more efficient decision process.

[28]See the valuable discussion in Charles de Visscher, *Theory and Reality in Public Interna-*

superior to particular advantage is natural law—the duty to protect life, liberty, and property. Thus it is only Liberal international law (law concordant with Liberal principles) that finds a categorical authority in Lockean international relations.

BENTHAM'S INSTITUTIONALIZED UTILITARIANISM

Jeremy Bentham completes the Lockean view of international organization. Bentham is a Utilitarian, a calculator of pleasures and pains, an advocate of the greatest happiness of the greatest number, and Locke is the great exponent of natural rights. Bentham nonetheless effectively addresses ways to overcome the "Inconveniences" that plagued Lockean international politics. Bentham, moreover, argues with a similar emphasis on personal decision and moral judgment and thus draws most closely on the effects of human nature. In doing so, he outlines the shape of an organized system of international cooperation and collective security.

Bentham, 1748–1832, was a man of contradictions. A polymath trained in law, he disdained the intricate traditions of the common law in favor of great systems of rational justice. He devised grand plans for social order and human progress, from model prisons to codes of laws, but also enjoyed a bit of scheming and entrepreneurship, as in his efforts to outfit a privateer against Napoleon. He criticized Locke's "dry, cold, languid, wearisome"[29] language. He regarded "natural rights," the foundation of all Locke's thought, as "nonsense on stilts."[30] Yet he completed Locke's view of international peace in his *Plan for an Universal and Perpetual Peace*, of 1789.[31]

Drawing on Liberal principles of individual welfare, free exchange, representative rule, and educable individuals, Bentham shared a view of the international inconveniences that Locke identifies: (1) Ignorance and bias in information, (2) partiality and negligence in adjudication, and (3) weakness and fear in execution reflect and then shape all politics, but they are particularly prevalent in the interstate condition.

Interstate anarchy lacks the social and political institutions that correct each of those tendencies. Highlighting what we now call the security dilemma and

tional Law (Princeton: Princeton University Press, 1968), pp. 138–63.

[29] *The Works of Jeremy Bentham*, ed. John Bowring (Edinburgh: 1845), vol. 10, p. 143, quoted by Isaiah Berlin, *Against the Current*, p. 130.

[30] Bentham, *Anarchical Fallacies* (1843), in *Bentham's Political Thought*, ed. Bhikhu Parekh (New York: Barnes and Noble, 1973), p. 269.

[31] Jeremy Bentham, *Plan for an Universal and Perpetual Peace* (1789), with an introduction by C. John Colombos, Grotius Society Publications No. 6 (London: Sweet and Maxwell, 1927). For an insightful overview of Bentham's ideas, S. Conway, "Bentham on Peace and War," *Utilitas* (May 1989), pp. 82–101, reprinted in Bhikhu Parekh, ed., *Jeremy Bentham:*

the consequent temptation to "preemptive war" and the susceptibility to domestically based "diversionary war," Bentham warned: "Measures of mere self-defense are naturally taken for projects of aggression. The same causes produce on both sides the same effects; each makes haste to begin for fear of being forestalled. In this state of things, if on either side there happen to be a Minister, or a would-be Minister, who has a fancy for war, the stroke is struck, and the tinder catches fire."[32]

Bentham's remedy was simply to supply what was missing. Beginning with weakness and fear, the third feature, he addresses them with collective security and disarmament. Disarmament (holding aside the arms necessary for dealing with pirates) will follow, he argues, when the causes of war are removed and so save the taxpayer large sums unnecessarily spent to the detriment of the public. He also builds, "as a last resort," a scheme of enforcement against the recalcitrant with a "contingent to be furnished by the several states for enforcing the decrees of the court." But he regards enforcement as likely to be unnecessary when the "Congress or Diet" formed to enforce the courts decisions under international law holds the authority to require that liberty of the press be permitted in all countries, so that the decisions of the international tribunal are promulgated in each country.[33]

Much more significant for Bentham therefore are his measures designed to deal with the second Lockean source of war, partiality in adjudication. His "Congress," constituted by each power sending two representatives, will have the capacity and duty to determine facts impartially, report its opinion, and circulate its opinion to all nations. He also proposes the establishment of a "Common Court of Judicature" designed to make sure that "the necessity for war no longer follows from difference of opinion" over rights claimed and duties owed. An impartial common adjudication will save the credit and honor (prestige) of each contending party, avoiding what would otherwise be seen as unwelcome deference to the partial will of another sovereign. This, he implies, should make those sovereigns more willing to abide by impartial fact-finding, arbitration, and judicial decisions, especially when those adjudications implement mutually endorsed, collectively codified international law.[34]

Bentham, however, realized that neither enforcement nor international judicial settlement would function effectively unless the deep causes for dispute were adequately addressed. To correct ignorance and bias, those deeper human failings, he therefore proposed the formation of a "Pacific or Philharmonic

Critical Assessments (New York: Routledge, 1993), pp. 966–85.

[32] Bentham, *Plan*, p. 43.

[33] Ibid., Proposition XIII:3, p. 31. But, as Conway notes, Bentham in his later writings backs even further away from forceful collective security, p. 977.

[34] For a discussion of Bentham's role in the development (indeed, the definition) of international law, see M. W. Janis, "Jeremy Bentham and the Fashioning of 'International Law,' "

Society" that would educate the public by undermining the passions of national glory, "religious antipathy," "unjust ambition," and the perceived "sincere and honest jealousy" of competitive interests.[35]

Vulgar prejudice, a product of passion, generates these prejudices, but so does pure ignorance. Fortunately the latter is correctable by the educative campaigns of bodies such as the peace society. First and foremost, the public must be made to realize that the objects for which wars are fought are neither desirable in themselves nor worth their cost in war.

Democracy assists the peace education effort by making officials responsible to the public, and it is the public that bears the (very large) costs of war while the elite reaps its (much smaller) benefits in, for example, "places" for official employment. But in a powerful critique of the effects of democratic representation per se, Bentham notes that the sanction of election is at best retrospective and often thus too late to prevent the aggression. It is, moreover, also too small a deterrent when weighed against the powerful interests of ministerial intrigue, pride of place, and government spoils. Lastly, the entire process of representation is regularly corrupted by secrecy. "Over measures of which you have no knowledge, you can apply no control," he tellingly remarks.[36] Alliances, agreements, more or less binding deals, not to speak of operations altogether covert are kept from the public, which then can have no influence on them.

The biggest problem, however, arises from the inability of representation to have the needed deterrent effect on aggressive, governmental intrigue even when government policy is public. When caught, ministers plead to the public: "It was your interest I was pursuing." Without a well-informed public, their plea will too often work. Much of Bentham's peace plan is thus directed at exposing the false conception of the value to be derived from imperial conquest and competitive tariffs. In doing so, he draws on his great predecessor Adam Smith, who attacked the arguments of the Mercantilists—the Realist political economists—and thereby outlined the shape of Liberal international political economy. I turn to his arguments and those of the other commercial Liberals in the following chapter, which examines how it is possible to create a material interest in peace.

CONCLUSION

When we compare Liberals with Realists, we can see much of Hobbesian rational unitary egoism in the Lockean "federative power," with its pursuit of "national advantage." In troubling times, Lockean "Inconveniences" might

American Journal of International Law 78 (1984), pp. 405–18.
[35] Bentham, *Plan*, p. 28.

well approach a nearly general state of war. But we also see one crucial difference. Lockean statespersons, like his citizens, are governed by the duties of natural law—life, liberty, and property. Lockean states then are distinguished, if Locke is correct, by a commitment to mutual trust under the law. In the bargaining literature, trust is crucial for stable agreements, and all rational egoistic bargainers will want to cultivate a reputation for it.[37] But Lockean bargainers, to take a further step, are committed to it by nature (or God).[38]

Bentham reinterprets human nature with a focus on utility and the effect of institutional changes domestically and internationally. In doing so, he outlines an early theory of international organization and collective security as supplements to the legalism Locke justifies. But he also relies on new conceptions of civil society and the interests of states, conceptions developed by the next set of Liberals, the commercial pacifists.

The late Cold War was full of surprises. Soviet communism had long stood up for the view that the world implacably divided in two: communist and capitalist. Nothing universal or impartial could join them. As a sign of the international revolution Soviet President Mikhail Gorbachev was about to unleash, we need therefore go no further than the great speech he gave before the United Nations on December 7, 1988. Reconciling Bentham's interests and Locke's rights-based law, the Soviet president announced to the assembled delegates: "As awareness of our common fate grows, every nation would be genuinely interested in confining itself within the limits of international law. Our ideal is a world community of states," he added, "with political systems and foreign policies based on law . . . to make the world safer for all of us."[39]

[36] Ibid., p. 32.
[37] Philip Heymann, "The Problem of Coordination: Bargaining and Rules," *Harvard Law Review* 86, 5 (March 1973) develops these points.
[38] See the seminal essay by John Dunn, "The Concept of Trust in the Politics of John Locke," in Richard Rorty, ed., *Philosophy in History* (Cambridge: Cambridge University Press, 1984).
[39] *New York Times*, December 8, 1988. Senator Moynihan sees the Soviet acknowledgment of the universality of international law as the revolution that ended the Cold War in *On the Law of Nations* (Cambridge, Mass.: Harvard University Press, 1990), chap. 6, "*Pacta Sunt Servanda!*"

C H A P T E R   S E V E N

Commercial Pacifism: Smith and Schumpeter

> . . . commerce and manufactures gradually introduced order and good government, and with them, the liberty and security of individuals, among the inhabitants of the country, who had before lived in a continual state of war with their neighbors, and of servile dependency upon their superiors. This though the least observed is by far the most important of all their effects.
>
> —Adam Smith, *Wealth of Nations*

> It may be stated as being beyond controversy that where free trade prevails *no* class has an interest in forcible expansion as such.
>
> —Joseph Schumpeter, "The Sociology of Imperialisms"[1]

COMMERCIAL PACIFISM RESTS on the view that market societies are fundamentally against war.[1] The very existence of free market democracies, such as the United States, Japan, our European allies and now possibly Hungary, Czechoslovakia, Poland, and perhaps a democratic Russia, makes for peace. This current of contemporary Liberalism also finds roots in classical Liberal theory.

The commercial pacifists—a second tradition of Liberal scholarship—focus on the pacifying international effects of markets and commercial capitalism.

[1] Adam Smith, *Wealth of Nations*, ed. R. H. Campbell and A. S. Skinner (Oxford: Oxford University Press, 1776/1976), bk. 3, chap. iv, p. 412; Joseph Schumpeter, "The Sociology of Imperialisms," *Imperialism and Social Classes* (Cleveland: World Publishing Co., 1955), p. 75. For a valuable discussion of contemporary aspects of Commercial Liberalism, see Robert Keohane, "International Liberalism Reconsidered," in John Dunn, ed., *The Economic Limits of Politics* (Cambridge: Cambridge University Press, 1989), pp. 165–94.

Commercial Pacifists

Human Nature	x
Domestic Society	xx
Interstate System	x

The tradition that Albert Hirschman has called *doux commerce* (soothing commerce) originates in the eighteenth-century attack on the Realist doctrine of relative economic power then advocated by the Mercantilists, who drew on the fundamental insights of Machiavelli, Hobbes, and other Realist theorists of war and peace.[2]

Although the commercial pacifists argued that representative government contributed to peace—when the citizens who bear the burdens of war elect their governments, wars become impossible—for them, the deeper cause of peace was commerce. Democracies had been more than war-prone in history. Thucydides's story of democratic Athens was familiar to all with classical educations. Passions could wreak havoc among democrats too. What was new was manufacturing and commerce—capitalism. Paine, the radical American democrat, announced: "If commerce were permitted to act to the universal extent it is capable, it would extirpate the system of war."[3] Paine built on and contributed to a growing recognition, systematically developed by Enlightenment philosophers, of a powerful insight: War does not pay for commercial manufacturing societies. The great Scottish philosopher-economist Adam Smith articulated that view most comprehensively. The Austrian economist Joseph Schumpeter extended it into a general theory of capitalist pacification.

ADAM SMITH

Adam Smith (1723–1790) wonderfully fits our image of the absentminded professor. He was shy and devoted to his mother, with whom he lived until her death, at which time an unmarried female cousin took him in. He wandered the streets and environs of Glasgow, often, it is said, muttering to himself. Appointed professor of logic at the University of Glasgow in 1751, he earned a reputation as an inspiring teacher, although his mind was easily distracted dur-

[2] Albert Hirschman, "Rival Interpretations of Market Society: Civilizing, Destructive or Feeble," *Journal of Economic Literature* 20 (December 1982). For another example of this tradition, see Montesquieu, *Spirit of the Laws*, bk. 20, chap. 1. For a discussion of Montesquieu's ideas, Stephen Rosow, "Commerce, Power and Justice: Montesquieu on International Politics," *Review of Politics* 46, 3 (1984), pp. 346–67.

[3] Paine, *Rights of Man*, chap. 5.

ing his lectures. He mastered theology, ethics, jurisprudence—all of which he taught—and Latin, Greek, French, and Italian. He achieved fame with the publication in 1759 of the *Theory of Moral Sentiments.* This treatise demonstrated how self-interested human beings could be motivated to pay heed to the virtues of benevolence and justice by means of an instinct for sympathy, which was the capacity to imagine oneself in another's place and to perceive one's own actions from the viewpoint of an "impartial spectator." Enjoying the company of a wide circle of brilliant friends, including David Hume, Edmund Burke, Samuel Johnson, and Edward Gibbon, he met the Physiocrats Turgot and Quesnay on his travels in France in the 1760s. The French economists persuaded him that wealth should be conceived of not as money but as the physical productive capacity of land. Back in Scotland, Smith broadened their ideas in what he planned to be a sequel to *Moral Sentiments,* and he published in 1776 *An Inquiry into the Nature and Causes of the Wealth of Nations.*[4]

Liberal Domestic Political Economy. The pursuit of wealth, according to Adam Smith, not only satisfied human interests but could, if well organized, contribute to moral perfection.[5] A system of "natural liberty" in which the state respects basic freedoms allows individuals a range of free rein (laissez-faire) to develop cooperative productive enterprises and satisfy their wants as consumers. Market exchange can produce a "natural progress of things toward improvement" because it encourages the efficient production of a division of labor and it induces individuals to consume and produce in ways that rationally adjust their activities to the intensity of their effective demands for goods versus money, work versus leisure, security versus risk, and present versus future consumption. Free market exchange thus can ensure that the consumer is "led by an invisible hand to promote an end which was no part of his intention."[6] The market generates a "public interest" that encompasses national wealth, a noncoercive society, and the freedom to choose and cooperate that emerges

[4]For Smith's life and influence, see Jerry Z. Muller, *Adam Smith in His Time and Ours: Designing the Decent Society* (Princeton: Princeton University Press, 1993) and Ian Ross, "Adams Smith (1723–1790): A Biographical Sketch," in Hiroshi Mizuta and Chohei Sigiyama, eds., *Adam Smith: International Perspectives* (London: St. Martins, 1993), pp. 1–26. A valuable comparison can be found in Edward M. Earle, "Adam Smith, Alexander Hamilton, Friedrich List: The Economic Foundations of Military Power," in *Makers of Modern Strategy* (Princeton: Princeton University Press, 1986). The edition of *Wealth of Nations* cited is the Glasgow edition (Oxford: Oxford University Press, 1976), ed. R. H. Campbell and A. S. Skinner, as reprinted by Liberty Classics (Indianapolis: 1981).

[5]For background on Adam Smith's moral philosophy: Donald Winch, Istvan Hont, and Michael Ignatieff, eds., *Wealth and Virtue: The Shaping of Political Economy in the Scottish Enlightenment* (Cambridge: Cambridge University Press, 1983), Robert E. Prasch, "The Ethics of Growth in Adam Smith's *Wealth of Nations,*" *History of Political Economy* 23, 2 (1991), pp. 337–51, and Muller. A useful collection of critical essay on Smith's economics can be found in Mark Blaug, ed., *Adam Smith,* vols. I and II, in the series *Pioneers of Economics* (Aldershot: Ed. Elgar Publishing, 1991).

[6]Smith, *Wealth,* pp. 443, 456.

when individuals have the option (and incentive) to make rational choices.

Smith is thus arguing not just for the economic superiority of laissez-faire. He is also a Liberal political and moral economist: Commerce can not only lead to individual material and psychic "happiness" but can also bring "perfection" by allowing the exercise of moral liberty—the freedom to choose—in a civil society. A society that permits "natural liberty" allows individuals to shape their own lives free from the need to submit to a feudal lord. The alternative to a free society, according to Smith, is paternalistic statism—ill informed, inefficient, usually corrupt, potentially violent, and morally degrading coercion.

The state of course has a legitimate role: It should do what the market cannot. States have three—and only three—duties: first, defense, "protecting the society from the violence and invasion of other independent societies . . . which can only be performed by means of a military force"; second, the administration of justice, "protecting, as far as possible, every member of the society from the injustice or oppression of every other member of it . . ."; and "third, and last," "erecting and maintaining those public institutions and those public works, which . . . though most advantageous . . . are such that the profit could never repay the expense to any individual or small group of individuals."[7] By this last Smith means what we would now call public goods, such as roads, bridges, and canals. Overseas commerce may need the security of forts and the assistance of an ambassadorial service. Religious instruction according to choice is of value to the society as a whole. And the youth, especially of the poor, will need state assistance to become properly educated in writing, reading, arithmetic, and the martial arts that are suited to the forming of an effective military force. Defense and the maintenance of the chief magistrate are charges that are best levied on the public as a whole through direct taxation; other public goods may call for general taxation, but only if local revenues or charges on the direct beneficiaries are not sufficient to meet their expenses. A bridge may be a public work, but it should be paid for, where feasible, by a local toll on users.

Liberal International Political Economy. Two of the hoariest myths of international political economy are that the Realist Mercantilists were interested only in power and the Liberals were interested only in wealth. The Mercantilists were said to focus only on maximizing a positive balance of payments (storing up gold the better to be secure), and the Liberal free traders, such as Smith, were said to have no appreciation for international security and to be prepared to trust all to free markets. Smith in his famous and devastating critique of the Mercantilists seems to have contributed to the first stereotype.

In a penetrating essay, Jacob Viner effectively frees the Mercantilists from the charge of power mania. Viner notes that the clearest formulation of what was to become the stereotypical Mercantilist view was that of Louis XIV's finance minister, Jean Baptiste Colbert, who said, "Trade is the source of

[7] Ibid., bk. V, chap. 1.

finance and finance is the vital nerve of war."[8] Colbert's statement has been used to illustrate the supposed mercantilist thesis that the purpose of trade is to generate a positive balance of payments and tariff revenue, hence an inflow of gold, which then may be used to finance wars, especially wars overseas. But the real object of Mercantilist policy, Viner has shown, was both power and wealth and was better represented in a comment by Lord Bolingbroke, an eighteenth-century British statesman: "By trade and commerce we grow rich and powerful and by their decay we are growing poor and impotent. As trade and commerce enrich, so they fortify, our country."[9]

It is equally wrong to see Smithian Liberals as neglectful of power or forgetful of the connection between security and wealth. Defense is the first duty of the sovereign and as such prior to "opulence." Smith's critique of the Mercantilists was based on their policies, not their ends of power and wealth. The real differences then between the Realists and Liberal political economists lie in their differing conceptions of the worlds in which states pursue their interests.

Specifically, Smith rejects two of the favorite policies of the Mercantilists: colonies and tariffs. In doing so, he argues that in rejecting colonialism and adopting free trade, rational Liberal political economists would thereby eliminate two potent causes of aggressive war. But his larger contribution lies in outlining an evolutionary model of the political economy of international security that explains the changing economics of defense and identifies a political economy conducive to peace.

Anti-Mercantilism. Smith denounces Mercantilism as advocating "beggaring all their neighbors," a view he sees as being foisted on a weak public equally by the "violence" of rulers and the "monopolizing spirit" of merchants and manufacturers. Mercantilism considers another's gain as one's loss. It makes "commerce, which ought naturally to be among nations, as among individuals, a bond of union and friendship . . . the most fertile source of discord and animosity."[10] This was the famous problem of relative gains versus absolute gains from trade.

Adam Smith addresses the relative gains problem in political economy in its three classic aspects. Relative gains govern either (1) because any external interference with domestic law and order is destabilizing, or (2) because trade can be manipulated advantageously and produces, in any case, very little mutual gain, or (3) because the insecurity of world politics means that only the relative gains are valued, since only they produce superiority vis-à-vis rivals.

Smith rejects the first view, associated with such Realists as Rousseau,

[8] Quoted in Eli Heckscher, *Mercantilism* (London: 1935), vol. II, p. 17, and Jacob Viner, "Power versus Plenty as Objectives of Foreign Policy in the Seventeenth and Eighteenth Centuries," *World Politics* 1 (October 1948), pp. 1–29.

[9] From Bolingbroke's "Idea of a Patriot King," *Letters on the Spirit of Patriotism* (London: 1752), p. 204, quoted in Viner.

[10] Smith, *Wealth*, I IV, vol. I. bk. IV, iii. c, p. 493.

because he sees international exchange as expanding the range of autonomous individual choice, which should be a fundamental purpose of social institutions and was indeed the key moral justification he proposed for market society.[11]

The second aspect, the economic problem, of relative gains involves the value of colonies and tariffs as sources of wealth. Colonies and tariffs are two aspects of the same problem for Smith. Both tend to privilege certain groups of producers and merchants over and above the true interests of consumers and the nation as a whole. Neither is inherently bad. Colonies expand the market and allow for a greater division of labor and hence greater efficiency and more product. Tariffs and other trade restrictions might be necessary for national security (to build a navy) or for temporarily subsidizing a foreign trade in a new and risky area.[12] But, generally, colonies and the trade restrictions associated with them are harmful. They stir up conflict with other countries. They cost money to the taxpayer in colonial military campaigns and in tariff administration. And they distort economic activity away from efficient allocations to the subsidized ones, reducing overall welfare by forcing consumers to buy dear (at home, one's own colonial imports, or in the colonies, metropolitan exports). This in turn reduces overall product by encouraging investors to allocate capital to artificially profitable (subsidized) production in place of the most productive investment.

Free trade—unsubsidized and unrestricted—is best for all, a view shared by most modern economists. Although an ideal decision maker possessed of perfect information in a world where no rival could retaliate might be able to allocate subsidies (or tariffs) optimally to take advantage of dynamic, high-wage industries with increasing returns to scale, the usual decision maker, who is faced with foreign rivals who are likely to retaliate, will find "strategic optimizing" to be unpromising. Japan and Sweden appear to have successfully pursued an optimum industrial policy in the early post–World War II period, but they succeeded in part because the industrial leader (the United States) was for strategic reasons not prepared to retaliate and they were investing in known, catch-up technology. Similar industrial strategies today are more perplexing in face of an unknown technological horizon, no leader, and likely retaliation.[13]

[11] See the discussion of Rousseau in chapter 4. For a contemporary discussion, see Stephen Krasner, "Global Communications and National Power: Life at the Pareto Frontier," *World Politics* 43, 3 (April 1991), pp. 336–66.
[12] Smith, *Wealth*, bk. IV, iii and IV, vii.
[13] The best discussions I have seen of these complicated issues are James Tobin, "The Adam Smith Address: On Living and Trading with Japan: United States Commercial and Macroeconomic Policies," *Business Economics* (January 1991), pp. 5–16, and Paul Krugman, *Rethinking International Trade* (Cambridge, Mass.: MIT Press, 1990). Tobin notes that although Krugman has made the best case for strategic trade, Krugman advocates it only under very specific circumstances, which Krugman did not find to hold for the United States in 1989, when he signed the "free trade" side of the Twentieth Century Fund study *The Free Trade Debate* (New York: Priority Press, 1989).

Free trade, however, does not solve the third problem of international *political* economy. Trade should generate mutual gains, but these gains need not be equal. For the pure (nonenvious) economist this is not a problem, but for a political economist it can be. What if the differential gains reduce security by, for example, advantaging a strategic rival? And what if all states are in a mutual state of war, balancing capacity against capacity, as the Realist argues they must? "In a world of competing states," the American political scientist Robert Gilpin has noted, "the nationalist considers relative gain to be more important than mutual gain."[14]

Pacific Evolution. The essential problem was determining when security was (and when it was not) a problem for international political economy. "The wealth of a neighbouring nation, however, though dangerous in war and politicks, is certainly advantageous in trade. In a state of hostility, it may enable our enemies to maintain fleets and armies superior to our own; but in a state of peace and commerce it must likewise enable them to exchange with us to a greater value, and to afford a better market, either for immediate produce of our own industry, or for whatever is purchased with that produce."[15] Wealthy France, by that account, should have been Britain's best market, and vice versa. Instead, of course, France in 1776 was Britain's greatest rival, and each raised great barriers to free trade against the other, which were justified by "national animosity" exacerbated by their closeness as neighbors and by the "mercantile jealousy" stirred by the "passionate confidence of interested falsehood" that rival merchants and manufacturers had foisted on the two publics. Their "real interests" lay in peace and free trade; their actual policies were bellicose and restrictive (IV, iii. c, p. 495).

Liberal political economists agree with Realist political economists on the importance of a political foundation for the international economy. Lacking such a foundation, economics becomes "politicized." Trade is dangerous, and economic dependence makes states insecure. Depoliticization, on the other hand, requires a political foundation. The Realists thus posited the need for hegemony—a dominating power that imposes interdependence and overcomes the tendency of equal states to prefer autarky to dependence. Liberals too sought a response to security-motivated searches for autarky, for hostilities resulting from insecurity would disrupt trade.

Could these insecurities and hostilities be curbed? Possibly. Smith is far from confident, but he does outline as a possible pacifier an evolutionary sociology of aggression, in which some societies are aggression-dominant and others peace-dominant and a history that evolves unevenly from the first to the second. He argues that "commerce and manufactures gradually introduced order and good government, and with them, the liberty and security of individuals, among the

[14] Gilpin, *Political Economy of International Relations*, 33.
[15] Smith, *Wealth*, bk. IV, iii.

inhabitants of the country, who had before lived in a continual state of war with their neighbours, and of servile dependency upon their superiors. This though the least observed," Smith added, "is by far the most important of all their effects."[16]

War, Smith seemed to believe, is a rational function of two factors: the spoils that successful aggression gains and the cost of war. The latter in turn is determined by the opportunity cost of war and the net costs of war (a function of the chance of winning, the direct costs, and the spoils of war). The larger the spoils, the lower the opportunity costs, and the higher the chance of victory, the more likely the war; and vice versa for peace.

The calculation changes according to the condition of society.[17] Among a nation of "hunters, the lowest and rudest state of society"—the society one finds among "the native tribes of North America"—every man is a warrior as well as a hunter. Hunting is a full-time occupation, and war takes away from hunting. The spoils offered by other hunting societies are slight, very much what the hunter already has or could obtain by further hunting. Other hunting tribes are likely to be as skilled at war as one another, and none of them generates large numbers of inhabitants or stable, hierarchical leadership. Aggression therefore makes little sense.

"Among nations of shepherds," such as the ancient Israelites, the Arabs, and the Tatars, on the other hand, aggression is much more attractive. War for them, united behind chiefs, is an efficient employment of their abundant leisure. Their flocks and families follow them in campaigns of conquest, some of which are driven by the need to discover fresh pasture and others by the search for the flocks and women that other pastoral nations afford. An outdoor life keeps them physically fit for battle, and pastoral economics allows great concentrations of forces, making them, unlike hunters, difficult to deter.[18]

Among nations of "husbandmen"—farmers—such as the ancient Greeks and Romans, military readiness comes easily. The life is healthy, and the technology simple, ditchdigging and fortification being close cousins. But for them the costs of war are significant. Time at war is time away from their fields and fixed

[16]Ibid. bk. 3, chap. iv:4, p. 412, quoted in Prasch, p. 348. Some contemporary international political economists have reversed Smith's argument. Where Smith examines the effects of economic development on the state and on international relations (trade and then war), they examine the effects of international trade and war on states and the domestic coalitions that rule them. See, for example, Peter Gourevitch, "International Trade, Domestic Coalitions and Liberty: Comparative Responses to the Crisis of 1873–1896," *Journal of Interdisciplinary History* 8 (1977), pp. 281–313, and Ronald Rogowski, *Commerce and Coalitions* (Princeton: Princeton University Press, 1989).

[17]We could almost say "stage" of society, but Smith also noted that reversals could occur. The fall of Rome led European civilization back from agricultural to pastoral society. *Wealth* bk. V, i, part 1.

[18]Smith approvingly cites Thucydides's observation (II:97) that the Scythians united could have conquered the ancient world, a remark prescient of the later success of the Huns and the Mongols.

GRAPH 7.1

Smith's Theory of War*

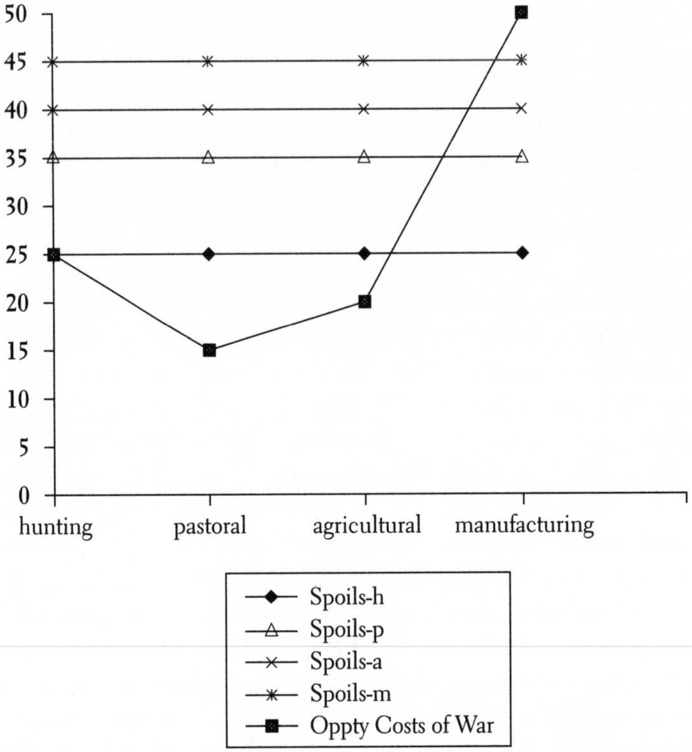

* Smith, *Wealth of Nations*, bk. V, chap. 1, 1, p. 698–708. This graph is adapted from one by Craufurd Goodwin in "National Security in Classical Political Economy," *History of Political Economy* 23 (1991), pp. 23–35.

homes. But if campaigns are fought after the seed has been sown and before the crop needs to be harvested, the opportunity costs of war are not too exorbitant. Then a fifth or more of the population can be spared for war.

But among a nation of "manufacturers" there is no leisure time. All is work, and every soldier is a laborer taken away from manufacturing. Manufacturing, moreover, unsuits laborers for the trade of soldier. Militias thus tend to be very unreliable, a militia of industrial laborers being much less capable than a militia of farmers. Sovereigns thus form professional standing armies, which must be paid in times of peace as well as war. War being so very costly, there then follows a natural incentive both to maintain peace and to neglect defense.

The neglect, however, is a serious danger of modern societies, Smith warns. Since the spoils of conquest rise with the state of civilization, manufacturing societies are natural prey for militaristic pastoralists and farmers. Modern societies must find a way to raise the net costs of aggression by reducing the chance of success. Standing professional armies fortunately do just that. Their superiority over militias is based on their ability to afford expensive weapons (firearms) and on the superior training that allows them to employ those more sophisticated weapons. Fortunately as well, Smith notes that their danger to civil liberty is much less than has often been assumed. The Roman professional armies destroyed their republic because they were a separate caste of soldiers. If the army is entrusted to the ruling classes, as it was in the Britain of Smith's day, it will protect the state and serve to educate unruly peoples. Even more, it will allow for civil liberty, because popular disturbances will be little threat to such a force.

We can infer that aggressive war is irrational for both hunting and industrial societies. Presumably, therefore, a world composed solely of hunting societies or industrial societies would tend to be at peace (if states were rational). In relations between the hunters and the industrialists—in worlds of pastoral or agricultural societies or perhaps especially the mixed worlds of uneven development—war would be a constant danger.

Modern anthropologists have touched on the issues Smith identified (though rarely making specific reference to his work). Anthropologists have identified physical sources of warlike behavior, suggesting war as a response to protein deficiency, and institutional sources, arguing that war is produced by the absence of peacemaking capabilities.[19] They have also discussed in some depth the effect of socioeconomic forces of the sort Adam Smith considered. Some of his views are confirmed; some not. Some hunting societies, despite mythic reputations for aggressiveness, are in the views of some scholars actually peace-oriented, as has been asserted of the Iroquois nations.[20] Other hunters and gatherers unfortunately do not appear to have been as peace-prone as Smith seems to imply. Armed intergroup conflict is a normal method of settling disputes and acquiring resources, other anthropologists have noted. But war is not a normal condition. Small in numbers, these tribes had to marry their enemies.[21]

[19] Marvin Harris, *Culture, People and Nature* (New York: Harper and Row, 1980) and K. F. Koch, *War and Peace in Jalemo* (Cambridge, Mass.: Harvard University Press, 1974).

[20] Mathew Dennis, *Cultivating a Landscape of Peace* (Ithaca: Cornell University Press, 1995) and Neta Crawford, "Cooperation among Iroquois Nations," *International Organization*, 48, 3 (1994), pp. 345–85. Smith neglects a factor some modern anthropologists have found to be significant: gender. Tribes in which males dominate or the primary gods are male tend to be more warlike than those in which the gender balance is more equal, according to Dorothy McGuigan, ed., *The Role of Women in Conflict and Peace* (Ann Arbor: University of Michigan Press, 1977). The causality might, however, run the other way: warlike societies may favor male predominance.

[21] E. E. Evans-Pritchard and M. Fortes, eds., *African Political Systems* (Oxford: Oxford University Press, 1940), preface, and Max Gluckman, "Rituals of Rebellion in South-East Africa," *Order and Rebellion in Tribal Africa* (London: Cohen and West, 1963), pp. 110–36.

Pastoralists, as Smith claims, may well have been much more aggressive. Smith himself probably had in mind the warlike record of the Huns, the Mongols, and perhaps even the Scottish highlanders. It is difficult to tell how representative the Blackfoot hunter/pastoralists' raiding party was, but in one account it resonates with Smith's speculations: "Each raiding party . . . might never see action again as a military unit. Its members were motivated much less by tribal patriotism than by hope of personal gain—the economic security and social prestige that possession of a goodly number of horses would bring them. The killing of enemy tribesmen and the taking of scalps were not major objectives of these raids. Many of the most active Blackfoot horse raiders were members of poor families who were ambitious to better their lot. . . . [But] there were also rich young men who loved the excitement of these raids and coveted the prestige that could be gained through success in war."[22]

Among the pastoralist Boran of East Africa, it was said: "To be a stock herder and to be a warrior then are not separate occupations, because being the former involves being the latter. A herder must not only guide the stock in his charge to good and safe pastures but he must also protect them from predators and raiders. . . ."[23]

Preindustrial agricultural societies, such as those of European feudalism, displayed a strong propensity toward war. So too did the pre-Hispanic Mixteca of modern Mexico, who fought generation after generation for the possession of land, each new claimant clan justifying its aggression by asserting an ever more direct descent from the original gods of the land.[24] The Hawaiian agrarian monarchy bifurcated the calendar year into periods of peace and war. They achieved peace during half the year, when the fertility god, Lono, held sway

[22] John C. Ewers, "Blackfoot Raiding for Horses and Scalps," in P. Bohannon, ed., *Law and Warfare: Studies in the Anthropology of Conflict* (Garden City: Natural History Press, 1967), pp. 327–44, p. 329 for quote; quoted and discussed in M. Margaret Clark, "The Cultural Patterning of Risk-Seeking Behavior: Implications for Armed Conflict" in Mary LeCron Foster and Robert A. Rubinstein, eds., *Peace and War: Cross-Cultural Perspectives* (New Brunswick, N.J.: Transactions Books, 1986), pp. 79–90.

[23] P. T. W. Baxter, "Boran Age-sets and Warfare," in Katsuyoshi Fukui and David Turton, eds., *Warfare among East African Herders*, (Kyoto: National Museum of Ethnology, 1977) pp. 77–78; quoted in Walter Goldshmidt, "Personal Motivation and Institutionalized Conflict," in Foster and Rubinstein, *Peace*, pp. 3–14. But Marshall Sahlins, in "The Segmentary Lineage: An Organization of Predatory Expansion," *American Anthropologist* 63, 2 (1961), pp. 332–45, finds that social structure (how the tribe is organized) is more important than mode of production. Both agriculturalists and pastoralists aggressed when they had segmentary lineage structures, which encouraged division and the search for new lands for the newly segmented tribal unit. In the famous case of persistent aggressive expansion by the Nuer of the Sudan a combination of factors was at work in which cattle shortage was a product of the demands of prestigiously large payments of bride wealth more than absolute land shortage or population pressure per se. See Raymond C. Kelly, *The Nuer Conquest* (Ann Arbor: University of Michigan Press, 1985), pp. 226–52.

[24] Jill Leslie Furst, "Land Disputes and the Gods in the Pre-Hispanic Mixteca," in Foster and Rubinstein, pp. 93–104.

(and the king was controlled), and they warred during the other half, when the virility god, Ku, ruled (and the king was active).[25]

An interesting, though far from comprehensive, study by Ronald Cohen of the "industrialization makes peace" thesis confirms its major propositions.[26] Cohen's sample (albeit very limited) of four preindustrial and five industrial societies suggestively highlights three generalizations: (1) Cultures are not static and deterministic with respect to war; countries change; (2) preindustrial societies are much more war-prone than industrial societies (Table 7.1); and (3) there is a slight tendency for a regime, or type of society, to become less war-prone over time, whether it is preindustrial or industrial (Table 7.2).

While the anthropological data are encouraging—Smith's commercially pacific manufacturing does seem to make a difference—they offer little ground for complacency. The two most destructive wars—World Wars One and Two—were fought among industrial societies. For modern societies, industrialization, rather than remove the incentive to fight, magnified the capacity to inflict pain.

Adam Smith's message for the international political economists of the dawning age of manufacture was thus at best one of cautious hope. Perhaps, he suggests, relations among industrial societies would be peaceful if they realized how uneconomic aggressive war could become.[27] He realized that France and Britain in 1776 were each other's greatest enemy, but this may have been either because both were in transition from agricultural to manufacturing societies or because both were very susceptible to irrational passions. The progress of society in both dimensions, social and moral, was the key. Adam Smith set out to discover the social foundations of moral behavior. Commerce and armies together could, he argued, push societies from servile dependency and a continual state of international war to something better, a civil society enjoying natural freedom and a prospect of peace.

JOSEPH SCHUMPETER

Joseph Schumpeter (1883–1950) offers us a modernized and more complete version of the Smithian tradition when he considers the international effects of capitalism and democracy. Schumpeter's "The Sociology of Imperialisms,"

[25] Clifford Geertz, "Culture War," *New York Review of Books* XLII, 19 (November 30, 1995), pp. 4–6, citing Ganath Obeyesekere, *The Apotheosis of Captain Cook* (Princeton: Princeton University Press, 1995) and Marshall Sahlins, *How "Natives" Think, about Captain Cook, for Example* (Chicago: University of Chicago Press, 1995).

[26] Ronald Cohen, "War and War-proneness in Pre- and Postindustrial States," in Foster and Rubinstein, pp. 253–67. Cohen is assessing the arguments of Comte's industrialization thesis rather than Smith's manufacturing thesis, but the data serve to confirm Smith's views as well.

[27] So too by implication would relations among hunting societies. Smith here seems to prefigure Marx's own highlighting of structural affinities between premodern "primitive communism" and postcapitalist true "communism."

TABLE 7.1[28]

Frequency of Wars per Decade

	Preindustrial				Industrial				
Country	Sokoto	Borneo	India 1707–1771	France 14th c.	France	U.K.	USSR	U.S.	Germany
Wars per decade	13.6	7.5	12.7	8.5	3.5	5.6	2.8	.86	.74
Mean wars per decade	10.6				2.7				

TABLE 7.2

Wars per Decade over Time

	Preindustrial				Industrial				
Country	Sokoto 19th c.	Borneo 19th c.	India 1707–1771	France 14th c.	France	U.K.	USSR	U.S.	Germany
Early	23	>10			4.4 (1816–1900)	6.1	1.7	.83	.83
			12.7	8.5					
Late	4.1	>10			2.5 (1901–1980)	4.6	1.8	.88	.63

[28]Tables 7.1 and 7.2 are from Cohen, p. 262. Cohen's data are drawn from Melvin Small and David Singer, *Resort to Arms: International and Civil Wars 1816–1980* (Beverly Hills: Sage, 1982) and Quincy Wright, *A Study of War*.

published in 1919, makes a coherent and sustained argument concerning the pacifying effects of Liberal institutions and principles.[29] Unlike some of the earlier Liberal theorists, who focused on a single feature (such as trade or industrialization) or failed to examine critically the arguments they were advancing, Schumpeter saw the interaction of capitalism and democracy as the foundation of Liberal pacifism, and he illustrated his argument in a sociology of historical imperialisms.

Educated in Austria, Schumpeter made a career first as entrepreneur, then as a scholar in the United States. His major contribution to economics lies in the theory of entrepreneurship as a source of economic growth. Ironically, although he became noted for his attack on Marxism-Leninism, he too thought capitalism would, after it had spread and developed the globe, decline into Socialist stagnation through the restrictions on entrepreneurship and the social welfare demands imposed upon it by democratic governments.

Before that gloomy day arrived, however, capitalism would develop the entire globe, dissolve the imperialist forces that swamped Europe in the late nineteenth century, and create a flood of pacifism that would transform the shape of world politics. The capitalist disposition, Schumpeter declares, was the necessary and sufficient cause of peace and anti-imperialism. But how does he justify this bold claim when it was the seemingly capitalist societies of late-nineteenth-century Europe and North America that divided the globe in an imperial scramble of unprecedented proportions and spiraled their rivalries into the disaster of World War I?

Imperialisms

It is important to note that he slips two idiosyncratic concepts into his argument. (Here is where he puts the "rabbit" *into* the hat.) First, he defines "imperialism" as "an objectless disposition on the part of a state to unlimited forcible expansion."[30] He excludes all imperialisms that were objectful imperialisms (e.g., defensive or motivated by concrete material objects, such as land, trade, etc). He also excludes all imperialisms that were mere "catchwords"—minor political slogans, not part of the inherent substance of the society's economy, such as was, he claimed, British imperialism under Disraeli and Gladstone in the late nineteenth century. (It is not too surprising that having excluded the imperialism of the largest capitalist economy of the century by definition, he exonerates capitalism.)

He thus traces the roots of modern, "objectless," imperialism to three

[29] Schumpeter, "The Sociology of Imperialisms," pp. 3–98. Schumpeter is also building directly on the ideas of the French sociologist Auguste Comte. For a discussion of a variety of industrialization theorists, see Raymond Aron, *War and Industrial Society* (London: Oxford University Press, 1958).

[30] Schumpeter, p. 6.

sources, each a social atavism. Modern imperialism results from the combined impact of a "war machine," warlike instincts, and export monopolism.

He illustrates these imperialist forces in six typical models.

1. ***The Egyptian War Machine.*** Stable, peaceful, agrarian Egypt was invaded by the Hyksos, Schumpeter recalls. The Egyptians formed an army of national resistance. But this army of ancient Egypt, created to drive the Hyksos out of Egypt, took over the state and pursued militaristic imperialism. Once necessary, the war machine later developed a life of its own and took control of the state's foreign policy. "Created by the wars that required it, the machine now created the wars it required."[31] And so, Schumpeter tells us, it fought wars for the sake of glory and booty, for the sake of warriors and monarchs—wars *gratia* warriors.[32]

2. ***Warrior Nations.*** Schumpeter adds that sometimes entire nations gear their way of life to war, creating a warlike disposition, "instinctual elements of bloody primitivism." This is the natural ideology of a war machine, but it also exists independently.[33] The Persians, he says, were a warrior nation from the outset.

3. ***Religious Imperialism.*** Divine commands could also drive a nation on an imperialist course. The god Assur demanded the destruction of nonbelievers, and the Assyrian military priesthood undertook to fulfill those commands.

4. ***Alexandrine Imperialism.*** The imperialism of one man also characterizes some imperial adventures. Alexander the Great's charisma and personal ambition dragged the Macedonians into imperial conquest.

5. ***Roman Imperialism.*** The Roman senators pursued Mediterranean imperialism in order to supply the slaves their plantations required and to acquire the military glory that their careers required *(cursus honorum)*.

6. ***Imperialism of the Court Nobilities.*** Both Louis XIV and Catherine the Great found imperial expansion not merely a useful way to enhance their own glory but also a valuable safety valve with which to keep their unruly court nobilities employed.

So what do all these imperialisms have to do with the modern nineteenth- and twentieth-century imperialisms of Germany, France, Italy, and Russia? Paradoxically Schumpeter tells us: Nothing and everything.

The absolute monarchies were the last clear-cut imperialisms. Nineteenth-century imperialisms merely represent the vestiges of the imperialisms created by Louis XIV and Catherine the Great. Capitalism and democracy are forces

[31] Ibid., p. 25.

[32] Schumpeter is suggesting something resembling a military-industrial complex of the sort President Eisenhower warned the United States about in his farewell address.

[33] Schumpeter, pp. 25–32.

for peace. Indeed, they are antithetical to imperialism. And the further capitalism and democracy develop, the more imperialism will disappear.

Capitalism produces an unwarlike disposition; its populace is "democratized, individualized, rationalized."[34] The disciplines of industry and the market train people in "economic rationalism"; the instability of industrial life necessitates calculation. Capitalist pluralism also "individualizes" as "subjective opportunities" replace the "immutable factors" of traditional, hierarchical society. Rational individuals then demand democratic governance.

And democratic capitalism leads to peace. As evidence, Schumpeter claims that (1) throughout the capitalist world an opposition has arisen to "war, expansion, cabinet diplomacy"; (2) contemporary capitalism is associated with peace parties; and (3) the industrial worker of capitalism is "vigorously anti-imperialist." In addition, (4) the capitalist world has developed the means of preventing war, such as The Hague Tribunal, and (5) the least feudal, most capitalist society—the United States—has demonstrated the least imperialistic tendencies. As evidence, Schumpeter notes (without irony) that the United States left more than half of Mexico unconquered in the war of 1846–1848.[35]

His explanation for Liberal pacifism is simple. Citizens have become rational materialists and have eschewed psychological militarism and chauvinism. The people's energies are daily absorbed in production. When free trade prevails, "no class" gains from forcible expansion. Trade restrictions merely raise the cost of commodities. Under free trade, foreign raw materials and foodstuffs are as accessible to each nation as though they were in its own territory. Only war profiteers and military aristocrats would therefore gain from wars. No majoritarian democracy would pursue a minority interest and tolerate the high costs of imperialism. And where the cultural backwardness of a region makes normal economic intercourse dependent on colonization, it does not matter (if one assumes free trade) which of the "civilized" nations undertakes the task of colonization.[36]

Modern (nineteenth-century) imperialism therefore rests on three atavisms: an atavistic war machine, militaristic attitudes left over from the days of monarchical wars, and export monopolism, which is nothing more than the economic residue of monarchical finance. The export monopolists are an atavism of the absolute monarchies, for they depend completely on the tariffs imposed by the monarchs (and their militaristic successors) for revenue.[37] Lacking a popular mandate, monarchs need revenues that they can collect easily and hide from domestic consumers; hence tariffs on foreign imports. Behind these tariffs, domestic producers reap monopoly profits and seek markets in which to dump

[34] Ibid., p. 68.
[35] Ibid., pp. 95–96.
[36] Ibid., pp. 75–76.
[37] Ibid., pp. 82–83.

their excess production. So, under export monopolism, export monopolists push for imperialist expansion as a way to expand their closed markets. Without tariffs, monopolies would be eliminated by foreign competition, so they ally with the war machine for political support. In the modern era, therefore, these imperialists gratify merely their private interests, and thus from the national perspective, their imperialistic wars are "objectless." Fortunately the superior efficiency of free competitive capitalism dooms these monopolists, their imperialism, and war—in the long run.

Later in his career, in *Capitalism, Socialism, and Democracy,* Schumpeter acknowledges that "almost purely bourgeois commonwealths were often aggressive when it seemed to pay—like the Athenian or the Venetian commonwealths."[38] But he stuck to his (pacifistic) guns, restating the view that capitalist democracy "steadily tells . . . against the use of military force and for peaceful arrangements, even when the balance of pecuniary advantage is clearly on the side of war which, under modern circumstances, is not in general very likely."[39]

Contemporary Commercial Pacifism

Schumpeter's arguments are difficult to evaluate. In a provocative analysis that resonates well with the spirit of Schumpeter, Richard Rosecrance has identified the vital consequences of the grand strategic choice between becoming a "trading state" and a "military state" with a discussion of the "atavistic" quality of the choices made by the postwar superpowers, the United States and the USSR.[40] In partial tests of quasi-Schumpeterian propositions, Michael Haas discovered a cluster that associates democracy, development, and sustained modernization with peaceful conditions.[41] But J. D. Singer and M. Small have discovered that there is no clearly negative correlation between democracy and war in the period 1816–1965, the period that would be central to Schumpeter's argument.[42]

Yet recently John Mueller in his *Retreat from Doomsday* has made a serious and provocative case for seeing world politics as not merely changing but as transformed before our very unseeing eyes.[43] War, he says, has become obsolescent. A durable, long peace among the developed industrial powers has changed international relations. The obsolescence of war—the transformation

[38] J. Schumpeter, *Capitalism, Socialism, and Democracy* (New York: Harper Torchbooks, 1950), pp. 127–28.

[39] Ibid., p. 128. He notes that testing this proposition is likely to be very difficult, requiring "detailed historical analysis." But the bourgeois attitude toward the military, the spirit and manner by which bourgeois societies wage war, and the readiness with which they submit to military rule during a prolonged war are "conclusive in themselves" (p.129).

[40] Richard Rosecrance, *The Rise of the Trading State* (New York: Basic Books, 1986).

[41] Michael Haas, *International Conflict* (New York: Bobbs-Merrill, 1974), pp. 464–65.

[42] Small and Singer, "The War-proneness of Democratic Regimes."

[43] John Mueller, *Retreat from Doomsday* (New York: Basic Books, 1989), chaps. 1–3.

of great power politics—is, he argues, a function of two developments. First, the physical costs of war, its very destructiveness, have made it intolerable since as early as the turn of the century and clearly since World War I. War has become "rationally unthinkable." Second, the psychic cost of war has increased. War has become "sub-rationally unthinkable." War is simply ridiculous. Hitler and Mussolini were therefore ridiculous aberrations, and they caused World War II. Instead, Mueller declares that war has become obsolete, as did dueling in the nineteenth century.

Dueling became ridiculous, as Mueller says, in the middle of the nineteenth century; before that it was very much required by honor. But we have to remember that dueling was outlawed before it became ridiculous. At the time of its being made illegal, truly harmful libels, slanders, and assaults could be addressed in the courts and punished by the law. Therefore only the petty insults and the minor bumping and pushing were left to the court of public opinion. In other words, dueling was not replaced merely by a change of public opinion but by a set of effective public institutions with the capacity to enforce the prohibition against murder and manslaughter. Dueling became a crime before it became absurd. International relations lacks just such a court and such a mechanism of enforcement that could address the causes of war and thereby make war truly as unthinkable as dueling is today.

The causes of war, moreover, are not just injured pride. Wars are also created by competition for scarce goods and by the very fear of war itself. Just as Sparta decided at the origin of the Peloponnesian War to strike before it became even weaker in the future, so wars, particularly nonnuclear wars, could still be driven by a form of rational calculus.

Lastly, not all democracies need be the same. The Rousseauian citizen, for example, cedes all rights to his fellow citizens, retaining only the right to equal consideration. In order to be completely self-determining, Rousseau requires that there be no limit but equality on the sovereignty and authority of the General Will. The resulting communitarianism is intense; every aspect of culture, morality, and social life is subject to the creation and the re-creation of the national citizenry. The tendency to enhance domestic consciousness through external hostility and what Rousseau calls *amour propre* would be correspondingly high.[44]

A study by R. J. Rummel of "libertarianism" and international violence is the closest test that Schumpeterian pacifism has received.[45] "Free" states (those

[44] Drawing on historical evidence of the early twentieth century, Van Evera (1990) reaches a similar conclusion about the dangers of militaristic nationalism. The comparison detailed here, however, suggests an even wider indictment of the danger of nationalism among democracies.

[45] R. J. Rummel, "Libertarianism and International Violence," *Journal of Conflict Resolution* 27, 1 (March 1983), pp. 27–71.

enjoying political and economic freedom) have considerably less conflict at the level of economic sanctions or above (more violent) than do "nonfree" states. The free, the partly free (including the democratic Socialist countries, such as Sweden), and the nonfree accounted for 0.24, 0.26, and 0.61 of the violence respectively.

These correlations are impressive but not conclusive for the Schumpeterian thesis. The data set is limited, in this test, to 1976–1980. It includes (for example) the Russian-Afghan War, the Vietnamese invasion of Cambodia, China's invasion of Vietnam, and Tanzania's invasion of Uganda, but it just misses the U.S. quasi-covert intervention in Angola (1975) and its not-so-covert war against Nicaragua (1981–1990). More important, it excludes the Cold War period with its numerous interventions and the long history of colonial wars (the Boer War, the Spanish-American War, the Mexican intervention, etc.) that marked the history of Liberal, including democratic capitalist, states.

The discrepancy between the warlike history of Liberal states and the pacifistic expectations of Schumpeter and the commercial Liberals highlights three extreme assumptions. First, his "materialistic monism" leaves little room for noneconomic objectives, whether espoused by states or individuals. Glory, prestige, ideological justification, and the pure power of ruling do not shape policy. These nonmaterial goals leave little room for positive-sum gains, such as the comparative advantages of trade. Second, his democratic states are all the same. The political life of individuals seems to have been homogenized at the same time as they were "rationalized, individualized, and democratized." Citizens, capitalists, and workers, rural and urban, all seek material welfare. Schumpeter seems to presume that no one wants to rule. He also presumes that no one is prepared to take those measures (such as stirring up foreign quarrels to preserve a domestic ruling coalition) that enhance one's political power, despite detrimental effects on mass welfare. Third, just as domestic politics is homogenized, so too is world politics. Materially monistic and democratically capitalist, all states evolve toward free trade and liberty together. Countries differently constituted seem to disappear from Schumpeter's analysis as "civilized nations" govern "culturally backward regions."

TWO LIBERALISMS

Locke and Bentham, on the one hand, and Smith and Schumpeter, on the other, offer us a fascinating set of choices within the Liberal tradition. Their arguments have important policy implications. In the post–World War Two era, West Germany and Japan appeared to choose a Smithian-Schumpeterian nonmilitary route to influence, becoming "trading states" and rising very quickly in the world economy, in part because they did not bear the burden of defense expenditures. Is their choice stable? Was their security simply provided at the expense of the United States, and if so, will the end of the Cold War require them to become war states once again? Can states survive by specializing in trade, or must they achieve military political security first? Are "clubs [still] trumps"?

These theorists also advance the dialogue on international theory. Locke looks back to Hobbes; Schumpeter, as we shall see, has built on Marx and Lenin while criticizing them. Bentham adds institutions that resolve gaps in Locke's international politics. Smith articulates the social and economic foundations on which Schumpeter builds.

Locke portrays for us an international condition of troubled peace, only one step removed from the Realist state of war and one fraught with "Inconveniences" that could deteriorate into war through the combined effects of bias, partiality, the absence of a regular and objective system of adjudication and enforcement. Schumpeter offers us an image of capitalist pacifism that starkly contrasts with the imperialism of the autocrats and the permanent state of war of the Realists. Bentham and Smith are complicated theorists who bridge Lockean Liberalism and Schumpeterian capitalist democracy.

The contrast between a Realist such as Hobbes and a First Image Liberal such as Locke is clear. Locke's international system, like Hobbes's, is anarchic. His state is based on representation and ultimately on consent, while Hobbes's is indifferent to these matters as long as the state is sovereign. Locke's citizens, like Hobbes's, are rational, independent individuals. The difference then lies in the importance Locke attributes to the duties to protect life, liberty, and property that he thought accompanied citizens' rights to the same. It is these duties that lead just commonwealths to maintain peace with one another, provided, that is, their natural partiality and the poorly institutionalized character of world politics do not overcome their duties to accommodate.

The contrast between Hobbes and Schumpeter is equally clear. Both regard the international system as anarchic. Both regard their citizens as individualistic, rational, egoistic, and usually materialistic. But Schumpeter sees the combination of democracy and capitalism as opening up a revolutionary transformation of domestic state and social structure. These societies are as self-interestedly, deterministically pacific as Hobbes's Leviathans were bellicist. Hobbesian Leviathans, after all, were merely Hobbesian individuals writ large, with all their individual competitiveness and egoism. Schumpeter's state is a structured whole, distinct from its parts, transformed as it were by an "invisible hand" (to borrow the classic commercial metaphor from Adam Smith). Market capitalism and democratic majoritarianism make individual material egoism and competitiveness into social pacifism. Markets make for collective solutions (equilibrium prices) separate from the motives of individual producers (sell dear) and consumers (buy cheap). Majorities constitute a combined interest through logrolling and least common denominators different too from individual interests. Democratic capitalism means free trade and a peaceful foreign policy simply because they are, Schumpeter claims, the first best solutions for rational majorities in capitalist societies.

The contrast between Locke and Schumpeter thus emerges as the contrast between First and Second Image Liberals. Schumpeter makes the peace, which is a duty of the Lockean Liberal statesman, into the structured outcome of capitalist democracy. Both highlight for us powerful elements of Liberal world politics. But if there is a long state of peace between Liberal republics, Locke offers us a weak explanation for it. (How do they avoid partiality and bias so regularly in these relations?) He also misses the persistent state of war between Liberals and non-Liberals. (Why are the Liberals so regularly more partial here?) Schumpeter misses the Liberal sources of war with non-Liberals, unless we should blame all these wars on the non-Liberals.

Kant and the Liberal internationalists try, as we see next, to fill these gaps as they illustrate for us the larger potential of the Liberal tradition.

CHAPTER EIGHT

Internationalism: Kant

> It can be shown that this idea of federalism, extending gradually to encompass all states and thus leading to perpetual peace, is practicable and has objective reality. For if by good fortune one powerful and enlightened nation can form a republic (which is by nature inclined to seek perpetual peace), this will provide a focal point for federal association among other states. These will join up with the first one, thus securing the freedon of each state in accordance with the idea of international right, and the whole will gradually spread further and further by a series of alliances of this kind.
>
> —Immanuel Kant, "Perpetual Peace"[1]

WHAT DIFFERENCE DO Liberal principles and institutions make to the conduct of the foreign affairs of Liberal states? Despite the contributions of Locke and the Institutionalists, on the one hand, and Smith and the commercial pacifists, on the other, a thicket of conflicting judgments suggests that the legacies of Liberalism have not been clearly appreciated. For many citizens of Liberal states, Liberal principles and institutions have so fully absorbed domestic politics that their influence on foreign affairs tends to be either overlooked altogether or, when perceived, exaggerated. Liberalism becomes either unselfconsciously patriotic or inherently "peace-loving." For many scholars and diplomats, the relations among independent states appear to differ so significantly from domestic politics that influences of Liberal principles and domestic Lib-

[1] Immanuel Kant, "Perpetual Peace," *Kant's Political Writings* (1795), trans H. B. Nisbet and ed. Hans Reiss (Cambridge: Cambridge University Press, 1970), p. 104.

eral institutions are denied or denigrated. They judge that international relations are governed by perceptions of national security and the balance of power; Liberal principles and institutions, when they do intrude, confuse and disrupt the pursuit of balance of power politics.

Although Liberalism is misinterpreted from both these points of view, a crucial aspect of the Liberal legacy is captured by each. Liberalism is a distinct ideology and set of institutions that have shaped the perceptions of and capacities for foreign relations of political societies that range from social welfare or social democratic to laissez-faire. It defines much of the content of the Liberal patriot's nationalism. Liberalism does appear to disrupt the pursuit of balance of power politics. Thus its foreign relations cannot be adequately explained (or prescribed) by a sole reliance on the balance of power. But contrary to the pacifists, Liberalism is not inherently "peace-loving," nor is it consistently restrained or peaceful in intent. Furthermore, Liberal practice may reduce the probability that states will successfully exercise the consistent restraint and peaceful intentions that a world peace may well require in the nuclear age. Yet the peaceful intent and restraint that Liberalism does manifest in limited aspects of its foreign affairs announce the possibility of a world peace this side of the grave or of world conquest. Liberals, contrary to the Institutionalists, have created something considerably more stable than a troubled peace constantly threatening an outbreak of war. They have strengthened the prospects for a world peace established by the steady expansion of a separate peace among Liberal societies.

This chapter highlights the differences between Liberal practice toward other Liberal societies and Liberal practice toward non-Liberal societies. It argues that Liberalism has achieved extraordinary success in the first and has contributed to exceptional confusion in the second. Appreciating these Liberal legacies calls, first, for another look at one of the greatest of Liberal philosophers, Immanuel Kant, for he is a source of insight, policy, and hope.

IMMANUEL KANT

Just as Locke is the theorist of individualist (Image I) statesmanship, and the commercial pacifists of societal (Image II) forces, Kant is the Liberal theorist of international interaction (Image III), distinguishing outcomes by differences in interaction. He highlights how the interacting pair (dyad) makes for outcomes that cannot be predicted by a dispositional analysis of the foreign policies of Liberal states. Peace holds only in the interaction between Liberals, he argues, not in relations between Liberals and non-Liberals. The peace they enjoy is, moreover, a state of peace, not merely successful deterrence or an absence of opportunity for war.

Kant

Human Nature	x
Domestic Society	x
Interstate System	xx

His life (1724–1804) gave little inclination of the revolution he was to ignite in the tradition of philosophy in the West. Born in Königsberg, a subject of Prussia, the son of a poor saddlemaker, he earned his tuition to the university by writing essays for his less assiduous fellow students and by winning at billiards (i.e., pool sharking). He took a graduate degree in physics, with a dissertation in kinetics, and began a long, exhausting and undistinguished career as a *privat docent* (tutor), teaching anything from anthropology to the sciences. At fifty-seven he suddenly burst upon the world with the publication of the *Critique of Pure Reason*, and over the next ten years he wrote the various critiques and other studies that were to lay the foundations of rigorous philosophy for the next two centuries.

Short (five feet), frail, and amazingly punctilious (housewives of Königsberg were reported to set their clocks by the regularity of his daily walk), Kant led a life almost solely of the mind. Still, he was in reliable contact with the currents of his day, reacting to both public and intellectual events. Indeed, it was the arrival of Rousseau's *Émile* that occasioned the only known, avoidable lapse in his schedule; he was so startled by the brilliance of Rousseau's arguments that he lost track of his time and resolved to respond to the Genevan. He did so by developing a moral theory that made a categorical imperative for individuals what Rousseau saw as the General Will of a society.

"Perpetual Peace"

Kant's "Perpetual Peace," a mature work, written in 1795 after he had established his system of philosophy, predicts the ever-widening pacification of a Liberal pacific union. It also explains that pacification, and at the same time suggests why Liberal states would not, regretfully, be pacific in their relations with non-Liberal states. Kant argues that perpetual peace will be guaranteed by the widening acceptance of three "definitive articles" of peace. When all nations have accepted the definitive articles in a metaphorical "treaty" of perpetual peace he asks them to sign, perpetual peace will have been established.

The importance of Immanuel Kant as an theorist of international ethics has been well appreciated.[2] Moreover, the ultimate aim of Kant's theory is to estab-

[2] A partial list of significant studies on Kant's international theory includes: A. C. Armstrong, "Kant's Philosophy of Peace and War," *Journal of Philosophy* 28 (1931), pp. 97–204; Karl Friedrich, *Inevitable Peace* (Cambridge, Mass.: Harvard University Press, 1948); Gallie, *Phi-*

lish the grounds on which a "moral politician"—"someone who conceives of the principles of political expediency in such a way that they [*sic*] can co-exist with morality"—can adopt a strategy of peace as a practical duty. To show that the duty is practical, Kant wants to demonstrate that it is not impossible. He does this by showing that it can be imagined to follow logically from human beings' pursuing their rational self-interest in the circumstances of the world as we know it.[3]

Kant's analytic theory of international politics is thus crucial to his project of eventual universal peace. "Perpetual Peace" helps us understand the interactive nature of international relations. Methodologically he tries to teach us that we cannot study either the systemic relations of states or the varieties of state behavior in isolation from one another. Like George and Martha in Edward Albee's *Who's Afraid of Virginia Woolf?*, the behavior of state A and state B cannot be understood in isolation from its pair.[4] Kant's states continue to live in international anarchy—in the sense that there is no world government—but this anarchy is tamed and made subject to law rather than to fear and threat of war. Kant's theory is, moreover, a theory of state interest and of what does and what does not constitute a threat. Just as the superior capability of another state would be inherently threatening in Hobbes's Structural Realists, so autocratic regimes would be assumed to be inherently threatening to Kantians. Rather than an alternative to rational national interest theory, Kant offers a specifica-

---

losophers of Peace and War; William Galston, *Kant and the Problem of History* (Chicago: University of Chicago Press, 1975); Pierre Hassner, "Immanuel Kant," in Leo Strauss and Joseph Cropsey, eds. *History of Political Philosophy* (Chicago: Rand McNally, 1972); Hinsley, *Power and the Pursuit of Peace;* Hoffman, "Rousseau on War and Peace"; George A. Kelly, *Idealism, Politics, and History* (Cambridge: Cambridge University Press, 1969); Patrick Riley, *Kant's Political Philosophy* (Totowa, N.J.: Rowman and Littlefield, 1983); Kenneth Waltz, "Kant, Liberalism, and War," *American Political Science Review* 56 (1962), pp. 331–40; Yirmiahu Yovel, *Kant and the Philosophy of History* (Princeton: Princeton University Press, 1980); Susan Shell, *The Rights of Reason* (Toronto: University of Toronto Press, 1980); Howard Williams, *Kant's Political Philosophy* (Oxford: Basil Blackwell, 1983); Roger Sullivan, *Immanuel Kant's Moral Theory* (Cambridge: Cambridge University Press, 1989); Sissela Bok, A *Strategy for Peace* (New York: Pantheon, 1989); and Pierre Laberge, "Kant on Justice and the Law of Nations," in Terry Nardin and David Mapel, eds., *The Constitution of International Society (forthcoming).*

[3]"On the Disagreement between Morals and Politics in Relation to Perpetual Peace," in "Perpetual Peace," p. 118. I will cite Kant's works from Immanuel Kant, *Kant's Political Writings,* ed. Hans Reiss, trans. H. B. Nisbet (Cambridge: Cambridge University Press, 1970). I cite "Perpetual Peace" (1795) as PP; "The Idea for a Universal History with a Cosmopolitan Purpose" (1784) as UH; "The Contest of Faculties" (1798) as CF; "The Metaphysics of Morals" (1797) as MM.

[4]This was the minimum condition argued by Kenneth Waltz to be essential to a systemic, structural model of world politics. The analogy to Albee's play is Waltz's as well; see *Theory of International Politics,* where Waltz's quotes, "That which is George or Martha, individually, does not explain what is compounded between them, nor how" (p .75).

tion of what does (and should) constitute the public interest that a Liberal state should (and usually does) rationally pursue.

Kant, like Hobbes, begins with the state of nature, which is a state of war. "States," he bluntly says, "like lawless savages, exist in a condition devoid of right . . . this condition is one of war. . . ."[5] International law constitutes no guarantee of justice in these circumstances. States therefore have the right to make war in this condition when they are injured (and legal proceedings do not provide satisfaction). But they also may make war (1) when they "believe" they are injured (and legal proceedings fail to satisfy the grievance) or (2) when the state experiences a "threat" as another state makes preparations for war or (3) when another state achieves an alarming increase in power.[6] From this last consideration follows the right to maintain a balance of power.

The rights of peace include neutrality, rights to guarantees, and defensive alliances. During war all means of conflict *(jus in bello)* are allowed except those that render one's own citizens "unfit to be citizens" of a possible eventual peace based on international law. Thus spies, assassins, poisoners, sharpshooters, propaganda: All are banned. So too are war aims *(jus ad bellum)* that involve punishment, permanent conquest, subjugation, or extermination. Just wars are defensive in nature. Conquest for the sake of reforming an unjust enemy states is permitted, forcing them "to accept a new constitution of a nature that is unlikely to encourage their warlike inclination."[7] But no peace should constitute a violation of the fundamental rights of the citizens of a conquered state.[8]

The state of war requires decisions on the basis of right, but it does not allow for security or welfare. The will to subjugate is always present, and the production of armaments for defense ("which often makes peace more oppressive and destructive of internal welfare than war itself") can never be relaxed. Only a true "state of international right" can establish peace. The "European balance of power" is nothing more than an illusion, like Swift's famous house constructed in such perfect harmony (balance) that as soon as a sparrow landed on it, it collapsed. Peace has to be founded on a different basis.[9] Thus, for example, the United States and the USSR were peaceful in their Cold War relations, experiencing very few direct casualties. And Venezuela and Argentina have never fought a war against each other, nor have Iceland and Indonesia. But nuclear deterrence goes a long way to account for the "peace" of the first, and distance and lack of capacity a long way to account for the second and third.

[5] Kant, MM, para. 54, p. 165.
[6] Ibid., para. 56, p. 167.
[7] Ibid., para. 60, p. 170.
[8] Ibid., para. 57, pp. 168–69.
[9] That is, it has to be constructed by changes in domestic structures and international relations among states.

None of these sets of relations escaped from the state of war. The Kantian peace, on the other hand, is a state of peace, experienced while relations are close and interdependent and irrespective of arms levels or technologies

Preliminary Articles. Kant begins with a set of six preliminary articles designed to build confidence among states still in the state of war.[10]

1. No peace treaty will be considered valid if it harbors a secret intent to resume war at some more favorable opportunity. True peace agreements should be distinguished from truces if states are going to learn to trust each other.
2. No independent state should be subject to conquest, purchase, or inheritance. This provision is designed to establish the norm of "territorial integrity."
3. Standing armies will be gradually abolished.
4. No national debt will be incurred with the purpose of enhancing international power. This provision is designed to limit the incentives to engage in war by requiring that wars be fought from current revenues.
5. No state will forcibly interfere in the constitution or government of another. Supplementing the second provision, this guarantees "political independence"—the second of the two principles underlying modern sovereign equality.
6. No state will commit war crimes—use poisoners, assassins, promote subversion—because these are acts that destroy the mutual confidence a future peace will require.

Together these principles are designed to build the mutual confidence and respect that establishing a true peace will require. Well-intentioned, "enlightened despots" (Kant praises his own Frederick the Great) should seek to further these principles, and they sometimes have.[11] But these principles alone are not likely to be effective in the state of war, when confusion and powerful incentives for aggression are prevalent. What is needed, Kant argues, is an institutionalization—a constitutionalization—of peace. The continuing dangers of the state of war make it "necessary to establish a federation of peoples [to] protect one another against external aggression . . . [going beyond an] alliance which can be terminated at any time, so that it has to be renewed periodically."[12]

[10] Kant, PP, pp. 93–97.

[11] Kant remarks on Frederick, ibid., p. 102. This point was drawn to my attention by Dr. Dominique Leydet.

[12] Kant, MM. para. 54, p. 165. In 1792 Madison came to the same insight Kant developed. Madison criticized "Jean-Jacques Rousseau's" plan for collective security. Actually, as noted in chapter 4, this was the Abbé de St.-Pierre's plan, which Rousseau had presented and dissected. Madison wrote: "Instead of beginning with an external application, and even precluding internal remedies, he [Rousseau/St.-Pierre] ought to have commenced with, and chiefly relied on, the latter prescription. . . . As the first step towards a cure, the government itself must be regenerated. Its will must be made subordinate to, or rather the same with, the will of the community." Quoted in Marvin Meyers, ed., *The Mind of the Founder* (Hanover: University Press of England, 1981), p. 192, and drawn to my attention by Stanley Kober.

The Definitive Articles. The first definitive article requires that the civil constitution of the state be republican. By "republican" Kant means a political society that has, from a formal-legal point of view, solved the problem of combining moral autonomy, individualism, and social order. A private property and market-oriented economy partially addresses that dilemma in the private sphere. The public, or political, sphere is more troubling. Kant's answer is a republic that preserves juridical freedom—the legal equality of citizens as subjects—on the basis of a representative government with a separation of powers. Juridical freedom is preserved because the morally autonomous individual is by means of representation a self-legislator, making laws that apply equally to all citizens including himself. Tyranny is avoided because the individual is subject to laws he does not also administer.[13]

Liberal republics will progressively establish peace among themselves by means of the pacific federation, or union *(foedus pacificum)*, described in Kant's second definitive article. The pacific union will establish peace within a federation of free states and securely maintain the rights of each state. The world will not have achieved the "perpetual peace" that provides the ultimate guarantor of republican freedom until "a late stage and after many unsuccessful attempts."[14] Then, right conceptions of the appropriate constitution and great and sad experience will have taught all the nations the lessons of peace. Not until then will individuals enjoy perfect republican rights or the full guarantee of a global and just peace. In the meantime, the "pacific federation" of Liberal republics—"an enduring and gradually expanding federation likely to prevent war"—brings within it more and more republics (despite republican collapses, backsliding, and disastrous wars), creating an expanding separate peace.[15] And Kant emphasizes: "It can be shown that this idea of federalism, extending gradually to encompass all states and thus leading to perpetual peace, is practicable and has objective reality. For if by good fortune one powerful and enlightened nation can form a republic (which is by nature inclined to seek peace), this will provide a focal point for federal association among other states. These will join up with the first one, thus securing the freedom of each state in accordance with the idea of international right, and the whole will gradually spread further and further by a series of alliances of this kind."[16]

[13] Kant, PP. pp. 99–102; and see Riley, chap. 5.
[14] Kant, UH, p. 47.
[15] Kant, PP. p. 105. Some have suggested, following the UH, that peace will be achieved only when all states have become republican. I think Kant meant that the peace would be established among Liberal regimes and would expand by ordinary political and legal means as new Liberal regimes appeared. By a process of gradual extension the peace would become global and then perpetual; the occasion for wars with non-Liberals would disappear as non-Liberal regimes disappeared. This interpretation suggests that "peace comes piece (peace) by piece (peace)" and that the UH should be read in light of the later and more complete "Perpetual Peace."
[16] Ibid., p. 104.

The pacific union is neither a single peace treaty ending one war nor a world state or state of nations. Kant finds the first insufficient. The second and third are impossible or potentially tyrannical. National sovereignty precludes reliable subservience to a state of nations; a world state destroys the civic freedom on which the development of human capacities rests.[17] Although Kant obliquely refers to various classical interstate confederations and modern diplomatic congresses, he develops no systematic organizational embodiment of this treaty, presumably because he does not find institutionalization necessary.[18] He appears to have in mind a mutual nonaggression pact, perhaps a collective security agreement, and the cosmopolitan law set forth in the third definitive article.[19]

The third definitive article establishes a cosmopolitan law to operate in conjunction with the pacific union. The cosmopolitan law "shall be limited to conditions of universal hospitality." In this Kant calls for the recognition of the "right of a foreigner not to be treated with hostility when he arrives on someone else's territory." This "does not extend beyond those conditions which make it possible for them to attempt to enter into relations [commerce] with the native inhabitants."[20] Hospitality does not require extending to foreigners either the right to citizenship or the right to settlement, unless the foreign visitors would perish if they were expelled. Foreign conquest and plunder also find no justification under this right. Hospitality does appear to include the right of access and the obligation of maintaining the opportunity for citizens to exchange goods and ideas, without imposing the obligation to trade (a voluntary act in all cases under Liberal constitutions). Liberal republican states, Kant suggests, would establish a peace among themselves while remaining in a state of war with nonrepublics.

LIBERAL INTERNATIONALISM

The historical record of Liberal international relations seems to support Kant's speculations. Liberal principles and institutions seem to have had three striking effects on the foreign affairs of Liberal states. They have created incentives for

[17] Kant, UH, p. 50.
[18] See Schwarz (1962), p. 77, and Riley (1983), chap. 5.
[19] Kant's *foedus pacificum* is thus neither a *pactum pacis* (a single peace treaty) nor a *civitas gentium* (a world state). He appears to have anticipated something like a less formally institutionalized League of Nations or United Nations. One could argue that these two institutions in practice worked for Liberal states and only for Liberal states. But no specifically Liberal "pacific union" was institutionalized. Instead Liberal states have behaved for the past 200 years as if such a Kantian pacific union and Treaty of Perpetual Peace had been signed.
[20] Kant, PP, p. 106.

a separate peace among Liberal states, for aggression against non-Liberals, and for complaisance in vital matters of security and economic cooperation.

The first of the effects of Liberalism on the foreign relations of Liberal states is the establishment of a peace among them.[21] During the nineteenth century the United States and Great Britain engaged in nearly continual strife, including one war, the War of 1812. But after the Reform Act of 1832 defined actual representation as the formal source of the sovereignty of the British Parliament, Britain and the United States negotiated their disputes despite, for example, British grievances against the North's blockade of the South, with which Britain had close economic ties. Despite severe Anglo-French colonial rivalry, Liberal France and Liberal Britain formed an entente against illiberal Germany before World War I. And in 1914–1915 Italy, the Liberal member of the Triple Alliance with Germany and Austria, chose not to fulfill its treaty obligations under the alliance to support its allies. Instead it joined in an alliance with Britain and France that had the result of preventing it from having to fight other Liberal states, and it then declared war on Germany and Austria. And despite generations of Anglo-American tension and Britain's wartime restrictions on American trade with Germany, the United States leaned toward Britain and France from 1914 to 1917, before entering the war on their side.

Nowhere was this special peace among Liberal states more clearly proclaimed than in President Woodrow Wilson's War Message of April 2, 1917: "Our object now, as then, is to vindicate the principles of peace and justice in the life of the world as against selfish and autocratic power and to set up amongst the really free and self-governed people of the world such a concert of purpose and of action as will henceforth ensure the observance of those principles."[22] Even in the quiet recesses of secret diplomacy, Liberalism has shaped the discourse of statesmen at crucial times of national emergency. In October 1938, as fears of war rose in Europe, President Roosevelt sent a special message to Britain. He asked the special envoy, Colonel Arthur Murray, in Murray's words, "to convey . . . to the Prime Minister . . . an assurance—in the

[21] Clarence Streit, *Union Now: A Proposal for a Federal Union of the Leading Democracies* (New York: Harper's, 1938), pp. 88, 90–92, seems to have been the first to point out (in contemporary foreign relations) the empirical tendency of democracies to maintain peace among themselves, and he made this the foundation of his proposal for a (non-Kantian) federal union of the fifteen leading democracies of the 1930s. D. V. Babst, "A Force for Peace," *Industrial Research* (April 1972), pp. 55–58, performed a quantitative study of this phenomenon of "democratic peace." And R. J. Rummel did a similar study of "libertarianism" (in the sense of laissez-faire), focusing on the postwar period in "Libertarianism and International Violence." I use Liberal in a wider (Kantian) sense in my discussion of this issue in "Kant, Liberal Legacies, and Foreign Affairs," Part I (1983). In that essay I survey the period from 1790 to the present and find no war among Liberal states. Recent work on the thesis of democratic peace is covered later in the chapter.

[22] Woodrow Wilson, *The Messages and Papers of Woodrow Wilson*, ed. Albert Shaw (New York: Review of Reviews, 1924), p. 378.

event of hostilities and the United States being neutral—of his [Roosevelt's] desire to help in every way in his power. . . . He [Roosevelt] said he wished the Prime Minister to feel he had, in so far as he, the President, was able to achieve it, 'the industrial resources of the American nation behind him in the event of war with the dictatorships.' "[23]

Beginning in the eighteenth century and slowly growing since then, a zone of peace, which Kant called the pacific federation or pacific union, began to be established among Liberal societies. (More than sixty Liberal states currently make up the union. Most are in Europe and North America, but they can be found on every continent.)

Of course the outbreak of war in any given year between any two given states is a low-probability event. But the occurrence of a war between any two adjacent states, considered over a long time, would be more probable. The near absence of war between Liberal states, whether adjacent or not, for almost two hundred years thus may have significance. More significant perhaps is that when states are forced to decide on which side of an impending world war they will fight, Liberal states all wind up on the same side, despite the complexity of the paths that take them there. And we should recall that medieval and early modern Europe were the warring cockpits of states, wherein France and Britain and the Low Countries engaged in nearly constant strife. Then in the late eighteenth century there began to emerge Liberal regimes. At first hesitant and confused, and later clear and confident as Liberal regimes gained deeper domestic foundations and longer international experience, a pacific union of these Liberal states became established. These characteristics do not prove that the peace among Liberals is statistically significant or that Liberalism is the peace's sole valid explanation.[24] But they do suggest that we consider the possi-

[23] From Barbara Farnham, *Roosevelt and the Munich Crisis: A Study of Political Decision-Making* (Princeton: Princeton University Press, forthcoming 1996). One can presume that Roosevelt's motivation, as in most political events, was complex. He did not categorically support every foreign policy of a democracy (nor should he have). He, for example, questioned the legitimacy of the British Empire. America had failed to support the democracies financially in the 1920s. Roosevelt was concerned as well to avoid a Nazi conquest of Europe and the threat a united Nazi Europe would pose to the United States. "On the Atlantic," the president also said, "our first line is the continued independent existence of a very large group of nations." (From a January 1939 briefing to the Senate Military Affairs Committee, quoted in John MacVicar Haight, *American Aid to France, 1938–1940* [New York: Atheneum, 1979], p. 98.) But Roosevelt's aim was not to establish a balance of power in Europe between Nazi Germany and democratic Britain and France but to defeat the Nazi forces altogether. See also Haight, pp. 30–31.

[24] Babst (1972) did make a preliminary test of the significance of the distribution of alliance partners in World War I. He found that the possibility that the actual distribution of alliance partners could have occurred by chance was less than 1 percent (p. 56). But this assumes that there was an equal possibility that any two nations could have gone to war with each other, and this is a strong assumption. Rummel (1983) has a further discussion of significance as it applies to his libertarian thesis.

TABLE 8.1

The Liberal Community
(By date "Liberal")[1]

Period		Total Number
18th century	Swiss Cantons[2] French Republic 1790–1795 United States,[2] 1776–	3
1800–1850	Swiss Confederations, United States France, 1830–1849 Belgium, 1830– Great Britain, 1832– Netherlands, 1848– Piedmont, 1848– Denmark, 1849–	8
1850–1900	Switzerland, United States, Belgium, Great Britain, Netherlands Piedmont, –1861, Italy 1861– Denmark, –1866 Sweden, 1864– Greece, 1864– Canada, 1867–[3] France, 1871– Argentina, 1880– Chile, 1891–	13
1900–1945	Switzerland, United States, Great Britain, Sweden, Canada Greece, –1911, 1928–1936 Italy, –1922 Belgium, –1940; Netherlands, –1940; Argentina, –1943 France, –1940 Chile, –1924, 1932 Australia, 1901	29

TABLE 8.1 (continued)

Period		Total Number
	Norway, 1905–1940 New Zealand, 1907– Colombia, 1910–1949 Denmark, 1914–1940 Poland, 1917–1935 Latvia, 1922–1934 Germany, 1918–1932 Austria, 1918–1934 Estonia, 1919–1934 Finland, 1919– Uruguay, 1919– Costa Rica, 1919– Czechoslovakia 1920–1939 Ireland, 1920– Mexico, 1928– Lebanon, 1944–	
1945[4]	Switzerland, the United States, Great Britain, Sweden Canada, Australia, New Zealand, Finland, Ireland, Mexico Uruguay, –1973; 1985– Chile, –1973; 1990– Lebanon, –1975 Costa Rica, –1948, 1953– Iceland, 1944– France, 1945– Denmark, 1945– Norway, 1945– Austria, 1945– Brazil, 1945–1954, 1955–1964; 1985– Belgium, 1946– Netherlands, 1946– Italy, 1946– Philippines, 1946–1972; 1987– India, 1947–1975, 1977– Sri Lanka, 1948–1961, 1963–1971, 1978–1983, 1988– Ecuador, 1948–1963, 1979–	68

Period		Total Number
	Israel, 1949–	
	West Germany, 1949–	
	Greece, 1950–1967, 1975–	
	Peru 1950–1962, 1963–1968, 1980–	
	Turkey, 1950–1960, 1966–1971; 1984–	
	Japan, 1951–	
	Bolivia, 1956–1969, 1982–	
	Colombia, 1958–	
	Venezuela, 1959–	
	Nigeria, 1961–1964, 1979–1984	
	Jamaica, 1962–	
	Trinidad and Tobago, 1962–	
	Senegal, 1963–	
	Malaysia, 1963–	
	Botswana, 1966–	
	Singapore, 1965–	
	Portugal, 1976–	
	Spain, 1978–	
	Dominican Republic, 1978–	
	Ecuador, 1978–	
	Peru, 1980–1990	
	Honduras, 1981–	
	Papua New Guinea, 1982–	
	El Salvador, 1984–	
	Argentina, 1983–	
	Uruguay, 1985–	
	Mauritius, 1987–	
	South Korea, 1988–	
	Taiwan, 1988–	
	Thailand, 1988–	
	Pakistan, 1988–	
	Panama, 1989–	
	Paraguay, 1989–	
	Madagascar, 1990–	
	Mongolia, 1990–	
	Namibia, 1990–	
	Nepal, 1990–	

TABLE 8.1 (continued)

Period		Total Number
	Nicaragua, 1990–	
	Poland, 1990–	
	Hungary, 1990–	
	Czechoslovakia, 1990–	

[1]I have drawn up this *approximate* list of Liberal regimes (including regimes that were Liberal democratic as of 1990) according to the four "Kantian" institutions described as essential: market and private property economies; polities that are externally sovereign; citizens who possess juridical rights; and "republican" (whether republican or parliamentary monarchy), representative government. This last includes the requirement that the legislative branch have an effective role in public policy and be formally and competitively (either inter- or intraparty) elected. Furthermore, I have taken into account whether male suffrage is wide (that is, 30 percent) or, as Kant would have had it (MM, p. 139), open to "achievement" by inhabitants (for example, to poll tax payers or householders) of the national or metropolitan territory. (This list of Liberal regimes is thus more inclusive than a list of democratic regimes, or polyarchies [G. Bingham Powell, *Contemporary Democracies* (Cambridge, Mass.: Harvard University Press, 1982), p. 5]).) Female suffrage is granted within a generation of its being demanded by an extensive female suffrage movement, and representative government is internally sovereign (for example, including and especially over military and foreign affairs) as well as stable (in existence for at least three years). Arthur Banks and William Overstreet, eds., *A Political Handbook of the World, 1982–83* (New York: McGraw-Hill, 1983); United Kingdom, Foreign and Commonwealth Office, *A Yearbook of the Commonwealth 1980* (London: HMSO, 1980), *The Europa Yearbook for 1985* (London: Europa Publications, 1985), 2 vols.; William Langer, ed., *The Encyclopedia of World History* (Boston: Houghton Mifflin, 1968); U.S. Department of State, *Country Reports on Human Rights Practices* (Washington, D.C.: Government Printing Office, 1981); Raymond Gastil, *Freedom in the World 1985* (New York, Freedom House, 1985); R. Bruce McColm and Freedom House Survey Team, eds., *Freedom in the World 1990–1991* (New York: Freedom House, 1991); and James Finn et al., *Freedom in the World 1994–1995* (New York: Freedom House, 1995).

[2]There are domestic variations within these Liberal regimes. For example, Switzerland was Liberal only in certain cantons; the United States was Liberal only north of the Mason-Dixon line until 1865, when it became Liberal throughout. These lists also exclude ancient "republics," since none appears to fit Kant's criteria (Stephen Holmes, "Aristippus in and out of Athens," *American Political Science Review* 73, 1 [1979], pp. 113–28).

[3]Canada, as a commonwealth within the British Empire, did not have formal control of its foreign policy during this period.

[4]Selected list, excludes Liberal regimes with populations less than one million. These include all states categorized as "Free" by Freedom House and those "Partly Free" (at least 4 on the political scale and 5 on the civil liberties scale).

bility that Liberals have indeed established a separate peace—but only among themselves.

This is a feature, moreover, that appears to be special to Liberal societies. Neither specific regional attributes nor historic alliances or friendships account for the wide reach of the Liberal peace. The peace extends as far as, and no farther than, the relations among Liberal states, not including non-Liberal states in an otherwise Liberal region (such as the North Atlantic during the 1930s) or excluding Liberal states in a less Liberal region (such as Central America or Africa).

Relations among any group of states with similar social structures or with compatible values or pluralistic social structures are not similarly peaceful.[25] Feudal warfare was frequent and very much a sport of the monarchs and nobility. There have not been enough truly totalitarian, fascist powers (nor have they lasted long enough) to test fairly their pacific compatibility, but fascist powers in the wider sense of nationalist, military dictatorships fought one another in the 1930s in Eastern Europe. Communist powers have engaged in wars more recently in East Asia when China invaded Vietnam and Vietnam invaded Cambodia. We have not had enough democratic Socialist societies to consider the relevance of Socialist pacification. The more abstract category of pluralism does not suffice. Certainly Germany was pluralist when it engaged in war with Liberal states in 1914; Japan as well in 1941. But they were not Liberal. Peace among Liberals thus appears to be a special characteristic.

Here the predictions of Liberal pacifists are borne out: Liberal states do exercise peaceful restraint, and a separate peace exists among them. This separate peace provides a solid foundation for the United States' crucial alliances with the Liberal powers (NATO, the Japanese alliance, ANZUS). This foundation appears to be impervious to the quarrels with allies that have bedeviled many U.S. administrations. It also offers the promise of a continuing peace among Liberal states. And as the number of Liberal states increases, it announces the possibility of global peace this side of the grave or world conquest.

Liberalism also carries with it a second effect—what Hume called "imprudent vehemence," or aggression against non-Liberals.[26] Peaceful restraint seems

[25]There is a rich contemporary literature devoted to explaining international cooperation and integration. Karl Deutsch *et al.*, *Political Community and the North Atlantic Area* (Princeton: Princeton University Press, 1957) develops the idea of a "pluralistic security community" that bears a resemblance to the pacific union, but Deutsch limits it geographically and finds compatibility of values, mutual responsiveness, and predictability of behavior among decision makers as its essential foundations. These are important, but their particular content, Liberalism, appears to be more telling. All three traits characterized the eighteenth-century state of war and balance of power. Joseph Nye in *Peace in Parts* (Boston: Little, Brown, 1971) steps away from the geographic limits Deutsch sets and focuses on levels of development; but his analysis is directed toward explaining integration—a more intensive form of cooperation than the pacific union.

[26]Hume, "Of the Balance of Power," *Essays: Moral, Political, and Literary*, pp. 346–47. With "imprudent vehemence," Hume refers to the reluctance to negotiate an early peace with France and the total scale of the effort devoted to persecuting that war, which together were responsible for over half the length of the fighting and an enormous war debt. Hume of course is not describing fully Liberal republics as defined here, but the characteristics he describes do seem to reflect some of the Liberal republican features of the British eighteenth-century constitution (the influence of both popular opinion and a representative [even if severely limited] legislature). He contrasts these effects with the "prudent politics" that should govern the balance of power and with the special but different failings characteristic

TABLE 8.2

International Wars Listed Chronologically*

British-Maharattan (1817–1818)	Franco-Mexicuuan (1862–1867)
Greek (1821–1828)	Ecuadorian-Colombian (1863)
Franco-Spanish (1823)	Second Polish (1863–1864)
First Anglo-Burmese (1823–1826)	Spanish-Santo Dominican (1863–1865)
Javanese (1825–1830)	Second Schleswig-Holstein (1864)
Russo-Persian (1826–1828)	Lopez (1864–1870)
Russo-Turkish (1828–1829)	Spanish-Chilean (1865–1866)
First Polish (1831)	Seven Weeks (1866)
First Syrian (1831–1832)	Ten Years (1868–1878)
Texan (1835–1836)	Franco-Prussian (1870–1871)
First British-Afghan (1838–1842)	Dutch-Achinese (1873–1878)
Second Syrian (1839–1840)	Balkan (1875–1877)
Franco-Algerian (1839–1847)	Russo-Turkish (1877–1878)
Peruvian-Bolivian (1841)	Bosnian (1878)
First British-Sikh (1845–1846)	Second British-Afghan (1878–1880)
Mexican-American (1846–1848)	Pacific (1879–1880)
Austro-Sardinian (1848–1849)	British-Zulu (1879)
First Schleswig-Holstein (1848–1849)	Franco-Indochinese (1882–1884)
Hungarian (1848–1849)	Mahdist (1882–1885)
Second British-Sikh (1848–1849)	Sino-French (1884–1885)
Roman Republic (1849)	Central American (1885)
La Plata (1851–1852)	Serbo-Bulgarian (1885)
First Turco-Montenegrin (1852–1853)	Sino-Japanese (1894–1895)
Crimean (1853–1856)	Franco-Madagascan (1894–1895)
Anglo-Persian (1856–1857)	Cuban (1895–1898)
Sepoy (1857–1859)	Italo-Ethiopian (1895–1896)
Second Turco-Montenegrin (1858–1859)	First Philippine (1896–1898)
Italian Unification (1859)	Greco-Turkish (1897)
Spanish-Moroccan (1859–1860)	Spanish-American (1898)
Italo-Roman (1860)	Second Philippine (1899–1902)
Italo-Sicilian (1860–1861)	Boer (1899–1902)
	Boxer Rebellion (1900)

---

of "enormous monarchies." The monarchies are apparently worse; they risk total defeat and collapse because they are prone to strategic overextension, bureaucratic and ministerial decay in court intrigue and praetorian rebellion (pp. 347–48). In this connection one can compare the fates of Britain with its imprudence with Louis XIV's or Napoleon's France or, for that matter, Hitler's Germany or Mussolini's Italy or Brezhnev's Soviet Union. Overextension to the extent of destruction is clearly worse, from the strategic point of view, than a bit of imprudence.

Ilinden (1903)
Russo-Japanese (1904–1905)
Central American (1906)
Central American (1907)
Spanish-Moroccan (1909–1910)
Italo-Turkish (1911–1912)
First Balkan (1912–1913)
Second Balkan (1913)
World War I (1914–1918)
Russian Nationalities (1917–1921)
Russo-Polish (1919–1920)
Hungarian–Allies (1919)
Greco-Turkish (1919–1922)
Riffian (1921–1926)
Druze (1925–1927)
Sino-Soviet (1929)
Manchurian (1931–1933)
Chaco (1932–1935)
Italo-Ethiopian (1935–1936)
Sino-Japanese (1937–1941)
Changkufeng (1938)
Nomohan (1939)
World War II (1939–1945)
Russo-Finnish (1939–1940)
Franco-Thai (1940–1941)
Indonesian (1945–1946)
Indochinese (1945–1954)
Madagascan (1947–1948)
First Kashmir (1947–1949)
Palestine (1948–1949)
Hyderabad (1948)
Korean (1950–1953)
Algerian (1954–1962)
Russo-Hungarian (1956)
Sinai (1956)
Tibetan (1956–1959)
Sino-Indian (1962)
Vietnamese (1965–1975)
Second Kashmir (1965)
Six-Day (1967)
Israeli-Egyptian (1969–1970)
Football (1969)
Bangladesh (1971)
Philippine-MNLF (1972–)
Yom Kippur (1973)
Turco-Cypriot (1974)
Ethiopian-Eritrean (1974–)
Vietnamese-Cambodian (1975–)
Timor (1975–)
Saharan (1975–)
Ogaden (1976–)
Ugandan-Tanzanian (1978–1979)
Sino-Vietnamese (1979)
Russo-Afghan (1979–)
Iran-Iraqi (1980–)

*The table is from Melvin Small and J. David Singer, *Resort to Arms* (Beverly Hills: Sage, 1982), pp. 79–80. This is a partial list of international wars fought between 1816 and 1980. In Appendices A and B Small and Singer identify a total of 575 wars in this period, but approximately 159 of them appear to be largely domestic or civil wars.

This definition of war excludes covert interventions, a few of which have been directed by Liberal regimes against other Liberal regimes. One example is the United States' effort to destabilize the Chilean election and Allende's government. Nonetheless, it is significant that such interventions are not pursued publicly as acknowledged policy. The covert destabilization campaign against Chile is recounted by the U.S. Congress, Senate Select Committee to Study Governmental Operations with Respect to Intelligence Activities, *Covert Action in Chile, 1963–73*, 94th Congress, 1st Session (Washington, D.C.: Government Printing Office, 1975).

The argument (and this list) also exclude civil wars. Civil wars differ from international wars not in the ferocity of combat but in the issues that engender them. Two nations that could abide each other as independent neighbors separated by a border might well be the fiercest of enemies if forced to live together in one state, jointly deciding how to raise and spend taxes, choose leaders, and legislate fundamental questions of value. Notwithstanding these differences, no civil wars that I recall upset the argument of Liberal pacification.

to work only in the Liberals' relations with other Liberals. Liberal states have fought numerous wars with non-Liberal states.

Many of these wars have been defensive and thus prudent by necessity. Liberal states have been attacked and threatened by non-Liberal states that do not exercise any special restraint in their dealings with Liberal states. Authoritarian rulers both stimulate and respond to an international political environment in which conflicts of prestige, interest, and pure fear of what other states might do all lead states toward war. War and conquest have thus characterized the careers of many authoritarian rulers and ruling parties, from Louis XIV and Napoleon to Mussolini's Fascists, Hitler's Nazis, and Stalin's Communists.

But imprudent aggression by the Liberal state has also characterized many of these wars. Both Liberal France and Britain fought expansionist colonial wars throughout the nineteenth century. The United States fought a similar war with Mexico in 1846–1848, waged a war of annihilation against the American Indians, and intervened militarily against sovereign states many times before and after World War II. Liberal states invade weak non-Liberal societies and display exceptional degrees of distrust in their dealings with powerful non-Liberal states.[27]

Nonetheless, establishing the statistical significance of Hume's assertion appears remarkably difficult. The best statistical evidence indicates that "libertarian" or "democratic" states (slightly different measures) are not less war-prone than nonlibertarian or nondemocratic states. Indeed, in these measures they appear to be more war-prone.[28] War proneness is not, however, a measure of imprudent aggression since many wars are defensive. But that does not mean that we can simply blame warfare on the authoritarians or totalitarians, as many of our more enthusiastic politicians would have us do.[29] Liberal states ("liber-

[27] For a discussion of the historical effects of Liberalism on colonialism, the U.S.-Soviet Cold War, and post–World War Two interventions against non-Liberal regimes, see "Kant, Liberal Legacies, and Foreign Affairs," Part 2 (1983) and the sources cited there.

[28] See Melvin Small and J. David Singer, "The War-proneness of Democratic Regimes," *Jerusalem Journal of International Relations* 1 (December 1976), pp. 50–69; Steve Chan, "Mirror, Mirror on the Wall. . . . Are Freer Countries More Pacific?," *Journal of Conflict Resolution* 28 (December 1984), pp. 617–48; and Erich Weede, "Democracy and War Involvement," *Journal of Conflict Resolution* 28 (December 1984), pp. 649–64. These quantitative studies counter Rummel's (1983) view that libertarian states are less prone to violence than nonlibertarian states, which he based on a sample of 1976–1980 data not representative of the war year data of 1816–1980 of Chan or the 1960–1980 data of Weede.

[29] There are, however, serious studies that show that Marxist regimes have higher military spending per capita than non-Marxist regimes (James Payne, "Marxism and Militarism," *Polity* [1987]). But this should not be interpreted as a sign of the inherent aggressiveness of authoritarian or totalitarian governments or—with even greater enthusiasm—the inherent and global peacefulness of Liberal regimes. Marxist regimes, in particular, represent a minority in the current international system; they are strategically encircled, and because of their lack of domestic legitimacy, they might be said to "suffer" the twin burden of needing

tarian") acted as initiators in 24 out of the 56 interstate wars in which they participated between 1816 and 1980 while non-Liberals were on the initiating side in 91 out of 187 times.[30] Although non-Liberal states initiated a higher percentage of interstate wars, Liberal metropoles were the overwhelming participators in "extrasystemic wars," colonial wars, which we can assume to have been by and large initiated by the metropole (see below). Furthermore, the United States intervened in the Third World more than twice as often in the period 1946–1976 as the Soviet Union did in 1946–1979.[31] Relatedly, the United States devoted one-quarter and the Soviet Union, one-tenth, of their respective defense budgets to forces designed for Third World interventions (where responding to perceived threats would presumably have a less than purely defensive character).[32]

Although Liberal initiation of wars suggests some basis for Hume's assertion, it does not resolve the claim he made. Initiation or response may reflect either aggressive or defensive policy, in that an aggressive policy may provoke a rival to initiate a war and a defensive policy may require preemption. Hume appears to suggest that Liberal policy has a tendency to be unnecessarily aggressive. To assess his assertion, we need to take into account the specific circumstances—the threats with which the state is faced, its resources, and its goals—and doing this requires a historical understanding of time and place. If Liberals were always aggressive or always nonaggressive in relations with non-Liberals, we could reasonably argue that they are also unnecessarily aggressive, or were not. Thus we were able to support the existence of something special in Liberal foreign relations with other Liberals. But relations with non-Liberals appear more complicated. Unless we can normalize not just the number but the situations of Liberal relations with non-Liberals and non-Liberal relations with non-Liberals, the best we can do, if we can do that, is illustrate imprudent vehemence.

We should recall as well that authoritarian states also have a record of imprudent aggression. It was not semi-Liberal Britain that collapsed in 1815, but Napoleonic France. It was the Kaiser's Germany that dissolved in 1918, not republican France and Liberal Britain and democratic America. It was imperial

---

defenses against both external and internal enemies. Andreski, "On the Peaceful Disposition of Military Dictatorships" moreover, argues that (purely) military dictatorships, because of their domestic fragility, have little incentive to engage in foreign military adventures.

[30] Chan (1984), p. 636.

[31] Walter Clemens, "The Superpowers and the Third World," in Charles Kegley and Pat McGowan, *Foreign Policy: USA/USSR* (Beverly Hills: Sage, 1982), pp. 117–18.

[32] Barry Posen and Stephen Van Evera, "Overarming and Underwhelming," *Foreign Policy* 40 (1980), pp. 99–118, and "Reagan Administration Defense Policy," in Kenneth Oye, Robert Lieber, and Donald Rothchild, eds., *Eagle Defiant* (Boston: Little, Brown, 1983), pp. 86–89.

Japan and Nazi Germany that disappeared in 1945, not the United States or the United Kingdom.[33] It is the contrast with ideal rational strategy and even more the comparison with Liberal accommodation with fellow Liberals that highlight the aggressive imprudence of Liberal relations with non-Liberals.

Most wars, moreover, seem to arise out of calculations and miscalculations of interest, misunderstandings, and mutual suspicions, such as those that characterized the origins of World War I. But we can find expressions of aggressive intent and apparently unnecessary vehemence by the Liberal state characterizing a large number of wars.[34]

In relations with powerful non-Liberal states, Liberal states have missed opportunities to pursue the negotiation of arms reduction and arms control when it has been in the mutual strategic interest, and they have failed to construct wider schemes of accommodation that are needed to supplement arms control. Prior to the outbreak of World War I, this is the charge that Lord Sanderson leveled against Sir Eyre Crowe in Sanderson's response to Crowe's classic memorandum on the state of British relations with Germany.[35] Sanderson pointed out that Crowe interpreted German demands to participate in the settlement of international disputes and to have a "place in the sun" (colonies) of a size not too dissimilar to that enjoyed by the other great powers, as evidence of a fundamental aggressiveness driving toward world domination. Crowe may well have perceived an essential feature of Wilhelmine Germany, and Sanderson's attempt to place Germany in the context of other rising powers (bumptious but not aggressively pursuing world domination) may have been naive. But the interesting thing to note is less the conclusions reached than Crowe's chain of argument and evidence. He rejects continued accommodation (appeasement) with Germany not because he shows that Germany is more bumptious than France and not because he shows that Germany has greater potential as a world hegemon than the United States, which he does not even consider in this connection. Instead he is (legitimately) perplexed by the real uncertainty of German foreign policy and by its "erratic, domineering, and often frankly aggressive spirit," which accords with the well-known personal characteristics of "the present Ruler of Germany."

[33] See David Lake, "Powerful Pacifists," *American Political Science Review* 86, 1 (1992), pp. 24–37. This does not necessarily mean that the non-Liberals are strategically inferior or less capable of mobilizing the resources needed to win. Non-Liberal Russia bore the burden of both those sets of victories. The Liberal advantage in World Wars I and II was in not fighting each other, but in being resistant to defection to the non-Liberal camp.

[34] The following paragraphs build on arguments I present in "Kant, Liberal Legacies, and Foreign Affairs," Part 2.

[35] Memoranda by Mr. Eyre Crowe, January 1, 1907, and by Lord Sanderson, February 25, 1907, in G. P. Gooch et al., eds., *British Documents on the Origins of the War, 1898–1914* (London: HMSO, 1928), vol. 3, pp. 397–431.

Similar evidence of deeply held suspicion appears to characterize U.S. diplomacy toward the Soviet Union. In a fascinating memorandum to President Wilson written in 1919, Herbert Hoover (then one of Wilson's advisers) recommended that the president speak out against the danger of "world domination" that the "Bolsheviki"—a "tyranny that is the negation of democracy"—posed to free peoples. Rejecting military intervention as excessively costly and likely to "make us a party in reestablishing the reactionary classes in their economic domination over the lower classes," he proposed a "relief program" designed to undercut some of the popular appeal the Bolsheviks were garnering both in the Soviet Union and abroad. Although acknowledging that the evidence was not yet clear, he concluded: "If the militant features of Bolshevism were drawn in colors with their true parallel with Prussianism as an attempt at world domination that we do not stand for, it would check the fears that today haunt all men's minds." (The actual U.S. intervention in the Soviet Union was limited to supporting anti-Bolshevik Czechoslovak soldiers in Siberia and to protecting military supplies in Murmansk from German seizure.)[36]

In the postwar period, and particularly following the outbreak of the Korean War, U.S. diplomacy equated the "International Communist Movement" (all Communist states and parties) with "Communist imperialism" and with a domestic tyranny in the USSR that required a Cold War contest and international subversion as means of legitimizing its own police state. U.S. Secretary of State John Foster Dulles most clearly expressed this conviction, together with his own commitment to a strategy of "liberation," when he declared: "[W]e shall never have a secure peace or a happy world so long as Soviet communism dominates one third of all the peoples that there are, and is in the process of trying at least to extend its rule to many others."[37]

Opportunities for splitting the Communist bloc along cleavages of strategic national interest were delayed. Burdened with the war in Vietnam, the United States took ten years to appreciate and exploit the strategic opportunity of the Sino-Soviet split. Even the signal strategic, "offensive" success of the early Cold War, the defection of Yugoslavia from the Soviet bloc, did not receive the wholehearted welcome that a strategic assessment of its importance would have

[36] Herbert Hoover to President Wilson March 29, 1919, excerpted in Thomas Paterson, ed., *Major Problems in American Foreign Policy* (Lexington, Mass.: D. C. Heath, 1978), vol. 2, p. 95.

[37] U.S. Senate, *Hearings before the Committee on Foreign Relations on the Nomination of John Foster Dulles, Secretary of State Designate, 15 January 1953*, 83d Congress, 1st Session (Washington, D.C.: Government Printing Office, 1953), pp. 5–6. John L. Gaddis has noted logistical differences between laissez-faire and social welfare Liberals in policy toward the Soviet Union. In U.S. policy, until the advent of the Reagan administration, the fiscal conservatism of Republicans led them to favor a narrow strategy; the fiscal liberality of Democrats led to a broader strategy. See *Strategies of Containment.*

warranted.[38] Both relationships, with Yugoslavia and China, became subject to alternating, largely ideologically derived moods: Visions of exception (they were "less ruthless," more organic to the indigenous, traditional culture) sparred with bouts of liberal soul-searching ("we cannot associate ourselves with a totalitarian state").

Imprudent vehemence is also associated with Liberal foreign policy toward weak non-Liberal states; no greater spirit of accommodation or tolerance informs Liberal policy toward the many weak non-Liberal states in the Third World. This problem affects both conservative Liberals and welfare Liberals, but the two can be distinguished by differing styles of interventions.[39]

Protecting "native rights" from "native" oppressors, and protecting universal rights of property and settlement from local transgressions, introduced especially Liberal motives for imperial aggression. Ending the slave trade destabilized nineteenth-century West African oligarchies, yet encouraging "legitimate trade" required protecting the property of European merchants; declaring the illegitimacy of "suttee" or of domestic slavery also attacked local cultural traditions that had sustained the stability of indigenous political authority. Europeans settling in sparsely populated areas destroyed the livelihood of tribes that relied on hunting. The tribes defensively retaliated in force; the settlers called for imperial protection.[40] The protection of cosmopolitan Liberal rights thus bred a demand for imperial rule that violated the liberty of Native Americans, Africans, and Asians. In practice, once the exigencies of ruling an empire came

[38]Thirty-three divisions of armed soldiers, the withdrawal of the Soviet bloc from the Mediterranean, political disarray in the Communist movement: These advantages called out for a quick and friendly response. An effective U.S. ambassador in place to present Tito's position to Washington, the public character of the expulsion from the Cominform (June 1948), and a presidential administration in the full flush of creative statesmanship (and an electoral victory) also contributed to Truman's decision to rescue Yugoslavia from the Soviet embargo by providing trade and loans (1949). Nonetheless (according to Yugoslav sources), this crisis was also judged to be an appropriate moment to put pressure on Yugoslavia to resolve the questions of Trieste and Carinthia, to cut its support for the guerrillas in Greece, and to repay prewar (prerevolutionary) debts compensating the property owners of nationalized land and mines. Nor did Yugoslavia's strategic significance exempt it from inclusion among the countries condemned as "Captive Nations" (1959) or secure most-favored-nation trade status in the 1962 Trade Expansion Act. Ideological anticommunism and the porousness of the American political system to lobbies combined (according to George Kennan, ambassador to Yugoslavia at that time) to add these inconvenient burdens to a crucial strategic relationship. (John C. Campbell, *Tito's Separate Road* [New York: Council on Foreign Relations/Harper and Row, 1967], pp. 18–27; Suctozar Vukmanovic-Tempo, in Vladimir Dedijer, *The Battle Stalin Lost* [New York: Viking, 1970], p. 268; George F. Kennan, *Memoirs, 1950–1963* [Boston: Little, Brown, 1972], chap. 12).

[39]See Robert A. Packenham, *Liberal America and the Third World* (Princeton: Princeton University Press, 1973) for an interesting analysis of the impact of Liberal ideology on American foreign aid policy, esp. chap. 3 and pp. 313–23.

[40]Alexis de Tocqueville, *Democracy in America* (New York: Vintage, 1945), vol. I, p. 351. Tocqueville describes how European settlement destroys the game; the absence of game

into play, Liberal imperialism resulted in the oppression of "native" Liberals seeking self-determination in order to maintain imperial security, to avoid local chaos and international interference by another imperial power attempting to take advantage of local disaffection.

Thus nineteenth-century Liberals, such as British Prime Minister William Gladstone, pondered whether Egypt's protonationalist Arabi rebellion (1881–1882) was truly Liberal nationalist (they discovered it was not) before intervening to protect strategic lifelines to India, commerce, and investment.[41] These dilemmas of Liberal imperialism are also reflected in U.S. imperialism in the Caribbean, where, for example, following the Spanish-American War of 1898, Article III of the Platt Amendment gave the United States the "right to intervene for the preservation of Cuban independence, the maintenance of a government adequate for the protection of life, property, and individual liberty. . . ."[42]

The record of Liberalism in the non-Liberal world is not solely a catalog of oppression and imprudence. The North American West and the settlement colonies—Australia and New Zealand—represent a successful transplant of Liberal institutions, albeit in a temperate, underpopulated, and then depopulated environment and at the cost of Native American and Aboriginal rights. Similarly, the twentieth-century expansion of Liberalism into less powerful non-Liberal areas has also had some striking successes. The forcible liberalization of Germany and Japan following World War II and the long covert financing of Liberal parties in Italy are the more significant instances of successful transplant. Covert financing of Liberalism in Chile and occasional diplomatic

---

reduces the Indians to starvation. Both then exercise their rights to self-defense. But the colonists are able to call in the power of the imperial government. Palmerston once declared that he would never employ force to promote purely private interests—whether commercial or settlement. He also declared that he would faithfully protect the lives and liberty of English subjects. In circumstances such as those Tocqueville described, Palmerston's distinctions were irrelevant. See Kenneth Bourne, *Palmerston: The Early Years* (New York: Macmillan, 1982), pp. 624–26. Other colonial settlements and their dependence on imperial expansion are examined in Ronald Robinson, "Non-European Foundations of Imperialism," in Roger Owen and Bob Sutcliffe, eds., *Studies in the Theory of Imperialism* (London: Longmans, 1972).

[41] Gladstone had proclaimed his support for the equal rights of all nations in his Midlothian Speeches. Wilfrid Scawen Blunt served as a secret agent in Egypt keeping Gladstone informed of the political character of Arabi's movement. The Liberal dilemma in 1882—were they intervening against genuine nationalism or a military adventurer (Arabi)?—was best expressed in Joseph Chamberlain's memorandum to the cabinet, June 21, 1882, excerpted in J. L. Garvin and J. Amery, *Life of Joseph Chamberlain* (London: Macmillan, 1935), vol. 1, p. 448. And see Peter Mansfield, *The British in Egypt* (New York: Holt, Rinehart and Winston, 1971), chaps. 2 and 3; Ronald Hyam, *Britain's Imperial Century: 1815–1914* (London: Batsford, 1976), chap. 8; and Robert Tignor, *Modernization and British Colonial Rule in Egypt* (Princeton: Princeton University Press, 1966).

[42] The Platt Amendment is excerpted in Paterson, p. 328.

démarches to nudge aside military threats to non-Communist democratic parties (as in Peru in 1962, South Korea in 1963, and the Dominican Republic in 1962[43] and again in 1978) illustrate policies that, though less successful, were directed toward Liberal goals. These particular postwar Liberal successes also are the product of special circumstances: the existence of a potential Liberal majority, temporarily suppressed, which could be readily reestablished by outside aid or unusually weak oligarchic, military, or Communist opponents.[44]

At other times in the postwar period, when the United States sought to protect Liberals in the Third World from the "Communist threat," the consequences of Liberal foreign policy on the non-Liberal society often became far removed from the promotion of individual rights or of national security. In Vietnam and elsewhere, intervening against "armed minorities" and "enemies of free enterprise" meant intervening for other armed minorities, some sustaining and sustained by oligarchies, others resting on little more than U.S. foreign aid and troops. Indigenous Liberals simply had too narrow a base of domestic support. These interventions did not advance Liberal rights, and to the extent that they were driven by ideological motives they were not necessary for national security.

To the conservative Liberals, the alternatives are starkly cast: Third World authoritarians with allegiance to the Liberal, capitalist West or "Communists" subject to the totalitarian East (or leftist nationalists, who, even if elected, are but a slippery stepping-stone to totalitarianism).[45] Conservative Liberals are prepared to support the allied authoritarians. The Communists attack property in addition to liberty, thereby provoking conservative Liberals to covert or overt intervention, or "dollar diplomacy" imperialism. The interventions against Mossadégh in Iran, Arbenz in Guatemala, Allende in Chile, and the Sandinistas in Nicaragua appear to fall into this pattern.[46] President Reagan's simultane-

[43] During the Alliance for Progress era in Latin America, the Kennedy administration supported Juan Bosch in the Dominican Republic in 1962. See also William P. Bundy, "Dictatorships and American Foreign Policy," *Foreign Affairs* 54, 1 (October 1975), pp. 51–60.

[44] See Samuel Huntington, "Human Rights and American Power," *Commentary* (September 1981), pp. 37–43, and George Quester, "Consensus Lost," *Foreign Policy* 40 (Fall 1980), pp. 18–32, for arguments and examples of the successful export of Liberal institutions in the postwar period. A major study of the the role of democratic expansion in U.S. foreign policy is Tony Smith, *America's Mission* (Princeton: Princeton University Press, 1994).

[45] Kirkpatrick, "Dictatorships and Double Standards." In 1851 the Liberal French historian Guizot made a similar argument in a letter to Gladstone urging that Gladstone appreciate that the despotic government of Naples was the best guarantor of Liberal law and order then available. Reform, in Guizot's view, meant the unleashing of revolutionary violence (Philip Magnus, *Gladstone* [New York: Dutton, 1964], p. 100).

[46] Richard Barnet, *Intervention and Revolution: The United States in the Third World* (New York: Meridian, 1968), chap. 10; and on Nicaragua, see the *New York Times*, March 11, 1982, for a description of the training direction, and funding (twenty million dollars) of anti-Sandinista guerrillas by the United States.

ous support for the military in El Salvador and guerilla "freedom fighters" in Nicaragua also tracks this pattern, whose common thread is rhetorical commitment to freedom and operational support for conservative, free enterprise.

To the social welfare Liberals, the choice is never so clear. Aware of the need for state action to democratize the distribution of social power and resources, they tend to have more sympathy for social reform. This can produce on the part of "radical" welfare Liberals a more tolerant policy toward the attempts by reforming autocracies to redress inegalitarian distributions of property in the Third World. This more complicated welfare Liberal assessment can itself be a recipe for more extensive intervention. The large number of conservative oligarchs or military bureaucracies with which the conservative Liberal is well at home are not so congenial to the social welfare Liberal, yet the Communists are still seen as enemies of liberty. Left Liberals justify more extensive intervention first to discover, then to sustain Third World social democracy in a political environment that is either barely participatory or highly polarized. Thus Arthur Schlesinger recalls President Kennedy musing shortly after the assassination of Trujillo (former dictator of the Dominican Republic): "There are three possibilities in descending order of preference, a decent democratic regime, a continuation of the Trujillo regime [by his followers] or a Castro regime. We ought to aim at the first, but we can't really renounce the second until we are sure we can avoid the third." Another instance of this approach was President Carter's support for the land reforms in El Salvador, which was explained by one U.S. official in the following analogy: "There is no one more conservative than a small farmer. We're going to be breeding capitalists like rabbits."[47] President Clinton's administration seems to have succumbed to a similar dose of optimistic interventionism in its conviction that nations could be rebuilt democratically in both Somalia and Haiti, although democracy had never existed in the first and was led in the second by Jean Bertrand Aristide, a charismatic Socialist and an eloquent critic of American imperialism.

The third effect apparent in the international relations of Liberal states is Hume's second assertion: "supine complaisance." This takes two forms: One is a failure to support allies; the other is a failure to oppose enemies.

Where Liberal internationalism among Liberal states has been shortsighted is in preserving its basic preconditions under changing international circumstances, particularly in supporting the Liberal character of its constituent states. The Liberal community of nations has failed on occasion, as it did in regard to Germany in the 1920s, to provide timely international economic support for

[47] Arthur Schlesinger, *A Thousand Days* (Boston: Houghton Mifflin, 1965), p. 769, and quoted in Barnet, *Intervention and Revolution*, p. 158. And for the U.S. official's comment on the Salvadoran land reform, see L. Simon and J. Stephen, *El Salvador Land Reform 1980–1981* (Boston: Oxfam-America, 1981), p. 38.

Liberal regimes whose market foundations were in crisis.[48] It failed in the 1930s to provide military aid or political mediation to Spain, which was challenged by an armed minority, or to Czechoslovakia, which was caught in a dilemma of preserving national security or acknowledging the claims (fostered by Hitler's Germany) of the Sudeten minority to self-determination. Farsighted and constitutive measures seem to have been provided by the Liberal international order only when one Liberal state stood preeminent among the rest, prepared and able to take measures, as did Britain before World War I and the United States following World War II, to sustain economically and politically the foundations of Liberal society beyond its borders. Then measures such as British antislavery and free trade and the U.S. loan to Britain in 1947, the Marshall Plan, NATO, GATT, the IMF, and the liberalization of Germany and Japan helped construct buttresses for the international Liberal order.[49]

Ideologically based policies can also be self-indulgent. Oligarchic or authoritarian allies in the Third World do not find consistent support in a Liberal policy that stresses human rights. Contemporary conservative critics claim that the security needs of these states are neglected, that they fail to obtain military aid or more direct support when they need it (the shah's Iran, Humberto Romero's El Salvador, Somoza's Nicaragua, and South Africa). Equally disturbing from this point of view, Communist regimes are shunned even when a détente with them could further United States strategic interests (Cuba, Angola). Welfare Liberals particularly shun the first group, while laissez-faire Liberals balk at close dealings with the second. In both cases our economic interests or strategic interests are often slighted.[50]

[48] France and Britain were insisting on prompt payment of wartime reparations, just as the United States was insisting on propmpt repayment of wartime loans. The U.S. government formally refused to consider the problem in a comprehensive light. American bankers stepped in, but in light of the needs for financial accommodation, the Dawes and Young plans were helpful but still feeble stopgaps to finance German reparations and Allied debts with lower-interest packages of loans. Two contemporary classics that discuss the problem are Arnold Wolfers, *Britain and France between Two Wars* (1940) and Harold G. Moulton and Leo Pasvolsky, *War Debts and World Prosperity* (1932).

[49] Kindleberger, *The World in Depression;* Robert Gilpin, *U.S. Power and the Multinational Corporation;* Krasner, "State Power and the Structure of International Trade"; and Fred Hirsch and Michael W. Doyle, "Politicization in the World Economy" in Hirsch, Doyle and Edward Morse, eds. *Alternative to Monetary Disorder* (New York: Council on Foreign Relations/McGraw-Hill, 1977).

[50] Kirkpatrick points out our neglect of the needs of the authoritarians. Theodore Lowi argues that Democratic and Republican policies toward the acquisition of bases in Spain reflected this dichotomy; "Bases in Spain," in Harold Stein, ed. *American Civil-Military Decisions* (University: University of Alabama Press, 1963), p. 699. In other cases where both the geopolitical and the domestic orientation of a potential neutral might be influenced by U.S. aid, Liberal institutions (representative legislatures) impose delay or public constraints and conditions on diplomacy that allow the Soviet Union to steal a march. Warren Christopher has suggested that this occurred in U.S. relations with Nicaragua in 1979. Warren Christopher, "Ceasefire between the Branches," *Foreign Affairs* (Summer 1982), p. 998.

A second manifestation of complaisance lies in a reaction to the excesses of interventionism. A mood of frustrated withdrawal affects policy toward strategically and economically important countries. Just as interventionism seems to be the typical failing of the Liberal great power, so complaisance characterizes declined or "not quite risen" Liberal states.[51] Especially following the exhaustion of wars, representative legislatures may become reluctant to undertake international commitments or to fund the military establishment needed to play a geopolitical role. Purely domestic concerns seem to take priority, as they did in the United States in the 1920s and may be doing in the 1990s. Rational incentives for "free riding" on the extended defense commitments of the leader of the Liberal alliance also induce this form of complaisance. During much of the nineteenth century the United States informally relied upon the British fleet for many of its security needs. Today the Europeans and the Japanese, according to some American strategic analysts, fail to bear their "fair" share of alliance burdens.

Liberalism, if we take into account both Kant and Hume, thus carries with it three legacies: peace among Liberals, imprudent vehemence toward non-Liberals, and complaisance toward the future. The first appears to be a special feature associated with Liberalism, and it can be demonstrated statistically. The latter two cannot be shown to be special to Liberalism, though their effects can be illustrated historically in Liberal foreign policy. And the survival and growth in the number of Liberal states suggests that imprudent vehemence and complaisance have not overwhelmed Liberalism's efficacy as form of governance.

THE LOGIC OF A SEPARATE PEACE

How can we explain the legacies of Liberalism on foreign affairs? Perpetual peace, for Kant, is an epistemology, a condition for ethical action, and (most importantly) an explanation of how the "mechanical process of nature visibly exhibits the purposive plan of producing concord among men, even against their will and indeed by means of their very discord."[52] Understanding history requires an epistemological foundation, for without a teleology, such as the promise of perpetual peace, the complexity of history would overwhelm human

[51] Ideological formulations often accompany these policies. Fear of bolshevism was used to excuse not forming an alliance with the Soviet Union in 1938 against Nazi aggression. And Nazi and fascist regimes were portrayed as defenders of private property and social order. But the connection Liberals draw between domestic tyranny and foreign aggression may also operate in reverse. When the Nazi threat to the survival of Liberal states did require a Liberal alliance with the Soviet Union, Stalin became for a short period the Liberal press's "Uncle Joe."

[52] Kant, PP, p. 108; UH, pp. 44–45.

understanding.[53] But perpetual peace is not merely a heuristic device with which to interpret history. It is guaranteed, Kant explains in "Perpetual Peace" 's "First Addition" ("On the Guarantee of Perpetual Peace"), to result from men fulfilling their ethical duty or, that failing from a hidden plan.[54] Peace is an ethical duty because only under conditions of peace can all humans treat one another as ends.[55] For this duty to be practical, Kant needs of course to show that peace is in fact possible. The widespread sentiment of approbation that he saw aroused by the early success of the French revolutionaries showed him that we can indeed be moved by ethical sentiments with a cosmopolitan reach.[56] This does not mean, however, that perpetual peace is certain ("prophesyable"). Even the scientifically regular course of the planets could be changed by a wayward comet's striking them out of orbit. Human freedom requires that we allow for much greater reversals in the course of history. We must in fact anticipate the possibility of backsliding and destructive wars (though these will serve to educate nations to the importance of peace).[57]

But in the end our guarantee of perpetual peace does not rest on ethical conduct, as Kant emphasizes in "Perpetual Peace":

> We now come to the essential question regarding the prospect of perpetual peace. What does nature do in relation to the end which man's own reason prescribes to him as a duty, i.e. how does nature help to promote his moral purpose? And how does nature guarantee that what man ought to do by the laws of his freedom (but does not do) will in fact be done through nature's compulsion, without prejudice to the free agency of man? . . . [T]his does not mean that nature imposes on us a duty to do it, for duties can only be imposed by practical reason. On the contrary, nature does it herself, whether we are willing or not: *facta volentem ducunt nolentem tradunt.*[58]

[53] UH, pp. 51–53.

[54] In the MM Kant seems to write as if perpetual peace were only an epistemological device and perpetual peace, while an ethical duty, empirically merely a "pious hope" (pp. 164–75). (Even here, though, Kant finds that the pacific union is not "impracticable," p. 171.) In the UH, Kant writes as if the brute force of physical nature drives men toward inevitable peace. Yovel (1980) argues that PP reconciles the two views of history, from a postcritical (post–*Critique of Judgment*) perspective (p. 168ff). "Nature" is human-created nature (culture or civilization). Perpetual peace is the "a priori of the a posteriori" (a critical perspective that then enables us to discern causal, probabilistic patterns in history). Law the "political technology" of republican constitutionalism are separate from ethical development. But both interdependently lead to perpetual peace: the first through force, fear, and self-interest, the second through progressive enlightenment, and both together through the widening of the circumstances in which engaging in right conduct poses smaller and smaller burdens.

[55] Kant, UH, p. 50.

[56] Kant, CF, pp. 181–82. This view is defended by Yovel, pp. 153–154.

[57] Kant, UH, pp. 47–48.

[58] Kant, PP, p. 112.

The guarantee thus rests, Kant adds, on the probable behavior not of moral angels but of "devils, so long as they possess understanding."[59] In explaining the sources of each of the three Definitive Articles of the perpetual peace, Kant then tells us how we (as free and intelligent devils) could be motivated by fear, force, and calculated advantage to undertake a course of actions whose outcome we can reasonably anticipate to be perpetual peace. But while it is possible to conceive of the Kantian road to peace in these terms, Kant himself recognizes and argues that social evolution also makes the conditions of moral behavior less onerous, hence more likely.[60] In tracing the effects of both political and moral development, he builds an account of why Liberal states do maintain peace among themselves and of how it will (by implication, has) come about that the pacific union will expand. He also explains how these republics would engage in wars with nonrepublics and therefore suffer the "sad experience" of wars that an ethical policy might have avoided.

The first source derives from a political evolution, from a constitutional law. Nature (Providence) has seen to it that human beings can live in all the regions where they have been driven to settle by wars. (Kant, who once taught geography, reports on the Lapps, the Samoyeds, the Peschneras.) "Asocial sociability" draws men together to fulfill needs for security and material welfare as it drives them into conflicts over the distribution and control of social products.[61] This violent natural evolution tends toward the Liberal peace because "asocial sociability" inevitably leads toward republican governments and republican governments are a source of the Liberal peace.

Republican representation and separation of powers are produced because they are the means by which the state is "organized well" to prepare for and meet foreign threats (by unity) and to tame the ambitions of selfish and aggressive individuals (by authority derived from representation, by general laws, and by nondespotic administration).[62] States that are not organized in this fashion fail. Monarchs thus encourage commerce and private property in order to increase national wealth. They cede rights of representation to their subjects in order to strengthen their political support or to obtain willing grants of tax revenue.[63]

[59] Ibid.
[60] Kant, CF, pp. 187–89. See George Kelly, pp. 106–13, for a further explanation.
[61] Kant, UH, p. 44–45; PP, pp. 110–11.
[62] Kant, PP, pp. 112–13.
[63] Hassner, pp. 583–86. The Kantian pacific union has in in fact expanded steadily, but whether we can anticipate its continued expansion much beyond the current numbers of Liberal democracies has been called into question by Samuel Huntington, in "Will More Countries Become Democratic?," *Political Science Quarterly* 99 (Summer 1984), pp. 193–218, an issue that he revisits in a more optimistic vein in *The Third Wave: Democratization in the Late Twentieth Century* (Norman: University of Oklahoma Press, 1991).

Kant shows how republics, once established, lead to peaceful relations. He argues that once the aggressive interests of absolutist monarchies are tamed and once the habit of respect for individual rights is ingrained by republican government, wars would appear as the disaster to the people's welfare that he and the other Liberals thought them to be. The fundamental reason is this:

> If, as is inevitability the case under this constitution, the consent of the citizens is required to decide whether or not war should be declared, it is very natural that they will have a great hesitation in embarking on so dangerous an enterprise. For this would mean calling down on themselves all the miseries of war, such as doing the fighting themselves, supplying the costs of the war from their own resources, painfully making good the ensuing devastation, and, as the crowning evil, having to take upon themselves a burden of debts which will embitter peace itself and which can never be paid off on account of the constant threat of new wars. But under a constitution where the subject is not a citizen, and which is therefore not republican, it is the simplest thing in the world to go to war. For the head of state is not a fellow citizen, but the owner of the state, and war will not force him to make the slightest sacrifice so far as his banquets, hunts, pleasure palaces and court festivals are concerned. He can thus decide on war, without any significant reason, as a kind of amusement, and unconcernedly leave it to the diplomatic corps (who are always ready for such purposes) to justify the war for the sake of propriety.[64]

These domestic restraints introduce republican caution, Kant's "hesitation," in place of monarchical caprice. Citizens become "co-legislative members" of the state and must therefore give their free consent through representatives not only to the waging of war in general "but also to every particular declaration of war."[65] Republican caution seems to save republics from the failings Hume saw as characteristic of "enormous monarchies," including "strategic over-extension," court intrigue, and praetorian rebellion.[66] Representative government allows for a rotation of elites, others have argued, and this encourages a reversal of disastrous policies as electorates punish the party in power with electoral defeat. Legislatures and public opinion further restrain executives from policies that clearly violate the obvious and fundamental interests of the public, as the public perceives those interests.[67] The division of powers among legislature,

[64] Kant, PP, p. 100.
[65] Kant, MM, para. 55, p. 167.
[66] See the discussion of Hume in footnote 6, above, pp. 347–48.
[67] For an argument that democracies can both defer to prudent leadership and make prudent judgments, see Kenneth Waltz, *Foreign Policy and Democratic Politics* (Boston; Little, Brown, 1967), pp. 288–97. Joseph Nye concludes that the U.S. record in postwar diplomacy is more mixed, finding that nuclear war has been successfully avoided, but that containing Soviet power and fostering moderation in and by the Soviet Union have been less successful

judiciary, and executive furthermore introduces salutary delay, time for reflection and adjustment in the foreign relations of republican states. In relations with fellow republics these delays are doubly compounded and thus can provide fertile opportunities to resolve disputes short of escalation and armed crisis.

Representation may also provide an effective signaling device, assuring foreign decision makers that democratic commitments are credible because rash acts and exposed bluffs will lead to electoral defeats. Able to make more credible commitments, democracies may thus be less likely to stumble into wars, especially with other democracies.[68] Tending to confirm this proposition is the observation that alliances among democracies endure longer than alliances among nondemocracies.[69] But a purely rational-egoist approach to democratic representation also reveals that elected decision makers have a stake in winning wars[70] and that democracies win 81 percent of the wars in which they are involved; autocracies only 43 percent.[71] This might account for the pattern we observe of many democratic wars but no (or very few) wars against fellow democracies. But if democracies can be rationally rapacious, it does not explain why we do not find more wars in which powerful democracies conquer much weaker democracies, why Luxembourg feels safe from France and Canada safe from the United States. Nor does rational, representative caution actually seem to produce prudence. Liberal publics can become disaffected from international commitments and choose isolationism or appeasement, as Britain and the United States did in the 1920s and 1930s. And republican caution does not end war or ensure that wars are fought only when necessary for national security. Many democratic and representative states have been war-prone, as was classical Athens or would have been Machiavelli's free republics.

If representation alone were peace-inducing, Liberal states would not be warlike or given to imprudent vehemence, as is far from the case. It does ensure that wars are only fought for popular, Liberal purposes. The historical Liberal legacy is laden with popular wars fought to promote freedom, protect private

("Can America Manage Its Soviet Policy?" in Joseph S. Nye, Jr, ed., *The Making of America's Soviet Policy* [New Haven; Yale University Press, 1984], p. 325–29).

[68] James Fearon, "Domestic Political Audiences and the Escalation of Political Disputes," *American Political Science Review* 88 (1994), pp. 577–92.

[69] Kurt Gaubatz, "Democratic States and Commitment in International Politics," *International Organization* 50 (1996), pp. 109–39.

[70] Bruce Bueno de Mesquita, Randolph Siverson, and Gary Woller find that victory in war reduces risk of leader removal by 25 percent in any year after the victory though increasing casualties by a factor of 10 (measured in battle deaths per 10,000) increases the risk of removal by 8 percent in each year afterward. Victorious initiators are the big winners, greatly reducing the rate of overthrow to about 1 percent from the base level of 10 percent, while victorious targets gain little. See their "War and the Fate of Regimes," *American Political Science Review* 86 (1992), pp. 638–46, and Bueno de Mesquita and Siverson, "War and the Survival of Political Leaders," *American Political Science Review* 89 (1995), pp. 841–55.

[71] Lake, "Powerful Pacifists."

property or support Liberal allies against non-Liberal enemies. Kant's own position is ambiguous. He regards most of these wars as unjust and warns Liberals of their susceptibility to them. At the same time, he argues that each nation "can and ought to" demand that its neighboring nations enter into the pacific union of Liberal states—that is, become republican.[72] Thus to see how the pacific union removes the occasion of wars among Liberal states and not wars between Liberal and non-Liberal states, we need to shift our attention from constitutional law to international law, Kant's second source.

Complementing the constitutional guarantee of caution, international law adds a second source, a guarantee of respect. The separation of nations that asocial sociability encourages is reinforced by the development of separate languages and religions. These further guarantee a world of separate states, an essential condition needed to avoid a "global, soul-less despotism." At the same time, they also morally integrate Liberal states, for "as culture grows and men gradually move towards greater agreement over their principles, they lead to mutual understanding and peace."[73] As republics emerge (the first source) and as culture progresses, an understanding of the legitimate rights of all citizens and of all republics comes into play, and this, now that caution characterizes policy, sets up the moral foundations for the Liberal peace. Correspondingly, international law highlights the importance of Kantian publicity. Domestically, publicity helps ensure that the officials of republics act according to the principles they profess to hold just and according to the interests of the electors they claim to represent. Internationally, free speech and the effective communication of accurate conceptions of the political life of foreign peoples is essential to establish and preserve the understanding on which the guarantee of respect depends.

We can speculate that the process might work something like this: The leaders and publics of domestically just republics, which rest on consent, presume foreign republics to be also consensual, just, and therefore deserving of accommodation. The experience of cooperation helps engender further cooperative behavior when the consequences of state policy are unclear but (potentially) mutually beneficial. At the same time, Liberal states assume that non-Liberal states, which do not rest on free consent, are not just. Because non-Liberal governments are perceived to be in a state of aggression with their own people, their foreign relations become for Liberal governments deeply suspect. Wilhelm II of imperial Germany may or may not have been aggressive (he was certainly idiosyncratic); Liberal democracies such as Britain, France, and the United States, however, assumed that whatever was driving German policy, reliable democratic, constitutional government was not restraining it. They

[72] Kant, PP, p. 106, p. 102.
[73] Ibid., p. 114.

regarded Germany and its actions with severe suspicion, to which the Reich reacted with corresponding distrust. In short, fellow Liberals benefit from a presumption of amity; non-Liberals suffer from a presumption of enmity. Both presumptions may be accurate. Each, however, may also be self-confirming.

Democratic Liberals do not need to assume either that public opinion directly rules foreign policy or that the entire governmental elite is Liberal. It can instead assume a third possibility: that the elite typically manages public affairs but that potentially non-Liberal members of the elite have reason to doubt that anti-Liberal policies would be electorally sustained and endorsed by the majority of the democratic public.

Third and last, cosmopolitan law adds material incentives to moral commitments, for over the long run commitments unsupported by material interests are unlikely to endure. The cosmopolitan right to hospitality permits the "spirit of commerce" sooner or later to take hold of every nation, thus impelling states to promote peace and to try to avert war. Liberal economic theory holds that these cosmopolitan ties derive from a cooperative international division of labor and free trade according to comparative advantage. Each economy is said to be better off than it would have been under autarky; each thus acquires an incentive to avoid policies that would lead the other to break these economic ties. Since keeping open markets rests upon the assumption that the next set of transactions will also be determined by prices rather than coercion, a sense of mutual security is vital to avoid security-motivated searches for economic autarky. Thus avoiding a challenge to another Liberal state's security or even enhancing each other's security by means of alliance naturally follows economic interdependence.

A further cosmopolitan source of Liberal peace is that the international market removes difficult decisions of production and distribution from the direct sphere of state policy. A foreign state thus does not appear directly responsible for these outcomes; states can stand aside from, and to some degree above, these contentious market rivalries and be ready to step in to resolve crises. The interdependence of commerce and the international contacts of state officials help create crosscutting transnational ties that serve as lobbies for mutual accommodation. According to modern Liberal scholars, international financiers and transnational and transgovernmental organizations create interests in favor of accommodation. Moreover, their variety has ensured that no single conflict sours an entire relationship by setting off a spiral of reciprocated retaliation.[74] Conversely, a sense of suspicion, such as that characterizing relations

[74] Karl Polanyi, *The Great Transformation*, chaps. 1 and 2; Zbigniew Brzezinski and Samuel Huntington, *Political Power: USA/USSR* (New York: Viking Press, 1963), chap. 9; Robert Keohane and Joseph Nye, *Power and Interdependence* (Boston; Little, Brown, 1977), chap. 7; Richard Neustadt, *Alliance Politics* (New York: Columbia University Press, 1970); Daniele

between Liberal and non-Liberal governments, can lead to restrictions on the range of contacts between societies. And this can increase the prospect that a single conflict will determine an entire relationship.

Immanuel Kant's 1795 essay "Perpetual Peace" offers a coherent explanation of important regularities in world politics: the tendencies of Liberal states simultaneously to be peace-prone in their relations with one another and unusually war-prone in their relations with non-Liberal states. Republican representation, Liberal respect, and transnational interdependence (to rephrase Kant's three definitive articles of the hypothetical peace treaty he asked states to sign) thus can be seen as three necessary and together sufficient causes of the two regularities. *Thus no single constitutional, international, or cosmopolitan source is alone sufficient, but together (and only together) the three sources plausibly connect the characteristics of Liberal polities and economies with sustained Liberal peace.* Alliances founded on mutual strategic interest among Liberal and non-Liberal states have been broken, economic ties between Liberal and non-Liberal states have proved fragile, but the political bonds of Liberal rights and interests have proved a remarkably firm foundation for mutual nonaggression. A separate peace exists among Liberal states.

But in their relations with non-Liberal states, Liberal states have not escaped from the insecurity of the world political system considered as a whole. Moreover, the very constitutional restraint, international respect for individual rights, and shared commercial interests that establish grounds for peace among Liberal states establish grounds for additional conflict irrespective of actual threats to national security in relations between Liberal and non-Liberal societies.

And in their relations with all states Liberal states have not solved the problems of international cooperation and competition. Liberal publics can become absorbed in domestic issues, and international Liberal respect does not preclude trade rivalries or guarantee farsighted collective solutions to international security and welfare.

TESTING THE LIBERAL PEACE

Liberalism is now widely regarded as having an important connection to international security. The twin propositions—that Liberal democratic republics do not seem to go to war with one another yet seem to be as war-prone as any other regime—are seen as the foundation of the great global changes of our time. The end of the Cold War fits in with the democratization of Russia.[75]

Archiburgi, "Immanuel Kant, Cosmopolitan Law, and Peace," *European Journal of International Relations* (1995), pp. 429–56.

[75] See James Lee Ray and Bruce Russett, "The Future as Arbiter of Theoretical Controver-

And in many local contests, such as the Falklands or Gibraltar, the dampening of once-bitter or violent conflict coincides with the emergence of mutual Liberal democratic respect. The Liberal peace, furthermore, takes on even greater significance as we observe the worldwide spread of democratic forms to every continent and region.

None of this has escaped the politicians. Drawing on Wilsonianism, Roosevelt's Four Freedoms, the Truman Doctrine, and, more recently, addresses by Presidents Reagan and Bush, President Bill Clinton's 1994 State of the Union Address affirmed that "democracies don't attack each other."[76] "Democratic enlargement" has become the doctrinal centerpiece of the Administration's foreign policy.

But the concern of social scientists is special. That significance was well expressed by Jack Levy, who observed a few years ago that "the absence of war between democracies comes as close as anything to an empirical law in international relations.[77] Liberalism is thus emerging as a powerful paradigm in the social scientific sense. Unusually—for international relations—it is a tested, causal theory. It has a causal argument that can generate lawlike hypotheses capable of being specified in such a way that they can in principle be disconfirmed.

One sign of the health of such a research program is that it attracts serious critical attention. By this measure the "Liberal Democratic Peace" is flourishing. The core association between peace and democracy has been extensively criticized and then defended, in both statistical and case study tests. The literature suggests that we need to pay special attention to three areas. We should elaborate—as a means of testing—the potential outcomes, or dependent variables. We should reexamine the causal model, adopting more careful ways to test it against relevant alternatives. And we should revisit its policy implications.[78]

Elaborate the Dependent Variables. An absence of war is not the same as a state of peace. A state of peace is the expectation that war is not a legitimate or likely recourse. That is what the Liberal model seeks to explain and what Immanuel Kant envisaged in his "Perpetual Peace." A state of peace thus is not the same as successful deterrence. It is a condition that should change expectations and attitudes and give rise to more extensive forms of dispute avoidance

sies: Predictions, Explanations, and the End of the Cold War," *British Journal of Political Science* (forthcoming).

[76] In the *New York Times*, January 26, 1994.

[77] Jack Levy, "Domestic Politics and War," *Journal of Interdisciplinary History* 18, 4 (Spring 1988), pp. 653–73.

[78] These suggestions of course draw on Imre Lakatos, "Falsification and the Methodology of Scientific Research Programs," in I. Lakatos and A. Musgrave, eds., *Criticism and the Growth of Knowledge* (Cambridge: Cambridge University Press, 1970).

and international collaboration. This is hard to measure. Recent valuable extensions—I can't name them all—have explored disputes short of war (Bremer); internal violence (Rudolph Rummel); peaceful territorial change (Arie Kacowicz); the effect of electoral cycles (Gaubatz); and great power cooperation (Benjamin Miller).[79] We should be expanding on the research in political economy, examining whether Liberal ideas, institutions, and interests make a difference in trade, investment, and financial disputes. Liberal institutions, principles, and interests should also provide a firm foundation for international law, leading Liberal states to abide by international law more reliably in dealings with one another than do other pairs of states.

To those areas we should add studies of: defense policies—which way do the weapons point and why?—intelligence cooperation—do liberals resist better the temptation to engage in covert activity (was the recent squabble with France the norm or an exception)?—foreign aid—is there a "democratic difference" of discriminating in favor of fellow democracies? Liberal democracy should make some difference over and beyond war. Does it?

Causal Argument and Testing.[80] One additional reason to expand our view of potential outcomes is (I suspect) that our current statistical tests of the "democratic peace" are full of false positives and false negatives. False negatives (absolving Liberalism) arise from the fact that there are many reasons not to go to war other than Liberalism. Distance, exhaustion, and deterrence resulting from an expectation that one will lose or that the costs of victory are too high are some of the obvious candidates. False positives (condemning Liberalism) arise from the circumstance that it is not at all clear that most lists of participating polities, including my own, are all Liberal republics. Many or some of the "democratic" conflicts and disputes may be among participatory polities but not among "Liberal republics."

Kant's theory held that a stable expectation of peace among states would be achieved once three conditions were met. We can rephrase them as:

1. *Representative, republican government.* This includes an elected legislature, separation of powers, and the rule of law. Kant argued that together those institutional features lead to caution because the government is responsible to

[79] Stuart Bremer, "Democracy and Militarized International Disputes, 1816–1965," *International Interactions* 18, 3 (1992), pp. 23–50; Rudolph Rummel, *Death by Government* (New Brunswick, N.J.: Transaction Publishers, 1994); Arie Kacowicz, *Peaceful Territorial Change* (Columbia: University of South Carolina, 1994); Kurt Gaubatz, "Election Cycles and War," *Journal of Conflict Resolution* (1991); and Benjamin Miller, *When Opponents Cooperate* (Ann Arbor: University of Michigan Press, 1995).

[80] I would like to thank George Downs and Bruce Russett for their valuable advice on this section.

its citizens. This does not guarantee peace. It should select only those wars that the citizens will support.

2. A *principled respect for nondiscriminatory human rights.* This should produce a commitment to respect the rights of fellow Liberal republics (because they represent free citizens, who as individuals have rights that deserve our respect) and a suspicion of nonrepublics (because if those governments cannot trust their own citizens, what should lead us to trust them?)[81]

3. *Social and economic interdependence.* Trade and social interaction generally engender a mix of conflict and cooperation. Liberalism produces special material incentives for cooperation. Among fellow Liberals interdependence should not be subject to security-motivated restrictions and consequently tends to be more varied, less dependent on single issues, and less subject to single conflicts.[82]

Kant suggests that each principle is necessary and that together they are sufficient to establish a secure expectation of peace. The first principle specifies representative government responsible to a winning electoral coalition of voters; the second and third specify the coalition's ends and interests. Together the three generate an expectation of peaceful accommodation among fellow Liberals and hostility toward non-Liberals.

Not all participatory polities would meet Kant's criteria. Kant distrusted unfettered, democratic majoritarianism, and his argument offers no support for a claim that all participatory polities—democracies—should be peaceful either in general or between fellow democracies. Many participatory polities have been non-Liberal. For two thousand years before the modern age, popular rule was widely associated with aggressiveness (by Thucydides) or imperial success (Machiavelli). Today a list of Kantian republics would not include, for example, institutionalized representative democracies that are motivated by a public culture of indiscriminate empire mongering or racism or ethnic purity. The decisive preference of their median voter might well include "ethnic cleansing" against other democratic polities. Nor would they include autocracies, however enlightened and Liberal, because the autotocrats are not constrained by representative legislatures and the rule of law. [83] Their rule would not generate a

[81] The individual subjects of autocracies of course do not lose their rights. It's just that the autocrats cannot claim legitimately to speak for their subjects. Subjects retain basic human rights, such as the rights of noncombatants in war. The terror bombing of civilians—as in the bombings of Dresden, Tokyo, Hiroshima, and Nagasaki—constitute, in this view, violations of these rights and of Liberal principles and demonstrate weaknesses of Liberal models in these cases.

[82] These three points are all developed above in "Liberal Legacies."

[83] Kant himself had a weakness for seeing pacific potential in some enlightened despots, a point drawn to my attention by Dr. Dominique Leydet. Kant appears to hope that enlight-

strable expectation of Liberal respect. Nor would they include autarkic democracies that lack the material and social foundations of interdependent interests that can generate mautual knowledge and egoistic incentives in support of moral commitments.[84]

How to weed out the false positives? One way is a better data set of Liberal polities that excludes non-Liberal republics, which may be generating cases of the "inter-Liberal" conflict. How to weed out the false negatives, where the Liberal model may be getting undue credit for peace? Distinguishing Liberal peace from peace by non-Liberal means calls for process-tracing case studies and comparisons that weigh the Liberal model against non-Liberal theories of a similar scope.

Hard Cases

The Liberal peace is full of difficult cases. The collection of existing states cannot readily be sorted along a simple dichotomy: Liberal versus non-Liberal. In individual cases, passions and political and economic interests work against the pacifying tendencies of the Liberal peace.

Imperial Germany. This is a case of complicated identification. Not only was the Reichstag elected by universal male suffrage, but by and large, the state ruled under the law, respecting the civic equality and rights of its citizens. Moreover, Chancellor Bismarck began the creation of a social welfare society that served as an inspiration for similar reforms in Liberal regimes. However, the constitutional relations between the imperial executive and the representative legislature were sufficiently complex that various practices, rather than constitutional design, determined the actual relation between the government and the citizenry. The emperor appointed and could dismiss the chancellor. Although the chancellor was responsible to the Reichstag, a defeat in the Reichstag did not remove him, nor did the government absolutely depend on the Reichstag for budgetary authority. In practice Germany was a Liberal state under republican law for domestic issues. But the emperor's direct authority over the army, the army's effective independence from the minimal authority of the War Ministry, and the emperor's active role in foreign affairs (including the influential separate channel to the emperor through the military attachés) together with the tenuous constitutional relationship between the chancellor and the Reichstag made imperial Germany a state divorced from the control of its citizenry in foreign affairs.

---

ened despots will begin the process of establishing peace, even if despotic governments cannot sustain a secure peace.

[84]Kant's is a testable proposition. All three may not be necessary, and we might be able to develop a more parsimonious theory of democratic peace than the one he offers. But it appears to be the case in the modern period that there is a strong tendency for stable democracies to be Liberal and interdependent.

This authoritarian element not only influenced German foreign policy making but also shaped the international political environment (a lack of trust) the Reich faced and the domestic political environment that defined the government's options and capabilities (the weakness of Liberal opinion as against the exceptional influence of Junker militaristic nationalism). Thus direct influence on policy was but one result of the authoritarian element. Nonetheless, significant and strife-generating episodes can be directly attributed to this element. They include Tirpitz's approach to Wilhelm II to obtain the latter's sanction for a veto of Chancellor Bethmann-Hollweg's proposals for a naval agreement with Britain (1909). Added to this were Wilhelm's personal assurances of full support to the Austrians early in the Sarajevo crisis and his erratic pressure together with Moltke's on the chancellor throughout July and August 1914. These factors helped destroy whatever coherence German diplomacy might otherwise have had and led one Austrian official to ask, "Who rules in Berlin? Moltke or Bethmann?"[85]

British Nonintervention in the U.S. Civil War. Here liberal pacification was tested in a demanding manner.[86] The Civil War, which broke out in 1861, constituted not an easy but a difficult case for British Liberals. Southern propagandists (such as Hotze) working in London advertised the Southern cause as a war for self-determination, for the rights of small nations, for free trade against Northern tariffs, and for (incongruously and perhaps in appeal to British Conservatives) an aristocratic way of life as against the crass industrial democracy of the North.[87] Liberals, including even Gladstone and Russell, leaned South. Prime Minister Palmerston was cautious and looked for Southern victories to establish effective independence. Napoleon III, seeking Southern support for his adventure in Mexico, lobbied Britain for recognition.

Both the British constitutional state and its trading interest thus seemed to lean South. Public opinion was divided, with the elite generally pro-South and the radicals pro-North. Lincoln brilliantly turned the tide, however, and averted European recognition of the South with his Emancipation Proclamation in 1863. Cynics taunted the North Americans for only freeing the slaves they could not reach.[88] But the proclamation slowly at first, then with a gathering

[85] Gordon Craig, *The Politics of the Prussian Army* (New York: Oxford University Press, 1964), p. xxviii and chap. 6. For an excellent account of Bethmann's aims and the constraints he encountered, see Konrad H. Jarausch, "The Illusion of Limited War: Chancellor Bethmann-Hollweg's Calculated Risk, July 1914," *Central European History* 2 (1969).

[86] This case and the British-American War of 1812 are examined by John Owen, who insightfully emphasizes the importance of perceptions.

[87] James McPherson, *Battle Cry of Freedom* (New York: Oxford University Press, 1988), p. 548.

[88] The proclamation applied only to the states currently in rebellion and did not affect slaves held in the occupied border states.

tide mobilized the mass of Liberal middle-class and working-class support for the Union cause, leading young Henry Adams to enthuse: "The Emancipation Proclamation has done more for us here than all our former victories and all our diplomacy.[89]

The Fashoda Crisis of 1898. Here we can see the opposite: how popular passion worked against peace and against constitutional and economic interest.[90] Indeed, according to some scholars, passions, colonial uncertainty, and a long history of rivalry overwhelmed Liberal restraint and peace was rescued by the balance power.[91]

In 1893, 1894, and 1896 France sent expeditionary missions to the Sudan. Angered by having been dropped from the former Anglo-French condominium over Egypt when Britain intervened in 1882 and established sole control, the French Colonial Ministry was determined to grasp the upper Nile and perhaps obtain a stranglehold on North Africa all the way from the Atlantic to the Red Sea, slicing the equally ambitious (and fanciful) British ambitions of "Cape to Cairo" at the "waist." Unlike the earlier efforts, Marchand's 1896 expedition survived and reached the Nile in 1898. Meanwhile, fearing a French plot to dam and control the Nile, the British responded by sending Kitchener south from Egypt in a bloody campaign against the Mahdist forces that had expelled Egypt from the suzerainty it had long claimed over the Sudan. Kitchener met Marchand at Fashoda, and the crisis began.[92]

The crisis was greatly complicated by the hazy legal status of the Sudan and Britain's very indirect claim (through Egypt's claim) over it. The French regarded the region as *terra nullius* (we would say it belonged to the Sudanese). On the other hand, the crisis was greatly simplified by Britain's overwhelming military superiority—both locally (Marchand depended on Kitchener for supplies) and at sea.

[89] McPherson, p. 567.

[90] My views of this case have been greatly influenced by an excellent paper written by Ms. Hongying Wang, "Liberal Peace? A Study of the Fashoda Crisis of 1898" (American Political Science Association, 1992).

[91] See the article by Christopher Layne, discussed below, and Erik Yesson, "Power and Diplomacy in World Politics" (Ph.D. dissertation, Department of Politics, Princeton University, 1992). Other difficulties for the liberal thesis are raised by Hongying Wang, "Liberal Peace?" But for a contrast favoring Liberal explanations over Realist in the Fashoda and Spanish-American War crises, see James Lee Ray, "Comparing the Fashoda Crisis and the Spanish American War," International Studies Association, American Political Science Association, March 1994.

[92] Valuable sources on the incident include Darrell Bates, *The Fashoda Incident of 1898: Encounter on the Nile* (Oxford: Oxford University Press, 1984); G. N. Sanderson, *England, Europe, and the Upper Nile* (Edinburgh: 1965); Roger Brown, *Fashoda Reconsidered: The Impact of Domestic Politics on French Policy in Africa* (Baltimore: Johns Hopkins University Press 1970); Christopher Andrew, *Théophile Delcassé and the Making of the Entente Cordiale* (London: Macmillan, 1968); and R. Ned Lebow, *Between Peace and War.*

Contrary to Liberal expectations, war soon loomed on the horizon. Britain mobilized its fleet. The French right and its press demanded firmness. The British Tory-Unionist and Liberal-Imperialist factions demanded French withdrawal. The jingoist press on both sides called for standing firm. Although no one wanted war, neither seemed at first willing to back down.

The crisis was, however, eventually resolved through Liberal politics (but also with very good fortune). The good fortune, from the Liberal Anglo-French point of view, was simply the long-standing and widely shared French hostility to Germany. This hostility, reflecting the German conquest of Alsace-Lorraine, had not been strong enough to stand in the way of Franco-German colonial cooperation against Britain in the 1880s, but the prospect of going to war against Britain with only Germany as a potential ally was not a prospect that most of the French, elite or mass, appeared to welcome.

Also leaning against the war were three more directly Liberal internationalist factors. The elected leadership of both countries was decidedly "bourgeois Liberal" (if "bourgeois" can be used to describe the Marquess of Salisbury). Antijingoist, deeply concerned about political stability, hostile to the moods of mass democracy, imbued with the cosmopolitan culture of Europe, seeking to cultivate the growing economic interdependence of the two economies, both Salisbury and the French foreign minister, Théophile Delcassé, sought a close understanding between the two neighbors. Very importantly, throughout the crisis the French ambassador to London (Courcel) and Delcassé appeared to believe that Salisbury was doing everything he could to avoid war and that although he could not say so in public, he would be prepared to accommodate France elsewhere (in Morocco) after the crisis was resolved by a French withdrawal.[93] The Liberal press—the *Manchester Guardian* and the radical pro-Dreyfusard press in France—was thoroughly opposed to escalating the crisis. And the business elite on both sides of the Channel were appalled at the idea of war.[94]

In the end the two appear to have been very close to war. Indeed, without French resentment of Germany's conquest of Alsace-Lorraine, there might have been war. On the other hand, if the Sudan had been clearly delimited territory, there is little indication that the two sides would have felt themselves to have been so firmly in the right. Colonial disputes between Liberals elsewhere were resolved through negotiation. Both geopolitical and Liberal forces rescued the two from war.

[93] At the same time the French were told that Queen Victoria was also urging moderation on Salisbury and the cabinet. See Courcel to Delcassé, October 29, 1898, no. 465, Ministère des Affaires Étrangères, *Documents diplomatiques français*, 1st Série, Tome XIV (Paris: 1957), pp. 731, 751.

[94] See William Langer, *The Diplomacy of Imperialism* (New York: Knopf, 1951), pp. 552–53; Lebow (1981), p. 322; and Bates, pp. 154–55.

Covert Actions. The Liberal peace depends on accurate publicity. Both citizens and leaders need to be informed and the former needs to know what the latter is doing. But in covert actions this link is broken.[95] For example, in the early 1950s Jacobo Arbenz led a democratizing movement that sought to improve the lot of the poor worker in Guatemala's banana plantations and to increase popular participation in politics. He met with hostility from the large U.S. business firms, including United Fruit, which questioned his labor policies. When the dispute escalated to the point that the Arbenz government nationalized the plantations of United Fruit, the U.S. companies mobilized the efforts of the CIA against Guatemala, alleging that Arbenz was an agent of the Soviet bloc. Influenced by the companies and determined to avert "communism" in Central America, the Eisenhower administration began to plan for the armed overthrow of the Arbenz government. Engaging disaffected military officers and mobilizing a collection of subversive dirty tricks, the CIA succeeded in ousting Arbenz in 1954 and installing the pro-U.S. regime of Colonel Carlos Castillo-Armas. The Arbenz regime was far from an established Liberal democracy; it was, however, much closer to democratic and Liberal principles than the regime with which the United States replaced it.[96] The American public knew little more than the Cold War propaganda orchestrated by United Fruit and its corporate allies, which painted Arbenz as a Soviet agent and kept the public uninformed about U.S. subversion.[97]

Unfortunately, despite major advances in public disclosure and constitutional control, the CIA still engages in operations inimical to the stability and spread of a Liberal peace. In 1995 the French government revealed a CIA attempt to bribe its trade negotiators, and in March 1995 it was revealed the CIA had kept information concerning its continued support for Guatemalan military intelligence and death squads secret from not only the public but also the U.S. State Department, which had assured the public that such links had ended.[98]

The Logic of Critical Cases. Recent research has offered a valuable exploration of similarly hard cases, where war nearly occurred; others have deepened the Liberal paradigm by showing how the process of the Liberal peace might

[95] For an analysis of the problem, see Stansfield Turner, *Secrecy and Democracy* (1985), p. 179, and Harold Koh, *The National Security Constitution: Sharing Power after the Iran-Contra Affair* (1990) and a general discussion of constitutional control in Lori Damrosch, "Constitutional Control over War-Powers: A Common Core Accountability in Democratic Societies," *University of Miami Law Review* 50, pp. 801–19.

[96] It should be noted that Arbenz later acknowledged that he was and had been a communist at heart.

[97] For a good brief account, see Barnet, *Intervention and Revolution*, pp. 229–36, and for U.S. policy making, see Richard Immerman, *The CIA in Guatemala*.

[98] Sam Dillon and Tim Weiner, "In Guatemala's Dark Heart, CIA Lent Succor to Death," *New York Times*, April 2, 1995.

have worked. Together these illustrate the progressive development of the Liberal research program.

One critic chose his cases as episodes when supposed liberals came close to war.[99] In the Venezuela dispute between the United States and the United Kingdom in 1895, the conflict over the Ruhr in 1936, and the Fashoda crisis of 1898 the logic of power seemed to replace the Liberal logic of accommodation. At the minimum the disputes should succeed in warning Liberals of the dangers of imperial pursuits of principled settlements (the Venezuelan dispute), unprincipled and punitive peace settlements (the Ruhr crisis), and the contest over undefined colonial assets (Fashoda).

While these cases serve as valuable warnings, they are not as effective as tests of the Liberal theory. A theory is a coherent causal relation that presents a possible causal explanation of an outcome or set of outcomes (formulated as hypotheses) that in principle can be disconfirmed by evidence. A case study can serve, as can statistical tests, either to confirm or to disconfirm theories. Most political theories, moreover, need process-testing case studies to determine whether the allegedly determining factors in a relationship were perceived by the actors. But case studies designed to test a theory should be selected not by the dependent variable (in this case peace or war) as one does when one seeks out near wars, but according to the independent variables—liberal republics and non-Liberal states. Hard cases are not the best tests of anything but iron laws. (Most advocates of Liberal theory took the trouble to point out exceptions to the peace proneness of Liberal republics or democracies.)

Moreover, when Liberals do get into hostile crises (militarized international disputes), they have already suffered a failure even if war does not result. The Liberal failure precedes the crisis. One of the most important signs of Liberalism at work will be not the war crises resolved but the issues and crises that did not arise. Kant focused on a state of peace distinguishing Liberal relations from the state of war characterizing Liberal–non-Liberal and non-Liberal–non-Liberal relations. Kant of course was drawing on Hobbes's famous Realist description of international relations not as war but as a state of war, which is "a tract of time, wherein the will to contend by battle is sufficiently known." "For," Hobbes continues, "as the nature of foul weather, lieth not in a shower or two of rain; but in an inclination thereto of many days together: so the nature of war, consisteth not in actual fighting; but in the known disposition thereto, during all the time there is no assurance to the contrary." War and peace are thus merely indicators of the "states" that permit them. States of peace are distinguished from states of war when judicial processes, not coercive bargaining, settle disputes and when third parties are trusted to mediate con-

[99] Christopher Layne, "Kant or Cant," *International Security* (Fall 1994), pp 5–49.

flicts.[100] Liberals do hope to have a backup mechanism, Liberal respect that precludes war even in crises, but relying on this backup unrealistically tempts human passions.

We can also use case studies to probe when Liberal politicians might be abusing Liberal principles to promote personal or ideological agendas.[101] Liberal intellectuals and leaders have interpreted political regimes in a biased fashion. Double standards abound. Left-wing Liberals have found democratic mandates in revolutionary dictatorships; Stalin became, briefly, "Uncle Joe." Right-wing Liberals have found Liberal potential in anti-Communist, capitalist dictatorships.[102] If the Liberal peace rested on enlightened Liberal intellectuals alone, its salience would presumably be much less. Constraining leaders, however, and contributing to the public reliability of the peaceful expectation are institutions of representative government and material interests that can control individual biases. Each of three Kantian conditions can be conceived of as a potential backup to each of the others. The system can allow for an occasional imperialist or racist or ethnocentric or simply erratic leader, provided his or her success and tenure in office rest on a calculation of what the interests of the represented majority will bear. Similarly, mass racism or ethnocentrism can be temporarily mitigated by Liberal statesmanship or commercial interests.

When it comes to testing the validity of the Liberal peace, therefore, we need to measure regimes better than some of the actual democratic leaders do, if only to identify where they may have made an error, mistaking favored or "like" regimes for "liberal" ones. This is because ideologies are not the only source of the peace and because we shall want to discover where their particular ideologies may have led them astray. Intersubjective measures play a particularly useful check on subjective interpretation in this connection since they go beyond the views of a single intellectual, leader, or country.[103] It may be the case that the Liberal peace is systematically misinterpreted and spurious and that it really is instead a "Teutonic," "Aryan," or "Anglo-Saxon"—or today "capitalist"—condominium resulting from "Anglo-Saxon" virtue or simple profit mongering, as

[100] For example, Anne Marie Slaughter Burley has shown the differing treatments accorded to Liberal and non-Liberal states in American courts and William Dixon has examined the management of conflict prior to the outbreak of a crisis. See Anne Marie Slaughter Burley, "Law among Liberal States: Liberal Internationalism and the Act of State Doctrine," *Columbia Law Review* 92 (1992), pp. 1907–96; and William Dixon, "Democracy and the Management of Conflict," *Journal of Conflict Resolution* 37, 1 (March 1993), pp. 42–68.

[101] Ido Oren, "The 'Democratic Peace' or Peace among 'Our Kind'?," *International Security* 20, 2 (Fall 1995), pp. 147–84.

[102] Doyle, "Kant, Liberal Legacies," pp. 327–28.

[103] For example, the proportion of the citizenry that can vote; the proportion of the society open to international trade, investment, and travel; the degree of control exercised by the legislature over public decisions, including foreign affairs; the condition of personal and civic rights and the attitudes of the citizenry on questions of human rights all can be studied intersubjectively, and should be. My list of Liberal regimes is a very rough approximation of such a measure.

some of the politicians and intellectuals of earlier and current times may have thought or think. The best way to find out is to test the counterproposition. Is there any evidence that the "Teutons" hang together? Have the capitalists?

If the Liberal thesis is anything like normal social science, we shall discover exceptions, inter-Liberal wars or inter-Liberal crises, with some of the latter resolved by luck (from the Liberal view) rather than by principled respect, institutional restraint, and commercial interest. In many other instances, Liberals suggest that differences will be managed long before they become violent disputes in the public arena. Rather than our writing case after case of nonevents, however, this is where the utility of statistically testing the significance of the liberal thesis will make itself clear.

A fairer test, for example, would select a small random sample of Liberal dyads, Liberal–non-Liberal dyads, and non-Liberal dyads and examine whether the Liberal thesis holds. To test the Liberal thesis on decision making, moreover, we will need a wider investigation than is typical of conventional diplomatic history or than is provided by me of the cases discussed above. We shall want to trace decision processes outside cabinets, through parliaments and pressure groups and to, sometimes, the public. We should look for distinctions between informed and uninformed publics (often aroused by crises), axiomatic and articulated assumptions,[104] and issues on or absent from the policy agenda.

Statistical Assessment

What is the correct statistical test of the international political significance of Liberalism? The ideal test would probe whether a Liberal state, replacing a non-Liberal state, would in its relations with other Liberals and non-Liberals behave the same way in the same circumstances for as long as would have a continuation of the original non-Liberal state—and vice versa. Such a proposition is not readily testable. We can control for contiguity, income, etc. across an entire sample,[105] but not for all those factors at once, together with geopolitical position. This is a key neglect; international history has been described as "geography in motion."[106] We will need to settle for something less. One (still-incomplete) test that would be interesting would be to compare for each country its war experience during its Liberal periods with that during non-Liberal periods.[107] History also provides its own test during world wars, when states are

[104] Ernest May, *"Lessons" of the Past: The Use and Misuse of History in American Foreign Policy* (New York: Oxford University Press, 1973).

[105] Zeev Maoz and Bruce Russett, "Alliance, Contiguity, Wealth and Political Stability: Is the Lack of Conflict among Democracies a Statistical Artifact?," *International Interactions* 17, 3 (1992), pp. 245–68.

[106] I have heard the tag most often from Robert Gilpin.

[107] This is the strategy employed by John Owen in the *International Security* 20 (Fall 1995) collection.

forced to chose on which side of an impending conflict they will fight; interestingly, Liberals tend to wind up on the same side (with a few anomalies).

Can we rely on statistical data sets for anomalies? Finland's formal status as a belligerent of the Allies in World War, II is driving much of the recent statistical differences. Ruling Finland out by the thousand battle deaths criterion of Singer and Small is a useful statistical convenience but does not resolve the issue.[108] If today the United States and Britain suddenly attacked each other and stopped before sustaining one thousand casualties, no advocate of the Liberal thesis should regard the theory as vindicated. Here is where we need careful case studies. A good place to begin would be Allied and Nazi relations with Finland. Was Finland regarded as an enemy by the Allies and, if so, in a way similar to how the other enemy states were regarded? If yes, then this should be regarded as a disconfirming case; if not, not.

Once we have identified the best criteria to construct data sets, there is a key role for statistical assessment. An article by Henry Farber and Joanne Gowa presents a valuable contribution to a more refined statistical testing of the "democratic peace" proposition. Drawing on evidence from 1816 to 1980,[109] they confirm the three major propositions: that "democracies" are as likely as any other regime to get into war, that they are significantly less likely to go to war with one another, and that they are less likely to get into militarized disputes with one another.[110] (The authors follow much of the literature in including all participatory polities irrespective of whether they are Liberal or not.)

The authors then proceed to segment the dependent variable—both war and dispute data—into five periods: "1) pre–World War I (1816–1913); 2) World War I (1914–18); 3) the interwar years (1919–38); 4) World War II (1939–45); and post–World War II (1946–80)."[111] Doing so, they discover that before 1914, although democratic states were less likely to engage in war with one another, this result is no longer statistically significant (it could have occurred by

[108] J. David Singer and Melvin Small, *Resort to Arms* (Beverly Hills: Sage, 1982).

[109] Henry S. Farber and Joanne Gowa, "Polities and Peace," *International Security* 20, 2 (Fall 1995), pp. 108–32.

[110] Ibid., pp. 119, 121. The authors are raising issues that should concern Liberals. Even if democracies get into fewer disputes, why democracies get into militarized disputes at all is a problem worth more attention. Perhaps they are more commercially interdependent—and thus have more to dispute about? Their disputatiousness may also be an ironic product of their success in avoiding war; militarized signaling may be employed simply because neither party assumes real war will result. Thus the Anglo-Icelandic Cod War, one of the most serious Liberal disputes of the Cold War period, which involved naval intimidation and bumping and may have resulted in a casualty, could have been a product of the assumption that the dispute would never go as far as real war. In this respect it resembles perhaps the bumping games (constrained by nuclear deterrence) that U.S. and Soviet submarines played during the Cold War.

[111] Ibid., p. 119.

chance). (The democratic probability of war is lower in every period but World War II, but the relationship is statistically powerful only during World War I and the Cold War.) Moreover, democratic states before World War I are more, not less, likely to get into low-level disputes with one another than are nondemocratic states with other nondemocratic states. (Democratic states are less likely to get into disputes in every period but the pre-1914 period, but only the period of World War II and the Cold War are statistically significant.) The results are interesting.

The reasons for segmenting the data, however, are less clear. Segmenting the data in that fashion makes no more sense than picking a random set of decades or half centuries, unless one is testing the democratic or Liberal model against some other model. It is worth paying some attention to their justifications.

The authors offer two reasons for breaking up the data set of democratic peace and war. First, they note that general wars such as World War I and World War II are different from dyadic wars. These wars are seen to involve systemic effects and attempts to "pass the buck" that operate over and above dyad-specific or domestic regime effects.[112] This may be so, but if so, these periods of general war should constitute an especially difficult time for Liberal cooperation. General systemic wars constitute especially severe tests of dyadic conceptions of war as states are pressured to choose sides on strategic alliance criteria ("the enemy of my enemy is my friend") rather than regime criteria. In World War II this produced the well-known anomaly of the formal state of war existing between the Liberal Allies and Liberal Finland, because Finland was an enemy of the non-Liberal Soviet Union, which was allied to the United States and Britain. Nonetheless, Liberal logic should resist systemic logic and hold up here. Why exclude those challenges?

A second reason offered for separating pre–World War I data from post–World War II data is unspecified differences in "processes underlying alliance formation [and] war outbreak," on the one hand, and "bipolarity and nuclear weapons," on the other. First, it is of course just these processes that we seek to test; what is the alternative set of processes? Second, one could and should test the Liberal or democratic model against other theories such as international structure—bipolarity and multipolarity, nuclear or conventional weapons. Indeed there have been—so far—no wars between atomic or nuclear-armed powers.[113] Nuclear deterrence thus might account for peace among the United

[112] Ibid., p. 114.

[113] Kenneth Waltz has elaborated the reasons for nuclear peace in Scott D, Sagan and Kenneth Waltz,*The spread pf Nuclear Weapons: A Debate* (New York: Norton, 1955). One exception to the nuclear peace might be the battles in 1969 between the USSR and the People's Republic of China along the Ussuri River Border. But casualty figures are uncertain in that conflict, and so was the status of China's deliverable nuclear weapons.

States, Britain, and France in the Cold War, and it widens the argument to incorporate U.S.-Soviet relations. Does it also account for fewer militarized disputes and as extensive cooperation? Doesn't it leave unaccounted for the preatomic peace among Liberal republics. More promisingly, do multipolar alliances perhaps generate interallied strife, and bipolar alliances interallied peace? Perhaps common security interests are stronger in alliances in bipolar systems, or perhaps the bipolar hegemons preserve the peace by policing the weaker allies. It would be worth testing whether bipolar peace is the true underlying cause of the peace among democracies in the U.S. bloc of the Cold War—and, presumably, an equivalent peace among Communist republics in the Soviet bloc?

None of the measures captures the temporal or institutionalized dimension of the Liberal peace. Liberalism claims to avert not merely war in any given year but any war among Liberal states as long as they are Liberal. It looks to the probability not that war was avoided by Britain and France in 1898 but that it was avoided continuously for as long as they both were Liberal. If we multiply the probabilities in each given year to find the joint probability over almost two hundred years, the probability that the Liberal peace is a statistical accident becomes remarkably small (2 preceded by a decimal point and twenty zeros, in Bruce Russett's calculation).[114] Wars, however, are not independent events. War in one year makes war in the next likely, as peace connects to peace, so the statistical measure is suspect. But not measuring the joint probability is equally suspect because it is that very jointness that is the essence of the Liberal claim.

The data, moreover, on democratic war and democratic disputes could just as well be a product of measurement error (the participatory polities were not Liberal) or uncontrolled factors—greater commerce, perhaps, among democracies. Interdependence is a source both of conflict and, for Liberals (by argument), of peace. If one controls for commerce, does the relationship between democracies and disputes change?[115] Or, perhaps, the pre-1900 disputatiousness of democracies is due to the incompleteness of Liberal democracy in the earlier era when the franchise was limited (*inter alia*, women were denied the franchise) and democratic principles were new. The best we can do is test theoretical models against each other. Until we have an alternative model, segmenting the data does not produce meaningful results.

[114] Bruce Russett, "The Democratic Peace—and yet It Moves," *International Security* 19, 4 (Spring 1995), pp. 164–75.

[115] John Oneal, Frances Oneal, Zeev Maoz, and Bruce Russett in "The Liberal Peace: Interdependence, Democracy and International Conflict, 1950–1985," *Journal of Peace Research* (February 1996), pp. 11–28, examine these questions and find that both interdependence and democracy contribute to peace.

Alternatives?

Some have suggested that the United States abandon the pursuit of democratic enlargement and instead recognize that states in fact pursue "common interests" over "common polities."[116] But "common interests" do not constitute an alternative model. The debate is not about whether states pursue their interests; it is about how to define and judge the interests of states. Realists (of a Structural persuasion) see those interests in terms of the balance of power; Liberals, in terms of Liberal accommodation; Marxists in terms of class warfare and solidarity. When we have to choose, is democratization a better long-term strategy for the United States than enhancing our position in the balance of power? It is over choices such as these that the debate should continue.

In the end, as with most theoretical disputes, the debate will turn on the alternatives. Liberal theory should not be compared with the statistical residual, a richly described case study, or "History" but with the comparative validity of other theories of similar scope. To do this, we need disconfirmable versions of the two other leading modern candidates, Realism and Marxism, which is in part the aim of this book.

FOREIGN POLICY DILEMMAS

Even if our answer favors democratization, Edward Mansfield and Jack Snyder have warned us that democratization is not enough.[117] Given all the instabilities of regime change, democratization may provoke more war. Their statistical analysis has recently been challenged, and the evidence is still in dispute.[118] But if Mansfield and Snyder are correct, Liberals have little to be surprised about, but much to worry about. Without Liberal principles and international interdependence, all of which take time, democratizing regimes may well be war-prone.

We have here a useful warning. Yet in the long run liberalization across nations seems to hold great promise. How does one get from here to there? Golden parachutes for ex-dictators and the military are one idea with a considerable history that may contribute to at least short-run stability.[119] Extending international institutions, or enhancing them, may be another answer.[120] Can

[116] Farber and Gowa (1995), p. 122.
[117] Edward D. Mansfield and Jack Snyder, "Democratization and the Danger of War," *International Security* 20, 1 (Summer 1995), pp. 5–38.
[118] Andrew Enterline, "Driving while Democratizing: A Rejoinder to Mansfield and Snyder," *International Security* 20, 4 (Spring 1996), pp. 183–207.
[119] Mansfield and Snyder, p. 6.
[120] See Jack Snyder, "Averting Anarchy in the New Europe," *International Security* 14, 4 (Spring 1990), pp. 5–41.

the promise of European Union membership and the presence of assistance and association be an institutional bridge over a difficult transition? Can similar institutional mechanisms become operative in Africa and Asia? These are well worth our attention.

Preserving the legacy of the Liberal peace without succumbing to the legacies of Liberal imprudence has proven to be both a moral and a strategic challenge. The bipolar structure of the international system and the near certainty of mutual devastation resulting from a nuclear war between the superpowers has created a "crystal ball effect" that has helped constrain the tendency toward miscalculation present at the outbreak of so many wars in the past.[121] But this "nuclear peace" appears to be limited to the superpowers. It has not curbed military interventions in the Third World. Moreover, it is subject to a desperate technological race designed to overcome its constraints and to crises that have pushed even the superpowers to the brink of war. We must still reckon with the imprudent vehemence and moods of complaisant appeasement that have almost alternately swept Liberal democracies.

Yet restraining Liberal imprudence, whether aggressive or passive, may not be possible without threatening Liberal pacification. Improving the strategic acumen of our foreign policy calls for introducing steadier strategic calculations of the long-run national interest and more flexible responses to changes in the international political environment. Constraining the indiscriminate meddling of our foreign interventions calls for a deeper appreciation of the "particularism of history, culture, and membership."[122] But both the improvement in strategy and the constraint on intervention in turn seem to require an executive freed from the restraints of a representative legislature in the management of foreign policy and a political culture indifferent to the universal rights of individuals. These in their turn could break the chain of constitutional guarantees, the respect for representative government, and the web of transnational contact that have sustained the pacific union of Liberal states.

Liberalism at the twentieth century's end looks remarkably robust. Ironically, so it did at the beginning. If nothing else, we should have learned something about peace, war, and cooperation from our very bloody twentieth century. We have paid a high tuition; let us hope we have learned that Liberal democracy is worth defending. The promise of peace may well be one more reason for doing so.

[121] Kenneth Waltz, "The Stability of a Bipolar World," *Daedalus* XCIII (Summer 1964), pp. 881–909, and Albert Carnesale, Paul Doty, Stanley Hoffmann, Samuel Huntington, Joseph Nye, and Scott Sagan, *Living with Nuclear Weapons* (New York: Bantam, 1983), p. 44.
[122] Michael Walzer, *Spheres of Justice* (New York: Basic Books, 1983), p. 5.

Conclusion: Liberals and Realists: Explaining Differences

LIKE THE REALISTS, Liberals display significant differences. The institutionalists (Locke and Bentham) focus on individual-level (Image I) determinants, the commercialists (Smith and Schumpeter) on societal-level (Image II), and the internationalists (Kant) on interstate (Image III) determinants of the state of war. Their conceptions of what describes the state of war also differ. For none of the Liberals does the state of nature (without government) produce the state of war; for each the state of war must be made known by aggressive acts or declared intentions to aggress. For all the Liberals—unlike the Realists—there exists the more or less firm possibility of a state of peace.

For Locke and Bentham, the state of peace is easily corrupted by the inconveniences of prejudiced and partial judgment, misinformation, and uncertainty; and the state of war and state of peace begin to merge. Individual citizens and statespersons whose perceptions and interest can corrupt peace can, if they are dedicated to the rule of law, defend the rights of life, liberty, and property and achieve a measure of international justice. They are, however, often likely to fail and may only succeed in preserving the security of their state.

For Smith and Schumpeter the state of war can be tamed by the development of commercial society or capitalist democracy, which rationalize and align individual interests with social interests through markets. The state of war is a product of autocratic imperialism and export monopolism, social formations that are atavistic after the process of free market capitalism has begun to take root. Indeed, it is the development of the market economy that in the long run will ensure that the warlike forces of traditional autocracies will evolve into extinction.

For the Kantian internationalists, the state of war is a potent structural force

Variants of Modern Liberalism

	Institutionalists	*Commercialists*	*Internationalists*
State of War	international homogeneous	international heterogeneous	international heterogeneous
State of Peace	"inconvenienced" uncertain, troubled	among capitalists	"pacific union" among republics
Actors	individuals	markets/societies	republics/nonrepublics
Source of State of War	prejudice misinformation	autocratic imperialism monopolism	autocratic diversion/ liberal crusading
Strategy of Peace	international law	free trade, capitalist development	republican enlargement

that can be overcome only by a process of constitutional evolution of world politics in which emerging republican governments establish among themselves a state of peace, a pacific union. By instituting reliable international law, collective security, and transnational "hospitality," republics create a new politics of peace whose expansion offers the prospect of an eventual perpetual and universal peace.

Liberalism, especially Kantian Liberalism, lays a special claim to what world politics is and can be: a state of peace. It also claims a special property right in what shapes the politics of Liberal states—liberty and democracy. But how special is the Liberal peace? Can it be equally well explained by Realist concerns, such as the balance of power? And how can we reconcile Machiavelli's love of liberty and Thucydides's and Rousseau's commitments to democracy with the Liberals' claim to their ownership? Or why should liberty and democracy produce war in the hands and minds of the Realists and peace in the hands and minds of the Liberals?

PEACE

Are Liberal principles and institutions the true source of the peace among Liberal states? Neither Realist theories of the balance of power nor Marxist theories of capitalist foreign policy account well for long periods of peace among states of one constitutional regime. Dispositional democratic theories or commercial capitalist theories or purely rational egoist theories explain at best the peace, which is only half the Liberal tradition that also includes the state of war with non-Liberals—imprudent vehemence and supine complaisance. Each can account for certain of the effects; none accounts for them considered together. Kant's theory, on the other hand, appears to be both necessary and sufficient to explain the Liberal peace.

Realists hold that the effects of differing domestic regimes (whether Liberal or not) are overridden by the international anarchy under which all states live. Hobbes does not bother to distinguish between "some council or one man" when he discusses the sovereign. Differing domestic regimes do affect the quantity of resources available to the state and the quality of its morale. But the ends that shape policy are determined for the Realist by the fundamental quest for power that shapes all politics or the competitive structure of the international system.

At the level of the strategic decision maker, Realists could argue that a Liberal peace could be merely the outcome of prudent diplomacy. Indeed, some, including Hobbes, have argued that sovereigns have a natural duty not to act against "the reasons of peace."[1] Individuals establish (that is, should establish) a sovereign to escape from the brutalities of the state of nature, the war of all against all, that follows from competition for scarce goods, scrambles for prestige, and fear of another's attack when there is no sovereign to provide for lawful acquisition or regularized social conduct or personal security. "Dominions were constituted for peace's sake, and peace was sought for safety's sake." The natural duty of the sovereign is therefore the safety of the people. Yet for the Hobbesian, prudent policy cannot be an enforceable right of citizens because sovereigns, who remain in the state of nature with respect to their subjects and other sovereigns, cannot themselves be subjects.[2]

The condition of the international system for Hobbesians remains, moreover, a state of war. Prudence can be enhanced by deterring technologies, transparency, geography, and a variety of other factors in complex games of chicken (as we saw in the discussion of Hobbesian Realism). Military technologies changed from offensive to defensive and from distinguishable to indistinguishable, yet the pacific union persisted and only among Liberal states. Hobbesian prudence recommends taking actions "whatsoever shall seem to conduce to the lessening of the power of foreigners whom they [the sovereigns] suspect, whether by slight or force."[3] If preventive wars are prudent, the Realists' prudence obviously

[1] Hobbes, *Leviathan,* chap. 13, para. 62, p. 186.
[2] Ibid., pp. 186–210, 212.
[3] Thomas Hobbes, "De Cive," p. 171.

cannot account for more than a century and a half of peace among independent Liberal states, many of which have crowded one another in the center of Europe.

Distance or weakness can sometimes make states peaceful simply because they lack the opportunity to engage in war. In Africa distance and weak states have made wars seem prohibitively expensive, and a political culture that valued postcolonial independence almost above all else took the prestige out of conquest. Together they seem to have produced a strong tendency toward interstate peace in the postwar period. Civil strife, on the other hand, has been frequent, and interstate wars have occurred: Tanzania invaded Uganda in 1979, Ethiopia has clashed with Somalia, and subversion and support for guerrillas had been ongoing in the confrontation between frontline states and apartheid South Africa. Nigeria and other West African states are now intervening in Liberia (with the full endorsement of the UN). Nonetheless, compared with early modern Europe—and twentieth-century Europe too—Africa in the postwar era has been an oasis of peace.[4] Much of Latin America—with a similar handful of exceptions—has benefited form an equivalent discrediting of war.[5] But this is not an explanation of the peace among Liberals, which is continuous and among the most wealthy and powerful states in the international system.

Raymond Aron has identified three other types of prudential interstate peace consequent upon the structure of the international system: empire, hegemony, and equilibrium.[6] An empire generally succeeds in creating an internal peace, but this is not an explanation of peace among independent Liberal states. Hegemony can create peace by overawing potential rivals. Although far from perfect and certainly precarious, United States hegemony, as Aron notes, might account for the interstate peace in South America in the postwar period during the height of the Cold War conflict. However, the Liberal peace cannot be attributed merely to effective international policing by a predominant hegemon—Britain in the nineteenth century, the United States in the postwar period. Even though a hegemon might well have an interest in enforcing a peace for the sake of commerce or investments or as a means of enhancing its prestige or security, hegemons such as seventeenth-century France were not peace-enforcing, and the Liberal peace persisted in the 1920s and 1930s, when international society lacked a predominant hegemonic power. This explanation overestimates both British and American hegemonic control. Neither Britain nor the United States was able to prevent direct challenges to its interests (colonial competition in the nineteenth century, Middle East diplomacy and con-

[4]Robert Jackson, *Quasi-States: Sovereignty, International Relations, and the Third World* (Cambridge: Cambridge University Press, 1990).
[5]Arie Kacowicz, "Explaining Zones of Peace: Democracies as Satisfied Powers," *Journal of Peace Research* 32, 3 (1995), pp. 265–76.
[6]Aron, *Peace and War*, pp. 151–54.

flicts over trading with the enemy in the postwar period). Where then was the hegemonic capacity to prevent all armed conflicts between Liberal regimes, many of which were remote and others strategically or economically insignificant? Liberal hegemony and leadership are important, but they are neither necessary nor sufficient to explain a Liberal peace.

Peace through equilibrium (the multipolar classical balance of power or the bipolar "Cold War") also draws upon prudential sources of peace. An awareness of the likelihood that aggressive attempts at hegemony will generate international opposition should, it is argued, deter these aggressive wars. But bipolar stability discourages polar or superpower wars, not proxy or small-power wars. And multipolar balancing of power also encourages warfare to seize, for example, territory for strategic depth against a rival expanding its power from internal growth. Neither readily accounts for general peace or for the Liberal peace.

Realism does, however, provide a plausible account of imprudent vehemence and supine complaisance, the other two effects associated with the foreign relations of Liberal states. Realism does not guarantee that states will be prudent. It only holds that imprudent states will not be successful. The international state of war offers many opportunities for aggression, and a concern with enhancing the balance of power can account for an interest in imperial expansion and for many of the Cold War interventions. The rational pursuit of narrow state interests can also explain incentives toward appeasement, particularly in multipolar systems, such as that of the 1930s, when Liberal and other states might reasonably doubt the willingness of other status quo states to come to the aid of a state willing to challenge the imperial ambitions of revisionist states.[7]

Thus Realist theories can account for aspects of certain periods of international stability. And they each can account for incentives toward imprudent aggression and complaisance. But the logic of the balance of power and international hegemony does not explain the separate peace maintained for more than 150 years among states sharing one particular form of governance, Liberal principles and institutions.

Most Liberal theorists also have offered inadequate guidance in understanding the exceptional nature of Liberal pacification. Lockean (Image I) Liberals acknowledge that purely ideological or normative commitments seem insufficient to account for the peace. Heads of state seem to need some institutional guarantee beyond a normative commitment to international rights in order to regularize a state of peace. The mutual respect and representative procedures of Liberal government seems to be what it takes to lock in the solidaristic sentiments of international law, and extensive economic interdependence may also help.

[7]Marxism offers an account of the Liberal (capitalist) peace. We shall consider its account of peace and criticisms of Liberal capitalist peace in chapter 10.)

Commercial (Image II) Liberals have argued that democratic states would be inherently peaceful simply and solely because in these states citizens rule the polity and bear the costs of wars. Unlike monarchs, citizens are not able to indulge their aggressive passions and have the consequences suffered by someone else.[8] Smith saw a strong tendency for manufacturing states to be peaceable. Schumpeter argued that laissez-faire capitalism contains an inherent tendency toward rationalism and that since war is irrational, Liberal capitalisms will be pacifistic. Others still, such as Montesquieu, claim that "commerce is the cure for the most destructive prejudices" and "Peace is the natural effect of trade."[9] While these developments can help account for aspects of the Liberal peace, they do not explain the fact that Liberal states are peaceful only in relations with other Liberal states.

LIBERTY

The Liberals were not the first philosophers to conceive of the value of human liberty or equality. What makes a Liberal a Liberal is making *equal, nondiscriminatory liberty* the center of one's political philosophy. What makes for international Liberal theory is an exploration of the significance of that choice for world politics.

Machiavelli, for example, gloried in the freedom of the citizens of his republics. It was what made Rome strong. But for Machiavelli, liberty is a means to an end, the glory, the imperial glory, of the republics he envisaged. So Thomas Macaulay, the great nineteenth-century Liberal historian, in his *Essays* remarked on Machiavelli's anti-Liberal, national republicanism: "The good of the body, distinct from the good of the members, and sometimes hardly compatible with the good of the members, seems to be the one object which he proposes to himself. Of all political fallacies, this has perhaps had the widest and most mischievous operation."

Locke is different (and differently dangerous). Locke says of all men: "[H]e and the rest of all mankind are one Community, make up one society distinct from all other creatures. And were it not for the corruption and vitiousness of degenerate Men, there would be no need for any other; no necessity that Men

[8]The absolute incompatibility of democracy and war was classically asserted by Paine in *The Rights of Man.* Randall Schweller, "Domestic Structure and Preventive War," *World Politics* 44 (January 1992) finds some evidence to support the view that democratic hegemons do not engage in preventive wars. And Carol Ember, Melvin Ember, and Bruce Russett in "Peace between Participatory Policies," *World Politics* 44 (July 1992) find that pacification is also evident in certain preindustrial tribal societies.

[9]This literature is surveyed and analyzed by Hirschman, "Rival Interpretations of Market Society: Civilizing, Destructive, or Feeble?"

should separate from this great and natural Community, and by positive agreements combine into smaller and divided associations."[10] He did not mean that states should be abolished or that national security was no longer a prime duty of statesmanship. He just meant that mankind itself was a community, greater in an important sense than Rome or any other single republic. Our understanding of the whole of mankind was what allowed us to understand our rights and thereby gave to us all a set of duties.

Locke is a bridge to the Realists in that he too saw the dangers of world politics, including the possibility of slipping from a state of peace to a state of war in the foreign relations of any state, whether Liberal or not. The federative power closely resembles the canonical unitary rational actor of Realism. Partiality, biased adjudication, weak enforcement all lay close to the state of peace that Liberals should maintain, thus occasioning a need for constant preparedness and strategic games playing. Statesmen, moreover, should pursue national "advantage." But their advantage is tempered, or fenced, by human rights. Competition, glory, and fear will, as they did for Thucydides and Hobbes, shape foreign policy because world politics is a troubled peace. But they do so, should do so, and will do so for authentic Liberals only to the extent they are compatible with a respect for the life, liberty, and property that gives Liberal states authority at home.

DEMOCRACY

Nor were the Liberals the first to conceive of the value of democracy either as a means or an end. Indeed, for two millennia between Thucydides and Machiavelli democracy was the great imperial model of government. But in the modern Liberal version it now becomes the great engine of peace.

Thucydides, Rousseau, Kant, and Schumpeter each are advocates (and theorists) of popular, or democratic, or representative republican government. Yet they expect democratic foreign relations to be (variously) imperialist, isolationist, internationalist, and pacific. How can we explain their differences and understand the multiple legacies of democratic foreign affairs?

The pattern of expected foreign relations of democratic states that they offer us can be seen in the table that distinguishes Thucydides's democratic imperialism, Rousseau's democratic isolationism, Kant's Liberal internationalism, and Schumpeter's Liberal pacifism. Each theory rests on fundamentally different views of the nature of man, the state, and international relations.

Let us examine the theorists by pairs.

[10] Locke, *Second Treatise*, para. 128.

Schumpeter and Kant. Schumpeter's man is rationalized, individualized, and democratized. He is also homogenized, pursuing material interests "monistically." Since his material interests lie in peaceful trade, he and the democratic state that he and his fellow citizens control are pacifistic. Schumpeter's "materialistic monism" leaves little room for noneconomic objectives, whether espoused by states or individuals. His states, moreover, are the same. The political life of individuals seems to have been homogenized at the same time as the individuals were "rationalized, individualized, and democratized." Citizens, capitalists and workers, rural and urban, seek material welfare. Schumpeter presumes that no one seems to want to rule. He also presumes that no one is prepared to take those measures (such as stirring up foreign quarrels to preserve a domestic ruling coalition) that enhance one's political power, despite detrimental effects on mass welfare. Just as ideal domestic politics are homogenized, so world politics too is homogenized. Materially monistic and democratically capitalist, all states evolve toward free trade and liberty together. Countries differently constituted seem to disappear from Schumpeter's analysis. "Civilized nations" govern "culturally backward regions."

Unlike Schumpeter's capitalist democracies, Kant's constitutional democracies, including our own, remain in a state of war with nonrepublics. Liberal republics see themselves as threatened by aggression from nonrepublics that are not constrained by representation. Liberal politicians often fail in their categorical moral duties and stir up foreign quarrels with non-Liberal states as a way of enhancing their own domestic power. And even though wars often cost more than the economic return they generate, Liberal republics are prepared to protect and promote—sometimes forcibly—democracy, private property, and the rights of individuals overseas in nonrepublics that, because they do not authentically represent the rights of individuals, have incomplete rights to noninterference. These wars may liberate oppressed individuals overseas; they also can generate enormous suffering.

Thucydides and Rousseau. Thucydides's citizens (unlike Schumpeter's) are splendidly diverse in their goals, both at home and abroad. Their characters are shaped in varying proportions by courage, ambition, fear, profit, caution, glory,

Foreign Relations of Democratic States

	Peace	*War*	*Imperialism*
with/			
Democratic	S, K	R, T	T
Nondemocratic	S	R, T, K	T, K

(S = Schumpeter; K = Kant; T = Thucydides; and R = Rousseau)

and patriotism. Although they are equal before the law and all citizens have a right to vote, their circumstances greatly differ, divided as they are among rich and poor, urban and rural. Internationally their states are driven by fear, honor, and self-advantage. States too are radically unequal in size, resources, and power. Such a people and such a state find imperialism useful, feasible, and valued. In a dangerous world, empire adds to the security, profit, and glory of the powerful majority, even if not of all the citizens. The *demos* makes naval power effective and cheap.

Rousseau's citizens of the Social Contract too are equal, rational, and free. But going beyond legal equality, social and economic equality distinguishes them from Thucydides's Athenians. Particular "wills," such as those that drove the Athenians to Sicily, would yield to the General Will—the rational, national, general interest—which Thucydides (Pericles) defined as precluding further imperial expansion. The exploitation of noncitizens in the empire (the source of so much national revenue) also would be unacceptable in a Rousseauian republic that demands that all men be free, ruling and being ruled on an equal basis. This obviously precludes slavery. It also requires that every other form of political rule that does not give an equal voice to all affected has to be excluded from a free democracy. That is why Rousseau's democracy has to be small. Nor, lastly, would Rousseau allow the extensive commerce that made empire both valued and feasible. The Rousseauian democracy is free, independent, and isolationist.

Rousseau and Kant. Kant's citizens, like Rousseau's, are free, politically equal, and rational. The Kantian state thus is governed publicly according to law, as a republic. Kant's constitutional democracy thus also solves the problem of governing equals. But his citizens are different in two respects. They retain their diverse individuality, whether they are the "rational devils" he says that we egoists often find ourselves to be or the ethical agents, treating other individuals as ends rather than as means, that we can and should become.

Given this diversity, Kantian republics are experiments in how "[t]o organize a group of rational beings who demand general laws for their survival, but of whom each inclines toward exempting himself, and to establish their constitution in such a way that, in spite of the fact that their private attitudes are opposed, these private attitudes mutually impede each other in such a manner that their public behavior is the same as if they did not have such evil attitudes."[11]

Like Rousseau's direct democracy, Kant's constitutional democracy exercises democratic caution in the interest of the majority. But unlike Rousseau's Gen-

[11] Kant, PP, p. 453. For a comparative discussion of the political foundations of Kant's ideas, see Judith Shklar, *Ordinary Vices* (Cambridge, Mass.: Harvard University Press, 1984), pp. 226–49.

eral Will, Kant's republics are capable of appreciating the moral equality of all individuals. The Rousseauian citizen cedes all rights to his fellow citizens, retaining only the right to equal consideration. In order to be completely self-determining, Rousseau requires that there be no limit but equality on the sovereignty and authority of the General Will. The resulting communitarianism is intense; every aspect of culture, morality, and social life is subject to the creation and the re-creation of the national citizenry. The tendency to enhance domestic consciousness through external hostility and what Rousseau calls *amour propre* would be correspondingly high. Just as individuality disappears into collective consciousness, so too does an appreciation for the international rights of foreign republics.[12] These international rights of republics derive from our ability to reconstruct in our imagination the act of representation of foreign individuals, who are our moral equals. Kant appears to think that the General Will, which Rousseau thinks can be realized only within the community, can be intuited by each individual as the categorical imperative. Rousseau's democracy—for the sake of intensifying national identity—limits our identification to fellow citizens.

This imaginative act of Kantian cosmopolitan identification benefits from the institutional process of republican government. Constitutionally divided powers among the executive, legislature, and the judiciary require public deliberation and sometimes compromise and thereby mitigate the effect of particular passions or hasty judgment. Rousseau's direct democracy, while deliberative, appears to slight the value of republican delay.

Moreover, for the sake of equality and autonomy, Rousseau's democracy precludes the private ties of commerce and social interaction across borders that lead to both domestic diversity and transnational solidarity. These material ties sustain the transnational, or cosmopolitan, identity of individuals with one another that serves as the foundation of international respect, which in turn is the source of the spirit of international law that requires tolerance and peace among fellow constitutional democracies (while exacerbating conflict between constitutional democracies and all other states).

Rousseau shares with Kant the idea of democratic rationality. Rousseau, however, excludes both the moral individualism and the social pluralism that provide the foundations for Kant's "international" and "cosmopolitan" laws, and thereby precludes the Liberal peace.

Comparing the Realists Thucydides and Rousseau, on the one hand, with

[12]Drawing on historical evidence of the early twentieth century, Van Evera, "Primed for Peace" reaches a similar conclusion about the dangers of militaristic nationalism. The comparison detailed here, however, suggests an even wider indictment of the danger of nationalism among democracies.

the Liberals Kant and Schumpeter, on the other, we can say that whatever the differences in their special views of man and the nature of domestic politics, the first two agree that the *polis* or state either does or should command all force and command all loyalty. Differences among actual states and personal values are then contained by their similar degree of national authority. There is thus no room for the individualism and domestic diversity that Kant finds to be at the root of the transnational loyalties and transnational interests that make a republican peace. Nor is there room for the simple transnational materialism Schumpeter sees as governing the interests of pacific democratic majorities. The democracies of Thucydides and Rousseau remain in a state of war.

To the extent that these theoretical distinctions tap the actual range of diversity in the development of contemporary democracies, they offer us some useful warnings about the international implications of the current trend toward democratization. While majority rule may be a necessary condition of a state of peace, it is not a sufficient condition. Autarky and nationalism can undermine democratic peace. To establish peace among themselves, democracies must also define individual rights in such a way that the cosmopolitan rights of all mankind are entailed in the moral foundations of the rights of domestic citizens. And they must allow the material ties of transnational society to flourish among themselves.

PART THREE

SOCIALISM

INTRODUCTION

A Great Betrayal?— 1914, Marxism, and Leninism

ON AUGUST 4, 1914, the German Social Democratic Party members of the Reichstag voted unanimously for war credits. So too in Austria, France, Belgium, and Britain the Socialist parties lined up behind their national governments in support of the war. At international meetings of these Socialist parties at Stuttgart (1907), Copenhagen (1910), and Basel (1912), their organization (the Second International) had pledged itself against militarism and in favor of concerted action to make war on war. So it seemed that on August 4 the solidarity of the international proletariat rang hollow.[1] V. I. Lenin, who was soon to lead the Communist movement, roundly condemned them: "The conduct of the leaders of the German Social Democratic Party of the Second International (1889–1914) who have voted the war budget and who repeat the bourgeois chauvinistic phrases of the Prussian Junkers and of the bourgeoisie is a direct betrayal of Socialism."[2]

[1] I have found the following especially valuable: Georges Haupt, *Socialism and the Great War* (Oxford: Clarendon, 1972), chap. 4; Peter Gay, *The Dilemma of Democratic Socialism: Eduard Bernstein's Challenge to Marx* (New York: Collier, 1962), pp. 276–80; James Joll, *The Second International, 1889–1914* (London: Weidenfeld and Nicolson, 1955), chap. 7; William Walling, *The Socialists and the Great War* (New York: Henry Holt and Company, 1915), chap. 10; and S. F. Kissin, *War and the Marxists* (Boulder, Colo.: Westview Press, 1989).

[2] This was the second of the Seven Theses against War, which Lenin announced in Bern to the handful of his Bolshevik fellow exiles on September 6 or 7, 1914, quoted in Bertram Wolfe, *Three Who Made a Revolution* (New York: Dell Publishing Co., 1964), pp. 635–36. Note the birth and *death* dates for the Second International. See Georges Haupt, *Aspects of International Socialism: 1871–1914* (Cambridge: Cambridge University Press, 1986), chap. 5, for a thorough account of Lenin's relations with the Second International just prior to the First World War.

The Socialists seemed simultaneously to betray international Socialism and to refute the Marxist theory of international politics. When Socialists failed to behave as they seemed to have said they would, when in fact Socialists joined the capitalists—that is, when both behaved like nationalists—what was there in Marxism to warrant a separate theory? Many of our leading international relations theorists have answered, "Very little."

In this part I want to suggest that it is time for a change of view. The Socialists of 1914, panicked and confused as they may have been, may have betrayed the cause of peace, but their actions did not refute Marxist theory. Marxism did not preclude the defense of the nation. Nor did it require opposing every policy adopted by a bourgeois government. Leninism was not Marxism. The "Marxist-Leninist" tradition of course has common roots in Marxist philosophy, but its explanations and judgments are at least as diverse as the differences between Machiavelli and Hobbes or Locke and Schumpeter. Neither was Marxist internationalism identical with nationalism or the Realists' pursuit of the "national interest." Nowhere in power, unable to prevent the war, the Marxists followed their governments when their governments adopted policies with which Marxists should not have disagreed. Where the two conflicted, as (I shall explain later) they did concerning imperialism in the Balkans for Austrians, Hungarians, and Russians and concerning support for the war in August 1914 for Italians, Russians, and Serbians, the Marxists acted as Marxists.

In this part I shall use the case of the Socialists of 1914 in order to illustrate Marx's theory and distinguish it from Lenin's theory. Socialist theory focuses on the material conditions of life and on the classes—workers and capitalists, and financiers, landowners, merchants, small farmers, peasants—that have defined their interests in relation to jobs and wealth. Where Realists focus on the state and political leaders and consider security and power to be the first goals of international relations and where Liberals focus on representation, the individual, and his or her rights, Socialists focus on class and the material interests those classes embody.

In the first chapter I draw on the writings of Marx and Engels in order to reconstruct a description of Marxist international theory that captures its views on internationalism, imperialism, peace, and war. In the following chapter on Lenin, I distinguish Lenin from the Marxist tradition and develop his major insights from *Imperialism: The Highest Stage of Capitalism*. In the conclusion I then show how the decisions of the Socialists of 1914 were consistent with Marxist internationalism, not with Leninism and not with some important versions of Realism and Liberalism. That consistency suggests how individuals or states imbued with class consciousness might pursue the contest of world politics in ways distinct from those of Realists or Liberals.

THE ISSUE: 1914 AND THE SOCIALIST TRADITION

Lenin's condemnation of the Socialists has echoed through our time. In his speech before the Twentieth Party Congress of the Communist Party of the Soviet Union in 1956, Nikita Khrushchev reaffirmed Lenin's condemnation: "Before World War I the main force opposed to the threat of war—the world prolteriat—was disorganized by the treachery of the leaders of the Second International."[3] Professional historians also concur in the significance of 1914, if not in the specific judgment.[4] Julius Braunthal concludes the first volume of his magisterial *History of the International* thus: "The bond of brotherhood between the nations had been broken and the spirit of international solidarity of the working classes superseded by a spirit of national solidarity between the proletariat and the ruling classes."[5]

Historians have also highlighted the confusion and fear that surrounded that epic moment. Anticipating the imposition of a state of siege as an excuse to suppress the party, the German Social Democratic Party sent its leaders Ebert and Braun to Switzerland in order to safeguard the party's treasury. The party feared being abandoned by the mass of the patriotic working class if it chose to stand against a war that many of the workers saw as an act of self-defense, a view reinforced everywhere by governments that subjected Socialists to barrages of propaganda.[6] The leaders in Germany contemplated the prospect of contributing to a Russian invasion, just as the French feared a German invasion if the working class heeded a call for strikes.[7]

For many social scientists the betrayal of Socialist solidarity implied the refutation of Marxist theory. "So far as the majorities of the Marxist parties were concerned," Joseph Schumpeter writes, "socialism at the crossroads (1914) had

[3]In G. F. Hudson, Richard Lowenthal, and R. MacFarquhar, eds., *The Sino-Soviet Dispute* (New York: Praeger, 1961), pp. 43–44.
[4]James Joll has found that "[t]he Socialist world was never to be the same again after 1914 . . . international solidarity was broken . . . and the new Communist parties were able to charm away much of the mass support which had been the Social Democrat's strength." Joll, p. 184.
[5]Julius Braunthal, *History of the International*, vol. 1, *1864–1914*, trans. Henry Collins and Kenneth Mitchell (New York: Praeger, 1967), p. 355.
[6]Carr, *Nationalism and After*: "The socialization of the nation has as its natural corollary the nationalization of socialism," p. 20, and he added, "International socialism ignominiously collapsed," p. 21. See Franz Borkenau (1939), *World Communism* (Ann Arbor: University of Michigan Press, 1962) and his *Socialism, National or International* (1942) on the nationalization of Socialism. Valuable surveys of and contributions to the state of the recent literature on the strategic causes of World War One can be found in Steven Miller, ed., *Military Strategy and the Origins of the First World War* (Princeton: Princeton University Press, 1985) and Peter Gellman, "The Elusive Explanation: Balance of Power Theories and the Origins of World War One," *Review of International Studies* 15 (Spring 1989), pp. 155–82.
[7]Gay, pp. 278–79; Carl Schorske, *German Social Democracy: 1905–1917* (New York: Harper Torchbooks, 1972), pp. 288–91.

in fact not stood the test. It had not chosen the Marxist route."[8] Many leading philosophical commentators on Marx agree: Socialist soldiers voted for nationalism and against Marxist internationalism, with their feet (so to speak) by marching to the trenches of World War I.[9] In the leading introductory text in international relations theory, Kenneth Waltz concurs. International relations scholars have frequently noted the fact that Communist states have fought each other (as China did in invading Vietnam). Waltz's critique is more fundamental. According to Waltz, Marxism is one of the domestic images that fail to explain the phenomenon of war. Realist theory, conversely, by taking into account the effects of international anarchy on a pervasive sense of international insecurity, accounts both for the persistent "state of war" among all independent states and for the efforts by those states to enhance national security through the balance of power. Given the Socialist view, Waltz argues, that capitalist states cause war and that Socialist revolution will bring peace, the failure of the Socialist parties to oppose, not their failure to prevent, the outbreak of war is what constitutes an indictment not only of the parties themselves but of the theories on which they were ostensibly based.[10]

[8]Schumpeter, *Capitalism, Socialism, and Democracy*, p. 353.

[9]See the discussion in G. A. Cohen, *Karl Marx's Theory of History: A Defence* (Princeton: Princeton University Press, 1978), p. 239, and his "Reconsidering Historical Materialism," in *Marxism Today: Nomos*, ed. J. Roland Pennock, (New York: New York University Press, 1983), vol. 24, and Jan Elster, *Making Sense of Marx* (Cambridge: Cambridge University Press, 1985), p. 397. Kolakowski concurs in this judgment, seeing the Socialists as having been overwhelmed by national patriotism and having revealed that "the international solidarity of the proletariat—its ideological foundation—was an empty phrase." Leszek Kolakowski, *Main Currents of Marxism*, vol. 2, *The Golden Age* (Oxford: Oxford University Press, 1978), p. 29. And Julius Braunthal, *History of the International*, vol. 2, *1914–1943*, trans. John Clark (New York: Praeger, 1967), p. 1: "In the spirit of Marxism it [the International] had proclaimed itself the irreconcilable opponent of the bourgeois-capitalist state. But on 4 August almost all Socialist parties in the belligerent countries pledged themselves to the defense of the very bourgeois-capitalist states whose destruction had hitherto been their aim."

[10]Although Waltz carefully notes that his summary compresses many interesting points of Marx's ambiguous statements on world politics, he supports this synopsis while identifying the valuable distinction between Socialist policy toward the war and Socialist responsibility for the war. In Waltz, *Man the State and War*, pp. 125–26, 129: "On first thought it would seem that the socialist view of war and peace is nothing more than this: that capitalist states cause war; that to revolutionize states, to destroy capitalism and institute socialism, will bring peace. Further it might appear that the behavior of the various socialist parties during the First World War—not their failure to prevent war, but their failure to oppose war—is in one way or another an indictment of the socialist parties and the theories on which they were ostensibly based. . . . [T]here nevertheless grew among the socialists the conviction that social democracy would serve as an effective instrument against war. It did not. The German party, the largest of the socialist parties, not only failed to oppose the war that began in August of 1914 but on the fourth of that month unanimously supported the granting of war credits to the bourgeois German government. . . . The socialist parties in other states that became involved in the war supported their governments." Waltz's criticism is thus different from the one made by Merle Fainsod, *International Socialism and the World War* (Cambridge, Mass.: Harvard University Press, 1935), p. 38. Fainsod focused on the International's

Having failed the acid test of 1914, Marxism and Leninism have often been dismissed as contributing little to the theory of international relations. We treat Marxist and Leninist theories as significant contributions to international political economy.[11] Indeed, Lenin has been credited with originating what has been called the dependency approach to the contemporary international political economy of relations between the developed and the developing countries. But we discount their general relevance to international relations theory, particularly international security.[12] According to some, Marxism fails to acknowledge the autonomy of the international state of war and therefore generates intractable contradictions when it seeks to explain relations among states.[13] According to others, Marx and Engels, who enjoyed lifetimes bounded by the regulated "peace" of nineteenth-century international politics, paid little attention to international security matters.[14] Furthermore, the Soviets themselves stepped away from Marxist international theory; prominent texts on Soviet foreign policy argued extensively for the declining significance of Marxist theory and practice.[15]

Despite the validity of many of the criticisms that have been made of Marxist and Leninist theory, their failings are not due to lack of interest in world politics. Lenin clearly stands out as someone who paid overwhelming attention to international relations. Nor can it be for lack of interest that Marx and Engels fail as theorists of international relations. Engels wrote more on international

---

failure to avert war (p. 18) and attributed the crisis of international Socialism to the doctrinal differences and organizational weakness of the Second International. In fact, the Socialist parties and their organization of international socialism were unsuited to rapid crisis decision-making, as evidenced by the fact that the SPD delegate to the French Socialists during the July crisis was unable to assure them in advance of what position his party would take in the Reichstag vote. Waltz is making a more fundamental criticism of Socialist internationalism.

[11] C. Chase-Dunn, "Interstate System and Capitalist World Economy," *International Studies Quarterly* 25, 1 (March 1981), pp. 19–42, and Gilpin, *The Political Economy of International Relations*, chap. 2.

[12] "Neither Marx, Lenin, nor Stalin made any systematic contribution to international theory," Martin Wight has argued (1966, p. 25). Hayward Alker and Thomas Biersteker, "The Dialectics of World Order," *International Studies Quarterly* 28 (1984), pp. 121–42; K. J. Holsti, *The Dividing Discipline* (Boston: Allen and Unwin, 1985), p. 75; and Andrew Linklater, "Realism, Marxism and Critical International Theory," *Review of International Studies* 12 (1986), pp. 301–12.

[13] Martin Wight and Hedley Bull divided international relations theory into three categories, the Hobbesian, Kantian, and Grotian. "Marxian" theory is absent from their list (Bull, 1977).

[14] Gallie, *Philosophers of Peace and War*, p. 99; R. N. Berki, "On Marxian Thought and the Problem of International Relations," *World Politics* 24 1 (October 1971), pp. 80–105; and V. Kubalkova and A. A. Cruickshank, *Marxism and International Relations* (Oxford: Clarendon Press, 1985), p. 27.

[15] Zimmerman (1971); Margot Light, *The Soviet Theory of International Relations* (Brighton: Wheatsheaf, 1988); and Allen Lynch, *The Soviet Study of International Relations* (Cambridge: Cambridge University Press, 1987).

relations, particularly on military and diplomatic matters, than on any other issue—almost two thousand pages.[16] And Marx himself could not have been more emphatic about his appreciation of the subject and its importance to the success of the international workingman's movement. In his "Inaugural Address to the Workingman's International Association" (the First International), Marx urged the working classes "to master themselves of the mysteries of international politics; to watch the diplomatic acts of their respective governments; to counteract them, if necessary, by all means in their power; when unable to prevent, to combine in simultaneous denunciations, and to vindicate the simple laws of morals and justice, which ought to govern the relations of private individuals, as the rules paramount of the intercourse of nations."[17]

Marx and Engels and Lenin not only preached foreign policy but also practiced (as theorists and activists) what they preached. Marxist and Leninist approaches to international political theory contain insight and error, coherence and inconsistency. Here I propose to concentrate on their insight and coherence, their neglected strengths.

In our times seemingly so fond of proclaiming an "end of history," the Marxist-Leninist tradition has been subjected to wide attack and much contempt. Missing the irony of using so Marxist (and Hegelian) a concept as the end of history for the purpose of dismissing the tradition that conceived of it, we have overemphasized Marxism's failings. We recall that Marx himself was wildly optimistic concerning the prospects for social revolution, greeting each crisis—1848, 1870—as if the revolution had at last arrived. We all have almost accepted that the labor theory of value is either a banal ontological statement (without human beings nothing would have value) or an extremely narrow, inaccurate model of the determination of price.[18]

The value of Marxism-Leninism for international relations theory is nonetheless quite large.

1. This tradition highlights the importance of socioeconomic factors in international relations and does so in a way that is distinct from the Mercantilism of the Realists and the market capitalism of the Liberal commercialists.

2. It adds an insightful focus on the inequality of the world political system. Despite the legal norm of sovereign equality, the reality of world politics is

[16] Gallie, p. 67. Sigmund Neumann and Mark von Hagen, "Engels and Marx on Revolution, War, and the Army in Society," in Peter Paret, Gordon Craig, and Felix Gilbert, eds., *Makers of Modern Strategy* (Princeton: Princeton University Press, 1986), which makes a strong case for the relative importance of Engels (as against Marx) in the development of a Marxist theory of military strategy.

[17] Marx, *The Marx-Engels Reader*, ed. Robert C. Tucker (New York: Norton, 1978), p. 519.

[18] Inaccurate in that it neglects, on the supply side, the independent value and scarcity of land, capital and entrepreneurship, and of course demand.

radically unequal in economic terms. In 1991, for example, the income gap between the richest fifth and, the poorest was 61.1 to 1.[19]

3. The Marxist-Leninist tradition offers us the most specified and complete dynamic theory of world politics. Rather than equilibrium theories of the balance of power, or comparative static theories of the effects of Liberal democratic institutions, it portrays and seeks to explain a pattern of change, of development.

4. It also offers us a fascinating and original conception of what world politics is about. It portrays a state of war and peace determined by the conflicts and solidarities among distinct units that are not states or constitutional orders or individual statespersons, but instead are classes—typically capital (C) and labor (L). Their politics of war and peace, moreover, takes place transnationally; across borders, not merely between or within them. The world political map therefore resembles alliances from one class to another of the following sort:

C = Capitalists; L = Labor; ( ) = state;
| = relations of domination; – = relations of cooperation

5. The Marxist-Leninists provide us with a provocative set of linkages to and differences from the other two classical traditions. Marx, like Rousseau and Schumpeter, is primarily an Image II (societal structure) thinker; Lenin, like Hobbes (especially) or Kant, is more an Image III (international structure) thinker. Overall the Marxists-Leninists share with Machiavelli a vision of the state of war and peace that crosses borders and that applies as much within states as to relations between them. Marx, on the other hand, is somewhat closer to the Liberals, seeing a more heterogeneous state of peace and war; Lenin closer to the Realists, sees a much more homogeneous state of war among independent countries.

6. Lastly, as Communist parties continue to hang on to power in China, Vietnam, Romania, and Cuba and (surprisingly) communist and socialist parties return to power through election in Bulgaria, Hungary, Poland, and perhaps Russia, understanding the legacies of Marxism-Leninism for world politics may tell us something more about how the world works.

[19] But many poor countries improved their rates of literacy (to over 60 percent) and reduced chronic malnutrition. See United Nations Development Program, *Human Development Report 1994* (New York: Oxford University Press, 1994), p. 35.

CHAPTER NINE

Development and Class Solidarities: Marx and Engels

> As long as we [the Germans] help, therefore, to oppress the Polish nation, as long as a part of Poland remains chained to Prussia, as long as we ourselves remain chained to Russia, we shall be unable to radically break patriarchal and feudal absolutism in our own realm. The re-establishment of a democratic Poland is the most essential condition for the reconstruction of a democratic Germany.
>
> —Karl Marx, "The Polish Question before the Frankfurt Assembly"[1]

KARL MARX (1818–1883) AND Friedrich Engels (1820–1895) are perhaps best known for the materialist conception of history in which the conditions of production shape all other areas of society—institutions, laws, ideas, and morality. But their conception is not crude or one-dimensional. We need only recall that Engels was a successful merchant and manufacturer. Marx was the son of an accomplished middle-class Liberal lawyer married to the daughter of a German baron, the baron being an utopian Socialist. Marx studied Hegelian idealism, rejected a university career, and entered journalism. His radical views soon provoked the authorities, and he was forced to flee from Germany to Paris and then to London, where he pursued active revolutionary politics, freelance journalism, and scholarship. He discovered that ideas were more the product than the cause of history and history must be changed. As Engels said in his eulogy for his lifelong friend, Marx was "before all else a revolution-

[1] Karl Marx, "The Polish Question before the Frankfurt Assembly," quoted in Demetrio Boersner, *The Bolsheviks and the National and Colonial Question* (1917–1928) (Geneva: Droz, 1957), p. 3.

ist."[2] Marx's thoughts on world politics contain four elements: the internationalist foundation, the theory of development, imperialism (the spread of capitalism), and war and peace (relations among capitalist societies). Overall he develops the impact of social and economic forces on world politics, as did Rousseau and classical eighteenth-century commercial Liberals, such as Bentham, Smith, and Ricardo, on whom he builds.

Marx's Socialism

Human Nature	x
Domestic Society	xx
Interstate System	x

INTERNATIONALISM

Marx held that Socialists should engage in an ethical international politics in which, even though the *arena* of political action had to be national (where that was possible), the *object* of political action had to be international.[3] In order, therefore, to determine what was feasible and what was desirable, Marxist political judgment should take into account two factors: the stage of development toward Socialism of the country in question and the relative position of that country within the world capitalist system.

Despite Marx's scientific treatment of historical materialism, he accepted the

[2] See the introduction to Marx in Robert C. Tucker, *The Marxian Revolutionary Idea* (New York: Norton, 1969), p. 3ff. Also particularly helpful among the many introductions to Marxist thought is George Lichtheim, *Marxism* (New York: Praeger, 1964).

[3] Solomon Bloom, for example, concludes his seminal study of Marx's views on nationalism with the observation that Marx's work was dominated by humanitarian and internationalist commitments (*The World of Nations* [New York: Columbia University Press, 1941], pp. 194–95). But whether Marx was in fact a moralist has been the subject of an unusually interesting debate in recent years. All try to reconcile Marx's simultaneous dismissal of morality and his constant moral indignation. Most agree that he was neither a Hegelian idealist nor a hedonistic materialist. Between these wide extremes G. A. Cohen, "Reconsidering Historical Materialism," Alan Gilbert, *Marx's Politics: Communists and Citizens* (New Brunswick, N.J.: Rutgers University Press, 1981) and "The Storming of Heaven: Politics and Marx's Capital," in J. Roland Pennock and John W. Chapman eds., *Marxism* (New York: New York University Press, 1983), pp. 119–68; and Steven Lukes, *Marxism and Morality* (New York: Oxford University Press, 1985) make a case for Marxist morality or, as in Lukes, "an ethics of liberation." In an interesting essay, Alan Ryan, "Justice, Exploitation and the the End of Morality," in David Evans, ed., *Moral Philosophy and Contemporary Problems* (Cambridge Cambridge University Press, 1988) criticizes these views yet endorses an ethics of striving toward Socialism as a good description of Marx's position. I try to keep my interpretation of Marx's position on internationalism within these wide bounds.

possibility of making what we would call moral judgments. Although dominant notions of justice tend to be tied to modes of production and class position, Marx urged workers to condemn the capitalism that fettered them. They should seek to push toward Socialism wherever they could make progress.[4] Further elaborating moral restraints, Marx declared that Socialists should oppose both direct violence against those not deserving it as well as indirect violence against those being oppressed by an unjust society, for a long train of deaths caused by the persistence of social inequality is morally equivalent to violence.[5]

According to Marx, justice can therefore require inflicting necessary violence on those who are unjustly violent, even when that unjust "violence" is mere exploitation (the "legal" defense of capitalist ownership). But Marx expressed no sympathy for romantic rebels. Reformist politics are essential to effective revolutionary progress, and Socialists must cooperate with all progressive forces. In a prerevolutionary situation these forces can include a wide range of classes, including the bourgeoisie against the monarchy in 1848 and the petty bourgeoisie against the bourgeoisie in 1875.[6]

It is widely recognized among Marxist scholars that the immediate arena for a Marxist moral politics would be the national state, but the object of Socialist struggle for Marx was international.[7] Marx granted that "it is perfectly obvious that to be able to fight at all, the working class must organize at home as a class and that its own country is the immediate arena of struggle." Yet in assessing the prospects for the advance of Socialism in Bismarck's Germany, he rejected moderate plans for Socialist progress in one country ("Critique of the Gotha Program," 1875).[8] Marx was suspicious of the willingness of the moderates to

[4] See the discussion in Tucker, *The Marxian Revolutionary Idea*, pp. 42–46, Ziyad I. Husami, "Marx on Distributive Justice," *Philosophy and Public Affairs* 18, 1 (1978), p. 32, and *Making Sense of Marx*, 229. For a description of Marxism's central theoretical enterprise as the attempt to achieve a scientific conception of history, see Tony Smith, *Thinking Like a Communist* (New York: Norton, 1987), chap. 2.

[5] See John Harris, "The Marxist Conception of Violence," *Philosophy and Public Affairs* vol. 3, 4 (1974), pp. 193–94, and Chris Brown, " "Marxism and International Ethics," in Terry Nardin and David Mapel, eds., *Traditions of International Ethics* (Cambridge: Cambridge University Press, 1992), pp. 225–49. A good example of this form of this kind of Marxist moral reasoning is Barrington Moore Jr., *The Social Origins of Dictatorship and Democracy: Lord and Peasant in the Making of the Modern World* (Boston: Beacon Press, 1966), chap. 6 and pp. 103–04, 505–08, on the comparison between revolutionary violence and the tragic toll of preventable deaths, such as by starvation, that unjust societies regularly grind out.

[6] See "Manifesto" in Marx (1978), p. 499, and "Letter to Bebel," Marx, *Selected Works* (Moscow: Progress Publishers, 1968), p. 337.

[7] Eminent Marxist internationalists, such as Jean Jaurès, leader of the prewar French, Socialists, defended national development as the route to Socialist internationalism. Miklos Molnar, *Marx, Engels et la Politique internationale* (Paris: Gallimard, 1975) and Boersner, *The Bolsheviks and the National and Colonial Question (1917–1928)* are two of the most valuable commentators on this version of Marx's internationalism.

[8] In Marx (1978), p. 533.

ally with Bismarck against the bourgeois Progressive Party. Marx preferred to support an evolution to Socialism in stages and therefore favored an alliance with the democratic constitutionalist reformers of the Progressive Party even though the social policies of the Progressives were more hostile to legislation protecting union rights and social welfare than were those of Bismarck, who sought to exchange official tolerance for political support. Marx feared a Socialist alliance with the Bismarckian government because of the government's militaristic nationalism and international oppression of the just demands for national independence and social progress of the Poles and other East European peoples whom the Prussian Junkers, together with reactionary Russia and Austria-Hungary, were determined to suppress.[9] Marx thus applauded when the Socialist leader Karl Liebknecht opposed the annexation of Alsace-Lorraine during the Franco-Prussian War of 1870–1871.

By similar internationalist reasoning, Marx singled out for special praise the role played by the British working class in opposing (supposed) plans for intervention by the British government in favor of the American South during the U.S. Civil War. Despite their suffering (caused by the cotton embargo imposed by the bourgeois democratic American North), British workers sensed that "disregard of that bond of brotherhood which ought to exist between the workmen of different countries, and [to] incite them to stand firmly by each other in all their struggles for emancipation, will be chastised by the common discomfiture of their incoherent efforts" ("Inaugural Address to the International Workingmen's Association," 1864).[10] Expressing Socialist solidarity meant standing against slavery and with the workingmen of the American democratic North, whose livelihood, according to Marx, was threatened by the extension of slavery. Succumbing to a foreign policy that stirred up national prejudices and engaged in "piratical wars" would, contrarily, drag down the efforts of the proletariat to liberate itself by undermining Socialist solidarity within and between industrial countries.[11]

In this context, then, we can make Marxist sense of Engels's otherwise bizarre fulminations or, as commonly interpreted, merely nationalistic prejudices directed against the Czechs and the southern Slavs during the failed revolutions of 1848–1849. The Poles and Hungarians represented to Marx and Engels the forces of democratic and inevitably nationalist progress in Eastern Europe. Their progress, moreover, was inseparable from that of the fate of international progress toward Socialism, as Marx notes in the "The Polish Question before

[9] Ibid., pp. 533–34, and G. D. H. Cole. A *History of Socialist Thought*, vol. I, *Marxism and Anarchism, 1850–1890* (London: Macmillan, 1954), pp. 84–85.
[10] Marx (1978), p. 519.
[11] Molnar, p. 306, and Gilbert, "Marx on Internationalism and War," pp. 353–54. For valuable discussion on the Marxist view of nationalism, see Walker Connor, *The National Question in Marxist-Leninist Theory and Strategy*, (1984), esp. chaps. 1 and 2.

the Frankfurt Assembly": "As long as we [the Germans] help, therefore, to oppress the Polish nation, as long as a part of Poland remains chained to Prussia, as long as we ourselves remain chained to Russia, we shall be unable to radically break patriarchal and feudal absolutism in our own realm. The reestablishment of a democratic Poland is the most essential condition for the reconstruction of a democratic Germany."[12]

Although the Czechs and the South Slavs were also engaged in nationalistic revolts, their revolts had a different *international* significance for Marx. The mid-nineteenth-century Polish and Hungarian Liberals were rebelling directly against imperial oppressors—against the Russians, the Prussians, and the Habsburg kaiser, who since the partitions of the eighteenth century had ruled Poland and Hungary and thereby imposed a conservative order on all Europe. The Czechs, on the other hand, were rebelling against the German Austrians; the South Slavs, against the pretensions of Hungarian Liberals. By rebelling against rebels—the progressive nationalists in Hungary and Austria—they were indirectly aiding the imperialists.[13] "Objectively," from an internationalist perspective, their nationalisms were reactionary; they were setting back the overall cause of international liberation.

Political action, for Marxists, should promote the progress of Socialism. This meant (and means) making a political judgment that incorporated considerations both specific to the country in question (its stage of development) and relative to that country's position in the world political economy (its international relations).[14] Under the world-embracing impact of capitalism such dualistic judgments had become inescapable. It was internationalism therefore that distinguished the Communists from other working-class parties, Marx declares in the *Manifesto*. Large-scale capitalist industry, by creating the world market, established a "universal interdependence of nations."[15] "It is a world revolution," Engels announces, "and will, therefore, have the whole world as its arena" (from Engels, "Principles of Communism," 1847). Marxists therefore sought (and still seek) a scientific understanding of how the stages of progress develop and of how societies at similar and different stages relate to one another.

[12] Quoted in Boersner, p. 3.
[13] For discussion, see ibid., pp. 5–10.
[14] Here I follow Boersner, who stresses the necessity of a twofold judgment and the possibility that they might be in contradiction. I read Bloom (pp. 205–07) as saying that the stage of development is sufficient. See also Martin Berger, *Engels, Armies, and Revolution* (Hamden, Conn.: Archon Books, 1977), pp. 72–73, who explains Engels's positions in light of his consistent concern for revolution.
[15] Marx (1978), p. 476.

DEVELOPMENT AND PROGRESS

Marx's description of his contribution to the scientific understanding of development was not the discovery of class, which was familiar to Ricardo and many of the other classical political economists. "My contribution," Marx notes in the "Letter to Wedemeyer" (1852), "has been to prove: (1) that the existence of class conflict is confined to particular historical periods in the development of production (e.g. not in primitive or true communism); (2) that the class struggle necessarily leads to the dictatorship of the proletariat; and (3) that this dictatorship of the proletariat constitutes the transition to the abolition of all classes, to a classless society."[16]

In the "Preface" Marx announces: "In broad outlines Asiatic, ancient, feudal, and modern bourgeois modes of production can be designated as progressive epochs in the economic formation of society."[17] The four are the class societies. They are preceded by "primitive communism" (tribal communitarianism), which generates almost no surplus,[18] and they lead to the last mode of production, communism, under which abundance and complete autonomy—self-realization—will be achieved. Together the class societies constitute a pattern of historical evolution. They also constitute progressive developments in the social forces of production, the latter representing greater production of surplus and greater freedom for the worker."[19] Driving these stages of progress, productive forces undermine established class relations, relations succumb to internal contradictions (class struggles), and relations fall before external conquest—that is, to imperialism."[20]

Marx said very little about the "Asiatic" mode of production, and what he

[16] Marx, *Selected Works*, p. 679.

[17] Marx (1978), p. 5.

[18] Primitive communism is discussed by Engels in *The Origin of the Family, Private Property and the State* (1884) (Harmondsworth: Penguin, 1985).

[19] Cohen, *Karl Marx's Theory of History*, p. 198.

[20] Marx argued in the *Manifesto* (1848) that class struggles drive history, but in the "Preface" to *The Contribution to the Critique of Political Economy* (1859) he gave that role to forces of production (technical change and increasing productivity). Not surprisingly he has provoked a heated debate on this crucial issue of the dynamics of development; see Stanley Moore, "Marx and Lenin as Historical Materialists," *Philosophy and Public Affairs* 4, 2 (Winter 1975); Richard Miller, "The Consistency of Historical Materialism," *Philosophy and Public Affairs* 4, 4 (Summer 1975); and Gary Young, "The Fundamental Contradiction of Capitalist Production," *Philosophy and Public Affairs* 5, 2 (Winter 1976). Young attempts to resolve the dispute by proposing that the key contradiction is not between forces of production (driving change) and relations of production (class structures, limiting change) but between those forces of production that are realizable under a mode of production and the relations of production of that mode (Young p. 204). Young's resolution may reconcile Marx's theoretical contradiction, but it doesn't explain the concrete process Marx described to account for the historical stages of development.

did say is a caricature of the actual history of ancient Eastern society.[21] His general conception (later elaborated by Karl Wittfogel in *Oriental Despotism*) was that in an arid climate needing irrigation but lacking advanced technology, only a centralized, despotic bureaucracy could ensure production.[22] Until they were overrun by modern imperialism, these societies were stagnant; increases in production were available only through lateral expansion, not through any increase in efficiency. The ancient slavery of Greece and Rome was also stagnant and inefficient. The slave had no incentive to economize in the use of raw materials and tools that were not his own, and the owner had little incentive to invest when prestige and power lay in conspicuous consumption of luxuries, both private and public.[23] Under feudalism the laborer was both partly free from the legal restrictions of slavery and a part owner of the means of production. Both of these served to increase efficiency and advance production. But domination by military castes, the small scale of "petty production," and the remaining restrictions of serfdom retarded both efficiency and production.

Marx's account of the next transition, from feudalism to capitalism, seems to vindicate class struggle, rather than forces of production, as the motor of progress.[24] Following Francis Bacon, Marx declares that "gunpowder, the compass, and printing" were the three inventions that ushered feudalism out and bourgeois society in. Cannon destroyed the power of the feudal nobility and created the centralized, national state. Printing opened the mind to critical inquiry and science. Only the compass, precursor of maritime discovery and thus of imperial plunder and the expansion of the world market, had a specifically economic significance. Merchants under "late" feudalism could invest their trade profits directly into manufacture and thus initiate capitalist production. But here again, Marx argues, class struggles in the form of the bourgeois capture of the state must play a vital role. Before merchants could build factories and transform society, they must have had laborers to hire. Laborers had to be freed from feudal restrictions on their persons. They had to have been "freed" as well from their partial ownership of the means of production, their tools as guild members or their land as peasants. The "secret of primitive accumulation" lay in the expropriations of the enclosure movement, which drove peasants from the land into factories.[25]

[21] For a useful discussion of the problem, see Perry Anderson, *Lineages of the Absolutist State* (London: New Left Books, 1974).
[22] Marx, *New York Herald Tribune*, June 25, 1853, in Marx (1978), p. 655.
[23] Anthony Brewer, *Marxist Theories of Imperialism* (London: Routledge and Kegan Paul, 1980), pp. 41–42; Elster, *Making Sense of Marx*, pp. 272–77.
[24] (Marx, the *1861–1863 Critique of Political Economy*), and see Elster, p. 287.
[25] Karl Marx and Friedrich Engels, *Capital*, trans. S. Moore and E. Aveling (New York: Modern Library, 1906), pp. 834–37, and Tucker, *The Marxian Revolutionary Idea*, pp. 95–102. In fact, it appears that the enclosure movement did not drive laborers from the land in large numbers. Population growth seems to have been the more significant source of the

The "Asiatic," ancient (slave), and feudal societies fell as productive forces, class struggles, and war tore them apart. Under modern conditions, within capitalism, the bourgeoisie evolved from a subordinate role, as merchant and financial capitalists within social orders dominated by the feudal nobility and their monarchical state, to a dominant role, as industrial capitalists within fully bourgeois, electoral democracies. In transitional stages, the bourgeoisie often joined in class alliances or alliances among fractions of classes, such as the notorious combination of a weak French bourgeoisie with the poor peasantry in an alliance dominated by Louis Bonaparte (so-called Bonapartism).[26]

With the achievement of civic equality, the organized parties of the working class began to find themselves in the final contest directly against the bourgeoisie.[27] This was an evolution still occurring during the lives of Marx and Engels. Russia still lay in the quasi-feudal stages; Germany in the middle; Britain, the United States, and France in the fully bourgeois stages. None had as yet experienced a Socialist revolution.

Although Marx anticipated that the prospective transition from capitalism to socialism (unlike the actual transition from feudalism to capitalism) would be driven more directly by the forces of production, his account of capitalist development nonetheless relied heavily on the politics of class struggle. Capitalism to Marx was the first truly "revolutionary" society, not only tearing apart the remnants of the feudal-monarchical order but constantly remaking its own instruments of production and battering down the walls of nonbourgeois societies overseas. In establishing its own rule, the bourgeoisie rooted out aristocratic privilege and substituted in its place formal legal equality and democratic rule. Economic competition forced efficiency as capitalists tried to prevent a fall in their profits. They invested in new machines and recruited new labor in order to produce more, which, in their competition with other capitalists, forced them to sell at a lower price. This then forced them to invest in more efficient machines, to drive down the wages of the proletariat, and to expand markets across the entire globe.[28]

A tendency to a fall in the rate of profit was not, moreover, the secret of the Socialist revolution.[29] Competition also produced concentration as more

---

industrial labor forces of early capitalism. For general criticisms of the social theory underlying Marxist views on development, see Theda Skocpol, *States and Social Revolutions* (Cambridge: Cambridge University Press, 1979) and Anthony Giddens, *The Nation-State and Violence*, vol. 2, *Contemporary Critique of Historical Materialism* (Cambridge: Polity Press; Oxford: Basil Blackwell, 1985).

[26] "The Eighteenth Brumaire of Louis Bonaparte," 1852, in Marx (1978), pp. 594–617.

[27] Brewer, pp. 48–49.

[28] Marx, in the "Manifesto" (1978), pp. 475–76.

[29] Even if capitalism did not face the class conflicts Marx describes, it would in the end suffer a crisis of accumulation resulting from an exhaustion of profit opportunities. This, however, as Albert Hirschman has argued, might take centuries to emerge ("Hegel, Imperial-

successful capitalists bought up less successful capitalists. Concentration then reduced the number of capitalists and weakened the bourgeoisie as a political class. At the same time it increased and strengthened the proletariat. It "socialized" the proletariat as more and more workers were assembled in larger and larger factories. Socialism would thus take over only when, Marx explains, "centralization of the means of production and socialization of labour at last reach a point where they become incompatible with their capitalist integument. . . . This integument is burst asunder. The knell of capitalist private property sounds. The expropriators are expropriated."[30]

This expropriation would be the Socialist revolution, the final step to the final stage of historical progress. Under bourgeois democracy, the revolution could occur through suffrage politics, according to Engels, who observed the steadily increasing electoral popularity of the German Social Democratic Party.[31] Under less democratic circumstances, a more violent revolution would be necessary, as it was during the Paris Commune. Established during the Franco-Prussian War of 1870–1871 with its democratically elected "dictatorship of the proletariat," it served for Marxists as the model for a potential Socialist revolution.[32] The success of either route would then be measured in the final liberation of labor under "true communism." The abundance provided by industrial productivity would enable workers to realize all their creative potential, being able to work according to their choice and consume according to their needs.[33] With the elimination of class struggle, finally, the state too would disappear.

---

ism, and Structural Stagnation," *Journal of Development Economics* 3, 1 [July 1976], pp. 1–6), or, as Solomon Bloom notes in one of Marx's speculations, might provoke an attack from a newly capitalist Asia on a recently socialized Europe (*The World of Nations*, p. 99).

[30] Marx and Engels, *Capital* (1906), p. 837.

[31] Engels, "Two Tactics of Social Democracy" in Marx (1978), p. 572.

[32] Engels, "Introduction" to *The Civil War in France* in Ibid., p. 628, and Shlomo Avineri *The Social and Political Thought of Karl Marx* (Cambridge: Cambridge University Press, 1968), pp. 240–49.

[33] For the two steps to complete communism, see Marx's *Critique of the Gotha Program* and Herbert Marcuse, *Soviet Marxism* (New York: Random House, 1961), chap. 1. Some have seen Marx's comments on the Russian village as an exception to his basic position that Socialism would become realizable only within mature industrial capitalism, after all the possibilities of the capitalist mode of production were exhausted (as 1861 the "Preface" suggests). The evidence for this is the letter to Vera Zasulich (1881). But in that "letter" (actually a later construction) Marx discusses the possibility that given the European development of capitalist forces of production, a Russian revolution inspired by Socialism might be able to preserve the communal features of the village and use them as a basis for an accelerated transition to Socialism ("Letter on the Russian Village Community" [1881] in Marx, *The Russian Menace to Europe*, ed. Paul Blackstock and Bert Hoselitz [Glencoe, Ill.: Free Press, 1952], pp. 218–26). This is difficult to reconcile with Marx's many condemnations of "quixotic" attempts at Socialist revolution (see Elster [1985], p. 289). But we might want to resolve the confusion by stating, as does Marx, that societies need not follow a

For Marxists, therefore, promoting progress had (and has) a determinate meaning. Progress would vary unevenly among countries depending on their stage of development, and it would vary across history, reflecting differences in world technical and social environments,[34] but at any given time promoting the progressive development of a country's social forces was a distinct beacon for political action. Marxist theory of development established categories and relationships, gave Socialists a vocabulary and grammar of progress. But it was not a sufficient guide to political action. Evaluating progressive policy was a matter of contestable judgment, particularly because progress also had a relative dimension. Progress toward Socialism was interdependent. The advance of some could set back the prospects of most, as Czech and South Slavic nationalisms had threatened to do in 1848. The retardation of others could also set back the advance of many, as Prussia's and Russia's oppression of Poland had set back the liberation of the German working class. Judging policy required an international assessment. This assessment in turn called for understanding the types of relations that develop among various social systems.

IMPERIALISM AND INDEPENDENCE

Marx's work lacked a developed theory of imperialism. It did, however, display brilliant commentary on the leading instances of imperial expansion in his day (concerning India and China particularly) and more general insights, which shaped how prewar Marxists understood relations with the non-European world. They included the following. Relations between capitalist and precapitalist societies tended to be characterized by imperialism, though imperialism of course also existed before capitalism. Capitalism did not require imperialism, though it was likely to engage in it. Imperialism was both a creative and a destructive force. The proletariat of industrial capitalism should oppose it when its regressive features outweighed its progressive ones, but they might not suc-

---

lockstep path to development; their overall state of development is more important than the particular order of the steps. Should, therefore, a self-consciously revolutionary industrial proletariat develop in Russia before Russian capitalism had overwhelmed the village community, it could rely upon the village community as an ally or, at the minimum, feel no compunction to capitalize village communism before resocializing it (see Bloom, p. 168).

[34] One cannot, for example, simply apply the lessons of class conflict under industrial capitalism to class conflicts in ancient Rome, under the slave mode of production. The expropriated peasantry of Italy were not in a position to engage in a Socialist revolution since the forces of production could not sustain this, even though they had lost control (as have modern industrial workers) of the means of production. Instead they became the corrupt clients of urban largess (see Marx, "Letter on the Economic Development of Russia" [1877], in Marx [1952], p. 217).

[35] Marx (1978), p. 477.

ceed until the bourgeoisie of the colonies was strong enough to throw off the imperial yoke and establish national independence.

Capitalism, Marx and Engels declare in the *Manifesto*, "create[d] a world in its own image."[35] The search for profit led to a search for ever-widening markets. The cheap prices of industrial commodities simply outcompeted the precapitalist hand manufactures of Asia and Africa; they "batter[ed] down all Chinese walls." Outcompeted economically, precapitalist society was also incapable of concerted political or military resistance. Pervasive localism—the lack of national identification—stifled an anti-imperial response as long as the "inhabitants [of India] gave themselves no trouble about the breaking up and division of kingdoms; while the village remains entire they care not to what power it is transferred, or to what sovereign it devolves."[36]

Capitalists benefited from imperial markets and thus sought to expand them. But capitalism did not require imperialism.[37] Imperialism was only one, and not the most significant one, among a number of ways in which capitalists could counteract the tendency for the rate of profit to fall. Much more significant than foreign and imperial trade was the cheapening through technical progress of the elements of constant capital (investment goods or means of production). Nor did imperialism consequently necessarily prolong bourgeois society, so to speak, "beyond its natural span." Socialism triumphed through the contradiction between socialized production and concentrated private ownership, not when capitalists experienced a profit squeeze.[38]

Imperialism created progress, but not because it benefited overall the proletariat of the industrial capitalist countries. Overseas trade tripled between 1843 and 1864, but "no new colonies, or new trade" or "prosperity three years in ten" would end the misery of the workers under industrial capitalism.[39] Thus, while individual workers could "benefit" ("three years in ten"), what we now call social imperialism made no sense to Marx. Nations did not exploit nations; classes exploited classes (see below, in the discussion of inter-Socialist foreign relations).

Imperialism also harmed the societies of the Asian and African periphery. Its effects in India were "devastating . . . palpable and confounding." Imperialism uprooted traditional Indian society without yet substituting in its place bour-

[36] Marx, "On Imperialism in India" in Ibid., p. 657.
[37] Marx, however, did emphasize the historical role of imperial markets in primitive accumulation: "The colonies secured a market for the budding manufactures, and, through the monopolies of the market, an increased accumulation. The treasures captured outside Europe by undisguised looting, enslavement, and murder, floated back to the mother-country and were there turned into capital" (Marx, *Capital* [1906], p. 826).
[38] See the discussion in Brewer, pp. 36–37.
[39] "Inaugural Address to the Workingmen's International Association," 1864 in Marx (1978), p. 513.

geois society, and this imparted "a particular kind of melancholy to the present misery of the Hindoo."[40]

But imperialism did constitute one of the two great engines of progress that, together with the domestic development of capitalism in the industrial countries, would drag mankind inexorably, though unevenly (country by country), toward its Socialist "destiny." It spread capitalism—precursor to Socialism—across the globe, ripping Asia and Africa from the stagnation of precapitalist modes of production and ending their indigenous "unspeakable cruelties" and rampant "superstition."[41] Destroying the old, it developed and revolutionized the countries it overran. Economically India received the beginnings of capitalism with the introduction of private property in land and with the arrival of British railroads, which radically cheapened the means of transport. Politically imperialism also unified the subcontinent, establishing a national network of communications and a unified army.[42] Imperialism, in short, created the national conditions that could make the native bourgeoisie a national bourgeoisie.[43]

But this did not mean that the proletariat should support imperialism. Later in life Marx came to realize that imperialism had political effects on the industrial metropole that sustained reactionary forces. Imperialism could foster chauvinistic, nationalist prejudices, such as those between English and Irish workers, thereby vitiating the solidarity between the two nations composing the British proletariat that would be needed for the emancipation of the working class.[44] Indeed, the emancipation of the British working class in these circumstances came to depend on a prior successful national revolt of Ireland against British imperialism.

Should Socialists come to power before the colonies had emancipated themselves, they would need to spur colonial development and encourage a transfer of power from colonial to national bourgeoisies. Some Socialists came to believe that imperialism could be justified if it helped the inhabitants of the colonies. The Dutch and others, including, in Britain, the Labour Party leader Ramsay Macdonald, argued that the Europeans should not simply abandon the colonies.[45] But Engels, warning Socialists of the danger of political corruption,

[40] Ibid., pp. 655, 663.
[41] Ibid., p. 658.
[42] "Future Results of British Rule in India" in Ibid., pp. 659–62.
[43] Marx and Engels therefore also applauded the victory of the United States over Mexico in the War of 1848 as a means of bringing vigorous U.S. capitalism to the great task of developing the Pacific basin (Engels, "Democratic Panslavism," in Marx [1952], pp. 70–71).
[44] Engels, "Letter to Marx, Oct. 24, 1869," in Boersner (1954), p. 11, and see the discussion in Bloom, p. 113; Elliot Goodman, *The Soviet Design for a World State* (New York: Columbia University Press, 1960), pp. 11–12; and Gilbert (1978), p. 359.
[45] Joll, *The Second International*, pp. 123–24.

rejected the extension of colonialism under proletarian auspices: "[T]he victorious proletariat can force no blessings of any kind upon any foreign nation without undermining its own victory by so doing."[46]

WAR AND PEACE

Cooperation and conflict, as sources of war and peace, characterized relations among countries not subject to imperial conquest, Marx and Engels argued. Military power depended on the mode of production both for its war matériel and organization.[47] Independent interstate relations would therefore be found among societies that could each protect itself from hostile neighbors; that meant among societies with similar modes of production. In an environment in which the international independence of states made war possible, these relations differed according to how their transnational modes of production related to each other—feudalist to feudalist, capitalist to capitalist, and, in anticipation, Socialist to Socialist—and according to which class faction—Bonapartist, "free-trading," or other—currently commanded the national state. These crosscutting ties among both states and classes created perplexing questions for how Socialist societies would relate to the remaining capitalists and how Socialist leaders operating within still-bourgeois societies would plan a strategy of international progress.

Insofar as they engage in a calculation of means, the leaders of all states and societies have been influenced by international strategic competition. Minimizing enemies, maximizing friends are but basic prudence. Marx therefore warned the Germans in 1870 that the "law of the old political system" would continue to apply, that the dismemberment of France (Alsace-Lorraine) would drive France into the arms of Russia.[48] But internally generated drives also shaped the goals of foreign policy. Precapitalist societies engaged in dreary

[46] Letter to Karl Kautsky in Marx (1968), p. 686.

[47] This was Engels's force theory, developed in the *Anti-Duhring*, excerpted in Bernard Semmel, ed., *Marxism and the Science of War* (Oxford: Oxford University Press, 1981).

[48] Marx, "Second Address of the General Council of the International Working Men's Association on the Franco-Prussian War" in Marx (1968), p. 271. See, as another example, Engels's 1890 essay "The Foreign Policy of Czarism" (in Marx [1952]). Marx's very odd essay on Anglo-Russian diplomacy, "The Secret Diplomatic History of the Eighteenth Century," written in 1856 (in *The Unknown Karl Marx*, ed. T. Payne [London: University of London Press, 1972]), is, however, difficult to reconcile with any version of historical materialism. Marx wrote this essay for an ultraconservative Tory journal that shared his strange view that Palmerston was a Russian agent. It asserted that Russia had gained its international power (all sham) by means of its subornation of foreign leaders—first among the Tatars, now among the British. Jerrold Seigel, *Marx's Fate: The Shape of a Life* (Princeton: Princeton University Press, 1978) offers very useful biographical context for this most difficult stage of Marx's life.

contests over natural resources; slave societies, in predatory, slave-hunting wars; and feudal societies, in conflicts of dynastic expansion.

Relations among bourgeois societies raised complex questions. Marx's most complete short statement on the issue deserves quotation:[49]

> The unification and fraternization of nations is a phrase used today by all parties, particularly the bourgeois free-trade men. Of course there does exist a certain kind of fraternization among the bourgeois classes of all nations. It is the fraternization of the oppressors against the oppressed, the exploiters against the exploited. Just as the bourgeois class of any one country unites and fraternizes against the proletarians of that country, despite competition and conflict among the members of the bourgeoisie themselves, so also the bourgeoisie of all countries fraternize and unite against the proletarians of all countries, despite their mutual conflict and competition in the world market. For nations really to unite, they must have a mutual interest. For their interest to become mutual, the present property relationships must be abolished, for they condition the exploitation of nations among themselves. To abolish the present property relationships is the interest of the working class. It alone, moreover, possesses the means to do it. The victory of the proletariat over the bourgeoisie is at the same time a victory over the national and industrial conflicts with which the various nations nowadays confront each other inimically. The victory of the proletariat over the bourgeoisie is therefore at the same time the liberation signal of all oppressed nations.

Would "fraternal" relations among the bourgeois states be peaceable, despite their conflicts and competition, as the relations within the bourgeoisie of a single state were peaceable despite their conflicts and competition? And if so, how and why?

In the current academic literature on Marxism views differ greatly. Some argue that Marx portrayed the bourgeoisie as inherently aggressive, ruthlessly competing for the last drop of profits. Only the temporary coincidence of interests in suppressing Socialist revolution would produce capitalist fraternity.[50] Others argue that bourgeois competition would be commercial, not militaristic, simply because militarism destroyed profits and social order, on which bourgeois dominance rested. Capitalist class solidarity then would be as fraternal as that of proletarian solidarity, which would, according to Marx, engender peace.[51]

[49] "International Class Conflict," a speech delivered in London in 1847 in Marx, vol. 1, *The Karl Marx Library, On Revolution*, ed. Saul K. Padover (New York: McGraw-Hill, 1971), p. 35.

[50] Kubalkova and Cruickshank, *Marxism and International Relations*, p. 34.

[51] Adam Ulam, *Expansion and Coexistence: Soviet Foreign Policy 1917–73* (New York: Praeger, 1968), pp. 133–35.

Let us distinguish between Marx's views on capitalism as a fully realized mode of production and his views on the bourgeois factions and alliances that dominated the incomplete bourgeois societies of nineteenth-century Europe.

Concerning the latter Marx noted the frequent interest of Bonapartist and other militaristic factions in stirring up wars to enhance their domestic support by externalizing tenuously balanced, suppressed class and ethnic conflicts. Where the bourgeoisie lacked hegemony, these clashes among classes and ethnic groups were ripe fields for the likes of Bismarck or Napoleon to exploit, turning the dependent bourgeoisie itself into a "roaring lion" of patriotism.[52] In these circumstances only the vital common interest of suppressing Socialist revolution served as a source of fraternal cooperation, such as that extended by Bismarck to the French bourgeoisie when he helped it crush the rising of French radicals and Socialists in 1871, the Paris Commune. (Bismarck released captured French soldiers so that they could participate in the siege of Paris.)[53]

Among more fully developed capitalist societies, on the other hand, more peaceable tendencies appeared to hold sway, as Marx declares in the *Manifesto*. "National differences and antagonisms among peoples are daily more and more vanishing, owing to the development of the bourgeoisie, to freedom of commerce, to the world-market, to uniformity in the mode of production and in the conditions of life corresponding thereto. . . . The supremacy of the proletariat will cause them to vanish still faster. . . . In proportion as the exploitation of one individual by another is put an end to, the exploitation of one nation by another will also be put an end to. In proportion as the antagonism between classes within the nation vanishes, the hostility of one nation to another will come to an end."[54]

If Socialism only accelerated a tendency toward peaceableness, that tendency must already have existed in bourgeois society.[55] Indeed, within Marxist theory there are substantial reasons why the bourgeoisie would be expected to resist militarism. Although a war might stimulate economic demand and thus raise profits, it would also impose financial costs. Since the proletariat receives an income only marginally above subsistence, capitalists would have to pay the taxes that militarism would impose. Unlike colonial wars, wars among powerful bourgeois societies would be especially costly. Since mature capitalists generate their profits primarily through commodity transaction and not through "primi-

[52] Marx, "Second Address" in Marx, *Selected Works*, p. 268.

[53] Marx, *The Civil War in France*, in Marx (1968), p. 279. An example of a much more sophisticated form of the politics of "international civil war," according to Arno Mayer's account (*Politics and Diplomacy of the Peacemaking* [New York: Knopf, 1967], chap. 1), is the contest between Woodrow Wilson and Lenin over the shape of post–World War One Europe.

[54] Marx (1978), pp. 488–89.

[55] For discussion, see Fainsod, *International Socialism and the World War*, p. 2.

tive accumulation," a policy of conquest would appear unattractive. As Engels noted late in his life, the army itself might become not merely a mass but a democratic and Socialist-leaning institution; general war might even become general revolution.[56] The economic interdependence of capitalist interests, moreover, could counteract whatever militaristic interests might be at work, as occurred (according to Marx) during the American Civil War: "The latter idea (forcibly breaking the Northern blockade) had been altogether abandoned, since, beside all other circumstances, Manchester (the aggrieved cotton capitalists) became aware that two vast interests, the monetary interest, having sunk an immense capital in the industrial enterprises of North America, and the corn trade, relying on North America as its principal source of supply, would combine to check any unprovoked aggression on the part of the British government.[57]

Relations among Socialists, Marx and Engels agree, would be much less contradictory. Here true peace and justice would rule.[58] "Antagonisms" and "hostility, "national and industrial conflicts" all would dissolve in the course of the liberation of the proletariat. Setting the ends for the states and then transcending those states altogether, enjoying abundance, removed from all exploitation, the proletariat would have nothing over which to fight either at home or abroad. Moreover, its class solidarity would appear to be more than the

[56] This point is developed in Neumann and von Hagen, "Engels and Marx on Revolution, War, and the Army in Society," p. 280, and Gallie, pp. 86–87.

[57] Marx, "The British Cotton Trade," October 14, 1861, in the *New York Herald Tribune* in Henry Christman, ed., *The American Journalism of Marx and Engels* (New York: New American Library, 1966), p. 224. This does not mean that either Marx or Engels found these tendencies to be a product of purely political or ideological harmony among Liberal republics, as a number of Liberals of the time and later have argued. Engels indeed opposed what he called "Democratic Panslavism" as an idealistic fiction and cited the war between the United States and Mexico in 1848 as evidence of the fiction of republican peace (few liberals would count them both Liberal republics, however) in Marx, *The Russian Menace to Europe*, ed. Paul Blackstock and Bert Hoselitz (Glencoe, Ill.: Free Press, 1952), pp. 70–71. Engels further asserted that "they [the bourgeoisie] can never go beyond the limitations of nationalism" (from Engels, "Das Fest der Nationen," quoted in Goodman, p. 7).

[58] For a differing view, see R. N. Berki "On Marxian Thought and the Problem of International Relations." *World Politics* 24, 1 (October 1971), pp. 80–105. He argues that Marx neglected and would be refuted by the persistence of exploitation between Socialist nations. Berki relies on analogies to resource conflicts characteristic of communities under "primitive communism." In footnotes above, I give some reasons why a Marxist would probably reject the transhistorical analogy, which neglects the development of industrial production and Socialist revolution. Some Socialist politicians (among them Lensch), however, did maintain that view and justified German imperialism on the grounds that Germany constituted a "proletarian nation" within international capitalism. Lensch then became in the course of World War I an enthusiastic proponent of German expansionism (see Abraham Ascher, "Radical Imperialists within German Social Democracy: 1912–1918," *Political Science Quarterly* 76, 4 (December 1961), pp. 555–75).

[59] Engels, "Das Fest der Nationen," as quoted in Goodman, pp. 7–8.

achievement of cooperation (such as would characterize capitalist egoists). Proletarians, Engels asserts, are by nature "devoid of national prejudices," and "their whole outlook and movement are essentially humanitarian and antinational."[59] Proletarians, he seems to argue, would experience a harmony of perceived interests—alternatively an altruism—first molded perhaps in the cauldron of socialized labor in the great capitalist factories.[60]

Relations between future Socialist revolutions and continuing capitalist societies received little attention from the early Marxists. They expected that the revolution would be worldwide and nearly simultaneous among the advanced capitalist countries of Britain, the United States, France, and Germany. The problem of Socialist-capitalist relations would not arise.[61] Marx did no more than muse that perhaps the extra-European world, remaining bourgeois after the European Socialist revolution, might be tempted to crush Socialism. But he and Engels also expected that the efficiency of advanced Socialist industrialism would furnish a "colossal productivity," making the semicivilized capitalist countries overseas of little threat to the flourishing of Socialism.[62]

Before the revolution Socialist leaders would want to choose strategies to promote progress and socialist solidarity. Operating within still-capitalist societies, they had to respect the progressive character of democratic nationalism. Marx chides Proudhon for attempting an utopian assertion of cosmopolitan anarchism. Proudhon utterly neglected, Marx charges, the vital role of national independence and bourgeois democracy in the crushing of the vestiges of feudalism and in the development of the proletariat.[63]

At the same time, Socialists would want to promote the peaceable resolution of conflicts among capitalist powers, since war would impose its severest burdens on the working class, whose members would make up the casualty lists of the mass armies and whose internationalist parties would be the first to suffer from the national chauvinisms that wars engendered.

Marx thus argues that in 1870 the German proletariat rightly declared its support for a German war of defense against the aggression of Napoleon III, even though that support meant temporarily, indirectly supporting the Bismarckian regime of Prussian, quasi-feudal, military despotism (Junkerism). The German workers during the Franco-Prussian War supported national defense against Napoleon, not a war against the French people, and they protested against "dynastic wars" and a punitive peace, earning Marx's praise on all

[60] Thus a purely egoistic account of solidarity seems to miss the dimension Engels stressed. It would need be something more than the solidarity Elster discusses, p. 347, "which is the ability to overcome the free-rider problem in realizing class interests."
[61] See Kubalkova and Cruickshank, p. 36.
[62] See the letters in Marx (1978), pp. 676–77.
[63] Marx's letter to Engels, June 20, 1866, as quoted in Boersner, p. 21.

accounts: "The German socialist workers did not allow themselves to become confused for a single moment. They did not show any hint of national chauvinism. They kept their heads in the midst of the wildest jubilation over the victory, demanding 'an equitable peace with the French republic and no annexations.' Not even martial law could silence them. No battle glory, no talk of German 'imperial magnificence,' produced any effect on them; liberation of the entire European proletariat was still their sole aim."[64]

THE PROBLEM OF 1914

No war of imperial conquest fought among the bourgeois societies of Europe could promote Socialist progress, but some defeats would be even more harmful than others. Britain, France, and the United States were the most advanced bourgeois democracies. But despite Germany's Junkerism, Engels affirms the importance of defending the best prospect of Socialist revolution in Europe, Germany during the 1890s. A Socialist Germany would of course restore the independence of Poland and Alsace-Lorraine, he assures. But if the French bourgeoisie were to attack Germany before the revolution, citing as a pretext Alsace-Lorraine, and to ally itself with the Russian tsar, "who is the enemy of the bourgeoisie of the whole of Europe," then the German working class should support war against them: "go for the Russians and their allies, whoever they may be."[65]

Let us compare Marx's usurping heir, Vladimir Lenin, on world politics.

[64] "Preface to the Peasant War in Germany," in Marx, *Selected Works*, p. 249.
[65] Engels, letter to Bebel, in Marx, *Correspondence* (New York: 1934), p. 488.

CHAPTER TEN

War and Revolution: Lenin

> [F]*ormerly* the main thing was to fight "against Tsarism" (and against certain small-nation movements that *it* was using for undemocratic ends), and for the greater revolutionary peoples of the West; the main thing *today* is to stand against the united, aligned front of the imperialist powers, the imperialist bourgeoisie and social-imperialists, and for the utilisation of all national movements against imperialism for the purposes of the socialist revolution.[1]
>
> —V. I. Lenin, "The Socialist Revolution and the Right of Nations to Self-Determination" (January–February, 1916)

VLADIMIR I. ULYANOV—Lenin (1870–1924)—was a party leader and a revolutionary much more than he was a philosopher. Indeed, none of our other philosophers was so political; he stands out even when we compare him to very political intellectuals such as Thucydides and Machiavelli. The son of a family in the professional and bureaucratic ranks, he was radicalized by the execution of his elder brother. Rejecting the populism (revolution of the peasantry) of his brother, he studied Marxism, wrote pamphlets, and then went abroad at the age of twenty-five to establish contact with the exiled Russian Marxists and the European Socialist movement. On his return to Russia and in the course of his participation in labor agitation in St. Petersburg, the Russian police arrested

[1]V. I. Lenin, "The Discussion on Self-Determination Summed Up," *National Liberation, Socialism and Imperialism: Selected Writings* (New York: International Publishers, 1968), p. 147.

him and then exiled him to Siberia, where he married Nadezhda Krupskaya, who had joined him in exile.

While he was in exile, he wrote the *Development of Capitalism in Russia* (1899), which revealed the political bankruptcy of populist Socialism. If the populists relied on a radical peasantry to bring communalism to Russia, they were gravely mistaken, Lenin argued ("Lenin" was the revolutionary pseudonym he adopted on his return). Capitalism was transforming rural Russia; the peasantry, far from being a united communal force, was becoming differentiated into capitalist farmers and a rural proletariat. But Lenin also rejected the reformist movement in the orthodox Russian Marxism that was the dominant strain of the Russian Social Democratic Workers' Party, the party that was to become Lenin's vehicle, rival, and victim. Its gradualist and reformist strategy of labor organization and working-class mobilization repelled him. He thought its plan to conduct parliamentary politics within a developing bourgeois parliamentary regime, until some date in the future when a Socialist parliamentary majority would lead the transformation to Socialism, was purely visionary and completely ineffective. Instead, freed from his Siberian exile, he left Russia and founded *Iskra* as a party newspaper that would combat reformism and would be the catalyst for a strategy of revolution, designed to seize power from the bourgeoisie with a dictatorship of the working class and the peasantry, led by a disciplined cadre of professional party leaders that he would lead.[2] He waged ferocious intraparty struggles over the next seventeen years, at times achieving majority control (whence "Bolshevik") over his more gradualist rivals (the "minority," "Mensheviks"), at other times finding himself a small majority even within his own Bolshevik faction of the party. He returned to Russia during the 1905 Revolution only to play an ineffectual role and see the reformist forces crushed by the tsarist state. The following years in European exile became another low point of his career, marked in 1914 by what he saw as the betrayal of all Socialism by the Democratic Socialist parties of Europe. All changed, of course, when as part of covert maneuver to destabilize the tsarist state, German authorities sent Lenin in a sealed train to the Finland Station in St. Petersburg in 1917 and the Russian Revolution was born.[3]

Despite the Marxist foundations, we see large differences between Lenin and the founders, Marx and Engels. In his international theorizing, Lenin makes a bridge to the Image III Hobbesian Realists, just as Marx did to the Image II Commercialist Liberals. Where Marx saw the competitiveness of the capitalists as a source of development and progress, Lenin saw it as a source of oppression

[2]This strategy is laid out in *What Is to Be Done?* (1901–1902).
[3]Adam Ulam's *The Bolsheviks* (New York: Macmillan, 1965) and Bertram Wolfe, *Three Who Made a Revolution* are two classics among the many valuable studies of Lenin's career.

and imperialism. Where Marx perceived a tendency toward transnational cooperation among capitalist states, Lenin found an inevitable trend toward war. Marx saw capitalist states as fractured "committees" of the bourgeoisie having neither a coherent single nor a coordinated national interest. They were not single actors making consistent policy. Lenin argued that bank capital created an organized and dominated capitalist order that led to the development of a unitary, superbureaucratic state, which gave it an apparatus for rational unitary calculations in both the political and economic realms. So he reestablished the centrality of the balance of power—not, however, a balance among states or nations but a balance of power among rival "financial oligarchies." He designed a ruthless strategy and a revolutionary party—a Socialist Leviathan—fit to overcome the bourgeois Leviathan he saw in the imperialist state.

Lenin's Communism

Human Nature	x
Domestic Society	x
Interstate System	xx

HOBSON, HILFERDING, LUXEMBURG, KAUTSKY, AND CO.

Although many of Lenin's ideas on imperialism can be traced to bourgeois writers on imperialism, such as Hobson, (Lenin effusively acknowledges this debt) the structure, the emphasis, and the interrelation of the parts all differ.[4] The Leninist contribution is both more tightly logical and less complete, a work of a more disciplined but less observant, less open mind. In part, the tighter logical construction owes a great deal to Lenin's reliance on Hilferding's insightful but unsystematic analysis of the institutional aspects of finance capital.[5] But an awareness of the scientistic certainty and revolutionary strategy that directs Lenin's arguments is more important to understanding Lenin and *Imperialism: The Highest Stage of Capitalism.*[6]

Imperialism is an unabashedly political tract designed to confute Kautsky's view that capitalism could evolve peacefully. Furthermore, Lenin aims to explain the political situation of the times: what he saw as the desertion of

[4]Louis Fischer, *Lenin* (New York: Harper and Row, 1964), p. 36. For excellent critical reviews of Marxist and Leninist economic theory, see Wolfgang Mommsen, *Theories of Imperialism* (New York: Random House, 1980) and Brewer, *Marxist Theories of Imperialism*, chaps. 2–5.

[5]Rudolf Hilferding, *Finance Capital*, trans. Morris Watnick and Sam Gordon, ed. Tom Bottomore (London: Routledge & Kegan Paul, 1981); the original German edition appeared in 1910.

[6]New York: International Publishers, 1939. Written in 1916 in Zurich, it was first published in Russia in 1917.

the Socialist parties from proletarian internationalism and their embrace of nationalism in the crisis of 1914. It is against Kautsky's position and in reaction to the Socialist desertion, which in differing ways made revolution (and thus Lenin) appear unnecessary, that Lenin wrote *Imperialism*.

Thus, before we examine Lenin's own theory, it seems useful to outline the background onto which Lenin projected his theory. Marx left a confusing legacy on the subject of imperialism. Sometimes he identified it with Napoleon III's antics; in other places he described it as an inevitable, progressive (if painful) economic development of the backward regions. But it was not of central significance to his theory of capitalism.[7] His general economic theories left room for more than one inference: Exports might restrain the downward plunge of profits; foreign investment might have a similar effect. Imperialism might aid either of the two, but no specific connection was systematically argued at the theoretical level.

The theoretical backdrops to Lenin's views on imperialism were the traditional templates of Realism and Liberalism. Realists had portrayed conquest as a natural result of a significant disparity in power between one state and another. Imperialism, as Thucydides had long before explained, was a rational strategy to enhance security, prestige, and interests (trade, population, territory, resources) when the costs of conquest were less than the gain. Frederick the Great had explained his seizure of Silesia in just those terms in the eighteenth century; in the nineteenth century the Prussian (later German) Chancellor Otto von Bismarck justified German expansion, and Prime Minister Benjamin Disraeli explained British expansion with a similar rhetoric.[8] Liberals had agreed that power disparity was a root cause but differed on what should motivate imperialism. Imperialism, J. S. Mill argued, might be justified as an educative force designed to promote freedom or eradicate vicious practices, such as the slave trade and suttee. Following Adam Smith, however, Liberals became skeptical that imperialism did serve national economic or therefore strategic interests. Only a corrupted capitalism would discover and then be ruled by a material, special interest in imperial colonialism.

Lenin was most influenced, as he handsomely acknowledged, by the radical Liberal John Hobson, whose *Imperialism: A Study* charted the radical critique from which Lenin borrowed. Radical Liberals pursued the explanation Smith and Bentham suggested. They focused on how conspiracies of special interests, compounded of munitions makers and financiers, governed an imperial engine that needed imperial expansion in order to discover markets and fields for

[7] E. M. Winslow, *The Pattern of Imperialism* (New York: Columbia University Press, 1948), pp. 126–27; T. Kemp, *Theories of Imperialism* (London: Dobson, 1967), pp. 27–28.

[8] A. J. P. Taylor, *Germany's First Bid for Colonies* (New York, 1970) See the discussion in Doyle, *Empires*, chaps. 11 and 12.

investment that, because of the unequal distribution of income, could not be satisfied at home.[9] None of this was inevitable, Hobson argued. Domestic markets could clear, and citizens could appreciate their true interests, if only the special interests could be prevented from using their financial power to corrupt elections and the state. Political corruption prevented the democratic public from adopting the social welfare policies that the domestic economy needed to absorb excess savings and to stimulate consumption.

Although Hobson shaped much of Lenin's approach, Lenin was also reacting directly to his Marxist precursors, the Austrian Rudolf Hilferding and the German Rosa Luxemburg. Hilferding made perhaps the most interesting contribution in the area of economic theory to the Socialist canon that was developed after Marx's death (in 1883).[10] He examined the new and crucial role of finance and monopoly—finance capital. On the basis of Marx's remarks concerning simple reproduction, Hilferding argued that capitalism could remain stable, provided proper portions were maintained between the capital goods and the consumption sectors of the economy. Thus, from a theoretical stance, expansion (imperialism) was a policy, not a necessity of capitalist growth.[11]

Moreover, since capitalism could not be regulated by the price mechanism, the distribution of money in an economy warranted careful investigation. Here Hilferding noted a new development. With the growing accumulation of finance capital and the formation of modern corporations, which replaced family-owned enterprises, capitalism underwent a decisive reversal. Ownership became separated from management, a rentier class emerged, and banks moved in to bridge the gap by promoting and reorganizing companies on the stock exchange. Thus, fundamentally, the "circulation process comes to dominate the production process." Banks create monopolies or cartels to regulate production and maintain high and stable prices. Banks engage in a similar strategy of control internationally as well.[12] Just as finance capital demands protectionism at home to preserve its cartel prices, so it demands control abroad to ensure the stability of investments as sources of profit. With the demise of industrial capitalism, its policy of international competition and free trade has similarly departed. Inevitably the existence of more than one center of finance

[9]John A. Hobson, *Imperialism: A Study* (1902) (Ann Arbor: University of Michigan Press, 1965), chap. 4.
[10]In a brilliant article Albert O. Hirschman suggests that Marx may have been particularly reluctant to develop a theory of economic imperialism, although he was certainly aware of Hegel's views on the role of foreign trade as a means of absorbing domestic overproduction. By solving the overproduction crisis, foreign trade would dim the prospects for domestic revolution. Hirschman, "Hegel, Imperialism, and Structural Stagnation." On Marx's view of colonialism and the changes made by later Socialists, see Lichtheim, *Marxism*, pp. 310–31.
[11]See Brewer, *Marxist Theories of Imperialism*, chap. 4.
[12]Winslow, p. 167.

capital engaging in protection and dumping leads to economic conflict; and the existence of economic conflict, to war.

In almost every respect Rosa Luxemburg represented Hilferding's opposite. She excoriated his use of Marx's simple model of capitalism.[13] To her, that model was a mere theoretical construct; extended reproduction was the accurate model of capitalism. She thus emphasized the "realization" problem, how to guarantee effective demand when capital goods expenditure itself creates more consumption goods and when workers could not consume all of the final product. She concluded that to realize surplus value, exports are necessary. Furthermore, these exports must be purchased "outside" the capitalist economy—in underdeveloped lands abroad or in a country's own primitive sectors (together constituting the "external economy").[14] Imperialism therefore is "the political expression of the accumulation of capital in its competitive struggle for what remains still open of the non-capitalist environment." Imperialism, in short, is a competition for noncapitalist consumers (and suppliers of raw materials).[15]

Hilferding saw imperialism as a capitalist policy; Luxemburg saw it as a necessity. The first found imperialism's roots in the particular organizational interests of finance capital; the latter, in capitalism in general. The former saw foreign investment as the mechanism of relief for falling profits; the latter held that only foreign trade would serve that function. Nonetheless, both Hilferding and Luxemburg were fully accepted as part of the theoretical landscape of Marxist imperialism.

Lenin borrowed ideas from Hilferding and Luxemburg in writing *Imperialism,* and he directed extended criticism at neither of them. Kautsky was the intellectual leader of social democracy and a strong critic of those seeking to revise the Marxist canon. Lenin attacks him ferociously in *Imperialism.* The reasons for this difference in treatment are as much political as theoretical.

Kautsky had written extensively about colonialism and had even gone to the length of claiming priority over Hobson in discovering the interests behind it.[16] His ideas, however, did not crystallize until 1914, when he defined imperialism as "the striving of every industrial nation to annex larger and larger agrarian regions, irrespective of what nations inhabit them." Kautsky placed imperialism upon the shoulders of expanding industrial capitalism allied with banking capi-

[13] Gold production was one exogenous "solution" for Marx. The magisterial source on Luxemburg's thought is J. P. Nettl, *Rosa Luxemburg* (New York: Oxford University Press 1966), vols. 1 and 2.
[14] Winslow, pp. 137, 168–71.
[15] Rosa Luxemburg, *The Accumulation of Capital* (London: 1951), p. 466, and Alan Hodgart, *The Economics of European Imperialism* (New York: Norton, 1977), pp. 36–38.
[16] Kautsky published "Der Imperialismus" in *Neu Zeit* in 1914.

tal, which sought to export producers' goods and to make foreign investments. His theoretical position in 1914 was an evolution from earlier views that an American scholar has described as being closer to Schumpeter's later ideas than to most Socialist explanations.[17] Previously Kautsky had stressed the role of preindustrial factors—aristocratic, military classes and their ties to banking—and a search for new land to conquer. Despite evolution from this early view (written before specifically Marxist theories were developed), he retained an emphasis on atavistic forces as causes and a (perhaps resulting) belief in a pacifist, evolutionary Socialist strategy. He expressed these pacifist leanings in attacks on the German Social Democratic Party's support for war. Furthermore, he argued that imperialism did not necessarily cause war. War is a policy, not a necessity, of capitalism. Capitalist countries could combine to exploit jointly the world in large international cartels engaging in what Kautsky called ultraimperialism.

A comparison of contemporary radical and Marxist theories of imperialism reveals Lenin's theory to be a mélange. Analytically it owed most to Hilferding and—as founder of the financial taproot approach—to Hobson. But the combination was new and very carefully designed to join finance capital to orthodox Marxian analysis. To Lenin, imperialism was finance capitalism seeking worldwide, inevitably warlike domination. Some of his animus against Kautsky can be appreciated at first glance when it is noted that Kautsky has the unique distinction of being a Socialist political competitor and failing to reach "correct" conclusions on the causes, consequences, and policies that Lenin associated with imperialism and its Socialist cure, revolution.

LENIN'S *IMPERIALISM*

Rarely have attempts to be so clear created as much confusion as Lenin's definition of "imperialism." The confusion is a product of the specific definition Lenin chose, the mind-set of the scholars of international politics who later examined it, and the general method of Lenin's argument.

Lenin's attempt to make his definition very clear lies in a summary of his argument in chapter 7 of *Imperialism:*

> If it were necessary to give the briefest possible definition of imperialism we should have to say that imperialism is the monopoly stage of capitalism. Such a definition would include what is most important, for, on the one hand, finance capital is the bank capital of a few big monopolist banks, merged with

[17] John Kautsky, "J. A. Schumpeter and Karl Kautsky," *Midwest Journal of Political Science* (1961), pp. 108–9.
[18] Lenin, *Imperialism*, pp. 88–89.

> the capital of the monopolist combines of manufacturers; and on the other hand, the division of the world is the transition from a colonial policy which has extended without hindrance to territories unoccupied by any capitalist power, to a colonial policy of monopolistic possession of the territory of the world which has been completely divided up. But very brief definitions, although convenient, for they sum up the main points, are nevertheless inadequate, because very important features of the phenomenon that has to be defined have to be especially deduced.[18]

He adds that a more complete definition has to embrace the following five "essential features":

> 1) The concentration of production, and capital developed to such a high stage that it created monopolies which play a decisive role in economic life.
> 2) The merging of bank capital with industrial capital and the creation, on the basis of "financial capital," of a "financial oligarchy."
> 3) The export of capital, which has become extremely important, as distinguished from the export of commodities.
> 4) The formation of international capitalist combines which share the world among themselves.
> 5) The territorial division of the world among the greatest capitalist powers is completed.[19]

To the scholar seeking to understand the conquest of Africa and Asia, Lenin's definition often appears to say that imperialism is a product of the highest stage of capitalism, monopoly capitalism.[20] This same scholar will soon note that there were empires before capitalism, nineteenth-century imperialism before monopolies, and nonmonopolistic, as well as noncapitalistic, imperial powers at the time Lenin wrote. But Lenin himself mentions those three items in his *Imperialism* without these facts in the least affecting his argument.[21]

Part of this confusion is resolved when we realize that Lenin said what he meant. Finance capital, the monopoly stage of capitalism, is for him the *definition,* not the explanation, of "imperialism." In short, Lenin's theory is not an analysis of international politics but a description of capitalist development in

[19] Ibid., p. 89.
[20] Langer, *The Diplomacy of Imperialism,* pp. 68–69. In a number of respects, Langer's account remains the best short critique of economic imperialism.
[21] Lenin, *Imperialism.* pp. 82, 86, 124. Eric Stokes, "Late Nineteenth Century Colonial Expansion and the Attack on the Theory of Economic Imperialism: A Case of Mistaken Identity," *Historical Journal,* XII, 2 (1969), pp. 285–301, argues that economic imperialism was really a theory of interindustrial state conflicts. He correctly emphasizes Lenin's attention and inclusion of industrial conflicts, public and private, in *Imperialism.* But Lenin specifically included political division and redivision of overseas colonies as an essential feature of "imperialism."

its "highest stage." The ruling of foreign territories, the traditional "imperialism," bears the same relationship to Lenin's conception of imperialism as barking does to terriers. Not all terriers bark, and not all barks are produced by terriers, but one of the "characteristic features" of terriers is that they do bark.

Another confusing part of Lenin's analysis is his method of explanation by "general characteristics," "fundamental attributes" or "general picture."[22] He has not presented a statistical correlation of the five essential characteristics on a worldwide basis or argued that any particular country shows their "real" operation. His method is to examine "the whole of the data concerning the basis of economic life in all the belligerent countries [of World War I] and the whole world." To show what is characteristic, he combines what has happened and does happen with what, to an orthodox Marxist, must happen. Examples from all over the world illustrate "what happens," as the "general picture" reveals why they were examples in the first place. The circularity of this general analysis makes it difficult to test, although specific points and the internal logic of the analysis are susceptible to closer examination.

One is then left with two possibilities: to attempt to treat Lenin as he himself defined his position or to reinterpret him to obtain a "Leninist" view of international politics. Both involve later difficulties, and neither resolves the "barking terrier" problem mentioned earlier.

If Lenin's definition of imperialism is taken as a definition, including the five characteristic features, then his work is practically irrelevant to an understanding of imperialism in the common sense of that term. He has given a description of how finance capital might work, not an explanation of it. Only in three paragraphs of the first chapter does he explain the origins of monopoly, and these are mere citations from the work of bourgeois economists. Banks are shown to be related through interlocking directorates; together they do need to export capital, and economic and political divisions of the world do historically take place.[23] Why does this "imperialism" occur? It is the inevitable product of capitalist development, thereby leading us back to the first chapter on the reasons for monopoly. Thus on three paragraphs does the whole explanation rest.[24]

This is an interesting description of a late phase of international capitalist evolution (especially considering the fact that Russian censors barred political tracts, while allowing economic tracts). But Lenin himself indicated that he meant *Imperialism* to be more than an economic treatise. In the "Preface to the French and German Editions," he claims, "In the pamphlet [*Imperialism*] I proved that the war of 1914–18 was imperialistic (that is, an annexationist,

[22] Lenin, *Imperialism*, pp. 9, 88.
[23] Ibid., pp. 18, 26.
[24] Ibid., p. 88.
[25] Ibid., pp. 9, 10.
[26] Ibid., p. 75.

predatory, plunderous war) on the part of both sides; it was a war for the division of the world, for the partition and re-partition of enemies, 'spheres of influence' of finance capital, etc.," and later, ". . . imperialist wars are absolutely inevitable under such an economic system, as long as private property in the means of production exists."[25] Manifestly Lenin did aim to explain imperialism in the usual expansionist, or Hobsonian, sense by his analysis and description. But if so, merely by defining "imperialism" as monopoly capitalism, he cannot claim to have proved it.

Another tack would be to break up Lenin's definition and create an analytical model with dependent and independent variables, into "barks" and "terrier," and examine the nature of the connections between the two. Since Lenin gives the lead in this endeavor in his own "Preface," it does not seem totally illegitimate. One method would be to isolate the fifth of his essential characteristics, the territorial division of the world, but this is clearly inadequate because Lenin argues with some vehemence against just such a division as a Kautskyite obfuscation.[26] A better choice would be joining the fourth and fifth as dependent variables—the economic and territorial divisions of the world in the last stage of capitalism. In this stage a complete division of the world occurs between capitalist combines, such as in the German-American amalgam of AEG and General Electric in the electrical industry. At the same time and "parallel" to this economic division there follows a territorial division that completes the political division of the globe between the great powers. This territorial division is "closely associated with," "bound up with," the economic division.[27] It is accomplished not merely by colonial annexations, although the division of Africa and Asia is one of the characteristic features of the epoch. Informal rule over formally independent countries by political manipulation, bribery, threats (such as that exercised by "Britain over Argentina") also establishes control adequate for the monopolies.[28] Unlike Hobson and many other Liberals and Realists, Lenin thus has not compressed his concept of imperial control to the exclusion of informal but no less effective methods of actual control.

The Sources of the Two Divisions

Lenin sees imperialism (interpreted as the economic and political division of the world) as the product of institutions and forces. The institutions are monopoly capital, composed of the merger of industrial and bank capital, and the state, a reflection of those economic institutions. The forces are exerted by and through the institutions.[29]

Extracting his main examples from Germany and the United States and

[27] Ibid., pp. 70, 75.
[28] Ibid., p. 85.
[29] My views on Lenin's work have benefited from suggestions made by Dina Spechler.

noting similar tendencies in Britain, Lenin in his first chapter outlines the growth of monopoly, concentrated production. Companies expanded their capital base and merged their holdings in order to level out fluctuations in production and to weather recurrent financial crises. By the turn of the century large firms had become the dominant form of industrial enterprise.[30]

This was a familiar analysis of late-nineteenth-century monopoly growth, but in a discussion of the new role of banks Lenin moves to more interesting interpretations. Here he shows the increasing concentration of the banks themselves—the nine German banks, four British, and the big three of France.[31] These huge banks acquire funds that must be invested profitably, and in the process of investing, they outmode the regular mechanism of the stock exchange and transform the usual financial services they offer corporations into distinct forms of control manifested in seats on the boards of directors of their client companies. Seeking secure investments, they demand careful management, noncompetition with their other investments, and even, where it appears safe, mergers to reduce unwanted fluctuations in stock values caused by competition.[32] The result is a single financial oligarchy of capitalists dominating each country and operating through the coordinating control that banks exercise over corporations. This creates a new stage of capitalism: Financial, or Monopoly, Capitalism.

Finance capitalism serves as a channel for three international pressures or forces. The first economic force is the search for profitable investment necessitated by a "superabundance" of capital in the advanced capitalist economies that are now constructed along monopoly lines.[33] The necessity for exporting capital arises from the fact that in a few countries capitalism has become "overripe," and (owing to the backward state of agriculture and the impoverished state of the masses) capital cannot find "profitable" investment.[34] Lenin argues that capital cannot invest in either agriculture or the masses because investing there would involve lower profits for capitalists. Under the "old capitalism when free competition prevailed," the export of goods was the dominant transaction. Now under monopoly capitalism with its tariffs limiting the international exchange of commodities, the export of capital predominates. As an example of the extent and complexity of the search for profitable overseas investment, he cites the Deutsche Bank's floating of the Siberian Commercial Bank's shares from which the German bank "skims the cream."

Second, Lenin holds that underconsumption drives monopolies to seek mar-

[30] Lenin, *Imperialism*, pp. 17–19.
[31] Ibid., p. 33.
[32] Ibid., pp. 39, 41.
[33] Ibid., pp. 53, 65. He uses railways as a leading example.
[34] Ibid., p. 63.

kets in the undeveloped areas of the world. Even though trade is not the predominant form of international exploitation, concentrated industries do find that exports are one mechanism by which the tendency of the rate of profit to fall can be momentarily slowed. Moreover, capital export complements trade by creating certain advantages for home country exporters. When loans are tied to the purchase of home-produced goods, exports are secured for the monopoly industries.

Third, in order to secure a monopoly, control of markets and sources of raw materials is sought.[35] Occasionally agreements divide the world market, as happened in the electrical trust formed by AEG and General Electric. But usually there is a continual "struggle for redivision," such as that characterizing the international oil industry and the contest between Standard Oil and the Baku fields of Rothschild and Nobel.[36] One of the clearest forms of this expand-or-be-absorbed monopoly pressure is the connection between colonialism and the search for raw materials. "These monopolies are most firmly established when all sources of raw materials are controlled by one group. . . . Colonial possession alone gives complete guarantee of success to the monopolies against all the risks that the latter will defend themselves by means of a law establishing a state monopoly [as Germany did when it established a state cartel in oil]."[37]

Even if the bank and industrial monopolies form the crucial institutions of imperialism, the state also plays an important role. Unfortunately Lenin had to write an "economic study" in order to pass the Russian censors, and his resort to "Aesopian" language (fables as a mask for messages) was not conducive to political analysis. However, he does comment on imperialism's relation to politics in *Imperialism,* and he presents ideas on the state in other writings. Both the general nature of the state and the particular characteristics of the imperialist state are important to his understanding of its role in imperialism.

Lenin, drawing heavily upon Engels's *The Origins of the Family, Private Property, and the State,* outlines his ideas on the relationship between state and society in *State and Revolution* (August 1917). Following Engels, he argues that the state is the product of society at a certain stage of development when class antagonisms become irreconcilable. "Standing above society," the state ". . . arose in the midst of the conflict of these classes; it is, as a rule, the state of the most powerful, economically, dominant class, which by virtue thereof becomes also the dominant class politically, and thus acquires new means of holding down and exploiting the oppressed class."[38] Even in democratic republics, the

[35] Ibid., p. 66, for exports; p. 82, raw materials.
[36] Ibid., pp. 76, 91.
[37] Ibid., p. 82.
[38] Lenin, *State and Revolution* (New York: International Publishers, 1919), p. 8.

capitalist class exercises control through the corruption of officials, an informal alliance of the stock exchange and the government, the capitalist ownership of the press, and restriction of the suffrage.[39]

Just as imperialism represents a stage in the evolution of capitalism, so the imperial state is a special development of the state. Two institutions are characteristic of state machinery: "bureaucracy and a standing army." Imperialism in particular shows an unprecedented growth of the "state machinery" and of its bureaucratic and military apparatus, side by side with the increase of repressive measures against the proletariat alike in monarchical and the freest republican countries.[40] This growth of the state, which reflects increased class antagonisms, has important points of contact with imperialism. First, the economic foundations of the state shift toward "parasitism" (here Lenin is following Hobson). The imperialist state becomes a "rentier state," collecting interest for its dominant class of capitalist investors. Second, the top levels of the working class—"the aristocracy of labor"—become politically subservient as they reach bourgeois status through their share in imperialist superprofits.[41] Adding to this corruption is the development the British imperialist Cecil Rhodes noted (which Lenin cites): empire has turned into a "bread and butter question," an opportunity for settlement and an expansion of markets that together increase popular welfare and indirectly stave off revolution. Third, the state as an institution is transformed. Its size and power increase. To relieve domestic popular discontent, it employs mercenary armies (Lenin follows Hobson again), and to maintain popular support, it encourages "social chauvinism," or national hatreds and lusts for conquest. These three sources form the imperialist state. This state then must satisfy the forces on which it is built by imperial expansion, which economically satisfies the bondholders and the bribed working class and psychologically feeds social chauvinism.[42]

Revolution

Lenin not only described a solution to imperialism, as Hobson did, but took the first steps toward achieving it. His solution was, of course, revolution; but it was somewhat more complicated than is sometimes assumed. Revolution at home is necessary for emancipating the colonies since emancipation is " 'impracticable' under capitalism," but reflecting the international systemic character of Lenin's *Imperialism*, national liberation abroad is also needed to stage successfully a revolution at home: "The social revolution can come only in the form of an epoch in which are combined civil war by the proletariat

[39] Ibid., pp. 13, 72.
[40] Ibid., p. 29.
[41] Lenin, *Imperialism*, pp. 100–01, 104.
[42] Ibid., pp. 108–09.

CHART 2

Lenin's Imperialism—the Monopoly Stage of Capitalism

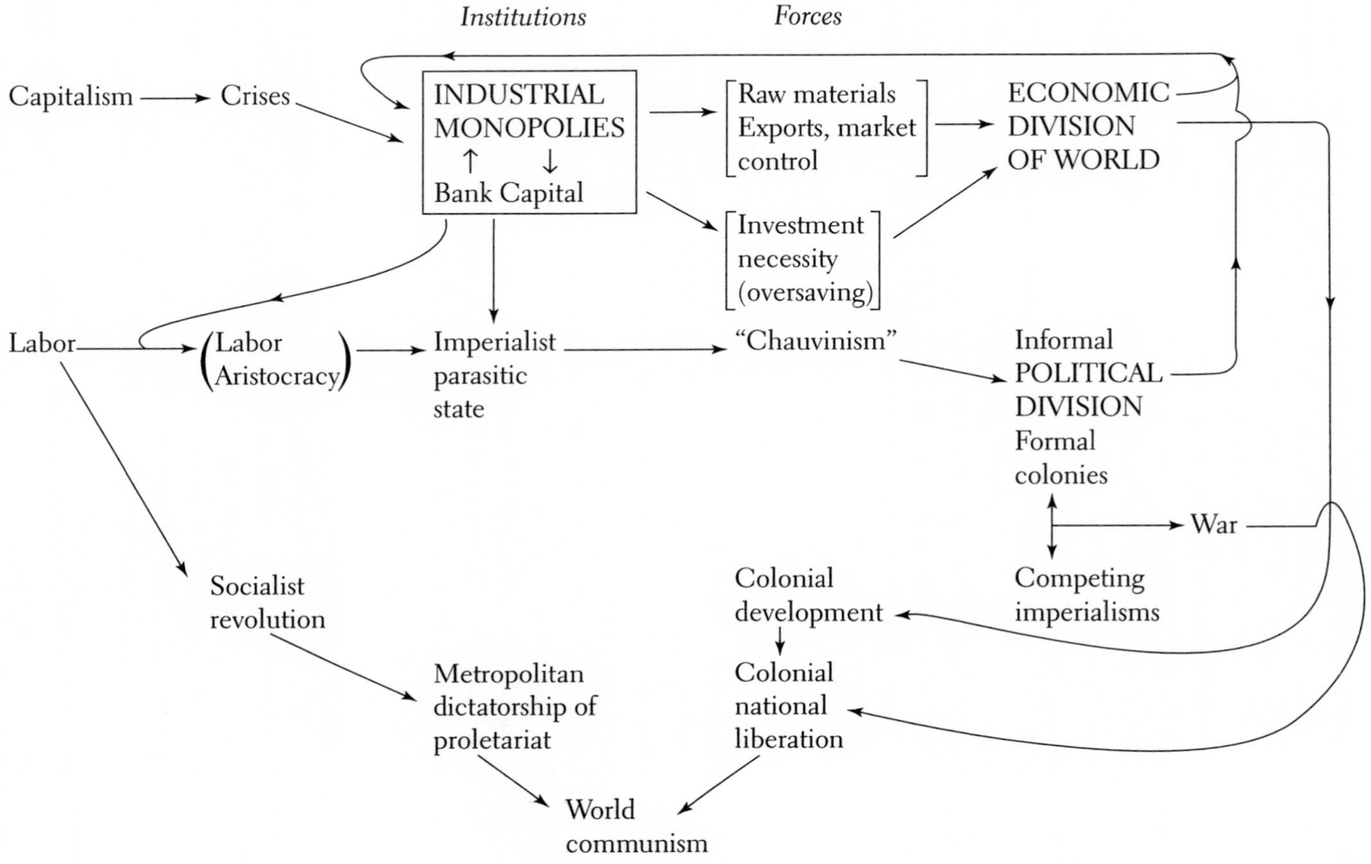

against the bourgeoisie in the advanced countries and a whole series of democratic and revolutionary movements, including the national liberation movement, in the undeveloped, backward and oppressed nations."[43]

Capitalism, according to Lenin, should evolve in a way that ensures that both of the two sets of revolutions that must occur will occur. With Marx, Lenin believed that capitalism is both destructive and creative in the colonial areas. Their feudal and colonial stages of production would be transformed by the world market and by international investment into industrial capitalism. The emergence of capitalism would then lay the objective foundations for a bourgeois, national revolution. In the capitalist metropolis, the process of concentration of industry and the increasing misery of the working class would lead to conditions more and more ripe for a Communist-led revolution under a "dictatorship of the proletariat." But if the combination of a national bourgeois revolution in the colonial peripheries and a Communist revolution in the metropolis fails to occur, a serious danger confronts the revolutionary process. Metropolitan troops could be used to quell the colonial rebellion; colonial troops could be used to suppress the working-class rebellion in the metropole.[44]

Peace and Evolution?

In *Imperialism*, Lenin devotes the chapter before the concluding summary to the question of peaceful evolution. Is it possible? Can imperialism maintain peace, as Kautsky argued, long enough to evolve into social democracy and national liberation? Lenin's answer is, as usual, unequivocal: peace is impossible, and there can be no evolution toward social democracy.

Kautsky held that "ultraimperialism" can be a stage beyond imperialism in which capitalists form alliances to reduce economic and political competition in the world economy.[45] But Lenin replies that any slackening of competition is merely a truce since capitalism develops unevenly. Why? Objective reality gives us highly developed capitalist nations side by side, with a number of economically slightly developed or totally undeveloped nations. Relative forces change, and an alliance of yesterday, reflecting an equilibrium of forces yesterday, cannot be maintained in the future. When the relationships of force change, states and imperialist monopolies will seek to prevent their decline by force; others will seek to promote their own rise by force. Furthermore, Kautsky's notions of reform and evolution toward social democracy are no more than a "reactionary ideal" that seeks to move from monopoly back to peaceful

[43] Lenin, "The Socialist Revolution and the Rights of Nations to Self-Determination" *Selected Works* (London: Lawrence-Wishart, 1968), pp. 158–59; and for quotation, "A Caricature of Marxism and Imperialist Economism," *Collected Works* (August–October 1917), vol. 23, p. 60.
[44] Lenin, *State and Revolution*, p. 74.
[45] Lenin, *Imperialism*, p. 119.

competition. He forgets, Lenin admonishes, that it was just that peaceful competition that developed into monopoly. The ideals of neither "English parsons" (Hobson) in favor of democratic reform nor German Marxists (Kautsky) are relevant or correct. Capitalism cannot evolve into democratic competition or maintain peace by an alliance of national monopolies.[46]

Lenin's theory, in summary, holds: (1) Imperialism is an essential feature of the informal division of the world, just as colonial conquest is an equivalent feature of the formal division of the world. (2) Metropolitan dispositions are the source of imperialism. (3) Among these, finance, parasitic interests, and the working-class aristocracy are necessary parts and fundamentally "bound up with" the monopoly stage of capitalism. (4) The driving economic forces are oversaving and the imperative of monopoly to control raw materials and markets.

All of imperialism's parts are, by argument, products of capitalism, the sole root cause. The parts form a single whole. The imperial oligarchy Lenin identifies is a powerful, completely unitary, rational actor. All the parts of Lenin's theory are logically interconnected to one another. To maintain the inevitability of revolution, the working class must be potentially revolutionary, but to explain the present strength of the imperialist state, more than capitalist coercion must be at work. Lenin's answer lies in an emphasis on the "labor aristocracy" bought with imperialist superprofits. Lenin argues necessities, not tendencies. Given his description of monopoly capitalism, all else follows.

Lenin's Political Economy

For Lenin, imperialism is not caused by but *is* finance capital, and international domination is just one of its by-products. But then how do we identify or test for its presence? Perhaps the strongest criticism that can be made of any theory is that it is untestable or tautological. Lenin's imperialism, which he defined as the highest stage of capitalism, is certainly that. However, many of his separate ideas are powerful and insightful, and they are combined in original ways.

In *The Theory of Capitalist Imperialism,* D. K. Fieldhouse, a leading scholar of empires, argues that the most telling criticisms are chronological, geographical, and historical.[47]

Considering the chronology of imperialism, the critics say, "imperial expansion occurred too early to fit the emergence of 'finance capitalism.' "[48] That is, the "new imperialism" of the late nineteenth century (1870–1900) came before, not after, monopoly capitalism or finance capital. Lenin states: "For

[46] Ibid., p. 119.
[47] D. K. Fieldhouse, *The Theory of Capitalist Imperialism* (London: Longmans, 1967), pp. 189–94.
[48] Ibid., p. 140.

Europe, the time when the new capitalism definitely superseded the old can be established with fair precision: it was at the beginning of the twentieth century."[49] He recognized that the great period of colonial expansion was 1886–1900. To the critics here was a clear discrepancy.

But Lenin never argues that all colonies, or forms of colonialism, were the special products of monopoly capital: "Colonial policy and imperialism existed before this latest stage of capitalism, and even before capitalism. Rome, founded on slavery, pursued a colonial policy and achieved imperialism. But 'general' arguments about imperialism which ignore, or put into the background, the fundamental difference of social-economic systems, inevitably degenerate into absolutely empty banalities, or into grandiloquent comparisons like 'Greater Rome and Greater Britain.' Even the colonial policy of capitalism in its previous stages is essentially different from the colonial policy of finance capital."[50]

Furthermore, Lenin identifies "an intensification of colonial policy" as the key sign for which to look. Thus the existence of colonialism before finance capital is not an adequate criticism as it stands; one should look for its intensification, not merely its existence.

In this search, however, Lenin leads the reader astray. He first describes the stage of "free competition," at its peak in the 1860s and 1870s in Europe and in Britain in the 1840s and 1860s, as an age of anti-imperialism. He says 1876 marks the completion of the "pre-monopolist stage of development." Next, although admitting Britain's greatest colonial expansion occurred between 1860 and 1889, he concludes that "it is precisely after the period [of free competition 1860–1880]" that the "boom" in colonial annexations begins and that "the struggle for the territorial division of the world becomes extraordinarily keen."[51] In other words, he says the "intensification" follows the "free competition" stage and occurs after 1876. But although Lenin thinks that he has proved his assertion at this point, his analysis is less than complete.

Free competition held sway between 1840 and 1880 (in Britain and Europe), monopoly "definitely" superseded competitive capitalism after 1900, and colonialism intensified after 1876. This does not show colonialism to be "bound up with" monopoly. Logically imperialism could be: (1) a late stage of moribund free competition, (2) an early product of embryonic monopoly, or (3) the product primarily of Britain, which went through its stages more rapidly. Empirically the last does not hold; even though capitalism came early, monopoly came late to Britain (and Lenin does not argue this third hypothesis). Thus, from Lenin's own analysis, it could be either free competition or monopoly

[49] Lenin, *Imperialism*, p. 20.
[50] Ibid., pp. 81–82.
[51] Ibid., pp. 27–28, 79, 77.

that is responsible. The intensification of 1880–1900 accords with either factor (though more closely with moribund free competition), and Lenin does not offer an adequate argument to distinguish the two.

This represents a distinct failure in Lenin's argument since his intensification is not fully "bound up with" monopoly, but it should be remembered that the thrust of Lenin's theory was that the monopoly stage led to "intensification" of imperialism, not that the actual annexation period was produced by monopoly. The real issue for a Leninist thus has only been skirted.

Before we examine it more directly, let us consider the geographic critique. Critics point out that many nonmonopoly capitalist powers were imperialistic; among this group were Russia, Spain, and Portugal. This was recognized by Lenin and dismissed along with his reference to Rome. There are, he implies, other grounds for colonialism than monopoly capital. Lenin is arguing that monopoly capital produced colonialism, not that all colonialisms are the product of monopoly capital. Critics also point to the disparity between capital outflow, one of Lenin's forces, and new colonies acquired primarily in Africa and Asia. They do not correspond.

But oversaving for Lenin is just one of the motive forces. More important is the monopoly imperative to control sources of raw materials and potential markets (even if currently unproductive) to keep them out of the hands of competitors. Furthermore, Lenin saw formal annexations as just part of the imperial product. Informal acquisitions, such as Argentina and Turkey, were equally important, and both of these were mere overflow from the true arena of competition: the economic (monopoly) division of the whole world, not just the undeveloped portions of it. The lack of correlation should not only be untroubling for a Leninist, but also be reassuring. It might nevertheless be troubling to someone seeking to understand the domination of the undeveloped world and expecting Lenin to have provided an explanation for it.

Thus Lenin does have responses to the "geographic" and "chronological" criticisms of his imperialism, but each of his responses take us a step farther away from an understanding of the domination or control of one country by another. If he is only explaining the latest instance and not the many previous instances of imperialism—and, at that, only the capitalist, not the autocratic or other variants of empire building—someone interested in explaining imperial domination can fairly doubt that he has truly captured its most important sources. Monopoly capitalism, by his admission, is not necessary to the existence or explanation of empires: neither in the past nor in the present. Lenin is not really attempting to explain empires (despite *Imperialism*). Thucydides, two millennia before, gave us a more convincing account of how and why empires could be formed. Instead Lenin is examining a new stage of capitalism, one that also involves a new variety of domination. But international domination per se is not his interest; it is, he argues, a necessary by-product that in turn has interesting implications for his concern, monopoly capitalism. He directs his attention not at an old wine in new bottles but at a new wine, some of which is in old imperial bottles.

It makes sense therefore for critics also to meet him on his own ground—to examine how essential political division was to monopoly capital—rather than whether monopoly capital was the unique and necessary cause of colonialism, a claim Lenin specifically denied. If by so doing, Lenin appears more irrelevant to an understanding of empires, our examination becomes more relevant to an understanding of Lenin. Was monopoly capitalism a sufficient, even though not a necessary, cause of imperialism (considered as international domination)?

His explanation makes some logical sense; political division could support economic division, and both could be necessary features of monopoly capitalism. But this contention needs to be examined more critically. Lenin's prime example for much of his pamphlet is the United States. It can serve us as well as an instance of the historical association of monopoly and imperialism. It can also help us answer three questions. Were there monopolies in the sense Lenin described? Were these monopolies in control of the state? Was imperial expansion one of their essential interests?

Modern scholarship seems to offer support for much of Lenin's analysis. J. P. Morgan's career illustrates many features of Leninist theory. Acting frequently as an agent for British capital, whose investment proxies he held, Morgan grew to exercise enormous influence over U.S. industry. From his strategic position as an international investment banker, he placed foreign investments in the United States and found foreign lenders for American firms seeking to borrow. Following the crisis of 1893, he took a leading role in reorganizing—concentrating and trustifying—the major eastern railroads. This resulted in Morgan's exercising a "veto power" over their management.[52] He also helped form the U.S. Steel Company and thus exercised a striking influence over half of American steel production. In 1902 he organized the International Merchant Marine. International Harvester was formed that same year under his aegis, and it controlled 80 percent of the production in that industry. After the 1907 bank panic he consolidated and enlarged the First National Bank, of which he was the second largest stockholder, and acquired control of Equitable Insurance. Alliances also were established with the National City Bank.[53]

Altogether this is a picture strikingly close to the merging of bank and industrial capital under the control of the banks that Lenin described. The relations of finance with the state superstructure also bore some similarities to Lenin's view. The control Morgan could exercise in public finance was illustrated by

[52] Frederick Lewis Allen, *The Great Pierpoint Morgan* (New York: Harper and Row, 1965), pp. 37, 79.
[53] Ibid., pp. 136, 144, 153, 186, 217–18.

the gold bond transaction with the Cleveland administration in 1895 when the U.S. government was required to accept the financial terms Morgan and his partners dictated. Morgan's interest in politics took two forms. The first was corruption, as demonstrated in his conviction that all local politicians, such as the bosses Platt and Tweed, could be bought. The second was general support for, influence over, and symbiosis with a political party, as shown in his happy relations with Mark Hanna, the trustworthy boss of the Republican Party whom Morgan kept pledged to the international gold standard.[54]

But even though the Republican Party was the party of business, not all Republicans were Mark Hannas. President Theodore Roosevelt demonstrated this to Morgan by prosecuting him in 1902 under the Sherman Antitrust Act for monopoly practices. And Morgan's Northern Securities Company, a holding company he set up with E. H. Harriman to establish control over the Northern Pacific Railroad, was dissolved by court order.[55] The significance of these events is that in a contest on an issue that was vital to "monopoly capitalism," monopoly lost.

Whatever symbiosis did exist was not total. The superstructure was not completely controlled. Neither was governmental policy free from the special interests of capital. The Sherman Act did not turn out to be the scourge of monopolies first imagined. And the dominant public reaction to Roosevelt's prosecution of Northern Securities was that of surprise. Perhaps it could be said that the symbiosis was viable, but monopolies did not govern its terms.

If one accepts a Leninist analysis of finance capital but concludes that the superstructure was not fully controlled (i.e., that it was subject to the pressures of vote getting and competing interests in a "bourgeois republic"), what should one conclude about imperialism?

If finance capital were not fully in control, clearly it could attain at most only its vital interests or its unopposed or allied interests from the state. (This was the situation in *Northern Securities.*) Imperialist "political division" could accord with finance capital's interests in obtaining full security from foreign competition for raw materials, investments, and markets. But is it a "necessary" outcome and thus a truly "essential characteristic" of imperialism? And even if exporting capital and competing for control of raw materials were vital for monopolies, did those investments need to be placed in foreign countries formally or informally controlled?

The United States did engage in imperialism in the Caribbean and in the Pacific. But before 1914 raw material or investment-generated imperialism can hardly be seen as vital to the U.S. economy (to its "financial oligarchy"). The United States was still a net raw material exporter. It was also still a net capital

[54] Ibid., chap. 6, p. 173.
[55] Ibid., p. 176.

importer. The newly imperialized areas (formally ruled Hawaii and the Philippines or the informally ruled Caribbean) were not the recipients of large flows of U.S. investment, absolutely or relatively.[56] Moreover, imperialist wars were likely to be (and were) met with some opposition from remnants of free competition advocates and from the "unbought" working class. Imperialism was not unopposed. Allied interests? They undoubtedly existed. They included bureaucratic classes, landowners seeking new territory, missionaries, and intellectuals (the "Geographers"). If allies or other causes are needed to explain imperialism, they are not subservient enough to monopoly capital to form mere superstructural phenomena. They need an allied and independent place in the explanation.

Thus analysis within Lenin's model of essential characteristics does not quite support his conclusions. If this failing was a product of Aesopianism, he did not see it as important enough to correct later. And if that is the case, Lenin's theory is less than a complete explanation of "political division," even in the monopoly stage.

Leninist Internationalism

Lenin's solution was simultaneous revolution at home and in the dependent territories. Was it feasible? Was it desirable? For Lenin, the feasibility of revolution rested on three contradictions: the continuing tension in the colonies between national liberation forces and imperialism, the strife in the metropolis between the proletariat and the bourgeoisie, and the rivalry between metropolitan imperialisms caused by uneven development.

The confrontation of proletariat and bourgeoisie faced two new difficulties not present when Marx wrote his more optimistic predictions of working-class liberation. First, although the contradictions between the mass of the workers and the capitalists were growing more extreme with increasing concentration of production (socialization of production without socialized ownership), the powers of the imperialist state as a class-based coercive mechanism had grown in equal proportion. Second, as an even more disturbing development, the "labour aristocracy"—leading elements of the workers themselves—had been bribed with imperialist superprofits to desert their revolutionary interests and to pursue bourgeois social democracy and "social chauvinism" ("socialist rhetoric, chauvinist reality").[57]

Three revolutionary forces help countervail those additions to the reactionary arsenal. The first is the party as the elite vanguard of the proletariat, a Leninist

[56] W. W. Rostow, *The World Economy: History and Prospect* (Austin: University of Texas Press, 1978), chaps. 14, 29. These two chapters survey the international economy and the place of the United States within that world economy.
[57] Lenin, *Imperialism*, pp. 108, 126.

addition to Marxism. With education and leadership it hopes to compensate for the defection of the labor aristocracy. A second factor is the increased threat of war among the imperialist states. Even though victories enhance the strength of social chauvinism, defeats discredit and weaken the imperialist state and thus offer an opportunity for revolution led by the Communist Party.[58] The third factor is a national bourgeois revolution in the colonial areas. Following Marx, Lenin sees imperialism as a force that will develop the undeveloped world and in that process create nationalist bourgeoisies in the colonial periphery. And since the nationalist bourgeoisie may acquire power before the vanguard of the proletariat in the underdeveloped countries, a bourgeois revolution is to be expected as the toppling force of international imperialism.[59]

In 1916, as the world war raged and divided the Socialists, Lenin reconsidered Marx's internationalism. Progress, Lenin argued, meant something very different after 1898, in the era of imperialism, from in 1848, when Marx assessed the bourgeois revolutions in the era of competitive capitalism. In 1848 Marx prescribed an internationalist logic, and Lenin commented: "Marx is known to have favoured Polish independence in the interests of *European* democracy in its struggle against the power and influence—or, it might be said, against the omnipotence and predominating reactionary influence—of tsarism."[60] At the time some national struggles for liberation were "objectively" reactionary; they set back the overall cause of revolutionary progress. (Marx had in mind the Czech and South Slav movements because they undermined the major Polish and Hungarian struggles against the leading imperialist powers, Russia and Austria.) But the period of imperialism "1898–1916" is a period of five or six "imperialist Great Powers each oppressing other nations . . . artificially retarding the collapse of capitalism and artificially supporting opportunism and social chauvinism in the imperialist nations which dominate the world." This period, Lenin announces with clear references back to Marx, requires a change of strategy: "*[F]ormerly* the main thing was to fight 'against Tsarism' (and against certain small-nation movements that *it* was using for undemocratic ends), and for the greater revolutionary peoples of the West; the main thing *today* is to stand against the united, aligned front of the imperialist powers, the imperialist bourgeoisie and the social-imperialists, and for the utilisation of all national movements against imperialism for the purposes of the socialist revolution."[61]

After the 1905 Revolution in Russia and following the emergence of finance capital and its domination of the bourgeois democracies—Germany, France,

[58] Lenin, *State and Revolution*. p. 20.
[59] Lenin, *Imperialism*, p. 65.
[60] Lenin, "The Discussion on Self-Determination Summed Up," p. 145.
[61] Ibid., p. 147.

the United States, and Britain—Russia was no longer the greatest reactionary threat; the advanced imperialist powers were. Those powers could no longer be transformed by democratic revolution from within. The working class had been corrupted by a labor aristocracy. The bureaucratic state was too powerful. Instead the combined attacks of war, colonial revolution from abroad, and domestic revolution led by disciplined party cadres in the advanced capitalist nations were required.

So-called Socialists (really "social chauvinists") were deluded or corrupted, Lenin argues, if they supported bourgeois democracies over autocracies or sought, as Kautsky allegedly did in 1916, to encourage Austria and Germany to negotiate for a peace that would have kept their empires intact.[62] Lenin preferred war, the best instrument to weaken the imperialist, bureaucratic state, allowing both metropolitan revolution and colonial rebellion.

It appears clear that timing would be crucial; one needs to have a metropolitan Socialist revolution coincide with a nationalist revolution led by the colonial bourgeoisie. Interestingly, Lenin remained confident of the national qualities of the colonial bourgeoisie, indicating a residue of Marxist optimism (as well as a lack of belief in the possibilities of peasant revolution). Before the nationalist revolution in the colonies, troops drawn from the colonies could be used to suppress metropolitan revolution. Before the Socialist revolution in the metropole, metropolitan troops would be sent out and national revolution in the colony would be crushed. All turns, as Lenin suggested, on the very fortuitous timing of metropolitan and colonial revolution. Their simultaneity is crucial but also improbable and difficult to achieve. Only a world war with its destructive impact on the state institutions of all the combatants could coordinate the revolutionary forces of history. Despite the weakening of states that World War I actually did accomplish, the Russian Revolution was attacked from Russia's "colonial" periphery and by the nonrevolutionary Western bourgeois states. Revolutionary timing was thus far from an academic issue for Russia's Bolsheviks in 1918, 1919, and 1920.

Moral judgments on the progressive character of national bourgeois revolutions are likely to stir little controversy in our period of the twentieth century. National revolutions seem to benefit all classes in the colony except the collaborators and feudal elements sometimes attached to imperial interests. (That widely shared judgment may be more questionable than we assume.) The metropolitan Socialist revolution offers more ground for dispute with its enormous stakes and its clear conflict of interest between the proletariat and the bourgeoisie. The metropolitan revolution, operating under the constraint of a dictatorship for a substantial period, destroys the capitalists, who naturally resist.

[62] Lenin, "The Socialist Revolution and the Right of Nations to Self-Determination: Theses," pp. 123–24.

Revolutionary "omelets" presuppose cracked "eggs."[63] Many will die to halt the wage slavery of capitalist societies and the domination and exploitation of undeveloped countries.

The moral trade-off, furthermore, is not a simple equation. The more successful the imperialist state, the larger the portion of the working class would be that could be kept bribed with "bread and circuses" and the less materially noxious the oppression would be at home (while being worse overseas). Under these circumstances the less pressing revolution would be in the metropole, the more oppressive imperialism would be internationally.[64] All this encouraged catastrophist reasoning among Lenin's beleaguered underground. Lacking confidence in the revolutionary character of working-class democracy, Lenin and his small band of Bolshevik followers had come to believe that making things worse—though war and collapse—had become the only way to making things better, by Communist revolution.

Conclusion

Whatever its scholarly failings, Lenin's pamphlet on imperialism was a political success. It helped steer the Bolshevik Party away from social democracy by associating social democracy's very existence and character with the charges of "social chauvinism," "imperialist tool," and "labor aristocracy." Kautskyism, though untainted by social chauvinism, was condemned for its naive, illogical "ultraimperialism." War would be the product of monopoly capitalism, Lenin announced, and historically World War I to many Socialists seemed to confirm his analysis. Imperialism could not be merely a "policy," as Kautsky claimed it was. The outbreak of "imperialist" war seemed (though unnecessarily) to confirm that it was inevitable. The descent into war's brutal destructions by the advanced nations of Europe seemed to confirm that judgment too. Lenin's predictive success as scientist of class warfare rested on his skill as an ideological politician, and together they helped separate the Communists from the evolutionary strategy and the democratic politics of the Social Democrats.

The failings of *Imperialism* as an analysis of empires were the bases for its political success. For Lenin, imperialism followed as a necessary stage in the development of capitalism. Rejecting multicausal explanations of imperial expansion, he asserted that imperialism (which included, as an essential characteristic, imperial expansion) had a single root cause: the evolution of capital-

[63] Lenin, *State and Revolution*, pp. 44–48, 73.

[64] Frantz Fanon appears to have been aware of this possible contradiction between the interests of the colonial masses and the proletariat in the metropolis. He hoped that if the metropolitan proletariat failed to perceive their long-run interests in the liberation of the masses in the periphery, the global depression engendered by a peripheral rebellion and rejection of world capitalism would soon make them aware of their mutual interests. Frantz Fanon, *Wretched of the Earth* (New York: Grove Press), pp. 80–81.

ism. Admitting multiple causes (causes that were not merely superstructural) left one with too many possibilities and too many "policies" for a Leninist politics that rested on a absolute claim to material truth. Social democratic confusion (and angst) would not have been a convenient political position either for a Leninist strategy or for the monopoly role claimed by the Bolshevik vanguard.

Conclusion: "Beyond Betrayal"—Marxists, Leninists, and Nationalists

UNLIKE REALISTS AND Liberals who have held state power, Marxist Socialists have yet to do so. Leninism, Stalinism, Maoism, Castroism, and the many other variants of Socialist doctrine have shaped state policy in the countries in which they successfully acquired revolutionary authority. But Marxists qua Marxists never have; so unlike the balance of power or the Liberal peace, Socialist solidarity and Marxist theory require an indirect test. Did Marxist Socialists at their greatest historical moment of influence so far, 1914, try to follow Marxist precepts? There is some reason to believe they did and thus some reason to believe Marxist ideas, as discredited as they have become in the Central European region of their birth, might have a significant claim on our understanding of how world politics might evolve. What might happen if—as seems to be happening in the middle 1990s in Poland, Hungary, Bulgaria, and perhaps Russia too—Marxist Socialism begins to win political power? After reviewing the key differences between Marxism and Leninism, I shall examine the choices made by Leninists and democratic Marxist Socialists in 1914, the moment of crisis that may reveal how democratic Socialists actually would play the game of world politics.

MARXISM AND LENINISM

Marxism-Leninism is frequently hyphenated as one ideology; however, like both the Realists and the Liberals, Socialists display significant differences. The Marxists tend to focus on societal-level (Image II) and the Leninists on interstate (Image III) determinants of the state of war. Their conceptions of what describes the state of war differ not only from Liberals and Realists but also between themselves.

Both Marxists and Leninists (and like only Machiavelli among the Realists) see the state of war as a condition that holds both within and between states. For Marx and Lenin, classes exist in a state of warlike competition in modern capitalist society, as do capitalist states in their international relations. Peace and solidarity, correspondingly, are a condition that holds among Socialists both at home and across international borders.

Marx's view of capitalism sees the competitive drives of capitalists governed by the actions of their "executive committee," the bourgeois republican state. The search for profits and the heavy costs of war often encourage capitalists to maintain a tentative bourgeois peace and cooperate, especially when the working classes seem to threaten a coordinated revolt as they appear to have done in 1848 and 1871. Marx's cure is a worldwide democratic Socialist revolution that, by abolishing class exploitation, will create a domestic state of peace governed by the rule of the people and an international association with other Socialist democracies.

Variants of Modern Socialism

	Marxists	*Leninists*
State of War	international and domestic; heterogeneous between classes	international and domestic; heterogeneous
State of Peace	among Socialists	among Communists
Actors	classes	finance capital/ Communist vanguards
Source of State of War	class exploitation	monopoly competition "uneven development"
Strategy of Peace	democratic revolution	war and revolution

Lenin sees a different dynamic and different actors in the fore. In the monopoly stage of capitalism, a unified financial oligarchy dominates all industry and the state, extracting super profits at home and abroad (through "imperialism").

The oligarchy bribes leading elements of the working class and establishes so powerful a police and military apparatus that it precludes both the democratic revolution Marx envisaged and any possibility of cooperative relations among monopoly capitalists across international borders. Only when—driven by uneven development—monopoly capitalists clash in war is the imperialist state weakened enough for a vanguard of Communists to lead a revolution, establish a dictatorship of the proletariat, socialize production, and develop peaceful relations with other revolutionary states.

MARXISM AND WAR

By August 4, 1914, Marxism had become a political movement and a set of Socialist doctrines with a bewildering variety of positions. No national movement lacked factions. Each faction claimed to have discovered the true meaning of Marxist doctrine for its time. Some argued that the growth in the influence of trade unions and Socialist parties demonstrated the efficacy of electoral social democracy (the Social Democrats in Germany); others, that the capitalists had so protected themselves with the military and bureaucratic apparatus of a coercive state that only violent revolutionary warfare would achieve Socialism (Lenin in Russia). Some believed that the development of finance capital constituted a new stage of aggressive, monopolistic, imperialistic capitalism (Luxemburg and Lenin); others, that finance capital constituted a force for ultraimperialist international cooperation (Kautsky). These differences in philosophy were compounded by dozens of other differences in strategy (reformist, catastrophist, etc.).

But the Socialist leaders of Europe shared an intellectual heritage of Marxist theory that transcended their factional squabbles. They also shared a membership in the Second International.[1] Neither heritage, however, served to suppress controversy. Indeed, both separately encouraged it. The intellectual heritage of

[1] Fainsod, *International Socialism and the World War*, pp. 8–15; Cole, *A History of Socialist Thought, vol. 2, Marxism and Anarchism, 1850–1890;* Lichtheim, *Marxism*, chaps. 5–7: Franz Borkenau, *World Communism;* and Michael Lowy, "Marxists and the National Question," *New Left Review* (March–April 1976), pp. 81–100, are particularly good surveys of the variety of rival doctrinal factions that had emerged within Marxism in Western Europe and Russia before 1914. Fainsod divides up the prewar Socialists into three factions (right, center, left), reflecting philosophical disputes on the meaning of historical materialism and tactical differences on many issues, including policies in responding to the outbreak of a war (pp. 15–17). German Marxism, however, according to Lichtheim, remained the most influential doctrine up to the outbreak of the war (p. 323). More important in distinction from Fainsod, I suggest that their philosophical differences could be contained by the common core of Marxist thought and that common core provides a sufficient explanation of the differing policies the Socialist parties adopted. L. Kolakowski, *Main Currents of Marxism*, vol. 2, *The Golden Age*, pp. 4–5, describes the common core of Marxism during its "golden age."

Marx and Engels on war and peace contained many areas of ambiguity, as the critics have noted so pointedly. And the competition to lead the Socialist international movement encouraged fierce debate.[2]

Marx and Engels's legacy of revolutionary theory, however, did include a core of ideas on national development, imperialism, and internationalism that most Socialists knew well and that, despite the many other differences and disputes, was sufficiently broad to contain their differences. It also characterized the publicly expressed views of the dominant factions of the Socialist parties of prewar Europe.

The Marxist interpretation of the Socialists that follows cannot refute those who, like many Realists, note the pressures of nationalism (because those pressures indeed existed), nor does it deny the threat posed by the imperialist state that the Leninists decried, nor can it altogether replace those historians who stress the divergences among parties and the roots of those divergences in particular political interests of each faction (because those divisions existed). But looking back on the Socialists today, we can see that together their doctrinal commitments and party interests can offer a credible alternative account for the stance each Socialist party adopted in the crisis of August 1914.

Recapitulating Marx's own Socialist theory, we can see that Marxist development theory stressed that bourgeois national democracy was a progressive stage through which the working class would realize Socialism. Marxist international theory stressed that imperialism could be a progressive (albeit violent) stage of development for precapitalist societies, even though its effects on industrial societies could be politically reactionary. Bourgeois class factions were prone to war, though the more advanced capitalist democracies contained tendencies that counteracted militarism and gave a promise of some efficacy to Socialists seeking to oppose war. But only Socialism promised both the liberation of the proletariat and peace.

The proper internationalist policy for Socialist leaders had to take into account the precapitalist conditions of much of Africa and Asia and specific capitalist conditions of contemporary Europe. After 1870 all the major powers were operating within a capitalist mode of production (Russia recently), but only France, Britain and the United States had fully sovereign bourgeois democracies. Germany, though better endowed with a Socialist movement than any of the other capitalist democracies, suffered from the autocratic vestiges of Prussian Junkerism.[3] Russia remained the most oppressive and took

[2]An extensive account of these competitions and the resulting spheres of ideological influence can be found in Borkenau, chap. 4.

[3]Marx, *The Marx-Engels Reader*, p. 562. Prewar Socialists were well aware of constitutional differences among bourgeois Liberal regimes. Although the German Socialist Party was Europe's largest, the Reich government was not fully responsible to the Reichstag. Civil

Socialism in 1914

	Members	*Votes*	*Socialist MPs*	*MPs*
Serbia		25,000	2	166
Belgium		600,000	39	185
France	90,700	1,397,337	101	595
Britain	1,559,082	370,802	42	670
Italy			77	508
Austria	145,500	1,041,000	82	516
Germany	1,085,905	4,250,329	110	397
Russia		800,000	14	442

The number of party members, votes in the general election, Socialist members of Parliament, and total number of members of Parliament are as of the last election before August 1914. Sources: Braunthal (1967, vol. 1, p. 351), Julius Braunthal, ed. *Yearbook of the International Socialist Movement* (London: 1956) and J. Bruce Glasier, *The Socialist Yearbook 1913* (London: 1913), and *Statesman's Yearbook 1915*.

particularly vigorous steps to suppress its nascent Socialist movement following the abortive democratic revolution of 1905.[4]

Not surprisingly, the Socialists of Europe were divided concerning a proper colonial policy. The Stuttgart Conference of the Second International (1907) condemned imperialism, as had earlier conferences, stressing its war-provoking effects.[5] But in the imperial countries currently ruling over precapitalist societies of Asia and Africa, Socialists' views divided. Bernard Shaw and other Fabians went so far as to endorse support for the Boer War, since the majority of South Africans would experience more progress under British rule, which was civilized, than under Kruger's allegedly obscurantist racial oppression.[6] In cases where imperialism did not promote progress, the European Socialists ringingly and consistently opposed the imperialist policies of bourgeois governments,

---

liberties were also somewhat tenuous. The conference of the Second International in 1907 was held in Stuttgart rather than in Berlin in order to avoid provoking the kaiser. Despite this, one of the deputies, a Mr. Quelch from Britain, was summarily expelled from Germany merely for describing the Hague conference of the great powers then meeting as a "thieves' supper." G. B. Shaw dramatically summed up the differences when he remarked in 1896 that though the German Social Democratic Party was far better developed than the British Socialist movement, Karl Liebknecht went to prison (for *lèse majesté*) for a remark that the British Conservative leader Sir Arthur Balfour could have made in Parliament to the applause of all Britain. See Joll, p. 76.

[4] J. P. Nettl, *The Soviet Achievement* (London: Thames and Hudson, 1967), pp. 29–31.

[5] Joll, pp. 196–98.

[6] Semmel, *Imperialism and Social Reform.*

including their own, in the Fashoda (1898), Moroccan (1905 and 1911), and Balkan crises.[7]

Equally unsurprisingly, the Socialists were united in the condemnation of war and in their determination to do all they could to prevent its outbreak or to end it on just terms as soon as possible, though specific measures against militarism "naturally differ[ed] in different countries" (the "Stuttgart Resolution.")[8] But none of these resolutions "repealed" the rights of democratic nations to resist aggression or the more general duty to resist imperialism and promote the progress of international Socialism.

Given these strictures concerning imperialism and militarism, where should Marxists in the various Socialist parties of Europe have stood on the issues of the international crisis of August 1914?

No true Marxist would have judged an imperialist war against Serbia to have been a step toward Socialist progress; the costs in lives, the stirring up of militarism, and the fact that Serbia was engaged in its own bourgeois nationalist development were fully sufficient to discredit any potential defense along progressivist lines.

Significantly, no defense of imperialism in the Balkans was made by any of the Socialist parties. The Austrian Socialists, while deploring the terroristic assassination of the archduke, condemned Austrian imperialism, just before their party publications were censored by the Austrian state.[9] The German Social Democratic Party staged demonstrations against Austrian imperialism.[10] The Social Democratic paper *Vorwärts* editorialized (July 25, 1914), "Not a single drop of the blood of a single German soldier must be sacrificed for the benefit of the war-hungry Austrian despots or for imperialist commercial interests," and exhorted, "Long live international solidarity." The Russian Socialist Party similarly denounced the tsarist policy of intervention and imperialistic interference in the Balkans in a letter to the Austrian Socialists written as early as 1913.[11]

Marxists should have found the rapid escalation to world war to have been an issue that provoked more divisive stands (internationally and in some cases internally) than had the question of imperialism. Marx's opposition to militarism, his recognition of the progressive role played by the national independence of bourgeois democracy, and his commitment to encouraging international progress could all come into conflict. The competing variables can be arrayed on the following four-dimensional policy matrix. Marx and Eng-

[7] Schorske, *German Social Democracy: 1905–1917*, pp. 69, 201, and Walling, *The Socialists and the Great War*, pp. 99–113.
[8] Quoted in Joll, p. 197.
[9] Walling, pp. 146–47.
[10] Schorske, p. 286.
[11] Walling, p. 111.

els would have argued that the Socialist Party should support the war as a war of national defense and/or international progress: (1) the stronger the Socialist Party, (2) the more advanced the bourgeoisie (e.g., industrial development and democratic state), (3) the clearer it was that the nation was attacked as opposed to attacking, and (4) the more repressive the most immediate opponent of the nation seemed. In the converse, the stronger would be the case that the Socialist Party should reject the war as an instance of pure imperialism or reactionary militarism. Again, these implications seem to have been by and large fulfilled.

From the safety of an ocean away, American Socialists saw the war in simple class terms. Eugene Debs argued for strict neutrality in a war fought by the working class at the orders of the ruling class in order to enable the latter to extend "their capacity for robbery." He further explained: "Despotism in Russia, monarchic Germany and republican America is substantially the same in its effects on the working class."[12] There was nothing to choose but noninvolvement.

The European Socialists did not think they had that luxury. In Serbia, the war's first victim, the two (!) Socialists in the parliament of 166 deputies maintained solidarity with fellow Socialists at home and abroad.[13] To all the other deputies, supporting the war was a clear case of Serbian national self-defense: Austria-Hungary had attacked Serbia. But to the Socialist deputies, the representatives of a weak Socialist Party, the Serbian working class, like the Bulgarians and the Albanians, was the victim of an oppressive Serbian state—a semicolonial regime, dependent on the tsar and Parisian finance—that had actively tolerated terroristic organizations aimed at Austria. The Austrian Socialists had denounced the attack on Serbia. The Serbian Socialists responded: "[T]here must be no war between the peoples of Austria-Hungary and the Serbian people." The vote for war was 164 in favor; 2 Socialists against.[14]

Belgium was Serbia's Marxist mirror image. In Belgium, also obviously attacked, the Socialists also entered the war united. An electoral democracy, with 39 Socialist deputies in a chamber of representatives of 185, neutral Belgium was invaded by Germany. The Socialists stopped their antiwar demonstrations on August 3 and declared that "in defending the neutrality and even the existence of our country against militarist barbarism we shall be conscious of serving the cause of democracy and of political liberty in Europe."[15]

[12] Quotes from Thomas Knock, *To End All Wars: Woodrow Wilson and the Quest for a New World Order* (Princeton: Princeton University Press, 1992), p. 53.
[13] The parliamentary statistics for Serbia and the other states noted below are taken from the *Statesman's Yearbook 1915*. An insightful history of these events can be found in Mayer, *Political Origins of the New Diplomacy*, pp. 99–109, 152–54, and S. F. Kissin, *War and the Marxists* (Boulder, Colo.: Westview Press, 1989), chap. 7.
[14] Braunthal (1967), vol. 2, p. 34.
[15] Walling, pp. 181–82; Braunthal (1967), vol. 2, p. 25.

The Socialist Decision Matrix

Summary of Factors That in Marxist Theory Should Have Influenced the Socialist Decisions of August 1914

	Soc	*Cap*	*Def/Agg*	*Threat*	*Net*	
Serbia	0	0	−1	−1	−2	
Belgium		1	2	2	1	6
France	2	2	1	1	6	
Britain	1	2	0	1	4	
Italy	1	1	0	0	2	
Austria	2	1	−1	1	3	
Germany	/*2	1	0/−2	1/−1	4/0	
Russia	1	0	0	−2	−1	

Please note that this table is illustrative only; none of the difficult judgments facing the Socialists of 1914 lent themselves to reliable quantification.

"Soc" (Socialism) indicates the relative strength of the local Socialist parties on a scale of 0–2; "Cap" indicates the degree of bourgeois capitalist democratic development on a scale of 0–2; "Def/Agg" indicates the extent to which the country was clearly attacked (+2) to mixed (0) to clearly aggressive (−2); "Threat" indicates whether defeat would be by a more (−2) to less (+2) progressive power.

The "Net" increases with the increased set of reasons from a Marxist point of view for the Socialist parties to support the decisions of their governments to go to war in August 1914. All parties with scores 3 or above voted for war; at 2, the Italians abstained; all at or below 0 opposed the war. The "*" for Germany compares the 1914 situation to the 1915–1916 and later situations.

The French Socialists also entered the war united. Enjoying a representation of 101 in an elected chamber of 595 deputies, they originally staged large demonstrations against French participation in the Balkan crisis and in support of French mediation efforts, which they had been assured were under way.[16] They did an about-face after Germany had invaded France, calling forth Socialist patriots to remember their "historic role" in 1793 and 1870 in the new struggle against German "militaristic imperialism" and for democratic "civilization."[17]

The British Socialists entered the war more divided.[18] Only seven members

[16] In addition to the 102 organized Socialists, the elections of May 1914 returned 30 independent Socialists.

[17] Walling, pp. 177–79.

[18] Douglas J. Newton, *British Labour, European Socialism and the Struggle for Peace, 1889–1914* (Oxford: Clarendon, 1985) sympathetically assesses the errors made and the difficulties faced by the British Socialists in 1914. He found a lack of rapport between the British trade union leadership and the more doctrinaire of both the British and the Continental Socialists. Moreover, the secrecy of prewar diplomacy and the speed of the crisis of August 1914 made effective opposition extremely unlikely (pp. 343–51).

of the thirty-nine-member Labour Party were Marxist Socialists. Still, all the Socialists and the Labour Party opposed involvement in the Balkans. National defense was not an immediate issue, and the rival imperialist powers, whether Austrian or Russian, deserved, in their view, no help from British Socialists.[19] But the invasion of Belgium split the Independent Labour Party Socialists and changed the Labour Party majority positions toward active or passive support for the war. The wanton aggression against Belgium offered them proof that the war had now become a war against antidemocratic, military autocracy, which was what they thought threatened Europe if Prussia were to conquer the Western democracies.[20]

In Italy the 77 Socialists (of the 508 members of the lower house) maintained neutrality. Emerging from a bruising general strike against the government, the Italian Socialists were understandably disaffected from official policy, as well as critical of imperialism in the Balkans by their country's ally (Austria). They condemned Austrian and German aggression and rejected any participation in the war on the side of Austria. When the bourgeoisie also turned against Austria and Germany, the Socialists, in conflict with their own government and not yet called upon to defend the nation from foreign attack, also rejected participation against Austria. When Austria later invaded Italy, the Socialists expressed their hostility to an Austrian victory, adopting the policy of "Neither Support nor Sabotage."[21]

In Austria, the Socialists held 82 out of 516 seats in the lower chamber; in Germany, 110 out of 397 seats.[22] The Austrian party initially opposed the imperialist war in the Balkans. But with the specter of defeat at the hands of what they saw as a (more) reactionary Russia, it changed its stand. In Hungary the Socialists, though facing severe repression by the state, also supported the war against "Russia . . . the land of slavery."[23]

A great deal rested on the crucial decision of the German Social Democratic Party (SPD). Despite the many successes of the SPD and the power of labor in Germany, their influence on public policy was limited. The Kaiser and the military establishment were free from parliamentary control (as is suggested by the Kaiser's plans to have the Socialists arrested in the event they opposed the war). But as elsewhere, so in Germany, the powerful SPD succumbed on August 4 to the fear of a Russian victory that would result from a victory by the

[19] Fainsod, p. 32.
[20] Walling, pp. 164–65; Braunthal (1967), vol. 2, pp. 27–29.
[21] Walling, pp. 198–99.
[22] The eighty-three Socialists in Austria included German Social Democrats, Polish Social Democrats, and Bohemian Social Democrats. Austria and Hungary, although represented in separate parliaments, maintained unified foreign affairs and defense under the Austro-Hungarian monarchy.
[23] Walling, p. 149.

Entente powers.[24] And they thereby included bourgeois France and Britain with the threat from reactionary Russia. Writing two months later, Emil Vandevelde (Belgian president of the International) grasped the dilemma German Marxists faced: "Had they voted against the war credits they would have given up their country to invasion by the Cossacks. Yet in voting for the credits they provided the Kaiser with weapons for use against Republican France and against the whole of West European democracy. Between these two evils they chose that which they judged to be the lesser."[25]

Demonstrating the authenticity of their dilemma, the Socialists later changed their view. As information on the aggressive and annexationist cast of the German war aims became clearer in 1915 and 1916, the SPD slowly began to split. With each new Reichstag vote, new members, first Karl Liebknecht and including eventually Eduard Bernstein, joined the opposition to a war that now seemed to be directed less at the Russian menace than at the democratic bourgeois societies (with their Socialist parties) of Western Europe.[26]

In Russia, object of the Central European panic, the Socialists held 14 seats and the Labor Party held 10 seats out of 442 in the Duma. The Socialists and other working-class organizations had been subjected to severe police repression before and after the 1905 revolution. Both the Labor Party and the Social Democratic Party (Menshevik and Bolshevik) denounced the war on August 8 and declared their "solidarity with the European proletariat." Both walked out of the Duma. The Labor Party (Kerensky), following the outbreak of actual hostilities and feeling the pressure of patriotic demonstrations in the streets, called upon its members to "protect your country to the end against aggression."[27] Some of the Mensheviks expressed support for national defense. But the leading factions of the Social Democrats at home—Social Revolutionaries, left Mensheviks, and Bolsheviks—and some of the leaders abroad (Martov and Trotsky) continued to agitate, the domestic leaders were arrested, and the party

[24] Gay, p. 277.

[25] Quoted in Braunthal (1967b), p. 15. Vandevelde, however, did not see that the same Marxist logic justified Russian Marxists in opposing the war rather than supporting Russia in order to aid the Western democracies, as Vandevelde wished. Indeed, some part of the support for this position may have stemmed from internationalist, as opposed to purely nationalist, sources, in that a defeat of Russia by Germany could have resulted in the defeat of Russia's Western allies, the progressive societies of France and Britain. At least this seems to have been Plekhanov's convoluted reasoning prior to the war. The Menshevik leader Lavin countered that Russian Social Democrats must struggle against "that other, and not less dangerous, enemy of the working class which is Russian absolutism" (letters quoted in Braunthal, [1967b], p. 26). For very good interpretations of the Russian dilemma, see Ziva Galili, *The Menshevik Leaders in the Russian Revolution* (Princeton: Princeton University Press, 1989), chap. 1, and R. Craig Nation, *War on War* (Durham: Duke University Press, 1989).

[26] Gay, pp. 284–88.

[27] Walling, p. 192.

then urged the soldiers to "struggle for peace."[28] This was magnified by a lonely voice from abroad when Lenin urged proletarian soldiers, Russian as well, to rebel against their capitalist-bourgeois oppression.

The Significance of Socialism

By seeing the Marxist Socialists in this way, we can reopen a long-closed door, reconsider our history, reevaluate our theories, rethink our policy axioms. If we compare theories, we can see the differences.

Structural Realist (Hobbesian) theory at its simplest assumes a unitary rational actor in an environment where security is a scarce good. Actors seek to increase their power where they can. They expand empires where cost-effective; they fight when necessary for security or power.

Leninist theory assumed that Communists should seek to weaken the imperialist state that oppressed them whenever and wherever they could. War, for them, was an opportunity to begin revolution.

Marx's own Socialist theory was more complicated, having to weigh contradictory goals. Many of the Socialist parties were divided over the true significance of Marxism and Marxist strategy for their country. They, like many of the leaders of other parties at the beginning and during course of the world war, also were undoubtedly guilty of national chauvinism, opportunism, and many other errors. I have no wish to discover once and for all what were their actual motives, which even the historians, deeply versed in their biographies and the documents of the period, find difficult to fathom. Nor do I wish to defend the wisdom of their actions or minimize their role in the onslaught of the war. They were too weak to overwhelm the forces of right-wing militarism. Yet they might have been strong enough to cast doubt on the resolve of France and Britain to stand up to the plans of the German expansionists, influential enough in Germany to cast doubt on the threat its arms race posed to the other European powers, and fierce enough everywhere in attacks on each of their own national governments' militarism to provide grist for the propaganda of foreign militarists.[29]

If, however, we think the "betrayal" of August 4, 1914, is a refutation of the Marxist approach to international strategy, we are too hasty.

Like Leninist strategy, Marxist theory did include the solidarity that should have led Russian and Serbian Socialists to vote against the war. It urged a resistance to the sort of militarism and imperialism that the great powers were

[28] Braunthal (1967), vol. 2, p. 32. But some of the arrested left-Menshevik and Bolshevik leaders later declared, under examination at their trial, that they did support Lenin's injunction to work for national defeat. See Edward H. Carr, *The Bolshevik Revolution, 1917–1923* (London: Macmillan, 1950), vol. 1, p. 67.

[29] R. J. Crampton, "August Bebel and the British Foreign Office," *History* 58 (June 1973), pp. 218–32.

Realists, Leninists, and Marxists in 1914

	War		*Imperialism in Balkans*	
	Yes	No	Yes	No
Britain	M R	l		M R L
France	M R	l		M R L
Belgium	M R	l		M R L
Germany	M R	l/M* L*	r	M L
Austria-Hungary	M R	l	r	M L
Serbia	r	M L		M R L
Russia	r	M L	r	M L

A catalog of the expected positions that would be taken by parties that were: r = Hobbesian Realist; m = Marxist; l = Leninist. Capital letters denote positions actually taken by the Socialist parties of Europe in the summer of 1914; * = position that should have been taken after 1915. (Liberal parties, one could add, should have voted against imperialism in the Balkans, for J. S. Mill's educative rationale would not fit there. They would have faced a complicated decision on war in August 1914, but the simplest choice would have been to vote for war in Britain, France, Belgium, and Serbia and against war in Germany and Austria-Hungary—in order to avoid fighting and to protect fellow Liberals and, possibly, to constrain aggression.)

inflicting on the Balkans. But it did not require undermining the bourgeois state at every opportunity.

Like Realist nationalist strategy, Marxism did not preclude the defense of the nation. Nor did it require opposing every policy adopted by a bourgeois government. But Marxist internationalism was not identical with nationalism. Nowhere in power, unable to prevent the war, the Marxists followed their governments when their governments adopted policies with which Marxists should not have disagreed. When the two conflicted, the Marxists acted as Marxists.

For the Belgian, French, and British Socialists in bourgeois democracies, the crisis seemed clear. A German and Austrian victory meant the loss of national freedom and domination by more reactionary, militaristic strains of Junkeristic capitalism. For the German and Austrian and Hungarian Socialists, defeat by Russia also meant a loss of national freedom and domination by even more reactionary tsarist oppression. All voted for war.

Marxist strategy was not thereby identical with Realist strategy, nor did nationalism thereby overwhelm Marxism. The two merely corresponded. When the two differed, the Marxists followed Marxist strategy. In 1913 and 1914 Russian, Austrian, German, and Hungarian Socialists each condemned their states' imperialism in the Balkans. In 1914 Serbian and Russian Socialists voted against the war. For these Socialists subject to reactionary and aggressive states, a national defeat might mean Socialist liberation. Lastly, when the German SPD began to realize in 1915 that a Russian victory was not likely and that their own government had misled them and had not acted defensively in 1914, it began to turn against the war, voting in increasing numbers with each new vote against the war policies and war budget of the German state. Here the Marxists acted as Marxists, and Socialism explains the Socialists better than Realism and nationalism.

PROSPECTS FOR SOCIALIST INTERNATIONALISM?

Marxists may have much to say to us about how we explain the past and future of international security. The experience of the Socialists raises a vital question. What if Europe had been different in 1914, more developed, or more evenly developed? Had the Socialists then been in power, would democratic, Marxist Socialist governments have chosen to start the war of August 1914?

The hypothetical question of course can have no uniquely valid answer, but it does highlight important threads in our models of peace and war. We know that direct democracies and democratic republics (governments responsible to a majority of a mass citizenry) frequently engage in war.[30] We also know that these states have even fought one another, as they did most famously in the classical Mediterranean world when Athens invaded the Sicilian democracies and Rome conquered Greece.[31] At its most effective, majoritarian rule, it appears, merely guarantees that the interests of a majority of the citizens govern state policy, whether those interests are pacific or bellicist.

At the same time, as we saw in the discussion of Liberal theory, there is credible evidence to suggest that Liberal representative states, while prone to war, do not war against one another. Respect for individual moral equality, accommodation of those republican governments that represent free individuals, and the variety of material interests engendered by free exchange, it seems, together guarantee, as Kant claimed they would, a peace among Liberal states.

But so-called Socialist or Communist states have fought one another, as China did Vietnam in 1979 and Russia did China (along the Ussuri in a very limited war) in 1969. Do the potentially pacific strands that Marxist Socialism displayed in 1914 dissolve once Socialists come to power, or are the so-called Socialist states the sorts of state that Marxist Socialists would have wanted to establish?

Again, one cannot definitively answer this question. But there are better rea-

[30] Small and Singer. "The War-proneness of Democratic Regimes," pp. 50–69, and see chap. 8 above.

[31] Thucydides, VII:55; and Polybius, 24, 11–12. And see chap. 1 above.

sons to question the democratic Socialist (Marxist) credentials of the existing Communist states than to question the pacific credentials of Socialism. Existing Communist states, including the Soviet Union, China, Cuba, and Vietnam since their revolutions and the various satellite states of Eastern and Central Europe, have been dictatorships of one party (or one leader) over societies characterized by an overwhelming concentration of authority and ownership in the hands of the state. But for Marx and the Second International Socialists, the essence of Socialism was the extension of democratic principles to the control of the economy, not the extension of capitalist (ownership) principles to the rule of the state. Marx allowed for a democratic electoral route to Socialism of the sort the "reformists" of the Second International were practicing in the prewar period. The Paris Commune was widely taken among the Marxists of the Second International as the exemplar of the revolutionary route to communism (the "first dictatorship of the proletariat"). It planned to decentralize the French state and declared its solidarity with all working-class movements (accepting "foreign" Socialists on its governing elected bodies). The Commune, moreover, "filled all posts—administrative, judicial, and educational—by election on the basis of universal suffrage of all concerned, subject to the right of recall at any time by the same electors. All officials, high and low, were paid only the wages received by other workers."[32] Indeed, in Marx's view, the one major flaw of the Commune was its failure to extend democracy to the workplace soon enough.[33]

While absolving Marxism of the militarism of Leninist, Stalinist, or Maoist state centralism,[34] this interpretation of Marxist Socialism also makes Marxism much less relevant to the first ninety years of the twentieth century.[35] Yet it may by that very fact have something more to tell us about the century's last ten years.

Observers of the democratic upheavals in Eastern Europe have noted a striking feature characteristic of these "revolutions,": the extraordinary ease with which the states collapsed and the widespread sense of solidarity enjoyed by

[32] Engels, "Introduction" to Marx's "The Civil War in France," p. 628, and see Marx's own description in "The Civil War in France," p. 632, in Marx (1978).

[33] There is an extensive literature on the meaning of the Paris Commune for Marxists. It is well surveyed in Hunt (1984), vol. 2, chaps. 4 and 5. The differences between Marxism and Leninism are effectively explored by Moore in *Marx on the Choice between Socialism and Communism.*

[34] James L. Payne, "Marxism and Militarism," *Polity,* 19 (Winter 1986), pp. 270–89, and Thomas R. Dye and Harmon Ziegler, "Socialism and Militarism," *PS: Political Science and Politics* (December 1989), pp. 800–13.

[35] This Marxist communism will better characterize a wide variety of failed revolutionary movements, including the Mensheviks, the Spartacists, and oppositional Euro-Communist political parties.

the now-successful oppositions.[36] The hollowness of the seemingly formidable Communist state can be accounted for by its dependence on Moscow. Withdrawals of the "legions," metropolitan-induced decolonizations, and other easy colonial collapses are not that uncommon.[37] But the hollowness of the state and the solidarity of the opposition around common themes of democracy and equality also find striking echoes in Marx's own prognostications concerning Communist revolution, whose preconditions, ironically, seem to have at last been achieved by the Communist Party dictatorships of the postwar period. The hallmarks of Marx's crisis of capitalism—extreme centralization of the ownership of the means of production, socialization of labor in large factories, economic stagnation, and immiserization of the population at large—all are remarkably apt descriptions of the course of events within the Communist states of Eastern Europe in the 1980s. When was a conjuncture so revolutionary in Marx's own sense ever attained in the modern history of capitalism?

To be sure, none of this prefigures the dawn of a Socialist millennium. However revolutionary the objective conditions might have been and however strong the sentiments of social egalitarianism are, it is impossible to neglect the fact that these revolutions are revolutions against the trappings of Communist institutions and ideology. The most sensible prediction is that outcomes will vary with national differences.[38]

Within this range it is impossible to rule out anything from military coups sparked by ethnic unrest to a variety of democratic regimes. The democratic regimes might include, for example, the "gold rush" capitalism now anticipated by some Western investors; Swedish-style social welfare; mixed-economy capitalism; and the democratic Socialism Marx predicted and struggled to achieve in his own time.

A heterogeneous regional society would then offer many grounds for international tension. Military coups would clearly disrupt efforts at regional arms control and economic integration (as they have in Latin America). Swedish social welfare states, on the other hand, would fit easily within the Liberal "zone of peace," as has Sweden itself. But if the experience of the last free interactions of Marxist democratic Socialist parties is to be our guide, demo-

[36]Timothy Garton Ash, "Eastern Europe: The Year of Truth," *New York Review of Books* (February 15, 1990), pp. 17–22.

[37]John Gallagher, *The Decline, Revival and Fall of the British Empire*, ed. Anil Seal (Cambridge: Cambridge University Press, 1982).

[38]A valuable survey of this variety of national circumstances can be found in Teresa Rakowska-Harmstone and Andrew Gyorgy, eds., *Communism in Eastern Europe* (Bloomington: Indiana University Press, 1979) and recent assessments of its significance in Ellen Comisso (1990) and Christiane Lemke and Gary Marks, eds., *The Crisis of Socialism in Europe* (Durham: Duke University Press, 1992).

cratic Socialist governments of the Marxist variety in today's Central and Eastern Europe would find themselves in a state of peace with one another. They would not, however, quite escape tensions and a potential state of class war with the Liberal democratic capitalists around them. In order to be authentic to itself, each government, whether Liberal capitalist or democratic Socialist, would eschew aggression. But none could regard the others without suspicion. Far from experiencing an end to history those committed first to equality could find themselves engaged in a protracted political struggle with those committed first to liberty.

PART FOUR

CONSCIENCE AND POWER

INTRODUCTION

Hard Choices and International Law

SO FAR WE have been considering how states do behave and why they behave the way they do. Now we turn to how states should and can behave and why they should do so. The two are inherently connected, as Reinhold Niebuhr once stated: "Politics will, to the end of history, be an arena where conscience and power meet, where the ethical and coercive factors of human life will interpenetrate and work out their tentative and uneasy compromises."[1]

How states do behave is affected by their values—those of the elites, citizens, or classes that compose them. Power and politics are purposive activities. What politicians want to do shapes what they wind up doing in the name of the state, individual freedom, or class solidarity, even if the outcome is not quite what they hoped it would be. We thus cannot explain outcomes without being aware of those purposes. Realism, Liberalism, and Socialism thus embody values, ends, for which statespersons strove and nations, individuals, and classes fought.

William Frankena's summary of a very widely shared modern conception of ethics as two principles—beneficence and equality—thus has explanatory significance.[2] We should do as much net good (beneficence) as we can, and as little evil, when the costs to ourselves are not disproportionate. We should give equal consideration to persons and distribute goods equally unless there are

[1] Reinhold Niebuhr, as quoted in Robert Fullinwider, "Notes from the Classroom," *GSPM Network* (Spring 1986), 1, 3, p. 1.

[2] William Frankena, *Ethics* (Englewood Cliffs: Prentice Hall, 1973), p. 52. For valuable demonstrations showing how and when specifically ethical considerations do shape foreign policy see Robert McElroy, *Morality and American Foreign Policy* (Princeton: Princeton University Press, 1992), and David Welch, *Justice and the Genesis of War* (Cambridge: Cambridge University Press, 1992).

good, relevant reasons to do otherwise. Together they suggest a set of norms that, at the minimum, require that we have morally relevant reasons when we fail to adopt beneficent action or discriminate in the treatment of individuals (who are assumed to be equal from a moral point of view).

Neither principle, however, is sufficient to resolve policy problems. Even if we assume that statespersons want to be moral, the particular content of moral choice is constrained, also shaped, by a conception of how the world does work and how states do behave. Beneficence and equality are formal principles of ethics that tell us only a little about the actual decisions that statespersons will need to make. Political decisions can share a universal foundation in modern conceptions of the dignity of the human being, in fundamental human rights, such as those of the integrity of the person prohibiting torture; in civil freedoms; and in the political and basic economic and social rights embodied in the Universal Declaration of Human Rights (1948). Still, applied ethics will vary, reflecting differing conceptions of politics. In the political arena, we need to identify conceptions of what the good is that we are enjoined to maximize, who are the objects that are to benefit from equal treatment, and who are the agents that are responsible for acting ethically.

In the international arena, which lacks a single sovereign source of law and order, we need a conception of what constitutes a threat against which we can legitimately do harm and discriminate in order to protect ourselves. These are the questions international political theories help us frame. In the nation state, the individual, and class, Realism, Liberalism, and Socialism give us different answers to these questions. The answers thus create the foundations for a variety of overlapping Realist, Liberal, and Socialist international ethics.

This part focuses on the hard choices required by the existence of international borders. We engage in world politics under conditions of anarchy, in that there exists no world government. Realists, Liberals, and Socialists of course interpret the significance of anarchy in differing ways; none, however, can deny its impact.

Here we examine two borders of anarchy issues: intervention and the distribution of wealth. I seek to identify the borders of anarchy and their complement, the legitimate claims of sovereignty. What are the legitimate claims of those who wish to exercise their rights to sovereign political independence, noninterference, and nonintervention against those who wish to interfere or intervene to pursue what they think are legitimate interests or necessary duties? What can any society lay claim to as belonging to it, its property or income, free from the just demands of others? What can poor societies claim against wealthy societies as part of their share of the common heritage of mankind? In other words, what should a border count "for" or how "high" should it be?

Interventions and redistributions are deeply controversial moral questions. We disagree about when they are prohibited and when, if ever, they are justified. Each of us probably has some tested intuitions on this subject. We have debated with friends the justice or lack thereof of the intervention in Vietnam, the Soviet intervention in Afghanistan, the U.S. invasions of Grenada and Panama, whether the UN should or should not have become more deeply involved in the states of the former Yugoslavia. We wonder what can justify the extraordinary differences in life chances—the health and material standard of living—that exist between the average person born in the United States and the average person born in Somalia, Bangladesh, or Zaire.

International theory can help us systematize and reexamine our intuitions. This is what we shall be doing in the next two chapters as we examine international intervention and the international distribution of income.

Even though the topics are controversial, that does not mean that states have not evolved standard answers to the issues. Indeed, since the modern international system emerged in the seventeenth century, traditional international law has given a distinct answer, emphasizing the sanctity, or "height," of the borders between states that protect sovereign rights to political independence and territorial integrity against all challenges. The issue for us and for our leaders is whether we should abide by or override these traditional rules of the road. Debates among those inspired by Realism, Liberalism, and Marxism played a key role in making those traditional rules. Realists, Liberals, and Marxists are debating whether to abide by, override, or revise them.

TRADITIONAL INTERNATIONAL LAW

The tradition of international law prohibits intervention. States have a right to political independence and territorial integrity, which also constitutes a sovereign right over all the resources within their borders. Treaties may limit those rights or extend them, giving the nationals of one state ownership of claims against the nationals of another. But treaties rest on sovereign consent.

In 1965 the UN General Assembly issued an expansive *Declaration on the Inadmissibility of Intervention into the Domestic Affairs of States* that seemed to prohibit all forms of coercive interference.

> No state or group of states has the right to intervene directly or indirectly, for any reason whatever, in the internal or external affairs of any other state.
>
> Consequently, armed intervention and all other forms of interference or attempted threats against the personality of the state or against its political, economic and cultural elements are in violation of international law. No state may use or encourage the use of economic, political or any other type of measure to coerce another state in order to obtain from it advantages of any kind. Also, no state shall organize, assist, foment, incite, or tolerate subversive

> terrorist or armed activities directed towards the violent overthrow of or civil strife in another state.[3]

But traditional law sees "nonintervention" as distinct from but compatible with a considerable amount of mutual influence, interdependence, or even "interference." States have been free to criticize, to refuse to sell to or buy from foreign countries (when not prohibited by treaties), and to encourage or discourage international investment for the purpose of competitive diplomacy and bargaining among states.[4] "Intervention," then, is reserved for the dictatorial use of force, overt or covert, against the territorial integrity and political independence of another independent state. A continuum of activities, it is best seen as barring all behavior ranging from economic blockades through various forms of subversion to outright invasion.[5]

The first presumption of traditional international law is that states are the sole members of internationl society.[6] They rule and govern international society, and no one else—neither institutions above the state, such as the League of Nations or United Nations, nor individuals or classes below the state—has the standing to question them. These laws of international society originated at the founding of the state system at the end of the sixteenth and early part of the seventeenth centuries, when, following a long and bloody series of wars among the kingdoms and republics of Europe, states arrived at an accommodation recognizing one another's sovereignty and equality (embodied in the great Treaty of Westphalia of 1648).[7] States themselves acquired the right to govern, for example, the religion of their subjects *(cuius regio eius religio)*. This meant that individuals lacked international standing to challenge the authority of the state and that those societies that were not recognized and organized as European states were excluded from the rights of states. Almost all of the Americas, Africa, and Asia were regarded as uncivilized, not as members of the society of states, *terra nullius* (therefore fair game for colonization).

[3] 20th GA. Resolution 2131, A6014, from Ian Brownlie, ed., *Basic Documents of International Law*, 3d ed. (Oxford: Oxford University Press, 1983), p. 40.

[4] Two classic discussions of the concept are: Manfred Halpern, "The Morality and Politics of Intervention," in Richard Falk, ed., *The Vietnam War and International Law* (Princeton: Princeton University Press, 1968) and John Vincent, *Nonintervention and International Order* (Princeton: Princeton University Press, 1974).

[5] See Quincy Wright, "Non-Military Intervention," in Karl Deutsch and Stanley Hoffmann, eds., *The Relevance of International Law* (Cambridge: Schenkman, 1968).

[6] The "legalist paradigm" is well summarized (and also revised) by Walzer, *Just and Unjust Wars*, pp. 60–63.

[7] Leo Gross, "The Peace of Westphalia: 1648–1948," *American Journal of International Law* 42 (1948), pp. 20–41. But as Stephen Krasner has noted, the sovereignty provisions were in many respects an "ideal" that the existing complexity of international relations—the continuing authority of the Holy Roman Empire in Central Europe and the limited effectiveness of national states—recognized but did not fully reflect for more than a century afterward.

Second, recognized states have a right to territorial integrity and political sovereignty. They as sovereign "persons" have a right to a certain piece of space that they can call their own and mark off with property rights, excluding all others. Their political sovereignty over this particular piece of territory gives them the right to decide what is good and bad, just and unjust, to make laws to govern property, to govern all relationships among all individuals. Many states today have signed conventions that limit their freedom. The UN Charter empowers the Security Council to act in the name of the international community on matters of international peace and security. The Genocide Convention prohibits genocide and requires all states to stop it should it occur. The Nonproliferation Treaty binds its members not to acquire nuclear weapons or, if they are currently recognized nuclear states, to pursue arms control. But these are amendments, not revolutions, in the legal order defined by states.

Third, any use of force against either the territorial integrity or the political sovereignty of a state is a criminal act called aggression. Indeed, it is, as Michael Walzer notes in his discussion of traditional international law (the "legalist paradigm"), the only criminal act of international law. Invasions, border crossings are all wrong, unless of course they are done at the request of the political sovereign for, let us say, the purpose of suppressing domestic rebellion.

Fourth, any act of aggression justifies two things: a war of self-defense on the part of the attacked sovereign, and any other state of the international society of states coming to the aid of the attacked state for the purposes of stopping the attack. Nothing but aggression can justify a war.

Fifth, once an aggressor has been defeated by either the attacked state or some coalition, then the aggressor can be punished. Territory can be taken away from the aggressor state, and a financial indemnity can be imposed upon it. What cannot be done under classic international law is that one state cannot reform another state: change its form of government in order to make it better, send its leaders to reeducation camps, or take any other such action that infringes upon the political sovereignty of the state. Traditionally, only collective punishments can be inflicted on aggressor states.

In the nineteenth and twentieth centuries, states began to accept, as ancillary principles, codes for how to fight just wars that avoid excessive harm, that protect the rights of noncombatants, that regulate appropriate behavior during sieges and blockades, that define the proper standards of surrender, and that (with Nuremberg) allow for the punishment of government leaders responsible for war crimes and the crimes of aggressive war and genocide.[8]

These are rules of the road, conventions developed over long periods of time, convenient principles of "backscratching." Each sovereign does for the other

[8] See Walzer, *Just and Unjust Wars,* chap. 18, for revisions of classic international law and Nuremberg principles of responsibility.

what it would most like to have done for itself over the long run. The actual evolution of these rules was shaped by the fact that they were rules that were thought generally useful by the monarchs of Europe as the monarchs pursued their own interests, seeking to avoid unnecessary clashes among themselves. (Indeed, these are just the sort of backscratching rules that might be developed by equally ruthless "monarchs," the leaders of organized crime.)

This is not to say that rules do not have ethical significance. Rules of the road reduce traffic fatalities. They also can represent acceptable compromises among diverse moralities.[9] They work especially well for issues too unimportant, too unclear, or too dangerous to contest. The rules, however, also rest on deeper political moralities that surface when issues are important and seem clear and actors sense power. Each of the rules and the code as a whole are capable of philosophic justification, but only partially. Each of our philosophies—just as it justifies, for example, nonintervention as a generally prudent strategy (by Realists) or as a just manifestation of moral respect (among fellow Liberals, by Liberals)—also opens up grounds for overriding the prohibition, for example, when security requires it (by Realists) or when a rescue of individual rights is necessary (in relations between Liberals and non-Liberals).

What should we, the citizens, make of the rules and accommodations that sovereigns have made?

[9]Terry Nardin, *Law, Morality and the Relations of States* (Princeton: Princeton University Press, 1983).

CHAPTER ELEVEN

International Intervention

> To give help to a brave people who are defending their liberties against an oppressor by force of arms is only the part of justice and generosity. Hence, whenever such dissension reaches the state of civil war, foreign nations may assist that one of the two parties, which seems to have justice on its side. But to assist a detestable tyrant . . . would certainly be a violation of duty.
>
> —Emmerich de Vattel, 1758[1]

HOW MIGHT THE principles of political independence and territorial integrity be justified? Nonintervention, the dominant norm of international law designed to protect those principles, has been justified by straightforward appeals to law and order that rest on the value of having rules of the road that reduce the probability of conflicts between those actors who prefer some coordination. But abstract ethical considerations such as those fail to include the purposes for which a state engages in or avoids conflict. Nor does ethics give us enough information about who the actors are, their interests, values, environment, and capacities. Political philosophies aim to fill in those blanks. They provide contingent justification for nonintervention but also permit intervention, though for differing reasons.

Principles of nonintervention and intervention have been justified, though in differing ways, by Realists, by Socialists, by Liberals. Although these princi-

[1] Quoted by Daniel Moynihan, *On the Law of Nations*, p. 175, and see Lloyd Cutler, "Noriega's Actions Gave Us Justification," *Washington Post*, December 24, 1989, p. C7, raises a similar question.

ples never have been formally justified as a single treaty according to set of philosophical precepts, they nonetheless throughout time have been justified by scholars, by politicians, by citizens who have sought to provide for us good reasons why we should abide by these conventional principles of classic international law and good reasons why we should, as Vattel suggests, sometimes override them.[2] After sketching the philosophic debates, I shall take up a most difficult little case, the 1983 invasion of Grenada, in which the principles are tested and the practice of conscience and power reveals the difficulties of both.

PRINCIPLES OF NONINTERVENTION AND INTERVENTION

Realists

In many respects the principles of nonintervention can be seen as a summary of the sort of principles that a cautious or "soft" Realist would most want to have govern the international system. For example, Hobbes demanded that his sovereigns seek peace wherever they safely could. Rousseau, commenting on the peace plan of the Abbé de St-Pierre, argued that responsible statesmen, particularly, of course, those who were democratic, would not want to engage in wars of aggression but instead would merely seek the security of their own state. In a speech in 1994 U.S. Senator Richard Lugar suggested how a moderate definition of national ambitions can limit interventionism. "The American people," he declared, "are not convinced that we have vital interests in invading Haiti, despite immigration, which we believe might continue even if Mr. Aristide was restored. . . . And we've really not had a policy of forcing democracy on a country, however despicable that regime might be."[3]

But if we probe deeper, we can see that these justifications are extremely contingent from an overall Realist point of view. Doubting the efficacy of international law and morality as foundations for a obligation of nonintervention, Realists tend to see all states as caught in a state of war in which the only source of security is self-help. Security drives states then to focus on relative capabilities and a consequent search for predominance that is unrestrained by any factor but prudence.

Thucydides noted a first challenge to nonintervention coming from what we

[2]An insightful study of the historical context of the doctrine of nonintervention is John Vincent, *Nonintervention and International Order.* For valuable overviews, see Gerald Graham, "The Justice of Intervention," *Review of International Studies* 13 (1987), pp. 133–46, and Jefferson McMahan, "The Ethics of International Intervention," in Kenneth Kipnis and Diana Meyers, eds., *Political Realism and International Morality* (Boulder, Colo.: Westview Press, 1987), pp. 75–101.

[3]Quoted in the *New York Times,* September 1, 1994. For more on the role of prudence in limiting Realist intervention, see Hoffmann, *Duties beyond Borders* and Smith, *Realist Thought from Weber to Kissinger,* chap. 9.

can describe as a "hard" Realist view, a view espoused by the Athenian generals Cleomedes and Tisias in command of the blockade of Melos.[4] The generals say that rules are fit only for relations among equals. Among unequals, when the strong confront the weak, the only rules that hold are the will of the strong and the obedience of the weak. And so the generals tell the Melians that they should not hope to be saved by the Spartans, their allies, or be saved by rules that would restrict the aggressive actions of states. Instead they have to confront the hard face of power, which is the Athenian fleet blockading the island. The generals add that for Athens this conquest is important. Melos may be a small island, but if a small island can successfully resist the might of Athens, other islands might be tempted to engage in similar rebellions. If this challenge were then to spread, Athens would lose its power. In order to deter challenges and enhance Athenian prestige, the generals claim that the Melian borders have to be overridden; the Melians must surrender or be destroyed.

Even though conquering Melos may have seemed the right thing to do in the view of the two Athenian generals, there's good reason for us to believe that this was not necessarily Thucydides's own view. He seemed to think the Athenian disaster in Sicily was its just consequence. His own view on intervention was more evident in an earlier debate on the fate of Mytilene, a subordinate ally of Athens. There a group of rebels against the Athenian empire sought to establish a self-determining, independent state. When they did so, they came up against the might of Athens.[5]

In the Athenian Assembly, Cleon, a hard-liner, lines up against Diodotus, a soft-liner and they debate the fate of the Mytileneans. What form of punishment, Cleon asks, is the correct fate for those who rebel against the alliance and law of Athens? He says the punishment must fit the crime: They seek to destroy Athens's power, on which its security, indeed, survival rests. The rebels must be killed—men, women, and children—in order to teach a lesson to all others who might be tempted to imitate them. Diodotus corrects Cleon's demands for vengeance and responds as the better Realist, regretting Cleon's harsh conclusion. Diodotus says that thinking about international politics as a matter of right and wrong, as a matter of just and unjust, legal and unlawful, confuses politics with a court of law and interferes with what should be a matter of prudence and rational self-interest. International politics should cover no more than the prudent calculation of long-run security. We have to think of what sort of message, we, the Athenians, send if we slaughter all of them as Cleon urges. Diodotus warns that we may intimidate the subject cities but we

[4]Thucydides, *The Peloponnesian War*, V, para. 87–116. For a valuable and more general discussion of Realist ethics, see J. E. Hare and Carey Joynt, *Ethics and International Affairs* (New York: St. Martin's Press, 1982), chap. 3.
[5]Thucydides, 3:1–50.

also will stir up resistance elsewhere in the empire or with potential allies. Thus Diodotus argues for a softer course. The soft course is not too soft—it involves the death of about a thousand Mytilinean rebels—but he advocates sparing the rest of the island in hopes of a future of imperial reconciliation and imperial stability.

In addition to considerations of prestige and imperial stability, preventive war provides a third reason to override the nonintervention principle. The great English polymath Francis Bacon, in his essay "Of Empire," provided this rationale and drew the policy implications with eloquence and force, urging "that princes do keep due sentinel that none of their neighbors do overgrow so (by increase of territory, by embracing trade, by approaches, or the like) as they become more able to annoy them than they were. . . . [F]or there is no question but a just fear of an imminent danger, though no blow be given, is a lawful cause of war."[6]

Principles of nonintervention seem to have a thin foundation in Realist ethics, which finds them valuable only to the extent they are useful from a national point of view. One cannot abide by the rules of sovereign equality, sovereign nonintervention, when security is at stake. Rousseau thought that security need not be at stake if statesmen isolated themselves from one another, as should an ideal Corsica. Cleon and the Athenian generals at Melos had an expansive notion of security that included the merest threat to prestige. Bacon included any threats to the relative balance of power. Diodotus had a less but still-expansive notion of security, including as it did the stability of the empire.

Today, for example, some Israelis argue that the occupied West Bank—a form of long-term intervention against the Palestinians—is Israel's biblical heritage. Others, Liberals, argue that Israel must respect the right to self-determination of the Palestinians and return authority over the land to the people who inhabit it. Realism enters the debate when arguments focus on holding the West Bank as a necessary measure for Israel's security. But other Israelis of course think Realism calls for a recognition that occupation provokes more regional hostility, and thus danger, than it assuages. Realist arguments, whether hard or soft, shape a debate either when their underlying assumptions are widely shared or when actions force two sides into a state of war. For when a debate becomes a matter only of "them or us," the Realists say and usually convince us that the answer has to be "us."

Socialists

Socialists tend to regard international politics, particularly international law, as a mere reflection of the much more fundamental class interests that truly gov-

[6]Francis Bacon, "Of Empire," in *The Works of Francis Bacon*, ed. J. Spedding (London: 1870), vol. 6, pp. 420–421.

ern international society. International society, according to Socialists, is akin to international civil war, where capitalists line up against workers, both domestically and internationally. State borders among nations are semifictions and not the fundamental dividing blocks of world politics. Nonetheless, national borders can and have played a progressive role in history. Marx himself saw reasons to support the development of the working class within a national framework. For that development to be successful, one had to appreciate the value of national sovereignty and therefore the value of national defense. So he hesitates only very rarely to condemn aggressive wars as he sees them occurring in his own times.[7]

When Marx considers a doctrine that should guide Socialists in their own choices for world politics, he wants to remind them that even though they have a duty to advance to the greatest extent that they can, the processes of Socialism on a worldwide front, this does not include a duty to crusade for Socialism. He warns that the liberation of the working class can be achieved only by the working class. One cannot create revolutions for others by prematurely attempting to put a working-class or union movement in political power. Socialist crusades would create the grounds for a enormous amount of suffering, a great deal of instability, and the defeat of that particular working class at the hands of social forces, capitalist and others, that it has not yet historically been able to master. Therefore, Marxists of the Second International, the pre-1914 Marxists and the post-1914 social democrats, often lined up in favor of the principle of nonintervention.

Leninism and Stalinism, by contrast, came to perceive the role of international revolution as an important tool not just in the promotion of Socialism worldwide but also in the defense of the one Communist state that was the Soviet Union. In the early revolutionary phase, Bolsheviks enthusiastically adopted an expansive program of revolutionary intervention. The Soviet soldiers who conquered Armenia hailed their achievement from the balcony of the Armenian parliament building with these cheers: "Long live Soviet Armenia! Long live Soviet Azerbaijan! Long live Soviet Russia! Georgia will soon be a Soviet, too. Turkey will follow. Our Red Armies will sweep across Europe. . . . Long live the Third International!"[8]

In order to defend Socialism in one country, Lenin and Stalin thought it necessary to adopt two contradictory policies. The first was to weaken the inherently aggressive forces of capitalism directed at the Socialist state. So Lenin on a number of occasions—and Stalin after him—interfered aggressively in the

[7] See the discussion in chapter 9 above and pp. 64–66 of Walzer, *Just and Unjust Wars* for a complicated account of Marx's motives.

[8] Reported by Oliver Baldwin, *Six Prisons and Two Revolutions* (London: 1925), quoted in Lord Kinross, *Ataturk: The Birth of a Nation* (London: Weidenfeld, 1993), p. 280.

TABLE

Views on Intervention

	Egalitarian			*Libertarian*
Nationalism	M		R E A L I S T S	
	A	Classic	International	Law
	R		LIBERALS	
	X		National Liberals	
	I	(Walzer)		
	S		(Mill)	
	T	Left Cosmopolitans		Right Cosmopolitans
Cosmopolitanism	S	(Luban)		(Arkes)

domestic politics of other states, not so much with armed force as with attempts at subversion. Some of the strategies adopted were justifiable in Marxist terms, such as the financial aid that the Soviets provided for the British workers in the General Strike of 1926. On the other hand, Soviet state and party interests sometimes precluded a revolutionary strategy, such as the Comintern's targeting of German Socialists, whose appeals for help against the growing Nazi movement were rejected by the Soviets.[9]

Once the Soviet Union acquired great power of its own after World War Two, interventionism became a practice that then turned into doctrine, the Brezhnev Doctrine. Following the forcible "Stalinization" of East European states after 1948 and then the interventions in Germany in 1953, Hungary in 1956, and Czechoslovakia in 1968, Brezhnev declared that the Soviet Union stood in a particularly privileged position as the guardian of the collective interest of the working class worldwide and particularly, of course, within the Soviet bloc.[10] The Communist Party of the Soviet Union thus claimed to act in the name of the worldwide working class in intervening against governments that it claimed were about to "betray" the interests of the working class.

Liberals: For and Against

Nonintervention has been a particularly important and occasionally disturbing principle for liberal political philosophers. On the one hand, Liberals have

[9] R. Craig Nation, *Black Earth, Red Star* (Ithaca: Cornell University Press, 1992), pp. 60–67. On p. 70, he notes that the Comintern "encouraged division on the left."
[10] For a general background on the bloc, see Zbigniew K. Brzezinski, *The Soviet Bloc* (Cambridge: Harvard University Press, 1967).

provided some of the very strongest reasons to abide by a strict form of the nonintervention doctrine, and on the other hand, those very same principles when applied in different contexts have provided justifications for overriding the principle of nonintervention.

Liberal Nonintervention. Although the principle emerged historically as a practice among the monarchical sovereigns of Europe, when democratic and Liberal governments came to power, they too adopted it. The Liberals contributed two new justifications for nonintervention.[11]

The most important value they saw in the principle was that it reflected and protected human *rights*. Nonintervention enabled citizens to determine their own way of life without outside interference. If democratic rights and liberal freedoms were to mean something, they had to be worked out among those who shared them and were making them through their own participation. The first precondition of democratic government is self-government by one's own people. Kant's "Perpetual Peace" made a strong case for respecting the right of nonintervention because it afforded a polity the necessary territorial space and political independence in which free and equal citizens could work out what their way of life would be.[12]

John Stuart Mill provides a second argument for nonintervention, one focusing on likely *consequences*, when he explains in his famous 1859 essay "A Few Words on Nonintervention" that it would be a great mistake to export freedom to a foreign people that was not in a position to win it on its own.[13] A people given freedom by a foreign intervention would not, he argues, be able to hold on to it. It's only by winning and holding on to freedom through local effort that one acquires a true sense of its value. Moreover, it is only by winning freedom that one acquires the political capacities to defend it adequately against threats both at home and abroad. If, on the other hand, Liberal government were to be introduced into a foreign society, in the "knapsack," so to speak, of a conquering Liberal army, the local Liberals placed in power would find themselves immediately in an difficult situation. Not having been able to win political power on their own, they would have few domestic supporters and many non-Liberal domestic enemies. They then would wind up doing one of three different things:

They would (1) begin to rule as did previous governments—that is, repress

[11] For a valuable discussion of motives, means, and consequences applied to international policy choices, see Joseph Nye, *Nuclear Ethics* (New York: Free Press, 1986), esp. chap. 3.

[12] See Immanuel Kant, "Perpetual Peace," particularly the preliminary articles of a perpetual peace in which he spells out the rights of nonintervention that he hopes will hold among all states even in the state of war. These rights take on a absolute character within the pacific union of republican states.

[13] John Stuart Mill, "A Few Words on Nonintervention," in *Essays on Politics and Culture*, ed. Gertrude Himmelfarb (Gloucester: Peter Smith, 1973), pp. 368–84.

their opposition. The intervention would have done no good; it simply would have created another oppressive government. Or they would (2) simply collapse in an ensuing civil war. Intervention therefore, would have produced not freedom and progress but a civil war with all its attendant violence. Or (3) the intervenors would have continually to send in foreign support. Rather than having set up a free government, one that reflected the participation of the citizens of the state, the intervention would have set up a puppet government, one that would reflect the wills and interests of the intervening, the truly sovereign state.[14]

In the course of British intervention in the Russian civil war (1918–1920) all these lessons were learned again, at considerable cost. In late May 1919 E. H. Carr concluded a memorandum comparing the practices of the Kolchak regime then sustained by the British intervention with those of the Bolshevik regimes against which Britain was intervening: "The reasons for thinking that a Kolchak regime would be an improvement on the present Bolshevist regime do not therefore stand very close examination. . . . [Kolchak's methods] do not differ sensibly from those of the Bolshevik's, in spite of any restraining influence which allied cooperation may exercise on him."[15] British statesmen looked for "saner elements of the Left"—will-o'-the-wisp moderates who would bring stability and progress, national legitimacy, and international accommodation. The dilemma, however, is clear. As Richard Ullman has noted, "Civil wars are polarizing experiences; leaders who can supply the discipline and efficiency necessary to win are not likely to be 'moderate' (although they may, by most people's lights, be 'sane') whether they come from the Right or the Left."[16] And national moderates who accommodate the full range of the intervenor's interests—interests that rise as the cost of the intervention rises—are very unlikely to be nationally legitimate.

Liberal Intervention. Liberal arguments in favor of overriding nonintervention fall into two camps depending on what value they attach to national distinctiveness and on how confident the intervenors are that foreigners can truly understand the circumstances of another people.

The *cosmopolitan* Liberals are radically skeptical of the principle of nonintervention, almost as much as are the Realists, though of course for different rea-

[14] A good discussion of consequentialist issues can be found in Anthony Ellis, "Utilitarianism and International Ethics," in Terry Nardin and David Mapel, eds., *Traditions of International Ethics* (Cambridge: Cambridge University Press, 1992), pp. 158–79. See also Fernando Teson, *Humanitarian Intervention* (Ardsley-on-Hudson, N.Y.: Transnational Publishers, 1988).

[15] E. H. Carr, "The Proposed Recognition of the Kolchak Government," May 26, 1919, FO 608/188, as quoted in Richard Ullman, *Britain and the Russian Civil War* (Princeton: Princeton University Press, 1968), p. 352.

[16] Ibid.

A Comparison of Policy on Empire and Intervention

	Empire (Long-term)	*Intervention* (Short-term)
Realists	For national interest—security, prestige, profit—with prudence	
Hard	x	x
Soft		x
Marxists	When "progressive" or "international class war"	
Leninists		x
Stalinists	x ("Brezhnev Doctrine")	x

Liberal Justifications for Intervention

	Em-pire	Pro-dem Civil Lib.	Basic Rts. Social Rts.	Protracted Civil War	Cold War	National Libera-tion	Counter-interven.	Humani-tarian
Rt. Cosmo. (Arkes)		x	x			x	x	x
Lt. Cosmo. (Luban)			x			x	x	x
Mill	x			x	x	x	x	x
Nat. Lib. (Walzer)						x	x	x

sons. The other group, the *national* Liberals, are firm defenders of nonintervention but would override the principle in certain exceptional circumstances.

The cosmopolitan position portrays nonintervention as a derivative or instrumental value. It holds only where it seems to protect principles believed to be more fundamental. We can divide these more fundamental principles into right-wing libertarian cosmopolitan principles and left-wing, egalitarian cosmopolitan principles. But both sets share a confident reading of the moral world, a "flat" world, where all is or should be the same, where we can clearly interpret the meaning and priority others attach to values and interest, such that we can directly judge for others just as we judge for ourselves. We can therefore know what are the justifiable ends and means—here, there, and everywhere.

Articulating just such a flat, confident moral universe, right-wing cosmopolitans hold that a morally adequate recognition of equal human freedom requires freedom from torture, free speech, privacy rights, and private property. It also demands democratic elections and an independent judiciary and, as a safeguard, a right of emigration. The entire package goes together, as Hadley Arkes has eloquently argued.[17] The third right, emigration, serves as an obvious safety valve. The second group of political rights—democratic elections and an independent judiciary—serves to protect the basic rights of free speech, privacy, and private property. Free governments are governments that protect all the basic rights and all the political rights. Totalitarian governments violate all those rights. They violate free speech, privacy, private property, democracy, and the independence of the judiciary. Authoritarian governments are not quite as bad as the totalitarians. They nonetheless violate the political rights of democratic elections and a free independent judiciary, while managing to preserve (partially) the rights of privacy and private property.[18]

The rights of cosmopolitan freedom are valuable everywhere for all people. Any violation of them should be resisted whenever and wherever it occurs, provided that we can do so proportionally, without causing more harm than we seek to avoid.[19] Applying these views to the history of American interventionism, Arkes says we justly fought in Vietnam to prevent the takeover of a flawed South Vietnamese democracy by totalitarian North Vietnamese communism. We justly fought, he says, for good ends and used good means, and our only fault was in not sticking it out to protect South Vietnam, Cambodia, and Laos from the terror of oppression that accompanied the communist victories.

Equally cosmopolitan but at the other end of the Liberal political spectrum is the left cosmopolitan view. David Luban argues powerfully that we can make an equally clear judgment about basic rights, but his basic rights are different.[20] Basic rights include both subsistence rights—that is, rights to food and shelter and clothing—and security rights—that is, rights to be free from arbitrary killing, from torture, and from assault. We all have a duty to protect these socially basic rights. They are the rights held by humanity and claimable by all against all human beings.

[17] Hadley Arkes, *First Things* (Princeton: Princeton University Press, 1986), esp. chaps. 11–13. Transformed in a political and expediential way, these views relate to those adopted by the Reagan administration in its defense of global "freedom fighters." See a valuable discussion of this by Charles Beitz, "The Reagan Doctrine in Nicaragua," in Steven Luper-Foy ed. *Problems of International Justice* (Boulder, Colo.: Westview Press, 1988), pp. 182–95.

[18] This distinction has been developed by Jeanne Kirkpatrick in "Dictatorships and Double Standards," but it also appears in traditional Liberal discourse.

[19] The best discussion of the practical applications of the proportionality issue that I have seen is Richard Ullman, "Human Rights and Economic Power: The United States versus Idi Amin," *Foreign Affairs* 56, 3 (April 1978), pp. 529–43. The author explains how carefully targeting sanctions on the government and bypassing the people could put pressure on the murderous Amin government.

[20] David Luban, "Just War and Human Rights," *Philosophy and Public Affairs* 9, 2 (Winter 1980), reprinted in Charles Beitz, ed., *International Ethics* (Princeton: Princeton University Press, 1985), pp. 195–216.

In international politics, this means that states that fail to protect those rights do not have the right to be free from intervention. The most complete form of nonintervention thus is claimable only by states that do not violate basic rights. Moreover, all states have a duty to protect and to intervene, if an intervention is necessary, in order to provide subsistence needs held by all human beings. Both these considerations are subject to standard proportionality: We should never do something that would cause more harm than it saves. One implication of this principle is that if 500 individuals were to die of torture in country X this year and we could militarily or otherwise intervene at a cost of 499 lives or less, intervention would be the right thing to do, and we would have a duty to do it. Correspondingly, if the only way that Haitians could provide subsistence for themselves is by sailing a boat to Florida, the United States has no right to stop them.

National Liberals, a third group of Liberals, reject both cosmopolitan worldviews. They favor a revision and not a radical revolution in the principle of nonintervention. For Michael Walzer, who builds on the argument of John Stuart Mill, the moral world is not flat and clearly interpretable by all but a series of moral hills and valleys. The particular values the national community develops are hard for foreigners to perceive. They are the product not of abstract philosophic judgment but of complicated historical compromises.[21] If they are contracts, they are Burkean contracts among the dead, the living, the yet to be born. We cannot freely unpack the compromises that they have made between principle and stability, between justice and security, nor do we as nonparticipants in those packings, in those historical contracts, have a clear right to do so.

J. S. Mill argued on those grounds that for "civilized" nations, his principles of consequentialist nonintervention hold. Interventions do more harm than good, with three now unusual exceptions.

First, reflecting the imperial metropolitan values of nineteenth-century Britain, Mill does not think that all peoples are sufficiently "civilized" to be fit for national independence. Some societies are not, he claims, capable of the "reciprocity" on which all legal equality rests partly because of political chaos, partly because these peoples (like children) are incapable of postponing gratification. Moreover, they would benefit from the tutelage and commercial development imperial rule could provide. The only rights such peoples have are the right to be properly educated and the right to become a nation.[22]

[21] These compromises are part of the "thick" texture of moral and political life that each nation forms for itself. Beyond the "thin" foundation of basic human rights that all nations should share, these "thick" moralities cover such issues as form of government, distributions of income, family law, education, and the status of religious practices. See Michael Walzer, *Thick and Thin: Moral Argument at Home and Abroad* (Notre Dame: University of Notre Dame Press, 1994).

[22] Mill, "Nonintervention," p. 376.

Second, some civil wars become so protracted and so seemingly unresolvable by local struggle that a common sense of humanity and sympathy for the suffering of the populations calls for an outside intervention to halt the fighting in order to see if some negotiated solution might be achieved under the aegis of foreign arms. Mill here cites the success of outsiders in calling a halt to and helping settle the protracted mid-century Portuguese civil war.

Third, in a system-wide internationalized civil war, a "cold war," such as that waged between Protestantism and Catholicism in the sixteenth century, nonintervention can neglect vital transnational sources of national security. If one side intervenes to spread its ideology, the other has a defensive right to do the same.

Mill's last three exceptions have been the most influential and have been adopted and developed by Michael Walzer, who, like Mill, acknowledges that sovereignty and nonintervention ultimately depend upon consent. If the people welcome an intervention or refuse to resist, something less than aggression has occurred.[23] But we cannot make those judgments reliably in advance. We should assume, he suggests, that foreigners will be resisted, that nationals will protect their state from foreign aggression. For even if the state is not just, it's their state, not ours. We have no standing to decide what their state should be. We do not happen to be engaged full-time, as they are, in the national historical project of creating it.

All the injustices, therefore, that do justify a domestic revolution do not always justify a foreign intervention. Following Mill, Walzer says that domestic revolutions need to be left to domestic citizens. Foreign interventions to achieve a domestic revolution are inauthentic, ineffective, and likely to cause more harm than they eliminate.

But there are some injustices that do justify foreign intervention, for sometimes the national self-determination that nonintervention protects and the harms that nonintervention tries to avoid are overwhelmed by the domestic oppression and suffering that borders permit. Building on John Stuart Mill's classic essay, Walzer offers us three cases in which intervention serves the underlying purposes that nonintervention was designed to uphold.[24]

The first case occurs when too many nations contest one piece of territory. When an imperial government opposes the independence of a subordinate nation or when there are two distinct peoples, one attempting to crush the other, then national self-determination cannot be a reason to shun intervention. Here foreigners can intervene to help the liberation of the oppressed people,

[23] Michael Walzer, "The Moral Standing of States: A Response to Four Critics," in Bertz, ed., *International Ethics*, ed., p. 221, n. 7.
[24] Walzer, *Just and Unjust Wars*, pp. 106–08, 339–42.

once that people has demonstrated through its own "arduous struggle" that it truly is another nation. Then decolonization is the principle that should rule, allowing a people to form its own destiny. One model of this might be the American Revolution against Britain; another in Mill's time was the 1848–49 Hungarian rebellion against Austria, and in our time the many anticolonial movements in Africa and Asia that quickly won recognition and, in a few cases, support from the international community.

The second instance in which the principle against intervention should be overridden is counterintervention in a civil war. A civil war should be left to the combatants. When conflicting factions of one people are struggling to define what sort of society and government should rule, only *that* struggle, not foreigners, should decide the outcome. But when an external power intervenes on behalf of one of the participants in a civil war, then another foreign power can counterintervene to balance the first intervention. This second intervention serves the purposes of self-determination, which the first intervention sought to undermine. Even if, Mill argues, the Hungarian rebellion was not clearly a national rebellion against "a foreign yoke," it was clearly the case that Russia should not have intervened to assist Austria in its suppression. By doing so, Russia gave others a right to counterintervene.

Third—and perhaps the most controversial case—one can intervene for humanitarian purposes, to halt what appears to be a gross violation of the rights to survival of a population. When we see a pattern of massacres, the development of a campaign of genocide, the institutionalization of slavery—violations so horrendous that in the classical phrase they "shock the conscience of mankind"—one has good ground to question whether there is any national connection between the population and the state that is so brutally oppressing it. Under those circumstances, outsiders can intervene. But the intervenor should have a morally defensible motive and share the purpose of ending the slaughter and establishing a self-determining people. (Solely self-serving interventions promote imperialism.) Furthermore, intervenors should act only as a "last resort," after exploring peaceful resolution. They should then act only when it is clear that they will save more lives than the intervention itself will almost inevitably wind up costing, and even then with minimum necessary force. It makes no moral sense to rescue a village and start World War III or to destroy a village in order to save it. Thus, even though one often finds humanitarian intervention abused, Michael Walzer suggests that a reasonable case can be made that the Indian invasion of East Pakistan in 1971, designed to save the people of what became Bangladesh from the massacre that was being inflicted upon them by their own government (headquartered in West Pakistan), is a case of legitimate humanitarian intervention. It allowed the people of East Pakistan to survive and form their own state.

A right to intervene does not, however, establish a duty to intervene. States retain the duty to weigh the lives of their own citizens as a special responsibility. If an intervention could be costless, then there might be a strong obligation to intervene. But rarely is that so, and statesmen have an obligation not to volunteer their citizens in causes those citizens do not want to undertake. This is the basis of the right of neutrality in most wars. National interests invariably will come into play and should do so to justify an intervention to the citizens whose sons and daughters are likely to bear the casualties. In contradistinction to the Realists, Liberals hold that national interests should not govern when to intervene, just whether a nation should intervene when it has a right to do so.

GRENADA[25]

Let us look at a difficult case. Few invasions raise quite the moral dilemmas that the U.S. invasion of Grenada did. It was clearly illegal. It was roundly denounced in a debate of the UN General Assembly, in which many allies of the United States condemned the invasion. But on October 25, 1983, and in the months that followed, many in the United States and in the Caribbean thought it was justified. Both Realists and Liberals can make a case for the invasion; both can also argue against. None of the arguments is simple, and that is why the case, although odd in the disparity of the power between the United States and Grenada, is so typical a case of hard choice in world politics.

The debate over justification took place in the light of considerable controversy. From the traditional legal point of view, the invasion violated the territorial integrity and political independence of Grenada. It trampled on the charters of the United Nations and the Organization of American States.[26] In addition, a U.S. president had once again usurped the constitutional powers of Congress to declare war, while barring the press from covering a campaign involving U.S. troops. Crucial allies in Europe were distressed by our failure to consult them. Many feared that the Reagan administration would exploit the domestic popularity of the successful invasion as support for further invasions, for intensifying the ongoing covert war against Nicaragua, and for its wider program of militaristic diplomacy.

We still do not fully know the actual course of events surrounding the U.S.

[25] I am grateful for the advice I received on an earlier version of this argument from Steven David, Arthur Day, Ann Florini, Samuel Huntington, and Richard Ullman. This section draws on parts of "Grenada: An International Crisis in Multilateral Security," in Arthur Day and Michael W. Doyle, eds. *Escalation and Intervention,* (Boulder, Colo.; United Nations Association/Westview Press, 1986).

[26] The treaty of the Organization of Eastern Caribbean States did not clearly authorize a collective security intervention against one of its members. The UN and OAS charters prohibit armed attack, other than in individual or collective self-defense, unless specifically authorized by the UN Security Council under Chapter VII.

invasion.[27] But it appears that between October 12 and 14, 1983, a coup in Grenada deposed and then arrested Maurice Bishop, prime minister of the People's Revolutionary Government (PRG), and installed Bernard Coard, Bishop's former deputy, as the new prime minister.[28] On October 19 soldiers from the Grenadian People's Revolutionary Army, in the course of a popular demonstration that had freed Bishop from house arrest, fired on the crowd, killing numerous civilians, and then executed Bishop, three of his former fellow ministers, and two trade union leaders. On the next day Hudson Austin, commanding general of Grenada's People's Revolutionary Army, announced the formation of a Revolutionary Military Council (RMC) and imposed a shoot-on-sight curfew. Concurrently a joint armed intervention was planned at a hurried set of meetings among the United States, Barbados, Jamaica, and five states (Antigua, Dominica, St. Kitts, St. Lucia, and St. Vincent) of the Organization of Eastern Caribbean States (OECS). Consultations with Sir Paul Scoon, Grenada's governor-general, led to a request for help from him, according to Prime Minister Tom Adams of Barbados, "well before" the invasion force landed in the early morning of Tuesday, October 25.[29] By October 28 all significant resistance from elements of the People's Revolutionary Army and from the Cuban construction workers who were helping build the controversial airport at Point Salines had been overcome. According to U.S. sources, forty-five Grenadians (including twenty-four civilians), twenty-four Cubans, and nineteen Americans were killed in the invasion and in its aftermath.[30]

After stormy hearings the UN General Assembly deplored the invasion as "a flagrant violation of international law." Resolution 38/7 was adopted with 9 votes against, 108 for, and 27 abstentions. Voting with the United States in opposition were only its Caribbean allies in the invasion, El Salvador, and Israel. The Third World bloc and the Soviet Union and its allies overwhelmingly voted for the resolution. All the Atlantic and Pacific allies of the United States abstained.

Sir Paul Scoon appointed an interim administration on November 9, and U.S. combat forces left the island on December 15, 1983. The United States

[27] In addition to the citations below, a valuable collection can be found in Scott B. MacDonald, Harald Sandstrom, and Paul Goodwin, eds., *The Caribbean after Grenada: Revolution, Conflict and Democracy* (New York: Praeger, 1988).

[28] According to U.K. House of Commons, Second Report from the Foreign Affairs Committee, *Grenada*, March 15, 1984, para. 16–17. Other reports from the island indicate that Coard may have resigned soon after the coup, judging that his presence as head of the coup would increase popular discontent. An impressively thorough account on which I draw in this exposition is Hugh O'Shaughnessy, *Grenada: Revolution, Invasion, and Aftermath* (London: Sphere Books, 1984).

[29] Quoted in the *New York Times*, October 28, 1983.

[30] U.S. Department of State and Defense, *Grenada: A Preliminary Report*, December 16, 1983.

nonetheless left behind three hundred "noncombat" military personnel and a "Caribbean Peacekeeping Force" (most of whom were withdrawn in June 1985). On December 3, 1984, the elections Sir Paul Scoon promised at last took place, putting Herbert Blaize, a familiar middle-class politician, in office. Despite evidence of substantial foreign funding in his electoral campaign, Mr. Blaize seemed to have gained the overwhelming support of the Grenadian electorate.[31]

A Caribbean Melos?

A hard Realist could have made the case that the invasion contributed to U.S. strategic prestige and removed a strategic thorn in U.S. dominance of the sea in its traditional "backyard." Indeed, to many in the Reagan administration, the Grenada invasion was reportedly a promising model for international and domestic political success. It avoided "another Iran" (another hostage crisis), "another Beirut" (where the United States appeared helpless), and "another Nicaragua" (another "outpost" for Cuba and the Soviet Union).[32] On the day after the General Assembly resolution condemning the invasion as a flagrant violation of international law, President Reagan announced that the condemnation "didn't disturb my breakfast at all."[33] Eliminating the possibility of a strategic "hostile triangle" in the Caribbean (Cuba, Nicaragua, and Grenada) had long been an administration aim. And the potential hostage issue—the U.S. medical students and other U.S. residents on the island—helped the administration win the support of 63 percent of the U.S. public (its highest approval rating in the preceding two years) and rout its Democratic critics.[34]

Some in the United States thus used the success as the reason for renewed official support for indirect intervention through insurrectionist groups.[35] Considering unilateral means against Nicaragua, White House officials mused, "If the Soviet Union metaphysically speaking is equated to an ancient, evil empire,

[31] Joseph Treaster, "Man in the News: A Centrist in Grenada," *New York Times*, December 5, 1984, p. A2, charges that foreign sources of funding tied to the U.S. Republican Party aided his electoral campaign.

[32] Bernard Gwertzman, "An Invasion Prompted by Previous Debacles," *New York Times*, October 26, 1983, p. A1.

[33] Richard Bernstein, "Behind U.N. Vote: How Much Anti-Americanism," *New York Times*, November 4, 1983, p. A18.

[34] An ABC/*Washington Post* poll reported in *Time* (November 21, 1983), p. 17. The approval rating specifically for the Grenada invasion rose to 65 percent of the American public, 27 percent disapproving. James Dickenson, "Bombing, Invasion in Eerie Focus," *Washington Post*, October 24, 1984.

[35] U.S. Ambassador Middendorf, in making this demand, referred to the Rio Treaty and invoked its provisions for economic sanctions and military intervention (Gary Lee, "US May Seek OAS Action," *Washington Post*, March 28, 1985). Senator Kasten discussed setting up a special fund for aid to "freedom fighters." See the articles by Joanne Omang and David Ottaway, "US Seems More Willing to Support Insurgencies" and "US Course Uncharted on Aid to Insurgencies," *Washington Post*, May 26, 27, 1985.

then to the extent we can, we ought to attack it by going to the colonies."[36]

The official State Department position as enunciated by Deputy Secretary Kenneth Dam focused on two additional threats raised by the crisis: to the lives of U.S. citizens and to stability of law and order in Grenada and the region.[37] Indeed, it does not appear to be the case that the coup leaders would simply have released the U.S. citizens. Planning for a "non-permissive evacuation" of U.S. citizens began as early as October 15, as news of the crisis in Grenada reached Washington. The events of the following week escalated the planning. As the difficulty of a forcible rescue of U.S. citizens became apparent, planning turned, in conjunction with the OECS, to a full-scale intervention to oust the RMC coup leaders. The diversion of the Lebanon task force and the mobilization of the Rangers and elements of the Rapid Deployment Force brought the requisite military force within reach. The United States did send envoys to Grenada to determine whether the RMC would permit an evacuation of American citizens. The envoys reported that the RMC appeared to be stalling, either purposefully or because it was losing control of a disintegrating political situation.[38] The RMC would permit standard departures, going through customs, etc., but not a special evacuation by ship or air. (Standard exit procedures, we can surmise, would avoid further arousing Grenadian citizens and could be used to place pressure on the Organization of Eastern Caribbean States [OECS] and the Caribbean Community [CARICOM] to lift their quarantine of Grenada.) Three hundred U.S. citizens out of the approximately thousand residents and medical students signed a petition requesting a special exit.[39] President Reagan gave the final go-ahead for the planned invasion after learn-

[36] Gerald Boyd, "Role in Nicaragua Described by the US," *New York Times*, August 9, 1985. Liberal critics of the administration, such as Congressman Solarz, endorsed intervention but sought to limit it, particularly to insurgents fighting foreign occupiers, such as in Afghanistan and Cambodia. While this limitation exempted Nicaragua and came closer to traditional (pre-UN) international law, it also opened the United States to indirectly intervening in support of factionalized groups (as in these two cases) that may be unable to establish not only civil governance but also independent governments capable of standing on their own without continuing U.S. military support (see the Omang and Ottaway article noted above).

[37] Deputy Secretary Kenneth Dam, "The Larger Importance of Grenada," address before the Associated Press Managing Editors Conference, Louisville, Kentucky, November 4, 1983. For discussion, see Robert Pastor, "The Invasion of Grenada," in Scott MacDonald, Harald Sandstom, and Paul Goodwin, eds., *The Caribbean after Grenada* (New York: Praeger, 1985).

[38] U.S. consular officers were advised that their aircraft landing at Grenville was fired upon by soldiers on the ground. They were placed under constant military escort. They observed widespread patrols of soldiers and a public atmosphere of apprehension following the murders and the shoot-on-sight curfew. After they reported their apprehensions to U.S. Ambassador Milan Bish in Barbados, the ambassador then recommended an immediate evacuation to avoid another Iranian-style hostage crisis. Source: interview at the U.S. State Department with Ambassador Charles Gillespie, September 14, 1984.

[39] An account of the U.S. decision process can be found in Assistant Secretary Langhorne Motley's statement (January 24, 1989) printed as Annex E, House of Commons Second Report, *Grenada*.

ing of the RMC's refusal to provide special measures for the evacuation of U.S. citizens. The bombing of the Marines in Lebanon during the weekend the Grenada crisis peaked recalled the political disaster President Carter had suffered over the seizure of the Iranian hostages in 1979. President Reagan, facing a disaster in Lebanon and a looming replay of the hostage crisis in Grenada, was heard to bewail, "I'm no better off than Jimmy Carter."[40]

Taking a longer view, we can see that following the Grenadian revolution of March 1979, two security "threats" seemed to motivate U.S. policy. Emphasizing the strategic factor, President Reagan announced that Grenada "was a Soviet-Cuban colony being readied as a major military bastion to export terrorism and undermine democracy."[41] On March 23, 1983, the president had identified what his administration thought was the dual threat that Grenada posed. The airport at Point Salines was, he charged, a military installation, a "power projection" being built by the "Cubans with Soviet financing." This militarization of Grenada threatened U.S. "national security" by putting at risk our geoeconomic and geostrategic interests in the "Caribbean . . . a very important passageway for our international commerce and military lines of communication. More than half of American oil imports now pass through the Caribbean."[42] The second threat was the ideological advance of communism. Secretary of State George Shultz amplified: "[A]s Grenada demonstrated, we must defend ourselves against the organized violence of communism."[43] And

[40] As reported in "Britain's Grenada Shut-out," *Economist* (March 10, 1984), p. 32.
[41] "Transcript of Address by President on Lebanon and Grenada," *New York Times*, October 28, 1983, p. A10.
[42] President Reagan, "Peace and National Security," televised address to the nation, Washington, D.C., March 23, 1983, p. 40, in the U.S. State Department, *Realism, Strength, Negotiation*, May 1984. These specific interests gained an increased significance from the Reagan administration's Grand Strategy—the need to wage a new cold war to protect an America perceived to be under extreme global strategic threat and locked in an ideological contest with the Soviet Union. For an influential statement of this view, see Richard Nixon, *The Real War* (New York: Warner, 1980), esp. chap. 1. Cole Blasier, *The Hovering Giant* (Pittsburgh: University of Pittsburgh Press, 1976) is a survey of U.S. policy toward the wider region. The geoeconomic and sea-lanes view can be found in Timothy Ashby, "Grenada: Threat to America's Oil Routes," *National Defense* (May–June 1981), pp. 52–54, 205. David Ronfeldt, *Geopolitics, Security, and U.S. Strategy in the Caribbean Basin* (R-2997-AF/RC) (Santa Monica: Rand, 1983) provides a sophisticated argument for the strategic value of U.S. hegemony (which he calls "collective hegemony") over the Caribbean. For an alternative view, see the testimony by Jorge Dominguez and Richard Feinberg in *Hearings on the Caribbean Basin Policy*, House of Representatives, Committee on Foreign Affairs, Subcommittee on Inter-American Affairs, 97th Congress, 1st Session, July 14–28, 1981. This section draws on my "Squaring the Circle of Crisis: President Reagan's Cold War in the Caribbean" paper presented at the Conference on Geopolitical Change in the Caribbean, C.E.E.S.T.E.M., San Jerónimo Lidice, Mexico, April 1982.
[43] Secretary Shultz, "Democratic Solidarity in the Americas," luncheon remarks for leaders of Barbados, Jamaica, and OECS members, Bridgetown, February 6, 1984, p. 133, in U.S. State Department *op. cit.*, May 1984. *The Economist* (March 10, 1984) reported a Reagan

in explaining his policy of "restoring deterrence," President Reagan indicated the Third World advances of communism that he proposed to deter against: "The simple fact is that in the late 1970's we were not deterring, as events in Angola and Afghanistan made clear."[44]

A strategic assessment requires, however, that we consider whether the same ends might have been achieved by more efficient, less costly means. Despite its eventual success, the military conduct of the invasion left much to be desired. Military intelligence was meager (the soldiers were reduced to using tourist maps). Because Grenada was within the U.S. Navy's Atlantic Command, the operation was inappropriately "navalized," according to the critics.[45] Marine-style beachheads were established at the opposite ends of the island, leading to a unnecessarily drawn-out combat directed toward the capital and political center of the island at St. George's. Simultaneous assault, a *coup de main*, some military strategists argue, would have been far preferable.

Could a stable accommodation have been worked out with the Grenadian regime that would have served basic U.S. security interests? Some have suggested the United States could (and should) have relaxed its interventionism and developed an accommodation with nationalist forces in the region.[46] Instead the March 1979 revolutionary coup led by Maurice Bishop in Grenada met an inconsistent but overwhelmingly hostile U.S. response. The U.S. consul on the island accurately reported the widespread relief that accompanied the New Jewel Movement (NJM) coup. But the U.S. ambassador in Barbados, Frank Ortiz, on his first visit to Grenada, only a month after the March 13 revolution, threatened the NJM with a U.S. campaign to cut off its American sources of tourists (a vital source of revenue to bridge Grenada's nineteen-million-dollar balance of trade gap) if the Grenadians established relations with Cuba.[47] At the same time he offered five thousand dollars in U.S. economic aid for two or three Grenadian development projects. The Grenadians perceived the sum as insulting and denounced U.S. imperialism. Grenada directly threatened no U.S. strategic or economic interests. The island's residents

---

adviser's comments on the invasion along these same lines: "The purpose was to deny the Russians/Cubans a feeling of potency in grabbing small vulnerable states in the region. It had to be nipped in the bud before it developed into another Cuba," p. 32.

[44] President Reagan, "America's Foreign Policy Challenges for the 1980s," address before the Center for Strategic and International Studies, Washington, D.C., April 6, 1984, p. 11, in U.S. State Department, op. cit., May 1984.

[45] Edward N. Luttwak, *The Pentagon and the Art of War* (New York: Simon and Schuster, 1984), pp. 51–58.

[46] See the essays in Richard Newfarmer, ed., *From Gunboats to Diplomacy* (Baltimore: Johns Hopkins University Press, 1984), particularly the essay on trends in U.S. diplomacy by James Kurth.

[47] See the account and the April 13 speech by Prime Minister Bishop in D. Sinclair Dabreo, *The Grenada Revolution* (St. Lucia: M.A.P.S., 1979), pp. 302–10.

seemed to prefer the radical Bishop regime to the preceding Gairy regime. Yet the Marxist-Leninist rhetoric of some of the People's Revolutionary Government (PRG) leaders and the mere establishing of relations with Cuba ignited U.S. political and ideological concern. This confused and hostile start was hard to overcome, even though Sally Shelton, Ortiz's replacement, attempted to reduce U.S. Grenadian tensions and reassure the Grenadians that we were not going to support Gairy's plans to stage an armed invasion from U.S. shores (illegal under U.S. law in any case).

Despite that effort to normalize relations, extraneous pressures interfered; the debacle in Iran, the Soviet "combat brigade" in Cuba, and a supposed Caribbean "circle of crisis" inclined the Carter administration increasingly toward hostility. Here, U.S. Liberal ideology may have encouraged an excessive confidence in the coercive efficiency of petty economic sanctions. The United States refused, for example, to permit Grenada to share in funds allocated for a program designed to help the region recover from Hurricane Allen.[48] The Reagan administration radically escalated the economic and military confrontation with Grenada. President Reagan cut off all U.S. aid in March 1981 and urged the EEC to deny Grenada a grant for its international airport.[49] This airport was the centerpiece of the PRG's plan for economic development through stimulating its tourist trade. The United States said the airport was uneconomic and designed for Soviet and Cuban military use. The United States did not make available evidence indicating that the airport was being prepared for military use.[50] Despite U.S. efforts to cut off funds, the airport received matériel and financing from Cuba, Libya, Venezuela, and later Europe and others.[51]

Official U.S. policy was one of "distancing" itself from Grenada as a way of

[48]Tim Shorrock, "Revo Out, US In," *Multinational Monitor* (December 1983). The NSC also, it is reported, considered but rejected a blockade of Grenada in the spring of 1980 (Michael Massing, "Grenada Before and After," *Atlantic Monthly* [February 1984], p. 81).

[49]In April 1981 the administration lobbied against an IMF loan that was supported on financial grounds by the director of the IMF, Jacques de Larosière, and in July of the same year attempted to stipulate that a four-million-dollar loan to the Caribbean Development Bank (of which Grenada is a full member) not be used in any part to fund loans to Grenada. The CDB, denouncing U.S. attempts at coercion, declined the loan under those conditions.

[50]Any airport suited for intercontinental jets, apparently, can be readily converted into a military air base. But the British contractors working on the airport (Plessey and Co.) said that they observed no specifically military construction. One can speculate that even a civilian international airport in Grenada would improve the airlift capacity of Cuba, reducing its costs and current dependence on the Soviet Union for the transport of men and matériel to Africa. After the airport was modified, it also could serve as a convenient base for extending Soviet air reconnaissance. But as the only airfield available to Cuba or the Soviet Union in the southern Caribbean, it would also make whatever air forces were stationed there extremely vulnerable in a crisis to U.S. interdiction or sabotage.

[51]U.S. admirals have noted the attractiveness of Grenada as a possible U.S. naval air station. Rumors also circulated in Grenada during 1982 to the effect that the Soviets had investigated

putting economic pressure on the NJM. But the Defense Department (or just the Navy?) gave the appearance of having more forcible measures in mind. In August 1981 a huge armada, the largest assembled since World War Two, churned the waters about Cuba. It also seemed to carry a none-too-subtle message for Grenada, for it included an amphibious landing on the island of Vieques (off Puerto Rico) code-named Amber, directed against "Amber and the Amberdines." Alarmed Grenadian officials noted topographic and other similarities between the landing exercise's simultaneous attack on two airports and Grenada, which has a district called Amber adjacent to one of its two airports, the controversial one being built with Cuban aid at Point Salines. (Grenadians also call their country Grenada and the Grenadines, in part to remind St. Vincent, their island neighbor, and the outside world that with their possession of Carriacou and other small northern islands, they too hold some of the Grenadine islands.)[52] In the spring of 1983 the CIA (apparently presenting the administration's plan) reportedly proposed to destabilize Grenada, but the proposal was rejected by the Senate Intelligence Oversight Committee.[53]

When, in June 1983, Prime Minister Bishop announced the formation of an electoral commission and visited the United States trying to avert the mounting confrontation, he met with Deputy Secretary of State Dam and National Security Adviser Clark. From the deputy secretary, Bishop received assurances that the United States would tolerate Grenada if it steered clear of a direct alliance with the Soviet bloc. From the national security adviser, on the other hand, Bishop received threats, apparently including the withdrawal of the American Medical School at St. George's (an important local source of revenue), unless Grenada agreed to change its form of government and to adopt policies in line with those of the United States.[54]

It may be the case that if the United States had embraced Bishop, he still would have fallen. Nonetheless, coercing him—narrowing his options—played into the hands of Coard and the military within Grenada determined to place the island on an authoritarian and pro-Soviet path. The United States helped

---

the possibility of using it as a submarine base. I have not found confirmation of this in the seized *Grenada Documents* (Washington, D.C.: U.S. State Department, 1984) of the PRG.

[52] Jackson Diehl, "Grenada Is at Ground Zero in Washington's Great Snubbing War," *Washington Post*, November 21, 1981.

[53] See Massing, p. 83, citing the *Washington Post*, February 27, 1983.

[54] See the minutes of the meeting between the three and a Grenadian aide in the U.S. State Department, *Grenada Documents*, Doc. 32:1–2. Judge Clark did not specify exactly how the United States would achieve these outcomes, but the State Department had been warning potential visitors to Grenada of dangers they might encounter on the island and of the inability of the United States to offer them diplomatic protection since we had refused to establish diplomatic relations with the PRG.

set the stage for the coup that engulfed Grenada in October, which in turn led to the intervention.

Despite the "success in a multilateral mode" hailed by Assistant Secretary of State Langhorne Motley,[55] the process of U.S. policy formation toward Grenada exhibited all the ills of ideological confusion, reliance on ineffective economic coercion, and bureaucratic competition. Something strategically more efficient can well be conceived, whether an accommodation with Bishop or a covert operation if the accommodation failed. But we cannot tell whether it would have worked. Given the polarizing pressures of the Cold War, a radical nationalist Grenada could have served as a logistics base for Cuban activities in Africa and provided facilities for the USSR that would have supplemented the Soviet relationship with Cuba. Both of these were hypothetical in 1983. Grenada, even if ruled by populist nationalists like Bishop, had good reasons to accommodate the United States, as Bishop repeatedly tried to do. The appeasement may have been in vain; for some, the invasion itself was the payoff of the Grenada crisis. UN condemnation soon faded, while the patriotic glow of the invasion restored the self-confidence of the U.S. national security managers and began to erase the Vietnam syndrome that had clouded the prestige of the U.S. military for the preceding ten years.

A Liberal Rescue?

A Liberal justification rests on different premises: not that the invasion added to U.S. prestige but that it rescued Grenadian citizens who deserved to be saved from a local catastrophe. (Their rescue, we should note, would then contribute to enlarging the Liberal community of nations, which served U.S. economic and strategic interests.) Liberal ideology appears in fact to have influenced U.S. strategic policy toward the Grenadian revolution, but much for the worse. What, therefore, should Liberal policy have been?

Could it have been justified, Liberals should ask, by what it did not for the United States or the states of the eastern Caribbean but for the Grenadians? Should we agree that the people of Grenada were rescued from the "thuggish" leaders of a coup that had not only executed Maurice Bishop but also, as Bishop declared just before his death, "turned its guns against the people"?

Many shrank from condoning this invasion. Even those who accepted the view that the people of Grenada were rescued say that endorsing an invasion

[55] See the House of Commons report, *Grenada*, Appendix. But even if the operation is judged to be legal under the provisions of the OECS Charter, it was not an operation by the OECS. It was planned and conducted by an ad hoc group of states, including most of the OECS, Jamaica, Barbados, and, most obviously from a military standpoint, the United States. In this respect the Grenada operation resembled the multinational force sent to Beirut. For the legal debate, see the articles by C. Joyner, John Norton Moore, and Detlev Vagts in the *American Journal of International Law* 78, 1 (January 1984), pp. 131–71.

and overriding the principle of nonintervention could set precedents so dangerous that we should never justify interventions, even if they appear to be "humanitarian." If we agree that the United States justly invaded Grenada, they say, the Soviets could have justified invading Afghanistan. The national Liberals warn that should humanitarian rescue, democratic enlargement, or cosmopolitan intervention become the rule, then the United States should invade Burma, Zaire, and dozens of other countries suffering from "brutal dictatorships." The Tanzanian invasion of Uganda that rid the Ugandans of Idi Amin and the Indian invasion of East Pakistan that rid the people of what is now Bangladesh are often said to have met the standard criteria for humanitarian intervention against "massacre" or "enslavement."[56] National Liberals prepared to accept those humanitarian interventions as justifiable exceptions to the principle of nonintervention object that Grenada was not a justifiable humanitarian intervention. Genocide was not occurring. Instead ordinary oppression was what the Grenadians faced. Left-wing cosmopolitans saw a populist regime undergoing domestic crisis, but the Reagan administration hardly seemed an appropriate rescuer. Some right-wing cosmopolitans had little difficulty endorsing an intervention whose aim was to establish democratic rule. But even cosmopolitan Liberals, prepared to endorse humanitarian rescues and prodemocratic interventions, warned that we should have waited and negotiated, explored diplomatic accommodation rather than rushed precipitately to military measures. Most significantly, they add, the United States didn't wait to obtain collective agreement from the Organization of American States and the United Nations. Thus we needlessly failed to fulfill the requirements of international law.

These are serious objections. Setting precedents and obtaining multilateral endorsement are important aspects of international order. Nonintervention is a vital rule for encouraging order in a world without international government. But there are deeper roots for Liberals for nonintervention. Nonintervention also rests on a respect for the rights of individuals to establish their own way of life free from foreign interference. These principles are shared by both national and cosmopolitan Liberals. When are those principled interests clear enough to create a common ground favoring a humanitarian-democratic rescue?[57]

[56] The words are Walzer's from *Just and Unjust Wars*.
[57] Interestingly, Michael Walzer, a "National Liberal," acknowledges the need to make such determinations: "If the invaders are welcomed by a clear majority of the people, then it would be odd to accuse them [the interveners] of any crime at all. But it is almost certain that such a welcome will be extended only in circumstances that make for the three exceptions that I take up below" (fn. 7 of Walzer, "The Moral Standing of States," pp. 216–37). The three standard exceptions are discussed above. I am arguing that there are additional circumstances, reflecting democratic endorsement, which I outline in the Grenada case. For another version of a democratic argument, see Michael Levitin, "The Law of Force and the Force of Law," *Harvard International Law Journal* 27 (1986), pp. 621–57.

First, the people actually need to be rescued. Their oppression must be clear to any humane observer, or they themselves or their representatives, through their actions or words, must have declared themselves to be oppressed and have called for a rescue. The oppression must be of such a character that national Liberals should endorse an invasion. That is, national liberation, counter-intervention, or massacre and enslavement are occurring or—the Liberal paradigm being extended—there are such other violations of human rights that the people of the oppressed country *make known their own desire for a rescue.*

Second, the rescue will reliably halt the suffering. It will end the killing or address starvation and establish authentic self-determination. Humanitarian intervention cannot be an excuse for imperial aggression and still be humane.

Third, the intervention must be proportional to the suffering endured and likely to be endured without an intervention. Countries cannot, any more than villages, be destroyed in order to be saved. Intervenors must be able to account morally for the expected casualties of an invasion both to their own soldiers and to innocent victims, the population of the country rescued.

When those conditions are satisfied, Liberals can claim to have taken emergency measures that permit a people to exercise the self-determination that their own government has denied them. Liberals also say that the rescue of this people in this instance outweighs the danger of denigrating a rule of international law because the purposes of law were served and the intervention was conducted as prudently as possible. Let us examine each of those criteria in the Grenadian crisis.

First, the strongest case that can be made for this invasion is neither massacre nor enslavement. A "massacre" and some "enslavement" did take place. Up to a hundred may have died when the coup leaders turned their guns on the demonstration in St. George's; the people did experience fear and a loss of liberty. But even when we consider the total population of Grenada, there was not enough of either of those injustices to justify a foreign intervention in the name of the Grenadian people. Instead the invasion might be justified by arguing that it did what the Grenadian people wanted done. It violated the territorial integrity and political independence of Grenada at the request of the Grenadians.

Defeat of course does not mean acceptance. The defeat of an island with a population of one hundred thousand, an area of 345 square kilometers, and a GDP per capita of $930 (1983) by a nuclear-armed superpower with a population two thousand times, and a GDP per capita more than ten times its size hardly constitutes a surprise in the annals of military history. But when we consider the potential for resistance on a thickly forested, mountainous island and a Grenadian army of almost one thousand regulars and more than twenty-five hundred militia, two aspects of the invasion make us realize there is something special to be explained. Military casualties were low: twenty-one Grenadian soldiers, nineteen U.S. soldiers.[58] The militia does not appear to have fought. And the people of Grenada gave an overwhelming welcome to the U.S. (and later Caribbean) soldiers. In one poll taken soon after the invasion, 91 percent welcomed the toppling of the coup by U.S. and Caribbean forces.[59] In a later, scientifically conducted poll taken in December 1983 and January 1984, 86 percent welcomed the multinational operation as "a good thing."[60]

The reasons for the welcome are not far to seek. Coard's coup of October 14 and General Austin's soldiers in the massacre of October 19 destroyed the hopes of Grenadians who had welcomed the New Jewel Movement's "revolution" of March 1979 as a step toward Socialist democracy. They also destroyed the hopes of the equally numerous (and generally older) Grenadians who had rejoiced in the fall of Sir Eric Gairy's bizarre and heavy-handed regime. These hopes had rested on the public commitments made by Maurice Bishop and his followers to create a new democracy from the village up to the national level.[61] Bishop had achieved an impressive degree of village participation. But he began to move Grenada toward electoral democracy only in June 1983, when he appointed an independent lawyer from Trinidad to head an electoral commission. Those less enthused by the prospects of Socialism retained considerable respect for a government with democratic promise and, by international standards, humane practices. Grenada, after the fall of Gairy and before the coup by Coard, experienced no revolutionary terror, even though the rights of a free press and a speedy trial had been curbed in order, Bishop claimed, to meet the threat of foreign intervention—a threat U.S. militaristic diplomacy seemed designed to stimulate.

During the summer of 1983 a long-running split in the NJM widened. The faction following Bishop's democratic vision and those following Coard's dictatorship of the party (a faction described on the island as Stalinist) accused each other of plotting a takeover. Coard's faction struck on October 14, placing Bishop under house arrest. Coard, though leader of the dominant faction in the party, had no apparent popular support. Coard then disappeared from view, leaving General Austin in charge of the army and thus the state that the party had created.

[58] The twenty-four Cubans killed were killed defending their own installations, not defending the RMC, according to Fidel Castro.

[59] Associated Press, "Weinberger Says U.S. Forces to Quit Grenada," *New York Times*, November 12, 1983, p. 1.

[60] Poll by St. Augustine Research Associates of Trinidad and Tobago reported in the *Nation* (Barbados), January 20, 1984.

[61] Bishop made formal commitments to the leaders of CARICOM to hold an election, as noted by Payne, *The International Crisis in the Caribbean*, p. 149. Selwyn Strachan, minister of national mobilization of the PRG, explained Bishop's strategy to me in January 1982, in Grenada.

Outraged by the arrest of their popular leader and led by Bishop's followers among the democratic faction, between three to ten thousand Grenadians (almost 10 percent of the population) marched on October 19 through the capital of St. George's to free Bishop. After the crowd had been welcomed by part of the garrison of the main fort, other troops obedient to Austin attacked the crowd, indiscriminately fired on it, and killed between twenty to one hundred civilians. The soldiers then seized Bishop and the other leaders of his faction present, stood them up against a wall, and, from our one eyewitness account, summarily executed them. A search designed to root out Bishop supporters soon followed.[62] It was this massacre and the threat of more like it that apparently led Grenada's governor-general, Sir Paul Scoon, to acquiesce in the call for an intervention urged upon him by Prime Minister Tom Adams of neighboring Barbados.

Second, there were good reasons to expect that a U.S. intervention, especially when accompanied by forces from Grenada's neighbors, would succeed in reestablishing democratic self-determination. Resistance was likely to be slight, partly because the people themselves sought to get rid of the military regime. And the traditional U.S. first choice in its intervention policy had been democratic governance, which was also the demand and policy of Grenada's neighbors. But does a local welcome allow us to endorse the Reagan administration—friend of such dictators as Haiti's Papa Doc Duvalier and the Philippines' Ferdinand Marcos and paymaster of the covert war on Nicaragua—in its self-appointed role as agent of humanitarian liberation? The answer is that we cannot, and we don't have to.

The liberation of Grenada did not rest on President Reagan's "goodwill" alone. Nor, despite all Washington's efforts, did it rest on stimulating an invitation. Sir Paul Scoon—a widely respected official who had cordial ties with both conservative and NJM islanders—and the elected leaders of five neighboring states of the Caribbean (Barbados, Dominica, Jamaica, St. Kitts-Nevis, and St. Lucia) all called for the invasion.[63] Each of these states has impeccably democratic credentials, but unlike the Reagan administration, each had also come

[62] See O'Shaughnessy, pp. 133–39, for an account of these events based on eyewitness interviews. For background information, see Reynold A. Burrowes, *Revolution and Rescue in Grenada* (New York: Greenwood Press, 1988); Peter M. Dunn and Bruce W. Watson, eds., *American Intervention in Grenada: The Implications of Operation "Urgent Fury"* (Boulder, Colo.: Westview Press, 1985); and Kai P. Schoenhals and Richard A. Melanson, *Revolution and Intervention in Grenada* (Boulder, Colo.: Westview Press, 1985).

[63] See the speech by the Barbadian Prime Minister J. M. G. Adams in House of Commons, 2d Report, *Grenada*, Appendix C. I also benefited from interviews from John Connell, deputy ambassador of Barbados to the United Nations (March 30, 1984) and Charles Fleming (St. Lucia Mission to the United Nations) and a U.S. State Department official (who wished to remain off the record).

to a neighborly accommodation with the Grenadian revolution.[64] Their endorsement (not Washington's military implementation) and their guarantee of Grenadian self-determination (not Reagan's) should have convinced us to condone this invasion as a way to rescue the Grenadian people and restore their self-determination.[65]

On October 21 the Organization of Eastern Caribbean States (OECS)—Grenada absent—quarantined Grenada and voted for armed intervention according to the provisions of Article 8 (concerning collective defense against "external" attack; Grenada, however, a member of the OECS, was the perceived threat). The OECS then requested the participation of regional and favorably inclined extraregional military forces. (It sounded out the United States, France, Canada, Venezuela, and the United Kingdom.) On the twentieth the United States had diverted its Lebanon-bound task force to Grenadian waters.[66] On the twenty-second and twenty-third, at the request of Barbados and St. Lucia, the Caribbean Community (CARICOM, composed of all the anglophonic states of the Caribbean) met to consider the crisis in Grenada. After they approved the quarantine of Grenada announced by the OECS two days before, all but one of the members of CARICOM agreed to the following initiative:[67]

[64]Those who criticize the invasion for having been unilateral or lacking in international consultation adamantly refuse to credit the moral and political judgment of Grenada's neighboring states in the Caribbean. Unlike the OAS or the UN, the Organization of Eastern Caribbean States lacked a clear legal mandate to engage in a collective security intervention. On this purely legal ground, the critics have a point. But the critics strangely seem also to prefer the political and moral judgment of distant states in Latin America and in Europe, Asia, and Africa to the judgment of Grenada's close neighbors, who called for the invasion. These are neighbors whose democratic practices reflected Grenadian hopes, whose security was proximately involved, whose economies were closely linked to that of Grenada, whose Afro-Caribbean citizens have friends and relatives in Grenada.

[65]What, then, should we make of the nonparticipation of other Caribbean neighbors: Belize, the Bahamas, Trinidad, St. Vincent, and Guyana? We do not know their reasons for not joining the intervention. But we can note that neither Bahamas nor Belize has forces to spare from its own very grave security problems (crime and the Guatemalans respectively). They are also the most distant. Trinidad and St. Vincent had long-standing disputes with Grenada over the ownership of the Grenadines (between St. Vincent and Grenada) and over political differences (the NJM had accused the *Trinidad Express* of engaging in propaganda destabilization). Their nonparticipation was at least fortunate. And Guyana would not have fitted well into an intervention justified as a restoration of democratic self-determination.

[66]House of Commons, 2d Report, op. cit., para. 26–31.

[67]Trinidad and Guyana, both of which later opposed the invasion, had condemned the coup and the killings and had voted for the Trinidad resolution at the CARICOM meeting. This resolution included a strong condemnation of the coup and the killings. Trinidad had unilaterally and immediately embargoed Grenada. But many Caribbean diplomats questioned the sincerity of Guyana's position, some going so far as to suggest Guyana, itself the target of an earlier CARICOM condemnation for corrupt and coercive electoral practices, had warned the RMC of the impending invasion.

> (a) the immediate establishment of a broad based civilian government of national reconciliation whose composition was acceptable to the Governor General. The primary function of that government would be the putting into place of arrangements for the holding of elections at the earliest possible date.
> (b) acceptance of fact finding mission comprising eminent nationals of CARICOM states.
> (c) the putting into place of arrangements to ensure the safety of nationals of other countries in Grenada and/or the evacuation where desired.
> (d) the acceptance of deployment in Grenada of a Peace-keeping Force, comprising contingents contributed by CARICOM states.[68]

Sensing that they could not obtain the support of all of CARICOM for prompt military action should the RMC not accept these demands and fearing that accepting CARICOM negotiations would entangle them in endless delays, the OECS, Barbados, and Jamaica walked out of the meeting. These conservative democracies, particularly those closely neighboring Grenada in the eastern Caribbean, were especially determined to rid themselves of what they saw as the brutal and ruthless regime then controlling Grenada.[69]

Third, the human costs of the Grenadian invasion could be expected to be proportional, much less than the sufferings the people were enduring and would likely endure without an intervention. The importance that Grenadians themselves put on democratic governance was perhaps best demonstrated by the willingness of thousands to challenge a heavily armed military coup. "No Bish, no revo," Grenadians on the street corners later explained to reporters. When the military turned its guns against the crowd and executed Bishop and his followers, General Austin's soldiers trampled on these hopes. The soldiers also broke the pattern of civil governance the NJM had established. In the days following the massacre, neither General Austin nor Mr. Coard made any attempt, according to all the reports we had and have, to arrest the soldiers who had conducted the massacre.

At the same time there was good reason to expect that resistance to an invasion would be slight. The Coard-Austin regime had no apparent support outside the army and the party cadres. While Cuban worker-soldiers might well have resisted any invasion supported by the United States, they were as yet small in numbers and had not fortified the island. An invasion endorsed by neighbors from the Caribbean and conducted with care for civilian lives—as this one appears to have been with the one glaring exception (avowedly acci-

[68] See the speech before Parliament by Prime Minister George Chambers of Trinidad and Tobago, Appendix D, of the House of Commons, 2d Report, *Grenada*.
[69] See the text of the letter, dated October 23, 1983, from the OECS to the United States requesting U.S. help in the *New York Times*, October 25, 1983.

dental) of the bombing of the mental hospital—could expect to meet with little resistance and few casualties. To Grenada's governor-general, to Grenada's Caribbean neighbors, the rescue seemed worth the risks.

Tanzania's invasion of Uganda in 1979 and India's invasion of East Pakistan in 1971 also displayed motives that were far from being purely disinterested. But suffering peoples were rescued in ways and by agents that gave rise to a reliable guarantee of self-determination. In both those cases the suffering endured by the rescued population was much greater than that endured by the Grenadians, but so it had to be to justify the much greater degree of resistance and larger number of casualties that these interventions involved. In very few other interventions would a "humanitarian intervention" have been humane. In Afghanistan the Soviets rescued one bloody Kabul faction from another. Neither had support outside the capital, and armed resistance was widespread.

Others who would accept humanitarian interventions, such as those in Uganda and East Pakistan, deny the justice of the invasion of Grenada. They say the invasion was precipitate and lacked international endorsement. These objections rest upon the generally persuasive view that precipitate and unilateral actions in a world armed with nuclear weapons endanger the survival of all of us. But Grenada was a particular case.

Should General Austin have had more time? All those sympathetic to Grenada should have wished that Coard and Austin would have denounced and arrested those responsible for the killings or, better still, that the Grenadian people themselves could have overthrown the coup. But neither Coard nor Austin, nor other officials who were part of the coup, criticized the killings. Instead they started to round up Bishop's supporters and declared a shoot-on-sight curfew.

Time then appears to have been slipping away from the people of Grenada. They had risked their lives to demonstrate against the coup; soldiers had attacked them. Despite some early disaffection, the professional soldiers cleaved to Austin. There was little enthusiasm for Austin, and Coard and some of his faction must have regretted the deaths of their NJM comrades. Still, the army composed of the poor and the young seemed to be settling into a professional subservience to General Austin. However weak they were as a national military force, they had shown themselves to be more than adequate as a coercive police force. And the party was settling into the bureaucratic and authoritarian definition of its role that Coard had favored.

Castro denounced the killing of Bishop and his ministers, but he did not withdraw Cuba's logistical support or its six hundred worker-soldiers. Moreover, as word of an impending invasion including U.S. troops leaked out, Cuban soldiers fortified the airfield. Fidel then told the Cuban worker-soldiers to come home with their construction tools or be buried by them. Under these circumstances, additional time could only mean additional fortification, additional troops from the outside (from Cuba?), and even an opportunity to round up U.S. citizens as hostages. Caribbean leaders were worried that a blockade strategy would have made civilians, their friends and relatives, the frontline victims of the confrontation. An invasion soon might have become morally disproportionate in Grenadian, Caribbean, and American casualties. General Austin would then have been secure; the people of Grenada, politically shackled. The rescuers of Grenada did act precipitately; the Grenadians were at the edge of a precipice.

That conclusion reveals both the justification and the moral dilemma at the root of the rescue/invasion of Grenada. Wasn't this, as many critics charge, an U.S. invasion? Why didn't the United States obtain agreement for a collective intervention from American friends in the Organization of American States or from the United Nations? The United States and Caribbean states could then have avoided flouting international law. But practically such agreement was impossible. Following on the crisis of the Falklands, the renewed Cold War, and the crisis in Lebanon, neither the OAS nor the UN was likely to act. In part their reluctance reflected fundamental weaknesses in those organizations. But it also reflected the longer-term failure of the United States to cultivate these institutions of multilateral diplomacy that might have made international cooperation in a crisis more likely. That failure was no accident. It was part of a Cold War designed to marginalize Communist opponents and, by the 1970s, their Third World sympathizers.

The invasion, which could be justified in the name of the basic human rights, welfare, and self-determination of the Grenadian people, also served to strengthen an antirevolutionary strategy adopted by the Reagan administration. Its steady object since 1981 had been to undermine the revolution, which had, it appears, a majority of support on the island. The invasion that rescued Bishop's followers was ironically the culmination of a policy designed to destroy Bishop's revolutionary movement.

International organizations with their constituted impartiality—which means multipartiality—are designed to avoid such dilemmas. In the post–Cold War era, the UN Security Council serves as a global jury of peers charged with making the difficult judgments concerning when "international peace and security" justifies overriding sovereign independence. The international community recognizes that "international peace" includes the prohibition of genocide. In the 1990s, moreover, the OAS formally, through its Santiago Commitment and Resolution 1080, declared that established democratic governments should not be overthrown, as President Aristide's government was in Haiti. Reflecting the significance of the multilateral difference—and the end of the Cold War—the UN Security Council then voted 12–0 in favor of U.S.-sponsored Resolution 940 authorizing the use of force to restore Haiti's elected

President Aristide to power.[70] Even more tenuously, the Security Council practice seems to endorse the view that state sovereignty does not preclude the rescue of populations from mass starvation, as was occurring in Somalia in late 1992.

CONCLUSIONS

Realists, Socialists, and Liberals each defend and each override the principle of nonintervention. The Realists do so to promote the national interest and especially national security; the Marxist, to promote Socialist revolution; the Liberals, to protect and promote human rights. Each of the differing types of Liberal—right-wing cosmopolitan, left-wing cosmopolitan, and national—justifies intervention using the same logic and arguments (with sign reversed) that it uses to justify when states should uphold nonintervention. Right-wing cosmopolitans want to protect from intervention democratic capitalist states; left-wing cosmopolitans want to protect from intervention all states that guarantee the basic rights of their citizens. The right-wing cosmopolitans justify interventions against any state that violates civil and economic liberties, including radical democratic (non-Liberal, democratic anticapitalist) states; the left-wing cosmopolitans, against those states that violate the basic social welfare rights of their citizens, whether Liberal, capitalist, or democratic or all three. The national Liberals raise the hurdles somewhat higher, leaving much more room for national struggle, variation, and oppression. They insist that revolutions are matters for domestic citizens. But when one people struggles to be free of the oppression inflicted by another, when a second state has already intervened in an ongoing civil war (and one needs to intervene to right the balance), and when a state turns against its own citizens and makes all notion of a national community ridiculous through its acts of slaughter or slavery, then the principle of nonintervention needs to be overridden in order to achieve the very purposes of national self-determination that the rule is designed to protect.

The complexity of hard cases, where conscience and power meet, erodes the distinct lines. Grenada illustrates well the complexities of applied Realism and applied Liberalism. Because the island was so weak, little security was at stake, and the pursuit of power became ambiguous. Because the crisis did threaten oppression but did not fit the typical Liberal exceptions to nonintervention, Liberal conscience was confused.

[70] For the general issue, see Thomas Franck, "The Emerging Right to Democratic Governance," *American Journal of International Law* 86 (January 1992), pp. 46–91; Tom Farer, "A Paradigm of Legitimate Intervention," in Lori Damrosch, ed., *Enforcing Restraint* (New York: Council on Foreign Relations, 1993), pp. 316–47; and Jason Kamras, "Towards a New Paradigm for Just Military Intervention," Princeton senior thesis (1995).

When, for the Realists, national survival is threatened either by or by not intervening, Realists give simple answers. Liberals tend to agree with them, with the proviso and presumption that no fellow Liberal state could pose such a threat. But where survival is not at stake, Realist arguments tend to rest on contingent assessments of alternative policy outcomes and nebulous estimates of prestige, as they did in U.S. policy toward Grenada. Liberals then will strongly disagree if the intervention violates their principles.

When, for the Liberals, nations need to be liberated from foreign yoke, foreign intervention, or genocide, all Liberals respond clearly and together. Realists tend to disagree; those are none of their concerns. When Liberals face powerful oppressors, such as was the USSR or is China, the differences among Liberals disappear. A cosmopolitan intervention to promote democracy or basic human rights is unlikely to be proportional except when the authoritarian oppression has led to genocide, and even then it may be so costly as to preclude anything but symbolic action or economic sanctions. When faced with a weak oppressor, Liberal differences in policy expand. Proportionality allows more room for choice because the costs of intervention are low. For many right-wing cosmopolitans, revolutionary Grenada was a legitimate target. For some left-wing cosmopolitans, post–1983 coup Grenada became one. For national Liberals Grenada's travails never reached any one of the three standard exceptions. But following the violent coup of October 1983, perhaps it should have. Grenada was special in a morally crucial respect. Its people seem to have called for a rescue, and that call bridged the differences in conscience and could have united national and cosmopolitan Liberals in a rescue. If so, such rescues by democratic appeal should constitute another broad Liberal exception to nonintervention. Indeed this exception seems now to be emerging as a standard of international law, but only when interventions are approved by multilateral consent.

The actual rescue of Grenada, however, served to support a policy of Cold War interventionism and Liberal imperialism that at least two of the Liberals, nationalists and left-wing cosmopolitans, found reprehensible. Such is the terrain of hard choice.

CHAPTER TWELVE

International Distribution

Michael W. Doyle and Peter Furia[1]

MR. DORGAN. If I might interrupt you, where in that list of goals is just the plain, unselfish responsibility to reach out with a helping hand to people who need help?

MR. BROWN. I am quoting his [Secretary of State James Baker's] five—

MR. DORGAN. I understand that—

MR. BROWN. (continuing) Statements [goals for United States foreign aid] and they are what they are.

MR. DORGAN. I understand . . . the use of our dollars to pursue macroeconomic reform and growth strategies in various areas, some of which is fine, but that doesn't necessarily always relate to the needs of the people who are hungry and impoverished in the lowest-income countries of the world . . . I was just curious, in terms of those strategies. If the money we provide in Congress is used by an administration with those strategies, where in those strategies represents the desire simply to reach out the hand of assistance to people who need help?

An Exchange between Congressman Dorgan of the Select Committee on Hunger and Mr. Brown of the U.S. State Department[2]

[1]Peter Furia did the empirical research for and wrote the first draft of the "Foreign Aid" section of this chapter and contributed valuable critical commentary on other parts of the chapter. The exchange quoted is from United States House of Representatives Select Committee on Hunger, *A.I.D. Priorities: Time for a Change?*, Hearings, House Document SN 101-22 (Washington, D.C.: Government Printing Office, July 25, 1990).

[2]World Bank, *World Bank Development Report* (1989), "Table 30: Income Distribution and ICP Estimates of GDP," pp. 222–23.

INTERNATIONAL INTERVENTIONS ARE in many ways ordinary topics in international relations. Thucydides discussed them at length in his history of the origins of the Athenian empire, the expedition to Mitylene, to Melos, and to Sicily. They are also part of the wider tradition of the just and unjust use of force. Thus they are part of the traditional discourse of international relations. International distributive justice, on the other hand, is different from the traditional practice of soldiers and diplomats. Soldiers don't usually worry about the economic conditions of their military opponents other than as a further object of rivalry and attack, such as in economic warfare or a siege.

Now, especially since the 1970s, it has become a contentious international issue. It arose with the debate over the New International Economic Order, when "Southern" (Third World) countries sought to renegotiate the distribution of control and income in the world economy. But we can trace back the issue somewhat earlier, to World War II and to diplomatic demands of Latin America, Nazi Germany, and Fascist Italy in the 1930s for a larger share, for a redistribution to the then "have-not" nations from the haves. And today international distribution is an issue because of what appears to be an unprecedented degree of inequality in the world economy.

In this chapter I examine that inequality, the responses our international political philosophies make to international inequality, and the policy debate over the actual evolution of foreign aid. Do the rich have a right to what they now own? Does the distribution of foreign aid respond to the debate over international economic justice? Does global inequality warrant a global New Deal?

GLOBAL INEQUALITY

How unequal is the world? A provocative (and impressionistic) story by *Fellowship* magazine in February 1974 stirred considerable interest in this issue. It asked its readers to imagine the globe—without borders—as a statistically sampled village of a hundred human beings. In that village of one hundred, it noted, six would be North Americans, nine Europeans, and three Japanese. They would have more than half the total village (global) income. The other eighty-two villagers would live on less than the other half. Sixty to seventy villagers (few in North America, Europe, or Japan) would be illiterate. Fifty villagers would be undernourished. The village would have the equivalent of one college education.

While impressive, such comparisons exaggerate the real purchasing power effect of differences in monetary income, because money delivers more necessary goods in a very poor economy. A 1989 World Bank study that attempted to control for that exaggeration by using purchasing power measures of real income nonetheless found that the differences in per capita national income (GDP) between the poorest group and the richest group of economies were on the order of fifty to one. This ratio is double the greatest disparities found within even the most unequal countries, between the richest and the poorest fractions of the population (highest 10 percent and lowest 20 percent, twenty-five to one in Brazil in 1989).[2] In 1992 some 1.4 billion people, more than a quarter of the world's population, lived in "absolute poverty." This is 400 million *(40 percent)* more poor than fifteen years before. One in 4 lives without the regular food, health care, and shelter needed to have a productive life. In 1960 the richest fifth of world population had thirty times the income of the poorest fifth; by 1989 the ratio was sixty to one.[3] Population growth, at 90 million per year, and unemployment, at 400 million in the South, compound these problems. To hold even the rate of unemployment requires 40 million new jobs per year, far beyond the current rate, while failure to contain population growth in the next ten years will result in an additional 4 billion human beings in the year 2050.[4]

The globe was not always this way. The fourteenth-century Arab traveler Ibn Batutah highlighted Cairo, Toledo, Damascus, Delhi, Cambay in India (all of which he visited) and mentioned the fame of Milan and Venice in Europe when he discussed the leading cities of the world. He also noted the beauty and comfort and safety of Timbuktu, in the Sahel of West Africa. Would anyone today equate the standard of living of a city in the Sahel with London, Paris, Tokyo, or New York?[5]

REDISTRIBUTION: FOR AND AGAINST

For contemporary Realist scholars, international economic justice among existing nations is not an important normative issue. They doubt the basis for global cosmopolitan international morality in the first place. Realist scholars find international redistribution somewhat utopian, as we shall hear. Marxist Socialists, on the other hand, while at least in theory concerned with the "workers of the world," consider international attempts at gradualist redistribution insufficient and perhaps something of a sham. Thus the issue has devolved almost by default primarily to the Liberals, with the two other schools serving as, occasionally, very effective critics.

Liberals

The Liberals present us with three major views. The first portrays inequalities as the product of imperial theft, a violation of global common law that then requires reparations. The second, an utilitarian view, focuses on global humani-

[3] UN Development Program, *Human Development Report 1992* (New York: Oxford University Press, 1992).
[4] UN Fund for Population Activities, *State of the World Population 1992* and *Population and the Environment: The Challenge Ahead* (UNFPA, 1992).
[5] Ibn Batutah, *Journals*, trans. H. A. R. Gibb (London: Hakluyt, 1958).

tarianism. The third examines international justice as an implicit contract among free individuals that should be judged by the standards of fairness.

1. ***Global Common Law.*** Present inequalities in this first view are said to be the result of imperial theft. The victims, or their grandchildren, demand reparations. This view, once held by many Third World radicals (among them the eminent Guyanese historian Walter Rodney), draws to our attention the documented history of slavery, land seizure in South Africa and Rhodesia, the widespread appropriation of mines and plantations, and the exploitation of cheap produce and products for consumers of Europe and North America.[6] Famous cases of the theft of Aztec and Inca gold and the crops produced by slave labor and other indentured and underpaid labor are too numerous to detail. Even where colonialism did produce some benefits—for example, education—these were designed in the first instance to serve the imperialists.

In the name of the descendants of those who suffered, contemporary Third World intellectuals demand reparations for theft and kidnap. The great-great-grandfathers were done wrong; the great-great-grandchildren seek recompense—with, on the conventional international lending principle, compounded interest, which (we should note) will be a large sum. This presents a plausible moral case, especially given the current poverty of some of the most exploited areas such as northeast Brazil, Zaire, Bangladesh, and parts of India.

But claims are complex for the following reasons.

a. Is there an international statute of limitations? Are citizens of the wealthy North responsible for the crimes of their great-great-grandfathers? If so, on this principle does Britain also owe reparations to the United States for colonialism? Does Rome to Britain? Mongols to Ukrainians?

b. If we do owe, how much do we owe? Consider what small sums stolen or borrowed in 1800 are now worth with compounded interest. For example, the real estate value of Manhattan (bought for twenty-four dollars in 1626) would now, it has been calculated, be worth less than the current value of the twenty-four dollars compounded annually at current interest rates of twenty-four dollars over 370 years.

c. Whom do we pay? Do you pay elites in the poor South who may be wealthier than U.S. or French or British taxpayers?[7]

d. If we want to make sure that the money actually reaches those most in need, how much interference is tolerable? Should we also make sure that those in the North most connected to the theft pay (those who inherited wealth from slaveowners or slave merchants, for example)?

[6] Walter Rodney, *How Europe Underdeveloped Africa* (Cambridge, Mass.: Harvard University Press, 1981) offers a Marxist explanation of global theft; Liberals too should be concerned about the alleged theft irrespective of what motivated it.

[7] A valuable discussion of a number of these issues can be found in Richard Cooper, "A New International Economic Order for Mutual Gain," *Foreign Policy* (Spring 1977), pp. 66–120.

The complications of international ownership led one U.S. senator (Hayakawa) to dismiss such claims (to the Panama Canal) with the widely quoted remark "We stole it fair and square." Liberal values do not permit fair and square thefts. Both sides of the debate thus score points. The absolute status of international property is far from morally secure, yet the moral complexity of reparations does recommend that we consider other avenues toward justice.

2. ***Utilitarianism.*** This offers a recrimination-free approach that focuses on the needs of the destitute. Peter Singer in a classic article argues that we should base our distribution of goods on values that are common to all mankind—i.e., saving lives, avoiding harm. Liberal and cosmopolitan in its assumptions, it treats all humanity and individuality as ends, irrespective of state borders or class division.[8]

Singer focuses on the most desperate problem of international distributive justice, the plight of the starving. He wrote in 1971, in the midst of the famine in Bengal, but many other disasters have come since, and there are more than enough crises for our continuing concern. He says that charity is not a sign of our generosity but an imperative duty. And this point he makes in an unforgettable analogy.

Imagine walking by a pool of shallow water and seeing a two-year-old child drowning in it. What should you do? Obviously, he notes, you should walk in and save the child. So, he adds, just that simply you should aid people starving in the world.[9] But then many would object that:

a. Starving people are foreigners, and some are on the other side of the world.
b. Other people don't provide aid. Why should I?
c. I can't end the starvation unless all the rich also aid.
d. Aid is costly. I don't have enough to spare and still meet my other needs.
e. It's government's—my country's—not my personal, responsibility.

Singer takes up each of the objections in turn.

a. *Foreigners.* Would it make a difference if the child in the pool was not yours? Or if it took place not in your hometown? Obviously not.

b. *Other people don't aid the starving, so why should I?* Would it make a difference if three other people were standing around and doing nothing?

c. *Too many people are starving; can't save all?* What if there are ten children drowning? Shouldn't you save as many as you can?

[8] Peter Singer, "Famine, Affluence, and Morality," *Philosophy and Public Affairs* 1, 3 (Spring 1972), p. 229–43, and Beitz, ed., *International Ethics*, pp. 247–61.

[9] Singer also grounds his argument in a utilitarian critique of northern government expenditures in the crucial famine year. What is the implication, he asks, given that Australia spent more money on the Sydney Opera House or Britain more on the development of supersonic transport aircraft than on famine relief, pp. 247–48?

d. *Too costly to aid starving?* If you are wearing your best dress or suit, should you still jump in? Of course.

e. *It is a government responsibility?* Yes, but if lifeguards aren't present, should you shrug your shoulders?

A stronger objection: What if it is truly costly? Suppose the children are swept away in a deep, raging river and rescue is a risk to your own life. Then, Singer at last acknowledges, it seems different. There is no moral obligation; instead rescue becomes an act for heroes. But how much risk, or cost, is less than life-threatening? Singer argues that for a pure utilitarian, the answer is: At least until your own life is at risk too. This means that you should, if necessary, reduce your real income to the poverty or starving line. Mother Teresa thus is doing the right thing, but are any of the rest of us? Singer then provides a more accommodating version of his ethic. He suggests that at least we should reduce our income significantly, in order to aid, that is, by 40, 30, 20 percent. Or even, less demandingly, we should do something: agitate, petition, and try to persuade the government to supplement our efforts to aid the world's desperate.

Powerful as this ethic is, it leaves many questions even for the well intentioned. Does it apply to lesser inequality, or does it hold only in an emergency?[10] To state the charge provocatively, do we have a moral obligation to act in order to prevent children from perhaps catching colds when their parents don't take them out of the safe but chilly pool of water? Moreover, in less than clear emergencies do not other principles begin to have relevant weight? For example, does foreign assistance disrupt local cultural stability? Are the right people being taxed to pay for the assistance (rich more than poor)? Is there an appropriate international institution to distribute the aid in a way that discourages paternalism, that ensures that no one state acquires unmerited international influence, that avoids coercion in the raising of aid and also exploitation of the generous? Does the child-adult analogy assign too much innocence to the South, too much authority to the North? These problems are the typical concerns that arise in moral political practice; they acquire additional weight as one moves away from emergency, life-and-death to "merely" chronic deprivation situations.

3. ***International "Justice as Fairness."*** Utilitarians appeal to preexisting common moral standards that should apply to each individual. Rawlsian advo-

[10] While Singer formulates his ethic in terms of emergencies and not in terms of lesser inequalities, the two are closely related in practice. Perhaps the simplest way to see this is to consider that even given a severe drought in the United States, there is little (if any) chance of Americans' experiencing famine conditions. Utilitarians should have no problem imploring us to care about the 90 percent of the forty thousand deaths per day in the world caused by nonemergency conditions of chronic hunger.

cates of rights-based "justice as fairness" explain how separate individuals could converge on agreed standards for what is fair for the overall distribution of rights and valued primary goods.

How do we decide what is a fair set of standards? John Rawls's *A Theory of Justice* says, as did Rousseau and Kant, that we should contemplate a hypothetical contract.[11] What would be agreed to by free individuals under conditions of impartiality, which he describes as a "veil of ignorance"? If individuals had to agree to govern their lives and prospects, not knowing who they were, their class, talents, race, religion, tastes, yet knowing that they would have to live together, be dependent on one another for protection, economic production, and the products of social cooperation, what principles of justice to regulate the basic features of public life would they choose?

Rawls says we would choose two basic principles, the first being Maximum Equal Liberty. Even from a self-interested point of view, we have a stake in equal liberty for all. In case it turned out that—after the "veil of ignorance" had been lifted—we were part of a minority, we wouldn't want to be oppressed by tyranny, even by a democratic majority tyranny. So we would insist on civil liberties, constitutional protections of free speech, religion, assembly, trial by jury, *habeas corpus*. Added to this, for matters not protected by basic liberties, we would want democratic government so that our voices would be equal. Second, we would require Equal Opportunity and the Difference Principle. We would want income distributed so that (1) it was open to fair competition (no discrimination) and (2) we all would receive equal income, unless differences in income helped the people at the bottom of the social ladder improve their conditions. That is, we would reward the long, hard work of surgeons with incomes high enough to attract enough skilled practitioners away from sunbathing into surgery (because unlike sunbathing, surgery helps unfortunates needing medical care). We all would want the Difference Principle because we too might turn out to be among the poorest, least able, severely ill, or handicapped, after the lifting of the "veil."

These potentially egalitarian principles, Rawlsians say, apply only to domestic society. International relations should be governed by traditional international law (the legalist paradigm, no aggression, etc.) and just redistribution should be saved for domestic consumption.[12]

[11] Rawls, *A Theory of Justice*.

[12] John Rawls's own view of international distributional duties is still (1996) under construction, but in its current formulation it rejects strong duties of distributional justice such as justice as fairness or global resource redistribution. He assumes that a complete scheme of justice is constructed domestically when potential citizens choose from behind a veil of ignorance the principles under which they are prepared to live. International justice then is constructed by "peoples" (not states) on the basis of the principles those peoples would want to govern the relations among independent peoples. Among the principles they would choose are nonintervention in order to secure their independence and a set of laws of war

Charles Beitz, Thomas Pogge, and others have, however, objected that Rawls assumes unwarrantedly that societies are self-sufficient in international relations. They argue instead that societies are interdependent. So like interdependent individuals, nations that trade, invest, borrow, yet are unequal must redistribute goods fairly. Moreover, they must consider that like the endowments or talents of the hypothetical domestic original condition, national natural resources are arbitrary from a moral point of view.[13] The United States has done nothing to deserve ownership of the fertile Great Plains, Mesabi iron ore, West Virginia coal fields, while only the advancing desert belongs to Sahelians.

By analogy, the world too needs a hypothetical social contract in order to redistribute justly the products of global social interdependence. We then should distribute goods as if we also did not know of which *country* we would find ourselves citizens. The implications are unclear. How much would the wealthy have to tax themselves in order to implement a global difference principle in which all incomes were distributed in such a fashion that inequalities were permitted only to the extent that they served the needs of the *world's* least advantaged? Although unclear, such a calculus would, it seems, give rise to a large duty to redistribute income to the poor across the globe.

Realist and Marxist Criticisms

The most famous Realist criticism of global redistribution must be Garret Hardin's "Living on a Lifeboat."[14] Rather than a global village, our metaphorical condition, according to Hardin, is that of survivors in lifeboats after a shipwreck. In the real world these lifeboats happen to be distributed to nations, and those objecting to that distribution, he adds, are free to surrender their seats to the many struggling in the water. But no one has a duty to surrender space or the lifeboat's provisions. Doing so might erode the present "safety margin," on which all in the boat depend. Even for a currently well-equipped boat, charity leads to long-run disaster through a "ratchet effect," as more consumers are saved and they then increase the burden on the next round of distributions. Even the mutual sharing of resources will produce a long-run "tragedy of the

---

to limit violence and to protect noncombatants when people do clash. Disabling differences in material circumstances would be addressed by duties of assistance designed to make sure that each "people" has the basic needs met for a healthy and politically free life. These duties would not include distributive justice, which is intrusive against the rights of self-determination that are the foundations of Rawls's conception of justice among peoples. Rawls develops these themes in "The Law of Peoples," in Stephen Shute and Susan Hardy, eds., *On Human Rights* (New York: Basic Books, 1993), pp. 41–82, and in three seminars on the Law of Peoples at Princeton University, April 1995 (manuscript).

[13] Charles Beitz, "Justice and International Relations," *Philosophy and Public Affairs* 4, 4 (Summer 1975) and pp. 282–311, of *International Ethics*; Thomas Pogge, "An Egalitarian Law of Peoples," *Philosophy and Public Affairs* 23, 3 (Summer 1994), pp. 195–224.

[14] Garret Hardin, "Living on a Lifeboat," *Bioscience* 24, 10 (October 1974), pp. 561–68.

commons." If resources (such as grazing on a village common) are shared, no one (no "owner") has an incentive to save or invest since the product of any investment would be shared by all. Pooling supplies among the lifeboats, Hardin suggests, produces a similar tragedy of rapid consumption.[15]

The ethics of Realism inform Hardin's lifeboat.[16] All states are at sea in some degree of peril, lesser or more, boats in a storm in various degrees of proximity to sinking. Realists ask, "Do we in the better national boats have the obligation to aid those in the frailer or currently sinking craft?" What if the foreign boats are poorly managed or reluctant to rely on our assistance? What if, even if the foreign boats are well managed and willing to accept assistance, taking in too many will sink our boat? Do we not have the right to aid our own first, or must we aid all in all boats at the same time? Have not our passengers commissioned us to their care first, and is that not a duty that should govern the conduct of crew and captain?

Furthermore, the world, according to the Realist, is not composed of children falling into shallow pools of water or out of well-provisioned lifeboats. Nor is it governed by a global social contract among free and rational individuals. That is, while children do fall into pools of water, people face starvation, and we can think of contractual justice, those images are not accurate models of the international world. National lifeboats are more likely to confront than to aid other national lifeboats, and both may prefer plunder to relying on charity. R. W. Tucker argues that the real world is not the global village of 100 described above but instead a system of 180 or so interdependent sovereign states.

These states interact in an anarchic system, each protecting its own territory and sovereignty, each suspicious of interference from others, which it regards as a sign of a threat to territory and sovereignty. Fear, then relative power, insecurity, the state of war, anarchy, and real power shape the actions of states. Therefore aid rarely reaches directly the children or the starving. Instead between them and all who would help—or harm—stand state institutions. It is through states that one must act, and therefore it is through addressing the

[15] Some recent commentary suggests that these problems of social decay, environmental stress, and mass starvation are multiplying across the less developed world, particularly in Africa. A dramatic treatment of these issues can be found in Robert Kaplan, "The Coming Anarchy," *Atlantic Monthly* (February 1994) pp. 44–76. It must be noted, however, that the broader predictions of Hardin's and Paul Ehrlich's "neo-Malthusian" growth have not come to fruition.

[16] Onora O'Neill, however, challenges Hardin's moral reasoning in "Lifeboat Earth," *Philosophy and Public Affairs* 4, 3 (Spring 1975). Going a step farther, pursuing the implications of Singer and Beitz, and questioning the basic assumptions of Hardin, O'Neill concludes that inequalities that result in starvation in today's world are like murder in a "lifeboat" if others on other "boats" have enough to survive. Even if others do not have enough to survive, if the procedures governing the determination of those who die are not fair (e.g., if not by lot), then even in this circumstance deaths are murders.

needs and goals of states that one can have any helpful impact on individuals.[17]

Tucker adds that we misconstrue the South (the Third World), where the needy live, if we think of them according to the "New Sensibility," a sentiment that focuses on the global needs and rights of all individuals, worldwide. Instead states in the Third World are driven not by the New Sensibility but by a "New Egalitarianism." They seek not an equality of all individuals, themselves becoming one minor part of worldwide Liberal social democracy. They seek an equality of states, where they equal the superpowers.

Many Southern statesmen may welcome the alleviation of poverty within their societies, but what they demand is an equal status, equal power, equal development of their state, becoming not like us domestically, but taking our place internationally. Northern (First World, Western) New Sensibility statesmen, who think otherwise, are therefore irresponsible and not adequately protecting the security or welfare of their populations against the threat of the next turn in the international cycle of hierarchy.

This is where and why Tucker came into the debate on the just structure of the international economic order as the Cassandra who wanted to be Paul Revere, whose warning to the West in 1973 to restore international hierarchy over the Persian Gulf in response to OPEC's "rebellion" (its embargo and price raises) went unheeded. He laments our lack of intestinal fortitude and writes to educate us on how the world truly is—a world of order before justice, where you are neither right nor wrong, good nor evil, but instead up or down, rulers or ruled.

As for Marxist objections to Liberal distributive justice across international borders, a few Marxists focus on the problem that redistributing may be counterproductive. If substantial redistribution of income to the very poor may serve to reinforce the unjust social order of world capitalism by assuaging—or buying off—dissent, reforms thereby prolong oppression. But capitalists are unlikely in any case to be so redistributive, and most Marxists argue that aid does not reach the poor in the first place. Besides, according to these critics, it took massive rearmament (i.e., much more than Marshall Plan assistance) to effect the stable reintegration of war-devastated Europe into the postwar capitalist order dominated by the United States.[18] Only when power, through social revolution,

[17] Robert W. Tucker, *The Inequality of States* (New York: Basic Books, 1975), chaps. 4, 5; for a systematic political-economic analysis, Stephen Krasner, *Structural Conflict: The Third World against Global Liberalism* (Berkeley: University of California Press, 1985).

[18] Fred Block, *The Origins of International Economic Disorder* (Berkeley: University of California Press, 1977), pp. 103–104. The Asian case involving massive U.S. purchases in East Asia in support of the Korean War is well documented by Bruce Cumings, "The Origins and Development of the Northeast Asian Political Economy," in E. C. Deyo, ed., *The Political Economy of the New Asian Industrialism* (Ithaca: Cornell University Press, 1987), p. 67. In addition, the United States spent $500 million per year in aid for Japan between 1950 and 1970. Between 1946 and 1978, the aid figures are $600 per capita for South Korea

changes, liberates, and equalizes social interaction will redistribution be useful—in order to mop up leftover inequalities.[19]

The Marxist Socialists likewise have no patience with Realist views of New Egalitarianism, Third World nationalism, and international pecking orders. They often think the national ambitions of the Third World developmentalists are no more than a fig leaf for the private ambitions of the Third World elites, lining their own pockets and those of their relatives is much more important than developing their countries. For all but a small authentically revolutionary set of Communist leaders (Mao, Ho Chi Minh, Castro) and (at least for some Marxists) an equally small set of revolutionary capitalist national bourgeoisie (South Korea, Taiwan, Singapore), Third World leaders marry a rhetoric of nationalism to a reality of collaboration with multinational corporations and plundering of their economies.[20]

Liberal Criticisms

The Liberal critics agree that one must justify who has a right to what in what boat but insist that we all need not wind up in the same one. Their debate over the moral significance of national borders has both moral and political aspects.

Liberal moral criticisms fall into differing camps. Locke and other conservative, laissez-faire Liberals found that property could be justly acquired without a state to authorize acquisition and that states that instituted money further solidified the ownership of property, however unequal the distribution. International property rights for a Lockean might now be regarded as ambiguous because land is no longer abundant, pollution (Lockean "waste") is widespread, and international money is thinly instituted. Locke is also famous for recommending the export of labor to labor-scarce countries as a solution to distributive concerns in overpopulated ones. Still, most contemporary Lockeans concentrate on opportunity to work and blame unjust inequality primarily on restrictions on labor mobility *within* Third World economies and only secondarily on international restrictions.[21]

---

and $425 per capita for Taiwan, which both also became part of the order of postwar U.S. capitalism.

[19] For insightful remarks on the significance of these issues in Marxist theory, see the comments at an APSA Roundtable by Alan Cafruny, summarized by Michael W. Doyle in "International Distributive Justice," *PS* (Fall 1986), pp. 857–59.

[20] These harsh criticisms were first and most eloquently presented in Fanon, *Wretched of the Earth.*

[21] An example of this line of reasoning would be William Loehr and John Powelson, *Threat to Development: Pitfalls of the New International Economic Order* (Boulder, Colo.: Westview Press, 1983). But for an insightful discussion of the ethics of immigration restrictions, see Joseph Carens, "Membership and Morality," in William Brubaker, ed., *Immigration and the Politics of Citizenship in Europe and North America,* (Washington, D.C.: University Press of America, 1989).

Politically, the commitment of Liberals, especially the laissez-faire Liberals, to the efficiency and the political advantages of international free trade is severely tested by the inflow of low-cost imports from newly industrializing countries of the Third World. These imports threaten domestic industries, which tend to be politically active and affiliated with the extremes of conservative or welfare Liberalism.[22]

The modern Kantians and related welfare Liberals raise a different set of moral concerns. International rights, they argue, must be founded on moral freedom and individual self-determination. One cannot separate the economic from the political features of a just social order, but freedom, overall, is prior to wealth, just as Rawls's Maximum Equal Liberty is prior to the Difference Principle. We don't want to sacrifice freedom and democratic self-determination for material well-being unless—Rawls and others have argued—the community finds itself in a state of desperation, such that the natural principle of justice should operate, determining that the basic minimum subsistence of all is the first duty of public justice.[23]

In cases of extreme inequality and political anarchy within a country, the welfare Liberals thus find justifiable a developmental, redistributing dictatorship to equalize opportunity as a necessary foundation for an eventually just Liberal society.[24] But additional problems arise with respect to both establishing a just global society and justly distributing resources in an unjust international society. The Liberal justification for a dictatorial redistribution on a national scale is that without it, authentically democratic Liberal politics and social economy are rendered ineffective. The enormous social inequalities of the international order might, however implausibly, suggest the same prescription should apply to the international order. Extended to global scale, however, this prescription runs up against a fundamental Liberal constraint. It is not clear that an effective global Liberal polity can be formed. Kant, for example, regarded global sovereignty, whether Liberal in aim or not, as equivalent to global tyranny because of the remoteness of the representation it would entail. So while the utilitarians have a different story, no Rawlsian or neo-Kantian Liberal would want to join a "Scheme of Global Social Cooperation" unless it included a complete global social contract.[25] This would need to cover a polity

[22] Two classic sources on economic policy and pressure groups are J. J. Pincus, "Pressure Groups and the Pattern of Tariffs," *Journal of Political Economy* 83 (August 1975), pp. 757–78, and L. Salamon and J. Siegfried, "Economic Power and Political Influence," *American Political Science Review* 71 (September 1977), pp. 1026–43.

[23] Isaiah Berlin, for example, suggests the prior importance of at least a minimum level of subsistence before personal and political liberty can be enjoyed in any state. See Berlin, *Four Essays on Liberty* (New York: Oxford University Press, 1969), introduction.

[24] Rawls, *A Theory of Justice*, pp. 352–53.

[25] Rawls's position is complex, however, resting as much as anything on his view that peoples from different cultures do not possess the (nonpolitical) cultural common ground to "con-

establishing order and Maximum Equal Liberty. But under the present regime of global intentions characterized by national independence and cultural diversity, this may not be possible. We then have no duty to ensure a global Difference Principle until it is possible to have a global polity guaranteeing Maximum Equal Liberty.

At the individual level, the priority of freedom reflects the assumption that it is freedom that makes life subjectively valuable. We re-create ourselves, and this is the highest human faculty. Thus obligations incurred in the name of freedom to distribute to the destitute at home or abroad have to have a cutoff that allows individuals to pursue a self-determining life. They should not be forced to be "moral saints" or be subject to "moral tyranny."[26] On the public, constitutional level, other factors come into play. If the maximum effective size of a deliberative legislature is about five hundred, a global constituency would have to be of the order of eight million persons. Confederal solutions that mix direct and indirect elections further attenuate the political life of the citizen or create the grounds for serious conflict between the local government and the remote confederation. In short, the redistribution that can be justified on Liberal-contractarian grounds does not stretch beyond Liberal government. Modern states may already be too large for effectively Liberal politics. It is even harder to argue that global government can be a Liberal aim. Global reformers need to be able to guarantee that a scheme of global natural justice to assist the poor will end in effective global equal liberty. Without the prospect of moral autonomy through representative government this form of international redistribution is not justified on Liberal grounds.

The dilemma of justly redistributing income in the existing international society of independent states is addressed by Brian Barry.[27] After rejecting "just requitals" (just prices) for past exploitation as being inadequate justice for poor societies lacking any resources whatsoever and after rejecting justice as "fair

---

struct" a just cosmopolitan order. Here a dissenting line of Liberal thought (one distinct from both Utilitarianism and global common law) is worth mentioning: Explicitly motivated by questions of development in the global South, Martha Nussbaum, Amartya Sen, and others have recently attempted to construct a universalistic philosophy of "human capabilities." The group's most recent edited volume includes an essay by Seyla Benhabib that stakes out what might be called the middle ground between Rawls and the cosmopolitanism of Pogge and Beitz. See Seyla Benhabib, "Cultural Complexity, Moral Interdependence and the Global Dialogical Community," in Martha Nussbaum and Jonathan Glover, eds. *Women, Culture and Development* (New York: Oxford University Press, 1995).

[26] See the classic article by Susan Wolf, "Moral Saints," *Ethics* (1982). For useful critical reviews of the literature see Andrew Walter, "Distributive Justice and the Theory of International Relations," *Australian Outlook* 37, 2 (August 1983), pp. 98–103, and Ronald Findlay, "International Distributive Justice," *Journal of International Economics* 13 (1982), pp. 1–14.

[27] Brian Barry, "Humanity and Justice in Global Perspective," in J. Roland Pennock and John W. Chapman, eds., *Ethics, Economics and the Law, Nomos* XXIV (New York: New York University Press, 1982), chap. 11.

play" (reciprocal obligations) for being ill suited to the minimally integrated international economy, he settles on justice as equal rights.[28] He follows H. L. A. Hart's argument that special rights (e.g., to property) presuppose general rights (to property) and that natural resources (or inherited endowments) cannot be justly acquired without consent. Without consent, all have an equal right to global resources, and there has been no global consent to the current international order. The contemporary rich countries therefore owe a share of their income or resources to poor countries. Moreover, they owe this share without the requirement that it be directed to the poorest in the poor countries because the rich have no right to impose conditions on income or property to which all have an equal right. If rich countries can dispose of global income autonomously, poor countries should have the same right.[29]

There are two objections that I think should be made against accepting Barry's principle of indiscriminate interstate justice, even when one accepts the principles underlying his argument. First, if justice is determined by the equal rights of individuals to global resources or inheritances, then rich countries acquire income justly only when they acquire it justly from individuals (for example, by international trade and democratically legislated taxation). Only just countries have rights over the autonomous disposition of national income. An unjust rich state has no right to dispose or hold income. A just rich country, conversely, has the right to dispose autonomously of national income, provided that national income represents its just share of global income. Any surplus is owed to individuals who are poor or to (just) poor states that have acquired a right to dispose of income or resources by the consent of their citizens. Neither unjust poor states nor unjust rich states should (by the argument of equal rights of individuals) have rights over global income. If there were justice among "thieves," it might call for distribution without condition from unjust rich states to unjust poor states. It is difficult to see, however, why that scheme should apply to the surplus of just rich states beyond that which they distribute to just poor states. (But it is important to remember that there do exist international and nongovernmental institutions, such as UNICEF and OXFAM, that form a trust for the global poor, channeling some money successfully even to poor individuals living in unjust poor states.[30]) The point is that an obligation of equal justice that would have required, say, Norway or Sweden to tax its citizens to provide direct transfers to a Somoza (Nicaragua) or Duvalier (Haiti)—or, for

[28] Ibid., p. 234. For additional considerations on the difficulties of extending Rawlsian justice to the international arena, see Christopher Brewin, "Justice in International Relations," in Michael Donelan, ed., *The Reason of States* (London: George Allen and Unwin, 1978), pp. 151–52, and Robert Amdur, "Rawls' Theory of Justice: Domestic and International Perspectives," *World Politics* 29, 3 (April 1977), pp. 438–61.
[29] Barry, p. 248.
[30] The very existence of such institutions thus can expand the range of obligations of distributive justice, a point that has been developed by Martha Nussbaum among others.

that matter, a Mobutu in Zaire today—in preference to funding the World Bank or UNICEF is morally unconvincing.

The second objection reflects the residual insecurity of the contemporary order. As long as there is no guarantee of international security, indiscriminate obligations of justice to redistribute substantial amounts of income and resources (including redistribution to potential security threats) cannot be justified.[31] Obliging Japan to tax itself for China, or Israel for Syria, or even the United States for Cuba threatens the rights of individuals within these taxed states to promote their territorial integrity and political independence.

It should be stressed that these two objections to the application of just redistribution should not apply to (1) cases of assistance to the destitute, particularly when they are reachable by neutral nonpolitical agencies, such as development nongovernmental organizations, and (2) social justice within the pacific union of Liberal states. The Liberal priority of freedom sets the parameters for global justice of both the individual and public varieties. We can do our personal reasonable bit in assisting the destitute and then shift obligations to a state that makes moral political decisions that take into account national security and welfare in a world where both are goods that need protection. Liberal states then have a hierarchy of duties of global justice. First, they have duties to aid the truly destitute everywhere on the globe within the limits of guaranteeing the national security of their own citizens. Second, they do not, however, have universal obligations to institute a global scheme of distributive justice. But, third, for Liberals, because states within the Pacific Union do rest on sufficient consent and do not constitute threats to one another, there are obligations of justice to distribute global resources and income from the Union's rich members to its poor members. These obligations supplement universal humanitarian obligations applicable globally to aid individuals whose poverty threatens their life.

In summary, the political obstacles are still daunting. If the disadvantaged are rightly the objects of social welfare, redistribution should be directed toward the vast preponderance of the world's poor in the developing countries of the global South, primarily in Africa and Asia. Brian Barry has provided a strong defense against skepticism concerning this obligation. But he also concludes that while it is hard to doubt that 0.25 percent of national income (the 1980s U.S. figure for foreign aid) is too low, there does not seem to be a clear limit on how much aid of the enormous amount needed is obligatory. One should add that since this aid is required by needy individuals (mostly) in the poorer

[31] This prohibition need not include small payments into multilateral institutions that (albeit via an intermediary) already result in some minor such redistributions; for example, some of Israel's contributions to UN institutions actually end up funding projects that benefit its enemies. The question of where to draw the line as it relates to the still-simmering debate over a more significant multilateral tax in exchange for the privilege of UN membership is an interesting one indeed.

developing countries of the South and is not clearly owed to their states, the political logistics of distributing humanitarian aid, short of imperial control, will prove difficult. Since this aid is due from individuals in the wealthy northern developed world, a theoretically limitless personal obligation to the world's poor threatens a form of politically unacceptable, tyrannical morality. Nor is the burden easily shifted to Liberal governments in the North. Political obstacles to taxing rich Liberal societies for humanitarian aid are evident. The income of the Northern poor places them among the world's more advantaged few. But the demand for redistributing income from the Northern countries to the Southern poor meets two domestic barriers: The poor within the North are clearly disadvantaged, and our democratic polities place the needs of disadvantaged voting citizens above those of more disadvantaged but foreign people. That said, in practice support for genuinely redistributive foreign aid is high among northern publics, and it may even be among disadvantaged groups within the North that such support is the highest.[32]

Unresolved questions thus include how to raise international revenue in a just fashion, how to distribute this revenue in an efficient manner, and how to maintain the support of democratic citizens for lengthy programs when some mismanagement is likely and when strategic ties to authoritarian allies make competitive demands on aid revenues. These not insignificant obstacles and the competitive moral logics of Realism and Marxism each enter the moral politics of actual foreign aid; together they can identify the moral and political contours of international distributive reform.

FOREIGN AID

Wars and even foreign interventions have been with us throughout the ages, but attempts at international redistribution have not. The distinction may not

[32]Throughout most of the northern countries, where, as we shall see, aid policies are relatively uninfluenced by balance of power concerns, public support for economic aid generally hovers around 75 percent. The case of the United States, where support for aid has historically been around only 55 percent, nonetheless also turns up some interesting findings: First, is that even a Cold War–era Chicago Council on Foreign Relations study (John E. Reilly, ed., *American Public Opinion and U.S. Foreign Policy* [Chicago: CCFR, 1983], p. 25) found support strong (68 percent) for aid that "helps the economies of other countries" but weak (30 percent) for that which "helps our economy at home" or "helps our national security (44%)." The most comprehensive survey ever undertaken on U.S. public attitudes toward aid, the ODC-Interaction Survey, prepared by Christine Contee, *What Americans Think: Views on Development and U.S. Third World Relations*, (New York: ODC, 1987), adds that American blacks support aid more highly than do whites and for much more strongly felt humanitarian reasons. (Support for aid also correlates consistently with youth and with gender and perhaps even inversely with wealth—albeit here the results for purely humanitarian aid are ambiguous.) Finally, it seems a majority of all northern publics are opposed to military aid, albeit only slightly (51 percent) in such countries as the United States.

be insignificant. For example, opponents of redistribution sometimes hold that recent efforts will prove a passing fancy of the late twentieth century. Advocates of redistribution, on the other hand, may excuse shortcomings of redistributive policy on account of the relative newness of attempts to achieve economic justice beyond state borders.

Before deciding who is correct, however, we must say just a bit more about what international redistribution is—or, more accurately, about what it has as yet been. Over the last fifty years international redistribution can basically be said to have entailed both bilateral and multilateral foreign economic assistance. As is well known, such assistance began in earnest with the United States' (by all accounts successful) Marshall Plan of aid to Western Europe after World War II. It is interesting to note that during congressional debate on the plan, Republican Senator George Malone branded it "the most amazingly brazen and preposterous scheme for a worldwide redistribution of wealth which has as yet been proposed."[33] But has aid lived up to any such billing?

Liberals, as we have seen, have mixed views on aid. Social Liberals suggest to us that, much like domestic welfare, foreign aid is a fundamental requirement of justice. Market (or laissez-faire) Liberals disparage aid for its economic distortions and thus parallel their critique of domestic welfare. Realists believe that aid, just as any other instrument of foreign policy, should enhance national security. They thus tend to question the redistributionist motivation for aid outright. Marxists, while also questioning Liberal motivations for aid, may make their greatest contribution in attacking aid's effectiveness. Even where they do concede the good intentions of Social Welfare Liberal donors, Marxists tend to believe that the financial and commercial interests of capitalism prevail over even the best-laid Liberal schemes of gradualist redistribution. But what does the actual record of aid tell us about the influence of these perspectives?

Liberal Views of Aid

Liberalism is an appropriate place to begin an analysis of foreign aid because it can speak to how a now well-entrenched international regime (particularly among Liberal democracies) has expanded to system-wide prominence.[34]

[33] Quoted in Carroll J. Doherty, "Support for Foreign Aid Wilting," *Congressional Quarterly* (May 16, 1992), p. 1356.

[34] The social Liberal perspective has produced much work on aid by authors from various countries. As for works in English, Olav Stokke's *Western Middle Powers and Global Poverty* (Motala: Motala Grafista, 1989), Louis Imbeau, *Donor Aid—The Determinants of Allocations to Third World Countries: A Comparative Analysis* (New York: Lang, 1989), and David Lumsdaine, *Moral Vision in International Politics* (Princeton: Princeton University Press, 1993) all provide book-length social Liberal accounts of aid motivation. Also noteworthy is Alain Noel and Jean Philippe Therien's recent article "From Domestic to International Justice: The Welfare State and Foreign Aid," *International Organization* 49, 3 (1995). Noel and Therien emphasize the social aspect of social liberalism as determinative for strong aid

Moreover, one might make several at least potentially testable Liberal conjectures in regard to aid: If the aid regime was one of laissez-faire Liberalism, then perhaps there would be very little, but some, aid, with "aid as welfare" flowing less frequently through conservative Liberal governments, just as these states are less inclined to spend on domestic social welfare. Second, any aid given would be focused on economically productive investments, promoting the development of property rights and perhaps representative government.[35] Multilateral agencies—specifically such international financial institutions as the World Bank—should be the favored efficient, apolitical disbursers.

Social welfare Liberals, on the other hand, might expect that foreign aid would be relatively large and that the richer the donor country, the more it should contribute. Social Liberal aid should, moreover, directed toward the poor: The poorer the country, the more, other things being equal, it should receive. And aid should focus on projects that are closest to the needs of the poor—for example, on health and education. Multilateral delivery of aid might be preferred to bilateral delivery, as more in keeping with the equal dignity of peoples and less subject to political manipulation. Left-wing, welfare, or social democratic governments should probably be more generous than right-wing, market, or laissez-faire–oriented governments. Lastly, substantial amounts of aid should have redistributive intranational effects within the recipient countries.

With these issues in mind, one might first consider some broad statistics from the Development Assistance Committee (DAC) countries all of which are Liberal states that, although making up only two-thirds of the total number of aid donors, account for around 95 percent of current contributions:[36]

---

performance. Two works by British authors—Paul Mosley, *Foreign Aid: Its Defense and Reform* (Lexington: University of Kentucky Press, 1987) and Roger Riddell, *Foreign Aid Reconsidered* (Baltimore: Johns Hopkins University Press, 1987)—make an impressive case regarding the *effectiveness* of aid. Arguably, the broad scope of these works and the fact that only one of these authors (Lumsdaine) advocated an American social Liberalism set apart from American-authored Realist and Marxist analyses of aid focusing on the U.S. aid program. Market Liberal works on aid are less common, but Hadley Arkes, *First Thing,* chap. 14, limits all aid to survival rights while Peter Bauer, "Foreign Aid: Rewarding Impoverishment?," *Swiss Review of World Affairs* (October 1985) rejects aid outright. Those interested in pursuing the right Liberal critique of aid further should see the thorough discussion by Riddell.

[35] Because we use the statistic provided by the OECD for "social and administrative aid" as a stand-in for all social aid (instead of including agricultural aid, disaster relief, food aid, etc.), the figures in Table 12 separate "democracy-exporting" right Liberals from "economic" right Liberals. While this is in some respects unfortunate for evaluation of the right Liberal perspective on aid, a desire to subsidize democratic states appears distinct from one to support privatization of Third World economies.

[36] Notably none of our three schools has as yet produced a globally contextualized analysis of aid from Arab and Communist countries. As we know from raw figures and limited case

Turning to the table (12.1), then, one might first note that there is a large discrepancy in relative generosity—on the order of seven to one—between the top donor, Denmark, and the bottom donor, the United States. The fact that the United States is second only to Japan in terms of absolute disbursements (as measured by the third column) may or may not be seen as mitigating its stinginess relative to GNP. Consistent with the predictions of the social Liberals, in any case, is that three social democratic states are the top performers.

Further interpretation of the assistance as a percentage of GNP figures might be aided by an analogy between foreign assistance and domestic welfare.[37] States are obviously more concerned with their own citizens than with those of other nations. Yet the evidence on aid shows that states are not insignificantly committed to "duties beyond borders" as well. On the subject of quantity, then, though overseas development assistance (ODA) seems of dismissable significance when compared with GNP, Liberals would have us note that almost half the DAC states spend between 2 and 3 percent or more of their overall government budgets on (as we shall see) predominantly morally driven international initiatives. Moreover, given that such levels of spending are still discretionary as of the present (as opposed to all of the fixed budgetary items with which countries contend), the allocation of 5 to 10 percent or more of such discretionary funds to international altruism would seem a significant departure from Realist and Marxist expectations about state behavior.[38]

Next, a comparison of column one with column two and column three with column four gives an idea of trends within the aid regime. Of all our findings, these may be the least auspicious for the Liberal case. For while in absolute terms aid has more than doubled in a single decade (in 1992 constant dollars), in the all-important relative measure it has either declined or held even, depending on whether one goes by a weighted or unweighted average (the

studies of Arab and Communist programs, however, aid from these states is rapidly declining while aid from Liberal regimes not in the DAC (Israel, India, Taiwan, Korea, etc.) continues to rise moderately.

[37] One needs to maintain perspective. One very obvious, if often forgotten, distinction between international aid and domestic welfare is that the former is far smaller in terms of quantity—particularly if conceived of in per recipient terms. It may be perverse to expect the global "war on poverty" to have met with full success, given its having funded at effectively one one-hundredth the strength of that in the United States. There are also considerable qualitative differences. Domestic welfare policies of northern states are undergirded by comprehensive, mandatory, and, for the most part, progressive taxation systems. While it is true enough that tax revenues of individuals in northern countries may occasionally end up funding southern infrastructure projects, just as (in much larger quantities) such revenues fund infrastructure in the home country, the analogy diminishes when we also compare international aid with the domestic loans, subsidies, and transfer payments dispersed directly by northern governments to their citizens.

[38] See *Development Co-operation*, pp. C5–C13.

TABLE 12.1[39]

General Statistics on Foreign Aid

(3 High Performers)	*%GNP/Rank*	*%'82–'83/Trend*	*Abs/Rank*	*Abs '82–'83*	GA/GE	*% Mult*
Denmark	1.03 (1)	0.75 (+)	1.3 bil (12)	400 mil (+)	99.8/99.8	43.7
Norway	1.01 (2)	1.06 (−)	1.0 bil (11)	571 mil (+)	99.3/99.5	35.9
Sweden	0.98 (3)	0.93 (+)	1.8 bil (9)	870 mil (+)	100/100	26.8
(3 Low Performers)						
Japan	0.26 (17)	0.31 (−)	11.3 bil (1)	3.3 bil (+)	43.8/76.6	21.1
Ireland	0.20 (20)	0.23 (−)	81 mil (20)	40 mil (+)	100/100	54.8
United States	0.15 (21)	0.25 (−)	9.7 bil (2)	8.1 bil (+)	97.9/99.1	26.6
(Major Powers Not Included)						
France	0.63 (5)	0.56 (+)	7.9 bil (3)	3.0 bil (+)	74.8/87.5	21.4
Germany	0.37 (9)	0.48 (−)	6.9 bil (4)	3.2 bil (+)	80.2/92.7	28.1
All DAC Countries	0.30	0.35 (−)	56.0 bil	26.9 bil (+)	77.1/90.6	27.2
(unweighted average)	0.45	0.45 (even)				

%GNP: aid as a percentage of donor's gross national product in '92–'93
(Rank): ordinal ranking of donor on this %GNP measure

%'82–'83: aid as a percentage of donor's gross national product in '82–'83
(Trend): increase or decrease in donor's %GNP between '82–'83 and '92–'93

Abs: absolute volume of donor's aid in '92–'93
(Rank): ordinal ranking of donor's aid on this absolute measure

Abs '82–'83: absolute volume of donor's aid in '82–'83
(Trend): increase or decrease in donor's absolute aid between '82–'83 and '92–'93

GA: percentage of a donor's aid given in the form of grants
GE: the percentage of "grant element" in a donor's aid (very low interest loans, etc.)

% Mult: the percentage of a donor's aid that is multilaterally disbursed

[39] A word should be said about why these eight countries were chosen for examination (out of the twenty-one in the DAC). The most accepted single measure of "aid performance" has long been the percentage of aid that a donor gives as a percentage of its GNP. Likewise, many argue that aid quantity and aid quality are highly correlated. Short of a random sample, our initial thought was that to be fair to all schools of thought on foreign aid, it would be best to examine the three highest-performing as well as the three lowest-performing donors. In additional concessions to Realism, however, we have settled a near tie between Japan, New Zealand, and Spain at the low end by including Japan (because of its major power status) and included data for two other major powers—France and Germany—that would otherwise have been excluded from our schema. Figures in all three tables are taken from the Development Assistance Committee of the OECD (DAC), *Development Co-operation* (1994) and the International Monetary Fund, *Direction of Trade Statistics Yearbook* (1994).

former of which is extrasensitive to backsliding on the part of large economies such as the United States, Germany, and Japan). While an absolute doubling is hardly insignificant if one thinks of budget allocation processes in donor states, it is clear that not all donors operate from a sense of cosmopolitan obligation to meet a minimum relative figure, as social Liberals often suggest they should.

The final set of figures listed among these "General Statistics" is for the proportion of multilateral as opposed to bilateral aid. While one might construct all sorts of hypotheses about what this distinction signifies, we are hesitant to draw too many conclusions. This is first of all because with the exception of Ireland and, to a lesser extent, Denmark, the countries examined exhibit no more than an 8 percent variation around the DAC mean of 27.2 percent multilateral aid. Now, one might hypothesize that a larger amount of aid channeled multilaterally supports the social Liberal case (it certainly cannot suggest Realist motivation), but must one then conclude that Sweden's below-average multilateralism makes it relatively more motivated by realpolitik than are other industrialized states? The question may ultimately be one of what *kind* of multilateral aid states choose to fund. There is certainly a difference between the social Liberal International Fund for Agricultural Development (IFAD) and the more right Liberal hard windows of the World Bank. Thus, given so little overall variance and a suspicion that model donors such as Sweden use bilateral aid for relatively *more* redistributionist purposes than they would have attained multilaterally, we offer this evaluative framework only as an impetus to further debate.

An additional caveat is perhaps in order. While the rise of redistributionist aid policies in donor countries has to some extent been correlated with left-wing, social welfare political actors, the rise to power of a rightist regime in a donor country has rarely, if ever, presaged a drastic blow to extant aid programs. An inverse "bicycle theory" argument about international regimes may thus apply—e.g., it is difficult for donor nations not to pursue an at least somewhat redistributionist aid policy in the first place (and even harder for them to turn away from one once it is initiated). This is presumably due to patterns of both domestic and international social learning upon which the Liberals also speculate. Yet one must again be wary, for particularly among the major powers, a right Liberal international social norm may recently have come to the fore: France has as yet bucked the trend toward major power aid retrenchment, and middle powers have also picked up much of the slack, but whether the steady climb from a world without aid of fifty years ago to today's full-fledged aid regime has reached a plateau remains an open question.

The greater ability of any strand of Liberalism to trace such behavior to domestic factors makes it particularly significant. But one must not forget the considerable differences among Liberal approaches to foreign aid. The handful of libertarian authors who focus directly on aid and claim there is a principled reason not to provide it (see note 34) is indeed a dfferent story. Yet for them, the "foreignness" of aid is irrelevant to what they see as the unwarranted imposition characteristic of all forms of redistribution, whether at home or abroad. In any event, all Liberal theories recommend some respect for public opinion, and it appears that the rightist view of humanitarian-redistributionist aid is, if nothing else, undemocratic. Supporting the social Liberal perspective is that evidence from public opinion surveys points to a consensus in society after society favoring primarily humanitarian and redistributionist goals for foreign aid programs. This is only slightly less true of the larger countries wherein such a societal consensus may go more or less unreflected in government policy.

Realist Views of Aid

On the surface, it would seem that foreign aid is as troubling or more troubling to Realist theory than is any other international practice. One would think that a strong Realist case that does not concede aid policy to be exceptional (or insignificant) must show not only that transferring resources to foreign countries actually maximizes the power of the donor but that this power maximization is optimal in relative terms. Such an enterprise would probably have seemed strange to Thucydides or Machiavelli—note that the Athenians hardly proffered development projects to Melos (!)—but a few scholars have nonetheless tried to account for aid within a more subtle and modernized Realist theory.

Perhaps the best-known attempt to do so appears in an early essay by Hans Morgenthau. By the author's own admission, this essay offers little more than a set of categorizations intended as a "preface" to a Realist theory of U.S. aid.[40] Moreover, though stopping short of the conclusion of his friend and sometimes collaborator Kenneth Thompson that "if there exists any sector of foreign policy based on the moral imperative, it would appear to be foreign assistance," Morgenthau does concede that no policy innovation "has proved more baffling to both understanding and action than foreign aid."[41]

What might a Realist aid regime look like? Realists might expect that aid would flow for the most part bilaterally from states to other states rather than multilaterally or through nongovernmental organizations (NGOs), in order to maximize political control. This prediction is borne out by Table 12.2. Not

[40] See Morgenthau, "Preface to a Political Theory of Foreign Aid," in Robert H. Godwin, ed., *Why Foreign Aid* (Chicago: Rand McNally & Co., 1963). Robert D. McKinlay takes up the empirical task in "The Aid Relationship: A Foreign Policy Model and Interpretation of the Distribution of Official Bilateral Economic Aid of the United States, United Kingdom, France and Germany 1960–1970," *Comparative Political Studies* (January 1979), pp. 411–463. Steven W. Hook updates and expands upon McKinlay in his interesting *National Interest and Foreign Aid* (Boulder, Colo.: Lynne Rienner, 1995).

[41] See Morgenthau, p. 70, and Kenneth W. Thompson, *Morality and Foreign Policy* (Baton Rouge: Louisiana State University Press, 1980), p. 93.

TABLE 12.2

Strong Endorsement of Social Aid

Scale: 1 means lowest priority and 10 means top priority
(Responses in percentages)

	1	*2*	*3*	*4*	*5*	*6*	*7*	*8*	*9*	*10*	*Av.*
Relief for victims of disasters like floods, droughts, and earthquakes	2	1	1	2	7	4	8	19	13	42	8.3
Giving money to Third World countries to pay their foreign debts	35	14	11	10	12	5	5	3	1	2	3.2
Building large projects, such as roads, dams, and hospitals	4	4	5	5	16	9	15	18	8	15	6.5
Using aid to help farmers in those countries buy seeds and basic equipment	3	2	3	4	9	6	12	19	15	26	7.6
Helping foreign governments analyze their economic systems and improve them	6	4	4	4	13	9	14	16	10	18	6.7
Sending American volunteers, like those in the Peace Corps, to work in other countries	4	2	3	5	8	7	11	20	11	28	7.4
Providing health care	3	2	2	3	9	7	11	19	13	30	7.7

borne out by Table 12.2, however, would be a Realist proposition that the superpowers might give proportionately more aid because of their more extensive global interests. Some further issues are taken into account in Table 12.3. Above all, it seems Realists would be attentive simply to who gives aid to whom. Specifically these recipients might have close security (military bases or perhaps postcolonial) links to the donors. While it is almost common knowledge that the Cold War–era United States was a security-motivated donor, what should one make of the thirty *other* aid donors out there?

It must first of all be said that almost no one disputes the Realists in regard to military aid, and as is reflected in the standard measurement of "official development assistance," the aid debate deals exclusively with nonmilitary transfers. Nonetheless, the Realist theorists who do discuss economic aid extrapolate a lesson that even this type of assistance is ultimately no less motivated by concerns for a donor's own military security.[42] We now examine a few "security correlates of aid" from the DAC countries.

For the Realists, the most important question of all is probably which states receive aid from which donors. For example, Robert Gilpin notes that the two largest recipients of bilateral U.S. economic assistance are not among the poorest countries of the world (that might indicate a genuine concern for redistribution) but rather, as shown here, Israel and Egypt which grant military privileges to the United States. Though Gilpin does not construct the case himself, one can easily imagine a Realist argument that aiding these two countries ensures a stable Middle East and in turn a steady supply of oil—arguably a prerequisite for the United States' other security concerns. The record of the top quantitative performers, on the other hand, seems essentially free of power political motivation. French aid to the former colonies (column three) and German aid to the former Yugoslavia do suggest political motivations, but each of these recipients would qualify on humanitarian grounds as well. Finally, Japan's focus on aid to Asia is particularly contentious, as it developed out of legally and morally mandated reparations payments stemming from military occupation in World War II. In our view (a fairly standard one) only the aid programs of the United States and France reflect a significant weight given to noneconomic geopolitical concerns. The balance of evidence from other donors seems not to support the Realist case in regard to aid motivation.[43]

[42] Realist theories asserting the pursuit of narrowly defined foreign *economic* interests via aid might be better evaluated using the statistics we present in Table 12.4.

[43] It can also be added that the few multinational analyses of aid that do call themselves Realist make significant revisions to that paradigm as commonly understood. For example, Steven Hook's recent *National Interest and Foreign Aid* sets itself the task of vindicating Morgenthau's Realist research program yet concludes by quoting the following observation of Robert C. North: "A potentially powerful transformation can occur, at the point where 'my problem' and the problem of 'my adversary' are recognized by both of us as 'our prob-

TABLE 12.3

Security Correlates of Foreign Aid

(3 High Performers)	*Top 3 Recipients*	*Of Top 15, Mil. Priv.*	*Of Top 15, Fmr. Col./Mil. Occup.*
Denmark	Tanzania, Uganda, Bangladesh	0	0
Norway	Tanzania, Mozambique, Zambia	0	0
Sweden	Ex-Yugoslavia, Tanzania, Mozambique	0	0
(3 Low Performers)			
Japan	Indonesia, China, Philippines	0	6
Ireland	Tanzania, Lesotho, Zambia	0	0
United States	Israel, Egypt, El Salvador	6/3	2
(Major Powers Not Included)			
France	Ivory Coast, Cameroon, N. Caledonia	2?	12
Germany	Egypt, Ex-Yugoslavia, India	0	1

Top 3 Recipients: the top 3 recipients of a donor's bilateral aid

Of Top 15, Mil. Priv.: among a donor's top 15 recipients, the number of recipients from which the donor receives significant military privileges (basing rights, etc.)

Of Top 15, Fmr. Col./Mil. Occup.: among a donor's top 15 recipients, the number of recipient countries that were occupied or colonized by the donor (within the modern era)

Socialist Views of Aid

As is the case with the classical Realists, foreign aid postdates the era of classical Marxist scholarship. Yet if we broadly extrapolate from Marx's writings on imperialism, it seems likely that inasmuch as even exploitative aid-induced growth "batters down all Chinese walls," Marx would at the same time condemn it and urge revolutionaries to take advantage of its progressive effects. Contemporary leftist critics of aid, on the other hand, are less ambivalent: They are more or less united in dismissing government-to-government assistance, not only as ineffective in alleviating poverty but as regressively redistributive. Like the Realists, however, these primarily American authors write primarily about American aid, and as a result, their criticisms may lack generalizability.[44]

That said, Socialist authors have nonetheless made a large and enduring contribution to our understanding of aid, particularly as regards their critique of, first, the economic orthodoxy of aid institutions and, second, international loan assistance and the resultant debt crisis.[45] Their critique is also notable for highlighting aid's destructive effects on the environment and the cultural and class insensitivities of "the development aid industry."[46]

The power of the Socialist critique could be demonstrated in a number of ways. The hard-line, "dependency," Marxist account, associated primarily with André Gunder Frank but also creeping into scholarly works devoted specifically to aid, is that imperialistic "trickle-down" assistance inhibits even medium-term economic growth outright.[47] The softer, more widely shared position is that capitalist aid achieves nothing resembling the type of growth that the global poor need. Aid instead might be tied to purchases from the donor and associated with providing infrastructure or other support for export promotion and donor direct foreign investment. Aid would be directed less at grass roots needs

---

lem.' " See Hook, p. 185. Moreover, in taking motivations of aid recipients into account, even some preeminent "hard" Realists such as Robert Tucker and Stephen Krasner have arrived at a view distinct from that of either Gilpin or Hook. Tucker and Krasner, as we saw, are centrally interested in unmasking the power-maximizing behavior of southern aid-recipient states. In turn, their greatest fear seems to be that northern states will become (or are becoming) model redistributionist aid donors, thereby overlooking the potentially tragic loss of power such aid concedes to (ostensibly) disorderly Third World regimes.

[44] To be sure, leftist critiques direct anger not only at the United States but at multilateral international financial institutions (IFIs), especially at the World Bank and the International Monetary Fund, but these are seen largely as agents of U.S. capital.

[45] This represents one strain within the Marxist paradigm that remains vibrantly proredistributionist. Though a complete dismissal of loan aid neglects the success of at least several of the East Asian newly industrialized countries (NICs)—who have received considerable nongrant assistance from Japan as well as from multilateral sources—the argument is nonetheless one of the strongest within the Marxist arsenal. Cheryl Payer's excellent book *Lent and Lost* (London: Zed Books, 1991) culls a Marxist case largely from financial establishment sources and advocates simple debt repudiation—in other words, a relatively massive redistribution from the North to particularly the African debtor countries. Yet in the evaluation of current aid allotments, it is also important to remember that if there has been one sea change in the modalities of development assistance over the last thirty years, it has been a shift from less than 50 to almost 80 percent of aid in the form of grants. Thus Payer's critique functions primarily as a historical one in regard to private loans made during the 1970s.

[46] David Korten, Robin Broad, and John Cavanaugh are notable among leftist environmentalist critics. The case against the development aid industry is stated in Teresa Hayter and Catherine Watson, *Aid: Rhetoric and Reality* (London: Pluto Press, 1985) and Graham Hancock, *Lords of Poverty* (New York: Atlantic Monthly Press, 1989).

[47] See, for example, André Gunder Frank, *Capitalism and Underdevelopment in Latin*

TABLE 12.4

International Political-Economic Correlates of Foreign Aid

(3 High Performers)	*LIC/LMIC/HMIC+*	*Tied %*	*% Soc./Econ. Inf.*	*Top 15 Ex % DCE's*	*Bi%SSA*
Denmark	53.8/8.5/1.1	na	46.3/6.6	6.2	62.9
Norway	63.4/12.2/1.3	10.4	23.8/12.3	11.5[48]	61.8
Sweden	52.4/16.9/1.4	10.9	26.1/10.3	11.7	49.6
(3 Low Performers)					
Japan	57.7/21.1/3.3	12.5	17.5/27.4	39.6	9.4
Ireland	49.1/8.5/0.7	na	47.9/8.3	6.5	85.0
United States	48.1/14.7/13.1	17.0	15.2/3.5	12.6	18.5
(Major Powers Not Included)					
France	38.4/28.3/12.4	39.3	34.3/12.3	27.9	55.0
Germany	51.2/24.5/3.6	38.6	23.8/13.3	25.3	24.8

LIC/LMIC/HMIC+: the percentages of country-allocated aid allocated to low-, low-middle-, and high-middle- or higher-income countries respectively (see note 48)

Tied %: the percentage of a donor's aid "tied" to purchases of goods or services from that donor

% Soc: the percentage of a donor's aid allocated for human and/or social development purposes

% Econ. Inf.: the percentage of a donor's aid allocated for the construction of economic infrastructure

and more at development that would support indigenous capitalist elites, resulting perhaps in the fact that gaps between rich and poor would be exacerbated by aid. As Table 12.4, "The International Political-Economic Correlates of Aid," indicates, the actual record is complicated.

The statistics in Table 12.4 indicate that the Socialists do have evidence to question the purity of the motives of almost every donor's aid program. For model donors (and for Ireland) only about 10 percent of the total is implicated in pecuniary self-interest. For France, Japan, Germany, and the United States (in that order of severity) a more significant amount of aid seems so motivated. Nonetheless, the statistics in the first column do indicate that every country's "allocated" aid goes primarily to low-income countries.[49] The "SSA" column, indicating aid to some of the very poorest countries, supports a similar conclusion but again raises flags about Japan, the United States, and Germany. Aid "tying" also varies, although this is an area where the United States and Japan perform extremely well. One might also note the significant share of aid that is "Social," contrasted with "Economic Infrastructural", these figures run somewhat against the Marxist interpretation, as may those on aid linkage to export markets. Here we expected across-the-board figures more similar to Japan's (just under 40 percent); in fact, most donors export between only 5 and 15 percent of their total developing country exports to their top fifteen aid recipients. While Socialists might explain this finding as simply depicting the globalization of capitalism, it at the very least counters claims that states tend to focus on, and dominate, a few trade and aid partners. Whatever the motive, the world economy appears to be too globalized readily to accommodate exclusive linkages.

As concerns the distributive effects of aid, it does seem that relative gaps between rich and poor within Southern countries have increased in the foreign

America (New York: Monthly Review Press, 1967). Various empirical dependency school studies are summarized in Mitchell Seligson, ed., *The Gap between Rich and Poor* (Boulder, Colo.: Westview Press, 1984). In evaluation of the hard-line account, it is instructive to compare concessional aid with perhaps the only thing the Marxists dislike more—namely, foreign direct investment (FDI). Here the conclusions of Dennis J. Encarnation and Louis T. Wells, Jr., "Evaluating Foreign Investment," in Theodore H. Moran, ed., *Investing in Development: New Roles for Private Capital* (Washington, D.C.: Overseas Development Council, 1986), p. 67, are suggestive: "Like Reuber, and like Lall and Streeten, we found that a majority (ranging from 55 to 75 percent, depending on our assumptions) of the proposed projects would increase the host country's national income." While this is hardly an unqualified endorsement of FDI, it would certainly require an extreme account (moreover, an extreme *rightist* one) to explain how aid policies designed specifically to increase recipient national income could not perform significantly better. For an empirical evaluation of the soft-line Socialist account, see Montek S. Ahluwalia et al., "Growth and Poverty in Developing Countries," *Journal of Development Economics* 6 (1979), pp. 299–341.

[48]The developing country export share of Norway's top *ten* recipients is only 1.6 percent.

[49]Because of the large amount of aid not allocated to specific countries, percentages do not add up to 100 percent.

aid era. This may be true not because of but in spite of aid, which—in addition to moving from rich to poor countries—seems in aggregate to have had a downwardly redistributive *intra*national effect.[50] Despite the growing gap in wealth, the poorest of the global poor have made gains in terms of health, nutrition, and literacy—notably, gains in large part because of the type of foreign assistance most popular in the North (see Table 12.2 above). Developing country infant mortality rates, for example, have dropped by almost 50 percent during the foreign aid era. Of course this aggregate fact does not negate, much less excuse, the economically regressive disasters caused by individual aid endeavors gone awry (or poorly conceived from the start), disasters the Socialist have done a particularly valuable job of uncovering.[51]

What are the viable Socialist alternatives to Liberal models of development? The Socialists themselves seem to have given up not only on violent revolution but on all existing economic models "Left" and particularly "South" of Sweden. There has been a major shift since 1977, when Frances Moore Lappé's *Food First*, perhaps the first major leftist critique of aid, took pains to establish just what was useful (noting also what was reprehensible) in the Chinese model of development. But though a certain reticence to pick new models is understandable, the latest generation of Socialist books on aid seems to suggest that worthwhile aid objectives can be achieved only through NGOs.[52] This argument is made despite the apparent fact that left-leaning developmentalist regimes—China, Eritrea, South Africa, perhaps even Brazil—have not entirely disappeared from the picture.

Crucial to this neo-Socialist view seems to be a sentiment that "the importance of [development aid's] quantity can be, and has been, overemphasized." In turn "it is bad enough that we [the United States] have already poured so much money down this [aid] drain."[53] While, at least in relative terms, "so much" does not really seem to characterize the past quantity of U.S. aid, it may well be true that the contemporary South cannot replicate the developmental feats of Marshall Plan Europe. In pointing this out, however, those on the left

[50] See Ahluwalia, Mosley, and Seligson.

[51] Indeed, even the long-term record of a program as significant as U.S. PL 480 food assistance, despite ostensibly being aimed at the most absolute of deprivations, may well be one of doing more harm than good to the Third World poor.

[52] See Stephen Hellinger, Douglas Hellinger, and Fred M. O'Regan, *Aid for Just Development* (Boulder, Colo.: Lynne Rienner, 1988).

[53] Ibid., pp. 176, 180. Broad and Cavanaugh echo the Hellingers' argument about the futility of aid and tie it even more directly to one regarding the moral priority of domestic obligations: "[A]t a time when the United States is strapped for cash to rebuild our own nation, it is prudent that we begin to see the Marshall Plan for what it was—the very exceptional case where throwing money at a problem actually worked because the task was rebuilding physical infrastructure in highly industrialized societies ravaged by war," Robin Broad and John Cavanaugh, *Plundering Paradise* (Berkeley: University of California Press, 1993), p. 69.

should accept a special responsibility to avoid a consequent danger identified by southern leaders such as Michael Manley, who alleges that particularly the American left's desire to "close the development gap" seems at times to have been superseded by a desire to entrench it.[54]

One source of compromise may lie in the fact that almost all radical reformers concede the existence of *some* good state aid programs. While the vital role of NGOs is likewise widely recognized, one doubts they can do *all* that needs to be done in helping the Southern poor achieve economic justice. Nor can NGOs finance the means of upholding country-wide standards of education and health, much less deal with structural causes of regressive exploitation and put a stop to the major (e.g., state and corporate) sources of environmental degradation. But the most crucial caveat to a "quality, not quantity," approach to aid may be the fact that even if one ignores net negative transfers from North to South, *current aid totals amount to just fourteen dollars per person in the global South per year.* While it is tempting to suggest a few things people *can* buy for fourteen dollars, suffice it to say that economic justice is not on the list. Ironically, this is all the more true if we evaluate redistributive efforts according to the exacting demands of Marxist or Social Liberal justice.

CONCLUSION

Altogether there are serious objections in principle and significant restrictions in practice to an effective regime of global distributive justice. Is anything left of the obligation to help the world's starving or to promote a more egalitarian world economic order? Our answer depends on which view of international ethics (Realist, Socialist, or Liberal) we hold and how absolutely we do so. We can, however, conceive of mixed views that satisfy many objections but still include real duties to redistribute wealth or to aid the starving.

If a prudent Realist puts security first, and relative power of state next, yet acknowledges a residual duty to aid the desperate, then she should follow Robert Gilpin's suggestion. Abstractly, he notes, you can help the global poor three ways: (1) exporting capital (but this weakens the economy at home); (2) importing products (but this puts domestic corporations out of business and workers out of jobs, and it increases dangerous dependence); or (3) importing the global poor (bring the poor to the jobs). The third adds population, which

[54] Though perhaps consistent with a doctrine of social anarchism, these critics depart sharply from the country's premier social anarchist Noam Chomsky, who suggests that the United States has enormous financial obligations to Third World states harmed by our policies during the Cold War. ("An Evening with Noam Chomsky," April 18, 1994, University of Minnesota.) Nor do these authors necessarily echo the views of even the most left-leaning and nonoperational NGOs.

adds to national power (reserve soldiers), and this is good Machiavellian Realism. Immigration was once thought to be economically disruptive. It was said to hurt the domestic poor through additional unemployment, but recent studies indicate otherwise. The Cuban influx into Miami in 1980s, for example, produced growth and no extra unemployment other than that borne temporarily by immigrants themselves.[55] But apart from the Haitians and the Mexicans, how many of the truly poor can reach a wealthy country?

Another possibility is a Liberal view that responds to Realist objections.[56] Let us assume that you accept the argument that there should be no global Difference Principle without a global polity, but that you also feel bound morally to alleviate suffering and the arbitrary character of global resource allocation. Furthermore, if you want to avoid moral tyranny, we can reason that after you have tithed yourself 5 to 10 percent of your income or so, states, not individuals, have the residual obligation to alleviate suffering. Then states can legitimately infer that their obligation is owed to the global poor, not to rival states. Since, however, they can reach the poor only through just states or (marginally) through NGOs, wealthy states are obliged to aid only to the extent that money actually reaches the poor. They can therefore discriminate both against unjust states and against hostile, threatening states. (A Kantian can assume all Liberal states are not threatening.) In periods of great danger, moreover, just wealthy states can discriminate against all, including the just and desperate, in favor of preserving survival first.

This amounts to a discriminate justice that responds to Realist objections. But it still leaves firm duties to aid the desperate when danger is low, when the poor inhabit pacific or nonthreatening states, when they can do so effectively through private means that hostile states cannot exploit. The current blooming of peace, democracy, and security in the world may thus raise, not lower, international moral obligations. Ironically, the peace dividend *should*, by this logic, become an aid dividend. In short, mixing Liberalism and Realism produces less obligation to cure the world's poverty, but a better prospect of alleviating some suffering.

[55] Peter Passell, "So Much for Assumptions about Immigrants and Jobs," *New York Times*, April 25, 1990, p. E4.

[56] Realism and Liberalism are also mixed via the frequent calls for an aid policy that reflects an "enlightened" conception of self-interest—e.g., one that responds to potential risks to human health and to the global environment. Whether there exists a significant distinction between such concerns and a "purer" altruism is much debated.

PART FIVE

FUTURES

Conclusion: Futures

THE DISCOVERY OF the hypothetical future is something like the actual discoveries of the past. It is said that the explorer Columbus saw above the surf of a Caribbean beach a streak of waving palms and declared that he had discovered a province of Cathay. The explorer projected an expectation, a vision, a theory, onto inherently ambiguous evidence. Slowly and at great cost, expectations and realities converged.

We too are explorers, explorers of the future. We see momentous changes: the end of the Cold War, the spread of freedom and democracy, the dissolution of the Soviet empire and then the Soviet Union, the integration of Europe, the rise of Japan, the relative economic decline and geopolitical rise of the United States, the emergence of China, the collapse of states in Africa and Eastern Europe, the collective defense of the Persian Gulf, and a renewed policy debate between internationalism and isolationism. We declare these changes to be a "new world order." And now we must ask what do we mean.

In this concluding part, I project forward our three visions of the new world order: Realism, Liberalism, and Socialism. What are their implications, and how does each account for the transformation of world politics—the revolutions of 1989 and 1990? I engage in these prognostications not to lay claim to a new continent but to help us sharpen our own skills at mapmaking. After describing their assessments of the recent transformations in the world system, I speculate on what difference these different visions of the new world order might make.

FORWARD TO THE PAST?

According to many in the Realist school of commentators, the "new world order" that we are entering will be a new rendition of the classical balance of power when three or more (ideally five) nearly equal states competed in flexible alliances.[1] According to Hobbesian structuralists, this is because states are always balancing power against power. What is new, therefore, following the collapse of the Soviet bloc and the relative decline of the United States, is the increase in the number of players, from two to many and therefore from bipolar to more "classical," eighteenth-century–style multipolar balancing. Rousseauian constitutional sociologists note that a decrease in heterogeneity of the world (after the demise of the Cold War) at last allows states to perceive their true national interests shining through the clearing fog of Communist and capitalist ideologies. And Machiavellian strategists, while agreeing with the previous two, add that statesmanship will be required if states are to play the balance of power game effectively. Whether for one reason or the other, leaders and alliances will change, they all agree. States will "rebalance" by arming (internal balancing) and by dissolving old alliances and forming new ones (external balancing), as they have time and again, in response to large shifts in the relative distribution of power among states in the international system.

When the Realists assess the future, they are rarely given to optimism. Indeed, just as the public is now arriving at the party to celebrate the good times of the end of the Cold War, so some Realists stand at the door to announce the party is over: The good times *were* the Cold War. Then it was, according to them, that we enjoyed bipolar stability, military equivalence, and nuclear deterrence. During that time statesmen could focus on just one rival; the likelihood of confusions was greatly reduced. The bipolar structure of the international system ensured that neither superpower—neither the Soviet Union nor the United States—was drawn into wars as a function of vital attempts to protect vulnerable allies.[2] Former Soviet power has collapsed, and Realists ask what that collapse might portend for the future.

The Present. Let us begin with the consequences for *internal balancing.* Commentators offer us three scenarios in what might be called a politically significant (albeit mathematically curious) arithmetic of the future. The first scenario is unipolarity, and here the bipolarity of "two" minus the collapse of

[1] For two valuable and provocative examples, see the essays by John Mearsheimer and Henry Kissinger, in Graham Allison and Gregory Treverton, eds., *Rethinking American Security* (New York: Norton, 1991).

[2] The probipolar Realist analysis of the Cold War is well developed through Waltz (1979); John Gaddis, *The Long Peace* (New York: Oxford University Press, 1987); and John Mearsheimer, "Back to the Future," *International Security*, 15, 1 (Summer 1990), pp. 5–56. Other Realist analysis, that of Deutsch and Singer, draws out the advantages of multipolar systems.

the Soviet "one" equals, arithmetically, "one," or unipolarity.[3] Here the United States is the only military and economic superpower left. But the Realists also warn us that these hopes of unipolar dominance are unlikely to be realized. Realist logic holds that self-help competition ensures pressure toward military equivalence. "Clubs are trumps," Hobbes long ago warned us. The economic superpowers of Japan and Germany/Europe will acquire the full panoply of military resources to match their economic might, converging on some common ratio of investment in security with the United States. These military resources are likely to include the most efficient producers of security, nuclear weapons. That is not a description of a unipolar distribution of basic capabilities.

Realist arithmetic therefore generates a second scenario. "Two" minus "one" is really "three"—that is, the United States, a hypothetically uniting "Europe," and Japan, or "four," if the CIS/Russia survives its current strains, or even "five," if China continues at the same rate of economic growth. This multipolar world will replicate a new struggle for dominance and perhaps be the fertile ground for a new cycle of hegemonic competition as we wait to see which of these powers emerges to govern the world twenty to thirty years from now.[4] The Realists, furthermore, warn us that whatever tendencies toward balanced stability the international system might have possessed have been regularly given a shock by attempts to create hegemony. Each of these attempts, successful and unsuccessful, at hegemony have been accompanied by system-wide wars of hegemonic transition, wherein a declining hegemon seeks to hold on to its power and rising states challenge its predominance. Britain and France warred throughout the seventeenth and eighteenth centuries before Britain finally emerged dominant after the Napoleonic Wars. Germany challenged Britain in World War I and again in World War II before the United States emerged as the leader of the West and was in turn challenged by the Soviet Union as the leader of the East.[5]

Indeed, Realists could well argue that the next turn on the cycle of hegemony will be "fought" the same way the last one was. Here we refer not to Germany's competition or challenge to Britain in the world wars but to the Soviet challenge to U.S. hegemony in the postwar period of the nuclear long peace. Our hegemonic war was a Cold War fought in bloody proxy wars in Vietnam and in Afghanistan and, at great financial cost, in arms races. It was a war of attrition, a war of exhaustion, in which the United States spent eleven

[3]Charles Krauthammer, in Allison and Treverton, 1992.

[4]For a thorough exposition of why this will be the case, see Layne, "The Unipolar Illusion: Why New Great Powers Will Arise."

[5]Gilpin, *War and Change in World Politics* and his "The Richness of the Tradition of Political Realism," in Robert Keohane, ed., *Neorealism and Its Critics* (New York: Columbia University Press, 1986).

trillion dollars and the USSR lost to the superior position, more coherent alliance, and productivity of the U.S. economy.[6] It was this loss, Realists could well assert, that led to the democratic revolutions of 1989, as the Soviets, exhausted, withdrew their legions from Eastern Europe and the colonialist shell states they left behind collapsed. We face a similar cold war, the Realists now warn us, a cold war in which Japan (or perhaps Western Europe) will challenge the declining hegemony now exercised by the United States. Thus the Realists tell us that if we are *lucky*, we will be able to replay the Cold War and compete without a nuclear holocaust.

But the Realists say that in yet a third scenario we may not be so lucky as to fight another cold war. The chances of luck indeed fall in multipolar systems as some of the structural theorists warn us. There will be much more danger of buckpassing as great powers, in a more complex multipolar world with their attention dispersed, fail to deter local aggressive expansion, which later (recall Japan and Germany in the 1930s) turns into global expansion. "Chain ganging" also spreads in a multipolar world because allies now count for relatively more power, and therefore states will fight to hold on to their allies.[7] An increased number of relevant actors increases the prospects of uncertainty step by step with the increase in the number of planners. Nuclear proliferation to four or five or more equivalent nuclear powers can undermine deterrence and threaten the nuclear peace by increasing the prospect of surprises and panics. There would then be three or four enemies to monitor and the increased danger of four or five ganging up on one. With greater numbers of nuclear powers, proliferation itself can become less controlled and include proliferation to "crazy states." Although multipolar systems also may generate crosscutting ties and thus dampen conflict, nuclear weapons may erode the effects of those ties.[8] In these last scenarios Realist arithmetic warns us that "two" minus "one" might become zero.

In light of the danger of equality, officials in the Bush administration sought to outline a unipolar strategy with a $1.2 trillion five-year defense plan to preclude any combination of states, whether foes or allies, from acquiring a regional dominance that would permit them to challenge the U.S. position as lone superpower.[9] Issued in the midst of the 1992 primary campaign, the draft

[6]The figure is Greg Treverton's from Allison and Treverton (1992). For a valuable discussion of the end of the Cold War, from a Realist point of view, see William Wohlforth, "Realism and the End of the Cold War," *International Security* 19, 3 (1995), pp. 91–129.
[7]Christensen and Snyder, "Chain Gangs and Passed Bucks."
[8]Deutsch and Singer.
[9]The memo by Undersecretary of Defense Paul Wolfowitz was leaked to the *New York Times;* see Patrick Tyler, "Lone Superpower Plan: Ammunition for Critics," *New York Times*, March 10, 1992, p. A12. It was promptly criticized by the isolationist Patrick Buchanan and by such internationalists as Democratic candidates Paul Tsongas and Bill Clinton. The Bush administration replied that the memo was only a preliminary draft.

policy guidance met heated criticism from both "isolationists," who were unwilling to write a blank check to defend allies around the globe, and from "internationalists," who were appalled at the policy's neglect of multilateral cooperation.

A global hegemonic strategy was not out of the question at the end of the Cold War. U.S. defense spending was $277 billion in 1993. Identifiable potential threats to the United States included (by popular estimate) Russia, whose defense spending was estimated at $29 billion; China, $22 billion; Iraq, $9 billion; North Korea, $2 billion; and Iran, Syria, and Cuba, $1.2 billion each. The total at $66 billion was less than one-quarter of U.S. spending. The United States and its (1993) allies spent $454 billion, seven times that disbursed by the perceived potential enemies, who spent $66 billion.[10] Expanding the view to a pure balance of power calculation would require us to balance against Japan at $40 billion; France, Britain, and Germany at $36, $35, and $31 billion respectively. Italy, Saudi Arabia, and South Korea were at $17, $16, and $12 billion respectively. The total of other nations in the top ten was $238 billion, $39 billion less than the United States alone.

Commentators, however, have noted that a hegemonic strategy was unlikely to be realistic in the longer run. Even in the short run, finding domestic support would be difficult.[11] In the longer run, power balances change. The United States too will need to adjust. All previous hegemony-threatening distributions met a counterpoise coalition, as did Spain in the sixteenth century, France in the seventeenth, and Germany in the twentieth. Is there any reason for a Realist to suspect that U.S. predominance will not?

We should therefore, according to Realist theory, look to the consequences of a revival of *external balancing*. Shifting alliances is the dominant strategy of multipolar systems where internal efforts are inevitably discounted by the higher number of potentially threatening states and external balancing offers fiscally free resources.[12] Under multipolar competition will we see a continuation of the traditional Cold War alliances or should we too expect a realignment, a diplomatic revolution?

The relationship of alliances in the Cold War period gives some indication that states could have made their choices between the United States and the Soviet Union as alliance hegemons on the basis of a balance of power calculation, rather than just on the basis of tugs of ideological solidarity or economic interests. As Table Part 5.3 indicates, Moscow was Washington's greatest threat (measured by capability divided by distance), and Washington was Moscow's. Moscow was also much more of a threat to Berlin, Paris, and London than was Washington. Yet there were many exceptions to balancing logic, including most

[10] See Franklyn Holtzman, "Pentagon Overkill," *New York Times*, letter, February 1, 1995.
[11] See Layne, "The Unipolar Illusion."
[12] Deutsch and Singer, pp. 390–406.

TABLE PART 5.1

Power Resources, 1985
(GNP in $Bil.; Defense Spending in $Bil.; Armed Forces in Mil. of soldiers)

	USA	*USSR*	*Japan*	*W. Ger*	*France*	*UK*	*China*	*Canada*
GNP	3297.8	1843.4	1137.7	698.9	564.2	507.4	401	299.4
Defense	217.2	258	11.5	23.6	23.8	27.4	34.5	6.4
Armed	2.22	4.40	0.241	0.496	0.578	0.333	4.10	0.081

Sources: ACDA, *World Military Expenditures and Arms Transfers 1985* (Washington, D.C., 1986), and Walt, *Origins of Alliances*, pp. 289–91.

TABLE PART 5.2

Distances between Capitals, in Km.

	Beijing	*Brussels*	*London*	*Mexico*	*Moscow*	*Ot-tawa*	*Paris*	*Tokyo*	*Wash.*
Berlin*	7375	654	934	9746	1612	6147	880	8942	6729
Washington	11170	6233	5915	3033	7842	733	6180	10925	
Tokyo	2104	9476	9585	11319	7502	10342	9738		
Paris	8236	262	341	9213	2492	5664			
Ottawa	10475	5691	5379	3603	7179				
Moscow	5809	2260	2506	10740					
Mexico City	12478	9264	8947						
London	8160	320							
Brussels	7983								

Source: Gary Fitzpatrick and Marilyn Modin, *Direct Line Distances* (Metuchen: Scarecrow Press, 1986).
* Berlin, rather than Bonn, for later comparison

TABLE PART 5.3

Threat Matrices, 1985
(GNP/Distance and Defense/Distance)

		Threat to:							
Threat by:		Washington	Moscow	Tokyo	Berlin*	Paris	London	Beijing	Ottawa
Washington	GNP		0.421	0.302	0.490	0.534	0.558	0.295	4.499
	Defense		0.028	0.020	0.032	0.035	0.037	0.019	0.296
Moscow	GNP	0.235		0.246	1.144	0.740	0.736	0.317	0.257
	Defense	0.033		0.034	0.160	0.104	0.103	0.044	0.036
Tokyo	GNP	0.104						0.541	
	Defense	0.001						0.005	
Berlin	GNP	0.104	0.434			0.794			
	Defense	0.004	0.015			0.027			

obviously Canada and Mexico. Either the balancers need to show that those two states were so hegemonically constrained as to lack the capacity to assess independently their own national security—by balancing against the United States and aligning with the less threatening (because more remote) USSR—or scholars should infer that they do not seem to have fully bought the logic of the balance of power. More important, there is little evidence that middle powers followed the logic systematically, that France balanced against Germany or Britain, for example, or the Peoples Republic of China against the USSR in 1949–1960. Instead in the Cold War the logic of power balance has been married to the competing logics of the ideological Cold War and economic interest: Liberal solidarity, Liberal imperialism, and Soviet imperialism.

Even the simple balancing calculations have been complicated by the radically more complicated factor of the meaning of distance, now that the distance-shrinking technologies of communications and long-distance logistics disturb all the direct ratios. President Kennedy, adopting an argument of Secretary of Defense McNamara, put it succinctly during the Cuban Missile Crisis when he said: "You may say it doesn't make any difference if you get blown up by an ICBM flying from the Soviet Union or one that was ninety miles away. Geography doesn't mean that much."[13] (The President then went on to stress the significance of the missiles for the regional, *psychological* balance of prestige.) Simple geographic distance may now be unimportant compared with the economic, organizational, and psychological costs of action, which would tend to shrink the globe to an universal immediacy.[14] Equipoise then would domi-

TABLE PART 5.4

Equipoise, 1985
(GNP in $Bil., Defense in $Bil., Armed Forces in Mil.)

			Ratio
GNP	Nato and Japan	7514.9	2.930
	Warsaw Pact	2564.7	
Defense	Nato and Japan	340.70	1.136
	Warsaw Pact	299.80	
Army	Nato and Japan	6.1670	1.061
	Warsaw Pact	5.8100	

[13]Quoted in Michael Beschloss, *The Crisis Years* (New York: HarperCollins, 1991), pp. 442–43.
[14]Albert Wohlstetter, "Illusions of Distance," *Foreign Affairs* 46, 2 (1968), pp. 242–55.

TABLE PART 5.5

Equipoise Balances in the 1990s*

	GNP	Ratio
Equipoise 1:		
U.S., Eur., Japan, PRC	18	9
CIS	2	
Equipoise 2:		
U.S., Eur., Japan	14	2.33
CIS, PRC	6	
Equipoise 3:		
Eur., CIS, PRC	12	1.5
U.S., Japan	8	
Equipoise 4:		
U.S., CIS, PRC	11	1.22
Eur., Japan	9	
Equipoise 5:		
Eur., Japan, CIS	11	1.22
U.S., PRC	9	
Equipoise 6:		
Eur., U.S.	11	1.22
Japan, PRC, CIS	9	
Equipoise 7:		
U.S., Japan, CIS	10	1
Eur., PRC	10	

*Paul Kennedy estimates GNPs in 1990s for a (united) Europe at $6 trillion, United States at 5, Japan at 3, and Russia/CIS at 2 in *Grand Strategies in War and Peace*, Yale University Press, p. 181. PRC/China is estimated at $4 trillion for 2000.

nate counterpoise. (For Cold War equipoise measures, see Table Part 5.4.) Or we may not be able to assess a balance of power short of doing a multifaceted analysis of the costs of exercising force at a distance, and then we will need an algorithm that combines the many faces of power. But as noted above, the future might also be simpler from a security point of view than the past as we move into a world where the ideological factor sinks and the relative weight of the two superpowers declines. Other factors, including webs of economic and political integration and rivalry, even then will complicate this world.[15]

Let us nonetheless assume for the purpose of analysis that we now move forward to a period in which the structural and sociological conditions of the classical balance of power are once again present. What would such a world look like? Will we see a continuation of the traditional alliances, or should we too expect a Diplomatic Revolution.

Paul Kennedy has phrased the problem starkly from a balance of power perspective as he commented on the burden the United States bore at the end of the Cold War: "It is not a good strategy for the long term to have a country with a five trillion dollar economy (US) contributing so much more for defense in order to protect allies possessing economies of six trillion dollars (the European Community) and three trillion dollars (Japan) from the threat posed by a country with an economy of a little over two trillion dollars (the USSR)."[16] But what new alliances will be formed in a more multipolar era? How will states re-balance?

The Middle Run. Let us accept a very rough, relative estimate of prospective GNPs of the great powers of the late 1990s as follows: a (by assumption united) European Union $6 trillion (1980s dollars), the United States at 5, PRC/China at 4, Japan at 3, and Russia/Commonwealth of Independent States (CIS) at 2. If we measure power in GNP and judge from an equipoise point of view, is it reasonable to suppose a continuation of the radically nonequipoised, recent Cold War alliance system with the United States, a uniting Europe, Japan, and the PRC (at 18) all ganged up against whatever unity and continuity the Russia/CIS (at 2) might be able to muster? (See Table Part 5.5—"Equipoise Balances in the 1990s.") A somewhat more equipoised arrangement would be a return to the old (pre-1960) Cold War (United States, Europe, and Japan against Russia and China), which would produce a power ratio of 2.33. A "Heartlands versus Rimlands"—Europe, the CIS, and China (Eurasia) against the United States and Japan (Equipoise 3)—offers another step toward balance. The next (Equipoise 4) resembles the Grand Alliance of World War Two, pits the United States, CIS, and PRC against Europe and Japan (Equipoise 4). Equipoise 5

[15] The two most plausible portraits of the future I have read are by Stanley Hoffmann, "Delusions of World Order," *New York Review of Books* (April 9, 1992), and Robert Jervis, "The Future of World Politics: Will It Resemble the Past?" *International Security* 16, 3 (1991–1992), pp. 39–73. Both speculate on the effects of a sophisticated mix of a number of new and indeterminate factors in world politics.

[16] Paul Kennedy, "American Grand Strategy Today and Tomorrow," *Grand Strategies in War and Peace,* p. 181. It clearly makes sense to add the factor of China to this strategic calculus. For a valuable account of the role of East Asia in generating strife in the years ahead, see Aaron Friedberg, "Ripe for Rivalry," *International Security* 18, 3 (Winter 1993), pp. 5–34.

joins the United States and PRC against Europe, Japan, and the CIS. Equipoise 6 sets Europe and the United States against Japan, China, and the CIS. (Culturally this happens to pit the "West" against "the rest.") But Equipoise 7 is the most equipoised of all, combining the United States, Japan, and the CIS against Europe and the PRC, a perfectly equipoised balance of 10 versus 10. It is a curious and original combination with few cultural resonances, though I know which alliance's chefs I would prefer! But is the logic of equipoise sustained by counterpoise?

Let us examine what we saw as the traditionally more direct, more powerful logic of distance-sensitive geopolitical counterpoising and its various threat matrices. (See Table Part 5.6, "Counterpoise Threats (Ts) in the 1990s.) Let us thus assume that despite all the changes in technology, geography still counts for security purposes, psychological distance mirrors geographic distance, and we can measure perceived political distance as the distance between capitals. Brussels (the European Community) will then be most threatening to Washington; Moscow (or should it be Minsk, the prospective CIS capital?) most threatening to Brussels, though only marginally so. Beijing is most threatening to Tokyo, and conversely, Tokyo is most threatening to Beijing. Brussels is by far the most threatening to Moscow. The United States, because of the blessings of the expanse of the Atlantic and Pacific oceans, is the least threatened great power (with, consequently, the greatest temptations to isolationism?).

Let us examine another measure of alliance determination, alliance *stability measures* (Table Part 5.7). The alliance threat quotient is the sum of the threats against which an alliance balances. Given the flexibility, and hence contingent reliability, of all alliances, threat quotients have the advantage of measuring the

TABLE PART 5.6

Counterpoise Threats (T's) in the 1990s
(GNP/Distance)

Washington Threat Matrix	
Brussels	0.96
Tokyo	0.27
Moscow	0.26
Beijing	0.36

Tokyo Threat Matrix	
Washington	0.46
Moscow	0.27
Brussels	0.63
Beijing	1.90

Beijing Threat Matrix	
Brussels	0.75
Tokyo	1.43
Washington	0.45
Moscow	0.34

Brussels Threat Matrix	
Washington	0.80
Tokyo	0.32
Moscow	0.88
Beijing	0.50

Moscow Threat Matrix	
Washington	0.64
Brussels	2.65
Tokyo	0.40
Beijing	0.69

TABLE PART 5.7

Threat Quotients and Alliance Stability in the 1990s

					Alliance Total	System Total
Counterpoise 1 ("New Cold War Continued")						
Washington	Brussels	Tokyo	Beijing			
0.26	0.88	0.27	0.34	=	1.75	
USSR						
4.38				=	4.38	
						6.13
Counterpoise 2 ("Old Cold War Revived")						
Washington	Brussels	Tokyo		=		
0.62	1.38	2.17			4.17	
Moscow	Beijing			=		
3.69	2.63				6.32	
						10.49
Counterpoise 3 ("Heartlands vs. Rimlands")						
Brussels	Beijing	Moscow		=		
1.12	1.88	1.04			4.04	
Washington	+	Tokyo		=		
1.22		2.80			4.02	
						8.06
Counterpoise 4 ("New Grand Alliance")						
Brussels	+	Tokyo		=		
2.18		2.63			4.81	
Washington	Beijing	Moscow		=		
1.23	2.18	3.05			6.46	
						11.27
Counterpoise 5						
Brussels	Moscow	Tokyo		=		
1.30	1.33	2.36			4.99	
Washington	+	Beijing		=		
1.49		2.52			4.01	
						9.00
Counterpoise 6						
Brussels	+	Washington		=		
1.70		0.89			2.59	
Tokyo	Beijing	Moscow		=		
1.09	1.2	3.29			5.58	
						8.17

Counterpoise 7				Alliance	System
Washington	Tokyo	Moscow	=		
1.32	2.53	3.34		7.19	
Brussels	+	Beijing	=		
2.00		2.22		4.22	
					11.41

sum of the individual strategic values of the alliance for the allied states. Threat quotients, as chapter 5 argues, also generate the best measure of the alliance stability of an international system, which is the difference between the sums of the threat quotients of the most valuable and next most valuable sets of possible alliances. This is because the higher the alliance threat quotient, the greater its strategic value, and the larger the difference between the threat quotients of the existing and any other potential alliance, the more resistant the system should be to a change in partners. Conversely, the smaller the difference of threat quotients, the more vulnerable the system should be to a diplomatic revolution. International systems in which military resources change should, if states play according to Realist rules, therefore experience diplomatic revolutions. (This is what the traditional "flexibility" of alliance patterns means.) Conversely, international systems that, from a balance of power view, embody alliances strategically inferior to possible alliances suggest that the game is not being played by Realist rules.

If we compare the "New Grand Alliance" (Counterpoise 4: Europe and Japan versus the United States, CIS, and China) to Counterpoise 5 (Europe, Japan, and the USSR versus the United States and China), we see that "New Grand Alliance" has a larger sum of threat quotients (11.27) than does Counterpoise 5 (9.00). The sum of the threat quotients of the competing alliances measures the *stability* of the system of alliances, larger sums indicating greater value, greater stability. The "New Grand Alliance" (Counterpoise 4) is a more stable interstate system than Counterpoise 5, which is more stable than Counterpoise 6. But Counterpoise 7 (Europe and China versus the United States, Japan, and Russia) is the most stable system of all (11.41). Interestingly, this geopolitical "hopscotch"—with the breadth of the Pacific standing for another country—would look most familiar to the classical strategists from Philippe de Commines with his fifteenth-century "checkerboard" to Prince Kavnitz and his Diplomatic Revolution of 1756.

The United States, Japan and Russia get stuck with a historically difficult set of allies, passionately disliked former enemies from World War II and the Cold War, while the two great protectionist trade powers will have to learn to rely on each other. There is great deal of stress hidden in these simple numbers.

TABLE PART 5.8

GDP in 2020, PPP Basis, in US$ Billions

GDP	China	USA	EU	Japan	India	Indonesia	S. Korea	Thailand
2020	20,000	13,470	12,390	5052	4802	4157	3412	2384
1995	3205.0	6920	6200	2595	1320	666	547	382

Sources: Central Intelligence Agency, *Factbook 1995*, World Bank Growth Estimates, cited on p. 11 in Richard Halloran, "The Rising East," *Foreign Policy* (Spring 1996), pp. 3–21. I have constructed the 2020 EU figure from 1994 data and the average rate of growth of EU economies in 1994. I have dropped Germany, which is predicted to have a GDP of $2687 billion in 2020.

TABLE PART 5.9

Threat Quotients (gdp/distance)

from\to	Beijing	Wash.	Brussels	Tokyo	New Delhi	Jakarta	Seoul	Bangkok	SUM
Beijing		1.79	2.51	9.51	5.28	3.85	20.88	6.08	49.9
Washington	1.21		2.16	1.23	1.12	0.82	1.2	0.95	8.69
Brussels	1.55	1.99		1.31	1.93	1.09	1.42	1.34	10.63
Tokyo	2.4	0.46	0.53		0.86	0.87	4.36	1.1	10.58
New Delhi	1.27	0.4	0.75	0.82		0.96	1.02	1.65	6.87
Jakarta	0.8	0.25	0.36	0.72	0.83		0.79	1.8	5.55
Seoul	3.56	0.3	0.39	2.94	0.73	0.65		0.92	9.49
Bangkok	0.72	0.17	0.26	0.52	0.82	1.03	0.64		4.16
SUM	11.51	5.36	6.96	17.05	11.57	9.27	30.31	13.84	

Long-Run Asia-Centric Balances. What will the balances look like in 2020? Here we must adopt even more uncertain data, the very tentative World Bank projections of GDP to 2020 (see Table Part 5.8). The most striking fact of these projections is the predominance of China, whose GDP is anticipated to be $20 trillion, almost as large as that of the United States at $13.5 trillion and the European Union (EU) at $12.4 trillion combined.[17] The second most striking fact in these projections is the regional predominance of East Asia. The top eight countries—China, United States, Japan, India, Indonesia, Germany, South Korea, and Thailand—include only two non-Asian countries. (If we assume an EU in 2020, it replaces Germany and ranks third, behind China and the United States.) If these theoretical projections turn out to be correct, Asia will hold roughly the position Europe held in the world in 1900. The matrix of threats undergoes an equivalent transformation (Table Part 5.9). Given the concentration of capability and proximity in Asia, Washington and Brussels (EU) experience remarkable security; Seoul and Tokyo, equally striking insecurity. Beijing's predominance makes it the most threatening power.

If we look first at the global balance of power among the big four (Table Part 5.10)—China, the United States, EU, and Japan—the only alignment close to *equipoise* balance pits East versus West (Equipose 2), in which Japan and China (together 25.1 trillion) balance Europe and the United States (together 25.9 trillion). We might well expect in this scenario that though driven by balancing logic, cultural superstructure might play an exacerbating role, identifying the conflict as a "West versus the rest" crusade. But if distance continues to play a geopolitical role—and we thus take into account threat considerations that discount capability by distance—a different, a *counterpoise*, balance results. Here (Table Part 5.11) we see that the most stable alliance system (the one that generates the most security through alliance against the greatest threats, a sum of 20.9) pits the continental heartlands (China and EU) against the geopolitical rimlands (the United States and Japan). Japan is able to acquire U.S. support against China; the United States obtains Japan's support against the EU. But although this is the single most stable alliance pattern, it is not strongly stable: Unipolar alignments against China or a checkerboard joining the People's Republic of China and the United States against Japan and the EU are all close rivals. The only alliance system ruled out is the favorite equipoise system, East versus West. As long as Japan has allies against China, anything goes, and flexible alliances are likely.

The regional balance in Asia is clearly bound to be unipolar and antihegemonic. As long as self-helping states seeking to enhance their independence govern (and thus balance rather than bandwagon), the only balance is one that

[17] Also striking is the absence of Russia. The World Bank's projection of Russian economic growth fails to allow for a recovery from the current crisis.

TABLE PART 5.10

Equipoise Measures: Big Four Alliances

			SUM	Ratio
Equipoise 1: Unipolar				
PRC				
20,000			20,000	
EU	US	Japan		0.646998
12,390	13,470	5052	30,912	
Equipoise 2: East-West				
PRC	Japan			
20,000	5052		25,052	
EU	US			0.968755
12,390	13,470		25,860	
Equipoise 3: Heartland-Rimland				
PRC	EU			
20,000	12,390		32,390	
US	Japan			1.748731
13,470	5052		18,522	
Equipoise 4: Checkerboard				
PRC	US			
20,000	13,470		33,470	
EU	Japan			1.918931
12,390	5052		17,442	

TABLE PART 5.11

Counterpoise Measures: Big Four Alliances

			Alliance	System
Counterpoise 1: Unipolar				
PRC				
5.16			5.16	
EU	US	Japan		18.97
2.51	1.79	9.51	13.81	
Counterpoise 2: East-West				
PRC	Japan			
2.76	2.54		5.3	
EU	US			10.59
3.04	2.25		5.29	
Counterpoise 3: Heartland-Rimland				
PRC	EU			
3.61	2.69		6.3	
US	Japan			20.9
3.78	10.82		14.6	
Counterpoise 4: Checkerboard				
PRC	US			
3.95	2.45		6.4	
EU	Japan			19.65
2.51	10.74		13.25	

TABLE PART 5.12

Equipoise Measures: East Asia

			SUM	Ratio
Equipoise 1: Unipolar				
PRC				
20,000			20,000	
Japan	India	Indonesia		1.009744
5,052	4,802	4,157	19,807	
S. Korea	Thailand			
3,412	2,384			

TABLE PART 5.13

Counterpoise Measures: East Asia

			Alliance	System
Counterpoise 1: Unipolar				
PRC				
9			9	
Japan	India	Indonesia		54
10	5	3.85	46	
S. Korea	Thailand			
21	6			

TABLE PART 5.14

Equipoise Measures: World

			SUM	Ratio
Equipoise 1: North-South				
PRC	India	Indonesia		
20,000	4,802	4,157		
S. Korea	Thailand		34,755	
3,412	2,384			1.124321
EU	US	Japan		
12,390	13,470	5,052	30,912	
Equipoise 2: East-West				
PRC	Japan	India		
20,000	5,052	4,802	39,807	
Indonesia	S. Korea	Thailand		
4,157	3,412	2,384		
EU	US			1.539327
12,390	13,470		25,860	
Equipoise 3: Heartland-Rimland				
PRC	EU			
20,000	12,390		32,390	
US	Japan	India		0.973345
13,470	5,052	4,802	33,277	
Indonesia	S. Korea	Thailand		
4,157	3,412	2,384		
Equipoise 4: Checkerboard				
PRC	Japan	Indonesia		
20,000	5,052	4,157	29,209	
EU	US	India		0.801168
12,390	13,470	4,802	36,458	
S. Korea	Thailand			
3,412	2,384			

TABLE PART 5.15

Counterpoise Measures: World

			Alliance	System
Counterpoise 1: North-South				
PRC	India	Indonesia		
5.16	3.91	2.78	22.22	
S. Korea	Thailand			
6.98	3.39			
EU	US	Japan		43.91
4.27	2.91	14.51	21.69	
Counterpoise 2: East-West				
PRC	Japan	India		
2.76	2.54	3.05	15.17	
Indonesia	S. Korea	Thailand		
1.91	2.62	2.29		
US	EU			23.34
3.37	4.8		8.17	
Counterpoise 3: Heartland-Rimland				
PRC	EU			
9.96	4.45		14.41	
US	Japan	India		70.88
3.78	10.82	7.21	56.47	
Indonesia	S. Korea	Thailand		
4.94	22.3	7.42		
Counterpoise 4: Checkerboard				
PRC	Japan	Indonesia		
8.31	6.82	4.55	19.68	
EU	US	India		67.45
3.4	2.5	6.86	47.77	
S. Korea	Thailand			
26.03	8.98			

joins them all against the predominant power of China. (see Tables Part 5.12 and Part 5.13.)

If we last turn to a worldwide balance in which all the top eight states participate, both equipoise and counterpoise considerations result in a heartland-rimland arrangement (Tables Part 5.14–Part 5.15). The EU and China face a wide rimland coalition of the United States, Japan, India, Indonesia, Korea, and Thailand, all of which surround the two heartland-continental states. This is a very stable alignment; its only rival is the checkerboard pattern in which the threat between Indonesia and Thailand and India drives Indonesia into an alignment with China and Europe. These alignments again correspond with no (currently anticipatable) ideological or cultural alignments. Their closest, stylized historical reference might be classical balancing and coalition formation of the turn of the nineteenth century and the alliance of small powers against Napoleonic imperialism or France, Britain, and the United States against the Axis powers and the USSR in 1941.

As were the earlier models, these numbers are only ideal rational abstractions, which assume that states calculate only their structural relative strategic capacities and put aside all considerations of moral principle, domestic structure, ideology, and economic interest. These therefore are not the only international futures predicted by Realists. Constitutionally (sociologically) inspired Realists of various stripes foresee a coming "clash of civilizations" in which religion once again comes to divide peoples into hostile blocs, while other constitutional Realists describe an emergence of global concert among the great powers.

The Hobbesian structural balance of power can provide some form of order and does so while operating under all the inherent confusion and insecurity of the state of war. But the balance of power, even at its best, is a poor form of international order to rely upon for international security. Once it may have ensured the survival of the great powers and somewhat reduced the number of wars, but it did so at the cost of a large investment in arms, the destruction of small powers, and a devastating series of great power wars. Statespersons have done and should continue to try to do better. The end of the Cold War and the decline of heterogeneity in the international system not only removes alliance handicaps but also presents the opportunity for leaders who are committed to peace and stability to try to build the diplomatic institutions of a revived Concert.[18] A classical balance of power is what we should look forward to in the 1990s only if states are at least rational power calculators—and if the more ambitious efforts we examine next fail.

[18] See the discussions by Charles Kupchan and Clifford Kupchan, "Concerts, Collective Security, and the Future of Europe," *International Security* (1991) and by Richard Rosecrance, "Regionalism and the Post–Cold War Era," *International Journal* 43, 3 (1992), pp. 375–93.

THE FUTURE OF A PACIFIC UNION

Liberalism is the second vision of a possible future. It too is coherent and offers a controversial future; it too may be correct. If history is not at an end and if a broad Liberalism containing contradictory philosophies, movements, states, and ways of life does continue to spread, this could change world politics in ways that are counter to the Realist expectation of a continuing minuet of finely balanced power.

Beginning with the origins of Liberalism in the late eighteenth century, Liberal states have with great success avoided getting into wars with one another. They are as warlike in their relations with non-Liberals as any other state is—perhaps even more prone to getting into imprudent crusades. But among themselves Liberals have established the separate peace Immanuel Kant described. This lack of war seems to be based on the features Kant identified: the restraint that representative institutions impose upon sometimes wayward governments, the respect that Liberal societies have for the freedom that each embodies, and the transnational ties of commerce, investment, and tourism that help create mutual understandings. But these very same ties—representation, a concern for individual rights, and trade—are the forces that make for sometimes imprudent aggression, suspicion, and a confused foreign policy in dealing with non-Liberals.

Over the centuries the Liberal peace has expanded and contracted as Liberal regimes arose and fell, but overall it has grown so that it now includes the sixty to seventy states that have established a democratic government governance and a respect for individual freedom.[19] As it grows, if it grows, it can create a new international history, a history of peace, in which the politics of force is replaced by the force of politics.

The Liberal account of the new world order and the "revolutions of 1989" focuses on the expansion of this Liberal "zone of peace." How has the pacific union expanded? What challenges lie ahead in the middle run of the 1990s? And what is the long-run promise of Liberalism in the century ahead? Kant expected the pacific union to expand erratically, with many setbacks in the short and middle runs. In the long run the Kantian liberal message is one of profound hope. In the short run it is an eloquent warning.

1989 and All That. For some Liberals, including Francis Fukuyama, the collapse of communism and the spread of Liberal democracy around the world in the late 1980s constituted an end to history, a permanent triumph of consumer capitalism and democracy under the irresistible onslaught of transnational modernization. Fukuyama argues that the struggle over alternative ways

[19] Sixty-eight in the most recent count of established (three plus years), large (million plus) Liberal republics, from chapter 8.

of life, of identity, meaning, or purpose has, or soon will, come to an end because it is now clear that there are no viable alternatives to Western Liberalism, no credible alternative paths to the good life. There will be plenty of archaic illiberalism, autocracy, dictatorship, stale Socialism left in what used to be the Third World. But no longer can they claim to be the wave of the future. They have given up the struggle. World politics will henceforth, with allowances for the backward areas, be a politics of boredom, of peaceful common marketization.[20] This has come to pass, he adds, for two major reasons: first, because Liberalism (political democracy and consumer capitalism) has resolved all the contradictions of life for which, throughout the course of history, individuals have been prepared to fight. With democracy, economic productivity, and the VCR, we have satisfied the cravings for both freedom and wealth. Liberalism has achieved a strikingly simultaneous combination of social and psychomoral stabilization. Second, communism, and all other rival forms of political identity, are finished because they have failed to satisfy both the desire for freedom and the desire for wealth.

The Kantian tradition offers a more skeptical—but still revolutionary—account of international liberalization. The Kantian peace train has two tracks. The first track is transnational commerce and the other transnational ties and economic developments that tend to operate on societies from "below." These forces individually mobilize and pluralize the sources of power in a society and thereby put pressure on authoritarian institutions, a pressure whose release lies in political participation in Liberal political institutions.[21]

Here the role of global civil society and international civil politics is particularly important. Tourism, educational exchanges, and scientific meetings spread tastes across borders. Contacts with the Liberal world seem to have had a liberalizing effect on the many Soviet and East European elites that visited the West during the Cold War, demonstrating both Western material successes (where they existed) and regimes that tolerated and even encouraged dissent and popular participation (when they did).[22] The international commitment to human rights, including the Helsinki Watch process, found a reflection in Gorbachev's "universal human values." The "Goddess of Liberty" erected in Tiananmen Square represented another transnational expression of ideas shared on a global basis.

Trade can have even more powerful effects. In the modern economy, fostering growth has meant at least a minimal engagement with the world economy.

[20] Francis Fukuyama, "The End of History," *National Interest* 16 (Summer 1989), pp. 3–18.
[21] See for sources of the social mobilization, political participation, institutional change hypotheses, Samuel Huntington, *The Third Wave* (Norman: University of Oklahoma Press, 1991), chap. 2.
[22] For an excellent survey of these factors, see Deudney and Ikenberry's essay "The International Sources of Soviet Change."

Even the USSR in its later days traded for 5 percent of its GNP.[23] Trade can distribute income to abundant factors of production (often discriminated against within the domestic market) in ways that serve to pluralize and put strain on established national distributions of income and power. These effects can have political consequences that enhance democratic governance by shifting the locus of domestic resources and, consequently, power.[24]

The second Kantian track is the international track of war. The pressure of war and military mobilization creates incentives for authoritarian rulers to grant popular participation as a way of increasing the popular contribution to the power resources of the states.[25] Thus states cede representation in return for the increased taxation they need to fight wars successfully, and republican institutions descend from "above."

In that light 1989 looks like a case of Liberal modernization, reflecting the transnational effects of economic development on social identities and political mobilization.[26] Significant (whether stabilizing or destabilizing) change in political institutions can be a product of social mobilization, itself stimulated by economic development. Political upheavals and transformations should thus tend to correlate with social mobilization, and societies that have experienced extensive economic development and social mobilization should thus be either inclusionary (democratic) or highly repressive ("totalitarian," perhaps, rather than merely traditionally "autocratic" or "authoritarian," which, in this view, should characterize less mobilized societies). Interestingly, this is just the logic that fits the postwar pattern upheavals in Eastern Europe. Czechoslovakia (together with East Germany, the most developed) was forcibly demobilized from its democratic regime in 1948. East Germany suppressed an upheaval in 1953. Hungary and Poland (the next two most economically developed) rebelled in 1956. Czechoslovakia rebelled again in 1968, Hungary began to adopt "goulash communism" in the 1970s, and Poland rebelled again in 1981. Romania and Bulgaria, the least economically developed members of the bloc, did not experience political rebellion until 1989.[27] "1989" appeared so striking, another 1848, in part because the earlier rebellions and upheavals were not

[23]Timothy Colton, *Dilemmas of Soviet Reform* (New York: Council on Foreign Relations, 1992).

[24]As Gourevitch and Rogowski have demonstrated in their studies, international trade can alter domestic distributions of power—the "second image" reversed factor. See Peter Gourevitch, *Politics in Hard Times* and Ronald Rogowski, *Commerce and Coalitions.*

[25]This is one of the themes of John U. Nef, *War and Human Progress* (New York: Norton, 1968).

[26]Karl Deutsch, *Nationalism and Social Communication* (Cambridge, Mass.: MIT Press, 1966) and Huntington, *Political Order in Changing Societies*, esp. chaps. 5 and 6.

[27]Valuable accounts of these crises can be found in Brzezinski, *The Soviet Bloc;* Journalist M., *A Year Is Eight Months* (New York: Anchor/Doubleday, 1983); Alain Touraine et al., *Solidarity* (Cambridge: Cambridge University Press, 1983).

allowed to play themselves out nationally. Communist "totalitarianism" appeared permanent not as Jeane Kirkpatrick[28] and others argued because it could permanently suppress dissent, but because the Communist states of Eastern Europe were part of a Soviet empire that controlled their political fate. What made 1989 so striking was that at last Gorbachev and his associates had arrived at a willingness to abandon the Soviet empire, thus allowing national development to proceed.[29]

Two-track internationalism helps account for the international process of change and for the democratic revolutions of 1989, but it is far from a complete model of democratization or explanation of the spread of democracy in Eastern Europe or elsewhere in the late 1980s. Its attention to transnational forces from below and international forces from above the state does parallel explanations of liberalization processes that focus on splits within the governmental elite (as in Hungary in 1989) as well as on collapses of the governmental elite in the face of popular mobilization (as in East Germany in 1989).[30] These transnational and international forces offer important incentives for democratic Liberal reform. They implicitly promise the opportunity to participate more fully in the Liberal world market without security restrictions and with the protection of GATT standards and access to IMF programs. They also promise membership in the Liberal "zone of peace" and the consequent reduction in insecurity and, possibly, defense expenditures. The incentives to internationalize and democratize are not, however, consistent or smooth. There is mounting evidence that free market capitalism may not be the quintessential capitalist answer to growth under the conditions of late-late capitalism. Instead the most striking rates of growth appear to be achieved by the semiplanned capitalist economies of East Asia—Taiwan, South Korea, Singapore, and Japan. Indicative planning, capital rationing by parastatal development banks and ministries of finance, managed trade, incorporated unions—capitalist syndicalism, not capitalist libertarianism—may better describe the wave of the capitalist future.[31]

Democratization, moreover, is a bumpy road. There is a contingent, strategic element in both the popular and governmental process in the decisions to transform (*reforma* for Juan Linz), replace (Linz's *ruptura*), or "transplace" an

[28] Kirkpatrick, "Dictatorships and Double Standards."

[29] Jorge Dominguez, *Insurrection or Loyalty: The Breakdown of the Spanish American Empire* (Cambridge, Mass.: Harvard University Press, 1980) notes a similar pattern in the collapse of the Spanish empire in the Americas between 1800 and 1825. I extend Dominguez's argument in Doyle, *Empires*, chap. 14.

[30] Adam Przeworski, *Democracy and the Market* (Cambridge: Cambridge University Press, 1991), p. 56.

[31] The review essay by Robert Wade, "East Asia's Economic Success," in the October 1992 *World Politics* effectively makes this case. Interestingly, Fukuyama's book also stresses this latter, more complicated perspective on development; his article lends itself to the more libertarian interpretation of economic development.

existing authoritarian regime.[32] With the right incentives, authoritarian and (we now know, even totalitarian) regimes can choose to lead a transformation. They can also collapse and suffer a replacement at the hands of a democratic opposition, or join with a democratic opposition in a mutual transplacement toward liberalization and then democracy. Are the public, collective incentives of Liberal internationalism sufficient to motivate an authoritarian elite to start a transformation, an opposition to risk a crushed replacement, or both to engage in a transplacement? Although it focuses on the need to account for incentives to act, the new literature on democratization also suggests that we need to consider what should be called misincentives. Would Gorbachev have undertaken liberalization (glasnost and then political perestroika) had he known through a crystal ball the outcome today (not to speak of that during his dangerous incarceration during the 1991 coup)? Gorbachev, it appears, sought a reformed communism, a market Socialism, and a revivified (and politically rewarded) popular democratic Communist Party, led presumably by himself, not the current stumble toward Western-style Liberal pluralism and IMF-dependent capitalism, led by his rival Yeltsin.[33] The process of transformation escaped his grasp before, during, and especially after the coup.[34]

A second process factor affecting the risks replacers are willing to bear is the simple concatenation of events, what has been called in other contexts the domino effect. The dominoes fell in Eastern Europe in 1989, and these had effects in the USSR too, stimulating both the coup and some valiant Muscovites to resist it. Actions that seem imprudent here and now appear reasonable when everyone else is doing it, even if it's being done elsewhere. Thus what took ten years in Poland took ten months in Hungary, ten weeks in East Germany, and ten days in Czechoslovakia.

Third, simple lack of information, uncertainty, is conducive to democratic transplacements. When societies know the lines of cleavage and the distribution of social power, all the steps of transformations and transplacements must be negotiated in detail in advance, short-circuiting the open-endedness of Liberal democratic contestation.[35] The very lack of knowledge of underlying social

[32]Huntington, *The Third Wave*, p. 114, and Juan Linz, "Crisis, Breakdown, and Reequilibration," in Juan Linz and Alfred Stepan, eds., *The Breakdown of Democratic Regimes*, (Baltimore: Johns Hopkins University Press, 1978), p. 35.

[33]See "On Socialist Democracy" in Mikhail Gorbachev, *Socialism, Peace, and Democracy* (London: Atlantic Highlands, 1987) and Marshall Goldman, *What Went Wrong with Perestroika* (New York: Norton, 1991), pp. 128–71.

[34]See David Shipler, "Report from Moscow: The Coup" and "After the Coup," *The New Yorker* (November 4 and 11, 1991), a two-part series on the coup and the Yeltsin aftermath, and see the review essay by Theodore Draper *New York Review of Books* (June 1, 1992).

[35]This is the striking conclusion of Przeworski's discussion of transitions to democracy, p. 88.

geography, after the years of straitjacketed communism, thus may have made for a willingness to jump into contestation in Eastern Europe and may have the same effect in Russia and Ukraine today.

Hurdles in the Middle Run. Liberals also tell us important insights about the middle run. There too they are optimistic. They offer us hope that if the next hegemonic challenger is Liberal, the hegemonic transition might be peaceful. Then we will suffer neither war nor the waste of resources in a cold war, and we might then enjoy another transition such as the peaceable one between Great Britain and the United States in the twentieth century. But they also offer us a pessimistic scenario in the middle run: what we tend to call the Japan problem, or, better, the U.S.-Japan problem. Japan is quasi-democratic, like the United States, but it is less purely capitalist then we are. Most important, culturally it is not yet, perhaps never will be, as Liberal as the United States now is—Japanism always seems more important than universal Liberalism. That is, while the Japanese polity is representative, its economy is, Liberal Americans think, too closely integrated to be one of arm's-length competition and a free and flat playing field. Its culture identifies community as something more important than individuality.

Like pre–World War One Germany, Japan may not be fully liberal. While Wilhelm II of Germany and Bethmann-Hollweg were sometimes idiosyncratic in the formulation of their policy, they were not noticeably more aggressive than the other governments of Europe at the time. The problem was that the other governments of Europe—particularly Britain and France—assumed that because Germany was not a fully representative Liberal state, it was bound to be dangerous. This lack of trust then made Germany feel insecure and threatened. It responded in ways that confirmed the expectations of Britain and France and thereby escalated tensions and contributed to the onslaught of World War I. We need to ask if the same thing will happen in U.S. relations with Japan, given recent evidence of increasing tensions.

In short there is plenty of room for the sort of spiraling misperception and rivalry that characterized the prewar Anglo-German antagonism. We will need institutions and multifaceted contacts to offset the economic tensions that are likely to be an increasingly important part of the relationship.

One possibility is a globally enhanced role for Japan in the UN that helps integrate Japan more closely into the Liberal community of nations with a status more equal to that enjoyed by the other great Liberal democratic powers. Another vital institutional support is bilateral. Defense cooperation is an especially effective place to begin, and the Kakizawa Initiative is an imaginative proposal. A leading LDP defense politician (the Diet member Koji Kakizawa) has recommended the establishment of jointly staffed defense units: joint crews on warships, air stations, army units, all assembled perhaps in a pan-Pacific peacekeeping force at the call of the UN. He wisely hopes to add intense security cooperation as a counterweight to the economic tensions that are sure to arise.

Another danger in the middle run identified for us by Liberalism is the danger of hegemonic decline. Even though the United States declined from roughly 40 percent of world GNP in the late 1940s to 25 percent of world GNP in the 1970s, the problem today is not one of further absolute economic decline. U.S. absolute and even relative decline has slowed since the 1970s. The real problem is the decline that took place between the late 1950s and the early 1970s. That is, the horse is already out of the barn, and the danger is one of who will provide the collective goods of world trade and growth. In whose interest is it to make the sacrifices needed for an entrepreneurial development of the world political economy considered as a whole? Once it was the U.S. interest, but no longer is it so clearly so. Thus it is not surprising that the Uruguay Round of talks on trade expansion stalled and there is a looming danger of regional trade blocs in the 1990s. Will there be a 1930s collapse into crisis? This is a serious question, for economic decline and the depressions that follow pose a danger to democratization today, as they did in the 1930s. Democracy, in short, needs economic security, and as we know, a failure of democracy could eliminate the security that we have enjoyed in relationships with our democratic allies.

Thus the decline of U.S. hegemonic leadership may pose dangers for the Liberal world. The danger is not that today's Liberal states will permit their economic competition to spiral into war or that a world economic crisis is now likely, but that the societies of the Liberal world will no longer be able to provide the mutual assistance they might require to sustain Liberal domestic orders if they were to be faced with mounting economic crises.

The Promise of Peace. If we stretch our intellectual horizon beyond our revolutionary and troubled past decade, Liberalism is an extraordinary beacon of hope. In all likelihood the past rate of *global* progress in the expansion of the pacific union has been a complex and inseparable combination of the effects of both the international and transnational tracks. But if we imagine that progress has been achieved solely by one track or the other, we can deduce the outer limits of the underlying logics of the transnational and international progresses toward peace.

Thus, if we rashly assume that the transnational track of commerce alone led to the expansion of the pacific union, we can project when all regimes will have become Liberal. If we follow the past arithmetic rate of increase (spilling over from country to country), which again triples in shorter and shorter periods, as it did between the nineteenth and the first half of the twentieth century and again between the first and second half of the twentieth century—and if the number of states remains fixed at roughly two hundred—then all states will

TABLE PART 5.16

The Pacific Union

	1800	1800–1850	1850–1900	1900–1945	1945–(1990)
Number of Liberal regimes	3	8	13	29	68
Transnational track		+5	+5	+16	+39
International track		>2x	<2x	>2x	>2x

be Liberal republican by 2050. On the other hand, we can follow the international track of war. Warlike periods, such as the first halves of the nineteenth century and twentieth century, more than double the number of Liberal regimes; pacific periods, like the second of the nineteenth century, less than double the number. If we assume the future resembles the late nineteenth century, when there were no great world wars but many small petty wars (having epidemiclike effects), and if the geometric rate of expansion of the pacific union is thus the same, then the union will not become global until just before 2100. If, contrarily, we assume a warlike future of great tension, akin to the early nineteenth or twentieth century, then all states will become republican just after 2050.

Both tracks help engender Liberal regimes, and thus eventually a widening of the peace, but neither the tracks nor the trip are smooth. The transnational ties create incentives for conflict as well as cooperation; the international track of war obviously presupposes war in the first place. Moreover, the future portrayed is obviously only an extrapolation of the past, a past characterized by no nuclear war, technological development that was trade- and growth-enhancing, and states with such limited surveillance capabilities that they were vulnerable to the threat and reality of popular uprisings. To put it mildly, changes in these characteristics could upset Kantian expectations.

Getting to There. If the problem of Realism is that states can, and have, done better than the balance of power; the problem of Liberalism is that states can, and have, done worse, and that some of those failures in the pursuit of peace and security are attributable to the influence of Liberal principles and Liberal institutions.

From the Liberal point of view, the most pressing danger of complaisance today is how to support the continued liberalization of Russia and what is left of a shaky association of quasi-independent republics in the middle of Eurasia.

Having to confront thousands of nuclear weapons in the hands of the possible "fascist situation" is a danger both in Russia and in the rest of the dissolving Commonwealth of Independent States today.[36] The second most pressing danger is how to avoid imprudent vehemence in managing a commercial and political rivalry with the most significant non-Liberal power, the fastest-growing, soon-to-be-giant economy of the People's Republic of China. Both challenges require sophisticated transformations—that is, expansions of the pacific union. Nothing could be more difficult; nothing could be more costly than failing at either. The alternative is a state of war and the balancing that Realists prescribe.

Liberal principles and economic interest do not allow the luxury of noninvolvement. The principles of the Universal Declaration of Human Rights through which Liberals identify themselves do not permit equanimity in the face of suffering and oppression, whether it be in Haiti, South Africa, Hitler's Germany, the West Bank territories of Israel, or Chechnya, or the People's Republic of China and its constrained existing (Tibet) and prospective (Taiwan, Hong Kong) provinces. Even if Liberal principles did not call us to universalism, our economic interests now do. The trade and investments of the Liberal world reach across the globe. The oil we and our closest economic partners in Europe and Japan rely upon still depends on Middle East supplies, as the crisis in the Persian Gulf reminded us. The Chinese economy is becoming the fourth great growth pole of the world economy and soon will be the largest growth pole.[37] These two interdependencies are becoming even more connected, as an emerging "oil deficit" in East Asia, affecting the entire region and drawing China as well as Japan into dependence on the Middle East, well illustrates.[38]

There are few direct interstate measures that foster the stability, development, and transnational spread of Liberal democratic regimes. Many direct

[36] See the warning made by Robert Strauss, former U.S. envoy to Russia, in Francis Clines, "U.S. Envoy Urges Debt Relief for Soviets," in *New York Times*, November 19, 1991, p. A14. A Marshall Plan, he notes is not the right model for a response. The Soviets are not ready for it. Neither we nor the Europeans are ready to help pay for it. The real need is for the equivalent of a UNRRA, providing relief and rehabilitation, emergency food and distribution help, medical supplies, and technical advice, until they decide what sort of economy they plan to create. Then World Bank loans or European Bank for Reconstruction and Development capital and perhaps private capital will help, though, as in all such cases, bootstrap development will be the key.

[37] World Bank, *Global Economic Prospects and the Developing Countries* (Washington, D.C.: World Bank, 1993), pp. 66–67. The "standard international price" (purchasing power adjusted) GDP of the Chinese economic area (CEA, including Hong Kong, and Taiwan) will reach $9.8 trillion as early as 2002, at which time the United States will reach 9.7, Japan 4.9, and Germany 3.1. The respective per capita GDP figures are (CEA) $7,300, (United States) 36,000, (Japan) 37,900, (Germany) 39,100.

[38] Kent E. Calder, "Asia's Empty Gas Tank," *Foreign Affairs* 75, 2 (March–April 1996), pp. 55–69.

efforts, including military intervention and overt or covert funding for democratic movements in other countries, discredit those movements as the foreign interference backfires through the force of local nationalism. (The democratic movement in Panama in the 1980s denounced U.S. political aid before the invasion and today suffers at home and abroad from its overt dependence on the United States.) Much of the potential success of a policy designed to foster democracy therefore rests on an ability to shape an economic and political environment that indirectly supports democratic governance and creates pressures for the democratic reform of authoritarian rule.

Politically there are few measures more valuable than an active human rights diplomacy, which enjoys global legitimacy and (if successful) can assure a political environment that tolerates the sort of dissent that can nourish an indigenous democratic movement. There is reason to pay special attention to those countries entering what Samuel Huntington has called the socioeconomic transition zone, countries having the economic development that has typically been associated with democracy.[39] For them, more direct support in the form of electoral infrastructure (from voting machines to battalions of international observers) can provide the essential margin persuading contentious domestic groups to accept the fairness of the crucial first election.

Economically, judged from the historical evidence of the 1920s and 1930s, democratic regimes seem to be more vulnerable to economic depression than authoritarian regimes. (This is why Liberals should target economic aid at the margin toward fledgling democracies.) But in periods of stable economic growth, democratic regimes seem to accommodate better over the long run those social groups newly mobilized by economic growth than do authoritarian regimes. Democracies expand participation better. They also allow for the expression of nonmaterial goals more easily, it seems, than do the more functionally legitimated authoritarian regimes. Economic growth thus may be the Liberals' best long-run strategy.

But these general strategies of democratization do not answer the particular challenges Russia and China present. In the short run, choices must be made that avoid the extremes of appeasement and provocation. Appeasing a China or Russia that turns aggressive would be the most dangerous outcome. But starting a new "crusading" cold war with China or a post-coup Russia would also constitute a distinct failure of diplomacy. The cost of the forty-five-year Cold War has to be calculated in the trillions; one estimate was eleven trillion

[39] For background material on the conditions of democratic development, see Huntington, "Will More Countries Become Democratic?" And see the comments of Larry Diamond on some suggestions made by Juan Linz in Diamond, "Beyond Authoritarianism and Totalitarianism; Strategies for Democratization," *Washington Quarterly* (Winter 1989), pp. 141–63.

dollars.[40] Starting an equivalent cold war against "market Leninism" in China will cost an equivalent sum, with even larger long-run dangers, given China's dynamism. Economically reinforcing democratization in Russia and engaging with authoritarian China in a way that encourages moderate foreign policy behavior, a growing respect for human rights, and a steady advance of popular participation are the preferable courses of action.[41] No one should underestimate the difficulties. China's claim on democratic Taiwan, its possible repression of democratic Hong Kong, its growing relationship with the U.S. enemies Iran and Iraq, its trade disputes with the United States, not to speak of its treatment of domestic dissent—all these merely sketch in the current (1996) range of challenges.

Liberal states of the industrial world have entered a nearly unprecedented condition of international security, and it appears to be significantly linked to the surge of Liberalism worldwide. But that good fortune is not guaranteed to persist, nor will it necessarily involve worldwide peace. Even if a war of the scale of the U.S.-UN Gulf War against Iraq is unlikely to be repeated soon, Grenadas and Somalias and Bosnias are likely to arise frequently in the new world order we are entering. If we want to avoid their becoming revivals of destructive imperialism or arenas of neglect, we will need to reinforce the steadying institutions of multilateral security, whether in the UN or regional organizations, ready to provide guidance and multilateral support.[42]

Moreover, it is very much in our hands whether the 1990s do in fact become another 1931, a brief moment before the collapse of collective security into complaisance (as occurred in the Manchurian incident of 1931) and then war. Another cold war with China or Russia—after a next, perhaps successful authoritarian coup—could reenact the European crisis of Liberal democracy that began with the Reichstag fire of 1933. Or instead will 1991 become a 1911—a paranoid rivalry with a fellow near-Liberal spiraling into extensive hostility? Will the U.S.-Japanese relationship follow on the model of the pre–World War I antagonism between Germany and Britain? Either challenge alone, or both together, could radically alter our pacific prospects and make whatever investments in institution building and development aid we now consider seem cheap in retrospect.

[40] Graham Allison and Greg Treverton in *Rethinking America's Security*, p. 40.

[41] Indeed, this was the strategy originally recommended by George Kennan as *political* containment. See George Kennan, *Memoirs: 1925–1950* (Boston: Little, Brown, 1967) and John Gaddis, "The Insecurities of Victory," in *The Long Peace* (1987), pp. 20–47.

[42] For an informative discussion of the extent and limits of the United Nations as an institution through which to promote international security, see Adam Roberts, "The United Nations and International Security," *Survival* 35, 2 (Summer 1993), pp. 2–29.

THE FUTURE OF AN OLD MOLE

Marx described revolution as an "old mole" burrowing away through history, ready to pop up when least expected.[43] Many in the West, however, and others in the East agree with George Bush's assessment that communism experienced its final demise—it "died this year"—in 1991.[44] But the President's announcement was premature.

Marxist-Leninism has a viable account of the present crisis and political support in large parts of the world. It too is coherent, and it may possibly be correct. It offers us radical possibilities as we think about this very uncertain new world to come. What it now seems to lack is what Marxism most had, a history of the future.

Classic Leninism portrayed a future world revolution stemming from two interacting crises. The crisis on the first road to national revolution lay in the "periphery," in wars of national liberation provoked by the revolutionary transformations and aggressions of an expanding global capitalism. These were the sorts of revolutions we have seen recently in Vietnam and Cuba and Angola. The second road is through the road of uneven development among the "core" imperialist powers. This produces cataclysmic global wars, such as World War I and World War II, which wrecked the oppressive edifice of imperialist states. They allowed revolutionary countries to break through and establish dictatorships of the proletariat, such as were achieved in the Soviet Union in the course of World War I and in Eastern Europe and the People's Republic of China in World War II.

Today neo-Marxists see other prospects as they contemplate what we face in the 1990s. One is gloomy; the other is happy, or at least progressive.

Global Exploitation. The gloomy future focuses on global exchange in the world system. It sees a world divided among three tiers of economies. The first tier is the leading core economies, United States, Japan, and West Germany, each of them with strong, dynamic productive economies and strong, well-ordered hegemonic states. Below them is a less advanced semiperiphery, including Latin America, the USSR itself, and Eastern Europe, where the economies are quite weak, less productive, less well diversified, more dependent sometimes, at least on technology, but where the states are strong, often authoritarian, and quite coercive. In the third, the bottom tier, is the periphery itself, Africa and South Asia, where both the economies and the states are weak, where the economies are dependent and not very productive, and where the states are subject to constant civil strife, military coups, and civil wars.[45]

[43] Karl Marx, "The Communist Manifesto," in Marx (1978).
[44] George Bush, "State of the Union Address," *New York Times*, January 29, 1992.
[45] The evolution of the three-tier system is comprehensively described in Immanuel Wallerstein, *The Modern World System*, vols. 1–4 (New York: Academic Press, 1974–1980) and

The connection among these three tiers is "dependency," described classically by Theotonio dos Santos as "a situation in which the economy of certain countries is conditioned by the development and expansion of another economy to which the former is subjected . . . when some countries (the dominant ones) can expand and can be self-sustaining, while other countries (the dependent ones) can do this only as a reflection of that expansion."[46] The significant result of this process is a reversal of the Marxist-Leninist dynamic of capitalist development in which the capitalist centers exploited but also dragged the colonial areas into modern bourgeois industry. Now the expansion of world capitalism serves to integrate through differentiation, not homogenization.

Reacting to the stagnation in world development that seemed to occur when no new industrial core economies developed after the rise of the United States, Japan, and Germany at the beginning of the twentieth century, dependency Marxists sought out the cause in a major revision of the Marxist theory of international development. World capitalism, they argued, develops not progress but instead "underdevelopment" in the dependent economies of the Third World periphery. Raw material–exporting economies become the "hewers of wood" for the advanced industrial economies. Dependence makes for the continuous replication of poverty in the periphery as a result of a combination of factors: exploitative prices shaped by monopolized trading channels controlled by the core economies, declining terms of trade between the raw material exports of the peripheries and the manufactured goods exports of the cores, restricted consumption by impoverished peripheral laborers caused by the limited opportunities for increases in their wages (itself the effect of the labor surplus of the subsistence economy as well as the lack of union organization), and lastly the monopoly of advanced technology held by core economies. All these economic factors are compounded by the political weakness of peripheral societies whose internal class divisions among landlords, comprador merchants (agents of core merchants), workers, and peasants engender weak states, incapable of effectively bargaining with the more integrated societies and powerful states of the core.[47]

The conflictual and exploitative tie of dependency that links core and periphery is matched by a dynamic tension among core economies. Economi-

its current implications are pursued in "Peace Stability and Legitimacy, 1990–2025/2050," in Geir Lundestad, ed., *The Fall of Great Powers* (Oslo: Scandinavian Press, 1994), pp. 331–49.

[46]Theotonio dos Santos, "The Structure of Dependence," *American Economic Review* 16 (1970).

[47]See Paul Baran and Paul Sweezy, *Monopoly Capital* (New York: Monthly Review Press, 1966), Frank, *Capitalism and Underdevelopment in Latin America*, and Samir Amin, *Unequal Development* (New York: Monthly Review Press, 1976). For an insightful critical survey, see Brewer (1980).

cally capitalism develops unevenly as Kondratieff cycles push the industrial economies through boom and bust periods of fifty to sixty years in length. Politically the competition of core economies is shaped by a cycle of hegemonies in which great powers—the Dutch in the mid-seventeenth century, Britain in the mid-nineteenth, and the United States in the mid-twentieth—temporarily dominate the world economy, providing order for the rent they extract. The current crisis has two sources. The years 1967 to 1973 marked the end of the long postwar boom and the beginning of the challenge to U.S. hegemony by Japan and Europe.[48]

The crisis of the 1980s had different effects on each of these three different tiers.[49] In the core states, the class structure of capitalism crushed workers and bankrupted welfare states as capitalist classes responded to the stagflation and then the boom of the 1980s by disemployment. This observation finds confirmation in the growing gap between classes that emerged in the United States between 1973 and 1993. (See Chart Part 5.1.) Here capitalist hegemony was increased. At the same time, a fierce rivalry emerged among the great multinational firms for market share. Some (including non-Marxist business gurus) suggest that this rivalry will lead to a very "cold peace" in which states back their national champions even into wars (inadvertently following a quasi-Leninist model); others, that these champions will form transnational alliances to acquire megacontracts to develop China and other parts of the developing world, creating in the process a global sweatshop in which labor everywhere suffers (inadvertently following Kautsky).[50]

In the 1970s and 1980s in the periphery, crises further eroded both the economy and the state, especially among the poorest states of Asia and Africa. In the semiperiphery during these same decades, the unevenness of development increased. The stronger economies—with enforced labor discipline, low wages, and an outward orientation—such as those of South Korea, Singapore, Taiwan, Chile, and the People's Republic of China, all surged ahead. The weaker economies, such as those in Eastern Europe and Latin America, fell back. But in both sets of economies, whether strong or weak, the crises tended to weaken the state, leading in Latin America, East Asia, and Eastern Europe to "democratization," which broke through in some, such as South Korea, Taiwan, Chile, and the states of Eastern Europe, leading to the political revolution of 1989. In other areas, however, democratic pressures were turned back by the state, as they were by Singapore and China (the post Tiananmen repression). Democratization in this analysis is a particularly weak form of state power that opens up

[48] Wallerstein (1994), pp. 331–32.

[49] I draw on comments made by Albert Bergesen presented at the ISA Conference in Vancouver, March 1991, at the panel on "Dependency and the World System."

[50] See, for the first view, Jeffrey Garten, *A Cold Peace* (New York: Times Books, 1992); for the second, Cyrus Friedheim, "The Global Corporation—Obsolete So Soon," World Economic Forum, Davos, 1993.

CHART PART 5.1

From the Picket Fence to the Staircase
U.S. Annual Rates of Growth of Household Income by Income Quintiles
(Where 1st Is Lowest; 5th, Highest)

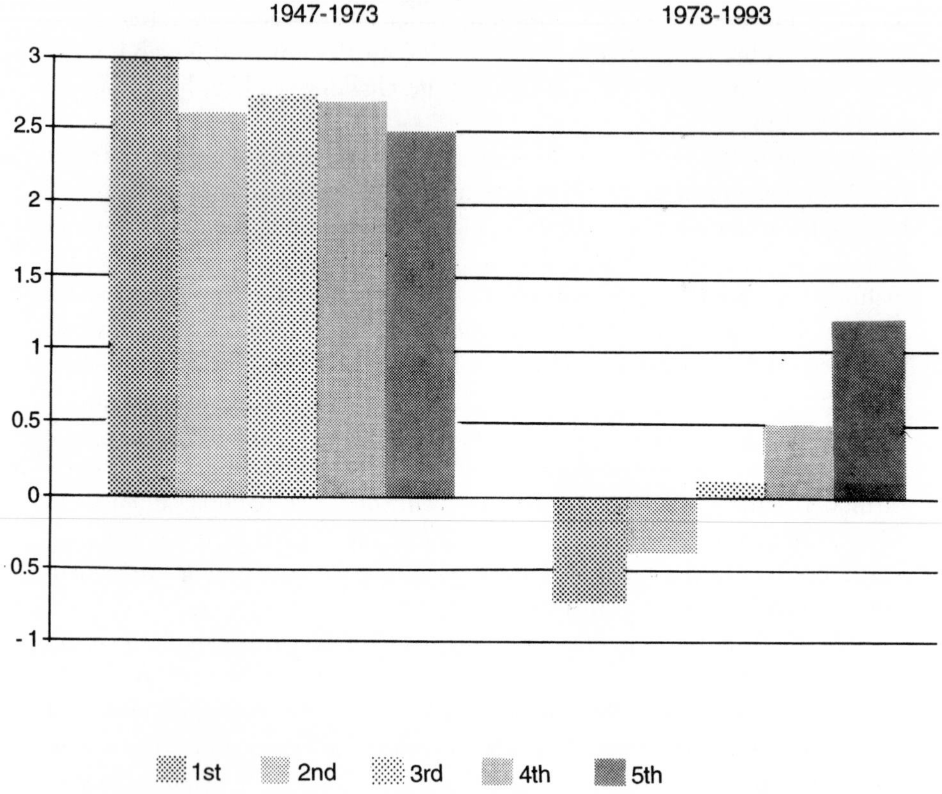

Source: John Cassidy, "Who Killed the Middle Class?," *The New Yorker* (October 16, 1995), p. 83.

the state to all sorts of private, confused, contradictory, and ultimately stalemating kinds of pressure. The semiperiphery needs strong states in order to mobilize savings into investment into growth and thereby onto a path that is equalizing rather than one that perpetuates and reinforces global capitalist hierarchy. Capitalism develops unevenly, and capitalist growth is the product of forcible extraction and class warfare. Yet international war no longer seems to hold the prospect of revolution. The Russian Revolution, itself a product of world war, heralded, Lenin hoped, a world revolution beginning in Europe and then spreading through decolonization across the globe. Instead communism in Russia was contained and then collapsed seventy years later, leaving itself and Eastern Europe to drop back into the capitalist fold.

CHART PART 5.2

Latin American and the Caribbean:
Net Capital Income and Net Transfer of Resources
(Billions of Dollars)

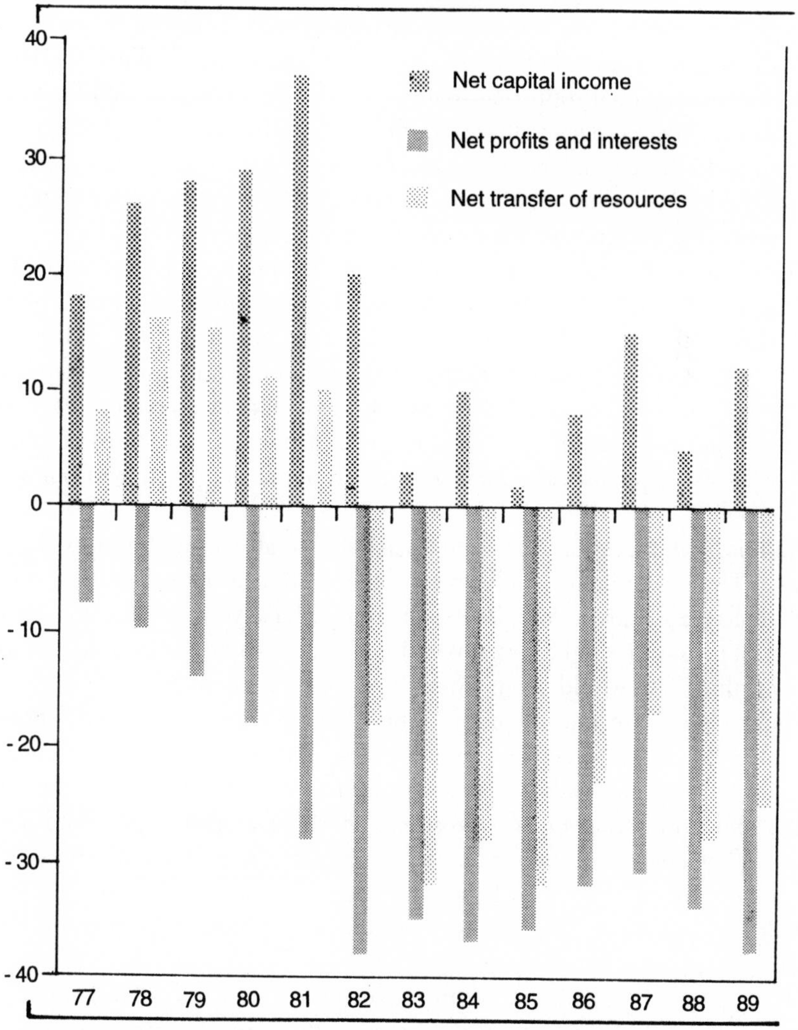

Source: Economic Commission for Latin America and the Caribbean ECLAC. Preliminary Balance of the Latin American and Caribbean Economy. December 1989.

Global Social Production. The neo-Marxist optimists, however, give us a new and different view. They focus not on the exchanges within the world system but on the modes of production, not on global trade imports and exports and flows of investment and dependence and interdependence, but on the very factory floor of capitalism.

Stimulated in part by the rise of the newly industrializing countries—South Korea, Taiwan, Hong Kong, Singapore, Malaysia, Thailand, and others—a group of Marxists has revived Marx's views on the destructive-creative effects of capitalist expansion. Dismissing Lenin's view that imperialism is the last stage of capitalism and dependency theory as nationalist mythology of the rebellious comprador class, Bill Warren stresses the revolutionary potential of foreign capital as an engine helping both to destroy feudal landlordism and to complement the efforts of national industrial bourgeoisie.[51] The postwar period for Warren has been an era of progress, albeit painful for the vulnerable classes. Capitalism, according to these scholars, has produced a significant advance toward a more interdependent and homogeneous capitalist society on a global basis and in so doing has created the basis for an eventual return to Socialist politics.

The long peace of the postwar period and the oppressive character of Stalinist regimes stimulated another neo-Marxist critique, one that focused on state Socialism ("state capitalism") in which the state, not the worker, is the owner of the means of production.[52] Rather than extend the principles of democracy to the economy and the workplace, which was Marx's own revolutionary vision of socialism and communism, Stalinism, as a premature Marxist revolution, extended the capitalist principles of ownership and the practice of oppression to the polity.

In this light, then, 1989 takes on a separate but also distinctly Marxist significance. The extraordinary hollowness of the Eastern European states—their so easy collapse—finds a Marxist explanation. Marx, you will recall, expected Socialist revolutions to be easy revolutions because capitalism would be eroded from within. This would occur when the extreme concentration of capital ownership reduced the rate of profits, when large factories socialized labor and revealed the working classes' common fate and solidarity in their common circumstances, and lastly when the dehumanizing conditions of mass wage labor and immiserization at subsistence levels of existence provoked a mass rising of the enormous, almost now universal proletariat. Ironically, these scholars ask, where more than in Eastern Europe and the USSR in the 1970s and 1980s had just those Marxist preconditions for revolution been more clearly met?

But the vision of an alternative future seems to have been cut off, not accelerated, by these democrats' revolts. The crisis they are now experiencing arises from a natural confusion. These are democratic socialist revolutions against communism. The revolutionaries must ask themselves, "Where do they go from here?," while facing the response of the proverbial Maine guide, who says, "You

[51] Bill Warren, *Imperialism: Pioneer of Capitalism* (London: New Left Books, 1980).
[52] Rudolph Bahro in his intriguing work *The Alternative in Eastern Europe*, published in 1970, explains this new vision of Socialism.

can't get there from here." Can one move democratically to socialism from communism when the institutions and principles of communism are so discredited among the ordinary people?

Socialist Futures. An insightful argument by Ellen Comisso takes up that issue.[53] Focusing on the work of the great Austrian libertarian economist Ludwig von Mises, she suggests that Socialism, in all its forms, is doomed economically and will continue to be rejected by democratic publics. Democratic Leninism, democratic Socialism, the historic forms of Yugoslav self-managed Socialism—none of these is a stopping point in the forced-march progress of Liberal modernization. None of these is an alternative to the choice between Liberalism and stagnation.

Socialists of all types want economic equality, but many now reject public ownership of the means of production. They, like Gorbachev, think they can reform Socialism through perestroika by having markets for goods, recognizing that markets make for more efficiency and thereby growth. But reforms in commodity markets, Mises said, were not enough to achieve productivity. An economic system also needs real capitalism, a market for capital. An efficient economy needs to ensure that resources—that is, capital—will be taken away from firms that are not profitable and given to the firms that are more profitable. For if the state centralizes the ownership of capital, industrial managers will have an incentive to mislead the state planner in order to get more capital, more resources. After the centralized state planner invests in these firms, each—that is, both the state planner and the firms—will acquire a bureaucratic stake in the survival of the other. Since the state cannot go out of business, then neither will the industrial entrepreneurs (until they go together). Capital will be wasted in inefficient and uncontrollable businesses, and therefore overall national productivity will fall, and therefore, von Mises implies, Socialism will not produce the products for which the modern consumer hungers.

But there are good grounds for us to reject economic Liberalism as a fully satisfactory explanation of the democratic liberalization of Eastern Europe and of the future of Socialist transformation. First, we should question the confidence in the traditional forms of capitalism that von Mises and other market capitalists display. We can, for example, envision a credible Socialist egalitarian form of the ownership of the means of productions that nevertheless relies on capital markets for social efficiency. Pension funds, for example, can compete for the investments of workers and can invest in the productive enterprises of the economy. These pension funds will attempt to maximize the long-run profits of their contributors, and therefore they will invest in the most efficient

[53] Ellen Comisso, "Crisis in Socialism or Crisis of Socialism," *World Politics* (July 1990). See also Valerie Bunce, "Rising above the Past: The Struggle for Liberal Democracy in Eastern Europe," *World Policy Journal* (Summer 1990).

firms and take away funds from those less efficient. Thus pension funds will be able to own the economy, but the funds themselves will be owned on an egalitarian basis by the workers and managers. This is not purely a foreign vision. The American business guru Peter Drucker has described how pension funds might even bring Socialism to America. But at the same time it is not a solely American vision. A whole line of scientists, theorists, and promoters of industrial democracy have envisioned how workers owning (with their managers) 50 percent or so of their firms would be able to rely on external funds, such as pension funds, to make up the discretionary capital they lack.[54] Moreover, in practice and for some purposes, communism and other forms of state-directed growth were *not an ineffective* mode of production, at least not until the 1980s.[55]

Neither are the democratic politics of Socialist modernization bankrupt. We should be concerned about the compatibility between democracy and capitalism that is assumed in much of this literature. A good case can be made that in the long run capitalism provides the dispersal of social power that effective democracy presupposes and that democracy is an especially effective mechanism with which to resolve differences within a society characterized by a pluralistic dispersal of social power. When liberal democrats consider Eastern Europe and the former Soviet Union, they can take a certain comfort from the observation that the values of democratic participation and toleration of dissent are supported by majorities in some recent polls. These same Russian polls indicate that a large majority is willing to tolerate income differentials based on people being allowed to "earn as much as they could."[56] (Is this enough to sustain a full-blown form of capitalist appropriation?) But Socialist values are far from dead. In a 1989 Soviet poll concerning the future of the economy, more than 60 percent of the sample said that they preferred the rationing of

[54] A discussion of these issues can be found in *Dissent* (Summer 1991), on market Socialism.

[55] Communism, Charles Maier has noted, like other forms of central planning, was an economic success between 1930 and 1970. In an era of large productive units and heavy industry, "Communism was the ideology of heavy metal." East and West European growth rates in the 1950s and 1960s were comparable and both quite good by global standards as both forged ahead, rebuilding and then extending heavy and light industry destroyed by the war. But in the 1980s the East European economies entered a profound economic crisis. In the 1970s and 1980s Communist states proved unable (unwilling) to shed these industrial workers and miners when their productivity fell; capitalist states of the West were able to disemploy the workforce of heavy industry and reemploy (though sometimes only their wives and children) in the growing service sector. The ten-year gap in industrial technology, Maier argues, doomed communism in Eastern Europe. See Charles Maier, *Why Did Communism Collapse in 1989?* Central and Eastern Europe Working Paper Series No. 7, Minda de Gunzburg Center for European Studies, Harvard University, January 1991.

[56] ROMIR Poll, December 1991 and January 1992, reported by Dr. Ellen Mickiewicz, *Findings of Four Major Surveys in the Former Soviet Union* (Carter Center, Emory University, 1992), p. 8.

basic essential commodities to relying upon market pricing. Concerning ownership, many (more than 66 percent) favored private farming, and some (more than 30 percent) would be happy to work for a multinational corporation in a joint venture in the Soviet Union. But more than half the Soviet public rejected the private ownership of businesses; these respondents regarded private enterprise as inherently corrupt and corrupting. Adam Przeworski, reflecting on the results of Polish polls, concludes, "The one value that socialist systems have successfully inculcated is equality, and this value may undermine pro-market reforms under conditions of democracy."[57] We do not yet know whether democratic sovereignty and consumer sovereignty are on the same course in the former communist economies.

Nor does Liberalism monopolize the political meaning of dignity in the modern world. In an interview he gave in May 1990 to *Time* magazine. Gorbachev defined what it meant to him to be a communist with dignity.[58]

> To be a communist, as I see it, means not to be afraid of what is new, to reject obedience to any dogma, to think independently, to submit one's thoughts and plans of action to the tests of morality and, through political action, to help working people realize their hopes, and aspirations and live up to their abilities. I believe that to be a communist today means first of all to be consistently democratic and to put universal human values above everything else . . . The Stalinist model of socialism should not be confused with true socialist theory. As we dismantle the Stalinist system, we are not retreating from socialism, but we are moving toward it.

In China today it looks as if even the Chinese Communist Party promises that China's youth is being asked to defer, not to abandon, the hope of freedom and equality.[59] In the dependent Caribbean, Dr. Cheddi Jagan, president of Guyana and the leading spokesman for democratic Socialism in the region, adds an eloquent plea for an alliance between progressive forces, from the Northern core and the Southern periphery, designed to overcome the current crisis that affects both: "In the North, the consequences of these disparities [between rich and poor] has been unemployment, homelessness, urban disorder, increase in crime especially among the youths, the rise of ultra-right movements, strident nationalism and fragmentation accompanied by racism and ethnic tensions. . . . In the South, the consequences of these divisions [between rich and poor

[57] Przeworski, p. 178.

[58] For a valuable discussion of the context of Gorbachev's transformation of Soviet foreign policy, see Steven Kull, *Burying Lenin* (Boulder, Colo.: Westview Press, 1992), esp. chap. 8.

[59] Such was the plea made by Ambassador Han Xu on August 21, 1989, in the *New York Times* when he said that the course of progress was not over, after the Tiananmen incident. Instead he pleaded for American patience, and gave in return a promise of progress and pluralism and a future of cooperation with a growing people's republic.

countries] has been the increase in crime and disease, hopelessness, emigration, environmental degradation, the illegal traffic and use of narcotic drugs."[60]

Jagan then called for "A New Global Human Order" inspired by a sense of Socialist solidarity to address the current crisis afflicting the poor countries of the South and the impoverished workers of the North.

Reform Socialism seeks to address a crucial contradiction residual in Liberalism—that is, the contradiction between liberty and social equality. So like the Realist and the Liberal, the Marxist can explain to us why a democratic revolution would take place, how such a revolution might take place, and even when such a revolution might take place. For the Realist it occurred when the Soviet empire collapsed and the American empire and hegemony declined. The new world order arrived when first the Soviets withdrew the legions and communism collapsed in Eastern Europe. For the Liberal it occurred when social modernization undermined, overstrained, and then broke the fetters of the authoritarian state. For the optimistic Marxist, the new order arrived when a class revolt overthrew state capitalism; for the pessimistic Marxist, when world capitalism entered a newly repressive cycle. Both seek democratic Socialist revolution, which pits them against the exclusively nationalist Realists and against the free market Liberals. Both Marxisms have a clear agenda in contemporary politics, but both have lost a sense of the course of history. The Leninists have had to come to realize that even though a war can damage world capitalism and permit a Bolshevik revolution, "Socialism" could not truly be established, much less survive, in one country. The progressive Marxist Socialists who have waited for the social production of modern industry to spread around the globe are condemned to patience in the wake of the spread of capitalism. But they have lost confidence in the old Marxist rule: The more advanced the capitalism, the more Socialist become the politics. The current global crisis—both unemployment and widening differences in incomes—sees not a strengthening but a decline of Socialism in Scandinavia and the weakening of social democrats and welfare state politics in Europe, Japan, and the United States. In the 1990s Socialism instead is emerging as the ideology of difficult transitions—in Eastern Europe, East Africa, India—from communism or colonialism to an open future. What Socialism seems to have lost is a sense of its future, a sense that was once the great claim on the allegiance of beleaguered Socialists everywhere.[61]

[60] Cheddi Jagan, "Appeal for an New Global Human Order" (November 1994) in a *New Global Human Order* by Cheddi Jagan (Georgetown, Guyana, 1994) pp. 4–5.

[61] This sense of the future was what led Rubaishev in Arthur Koestler's *Darkness at Noon* to confess to a crime he did not commit in order to protect a revolution that, although now corrupt, would some day create create social justice. See also the *New York Times* 1989 series on Socialists around the world.

TRANSFORMATIONS, RIVALRY, RECONCILIATION, AND ROTATIONS

The history of war has had a dreary regularity to it: battles, cycles of hegemony, bipolar and multipolar systems, the rise and fall of empires. There have been so few changes that many of us in the field of international relations begin our courses, as I began this book, with Thucydides's *The Peloponnesian War* not as a bit of antiquarian entertainment two and a half millennia old but as a relevant model of power politics, hegemonic transitions, and imperial overstretch. None of my colleagues teaching Middle East politics or comparative politics begins his or her courses with Herodotus's history of the Persian empire as a way to understand modern Iran.

The state of war preserves an old history. But new history—the history of change and development and liberation—begins with the politics of domestic peace, where changes of being and ways of life occur partly protected from the calamities of war. Can space for creative history be established among states? If so, our history is not the end of history but perhaps a different history. Unlike geographic discovery, our discovery is of a future that we can make, one in which we live not just as a matter of necessity but also as a matter of choice. As such, the future may encompass revolutionary transformations only dimly perceptible today. It may instead produce reconciliation's of Realism, Liberalism, and Socialism through amalgamation or demise. In either case it will call on an ethics of leadership, of choice, in which political leaders will seek to make the most of their and our visions. It is the creative aspect of their choosing that makes theories at best guidelines to, rather than accurate predictions of, the future.

Transformations. We should not assume that Realism, Liberalism, and Marxism will continue to have the role they have had in the modern era. Other collective identities challenge the state, the individual, and class. Religiosity, for example, is one. We all are familiar with the growing strife between radical Islam and Western Christianity. Civilizational divides loom, according to Samuel Huntington, that will shape future conflicts among Catholicism, Protestantism, Islam, Confucianism-Buddhism, Eastern Orthodoxy, and more.[62] The whole world, at the worst, could begin to resemble Bosnia, where Islam, Orthodoxy, and Catholicism have found fanatic adherents among Bosnians, Serbs, and Croats. But in the Western industrialized world today, given the rise of secularism, it's not so much which religion one ascribes to (with exceptions) as how much of any religion one ascribes to. The conflict is not primarily

[62] Huntington, "The Clash of Civilizations." And see Mark Juergensmeyer, *The New Cold War: Religious Nationalism Confronts the Secular State* (Berkeley: University of California Press, 1994).

between, let us say, Catholics, Protestants, and Jews but a conflict between those who have religion and those who have not.[63]

Clearly, the tension between nationality and liberty is also still real, even in the Liberal world.[64] This is the tension between collectivity and individuality, who we are as a group and who we are as individuals. The Europeans, we are told, are all Liberals. But are they French, German, Italian, and British Liberals, or will they be, should they be, really "European" Liberals? The European Maastricht Treaty of 1992, which included the possibility of giving real political power to a European center, raised this problem in a quite fundamental way. The reunification of Germany raised it even more profoundly. Not only does the unity of Germany challenge the identification of Germans, but even more strikingly it challenges the identity of all Europeans. The French, for example, regard it as one thing to become a European, one among other Europeans, but now a united Germany changes the very meaning of Europe that the Europeans are planning to join, because it now has a united and potentially dominant Germany at its center. The Japanese too are political Liberals of a sort, but they insist that Japanness outranks Liberalism, and so the tension between the two is likely also to generate a great deal of history, both within Japan and equally strikingly between Japan and its neighbors, particularly the United States.

Will gender evoke a redefinition of world politics in the way the development of the nation-state, the individual, and class did? Virginia Woolf once suggested as much in *Three Guineas:*

> "Our Country" . . . throughout the greater part of its history has treated me as a slave; it has denied me education or any share in its possessions. "Our" country still ceases to be mine if I marry a foreigner. "Our" country denies me the means of protecting myself, forces me to pay others a very large sum annually to protect me, and is so little able, even so to protect me. . . . Therefore if you insist upon fighting to protect me, or "our" country, let it be understood, soberly and rationally between us, that you are fighting to gratify a sex instinct which I cannot share; to procure benefits which I have not shared and probably will not share; but not to gratify my instincts, or to protect myself or my country. For . . . in fact as a woman, I have no country. As a woman I want no country. As a woman my country is the whole world.[65]

63 One religious leader, Hung Xu, has issued something like a manifesto, a pluralistic manifesto, an ecumenical manifesto, needless to say, to followers of Islam, Christianity, and Judaism, asking them all to join together to remake the world and save it from the oppression and corruption of egoism and materialism.

64 For a philosophic exploration of these tensions, and one possible resolution, see Yael Tamir, *Liberal Nationalism* (Princeton: Princeton University Press, 1993).

65 Virginia Woolf, *Three Guineas* (New York: Harcourt, Brace, 1938), pp. 108–09. This quotation was drawn to my attention by Katharine Moon, whose dissertation on camptown prostitution in Korea exposes the real effects of international politics on women's welfare and the heroic efforts that have been made by those Korean women to take control of their lives.

But we have yet to see a grand strategy of an independent feminist politics on a global scale, much less an actual political movement that expresses and promotes a female identity that redefines and reshapes relations among a newly defined set of units in world society. Instead we see gender-sensitive criticism of the abuses of the current international system, together with powerful claims on liberal, nationalist, and socialist movements to live up to the universal pretensions they espouse by including within them the true interests of women.[66]

Environmental consciousness is another form of contentious identity. The one "end-ism" that we often forget is the potential end of nature itself. Nature, it is argued, now needs our protection rather than offers us its shelter.[67] It needs our protection from market forces. How much burden should the old polluters—that is, the Industrial North—bear? How much should the new and future polluters of the South bear? Political strife thus arises not just among individual classes and nations but over radical new choices between generations on whether the earth shall bear a larger or lesser burden of pollution and whether it should be cleaned by us or our children.

These and other forms of collective identities challenge how we see ourselves. To the extent that they identify meaning and marshal interests, they push history forward. They ensure that we have not reached an end of history, but that history will continue with the strife, the cooperation, conflict, even the wars that we have had long ago and may continue to have in the future.[68] To the extent that radicals within each of them claim the allegiance of large numbers, these too could become "fighting creeds," and we should expect wars to continue. But even short of wars, they are the sorts of claims that drive people into politics in ways that change the world.

Rivalry. In the meantime, the traditional worlds of Realism, Liberalism, and (even) Socialism hold sway. Do we see a renewal of the balance of power and a struggle for hegemony, do we see a historic widening of the Liberal zone of peace, or do we see a renewal of transnational class conflict and the prospect of revolution? None of these futures is certain. There is evidence to support each of the three, but they give us policy choices that are different.

All three agree on the need for domestic and foreign reforms, both North and South. The Realists think the United States needs to improve productivity,

[66] The literature is now vast. Excellent surveys can be found in Fred Halliday, "Hidden from International Relations: Women and the International Arena," *Millennium* 17, 3 (Winter 1988); Jean Bethke Elshtain, *Women and War* (New York: Basic Books, 1987); J. Ann Tickner, *Gender in International Relations* (New York: Columbia University Press, 1992); and Cynthia Enloe, *Beaches, Bananas and Bases: Making Feminist Sense of International Politics* (Berkeley: University of California Press, 1989).

[67] Bill McKibben, *The End of Nature* (New York: Anchor, 1989).

[68] For interesting speculations along these lines, see Adda Bozeman, *Strategic Intelligence and Statecraft* (London: Brassey's, 1992). She focuses not on the obvious strife between Islam and Christianity but on the internal contest for the soul of the modern mind.

education, infrastructure, and balanced budgets for the sake of enhancing its national power in a threatening world of global competition. The Liberals think we need to do the same in order to enhance the prospects of justice and advance the wealth of the citizens of the society. They also want us to extend the reality of democracy to those who have not fully enjoyed it. The Marxists regard each of these matters perhaps as potentially dangerous reformism, but they also recognize that reforms that improve the lot of the powerless give them the resources with which to remake the social order and go beyond amelioration to the liberation of those who desperately need a larger share of the benefits of capitalist production.

The two now-dominant visions of Liberalism and Realism agree on one major U.S. grand strategy. Their agreement may be dangerous. Realism and Liberalism agree on the potential threat posed by China. With one quarter of the world's population and a GNP growing at 10 percent per annum, it poses as the classic hegemonic challenger as well as the single most powerful major restricter of human rights, democratic rule, and free enterprise. Both visions see a threat. Liberals advocate transforming China; Realists, to balancing, containing, or dividing it.

The three visions differ in important world policies. For U.S. Realists the collapse of the USSR might be taken as an opportunity to keep a former rival down or an opportunity for a diplomatic revolution. They suggest that we may need to balance against the rise of new powers, whether they be China, Japan, or a uniting Europe, and therefore to restrict trade in strategic goods, to limit cooperation, and perhaps to turn the CIA against the new rivals. They raise the hard choice of whether we should regard the liberal Japanese and the possibly uniting Europeans as potential enemies and invest our national resources in a competition to make sure that in any exchange we get more than they even at the cost of our all getting less.[69]

Liberalism would argue differently that we should intensify our cooperative links with Japan and Europe. We should trust their democratization and enhance and expand the framework of our security cooperation. For example, we should extend defense agreements beyond Japan and the Europeans to Russia and others of the new democracies that are becoming parts of the Liberal pacific union. Moreover, we should invest in Russia and Eastern Europe, taking the present crisis as an opportunity to help liberalize and democratize them. The cost of avoiding another cold war would be cheap at almost any price.

The democratic Socialists (and the social welfare Liberals) look to the pros-

[69] Some of these views resonate with the American public. See Michael Mastanduno, "Do Relative Gains Matter?" *International Security* 16, 1 (Summer 1991). But in other polls Japan and Europe consistently come out "warm" on the international political thermometer ratings, despite trade rivalry.

pects of the recent East European revolutions as one more step in the world liberation of the working class. This is a step that deserves the solidarity of all democratic workers. Our task for the future would be to lift the dead hand of intervention, coercion, and capitalist repression from the Third World, where suffering by the proletariat and the peasantry is now taking place. They would have us shift our vision South and change our policies so that first, we restrain ourselves from intervention; second, we recognize the basic humanity of all human beings; and third, we accept a commitment to preserving the freedom from starvation of the half of humanity that now suffers at a table so groaning with abundance in the North.

Reconciliation and Rotation. International political theories are structurally similar models of ends and means, intentions and consequences. We need to judge both ends and means for each doctrine. Realism is a doctrine, not of just pragmatism or consequences, but of ends. Realism and Socialism thus presuppose idealistic or ideal elements that include national glory and power and public security, for the first, and social solidarity, for the second. Liberalism, correspondingly, can be pragmatic and incorporate interests in security and commerce. We also need to judge policy makers on both ends and means, intentions and consequences, all of which can differ. Each of the three grand strategies emphasizes particular ends and consequences and tells us how to measure each. What we should ask is that statesmen learn to balance ends and consequences.[70]

Done well, policy defeats theory by inventing measures that bypass or reconcile theoretical contradictions. But pragmatism without criteria is not in a position to know when choices need to be made. Fortunately it is both necessary and possible to reconcile the three visions, but because the reconciliation is likely to be incomplete, we require an ethic of consequences, as judged by principle. Let me try to explain why, and then how.

A pluralistic model of world politics is not a contradiction to theoretical knowledge, but a basis for it. We as thinking human beings need not be, and for the most part are not, singular selves. Our modern identities are pluralistic, found in individual identity, nation, and class (whether ideal or real) as well as religion, race, and gender (which states have yet to embody). We cannot escape

[70] National Security Adviser Anthony Lake puts it well: "Do you judge foreign policy makers on the basis of their intentions or on the consequences of their actions? . . . In Vietnam, especially, the refuge was always taken in intentions; 'We are fighting for democracy, we are fighting for this; we are fighting for that—therefore, don't blame us.' And that's much too low a standard. On the other hand, to hold policy makers completely accountable is probably also unfair, because the consequences are so often uncertain. What we can ask—absolutely—is that they think about those consequences as hard as they can. And secondly, that they do so in real terms, which is to say the impact on human lives. That we can ask." Jason DeParle, "Inside Mr. Inside," *New York Times Magazine*, August 20, 1995, p. 57.

multiplicity's entering into our policy choices, nor, if we want to be true to ourselves, should we try to.[71]

Given a world of diverse moral identities within and between human beings, we need an ethics of statesmanship capable of accommodating our diverse moralities. Each of our visions of morality has a legitimate sway on our identities, interests, and duties. The tug of national solidarity, global human rights, and class identity and a commitment to the liberation of the disadvantaged poor: Each carries weight, as it should, in our complex moral world. "Where there is no completeness and no perfection to be found in morality," there we need "minimum procedural justice," Stuart Hampshire has argued. "This minimum justice plays the role of the scales, while considerations derived from different conceptions of the good can be seen as the weights that have to be assessed. The politician should establish the nature of the claims upon him in their own terms before he restates them in his own terms drawn from his own conception of the good. . . . This is the judicial function of practical reason in private deliberation, when there is a conflict of moral claims and not merely a question of means to ends. This function (domestically) in a decent society is discharged by parliaments, law courts, civil services, with some recognition and respect for the procedures of just judgment"[72] Recognition of this internationally would require a bias toward negotiation, international law, and recourse to multilateral bodies as preliminary signs of good faith.

This ethic does not resolve all hard choices. U.S. Realists will wonder how much prosperity they should sacrifice in deciding, for example, whether or not strategically to contain the dynamic economy of China. Liberals will wonder about similar trade-offs between human rights and trade and diplomatic cooperation with the People's Republic of China. But we will need to be clear about where there is and where there need not be a costly choice.

Sometimes a strategy is clear in theory, but ambiguous in practice. Realists face this concern when they assess the balance of power. It requires steadiness, patience, and long-term perspective on the external dimension of national interests. But foreign policy in a democracy must have a domestic constituency in the end, or it will not last beyond the machinations of the policy maker temporarily in office.[73] Not every diplomatic revolution, therefore, will be prudent policy, even if it might greatly advance our security relative to that of a potential rival. Triangulation and détente in the Nixon administration ran into these difficulties when Americans found it difficult to understand why they were losing fellow citizens fighting against Communism in Vietnam while the

[71] For discussion, see Walzer, *Thick and Thin*, chap. 5.

[72] Stuart Hampshire, *Innocence and Experience* (Cambridge, Mass.: Harvard University Press, 1989), pp. 186–87.

[73] This is discussed by Alexander George, *Presidential Decisionmaking in Foreign Policy* (Boulder, Colo.: Westview Press, 1980).

Administration was accommodating Moscow and Beijing, even though the diplomacy made perfectly clear geopolitical sense. The United States punished (to deter) small powers; divided great powers.

Sometimes the choice is clear but just costly. If some larger purposes are to be achieved, what Kant called "moral politics" rules. Those Liberals committed to freedom have made a bargain with their governments and need to live up to it. The major costs of a Liberal strategy are borne at home. Not merely are its military costs at the taxpayer's expense, but a liberal foreign policy requires adjustment to a less controlled international political environment, a rejection of the status quo in favor of democratic choice. Tolerating more foreign change requires more domestic reform. Avoiding an imperial presence in the Persian Gulf may require a move toward energy independence. Allowing for the economic development of the world's poor calls for an acceptance of international trade adjustment. The home front becomes the front line of Liberal strategy.

In other cases compromise is equally essential. Theory and practice both call out for adjustment. Machiavelli warned that sometimes the least bad must be considered the best. In order to avoid the extremist possibilities of abstract universalism, U.S. Liberal policy, for example, should be constrained by a geopolitical budget. Strategy involves matching what we are prepared to spend to what we want to achieve. It identifies our aims, resources, threats, and allies. While Liberal democracy therefore can identify our natural allies abroad, we must let our actual enemies identify themselves. One reason for this is that we cannot embark upon the "crusades" for democracy that have been so frequent within the Liberal tradition. In a world armed with nuclear weapons crusading is suicidal. And in a world where changes in regional balances of power could be extremely destabilizing for ourselves and our allies, indiscriminate provocations of hostility (such as against the People's Republic of China) could create increased insecurity (for Japan and ourselves). We simply do not have the excess strength that would free us from a need to economize on dangers, however worthy the cause or needy the individuals calling for our assistance. But an equally powerful second reason why Liberals should let enemies identify themselves is that Liberal values require a strategy of accommodation. If we seek to promote democracy because it reflects the rights of all to be treated with equal respect—irrespective of race, religion, class, or nationality—then equal respect must guide both our aims and our means. A strategy of geopolitical superiority and Liberal imperialism, for example, would require both increased arms expenditures and international subversion and have little (or more likely) a retrogressive effect on human rights in the countries that are our targets.

Lastly, we can sometimes be so fortunate that our goals will work with each other, and statesmen can "rotate" them. Theories emphasize differences in order to generate deeper understanding through testing and reformulation. The really real world is more complicated, and so, therefore, our statesmen should make policy that reconciles and—where that cannot be achieved—"rotates" our ends. "The prince," Rousseau informed us with perhaps his profoundest strategic insight, "always makes his schemes rotate: he seeks to command in order to enrich himself, and to enrich himself in order to command. He is ready by turns to sacrifice the one aim to the other, with a view to obtaining whichever of the two is most wanting at the moment. But it is only in the hope of winning them both in the long run that he pursues each of them apart. If he is to be master of both men and things, he must have empire and money at the same time."[74]

At the very height of the Cold War in 1958, the great French sociologist Raymond Aron tackled a similar challenge when he asked how to reduce the danger of war in order to achieve "a transition from non-total war, founded on mutual fear, to a peace based upon the desire for nonviolence." His answer was wise and theoretically eclectic: "The principal conditions appear to me to be three in number: a diminution of the gulf between the privileged minority and the mass of humanity which remains sunk in poverty; the constitution of nations ready to accept each other within an international community; and the end of the conflict between the two Great Powers and the two dominant ideologies, which implies that the various countries concerned would be ready to recognize the kinship between the different types of industrial civilization."[75] While the Cold War seems over, we have not yet reached all the ends he sought. In our approach to them, it is hard to argue with the proposition that both foreign aid which was designed to build bridges between the rich and the poor, and a growing willingness to acknowledge the political independence and territorial integrity of states (provided they were not engaging in aggression and gross violations of human rights), played a role in ending the Cold War. So, too, did the implicit promise of membership in a Liberal peace. More important from the Rousseauian point of view, they worked together. Aid built moral bridges across diverse cultures while the growth of an international community of independent states made aid seem less quixotic (why aid enemies?). Together both aid and community made that momentous revolution that reduced state communism by making the revolutions of 1989 less of a surrender and more of a reunion.

As we face the challenges of the turn of the next millennium, it is thus worth remembering that enemies *can* be contained, peace extended, and revolutions made.

[74] Rousseau, "Judgment on the Peace Project of the Abbé de St.-Pierre," p. 99.
[75] Aron, *War and Industrial Society*, p. 41.

Bibliography

Adams, Henry, ed. 1960. *The Writings of Albert Gallatin*, vol. 1. New York: Antiquarian Press.

Adcock, Frank Ezra. 1927. *Thucydides and His History*. Cambridge, England: University Press.

Akerlof, George. 1970. "The Market for Lemons: Qualitative Uncertainty and the Market Mechanism." *Quarterly Journal of Economics*, vol. 84 (August), pp. 488–500.

Alexandroff, Alan. 1981. *The Logic of Diplomacy*. Beverly Hills: Sage.

Alker, Hayward. 1981. "Dialectical Foundations of Global Disparities." *International Studies Quarterly*, vol. 25, no. 1, pp. 69–98.

——, and Thomas Biersteker. 1984. "The Dialectics of World Order." *International Studies Quarterly*, vol. 28, pp. 121–42.

Allen, Frederick Lewis. 1965. *The Great Pierpoint Morgan*. New York: Harper and Row.

Allison, Graham. 1971. *Essence of Decision*. Boston: Little, Brown.

——, and Gregory Treverton, eds. 1992. *Rethinking American Security*. New York: Norton.

Altfeld, M. 1984. "The Decision to Ally." *Western Political Quarterly*, vol. 37, no. 4 (December), pp. 523–44.

Amdur, Robert. 1977. "Rawls' Theory of Justice: Domestic and International Perspectives." *World Politics*, vol. 29, no. 3 (April), pp. 438–61.

Anderson, Perry. 1974. *Lineages of the Absolutist State*. London: New Left Books.

Andreski, Stanislav. 1980. "On the Peaceful Disposition of Military Dictatorships." *Journal of Strategic Studies*, vol. 3, pp. 3–10.

Andrew, Christopher. 1968. *Théophile Delcassé and the Making of the Entente Cordiale*. London: Macmillan.

Appleby, Joyce. 1978. *Economic Thought and Ideology in Seventeenth-Century England*. Princeton: Princeton University Press.

Archiburgi, Daniele. 1995. "Immanuel Kant, Cosmopolitan Law and Peace," *European Journal of International Relations*, vol. 1, no. 4, pp. 429–56.

Ardrey, Robert. 1966. *The Territorial Imperative*. New York: Atheneum.
Arkes, Hadley. 1986. *First Things*. Princeton: Princeton University Press.
Armstrong, A. C. 1931. "Kant's Philosophy of Peace and War." *Journal of Philosophy*, vol. 28, pp. 197–204.
Aron, Raymond. 1958. *War and Industrial Society*. London: Oxford University Press.
——. 1966. *Peace and War: A Theory of International Relations*, trans. Richard Howard and Annette Baker Fox. Garden City, N.Y.: Doubleday.
——. 1967. "What Is a Theory of International Relations?" *Journal of International Affairs*, vol.21, no. 2, pp. 185–206.
——. 1973. *The Imperial Republic*, trans. Frank Jellinek. Englewood Cliffs, N.J.: Prentice Hall.
Ascher, Abraham. " 'Radical' Imperialists within German Social Democracy: 1912–1918." *Political Science Quarterly*, vol. 76, no. 4, pp. 555–75.
Ashby, Timothy. 1981. "Grenada: Threat to America's Oil Routes." *National Defense*, vol. 83 (May–June), pp. 52–54, 205.
Ashcraft, Richard. 1986. *Revolutionary Politics and Locke's Two Treatises of Government*. Princeton: Princeton University Press.
Ashley, Richard K. 1981. "Political Realism and Human Interests." *International Studies Quarterly*, vol. 25, pp. 204–36.
——. 1984. "The Poverty of Neorealism." *International Organization*, vol. 38, no. 2 (Spring), pp. 225–86.
Avineri, Shlomo. 1968. *The Social and Political Thought of Karl Marx*. Cambridge, England: Cambridge University Press.
Axelrod, Robert. 1984. *The Evolution of Cooperation*. New York: Basic Books.
Babst, D. V. 1972. "A Force for Peace." *Industrial Research*, vol. 14 (April), pp. 55–58.
Bacon, Francis. 1870. "Of Empire," in J. Spedding, ed., *The Works of Francis Bacon*, vol 62. London: Longmans.
Bagby, Laurie. 1994. "The Use and Abuse of Thucydides." *International Organization*, vol. 48, no. 1 (Winter), pp. 131–53.
Bahro, Rudolph. 1970. *The Alternative in Eastern Europe*. London: NLB.
Baldwin, Oliver. 1925. *Six Prisons and Two Revolutions: Adventures in Trans-Caucasia and Anatolia, 1920–1921*. Garden City, N.Y.: Doubleday.
Banks, Arthur, and William Overstreet, eds. 1983. *A Political Handbook of the World*. New York: McGraw-Hill.
Baran, Paul, and Paul Sweezy. 1966. *Monopoly Capital*. New York: Monthly Review Press.
Barnet, Richard. 1968. *Intervention and Revolution: The United States in the Third World*. New York: Meridian.
Barnett, Michael and Jack Levy. 1991. "Domestic Sources of Alliances and Alignments: The Case of Egypt, 1962–1973." *International Organization*, vol. 45 (Summer), pp. 369–95.
Barry, Brian. 1982. "Humanity and Justice in Global Perspective,"in Roland J. Pennock and John W. Chapman, eds., *Ethics, Economics and the Law*, Nomos XXIV. New York: New York University Press.
——. 1983. "Some Questions about Explanation." *International Studies Quarterly*, vol. 27, no. 1 (March), pp. 17–28.
Bates, Darrell. 1984. *The Fashoda Incident of 1898: Encounter on the Nile*. New York: Oxford University Press.

Batutah, Ibn. 1958. *Journals*, trans. H. A. R. Gibb. London: Hakluyt.

Bauer, Peter. 1981. *Equality, the Third World, and Economic Delusion.* Cambridge, Mass.: Harvard University Press.

Baxter, P. T. W. 1977. "Boran Age-sets and Warfare," in Katsuyoshi Fukui and David Turton, eds., *Warfare among East African Herders.* Kyoto: National Museum of Ethnology.

Beitz, Charles. 1975. "Justice and International Relations." *Philosophy and Public Affairs*, vol. 4, no. 4 (Summer), pp. 282–311.

——, ed. 1985. *International Ethics.* Princeton: Princeton University Press.

——. 1988. "The Reagan Doctrine in Nicaragua," in Steven Luper-Foy, ed., *Problems of International Justice.* Boulder, Colo.: Westview Press.

Benhabib, Seyla. 1995. "Cultural Complexity, Moral Interdependence and the Global Dialogical Community," in Martha Nussbaum and Jonathan Glover, *Women, Culture and Development.* New York: Oxford University Press.

Bentham, Jeremy. 1789/1927. *Plan for an Universal and Perpetual Peace*, intro. C. John Colombos. Grotius Society Publications no. 6. London: Sweet and Maxwell.

——. 1843/1973. *Anarchical Fallacies*, in Parekh Bhikhu, ed., *Bentham's Political Thought.* New York: Barnes and Noble.

Berger, Martin. 1977. *Engels, Armies, and Revolution.* Hamden, Conn.: Archon Books.

Bergesen, Albert 1991. "Dependency and the World System." ISA Conference, Vancouver, March 1991.

Berki, R. N. 1971. "On Marxian Thought and the Problem of International Relations." *World Politics*, vol. 24, no. 1 (October), pp. 80–105.

——. 1981. *On Political Realism.* London: J. M. Dent.

Berlin, Isaiah. 1969. *Four Essays on Liberty*, Introduction. New York: Oxford University Press.

——. 1980. *Against the Current.* New York: Penguin.

Beschloss, Michael. 1991. *The Crisis Years.* New York: HarperCollins.

Bird, Kai. 1992. *The Chairman: John McCloy, the Making of the American Establishment.* New York: Simon and Schuster.

Blasier, Cole. 1976. *The Hovering Giant.* Pittsburgh: University of Pittsburgh Press.

Blaug, Mark, ed. 1991. *Pioneers of Economics*, vols. I and II, *Adam Smith.* Aldershot, England: Edward Elgar Publishing.

Block, Fred. 1977. *The Origins of International Economic Disorder.* Berkeley: University of California Press.

Bloom, Solomon. 1941. *The World of Nations.* New York: Columbia University Press.

Bluhm, William. 1965. *Theories of the Political System.* Englewood Cliffs, N.J.: Prentice Hall.

Boersner, Demetrio. 1957. *The Bolsheviks and the National and Colonial Question (1917–1928).* Geneva: E. Droz.

Bohlen, Charles. 1973. *Witness to History.* New York: Norton.

Bok, Sissela. 1989. *A Strategy for Peace.* New York: Pantheon.

Bolingbroke. 1749. "Idea of a Patriot King." *Letters on the Spirit of Patriotism.* London: Bolingbroke, H. A. Millar.

Borkenau, Franz. 1939/1962. *World Communism.* Ann Arbor: University of Michigan Press.

——. 1942. *Socialism, National or International.* London: Routledge.

Boulding, Kenneth. 1962. *Conflict and Defense.* New York: Harper Torch.

Bourne, Kenneth. 1982. *Palmerston: The Early Years.* New York: Macmillan.

Bowring, John, ed. 1845. *The Works of Jeremy Bentham,* vol. 10. Edinburgh: Nelson.

Boyd, Gerald. 1985. "Role in Nicaragua Described by the U.S." *New York Times,* August 9, 1985.

Bozeman, Adda. 1992. *Strategic Intelligence and Statecraft.* London: Brassey's.

Bradeen, Donald W. 1960. "The Popularity of the Athenian Empire." *Historia,* vol. 9, pp. 257–69.

Braunthal, Julius. 1967. *History of the International,* vol. 1, *1864–1914,* trans. Henry Collins and Kenneth Mitchell. New York: Praeger.

——. 1967. *History of the International,* vol. 2, *1914–1943,* trans. John Clark. New York: Praeger.

Bremer, Stuart. 1992. "Democracy and Militarized International Disputes, 1816–1965." *International Interactions,* vol. 18, no. 3, pp. 23–50.

Brenner, Robert. 1977. "The Origins of Capitalist Development: A Critique of Neo-Smithnian Marxism." *New Left Review,* vol. 104, pp. 25–92.

Brewer, Anthony. 1980. *Marxist Theories of Imperialism.* London: Routledge.

Brewer, John. 1989. *Sinews of Power.* London: Unwin Hyman.

Brewin, Christopher. 1978. "Justice in International Relations," in Michael Donelan, ed., *The Reason of States.* London: George Allen and Unwin.

Briggs, Herbert, ed. 1966. *The Law of Nations: Cases etc.* New York: Appleton-Century-Crofts.

Brilmayer, Lea. 1989. *Justifying International Acts.* Ithaca, N.Y.: Cornell University Press.

Broad, Robin, and John Cavanaugh. 1993. "Beyond the Myths of Rio: A New American Agenda for the Environment," *World Policy Journal* (Spring), pp. 65–72.

Brown, Chris. 1992. "Marxism and International Ethics," in Terry Nardin and David Mapel, eds. *Traditions of International Ethics.* Cambridge, England: Cambridge University Press.

——. 1992. *International Relations Theory: New Normative Approaches.* New York: Columbia University Press.

Brown, Roger. 1970. *Fashoda Reconsidered: The Impact of Domestic Politics on French Policy in Africa, 1893–1898.* Baltimore: Johns Hopkins University Studies in Historical & Political Science.

Brownlie, Ian, ed. 1983. *Basic Documents of International Law,* 3d ed. New York: Oxford University Press.

Bruell, Christopher. 1974. "Thucydides' View of Athenian Imperialism," *American Political Science Review,* vol. 68, no. 1, pp. 11–17.

Brzezinski, Zbigniew K. 1967. *The Soviet Bloc.* Cambridge, Mass.: Harvard University Press.

——. 1989. *The Grand Failure.* New York: Scribners.

——. 1989. "Will the Soviet Empire Self-Destruct?" *New York Times Magazine* (February 26), pp. 39–41.

——, and Samuel Huntington. 1963. *Political Power: USA/USSR.* New York: Viking Press.

Bueno de Mesquita, Bruce, and David Lalman. 1988. "Empirical Support for Systemic and Dyadic Explanations of International Conflict." *World Politics,* vol. XLI, no. 1 (October), pp. 1–20.

Bull, Hedley. 1977. *The Anarchical Society*. New York: Columbia University Press.
——. 1981. "Hobbes and the International Anarchy." *Social Research*, vol. 48, no. 4 (Winter), pp. 717–38.
Bunce, Valerie. 1990. "Rising above the Past: The Struggle for Liberal Democracy in Eastern Europe." *World Policy Journal* (Summer), pp. 395–430.
Bundy, William P. 1975. "Dictatorships and American Foreign Policy." *Foreign Affairs*, vol. 54, no. 1 (October), pp. 51–60.
Burckhardt, Jacob. 1965. *The Civilization of the Renaissance in Italy* (1878), trans. S. G. Middlemore. London: Phaidon Press.
Burke, John P., and Fred Greenstein. 1989. "Presidential Personality and National Security." *International Political Science Review*, vol. 10, no. 1, pp. 73–92.
Burley, Anne-Marie. 1992. "Law among Liberal States: Liberal Internationalism and the Act of State Doctrine." *Columbia Law Review*, vol. 92, no. 8 (December), pp. 1907–96.
Burrowes, Reynold. 1988. *Revolution and Rescue in Grenada*. New York: Greenwood Press.
Bush, George. 1992. "State of the Union Address," *New York Times*, January 29, 1992.
Butterfield, Herbert. 1954. "The Reconstruction of an Historical Episode: The History of the Enquiry into the Origins of the Seven Years War," *Man on His Past*. Cambridge, England: Cambridge University Press.
——. 1966. "The Balance of power," in H. Butterfield and M. Wight, eds., *Diplomatic Investigations*. London: George Allen and Unwin.
Calder, Kent E. 1996. "Asia's Empty Gas Tank." *Foreign Affairs*, vol. 75, no. 2 (March–April), pp. 55–69.
Campbell, John C. 1967. *Tito's Separate Road*. New York: Council on Foreign Relations/Harper and Row.
Carens, Joseph. 1989. "Membership and Morality," in William Brubaker, ed., *Immigration and the Politics of Citizenship in Europe and North America*. Washington, D.C.: University Press of America.
Carnesale, Albert, Paul Doty, Stanley Hoffmann, Samuel Huntington, Joseph Nye, and Scott Sagan. 1983. *Living with Nuclear Weapons*. New York: Bantam.
Carr, Edward H. 1945. *Nationalism and After*. New York: Macmillan.
——. 1950. *The Bolshevik Revolution, 1917–1923*, vol. 1. London: Macmillan.
——. 1951. *The Twenty Years' Crisis: 1919–1939*. London: Macmillan.
Carter, C. J. 1987. *Rousseau and the Problem of War*. New York: Garland.
Chan, Steve. 1984. "Mirror, Mirror on the Wall . . . : Are Freer Countries More Pacific?" *Journal of Conflict Resolution*, vol. 28 (December), pp. 617–48.
Chase-Dunn, C. 1981. "Interstate System and Capitalist World Economy." *International Studies Quarterly*, vol. 25, no. 1 (March), pp. 19–42.
Christman, Henry, ed. 1966. *The American Journalism of Marx and Engels*. New York: New American Library.
Christensen, Thomas, and Jack Snyder. 1990. "Chain Gangs and Passed Bucks." *International Organization*, vol. 44, no. 2 (Spring), pp. 139–68.
Christopher, Warren. 1982. "Ceasefire between the Branches." *Foreign Affairs*, vol. 60, no. 5 (Summer), p. 989–1005.
Churchill, Winston S. 1946. "Alliance of the English Speaking Peoples," March 5, 1946, *Vital Speeches*, vol. 12, no. 11, pp. 329–32.

——. 1950. *Triumph and Tragedy*. Boston: Houghton Mifflin.

Clark, Ian. 1980. *Reform and Resistance in the International Order*. Cambridge, England: Cambridge University Press.

Clark, M. Margaret. 1986. "The Cultural Patterning of Risk-Seeking Behavior: Implications for Armed Conflict," in Mary LeCron Foster and Robert A. Rubinstein, eds., *Peace and War: Cross-Cultural Perspectives*. New Brunswick, N.J.: Transactions Books.

Claude, Inis. 1957. *Swords into Plowshares*. New York: Random House.

——. 1962. *Power and International Relations*. New York: Random House.

Clausewitz, Carl von. 1976. *On War*, ed. Peter Paret and Michael Howard. Princeton: Princeton University Press.

Clemens, Walter C. 1982. "The Superpowers and the Third World," in Charles Kegley and Pat McGowan, eds., *Foreign Policy: USA/USSR*. Beverly Hills: Sage.

Cline, Ray. 1977. *World Power Assessment 1977*. Boulder, Colo.: Westview Press.

Coase, Ronald. 1960. "The Problem of Social Cost." *Journal of Law and Economics*, vol. 3 (October), pp. 1–44.

Cochrane, Charles. 1929. *Thucydides and the Science of History*. London: Oxford University Press.

Cogan, Marc. 1981. *The Human Thing: The Speeches and Principles of Thucydides' History*. Chicago: University of Chicago Press.

Cohen, David. 1984. "Justice Interest and Political Deliberation in Thucydides," *Quaderni Urbinati*, vol. 45, pp. 35–60.

Cohen, G. A. 1978. *Karl Marx's Theory of History: A Defence*. Princeton: Princeton University Press.

——. 1983. "Reconsidering Historical Materialism," in J. Roland Pennock, ed., *Marxism Today. Nomos*, vol. 24. New York: New York University Press.

Cohen, Ronald. 1986. "War and War-Proneness in Pre- and Postindustrial States," in Mary Foster and Robert Rubinstein, eds., *Peace and War: Cross-cultural Perspectives*. New Brunswick, N.J.: Transaction Books.

Cole, G. D. H. 1954. *A History of Socialist Thought*, vol. 2, *Marxism and Anarchism, 1850–1890*. London: Macmillan.

Colton, Tim. 1992. *Dilemmas of Soviet Reform*. New York: Council on Foreign Relations.

Comisso, Ellen. 1990. "Crisis in Socialism or Crisis of Socialism." *World Politics* (July), pp. 563–96.

Connor, W. Robert. 1984. *Thucydides*. Princeton: Princeton University Press.

Connor, Walker. 1984. *The National Question in Marxist-Leninist Theory and Strategy*. Princeton: Princeton University Press.

Contee, Christine. 1987. *What Americans Think: Views on Development and U.S. Third World Relations*. New York: Interfiction.

Conway, S. 1989. "Bentham on Peace and War," *Utilitas* (May), pp. 82–101, reprinted in Bhikhu Parekh, ed., *Jeremy Bentham: Critical Assessments*. New York: Routledge, 1993.

Cooper, Richard. 1977. "A New International Economic Order for Mutual Gain." *Foreign Policy*, no. 26 (Spring), pp. 65–120.

Cornford, Francis. 1907/1965. *Thucydides Mythhistoricus*. London: Routledge.

Cox, Richard. 1960. *Locke on War and Peace*. New York: Oxford University Press.

Craig, Gordon. 1964. *The Politics of the Prussian Army.* New York: Oxford University Press.

Crampton, R. J. 1973. "August Bebel and the British Foreign Office." *History*, vol. 58 (June), pp. 218–32.

Cranston, Maurice. 1957. *John Locke: A Biography.* London: Longmans.

Crawford, Neta. 1994. "Cooperation Among Iroquois Nations," *International Organization*, vol. 48, no. 3, pp. 345–85.

Crick, Bernard. 1970. "Introduction" to *The Discourses* by Machiavelli. London: Penguin.

Cumings, Bruce. 1987. "The Origins and Development of the Northeast Asian Political Economy," in E. C. Deyo, ed., *The Political Economy of the New Asian Industrialism.* Ithaca, N.Y.: Cornell University Press.

Cusack, Thomas. 1989. "The Management of Power in a Warring State System," in Richard Stoll and Michael Ward, eds., *Power in World Politics.* Boulder, Colo.: Lynne Rienner.

Cutler, Lloyd, 1985. "The Right to Intervene." *Foreign Affairs*, vol. 64, no. 1 (Fall), p. 111.

——. 1989. "Noriega's Actions Gave Us Justification." *Washington Post*, December 24, 1989, p. C7.

Dabreo, D. Sinclair. 1979. *The Grenada Revolution.* St. Lucia: M.A.P.S.

Dam, Kenneth. 1983. "The Larger Importance of Grenada," Address before the Associated Press Managing Editors Conference, Louisville, Kentucky, November 4 1983.

Damrosch, Lori. Forthcoming. "Constitutional Control over War-Powers: A Common Core Accountability in Democratic Societies." *University of Miami Law Review*, vol. 50, pp. 801–19.

Danto, Arthur, and Sidney Morgenbesser, eds. 1970. *Philosophy of Science.* Cleveland: World Meridian Books.

Darby, W. Evans. 1920. "Cardinal Alberoni's Proposed European Alliance for the Subjugation and Settlement of the Turkish Empire." Grotius Society, *Transactions*, vol. 5, no. 1, pp. 83–96.

David, Steven. 1991. "Explaining Third World Alignment." *World Politics*, vol. 43, no. 2 (January), pp. 233–56.

Day, Arthur, and Michael W. Doyle, eds. 1986. *Escalation and Intervention.* New York: United Nations Association/Westview Press.

de Grazia, Sebastian. 1989. *Machiavelli in Hell.* Princeton: Princeton University Press.

de Rivera, Joseph. 1968. *The Psychological Dimensions of Foreign Policy.* Columbus: Merrill.

de Ste. Croix, Geoffrey. 1954–55. "The Character of the Athenian Empire." *Historia*, vol. 3, pp. 1–44.

——. 1972. *The Origins of the Peloponnesian War.* Ithaca, N.Y.: Cornell University Press.

de Vischer, Charles. 1968. *Theory and Reality in Public International Law.* Princeton: Princeton University Press.

Dedijer, Vladimir. 1970. *The Battle Stalin Lost: Memoirs of Yugoslavia 1948–1953.* Nottingham, England: Spokesman.

Dehio, Ludwig. 1965. *The Precarious Balance.* New York: Vintage.

Dennis, Mathew. 1995. *Cultivating a Landscape of Peace.* Ithaca, N.Y.: Cornell University Press.

DeParle, Jason. 1995. "Inside Mr. Inside." *New York Times Magazine,* August 20, 1995, pp. 32–57.

Deudney, Daniel and John Ikenberry. 1991–1992. "The International Sources of Soviet Change." *International Security,* vol. 16, no. 3 (Winter), pp. 74–118.

Deutsch, Karl. 1957. *Political Community and the North Atlantic Area.* Princeton: Princeton University Press.

——. 1966. *Nationalism and Social Communication.* Cambridge, Mass.: MIT Press.

——, and J. David Singer. 1964. "Multipolar Systems and International Stability." *World Politics,* vol. 16, no. 3 (April), pp. 390–406.

Diamond, Larry. 1989. "Beyond Authoritarianism and Totalitarianism: Strategies for Democratization." *Washington Quarterly* (Winter), pp. 141–63.

Dingman, Roger. 1979. "Theories of, and Approaches to, Alliance Politics," in Paul Lauren, ed., *Diplomacy.* New York: Free Press.

Dixon, William. 1993. "Democracy and the Management of Conflict." *Journal of Conflict Resolution,* vol. 37, no. 1 (March), pp. 42–68.

Doherty, Carroll J. 1992. "Support for Foreign Aid Wilting under Glare of Domestic Woes," *Congressional Quarterly Weekly Report,* 50 (May 16), pp. 1351–57.

Dominguez, Jorge. 1980. *Insurrection or Loyalty: The Breakdown of the Spanish American Empire.* Cambridge, Mass.: Harvard University Press.

Donelan, Michael, ed. 1978. *The Reason of States.* London: George Allen & Unwin.

Doran, Charles. 1971. *The Politics of Assimilation: Hegemony and Its Aftermath.* Baltimore: Johns Hopkins University Press.

Dorn, Walter. 1940. *Competition for Empire, 1740–1763.* New York: Harper.

Downs, George, ed. 1994. *Collective Security beyond the Cold War.* Ann Arbor: University of Michigan Press.

——, and Keisuke Iida. 1994. "Assessing the Theoretical Case against Collective Security," in George Downs, ed., *Collective Security beyond the Cold War.* Ann Arbor: University of Michigan Press.

Doyle, Michael W. 1983. "Kant, Liberal Legacies, and Foreign Affairs," Parts 1 and 2, *Philosophy and Public Affairs,* vol. 12, nos. 3–4 (Summer and Fall), pp. 205–54, 323–53.

——. 1986. "Grenada: An International Crisis in Multilateral Security," in Arthur Day and Michael Doyle, eds., *Escalation and Intervention: Multilateral Security and Its Alternatives.* Boulder, Colo. and London: Westview Press/United Nations Association/Mansell Publishing, pp. 123–51.

——. 1986. "Liberalism and World Politics." *American Political Science Review,* vol. 80, no. 4 (December), pp. 1151–69.

——. 1986. "International Distributive Justice." *PS,* vol. XIX, no. 4 (Fall), pp. 856–59.

——. 1990. "Thucydidean Realism." *Review of International Studies,* vol. 16, no. 3 (July), pp. 223–37.

——, Fred Hirsch, and Edward Morse. 1977. *Alternatives to Monetary Disorder.* New York: Council on Foreign Relations/McGraw-Hill.

Doyle, William. 1978. *The Old European Order, 1660–1800.* Oxford: Oxford University Press.

Draper, Theodore. 1992. "Who Killed Soviet Communism?" *New York Review of Books* vol. 39, no. 11 (June 11), pp. 7–14.

Dunn, John. 1969. *The Political Thought of John Locke: An Historical Account of the Argument of the Two Treatises.* Cambridge, England: Cambridge University Press.

——. 1984. "The Concept of Trust in the Politics of John Locke," in Richard Rorty, ed., *Philosophy in History.* Cambridge, England: Cambridge University Press.

——. 1985. "Social Theory, Social Understanding, and Political Action," in John Dunn, *Rethinking Modern Political Theory.* Cambridge, England: Cambridge University Press.

Dye, Thomas R., and Harmon Ziegler. 1989. "Socialism and Militarism." *PS: Political Science and Politics,* vol. 22, no. 4 (December), pp. 800–13.

Earle, Edward M. 1986. "Adam Smith, Alexander Hamilton, Friedrich List: The Economic Foundations of Military Power," in *Makers of Modern Strategy.* Princeton: Princeton University Press.

Easton, David, ed. 1966. *Varieties of Political Theories.* Englewood Cliffs, N.J.: Prentice Hall.

Economic Commission for Latin America and the Caribbean (ECLAC). 1989. *Preliminary Balance of the Latin American and Caribbean Economy.* Santiago, Chile: ECLAC.

Elliott, John. 1963. *Imperial Spain 1469–1716.* New York: New American Library.

Ellis, Anthony. 1992. "Utilitarianism and International Ethics," in Terry Nardin and David Mapel, eds., *Traditions of International Ethics.* Cambridge, England: Cambridge University Press.

Elster, Jan. 1985. *Making Sense of Marx.* Cambridge, England: Cambridge University Press.

Elshtain, Jean Bethke. 1987. *Women and War.* New York: Basic Books.

Ember Carol, Melvin Ember, and Bruce Russett. 1992. "Peace between Participatory Polities." *World Politics,* vol. 44 (July), pp. 573–99.

Encarnation, Dennis J., and Louis T. Wells, Jr. 1986. "Evaluating Foreign Investment," in Theodore H. Moran, ed., *Investing in Development: New Roles for Private Capital.* Washington, D.C.: Overseas Development Council.

Engels, Friedrich. 1884/1985. *The Origin of the Family, Private Property and the State.* Harmondsworth, England: Penguin.

——. 1890/1952. "The Foreign Policy of Czarism," in Marx (1952).

——. 1940. "Introduction" to Marx's *The Civil War in France.* New York: International Publishers.

——. 1952. "Democratic Panslavism," in Marx (1952).

——. 1981. *Anti-Duhring,* excerpted in Bernard Semmel, ed., *Marxism and the Science of War.* Oxford: Oxford University Press.

Enloe, Cynthia. 1989. *Beaches, Bananas and Bases: Making Feminist Sense of International Politics.* Berkeley: University of California Press.

Enterline, Andrew. 1996. "Driving while Democratizing: A Rejoinder to Mansfield and Synder." *International Security,* vol. 20, no. 4 (Spring), pp. 183–207.

The Europa Yearbook. 1985. London: Europa Publications, 2 vols.

The Europa Yearbook. 1988. London: Europa Publications.

Evangelista, Matthew. 1988. *Innovation and the Arms Race.* Ithaca, NY: Cornell University Press.

Evans-Pritchard, E. E., and M. Fortes, eds. 1940. *African Political Systems.* Oxford: Oxford University Press.

Ewers, John C. 1967. "Blackfoot Raiding for Horses and Scalps," in P. Bohannon, ed., *Law and Warfare: Studies in the Anthropology of Conflict.* Garden City, N.Y.: Natural History Press.

Fainsod, Merle. 1935. *International Socialism and the World War.* Cambridge, Mass.: Harvard University Press.

Falk, Richard, ed. 1968. *The Vietnam War and International Law.* Princeton: Princeton University Press.

Fanon, Frantz. 1963/1965. *Wretched of the Earth.* New York: Grove Press.

Farber, Henry S., and Joanne Gowa. 1995. "Polities and Peace." *International Security,* vol. 20, no. 2 (Fall), pp. 108–32.

Farer, Tom. 1993. "A Paradigm of Legitimate Intervention," in Lori Damrosch, ed., *Enforcing Restraint.* New York: Council on Foreign Relations.

Farnham, Barbara. *Roosevelt and the Munich Crisis: A Study of Political Decision-Making.* Princeton: Princeton University Press (forthcoming).

Fichte, Johann G. 1800/1940. *L'État commercial ferme (Handelstaat),* trans. J. Gibelin. Paris: Librairie Générale de Droit et de Jurisprudence.

Fieldhouse, D. K. 1967. *The Theory of Capitalist Imperialism.* London: Longmans.

Findlay, Ronald. 1982. "International Distributive Justice." *Journal of International Economics,* vol. 13, pp. 1–14.

Finley, John. 1963. *Thucydides.* Ann Arbor: University of Michigan Press.

Finley, M. I. 1978. "The Fifth Century Athenian Empire: A Balance Sheet," in P. D. A. Garnsey and C. R. Whittaker, eds., *Imperialism in the Ancient World.* Cambridge, England: Cambridge University Press.

Fischer, Dietrich. 1984. *Preventing War in the Nuclear Age.* Totowa, N.J.: Rowman and Allanheld.

Fischer, Louis. 1964. *Lenin.* New York: Harper and Row.

——. 1972. *The Road to Yalta.* New York: Harper and Row.

Forde, Steven. 1992. "Varieties of Realism: Thucydides and Machiavelli." *Journal of Politics,* vol. 54, no. 2 (May), pp. 372–93.

Forrest, W. G. 1968. *A History of Sparta, 950–192 BC.* London: Hutchinson.

Forsyth, Murray. 1979. "Thomas Hobbes and the External Relations of States." *British Journal of International Studies,* vol. 5, pp. 196–209.

Fox, William T. R. 1959. "The Uses of International Relations Theory," in William Fox, ed., *Theoretical Aspects of International Relations.* Notre Dame: University of Notre Dame Press.

Franck, Thomas. 1992. "The Emerging Right to Democratic Governance." *American Journal of International Law,* vol. 86 (January), pp. 46–91.

Frank, André Gunder. 1967. *Capitalism and Underdevelopment in Latin America.* New York: Monthly Review Press.

Frankena, William. 1973. *Ethics.* Englewood Cliffs, N.J.: Prentice Hall.

Frederick II. 1752. *Political Testament of 1752.*

——. 1789. *A History of My Own Times, Part I,* trans. Thomas Holdcroft. London: Robinson.

——. 1789. *History of the Seven Years War, Part I, Posthumous Works II.* London: Robinson, 1789.

Frederick of Prussia. 1740/1981. *Anti-Machiavel,* trans. Paul Sonino. Athens: Ohio University Press.

Freud, Sigmund. 1924. "Why War?" *Collected Papers,* ed. James Strachey. New York: Basic Books.

Friedberg, Aaron. 1987–1988. "The Assessment of Military Power." *International Security,* vol. 12, no. 3 (Winter), pp. 190–202.

——. 1993. "Ripe for Rivalry," *International Security,* vol. 18, no. 3 (Winter), pp. 5–34.

Friedheim, Cyrus. 1993. "The Global Corporation—Obsolete So Soon," World Economic Forum, Davos.

Friedrich, Karl. 1948. *Inevitable Peace.* Cambridge, Mass.: Harvard University Press.

Fullinwider, Robert. 1986. "Notes from the Classroom." *GSPM Network,* vol. 1, no. 3 (Spring), p. 1.

Furst, Jill Leslie. 1986. "Land Disputes and the Gods in the Pre-Hispanic Mixteca," in Mary L. Foster and Robert A. Rubinstein, eds., *Peace and War: Cross-cultural Perspectives.* New Brunswick, N.J.: Transaction Books.

Gaddis, John Lewis. 1972. *The United States and the Origin of the Cold War.* New York: Columbia University Press.

——. 1982. *Strategies of Containment.* New York: Oxford University Press.

——. 1983. "The Emerging Post-Revisionist Synthesis on the Origins of the Cold War." *Diplomatic History,* vol. 7, no. 3 (Summer), pp. 171–91.

——. 1987. "How the Cold War Might End." *Atlantic Monthly* (November), pp. 88–100.

——. 1987. *The Long Peace.* New York: Oxford University Press.

——. 1988. "The Evolution of U.S. Policy Goals toward the USSR in the Postwar Era," in Seweryn Bialer and Michael Mandelbaum, eds., *Gorbachev's Russia and American Foreign Policy.* Boulder, Colo.: Westview Press.

Galili, Ziva. 1989. *The Menshevik Leaders in the Russian Revolution.* Princeton: Princeton University Press.

Gallagher, John. 1982. "The Decline, Revival and Fall of the British Empire," in Anil Seal, ed., *The Decline, Revival and Fall of the British Empire.* Cambridge, England: Cambridge University Press.

Gallie, W. 1978. *Philosophers of Peace and War.* New York: Cambridge University Press.

Galston, William. 1975. *Kant and the Problem of History.* Chicago: University of Chicago Press.

Garst, Robert, and Tom Barry. 1990. *Feeding the Crisis: U.S. Aid and Foreign Policy in Central America.* Lincoln: University of Nebraska.

Garten, Jeffrey. 1992. A *Cold Peace: America, Japan, Germany and the Struggle for Supremacy.* New York: Times Books.

Garton Ash, Timothy. 1990. "Eastern Europe: The Year of Truth." *New York Review of Books* (February 15), pp. 17–22.

Garvin, J. L., and J. Amery. 1935. *Life of Joseph Chamberlain.* London: Macmillan.

Gastil, Raymond. 1985. *Freedom in the World 1985.* New York: Freedom House.

Gaubatz, Kurt. 1991. "Election Cycles and War," *Journal of Conflict Resolution,* vol. 35, no. 2, pp. 212–244.

Gauthier, David. 1969. *The Logic of Leviathan.* Oxford: Clarendon.

Gay, Peter. 1962. *The Dilemma of Democratic Socialism: Eduard Bernstein's Challenge to Marx*. New York: Collier.

Geertz, Clifford. 1995. "Culture War." *New York Review of Books*, vol. XLII, no. 19 (November 30), pp. 4–6.

Gellman, Peter. 1988. "Hans J. Morgenthau and the Legacy of Political Realism." *Review of International Studies*, vol. 14, no. 4 (October), pp. 247–66.

——. 1989. "The Elusive Explanation: Balance of Power Theories and the Origins of World War One." *Review of International Studies*, vol. 15 (Spring), pp. 155–82.

George, Alexander. 1969. "The Operational Code: A Neglected Approach to the Study of Political Leaders and Decision-Making." *International Security*, vol. 13, pp. 190–222.

——. 1980. *Presidential Decisionmaking in Foreign Policy*. Boulder, Colo.: Westview Press.

Giddens, Anthony. 1985. *The Nation-State and Violence*, vol. 2, *Contemporary Critique of Historical Materialism*. Cambridge, England. Polity Press; Oxford: Basil Blackwell.

Gilbert, Alan. 1978. "Marx on Internationalism and War." *Philosophy and Public Affairs*, vol. 7, no. 4, pp. 353–54.

——. 1981. *Marx's Politics: Communists and Citizens*. New Brunswick, N.J.: Rutgers University Press.

——. 1983. "The Storming of Heaven: Politics and Marx's Capital," in Roland J. Pennock and John W. Chapman, eds. *Marxism*. New York: New York University Press.

Gilpin, Robert. 1975. *U.S. Power and the Multinational Corporation*. New York: Basic Books.

——. 1981. *War and Change in World Politics*. Cambridge, England. Cambridge University Press.

——. 1986. "The Richness of the Tradition of Political Realism," in Robert Keohane, ed., *Neorealism and Its Critics*. New York: Columbia University Press.

——. 1987. *The Political Economy of International Relations*. Princeton: Princeton University Press.

——. 1988. "The Theory of Hegemonic War." *Journal of Interdisciplinary History*, vol. XVIII, no. 4 (Spring), pp. 591–613.

——. 1991. "Peloponnesian War and Cold War," in Richard Ned Lebow and Barry Strauss, eds., *Hegemonic Rivalry*. Boulder, Colo.: Westview Press.

Gluckman, Max. 1963. "Rituals of Rebellion in South-East Africa," *Order and Rebellion in Tribal Africa*. London: Cohen and West.

Goldman, Marshall. 1991. *What Went Wrong with Perestroika*. New York: Norton.

Goldshmidt, Walter. "Personal Motivation and Institutionalized Conflict," in Mary L. Foster and Robert A. Rubinstein, eds., *Peace and War: Cross-cultural Perspectives*. New Brunswick, N.J.: Transaction Books.

Gooch, G. P., et al., eds. 1928. *British Documents on the Origins of the War, 1898–1914*, vol. 3. London: HMSO.

Good, Robert C. 1965. "National Interest and Moral Theory," in Roger Hilsman and Robert Good, eds., *Foreign Policy in the Sixties*. Baltimore: Johns Hopkins University Press.

Goodman, Elliot. 1960. *The Soviet Design for a World State*. New York: Columbia University Press.

Gorbachev, Mikhail. 1987. *Selected Speeches and Articles*, 2d ed. Moscow: Progress Publishers.

——. 1987. "On Socialist Democracy," *Socialism, Peace, and Democracy*. London: Atlantic Highlands.

——. 1988. "Address to the United Nations, December 7, 1988," excerpted in *New York Times*, December 8, 1988, pp. A1, A17.

Gourevitch, Peter. 1977. "International Trade, Domestic Coalitions and Liberty: Comparative Responses to the Crisis of 1873–1896." *Journal of Interdisciplinary History*, vol. 8, pp. 281–313.

——. 1986. *Politics in Hard Times*. Ithaca, N.Y.: Cornell University Press.

Graebner, Norman. 1969. "Cold War Origins and the Continuing Debate: A Review of Recent Literature." *Journal of Conflict Resolution*, vol. 13, no. 1 (March), pp. 123–32.

Graham, Gerald. 1987. "The Justice of Intervention." *Review of International Studies*, vol. 13, pp. 133–46.

Gray, Hanna. 1967. "Machiavelli: The Art of Politics and the Paradox of Power," in I. Krieger and Fritz Stern, eds., *The Responsibility of Power*. Garden City, N.Y.: Doubleday.

Grieco, Joseph. 1988. "Anarchy and the Limits of Cooperation." *International Organization*, vol. 42, no. 3 (Summer), pp. 485–508.

——. 1990. *Cooperation among Nations*. Ithaca, N.Y.: Cornell University Press.

Grin, John, and Lutz Unterseher. 1988. "The Spiderweb Defense." *Bulletin of the Atomic Scientists*, vol. 44, no. 7 (September), pp. 28–30.

Gross, Leo. 1948. "The Peace of Westphalia: 1648–1948." *American Journal of International Law*, vol. 42 (1948), pp. 20–41.

Gruen, Erich. 1972. *The Roman Republic*. Washington, D.C.: American Historical Association.

Guicciardini, Francesco. 1970. *The History of Florence* (1510), trans. Mario Dimandi. New York: Harper and Row.

Gulick, Edward V. 1967. *Europe's Classical Balance of Power*. New York: Norton.

Gutmann, Amy. 1980. *Liberal Equality*. Cambridge, England: Cambridge University Press.

Haas, Ersnt B. 1953. "The Balance of Power: Prescription, Concept or Propaganda." *World Politics*, vol. 5, no. 4 (July), pp. 442–77.

——. 1980. "Why Collaborate: Issue Linkage and International Regimes." *World Politics*, vol. 32, no. 3, pp. 357–405.

Haas, Michael. 1974. *International Conflict*. New York: Bobbs-Merrill.

Haight, John McVickar. 1970. *American Aid to France, 1938–1940*. New York: Atheneum.

Halle, Louis J. 1967. *The Cold War as History*. New York: Harper and Row.

Halliday, Fred. 1987. "State and Society in International Relations: A Second Agenda." *Millennium*, vol. 17, no. 2 (Summer), pp. 215–29.

Halpern, Manfred. 1968. "The Morality and Politics of Intervention," in Richard Falk, ed., *The Vietnam War and International Law*. Princeton: Princeton University Press.

Hammond, N. G. L. 1986. *History of Greece to 322 B.C.* Oxford: Clarendon.

Hampshire, Stuart. 1989. *Innocence and Experience*. Cambridge, Mass.: Harvard University Press.

Hancock, Graham. 1989. *Lords of Poverty: Free-Wheeling Lifestyles, Power, Prestige, and Corruption of the Multi-Million Dollar Aid Business.* London: Macmillan.

Hanson, Donald. 1984. "Thomas Hobbes's 'Highway to Peace.' " *International Organization,* vol. 38, no. 2 (Spring), pp. 329–54.

Hardin, Garret. 1974. "Living on a Lifeboat." *Bioscience,* vol. 24, no. 10 (October), pp. 561–68.

Hare, J. E., and Carey Joynt. 1982. *Ethics and International Affairs.* New York: St. Martin's Press.

Harris, John. 1974. "The Marxist Conception of Violence." *Philosophy and Public Affairs,* vol. 3, no. 4, pp. 193–94.

Harris, Marvin. 1980. *Culture, People and Nature.* New York: Harper and Row.

Hart, Jeffrey A. 1985. "Power and Polarity in the International System," in Alan Ned Sabrosky, ed., *Polarity and War: The Changing Structure of International Conflict.* Boulder, Colo.: Westview Press.

Hassner, Pierre. 1972. "Immanuel Kant," in Leo Strauss and Joseph Cropsey, eds., *History of Political Philosophy.* Chicago: Rand McNally.

Haupt, Georges. 1972. *Socialism and the Great War.* Oxford: Clarendon.

——. 1986. *Aspects of International Socialism: 1871–1914.* Cambridge, England: Cambridge University Press.

Healy, Brian and Arthur Stein. 1973. "The Balance of Power in International History." *Journal of Conflict Resolution,* vol. 17, no. 1 (March), pp. 33–61.

Heckscher, Eli. 1935. *Mercantilism.* London: George Allen & Unwin.

Hehir, J. Bryan. 1995. "Intervention: From Theories to Cases," *Ethics and International Affairs,* vol. 9, pp. 1–13.

Hellinger, Steve, Douglas Heilinger, and Fred O'Regan. 1988. *Aid for Just Development.* Boulder, Colo.: Lynne Rienner.

Heller, Mark. 1980. "The Use and Abuse of Hobbes." *Polity,* vol. 13, no. 1 (Fall), pp. 21–32.

Herodotus. 1987. *History* (425 B.C.E.), trans. David Grene. Chicago: Chicago University Press.

Herz, John. 1950. "Idealist Internationalism and the Security Dilemma." *World Politics,* vol. 2, no. 12, pp. 157–80.

Heymann, Philip. 1973. "The Problem of Coordination: Bargaining and Rules." *Harvard Law Review,* vol. 86, no. 5 (March), pp. 797–877.

Higonnet, Patrice. 1968. "The Origins of the Seven Years War." *Journal of Modern History,* vol. 40, no. 1 (March), pp. 57–90.

Hilferding, Rudolf. 1981. *Finance Capital,* trans. Morris Watnick and Sam Gordon; ed. Tom Bottomore. London: Routledge Kegan Paul.

Hinsley, F. H. 1967. *Power and the Pursuit of Peace.* Cambridge, England: Cambridge University Press.

Hirsch, Fred, and Michael W. Doyle. 1977. "Politicization in the World Economy," in Fred Hirsch, Michael W. Doyle, and Edward Morse, eds., *Alternatives to Monetary Disorder.* New York: Council on Foreign Relations/McGraw-Hill.

Hirschman, Albert. 1976. "Hegel, Imperialism, and Structural Stagnation." *Journal of Development Economics,* vol. 3, no. 1 (July), pp. 1–6.

——. 1982. "Rival Interpretations of Market Society: Civilizing, Destructive or Feeble." *Journal of Economic Literature,* vol. 20 (December), pp. 1463–84.

Hobbes, Thomas. 1651/1962. *Leviathan*, ed. Michael Oakeshott. London: Collier.
——. 1841. "De Cive," *The English Words of Thomas Hobbes*. London: J. Bohn.
Hobson, John A. 1902/1965. *Imperialism: A study*. Ann Arbor: University of Michigan Press.
Hodgart, Alan. 1977. *The Economics of European Imperialism*. New York: Norton.
Hoffman, Stanley, ed. 1960. *Contemporary Theory in International Relations*. Englewood Cliffs, N.J.: Prentice Hall.
——. 1965. *The State of War*. New York: Praeger.
——. 1966. "The Quest for World Order." *Daedalus*, vol. 124, no. 3 (Summer), pp. 1–26.
——. 1968. "The Balance of Power," in David Sills, ed., *The International Encyclopedia of the Social Sciences*, vol. 1. New York: Macmillan.
——. 1975. "Notes on the Elusiveness of Modern Power." *International Journal*, vol. 30, no. 2 (Spring), pp. 183–206.
——. 1977. "An American Social Science: International Relations." *Daedalus*, vol. 106, pp. 41–60.
——. 1981. "Notes on the Limits of 'Realism.' " *Social Research*, vol. 48, no. 4 (Winter), pp. 653–57.
——. 1981. *Duties beyond Borders*. Syracuse: Syracuse University Press.
——. 1992. "Delusions of World Order." *New York Review of Books* (April 9).
——, and David Fidler, eds. 1991. *Rousseau on International Relations*. Oxford: Clarendon.
Holmes, Stephen. 1979. "Aristippus in and out of Athens." *American Political Science Review*, vol. 73, pp. 113–28.
Holsti, K. J. 1985. *The Dividing Discipline*. Boston: George Allen and Unwin.
—— et al. 1973. *Unity and Disintegration in International Alliances*. London: Wiley.
Holtzman, Franklyn. 1995. "Pentagon Overkill." *New York Times*, letter, February 1.
Hook, Stephen. 1995. *National Interest and Foreign Aid*. Boulder, Colo.: Lynne Rienner.
Hopf, Ted. 1991. "Polarity, the Offense-Defense Balance, and War." *American Political Science Review*, vol. 85, no. 2, pp. 475–93.
Horn, D. B. 1970. "The Duke of Newcastle and the Origins of the Diplomatic Revolution," in J. E. Elliott and H. G. Koenigsberger, eds., *The Diversity of History*. London: Routledge Kegan Paul.
Howard, Michael. 1978. *War and the Liberal Conscience*. London: Temple Smith.
House of Commons Report. 1984. *Grenada, Second Report from the Foreign Affairs Committee*. London: HMSO.
Hudson, G. F. 1937. *The Far East in World Politics*. London: Oxford University Press.
——, Richard Lowenthal, and R. MacFarguhar, eds. 1961. *The Sino-Soviet Dispute*. New York: Praeger.
Huliung, Mark. 1983. *Citizen Machiavelli*. Princeton: Princeton University Press.
Hume, David. 1752/1963. "Of the Balance of Power," *Essays: Moral, Political, and Literary*. Oxford: Oxford University Press.
Huntington, Samuel. 1968. *Political Order in Changing Societies*. New Haven: Yale University Press.
——. 1981. "Human Rights and American Power." *Commentray*, vol. 72, issue 3 (September), pp. 37–43.

——. 1984. "Will More Countries Become Democratic?" *Political Science Quarterly*, vol. 99, no. 2 (Summer), pp. 193–218.

——. 1991. *The Third Wave: Democratization in the Late Twentieth Century*. Norman: University of Oklahoma Press.

——. 1993. "The Clash of Civilizations?" *Foreign Affairs*, vol. 72, no. 3 (Summer), pp. 22–50.

Hurwitz, Jon, and Mark Peffley. 1987. "How Are Foreign Policy Attitudes Structured? A Hierarchical Model." *American Political Science Review*, vol. 81 (December), pp. 1099–1120.

Husami, Ziyad I. 1978. "Marx on Distributive Justice." *Philosophy and Public Affairs*, vol. 8, no. 1, p. 32.

Hyam, Ronald. 1976. *Britain's Imperial Century: 1815–1914*. London: Batsford.

Ignatius, David. 1987. "They Don't Make Them Like George Marshall Anymore." *Washington Post*, National Edition (June 8), p. 25.

Ikenberry, John, David Lake, and Michael Mastanduno, eds. 1988. *The State and American Foreign Economic Policy*. Ithaca, N.Y.: Cornell University Press.

Imbeau, Louis. 1989. *Donor Aid—The Determinants of Allocations in Third World Countries: A Comparative Analysis*. New York: Lang.

Immerman, Richard. 1982. *The CIA in Guatemala*. Austin: University of Texas Press.

International Monetary Fund. 1981–present (annual). *Direction of Trade Statistics Yearbook*. Washington: IMF.

Isaacson, Walter, and Thomas Evan. 1986. *The Wise Men*. New York: Simon and Schuster.

Jackson, Robert. 1990. *Quasi-States: Sovereignty, International Relations, and the Third World*. Cambridge, England: Cambridge University Press.

Jagan, Cheddi. 1994. "Appeal for a New Global Human Order," *New Global Human Order*. Georgetown, Guyana: New Guyana Co.

James, Alan, ed. 1973. "The Balance of Power and International Order," *The Bases of International Order*. London: Oxford University Press.

Janis, M. W. 1984. "Jeremy Bentham and the Fashioning of 'International Law.' " *American Journal of International Law*, vol. 78, pp. 405–18.

Jarausch, Konrad H. 1969. "The Illusion of Limited War: Chancellor Benthmann-Hollweg's Calculated Risk, July 1914." *Central European History*, vol. 2, pp. 48–76.

Jervis, Robert. 1976. *Perception and Misperception in International Politics*, Princeton: Princeton University Press.

——. 1978. "Cooperation under the Security Dilemma." *World Politics*, vol. 30, no. 1 (January), pp. 167–214.

——. 1979. "Systems Theories and Diplomatic History," in Paul Lauren, ed., *Diplomacy*. New York: Free Press.

——. 1988. "Realism, Game Theory and Cooperation." *World Politics*, vol. 40, no. 3 (April), pp. 317–49.

——. 1991–1992. "The Future of World Politics: Will It Resemble the Past?" *International Security*, vol. 16, no. 3, pp. 39–73.

Johnstone, Ian. 1994. *Aftermath of the Gulf War: An Assessment of UN Action*. Boulder, Colo.: Lynne Rienner.

Joll, James. 1955. *The Second International, 1889–1914*. London: Weidenfeld and Nicolson.

Journalist, M. 1983. *A Year Is Eight Months.* Garden City, N.Y.: Anchor/Doubleday.
Joyner, C., John Norton Moore, and Detlev Vagts. 1984. "The United States Action in Grenada: Reflections on the Lawfulness of Invasion." *American Journal of International Law,* vol. 78, no. 1 (January), pp. 131–44.
Juergensmeyer, Mark. 1994. *The New Cold War: Religious Nationalism Confronts the Secular State.* Berkeley: University of California Press.
Kacowicz, Arie. 1994. *Peaceful Territorial Change.* Columbia: University of South Carolina Press.
——. 1995. "Explaining Zones of Peace: Democracies as Satisfied Powers." *Journal of Peace Research,* vol. 32, no. 3, pp. 265–76.
Kagan, Donald. 1969. *The Outbreak of the Peloponnesian War.* Ithaca, N.Y.: Cornell University Press.
——. 1995. *On the Origins of War.* Garden City, N.Y.: Doubleday.
Kahnemann, Daniel, and Amos Tversky. 1980. "Choices, Values, and Frames." *American Psychologist,* vol. 39, no. 4 (April), pp. 341–50.
Kamras, Jason. 1995. "Towards a New Paradigm for Just Military Intervention." Princeton University senior thesis.
Kant, Immanuel. 1970. *Kant's Political Writings,* ed. Hans Reiss and trans. H. B. Nisbet. Cambridge, England: Cambridge University Press.
Kaplan, Herbert. 1968. *Russia and the Outbreak of the Seven Years War.* Berkeley: University of California Press.
Kaplan, Morton A. 1957. *System and Process in International Politics.* New York: Wiley.
Kaplan, Robert. 1994. "The Coming Anarchy." *Atlantic Monthly,* vol. 273 (February), pp. 44–76.
Kateb, George. 1964. "Rousseau's Political Thought." *Political Science Quarterly,* vol. 76, no. 4, pp. 519–43.
Katzenstein, Peter, ed. 1978. *Between Power and Plenty.* Madison: University of Wisconsin Press.
——. 1986. *Small States in World Markets.* Ithaca, N.Y.: Cornell University Press.
Kautilya. 1951. *Arthasastra,* 4th ed., ed. and trans. R. Shamasastry. Mysore: Sri Raghuveer Printing Press.
Kautsky, John. 1961. "J. A. Schumpeter and Karl Kautsky." *Midwest Journal of Political Science,* vol. 20, pp. 108–09.
Kautsky, Karl. 1914. "Der Imperialismus." *Neue Zeit.*
Kavka, Gregory S. 1983. "Hobbes's War of All against All." *Ethics,* vol. 93, no. 2 (January), pp. 291–310.
——. 1986. *Hobbesian Moral and Political Theory.* Princeton: Princeton University Press.
Kelly, George A. 1969. *Idealism, Politics, and History.* Cambridge, England: Cambridge University Press.
Kelly, Raymond C. 1985. *The Nuer Conquest.* Ann Arbor: University of Michigan Press.
Kemp, T. 1967. *Theories of Imperialism.* London: Dobson.
Kennan, George. 1951. *American Diplomacy, 1900–1952.* Chicago: University of Chicago Press.
——. 1967. *Memoirs: 1925–1950.* Boston: Little, Brown.
——. 1972. *Memoirs, 1950–1963.* Boston: Little, Brown.

——. 1989. "After the Cold War." *New York Times Magazine* (February 5), pp. 32–33.

Kennedy, Paul. 1987. *The Rise and Fall of the Great Powers.* New York: Random House.

——. 1991. "American Grand Strategy Today and Tomorrow," in Paul Kennedy, ed., *Grand Strategies in War and Peace.* New Haven: Yale University Press.

Keohane, Nannerl. 1980. *Philosophy and the State in France.* Princeton: Princeton University Press.

Keohane, Robert. 1984. *After Hegemony: Cooperation and Disorder in World Political Economy.* Princeton: Princeton University Press.

——. 1986. "Realism, Neorealism, and the Study of World Politics," in Robert Keohane, ed., *Neorealism and Its Critics.* New York: Columbia University Press.

——. 1989. "International Liberalism Reconsidered," in John Dunn, ed., *The Economic Limits of Politics.* Cambridge, England: Cambridge University Press.

——, and Joseph Nye. 1977. *Power and Interdependence.* Boston: Little, Brown.

Khalil, Samir al-. 1989. *Republic of Fear.* New York: Pantheon.

Kim, Samuel. 1976. "The Lorenzian Theory of Aggression and Peace Research: A Critique," *Journal of Peace Research*, vol. 13, no. 4, pp. 253–76.

Kindleberger, Charles. 1973. *The World in Depression.* Berkeley: University of California Press.

Kinross, Lord. 1993. *Ataturk: The Birth of Nation.* London: Weidenfeld.

Kinzer, Stephen. 1994. "Where There's a War There's Amanpour." *New York Times Magazine* (October 9), pp. 56–59.

Kirkpatrick, Jeane. 1979. "Dictatorships and Double Standards." *Commentary*, vol. 68 (November), pp. 34–45.

Kissin, S. F. 1989. *War and the Marxists.* Boulder, Colo.: Westview Press.

Kissinger, Henry. 1964. *A World Restored.* Boston: Houghton Mifflin.

——. 1977. *American Foreign Policy.* New York: Norton.

——. 1992. "Balance of Power Sustained," in Graham Allison and Gregor Treverton, eds., *Rethinking American Security.* New York: Norton.

——. 1994. *Diplomacy.* New York: Simon and Schuster.

Knock, Thomas. 1992. *To End All Wars: Woodrow Wilson and the Quest for a New World Order.* Princeton: Princeton University Press.

Knutsen, Torbjorn. 1992. *A History of International Relations Theory.* Manchester, England: Manchester University Press.

Knorr, Klaus. 1973. *Power and Wealth.* New York: Basic Books.

Koch, K. F. 1974. *War and Peace in Jalemo.* Cambridge, Mass.: Harvard University Press.

Koestler, Arthur. 1983. *Darkness at Noon* (in Polish). Paryz: Instytut Literacki.

Koh, Harold. 1990. *The National Security Constitution: Sharing Power after the Iran-Contra Affair.* New Haven: Yale University Press.

Kolakowski, Leszek. 1978. *Main Currents of Marxism*, vol. 2, *The Golden Age.* Oxford: Oxford University Press.

Korten, David. 1990. *Getting to the Twenty-First Century: Voluntary Action and the Global Agenda.* W. Hartford, Conn.: Kumarian Press.

——. 1991–1992. "Sustainable Development: A Review Essay," *World Policy Journal*, (Winter), pp. 157–90.

Krasner, Stephen. 1976. "State Power and the Structure of International Trade." *World Politics*, vol. 28, no. 3 (April), pp. 317–47.

——. 1978. *Defending the National Interest: Raw Material Investments and U.S. Foreign Policy*. Princeton: Princeton University Press.

——, ed. 1983. *International Regimes*. Ithaca, N.Y.: Cornell University Press.

——. 1985. *Structural Conflict: The Third World against Global Liberalism*. Berkeley: University of California Press.

——. 1991. "Global Communications and National Power: Life at the Pareto Frontier." *World Politics*, vol. 43, no. 3 (April), pp. 336–66.

Kratochwil, Friedrich, and John Ruggie. 1986. "International Organization: A State of the Art on the Art of the State." *International Organization*, vol. 40 (Autumn), pp. 753–75.

Krauthammer, Charles. 1988. "Beyond the Cold War." *New Republic*, vol. 199 (December 19), pp. 14–19.

Krugman, Paul. 1990. *Rethinking International Trade*. Cambridge, Mass.: MIT Press.

Kubalkova, V., and A. A. Cruickshank. 1985. *Marxism and International Relations*. Oxford: Clarendon.

Kull, Steven. 1992. *Burying Lenin*. Boulder, Colo.: Westview Press.

Kupchan, Charles. 1994. "The Case for Collective Security," in George Downs, ed., *Collective Security beyond the Cold War*. Ann Arbor: University of Michigan Press.

——, and Clifford Kupchan. 1991. "Concerts, Collective Security and the Future of Europe." *International Security*, vol. 16, no. 1 (Summer), pp. 114–61.

Laberge, Pierre. Forthcoming. "Kant on Justice and the Law of Nations," in Terry Nardin and David Mapel, eds., *The Constitution of International Society*.

Lakatos, Imre. 1970. "Falsification and the Methodology of Scientific Research Programs," in Imre Lakatos and A. Musgrave, eds., *Criticism and the Growth of Knowledge*. Cambridge: Cambridge University Press.

Lake, David. 1992. "Powerful Pacifists." *American Political Science Review*, vol. 86, no. 1, pp. 24–37.

Langer, William. L. 1935/1951. *The Diplomacy of Imperialism*. New York: Knopf.

——. 1968. *The Encyclopedia of World History*. Boston: Houghton Mifflin.

Lappé, Frances Moore, 1979. *Food First*. New York: Ballantine Books.

Laslett, Peter. 1988. "Introduction to John Locke," *Two Treatises of Government*, ed. Peter Laslett. New York: Cambridge University Press.

Layne, Christoper. 1993. "The Unipolar Illusion: Why New Great Powers Will Arise." *International Security*, vol. 17, no. 4 (Spring), pp. 5–51.

——. 1994. "Kant or Cant: The Myth of Democratic Peace," *International Security*, vol. 19, no. 2 (Fall), pp. 5–49.

Lebow, Richard Ned. 1981. *Between Peace and War: The Nature of International Crisis*. Baltimore: Johns Hopkins University Press.

——. 1991. "Thucydides, Power Transition Theory and the Causes of War," in Richard Ned Lebow and Barry Strauss, eds., *Hegemonic Rivalry*. Boulder, Colo.: Westview Press.

Leckie, G. F. 1817. *Balance of Power*. London: Taylorwestview.

Lee, Gary. 1985. "U.S. May Seek OAS Action." *Washington Post*, March 28, 1985.

Lemke, Christiane, and Gary Marks, eds. 1992. *The Crisis of Socialism in Europe.* Durham, N.C.: Duke University Press.

Lenin, Vladimir I. 1917. "A Caricature of Marxism and Imperialist Economism." *Collected Works,* vol. 23 (August–October) p. 60.

——. 1917. *Imperialism: The Highest Stage of Capitalism.* New York: International Publishers.

——. 1919. *State and Revolution.* New York: International Publishers.

——. 1963. *What Is to Be Done?,* trans. S. V. and Patricia Utechin. Oxford: Clarendon.

——. 1968. "The Discussion on Self-Determination Summed Up," *National Liberation, Socialism and Imperialism: Selected Writings.* New York: International Publishers.

——. 1968. "The Socialist Revolution and the Rights of Nations to Self-Determination," *Selected Works.* London: Lawrence-Wishart.

Levin, Michael. 1970. "Rousseau on Independence," *Political Studies,* vol. 18, no. 4, pp. 496–513.

Levitin, Michael. 1986. "The Law of Force and the Force of Law." *Harvard International Law Journal,* vol. 27, pp. 621–57.

Levy, Jack S. 1983. *War in the Modern Great Power System, 1495–1975.* Lexington: University of Kentucky Press.

——. 1984. "The Offense/Defense Balance of Military Technology." *International Studies Quarterly,* vol. 28, pp. 219–38.

——. 1988. "Domestic Politics and War." *Journal of Interdisciplinary History,* vol. 4 (Spring), pp. 653–73.

——. 1989. "The Causes of War," in Philip Tetlock et al., eds., *Behavior, Society, and Nuclear War,* vol. 1. New York: Oxford University Press.

Lewis, Bernard. 1982. *The Muslim Discovery of Europe.* New York: Norton.

Lichtheim, George. 1964. *Marxism.* London: Routledge Kegan Paul.

Light, Margot. 1988. *The Soviet Theory of International Relations.* Brighton, England: Wheatsheaf.

Linklater, Andrew. 1986. "Realism, Marxism and Critical International Theory." *Review of International Studies,* vol. 12, pp. 301–12.

——. 1990. *Men and Citizens in the Theory of International Relations.* London: Macmillan.

Linz, Juan. 1978. "Crisis, Breakdown, and Reequilibration," in Juan Linz and Alfred Stepan, eds., *The Breakdown of Democratic Regimes.* Baltimore: Johns Hopkins University Press.

Liska, George. 1957. *International Equilibrium.* Cambridge: Harvard University Press.

——. 1986. "From Containment to Concert." *Foreign Policy,* no. 62 (Spring), pp. 3–23.

Locke, John. 1988. "Second Treatise," in *Two Treatises of Government,* ed. Peter Laslett. New York: Cambridge University Press.

Loehr, William, and John Powelson. 1983. *Threat to Development: Pitfalls of the New International Economic Order.* Boulder, Colo.: Westview Press.

Lorenz, Konrad. 1966. *On Aggression.* New York: Harcourt.

Lowi, Theodore. 1963. "Bases in Spain," in Harold Stein, ed., *American Civil-Military Decisions.* Tuscaloosa: University of Alabama Press.

Lowy, Michael. 1976. "Marxists and the National Question." *New Left Review*, no. 96 (March–April), pp. 81–100.

Luban, David. 1980. "Just War and Human Rights." *Philosophy and Public Affairs*, vol. 9, no. 2 (Winter), pp. 160–81.

Lukes, Steven. 1985. *Marxism and Morality*. New York: Oxford University Press.

Lumsdaine, David. 1993. *Moral Vision in International Politics: The Foreign Aid Regime 1949–1989*. Princeton: Princeton University Press.

Lundestad, Geir. 1990. *The American "Empire."* Oxford: Oxford University Press.

Luttwak, Edward N. 1984. *The Pentagon and the Art of War*. New York: Simon and Schuster.

Luxemburg, Rosa. 1951. *The Accumulation of Capital*. London: Routledge.

Lynch, Allen. 1987. *The Soviet Study of International Relations*. Cambridge, England: Cambridge University Press.

MacDonald, Scott B., Harald Sandstrom, and Paul Goodwin, eds. 1988. *The Caribbean after Grenada: Revolution, Conflict and Democracy*. New York: Praeger.

Machiavelli, Niccolo. 1950. *The Prince and the Discourses*, trans. Luigi Ricci and Christian Detmold and ed. Max Lerner. New York: Modern Library.

——. 1961. *Letters*, trans. Allan Gelbert. Chicago: University of Chicago Press.

——. 1970. *The Discourses*, trans. Leslie Walker, ed. Bernard Crisk. Harmondsworth, England: Penguin.

——. 1985. *The Prince*, trans. Harvey Mansfield. Chicago: University of Chicago Press.

——. 1988. *Florentine Histories*, trans. Laura Banfield and Harvey Mansfield, Jr. Princeton: Princeton University Press.

MacIntyre, Alasdair. 1988. *Whose Justice? Which Rationality?* Notre Dame: University of Notre Dame Press.

Macpherson, C. B. 1962. *The Political Theory of Possessive Individualism: Hobbes to Locke*. Oxford: Clarendon.

Madison, James. 1794/1986. *Papers of James Madison*, vol. 15, eds. W. Hutchinson and W. Rachel. Richmond: University of Virginia Press.

McMahan, Jefferson. 1987. "The Ethics of International Intervention," in Kenneth Kipnis and Diana Meyers, eds., *Political Realism and International Morality*. Boulder, Colo.: Westview Press.

Magnus, Philip. 1964. *Gladstone*. New York: Dutton.

Maier, Charles. 1970. "Revisionism and the Interpretation of Cold War Origins." *Perspectives in American History*, 4, pp. 313–47.

——. 1991. *Why Did Communism Collapse in 1989?* Central and Eastern Europe Working Paper Series no. 7, Minda de Gunzburg Center for European Studies, Harvard University (January).

Mansfield, Edward D., and Jack Snyder. 1995. "Democratization and the Danger of War." *International Security*, vol. 20, no. 1 (Summer), pp. 5–38.

Mansfield, Harvey C. 1970. "Machiavelli's New Regime." *Italian Quarterly*, vol. 13, pp. 63–95.

——. 1979. *Machiavelli's New Modes and Orders*. Ithaca, N.Y.: Cornell University Press.

——. 1983. "On the Impersonality of the Modern State: A Commentary on Machiavelli's Use of *Stato*." *American Political Science Review*, vol. 77, pp. 849–57.

Mansfield, Peter. 1971. *The British in Egypt.* New York: Holt, Rinehart and Winston.

Maoz, Zeev, and Nasrin Abdolali. 1989. "Regime Types and International Conflict, 1816–1976." *Journal of Conflict Resolution,* vol. 33 (March), pp. 3–36.

——, and Bruce Russett. 1992. "Alliance, Contiguity, Wealth and Political Stability: Is the Lack of Conflict among Democracies a Statistical Artifact?" *International Interactions,* vol. 17, no. 3, pp. 245–68.

March, James, and Johan Olsen. 1983. "Organizing Political Life: What Administrative Reorganization Tells Us about Government." *American Political Science Review,* vol. 77, issue 2 (June), pp. 281–96.

——. 1989. *Rediscovering Institutions.* New York: Free Press.

Marcuse, Herbert. 1961. *Soviet Marxism.* New York: Random House.

Marx, Karl. 1906. *Capital,* trans. S. Moore and E. Aveling. New York: Modern Library.

——. 1852. "The Eighteenth Brumaire of Louis Bonaparte," in Marx (1978).

——. 1853. *New York Herald Tribune,* June 25, in Marx (1978).

——. 1856/1972. "The Secret Diplomatic History of the Eighteenth Century," *The Unknown Karl Marx,* ed. T. Payne. London: University of London Press.

——. 1859. "Preface to *Critique of Political Economy,*" in Marx (1978).

——. 1877/1952. "Letter on the Economic Development of Russia" in Marx (1952).

——. 1935. *Correspondence.* New York: International Publishers.

——. 1952. *The Russian Menace to Europe,* ed. Paul Blackstock and Bert Hoselitz. Glencoe, Ill.: Free Press.

——. 1968. "Letter to Bebel," *Selected Works.* Moscow: Progress Publishers.

——. 1968. *The Civil War in France,* in Marx (1968).

——. 1971. *The Karl Marx Library, On Revolution,* vol. 1, Saul K. Padover. New York: McGraw-Hill.

——. 1978. *The Marx-Engels Reader,* ed. Robert C. Tucker. New York: Norton.

——, and Friedrich Engels. *The Communist Manifesto,* in Marx (1978).

Massing, Michael. 1984. "Grenada Before and After." *Atlantic Monthly* (February), p. 81.

Mastanduno, Michael. 1991. "Do Relative Gains Matter: America's Response to Japanese Industrial Policy." *International Security,* vol. 16, no. 1 (Summer), pp. 73–113.

Mastny, Vojtech. 1979. *Russia's Road to the Cold War.* New York: Columbia University Press.

May, Ernest. 1973. *"Lessons" of the Past; The Use and Misuse of History in American Foreign Policy.* New York: Oxford University Press.

Mayer, Arno. 1967. *Politics and Diplomacy of the Peacemaking.* New York: Knopf.

McElroy, Robert. 1992. *Morality and American Foreign Policy.* Princeton: Princeton University Press.

McGill, W. J. 1968. "The Roots of Policy: Kaunitz in Italy and the Netherlands, 1742–1746." *Central European History,* vol. 1, pp. 228–44.

——. 1971. "The Roots of Policy: Kaunitz in Vienna and Versailles." *Journal of Modern History,* vol. 43, pp. 228–44.

McGuigan, Dorothy, ed. 1977. *The Role of Women in Conflict and Peace.* Ann Arbor: University of Michigan Press.

McKay, Derek, and H. M. Scott. 1983. *The Rise of the Great Powers.* London: Longmans.

McKibben, Bill. 1989. *The End of Nature.* New York: Anchor.

McPherson, James. 1988. *Battle Cry of Freedom.* New York: Oxford University Press.

Mearsheimer, John. 1990. "Back to the Future." *International Security,* vol. 15, no. 1 (Summer), pp. 5–56.

——. 1992. "Disorder Restored," in Graham Allison and Gregory Treverton, eds., *Rethinking American Security.* New York: Norton.

Meiggs, Russell. 1972. *The Athenian Empire.* New York: Oxford University Press.

Meinecke, F. 1957. *Machiavellism.* New Haven: Yale University Press.

Mickiewicz, Ellen. 1992. *Findings of Four Major Surveys in the Former Soviet Union.* Carter Center, Emory University.

Midlarsky, Manus. 1988. *The Onset of World War.* Boston: Unwin.

Mill, John S. 1973. "A Few Words on Nonintervention," in Gertrude Himmelfarb, ed., *Essays on Politics and Culture.* Gloucester, Mass.: Peter Smith.

Miller, Benjamin. 1995. *When Opponents Cooperate.* Ann Arbor: University of Michigan Press.

Miller, Judith, and Lauie Mylroie. 1990. *Saddam Hussein and the Crisis in the Gulf.* New York: Times Books.

Miller, Richard. 1975. "The Consistency of Historical Materialism." *Philosophy and Public Affairs,* vol. 4, no. 4 (Summer), pp. 390–409.

Miller, Steven, ed. 1985. *Military Strategy and the Origins of the First World War.* Princeton: Princeton University Press.

Mindle, Grant. 1985. "Machiavelli's Realism." *Review of Politics,* vol. 47, no. 2, pp. 212–30.

Ministère des Affaires Etrangères. 1957. *Documents diplomatiques français,* lère série, tome XIV. Paris.

Modelski, George. 1964. "Kautilya." *American Political Science Review,* vol. 58 (September), pp. 554–57.

Molnar, Miklos. 1975. *Marx, Engels et la politique internationale.* Paris: Gallimard.

Mommsen, Wolfgang. 1980. *Theories of Imperialism.* New York: Random House.

Montesquieu. Charles de Secondat, baron of. 1748/1966. *Spirit of the Laws.* New York: Hafner.

Moon, Donald J. 1975. "The Logic of Political Inquiry," in Fred Greenstein and Nelson Polsby, eds., *Handbook of Political Science,* vol. 1, *Political Science: Scope and Theory.* Reading, Mass.: Addison Wesley.

Moore, Barrington, Jr. 1966. *The Social Origins of Dictatorship and Democracy: Lord and Peasant in the Making of the Modern World.* Boston: Beacon Press.

Moore, Stanley. 1975. "Marx and Lenin as Historical Materialists." *Philosophy and Public Affairs,* vol. 4, no. 2 (Winter), pp. 171–94.

——. 1980. *Marx on the Choice between Socialism and Communism.* Cambridge, Mass.: Harvard University Press.

Morgenthau, Hans. 1949/1967. *Politics among Nations,* 4th ed. New York: Knopf.

——. 1950. *Principles and Problems of International Politics.* New York: Knopf.

——. 1951. *Defense of the National Interest.* New York: Knopf.

——. 1952. "Another 'Great Debate': The National Interest of the United States." *American Political Science Review,* vol. 46, pp. 961–88.

——. 1962. "Preface to a Political Theory of Foreign Aid," in Robert G. Goldwin, *Why Foreign Aid?* Chicago: Rand McNally.

——, and Kenneth Thompson. 1950. *Principles and Problems of International Politics.* New York: Knopf.
Morrow, James D. 1988. "Social Choice and System Structure in World Politics." *World Politics,* vol. 41 (October), pp. 75–97.
——. 1991. "Alliances and Asymmetry." *American Journal of Political Science,* vol. 35, no. 4 (November), pp. 904–33.
——. 1993. "Arms vs. Allies" *International Organization,* vol. 47, no. 2 (Spring), pp. 207–33.
Mosley, Paul. 1987. *Foreign Aid: Its Defense and Reform.* Lexington: University of Kentucky Press.
Most, Benjamin, and Harvey Starr. 1984. "International Relations Theory, Foreign Policy Substitutability and Nice Laws." *World Politics,* vol. 36 (April), pp. 383–406.
Moul, William B. 1989. "Measuring the Balance of Power." *Review of International Studies,* vol. 15, no. 2 (April), pp. 101–22.
Moulton, Harold G., and Leo Pasvolsky. 1932. *War Debts and World Prosperity.* Washington, D.C.: Brookings Institution.
Mowat, R. B. 1923. *The European States System.* London: Oxford University Press.
Moynihan, Daniel. 1990. *On the Law of Nations.* Cambridge, Mass.: Harvard University Press.
Mueller, John. 1989. *Retreat from Doomsday.* New York: Basic Books.
Muller, Jerry Z. 1993. *Adam Smith in His Time and Ours: Designing the Decent Society.* Princeton: Princeton University Press.
Murray, Oswyn. 1988. "Greek Historians," in John Boardman, Jasper Griffin, and O. Murray, eds., *Greece and the Hellenistic World.* Oxford: Oxford University Press.
Nagel, Ernest. 1979. *The Structure of Science.* Indianapolis: Hackett.
Namier, Sir Lewis. 1942. *Conflicts.* London: Macmillan.
Nardin, Terry. 1983. *Law, Morality and the Relations of States.* Princeton: Princeton University Press.
Nathanson, Stephen. 1989. "In Defense of 'Moderate Patriotism.' " *Ethics,* vol. 99, no. 3 (April), pp. 535–52.
Nation, R. Craig. 1989. *War on War.* Durham, N.C.: Duke University Press.
——. 1992. *Black Earth, Red Star.* Ithaca, N.Y.: Cornell University Press.
Navari, Cornelia. 1982. "Hobbes and the Hobbesian Tradition in International Thought." *Millennium,* vol. 11, no. 3, pp. 203–22.
Nef, John U. 1968. *War and Human Progress.* New York: Norton.
Nettl, J. P. 1966. *Rosa Luxemburg,* vols. 1 and 2. New York: Oxford University Press.
——. 1967. *The Soviet Achievement.* London: Thames and Hudson.
Neumann, Sigmund, and Mark von Hagen. 1986. "Engels and Marx on Revolution, War, and the Army in Society," in Peter Paret, Gordon Craig, and Felix Gilbert, eds., *Makers of Modern Strategy.* Princeton: Princeton University Press.
Neustadt, Richard. 1970. *Alliance Politics.* New York: Columbia University Press.
Newfarmer, Richard, ed. 1984. *From Gunboats to Diplomacy.* Baltimore: Johns Hopkins University Press.
Newton, Douglas J. 1985. *British Labour, European Socialism and the Struggle for Peace, 1889–1914.* Oxford: Clarendon.
Niou, Emerson, and Peter Ordeshook. 1986. "A Theory of the Balance of Power in

International Systems." *Journal of Conflict Resolution*, vol. 30, no. 4 (December), pp. 685–715.

Niou, Emerson, Peter Ordeshook, and Gregory Rose. 1989. *The Balance of Power: Stability in International Systems.* New York: Cambridge University Press.

Nixon, Richard. 1980. *The Real War.* New York: Warner.

——. 1988. *1999: Victory without War.* New York: Simon and Schuster.

Noel, Alain, and Jean-Philippe Therien. 1995. "From Domestic to International Justice: The Welfare State and Foreign Aid." *International Organization*, vol. 49, no. 3, pp. 523–53.

Nozick, Robert. 1974. *Anarchy, State and Utopia.* New York: Basic Books.

Nussbaum, Martha. 1986. *The Fragility of Goodness: Luck and Ethics in Greek Tragedy and Philosophy.* New York: Cambridge University Press.

Nye, Joseph S. Jr. 1971. *Peace in Parts.* Boston: Little, Brown.

——, ed. 1984. "Can America Manage Its Soviet Policy?" *The Making of America's Soviet Policy.* New Haven: Yale University Press.

——. 1986. *Nuclear Ethics.* New York: Free Press.

——. 1988. "Neorealism and Neoliberalism." *World Politics*, vol. 40, no. 2, pp. 235–51.

O'Neill, Onora. 1975. "Lifeboat Earth." *Philosophy and Public Affairs*, vol. 4, no. 3 (Spring), pp. 273–92.

O'Shaughnessy, Hugh. 1984. *Grenada: Revolution, Invasion, and Aftermath.* London: Sphere Books.

Obeyesekere, Ganath. 1995. *The Apotheosis of Captain Cook.* Princeton: Princeton University Press.

OECD (Development Assistance Committee). 1994. *Development Co-operation*, no. 1. Paris: OECD.

Olson, Mancur. 1965. *The Logic of Collective Action.* Cambridge, Mass.: Harvard University Press.

Oneal, John, Frances Oneal, Zeev Maoz, and Bruce Russett. 1996. "The Liberal Peace: Interdependence, Democracy and International Conflict, 1950–1985." *Journal of Peace Research*, vol. 33, no. 1 (February), pp. 11–28.

Oren, Ido. 1995. "The 'Democratic Peace' or Peace among 'Our Kind'?" *International Security*, vol. 20, no. 2 (Fall), pp. 147–84.

Organization for Economic Cooperation and Development (OECD). 1972–present (annual reports). *Development Cooperation.* Paris: OECD.

Organski, A. F. K. 1958. *World Politics.* New York: Knopf.

Orwin, Clifford. 1989. *The Humanity of Thucydides.* Princeton: Princeton University Press.

Osgood, Robert E., and Robert W. Tucker. 1967. *Force, Order and Justice.* Baltimore: Johns Hopkins University Press.

Oye, Kenneth, ed. 1985. *Cooperation under Anarchy.* Princeton: Princeton University Press.

——, Robert Lieber, and Donald Rothchild, eds. 1983. *Eagle Defiant.* Boston: Little, Brown.

Packenham, Robert A. 1973. *Liberal America and the Third World.* Princeton: Princeton University Press.

Paine, Thomas. 1995. "The Rights of Man," *Complete Writings*, ed. Eric Foner. New York: Oxford University Press.

Papaligouras, Panaysis. 1941. *Théorie de la société internationale.* Geneva: Kundig.

Paterson, Thomas, ed. 1978. *Major Problems in American Foreign Policy.* Lexington, Mass.: D. C. Heath.

Payer, Cheryl. 1991. *Lent and Lost: Foreign Credit and Third World Development.* London: Zed Books.

Payne, Anthony. 1984. *The International Crisis in the Caribbean.* Baltimore: Johns Hopkins University Press.

Payne, James L. 1986. "Marxism and Militarism." *Polity*, vol. 19 (Winter), pp. 270–89.

Pecquet, Antoine. 1757. *L'Esprit des maximes politiques.* Paris: Chez Prault Père.

Perkins, M. L. 1967. "Rousseau on History, Liberty, and National Survival," in *Studies on Voltaire and the Eighteenth Century*, vol. 53, Theodore Besterman, ed. Geneva: Institut et Musée Voltaire.

Peters, Richard. 1956. *Hobbes.* Harmondsworth, England: Penguin.

Pincus, J. J. 1975. "Pressure Groups and the Pattern of Tariffs." *Journal of Political Economy*, vol. 83 (August), pp. 757–78.

Pipes, Richard. 1989. "Paper Perestroika." *Policy Review*, no. 47 (Winter), pp. 14–20.

Plato. 1930. *The Republic.* London: W. Heinemann; New York: G. P. Putnam's Sons.

Plutarch. 1960. "Pericles," *The Rise and Fall of Athens: Nine Greek Lives*, trans. Ian Scott-Kilvert. London: Penguin.

Pocock, J. G. A. 1975. *The Machiavellian Moment.* Princeton: Princeton University Press.

Pogge, Thomas. 1994. "An Egalitarian Law of Peoples." *Philosophy and Public Affairs*, vol. 23, no. 3 (Summer), pp. 195–224.

Polanyi, Karl. 1944. *The Great Transformation.* Boston: Beacon.

Polin, Raymond. 1984. *La Politique Morale de John Locke.* Paris: Presses Universitaire.

Popper, Karl. 1934/1959. *The Logic of Discovery.* New York: Academic Press.

———. 1961. *The Poverty of Historicism.* New York: Harper and Row.

Posen, Barry. 1984. *The Sources of Military Doctrine.* Ithaca, N.Y.: Cornell University Press.

———, and Stephen Van Evera. 1980. "Overarming and Underwhelming." *Foreign Policy*, vol. 40, pp. 99–118.

———, and Stephen Van Evera. 1983. "Reagan Administration Defense Policy," in Kenneth Oye, Robert Lieber, and Donald Rothchild, eds., *Eagle Defiant.* Boston: Little, Brown.

Pouncey, Peter. 1980. *The Necessities of War: A Study of Thucydides' Pessimism.* New York: Columbia University Press.

Powell, G. Bingham. 1982. *Contemporary Democracies.* Cambridge, Mass.: Harvard University Press.

Prasch, Robert E. 1991. "The Ethics of Growth in Adam Smith's *Wealth of Nations.*" *History of Political Economy*, vol. 23, no. 2, pp. 337–51.

Prescott, W. H. 1904/1968. *History of the Reign of Ferdinand and Isabella.* New York: AMS. 4 vols.

Reagan, Ronald. 1982. "Address to Parliament." *New York Times*, June 9.

Przeworski, Adam. 1991. *Democracy and the Market.* Cambridge, England: Cambridge University Press.

Pseudo-Xenophon. 1968. *The Constitution of the Athenians*, trans. G. W. Bowersock. Cambridge, Mass.: Harvard University Press.

Quester, George. 1980. "Consensus Lost." *Foreign Policy*, vol. 40 (Fall), pp. 18–32.

Rabinow, Paul, and William Sullivan, eds. 1979. *Interpretive Social Science: A Reader*. Berkeley: University of California Press.

Rakowska-Harmstone, Teresa, and Andrew Gyorgy, eds. 1979. *Communism in Eastern Europe*. Bloomington: Indiana University Press.

Range, Willard. 1959. *Franklin D. Roosevelt's World Order*. Athens: University of Georgia Press.

Rapkin, David, ed. 1990. *World Leadership and Hegemony*. Boulder, Colo.: Lynne Rienner.

Rau, Zbigniew. 1987. "Some Thoughts on Civil Society in Eastern Europe and the Lockian Contractarian Approach." *Political Studies*, vol. 35, no. 4 (December), pp. 573–92.

Rawlings, Hunter. 1981. *The Structure of Thucydides' History*. Princeton: Princeton University Press.

Rawls, John. 1971. *A Theory of Justice*. Cambridge, Mass.: Harvard University Press.

——. 1993. "The Law of Peoples," in Stephen Shute and Susan Hurley, eds., *On Human Rights*. New York: Basic Books.

Ray, James Lee. 1994. "Comparing the Fashoda Crisis and the Spanish American War." International Studies Association Convention.

——, and Bruce Russett. Forthcoming. "The Future as Arbiter of Theoretical Controversies: Predictions, Explanations, and the End of the Cold War." *British Journal of Political Science*.

Reagan, Ronald. 1984. "Peace and National Security," televised address to the nation, Washington, D.C., March 23, 1983, p. 40 in the U.S. State Department, *Realism, Strength, Negotiation*, May 1984.

——. 1984. "America's Foreign Policy Challenges for the 1980s." Address before the Center for Strategic and International Studies, Washington, D.C., April 6, 1984, p. 11 in U.S. State Department, op. cit., May 1984.

Riddell, Roger. 1987. *Foreign Aid Reconsidered*. Baltimore: Johns Hopkins University Press.

Ridolfi, Roberto. 1963. *The Life of Niccolo Machiavelli*, trans. Cecil Grayson. Chicago: University of Chicago Press.

Rielly, John, ed. 1987. *American Public Opinion and U.S. Foreign Policy*. Chicago: Council on Foreign Relations.

Riker, William. 1962. *The Theory of Political Coalitions*. New Haven: Yale University Press.

Riley, Patrick. 1983. *Kant's Political Philosophy*. Totowa, N.J.: Rowman and Littlefield.

Roberts, Adam. 1993. "The United Nations and International Security." *Survival*, vol. 35, no. 2 (Summer), pp. 2–29.

Robinson, Ronald. 1972. "Non-European Foundations of Imperialism," in Roger Owen and Bob Sutcliffe, eds., *Studies in the Theory of Imperialism*. London: Longmans.

Rodney, Walter. 1981. *How Europe Underdeveloped Africa*. Cambridge, Mass.: Harvard University Press.

Rogowski, Ronald. 1989. *Commerce and Coalitions*. Princeton: Princeton University Press.

Romilly, Jacqueline de. 1963. *Thucydides and Athenian Imperialism*, trans. Philip Thody. New York: Barnes & Noble.
Ronfeldt, David. 1983. *Geopolitics, Security, and U.S. Strategy in the Caribbean Basin* (R-2997-AF/RC). Santa Monica: Rand.
Roosevelt, Grace. 1990. *Reading Rousseau in the Nuclear Age*. Philadelphia: Temple University Press.
Rose, Gideon. 1996. "Soft Realism and Theories of Foreign Policy." Manuscript.
Rosecrance, Richard. 1986. *The Rise of the Trading State*. New York: Basic Books.
———. 1992. "Regionalism and the Post-Cold War Era." *International Journal*, vol. 43, no. 3 (Summer), pp. 375–93.
Rosenberg, Alexander. 1979. "Can Economic Theory Explain Everything?" *Philosophy of the Social Sciences*. vol. 9, no. 4, pp. 509–29.
Rosow, Stephen. 1984. "Commerce, Power and Justice: Montesquieu on International Politics." *Review of Politics*, vol. 46, no. 3, pp. 346–67.
Ross, Ian. 1993. "Adam Smith (1723–1790): A Biographical Sketch," in Hiroshi Mizuta and Chuhei Sigiyama, eds., *Adam Smith: International Perspectives*. London: St. Martin's Press.
Rostow, W. W. 1978. *The World Economy: History and Prospect*. Austin: University of Texas Press.
Rousseau, Jean-Jacques. 1756/1917. *State of War*, in *A Lasting Peace through the Federation of Europe*, trans. C. E. Vaughan. London: Constable, 1917.
———. 1756/1990. "State of War," trans. Grace Roosevelt, *Reading Rousseau in the Nuclear Age*. Philadelphia: Temple University Press.
———. 1761/1917. "Criticism of St. Pierre," in *A Lasting Peace, loc. cit.*
———. 1762/1950. *The Social Contract and the Discourses*, trans. G. D. H. Cole. New York: Dutton.
———. 1765/1953. "Constitutional Project for Corsica." *Political Writings*, trans. and ed. Frederick Watkins. Edinburgh: Nelson.
———. 1772/1953. "Poland," *Political Writings*, loc. cit.
———. 1953. *Political Writings*, trans. and ed. Frederick Watkins, introd. by Patrick Riley. Edinburgh: Nelson.
Rummel, Rudolph J. 1983. "Libertarianism and International Violence." *Journal of Conflict Resolution*, vol. 27, pp. 27–71.
———. 1994. *Death by Government*. New Brunswick, N.J.: Transaction Publishers.
Russett, Bruce. 1990. *Controlling the Sword*. Cambridge, Mass.: Harvard University Press.
———, and William Antholis. 1992. "The Imperfect Democratic Peace of Ancient Greece," in Russett, *Grasping the Democratic Peace*. Princeton: Princeton University Press.
Ryan, Alan. 1968. "Locke and the Dictatorship of the Bourgeoisie," in D. M. Armstrong and C. B. Martin, eds., *Locke and Berkeley*. London: Macmillan.
———. 1988. "Justice, Exploitation and the End of Morality," in David Evans, ed., *Moral Philosophy and Contemporary Problems*. Cambridge, England: Cambridge University Press.
Sagan, Scott D., and Kenneth Waltz. 1995. *The Spread of Nuclear Weapons: A Debate*. New York: Norton.
Sahlins, Marshall. 1961. "The Segmentary Lineage: An Organization of Predatory Expansion." *American Anthropologist*, vol. 63, no. 2 (April), pp. 322–45.

——. 1995. *How "Natives" Think, about Captain Cook, for Example.* Chicago: University of Chicago Press.

Salamon. L., and J. Siegfried. 1977. "Economic Power and Political Influence." *American Political Science Review*, vol. 71 (September), pp. 1026–43.

Sanderson, G. N. 1965. *England, Europe, and the Upper Nile.* Edinburgh: Edinburgh University Press.

Santos, Theotonio dos. 1970. "The Structure of Dependence." *American Economic Review*, vol. 60, no. 2 (May), pp. 231–36.

Saxonhouse, Arlene. 1985. *Women in the History of Political Thought.* New York: Praeger.

Scanlon, Thomas. 1982. "Contractarianism and Utilitarianism," in Amartya Sen and Bernard Williams, eds., *Utilitarianism and Beyond.* Cambridge, England: Cambridge University Press.

Schellenberg, James. 1982. *The Science of Conflict.* New York: Oxford University Press.

Schlatter, Richard, ed. 1975. *Hobbes' Thucydides.* New Brunswick, N.J.: Rutgers University Press.

Schlesinger, Arthur, Jr. 1965. *A Thousand Days.* Boston: Houghton Mifflin.

——. 1968. "Origins of the Cold War." *Foreign Affairs*, vol. 46, no. 1 (October), pp. 22–52.

Schoenhals, Kai, and Richard Melanson. 1985. *Revolution and Intervention in Grenada.* Boulder, Colo.: Westview Press.

Schorske, Carl. 1972. *German Social Democracy: 1905–1917.* New York: Harper Torchbooks.

Schumpeter, Joseph. 1950. *Capitalism, Socialism, and Democracy.* New York: Harper Torchbooks.

——. 1955. "The Sociology of Imperialisms." *Imperialism and Social Classes.* Cleveland: World Publishing.

Schwarz, Wolfgang 1962. "Kant's Philosophy of Law and International Peace," *Philosophy and Phenomenological Research*, vol. 23, pp. 71–80.

Schweller, Randall. 1992. "Domestic Structure and Preventive War." *World Politics*, vol. 44 (January), pp. 235–69.

Seigel, Jerrold. 1978. *Marx's Fate: The Shape of a Life.* Princeton: Princeton University Press.

Seligson, Mitchell, ed. 1984. *The Gap between Rich and Poor: Contending Perspectives on the Political Economy of Development.* Boulder, Colo.: Westview Press.

Semmel, Bernard. 1960. *Imperialism and Social Reform: English Social-Imperial Thought 1895–1914.* London: George Allen & Unwin.

Sharp, Gene. 1985. *Making Europe Unconquerable: The Potential of Civilian-Based Deterrence and Defense.* London: Taylor and Francis.

Shell, Susan. 1980. *The Rights of Reason.* Toronto: University of Toronto Press.

Shimshoni, Jonathan. 1990–1991. "Technology, Military Advantage, and World War I: A Case for Military Entrepreneurship." *International Security*, vol. 15, no. 3 (Winter 1990–1991), pp. 187–215.

Shklar, Judith. 1969. *Men and Citizens.* Cambridge, England: Cambridge University Press.

——. 1984. *Ordinary Vices.* Cambridge, Mass.: Harvard University Press.

Shorrock, Tim. 1983. "Revo Out, US In." *Multinational Monitor* (December).

Shultz, George. 1984. "Democratic Solidarity in the Americas," luncheon remarks for leaders of Barbados, Jamaica, and Organization of Economic Cooperation and Security Members, Bridgeton, February 6, 1984, p. 133, in U.S. State Department, op. cit., May 1984.

Simon, Herbert. 1982. *Models of Bounded Rationality.* Cambridge, Mass.: MIT Press. 2 vols.

Simon, L., and J. Stephen. 1981. *El Salvador Land Reform 1980–1981.* Boston: Oxfam-America.

Simowitz, Roslyn. 1982. "The Logical Consistency and Soundness of Balance of Power Theory." *Monograph Series in World Affairs,* vol. 19, book 3. Denver: University of Denver Press.

Singer, J. David. "The Levels of Analysis Problem in International Relations." *World Politics,* vol. 14 (1961), pp. 77–92.

——, and Melvin Small. "Wages of War, 1816–1980." ICPSR Study 19044.

Singer, Peter. 1972. "Famine, Affluence, and Morality." *Philosophy and Public Affairs,* vol. 1, no. 3 (Spring), pp. 229–43.

Namier, Lewis. 1942. *Conflicts.* London: Macmillan.

Siverson, Randolph. 1980. *Change in the International System.* Boulder, Colo.: Westview Press.

Skinner, Quentin. 1981. *Machiavelli.* New York: Hill and Wang.

Skocpol, Theda. 1979. *States and Social Revolutions.* Cambridge, England: Cambridge University Press.

Small, Melvin, and J. David Singer. 1976. "The War-proneness of Democratic Regimes." *Jerusalem Journal of International Relations,* vol. 50, no. 4 (Summer), pp. 50–69.

——. 1982. *Resort to Arms: International and Civil Wars 1816–1980.* Beverly Hills: Sage.

Smith, Adam. 1776/1976. *Wealth of Nations,* ed. R. H. Campbell and A. S. Skinner, reprinted by Liberty Classics, Indianapolis, 1981. Oxford: Oxford University Press.

Smith, Michael J. 1981. "Hans Morgenthau and the American National Interest in the Early Cold War." *Social Research,* vol. 48, no. 4 (Winter), pp. 766–85.

——. 1986. *Realist Thought from Weber to Kissinger.* Baton Rouge: Louisiana State University Press.

Smith, Tony. 1987. *Thinking Like a Communist.* New York: Norton.

——. 1994. *America's Mission.* Princeton: Princeton University Press.

Snidal, Duncan. 1991. "Relative Gains and the Pattern of International Cooperation." *American Political Science Review,* vol. 85, no. 3 (September), pp. 701–26.

Snyder, Jack. 1984. *The Ideology of the Offensive.* Ithaca, N.Y.: Cornell University Press.

——. 1990. "Averting Anarchy in the New Europe." *International Security,* vol. 14, no. 4 (Spring), pp. 5–41.

——. 1991. *Myths of Empire.* Ithaca, N.Y.: Cornell University Press.

Spykman, Nicholas. 1942. *America's Strategy in World Politics.* New York: Harcourt, Brace.

Stalin, Joseph. 1945. *The Great Patriotic War of the Soviet Union.* New York: International Publishers.

——. 1946. "New Five Year Plan for Russia," election address, February 9, 1946, *Vital Speeches,* vol. 12, no. 10 (March 1), pp. 300–04.

Starr, Harvey. 1972. *War Coalitions.* Lexington, Mass.: Lexington Books.

Steel, Ronald. 1988. "Moscow: End the Cold War." *New York Times,* December 11, op-ed page.

Stein, Janet Gross. 1992. "Deterrence and Compellence in the Gulf, 1990–91." *International Security,* vol. 17, no. 2 (Fall), pp. 147–79.

Stern, Fritz, and Leonard Krieger, eds. 1967. *The Responsibility of Power.* Garden City, N.Y.: Doubleday.

Stinchcombe, Arthur. 1968. *Constructing Social Theories.* New York: Harcourt, Brace and World.

Stokes, Eric. 1969. "Late Nineteenth Century Colonial Expansion and the Attack of the Theory of Economic Imperialism: A Case of Mistaken Identity." *Historical Journal,* vol. 12, no. 2 (1969), pp. 285–301.

Stokke, Olav. 1989. *Western Middle Powers and Global Poverty.* Motala: Motala Grafista.

Strauss, Leo. 1958. *Thoughts on Machiavelli.* Chicago: University of Chicago Press.

Streit, Clarence. 1938. *Union Now: A Proposal for a Federal Union of the Leading Democracies.* New York: Harper.

Suganami, Hidemi. 1989. *The Domestic Analogy and World Order Proposals.* Cambridge, England: Cambridge University Press.

Sullivan, Roger. 1989. *Immanuel Kant's Moral Theory.* Cambridge, England: Cambridge University Press.

Taft, Robert A. 1941. "Russia and the Four Freedoms." *Vital Speeches,* vol. 7, no. 19 (June 25), pp 584–86.

Tamir, Yael. 1993. *Liberal Nationalism.* Princeton: Princeton University Press.

Taylor, A. J. P. 1938. *Germany's First Bid for Colonies, 1984–85.* London: Macmillan.

——. 1954. *The Struggle for Mastery in Europe, 1848–1918.* Oxford: Clarendon.

Teson, Fernando. 1988. *Humanitarian Intervention.* Ardsley on Hudson, N.Y.: Transnational Publishers.

Thérien, Alain, and Jean-Philippe Thérien. 1995. "From Domestic to International Justice: The Welfare State and Foreign Aid." *International Organization,* vol. 49, no. 3, pp. 523–54.

Thompson, Kenneth W. 1980. *Morality and Foreign Policy.* Baton Rouge: Louisiana State University Press.

Thucydides. 1954/1972. *The Peloponnesian War,* trans. Rex Warner, intro. M. I. Finley. Harmondsworth, England: Penguin Books.

Tickner, J. Ann. 1992. *Gender in International Relations.* New York: Columbia University Press.

Tignor, Robert. 1966. *Modernization and British Colonial Rule in Egypt.* Princeton: Princeton University Press.

Tobin, James. 1991. "The Adam Smith Address: On Living and Trading with Japan: United States Commercial and Macroeconomic Policies." *Business Economics,* vol. 26, no. 1 (January), pp. 5–16.

Tocqueville, Alexis de. 1945. *Democracy in America,* vol. I. New York: Vintage.

Touraine, Alain, et al. 1983. *Solidarity,* trans. David Denby. New York: Cambridge University Press.

Truman, Harry S. 1947. "Our Responsibility: Foreign and Domestic Policies." *Vital Speeches of the Day,* vol. 13, no. 13 (April 5), p. 396.

Tucker, Robert C. 1969. *The Marxian Revolutionary Idea.* London: George Allen & Unwin.

Tucker, Robert W. 1952. "Professor Robert Morgenthau's Theory of Political Realism." *American Political Science Review,* vol. 46, pp. 214–24.

——. 1975. *The Inequality of States.* New York: Basic Books.

Tully, James. 1980. *A Discourse on Property: John Locke and His Adversaries.* New York: Cambridge University Press.

Turner, Stansfield. 1985. *Secrecy and Democracy.* Boston: Houghton Mifflin.

Twentieth Century Fund. 1989. *The Free Trade Debate.* New York: Priority Press.

Tyler, Patrick. 1992. "Lone Superpower Plan: Ammunition for Critics." *New York Times,* March 10, p. A12.

United Kingdom, Foreign and Commonwealth Office. 1980. *A Yearbook of the Commonwealth. 1980.* London: HMSO.

United Kingdom, House of Commons, Second Report from the Foreign Affairs Committee, *Grenada,* March 15, 1984, para. 16–17. London: HMSO.

Ulam, Adam. 1965. *The Bolsheviks.* New York: Macmillan.

——. 1968. *Expansion and Coexistence: Soviet Foreign Policy 1917–73.* New York: Praeger.

Ullman, Richard. 1978. "Human Rights and Economic Power: The United States versus Idi Amin." *Foreign Affairs,* vol. 56, no. 3 (April), pp. 529–43.

——. 1988. "Ending the Cold War." *Foreign Policy,* vol. 72 (Fall), pp. 130–51.

UN Development Program. 1992. *Human Development Report 1992.* New York: Oxford University Press.

UN Fund for Population Activities. 1992. *State of the World Population 1992* and *Population and the Environment: The Challenge Ahead.* UNFPA.

UNDP. 1994. *Human Development Report 1994.* New York: Oxford University Press.

U.S. State Department. 1981. *County Reports on Human Rights Practices.* Washington, D.C.: GPO.

——. 1984. *Grenada Document.* Washington, D.C.: GPO.

U.S. Departments of State and Defense. 1983. *Grenada: A Preliminary Report* (December 16).

Vagts, Alfred. 1948. "The Balance of Power: Growth of an Idea." *World Politics,* vol. 1, pp. 82–101.

Van Evera, Stephen. 1984. "The Cult of the Offensive." *International Security,* vol. 9, no. 1, pp. 58–107.

——. 1990. "Primed for Peace." *International Security,* vol. 15, no. 3 pp. 7–57.

Vasquez, John. 1983. *The Power of Power Politics: A Critique.* New Brunswick, N.J.: Rutgers University Press.

Vattel, Emerich de. 1758/1975. "Balance of Power," in Moorhead Wright, ed. *Theory and Practice of the Balance of Power: 1486–1914.* Totowa, N.J.: Rowman and Littlefield.

Vincent, R. John. 1974. *Nonintervention and International Order.* Princeton: Princeton University Press.

——. 1981. "The Hobbesian Tradition in Twentieth Century International Thought." *Millennium,* vol. 10, no. 2, pp. 91–101.

Viner, Jacob. 1948. "Power versus Plenty as Objectives of Foreign Policy in the Seventeenth and Eighteenth Centuries." *World Politics,* vol. I (October), pp. 1–29.

Viroli, Maurizio. 1988. *Jean Jacques Rousseau and the Well-Ordered Society*. New York: Cambridge University Press.

von Gentz, Friedrich. 1806/1975. "Fragments on the Balance of Power," in Moorhead Wright, ed., *The Theory and Practice of the Balance of Power*. Totowa, N.J.: Rowman and Littlefield.

Waddington, R. 1896. *Louis XV et le renversement des alliances*. Paris: Firmin-Didot.

Wade, Robert. 1992. "East Asia's Economic Success: Conflicting Perspectives, Partial Insights, Shaky Evidence." *World Politics*, vol. 44, no. 2 (January), pp. 270–320.

Wagner, R. Harrison. 1986. "The Theory of Games and the Balance of Power." *World Politics*, vol. 38, no. 4 (July), pp. 546–26.

Waldock, Humphrey. 1952. "The Regulation of the Use of Force by Individual States in International Law." *Recueil des Cours*, vol. 81, pp. 451, 467.

Walker, R. B. J. 1987. "Realism, Change, and International Political Theory." *International Studies Quarterly*, vol. 31, no. 1 (March), pp. 65–86.

——. 1993. *Inside/Outside: International Relations as Political Theory*. Cambridge, England: Cambridge University Press.

Wallerstein, Immanuel. 1974–1980. *The Modern World System*, vols. 1–4. New York: Academic Press.

——. 1994. "Peace Stability and Legitimacy, 1990–2025/2050," in Geir Lundestad, ed., *The Fall of Great Powers*. Oslo: Scandinavian Press.

Walling, William. 1915. *The Socialists and the Great War*. New York: Henry Holt and Company.

Walt, Stephen. 1988. *The Origins of Alliances*. Ithaca, N.Y.: Cornell University Press.

Walter, Andrew. 1983. "Distributive Justice and the Theory of International Relations." *Australian Outlook*, vol. 37, no. 2 (August), pp. 98–103.

Waltz, Kenneth. 1954. *Man, the State, and War: A Theoretical Analysis*. New York: Columbia University Press.

——. 1962. "Kant, Liberalism, and War." *American Political Science Review*, vol. 56, pp. 331–40.

——. 1964. "The Stability of a Bipolar World." *Daedalus*, vol. XCIII (Summer), pp. 881–909.

——. 1967. *Foreign Policy and Democratic Politics*. Boston: Little, Brown.

——. 1979. *The Theory of International Politics*. Reading, Mass.: Addison Wesley.

Walzer, Michael. 1973. "Political Action: The Problem of Dirty Hands." *Philosophy and Public Affairs*, vol. 2, no. 2 (Winter), pp. 160–80.

——. 1977. *Just and Unjust Wars*. New York: Basic Books.

——. 1983. *Spheres of Justice*. New York: Basic Books.

——. 1985. "The Moral Standing of States: A Response to Four Critics," in Charles Beitz, ed., *International Ethics*. Princeton: Princeton University Press.

——. 1987. *Interpretation and Social Criticism*. Cambridge: Harvard University Press.

——. 1994. *Thick and Thin: Moral Argument at Home and Abroad*. Notre Dame: University of Notre Dame Press.

Wang, Hongying. 1992. "Liberal Peace? A Study of the Fashoda Crisis of 1898." (Chicago) American Political Science Association.

Ward, Michael. 1982. *Monograph Series in Research Gaps in Alliance Dynamics, World Affairs*, vol. 19, book 1. Denver: University of Denver Press.

Warren, Bill. 1980. *Imperialism: Pioneer of Capitalism*. London: New Left Books.

Weart, Spencer. 1994. "Peace among Democratic and Oligarchic Republics," *Journal of Peace Research,* vol. 31, no. 3 (August), pp. 299–31.

Weede, Erich. 1984. "Democracy and War Involvement." *Journal of Conflict Resolution,* vol. 28 (December), pp. 649–64.

Welch, David. 1993. *Justice and the Genesis of War.* Cambridge, England: Cambridge University Press.

Weltman, John. 1974. "On the Obsolescence of War." *International Studies Quarterly,* vol. 18, no. 4 (December), pp. 395–416.

Wight, Martin. 1966. "The Balance of Power," in Herbert Butterfield and Martin Wight, eds., *Diplomatic Investigations.* London: George Allen and Unwin.

———. 1966. "Why Is There No International Theory?" *Diplomatic Investigations.* London: George Allen and Unwin.

———. 1973. "The Balance of Power and International Order," in Alan James, ed., *The Bases of International Order.* London: Oxford University Press.

———. 1977. *Systems of States.* Leicester: Leicester University Press.

———. 1978. *Power Politics,* intro. Hedley Bull and Carsten Holbraad. London: Royal Institute of International Affairs; New York: Holmes and Meier.

Wilkenfeld, Jonathan. 1968. "Domestic and Foreign Conflict Behavior of Nations." *Journal of Peace Research,* vol. 5, pp. 56–69.

Williams, Howard. 1983. *Kant's Political Philosophy.* Oxford: Basil Blackwell.

Williams, Michael. 1989. "Rousseau, Realism, and Realpolitik." *Millennium,* vol. 18, no. 2, pp. 185–203.

Wills, Garry. 1978. *Inventing America: Jefferson's Declaration of Independence.* Garden City, N.Y.: Doubleday.

Wilson, Woodrow. 1924. *The Messages and Papers of Woodrow Wilson,* ed. Albert Shaw. New York: The Review of Reviews.

Winch, Donald, Istvan Hont, and Michael Ignatieff, eds. 1983. *Wealth and Virtue: The Shaping of Political Economy in the Scottish Enlightenment.* New York: Columbia University Press.

Winslow, E. M. 1948. *The Pattern of Imperialism.* New York: Columbia University Press.

Wohlforth, William. 1987. "The Perception of Power." *World Politics,* vol. 39, no. 3 (April), pp. 353–81.

———. 1994–1995. "Realism and the End of the Cold War." *International Security,* vol. 9, no. 3 (Winter), pp. 91–129.

Wohlstetter, Albert. 1968. "Illusions of Distance." *Foreign Affairs,* vol. 46, no. 2, pp. 242–55.

Wolf, John B. 1970. *Toward a European Balance of Power, 1620–1715.* Chicago: Rand McNally.

Wolf, Susan. 1982. "Moral Saints." *Journal of Philosophy,* vol. 79 (August), pp. 419–39.

Wolfe, Bertram. 1964. *Three Who Made a Revolution.* New York: Dell Publishing.

Wolfers, Arnold. 1940. *Britain and France between Two Wars: Conflicting Strategies of Peace since Versailles.* New York: Harcourt, Brace.

———. 1994. *Discord and Collaboration.* Washington, D.C.: Foreign Policy Institute, Paul Nitze School of Advanced International Studies, Johns Hopkins University.

Wolin, Sheldon. 1960. *Politics and Vision.* Boston: Little, Brown.

Wood, Neal. 1965. "Introduction" to the *Art of War* by Machiavelli. New York: Da Capo/Bobbs-Merrill.

Woodruff, W. W. 1966. *Impact of Western Man*. New York: St. Martin's Press.

Woolf, Virginia. 1938. *Three Guineas*. New York: Harcourt, Brace.

World Bank. 1989. *World Development Report 1989*. New York: Oxford University Press.

——. 1993. *Global Economic Prospects and the Developing Countries*. Washington, D.C.: World Bank.

Wright, Moorhead, ed. 1975. *Theory and Practice of the Balance of Power: 1486–1914*. Totowa, N.J.: Rowman and Littlefield.

Wright, Quincy. 1942. *A Study of History*. Chicago: University of Chicago Press.

——. 1965. *A Study of War*. Chicago: University of Chicago Press.

——. 1968. "Non-Military Intervention," in Karl Deutsch and Stanley Hoffmann, eds., *The Relevance of International Law*. Cambridge, Mass.: Schenkman.

Yeats, W. B. 1983. *The Collected Poems of W. B. Yeats*, ed. Richard Finneran. New York: Collier.

Yesson, Erik. 1992. "Power and Diplomacy in World Politics." Ph.D. Dissertation, Department of Politics, Princeton University.

Young, Gary. 1976. "The Fundamental Contradiction of Capitalist Production." *Philosophy and Public Affairs*, vol. 5, no. 2 (Winter), pp. 196–234.

Young, Oran. 1980. "International Regimes: Problems of Concept Formation." *World Politics*, vol. 32 (April), no. 3, pp. 331–56.

Yovel, Yirmiahu. 1980. *Kant and the Philosophy of History*. Princeton: Princeton University Press.

Zakaria, Fareed. 1992. "Realism and Domestic Politics: A Review Essay." *International Security*, vol. 17, no. 1 (Summer), pp. 177–98.

Ziegler, David. 1981. *War, Peace and International Politics*. Glenview: Scott, Foresman/Little Brown.

Zinnes, Dina. 1967. "An Analytical Study of the Balance of Power Theories." *Journal of Peace Research*, vol. 4, pp. 270–88.

Zolberg, Aristide. 1969. *One Party Government in the Ivory Coast*. Princeton: Princeton University Press.

——. 1981. "Origins of the Modern World System: A Missing Link." *World Politics*, vol. 33, no. 2 (January), pp. 253–81.

Zumwalt, Elmo. 1976. *On Watch*. New York: Quadrangle.

Index

Page numbers in *italics* refer to charts.